MW00584430

ON WARRIORS' WINGS

ON WARRIORS' WINGS

Army Vietnam War Helicopters
and the Native Americans
They Were Named to Honor

——— • ———

David Napoliello

GLOBAL
COLLECTIVE
PUBLISHERS

Published by Global Collective Publishers
16 North Bryn Mawr Avenue, #1355
Bryn Mawr, Pennsylvania 19010, U.S.A.
www.globalcollectivepublishers.com

Hardback ISBN: 978-1-957831-08-4
eBook ISBN: 978-1-957831-09-1

Sharon, Donna, and David
Beloved wife and cherished children

CONTENTS

FORWARD

Whether fiction or non-fiction, every book begins at a different time and place than when the first words are put on the page. Frequently, the author draws inspiration from personal ideas or experiences, vivid memories of events gone by whose impact are significant and lasting. In the case of *On Warriors' Wings*, the first of several occasions that stimulated its writing occurred more than six decades ago, although the assimilation of several other experiential pillars that collectively shaped the book did not coalesce until almost a decade ago.

One's progress through life, its shape, and meaning congeal from the collection of experiences and interests that span the gamut of importance and impact. For *On Warriors' Wings,* I encountered three distinct formative experiences, which I call the pillars of this project. The first experiential pillar was my initial encounter with Army helicopters beginning in 1954. By that time, the Army had only twelve years' experience with rotary-winged aircraft, and its first combat use of helicopters was barely a decade past. The Army R-4 helicopter was a veteran of World War II, while the H-13 and H-19 were Korean War veterans, and the H-34 was making its initial flight in 1954.

As a grade-schooler in 1954, I was fascinated and mesmerized by what these latter three aircraft could do with a highly trained and skilled Army aviator at the controls. My father was stationed at Nelligen Kaserne, the Federal Republic of Germany, from late 1954 to 1957. The family was fortunate enough to live in Building 17, Stairwell A, Apartment 3 for the entire period. I say fortunate because five of the apartment's windows, including the picture window in the living room, had a direct view of the Nelligen Army Helicopter Port. I was excited to have an exclusive front-row seat for the helicopters' performances that were our next-door neighbors. Though I had several viewing options, my favorite was from the small window in the hallway half-bath. From there, while perched on top of the commode, I could see everything that the helicopters would do, from cranking up at the hangar, rolling down the taxiway to the runway, and finally lifting off. I could witness this entire evolution from that one window. The amazing H-13 pilots would hover at the hangar and then taxi to the runway with their skids a mere two feet or less off the ground for the entire trip. When we weren't gazing out the windows, the neighborhood kids and I would line the fence that separated the housing area from the airfield to watch the awesome helicopters do their thing with all their accompanying noise, wind, and dust. Also, with the airfield approach at 90° and departure at 270°, the helicopters could be seen arriving between and above the rooftops of Buildings 15 and 16 (which they were permitted to do). These mechanical wonders never ceased to astonish me. Before my dad's tour of duty ended, Sikorsky H-34s began arriving at Nelligen to join the H-13s and H-19s. With them, the aircrews started to do more training exercises which entailed the transporting of external loads. It was not uncommon to see equipment, containers, or cargo net loads hanging beneath the helicopters and heading off in one direction or another. In the years that followed, there would be numerous duty station changes, family relocations, and unfamiliar schools with new classmates to meet. And by the sixth grade, I was convinced that I wanted to follow in my father's footsteps. By college graduation, I had a regular Army commission in hand with my first choice branch selection, field artillery, and my chosen duty assignment, Vietnam.

One of the duties that befell the junior lieutenant in the battalion was to carry out the duties associated with "conversion day" or "C-day. This was the day when all allied military personnel were restricted to their installations while the entire country converted old Military Payment Certificates (MPC) to a newer version. The classified and unannounced exchange meant that a supply of new certificates had to be brought in so that every soldier, sailor, marine, and airman could make the one-for-one exchange in 24 hours. So along with countless other officers throughout the country, I was detailed to pick up the new, exchange it for the old, and deliver the latter for destruction on "C-day." Fortunately, an OH-6 *Cayuse* was my transportation for the day.

For the most part, my helicopter experiences in Vietnam were not particularly remarkable, and routine for life on a fire support base. The infrequent medevac flights hurried away injured cannoneers or the more infrequent wounded soldier. The occasional dedicated flights when the communications and electronics officer would venture out to our firebase to pick up and haul Freddie off for repair— Freddie was the nickname for our five cubic foot, 175-pound, portable field artillery digital automatic computer (FADAC). FADAC was a whiz for its day, processing one instruction every 7.8 microseconds. Although a dedicated gasoline generator powered it, it was vulnerable to electrical current fluctuations and hated heat and dust, so light observation helicopter (LOH) rides to the repair shop were common.

Later in my Vietnam tour, I served as an aerial observer conducting daylight observation of activities within the Demilitarized Zone (DMZ) and supporting ground forces in the northern extremes of the I Corps Tactical Zone (CTZ) with artillery, close air support, and Naval gunfire from an O-1 *Bid Dog*. Evenings were spent performing rocket visual reconnaissance (VR), searching for locations where enemy forces conducted rocket attacks on military installations and civilian towns. Once again, the *Cayuse* was our observation platform.

A helicopter-related exclamation point marked the end of my Vietnam tour. Helicopters ferried me throughout the combat zone's health care system and ultimately alighted aboard the U.S.S. *Repose* (AH-16) standing off the Demilitarized Zone (DMZ) before heading on to an aerial port of debarkation in Da Nang.

Essential for every soldier and marine who was caught in a most unfriendly place, these trips were carried out with such urgency that they felt like a blur. The Army and the Marine Corps aviators who conducted those trips were seen as angels of mercy and deserved all the accolades bestowed on them as their predecessors in earlier wars were and like their successors in battles and wars that would follow.

The experience of Vietnam heightened my appreciation for the helicopter's capabilities and its more important purpose for being, as well as its flexibility and adaptability, just as it did for more senior Army officials who gazed beyond the horizons for newer and better helicopters and the missions they could perform. It appeared that what could be done with a helicopter in Vietnam was only limited by the safety and the ingenuity of the aircrew and ground support personnel. Similarly, innovation and technical advancements would help fulfill their promise for the future.

Later as a battalion commander, I was once more dependent upon the capabilities of helicopters and their crews. My units' special weapons capability beyond the delivery of conventional fires was inextricably linked to the ability of the supporting aviation units, the surety of their personnel, and the skill of their pilots. They delivered those special munitions containers under the watchful eye of evaluation teams from command levels far beyond that found on a mere divisional installation. Once more, the benefactor of army aviation's uncompromising capabilities and standards, I enjoyed my association with helicopters and their absorbing story.

All surviving veterans of Vietnam have their own story to tell about their return and reception once home, but we shall not forget the stories of their comrades who did not return, those who gave their last full measure of devotion. Having retired from a second career as a defense industry executive charged with modernization programs for the Army and Marine Corps and ultimately with framing the corporation's global strategy, I was uniquely privileged to be invited by the Vietnam Veterans Memorial Fund (VVMF) staff to join in their campaign to erect the Education Center at The Wall in partnership with the National Park Service. Approved by Congress in 2003, the Education Center was to be dedicated to apprising future generations of the honor and sacrifices made by those who served their country during the Vietnam War. At the heart of the center's educational program was the aim of instilling the seven traits embodied in American service members of all eras: Loyalty, Duty, Respect, Service, Honor, Integrity, and Courage. On November 28, 2012, a ceremonial groundbreaking took place on the designated site of the center, on the National Mall at the corner of Constitution Avenue and 23rd Street. A unique feature of the museum was the plan to display many of the more than 400,000 artifacts that have been left at the Vietnam Veterans Memorial since its dedication in 1982.

The second pillar of this work was the informative and inspiring experience of my association with Native American tribes, leaders, and, most importantly, veterans. Many people and organizations were interested in seeing the Education

Center become a reality. One, in particular, was the American Indian Veterans Memorial Initiative (AIVMI), sponsored by the Seminole Tribe of Florida. Deeply rooted in the service of Native Americans in Vietnam and painfully aware of the lack of a national appreciation of the generations of service to the nation by their Native American ancestors, the AIVMI team also wanted to recognize their ancestors on the National Mall. Thus members of the Seminole Tribe spent several years working with Native American Vietnam veterans and tribal leaders from the 573 federally recognized Native American tribes raising awareness of their efforts to establish a Native American veterans memorial. They generously approached the leaders of VVMF, offering their support for the Education Center and their willingness to raise money for its construction. This gesture was one of those awakenings I experienced when I was charged with negotiating a cooperative, third-party fundraising agreement with AIVMI. The agreement would recognize them as official fundraisers for the center and set into motion the planning for an exhibit honoring Native American veterans of America's wars. With the agreement in place, AIVMI set off on their agreed-upon multi-million-dollar fundraising campaign, and concepts for the tribute exhibit began to emerge from discussions with prominent Native Americans interested in the project. In so doing, they embraced me and involved me in their programs and activities. Opportunities to meet and interact with Native American veterans of wars besides Vietnam were remarkable and inspiring. The second experiential pillar supporting *On Warriors' Wings* was thus firmly in place.

The final pillar of the book sprang from an episodic sentiment within the country concerning the stereotyping and characterization of Indigenous Americans. This was yet another cyclical eruption of the non-Native American segment of the population over what constituted a denigration of the Indigenous population. The target of the animus was the use of Native American or First Nation names and symbolisms for institutional representation like athletic team mascots or, worse yet, a Native American image coupled with it. The issue was not new but merely resurrected for a new time. As Carter Meland and David E. Wilkins note in their article "Stereotypes in sports, chaos in federal policy," from *The Star Tribune*: "Since the first Europeans made landfall in North America, native peoples have suffered under a vast array of stereotypes, misconceptions, and caricatures. Whether portrayed as 'noble savages,' 'ignoble savages,' 'teary-eyed environmentalists,' or, most recently, simply as 'casino-rich,' Native peoples find their efforts to be treated with a measure of respect and integrity undermined by images that flatten complex tribal, historical and personal experience into one-dimensional representations that tell us more about the depicters than about the depicted."[1]

During the 2012 reincarnation of the Native American name and mascot debate, the Army found itself, in some quarters, being painted with the broad brush-strokes of racial discrimination and defamation of Native Americans. The charges stemmed from the perceived disgraceful Army practice of bestowing potentially "hostile or abusive" names on its helicopters. The broad argument was that such a naming policy maintains harmful stereotypes that are discriminatory and hurtful by distorting the Native American past and thus prevent a better understanding of the fundamental contributions of Native Americans to the history of the United States.

Arguments on both sides of the debate have been spirited, emotional, and too frequently engaged in by non-Native Americans. There appears to be little consultation with the Indigenous peoples of the country and consideration of their opinions which should matter most in any resolution of this crisis. And because so many government agencies and their policies and regulations control the appropriateness, suitability, and conflict resolution of the use of trademarks, all branches of the federal government, in one manner or another, have had a say in the outcome. One of the sagest opinions for dealing with the question came from an enjoinder from the forty-fourth president of the United States, Barack Obama: "Consultation is a critical ingredient of a sound and productive Federal-tribal relationship."[2] From this final pillar comes the inquiry into the genesis and implementation of the Army naming policy and the role played by Native Americans and people protective of their rights, interests, and historical image.

While the time and the journey have been long to reach this project, I am optimistic that the result will be worthwhile and thankful that it did not consume the same number of years as getting to this point did.

INTRODUCTION

For more than 1,500 years, man dreamed about the possibility of flying like a bird, in the most literal sense. History is replete with the misadventures of man and his bird-imitating contraptions, vainly trying to "slip the surly bonds of earth."[1] With time, man learned that flight is achieved through a balance and equality among the forces of flight—lift, weight (gravity), thrust, and drag (friction)—the pairing of opposing forces. The helicopter attained flight when its lift was greater than its weight, and the realized thrust was greater than the drag.

Maintaining fixed-wing flight can thus be understood as a tug of war between the opposing forces of lift versus weight, thrust versus drag. When an aircraft's engine produces more thrust, it will accelerate, increasing airspeed over the wing, providing lift and greater altitude. With the plane moving faster, air resistance or drag increases, thus slowing the plane until thrust and drag are again in equilibrium. This combination maintains the aircraft at a constant speed but greater altitude—an airplane experiences more drag by reducing thrust, which slows the plane. A reduction in speed slows the air over the wing, causing the loss of lift and the plane's descent.

The basic idea of a helicopter, namely achieving flight through the rotation of a horizontal wing, dates back to a simple invention known as the "Chinese top"—a simple toy with a propeller-shaped blade horizontally attached to a vertical stick. It is also worth noting that the name helicopter is derived from the Greek phrase for "spiraling wing." Thus by spinning a control stick between the palms of one's hands, a pilot creates lift and causes the helicopter to soar into the air. The "Chinese top" appeared in European paintings dating back to 1463, and in 1483, Leonardo da Vinci included illustrations of his more sophisticated "rotary-wing" toy in his notebooks. These ideas and drawings lay dormant for another three centuries while technology caught up with the toy.

In 1784, two Frenchmen, naturalist Christian de Launoy and his mechanic, Bienvenu, found the solution to one of the perplexing problems of rotary-wing flight: torque. When the rotor of a rotary-wing vehicle spins in one direction, the vehicle's body rotates in the other. Placing a rotor on each end of the stick with a string under tension that was wound around the stick, Launoy and Bienvenu had a self-powered craft whose rotors spun in opposite directions. The rotors' resultant "contra rotation" canceled out the torque and added stability to the stick.

In the late nineteenth century, work on helicopters was hampered by the same predicament encountered by heavier-than-air flying machines—the lack of an engine with a sufficiently high power-to-weight ratio. In the 1860s, Viscount Gustave de Ponton d'Amécourt experimented with small flying coaxial rotary-wing aircraft models that used springs for power. A decade later, Alphonse Pénaud used wound-up rubber bands to power his helicopters and fixed-wing aircraft toys.

During the American Civil War, Union naval forces effectively blockaded most of the ports of the Confederacy, whose own navy proved inadequate to break the blockade. In 1862, architectural engineer William C. Powers of Mobile, Alabama, determined that an alternative to seaborne strikes would be to attack the blockade from the air.[2] Drawing upon the engineering ingenuity of Archimedes and Leonardo da Vinci, Powers conceived of what would become known as the "Confederate Helicopter." Coupling Archimedean screws to a steam engine, Powers attained lift and thrust. He mounted two such screws on the side of the craft to provide forward thrust, much like a propeller drives a ship. Two additional vertically mounted screws provided the helicopter with lift. Steering was accomplished by a rudder added to the rear of the craft. The designer had initially intended to create a model of his helicopter to be followed by a full-scale version, but the lack of financial resources and Confederate support relegated Powers' work to the drafting board and obscurity. Family lore has it that the plans for the helicopter were hidden to prevent them from falling into Union hands and becoming an aerial instrument for the destruction of the Confederacy.[3]

The advent of heavier-than-air flight followed the introduction of a practical internal combustion engine built by Niklaus Otto of Germany in 1876, and twenty-seven years later, the "Wright Flyer" was flown at Kitty Hawk, North Carolina. During the ensuing years, flight pioneers continued to work on both fixed-wing and rotary-wing aircraft, yet because fixed-wing aircraft were considered primitive, some aviation pioneers believed that rotary-wing aircraft held more promise.

Powered helicopter flight followed four years later when French aviation pioneer Louis Charles Breguet was able to lift his helicopter, the Gyroplane #1, one meter off the ground for an elapsed time of about a minute. It wasn't until later that year that Paul Cornu conducted the first untethered flight by a helicopter, which remained aloft for a few minutes at about one meter off the ground.

Before one could build what would be more identifiable as a real helicopter, many lingering issues needed to be resolved, and the early twentieth-century pioneers addressed them one by one. Among them was the community's coming to grips with the erroneous belief that power and not control was the most difficult challenge. However, it was the inability to define control requirements that would confound helicopter researchers for thirty years.[4]

In 1912, Russian Boris Yuriev tried to fly a helicopter of his creation. Although unsuccessful, his was the first helicopter to feature a large central rotor and a small side-mounted tail rotor to cancel torque. His new configuration was noteworthy, as it eventually became the heart of helicopter design.

Marquis Raúl Pateras Pescara from Argentina built several coaxial helicopters in the early 1920s that stayed in the air in a somewhat controlled flight for an extended period. His aircraft was the most advanced design of the time and continued to solve several underlying problems in helicopter design.

The first issue was "cyclic pitch control"—directional motion control. Pescara used a set of linkages that could change a blade's pitch while spinning to increase lift, shift sideways, and move forward. A second innovation was the concept of "autorotation." If a pilot lost engine power, the entire aircraft would fall to earth like a brick. Pescara determined that by keeping the rotor spinning as fast as possible during a helicopter's fall and then abruptly increasing the rotor pitch as it neared the ground, the impact on the earth could reduce the damage to the aircraft and possibly save the pilot's life.

Unlike the other helicopters of the period, Pescara's helicopter No. 3, did not achieve forward flight by the use of conventional propellers. Instead, Pescara was able to adjust the angle of attack of the rotor blade during operation by twisting it along the longitudinal axis, thus producing thrust in the desired direction as the imaginary rotor axis was tipped in the new direction of travel.

Further advances were made after the First World War, when Spanish aeronautical engineer Juan de la Cierva built the first practical rotary-wing aircraft. His "autogiro" (his patented spelling) was not a helicopter but rather a workable combination of a fixed-wing aircraft fuselage and a helicopter rotor mounted on top. The unpowered rotor spun from the wind caused by the craft's forward motion and the propeller's draw in the front. The spinning rotor shortened the autogiro's takeoff distance and enabled vertical landing using autorotation.

One of the obstacles confronting de la Cierva was a fundamental helicopter design issue known as "asymmetry of lift." If a helicopter moves forward, the rotor blade that moves forward generates more lift than the rotor blade that's moving backward, which caused fixed rotor blade helicopters to tip over. La Cierva's solution was to hinge the rotor blades to the hub, allowing them a degree of travel up-and-down and back-and-forth.

His first hinged blade autogiro was the "C-4", which flew on January 9, 1923. The C-4, a modified World War I French Hanriot fighter, retained the wings for flight control. Later de la Cierva autogyros removed the wings and added cyclic pitch control to steer the craft. Subsequent developments included an engine clutch that allows the rotor blades to spin up before liftoff, although the rotor would spin freely during flight.

His autogyros, licensed for manufacture in the United States, were nominally used by news outlets, and the Postal Service briefly experimented with them for mail delivery. A Kellett Company autogyro accompanied Admiral Richard E. Byrd, Jr on his 1933 expedition to the Antarctic. The U. S. Army Air Forces (USAAF) evaluated Kellett's machines but assessed no serious need for them.

Despite de la Cierva's untimely death on December 9, 1936, in a Dutch airliner crash near South London, he had nevertheless made significant advances in rotorcraft development, including the first practical production aircraft. Remarkably, his autogiro still survives in ultralight aircraft, such as the gyrocopters and gyro gliders sold for kit-builder flying enthusiasts.

Europe was not the only site of innovation and investigation into the nascent field of powered vertical flight. In 1921, U.S. Army aviators also began their intellectual fiddling with helicopters. In January of that year, the Army awarded a contract to Dr. Charles de Bothezat and Ivan Jerome for a vertical flight machine. Their offering was a quadcopter that made its first flight in October of the same year. Fourteen months later, on December 18, 1923, Army Major Thurman H. Bane piloted what by then became the H-1 in its first public demonstration flight. Bane kept the aircraft aloft for 1 minute and 42 seconds at a maximum height of six feet.[5] Although the Army continued flying the H-1 throughout the year, its interest in vertical flight aircraft waned.

Stimulated by the work of de la Cierva, French aircraft designer and builder Louis C. Bréguet established a separate rotary-wing business under the technical direction of René Dorand to further mature and advance helicopter technology and design. The first product of this collaboration was the purely experimental aircraft, the Gyroplane-Laboratoire. After almost four years of failure, Bréguet and Dorand achieved flight, and in 1937 won a French Air Ministry prize when their helicopter achieved specific flight and performance objectives.

While the Gyroplane-Laboratoire was a significant advancement in rotary-winged flight, the invention of the first practicable helicopter is often attributed to Professor Heinrich Focke of Germany, Professor Georg Wulf, and Dr. Werner Naumann who together founded the Focke-Wulf Flugzeugbau AG aircraft firm. In 1931, when Professor Focke was forced from the company by its financial backers, he turned to building and refining autogyros, ultimately working on his Model 61, of which two were made, the first model flying in the spring of 1936—the first practical, fully-controllable helicopter to take to the air. It was not easy to fly, but it could reliably do all the essential maneuvers of a modern helicopter.

The Model 61, reflecting its roots in autogyro design, was built on the fuselage of a Focke-Wulf FW-44 *Steiglitz* biplane with a rotor on each of two outriggers, one on each side of the fuselage. It had a 160 horsepower (hp) radial engine in the nose to drive the two contra-rotating rotors for powered flight. The small propeller affixed to the engine was used only to cool the radial engine.

Mostly unnoticed by the public and aviation elite, the Fa-61 became a public sensation in February 1938. It was flown by twenty-five-year-old aviatrix and Luftwaffe test pilot Hanna Reitsch[6] in the enclosed *Deutschland Halle* sports arena in Berlin at a huge Nazi gathering.[7] Included in the audience were Adolf Hitler and Charles Lindberg, as she flew the Fa-61 nightly for three weeks.[8]

Given the design and performance superiority of the Fa-61, its potential for the application of advancements allowed the company to use it as a basic platform for future developments. Because the German government was so impressed with the helicopter, it encouraged Henrich Focke to form a company dedicated to helicopter advancements and production. Along with partner-pilot Gerd Achgelis, Focke-Achgelis & Co. G.m.b.H. was formed and began developing a larger, heavier lift helicopter off the Fa-61 base. This was the Fa-223 *Drache* (Dragon). The most capable helicopter of World War II, it had a 1,000 horsepower piston engine and could carry a crew of two plus 2,820 pounds of internal or external load. The Fa-223 was also capable of carrying a forward-firing machine gun or being armed with bombs or mines. However, competing German military production priorities and the effects of Allied bombing limited the number of helicopters built.

While the Germans were pioneers in helicopter development and operations, the country's defeat in World War II meant that leadership in the post-war development of rotorcraft would pass to other countries, particularly the United States. Yet, unlike the airplane, the helicopter had no Kitty Hawk nor a single or group of aviation pioneers who could claim to be its father or inventor. The helicopter presented its inventors with complex problems of greater significance than those encountered and successfully assailed by the Wright brothers and their contemporaries four decades earlier.

In the United States, four pioneers who worked independently and along parallel lines solved the technological obstacles needed to bring the helicopter into reality and volume production for commercial and military use. We should note though, that the more realistic advent of helicopters stems from the accomplishments dating to the 1930s.

For the United States, domestic excellence in rotary-wing aviation was vested in the brilliance and imaginative ingenuity principally of four men. The four pioneers included Russian-born American Igor Ivanovich Sikorsky, a visionary whose aviation innovations spanned both fixed-wing and rotary-wing aviation technology. By having his company based in both aviation domains, Sikorsky was able to bring the best and most applicable advances and technology from both realms to his product lines, thus linking the "early birds" to the "whirlybirds."

The second American helicopter pioneer was Frank Piasecki. His ideas and showmanship propelled his company (later to become Vertol and today Boeing Helicopter) to the forefront as the world's supplier of big helicopters. His company mastered the issues of dual-engine helicopters with tandem rotors and opened the helicopter field to the large, medium, and heavy lift aircraft that were common in Vietnam and continue to be in use today.

Arthur Young was the technical and inspiration genius behind Bell Helicopter. Although not a scientist but rather an inventor, cosmologist, philosopher, astrologer, and author, Young took a holistic approach to his work and his most challenging invention. In 1928, the brilliant inventor began the quest for his great project—something that would challenge his competitive nature and take a long time. His invention, in time, became the Model 30 and the testbed for the Bell helicopters that followed, including its commercial helicopter, the Model 47. Besides making helicopters almost commonplace at the time, Young and Bell added the tilting rotor head and stabilizer bar that are fixtures on all helicopters in one form or another to this day.

The transition to commercial acceptance of helicopters gained impetus from Stanley Hiller, Jr. His company was the first to define and manufacture a civilian helicopter to meet the marketplace's needs. It is also worth noting that he was the first helicopter pioneer to succeed in the field without the benefit of either military contracts or corporate financial support. Collectively, the technological developments introduced by these men paved the way from the foundling beginning of helicopters in the United States to a rotary-wing industrial base, and ultimately to American-developed helicopters for its uniformed services.

The helicopter first appeared on the Army's horizon on January 10, 1941, when it entered into a $50,000 contract with Sikorsky for an S-47/VS-316 helicopter. After a few alterations to the design, the army experimental prototype XR-4 made its first flight on January 14, 1942, and five months later, on May 30, 1942, the Army would accept the helicopter for production and service. Between 1942 and 1944, Sikorsky would produce 131 R-4s for the Army Air Forces, Navy, Coast Guard, and the British Royal Navy and Air Force. The tactical missions for the R-4 included aerial observation, courier flights, artillery target location, and fire adjustment. With the addition of an external litter, the R-4 could also perform medical evacuation flights. And when modified with bomb racks, it could carry three 100-pound bombs or a single 325-pound depth bomb for anti-submarine warfare (ASW).

The R-4 conducted rescue operations during World War II in the China-Burma-India (CBI) Theater, including the first medical evacuation which was the rescue of the crew and passengers of a British 1st Air Commando Group Stinson L-1 *Vigilant*, piloted by Technical Sergeant Ed "Murphy" Hladovcak, with three British soldiers on board. The saga began when the L-1 crashed behind Japanese lines in northern Burma on April 21, 1944.[9]

On May 23, 1944, six ships configured as floating repair depots for damaged Army Air Forces aircraft set sail for the South Pacific. Each had two R-4s aboard. The R-4 was used to ferry aircraft repair parts between these floating Aviation Repair Units in the theater. Similarly, the R-4s of the 10th Air Force Air Jungle Rescue Unit were used to locate downed aircraft and recover the valuable instruments, equipment, and parts for reuse.[10]

The Marine Corps also took a focused interest in rotary-wing aviation; however, its focus was on the helicopter as a facilitator for amphibious landing, which was the operational specialty of the Corps in the years following World War II, and upon the delineation of service roles and missions. The Marines formed their first helicopter squadron, HMX-1, at the Marine Corps Air Station, Quantico, Virginia, on December 1, 1947.[11] Less than a year later, after experimenting with the Sikorsky HO3S-1 in amphibious operations and what would later be known as "vertical envelopment," the Marine Corps published the world's first manual on using helicopters in amphibious landings—entitled "Amphibious Operations—Employment of Helicopters (Tentative)." The Marine Corps manual was an invaluable asset when the Army began exploring the helicopter's exploitation for airmobile operations and organizations.

While the helicopter demonstrated its early life-saving potential during World War II, the French proved its versatility during the First Indochina War (1946–1954). Other evacuation ships included the Hiller 360, flown by the French and outfitted with two externally mounted stretchers. Notable among France's first medevac pilots was Valérie André, who made 129 rescue sorties recovering 165 wounded soldiers by the war's climactic end at Dien Bien Phu.[12] Following the French withdrawal from Vietnam, Valérie André found herself in Algeria flying medevac missions in the early 1960s during the French Algerian War (1954–1962). She flew an additional 236 missions aboard the Sikorsky H-19 and H-34 and the Alouette 2 helicopters.[13] She and her colleagues evidenced the wider global acceptance of the helicopter's life-saving utility.

The onset of the Korean War witnessed further U.S. Army experimentation with force mobility enhancements through the application of vertical lift. The Army's 2nd Helicopter Detachment began flying medical evacuation missions in Korea on January 1, 1951, using the four Bell H-13B *Sioux* that arrived with the unit on November 22, 1950. The 3rd and 4th Helicopter Detachments, each with their complement of four aircraft, arrived later in January 1951. With the twelve aircraft of these units, the H-13s shouldered the Army's medevac missions. The medevac helicopter began to shed light on what would become known years later as the all-important "golden hour": those precious sixty minutes between combat injury and the receipt of critical life-saving care at a forward medical facility.

Records of the military medical department reflect the substantial impact of the helicopter on casualty survivability rates. During World War II, seventy-one percent of combat-wounded would survive; that percentage would increase to seventy-four percent during the Korean War. In Vietnam, however, that rate would climb to eighty-one percent, primarily because of the helicopter.[14] This result is all the more significant when you consider that twenty percent of Vietnam wounded suffered serious, multiple wounds, a scale not experienced in either World War II or Korea. Medical evacuation pilots in Vietnam claimed that an injured service member could reach hospital treatment within a maximum of thirty to thirty-five minutes from the moment of being wounded,[15] with the average time being seventeen minutes.[16]

It would take a new aircraft arrival before aviation units undertook large resupply assignments and large troop movements. The Army sent its first Sikorsky H-19 *Chickasaw* helicopters to Korea with the 6th Transportation Company in early 1953. The H-19s played a crucial role in resupplying troops in the forward battle areas, bypassing some of Korea's most inhospitable terrain. This helicopter also provided airlift for the U.S. and allied prisoners of war exchanges after the armistice signing on July 27, 1953.

The Korean War brought advanced and standardized procedures in the helicopter's use that would maximize its potential, capabilities, and support to ground commanders in the coming war. Lieutenant General Maxwell Taylor, Eight Army Commander, illuminated a guiding beacon for Army aviation when he said, "The cargo helicopter, employed in mass, can extend the tactical mobility of the Army far beyond its normal capability. I hope that the United States Army will make ample provisions for the full exploitation of the helicopter in the future."[17]

With the cessation of operations in Korea, the Army returned its combat forces to the Continental United States (CONUS) and bases in other theaters. It also implemented a reduction in forces, downsizing through force personnel attrition. In the midst of all this personnel churn, the Army continued its after-action analyses of its wartime actions seeking strategic and tactical doctrine and force structure changes appropriate for the post-war environment. Some general principles from the Korean War experience and the post-war assessments emerged which transcend specific aircraft requirements. The Army's first Director of Army Aviation, Major General Hamilton H. Howze, when summarizing the future role of aviation, was clear about first principles of the aviation arm: "Army Aviation must never lose sight [...] that it exists only because it can serve the ground unit commander better than some other type of aviation support."[18] The immediate post-war period saw replacing current conventional fixed- and rotary-wing aircraft with product improvements of the same aircraft models.

By the end of the Korean War, the nation and the military services had about five years of experience with the organizational changes wrought by the National Security Act of 1947. The soundness of the new national security program and organization had been demonstrated. The service chiefs embodied in the Joint Chiefs of Staff (JCS) recommended to Defense Secretary James Forrestal their vision of the roles and missions, which were modified in 1953. However, by 1956, the department felt that with the development of new strategic concepts and new weapons, coupled with nine years of experience under the approved roles and missions, a need existed for clarification and a more precise interpretation of the roles and missions of the armed services.[19] The call for these changes did not impugn the primary roles and missions previously adopted. The changes intended to review five crucial problem areas, which included:

1. Use of aircraft by the U.S. Army,
2. Adequacy of airlift,
3. Air defense,
4. Air Force tactical support of the Army, and
5. Intermediate-range ballistic missile (IRBM).[20]

To frame the problem area of aircraft for the Army, the Department of Defense (DoD) defined the combat zone as extending 100 miles forward of the Forward Line of Own Troops (FLOT) and a similar 100 miles to the rear. Given these geographic dimensions, Army aircraft operating in this zone would perform the following missions:

1. Command, liaison, and communications,
2. Observation, visual and photographic reconnaissance, fire adjustment, and topographical survey,
3. Airlift of Army personnel and materiel, and
4. Aeromedical evacuation.[21]

Rotary-wing aircraft to perform these missions were limited to a maximum empty weight of 20,000 pounds unless an exception was provided for a specific plane by the secretary of defense after consultation with the newly created U.S. Air Force. Troop airlift capability for the Army was limited to small combat units or equipment to improve local mobility. Furthermore, enhanced army airlift capabilities should be accompanied by a corresponding reduction in other forms of army transportation in the defined combat zone.

On November 26, 1956, a DoD policy memorandum specifically excluded certain functions within the Army Aviation program. Those functions included:

1. Strategic and tactical airlift,
2. Tactical reconnaissance,
3. Interdiction of the battlefield, and
4. Close air support.[22]

Additionally, the Army was explicitly prohibited from establishing its aviation research facilities. Instead, it was to make maximum use of Air Force and Navy aircraft research and development capabilities performed on a reimbursable basis from within Army fiscal resources. The Army was to limit itself to developing requirements for Army aviation needs, evaluating vendor proposals, and conducting user testing of equipment. The policy memorandum also restricted the Army from developing and procuring new aircraft to meet its requirements. When they were suitable or modifiable, civilian, Navy and Air Force aircraft were used instead.

Some of those Army aircraft would see combat in Vietnam, and all would be influenced by four first-principal requirements.

1. Obtain satisfactory maintenance requirements in the forward combat area by procurement of simplified aircraft,
2. Aircraft must have short takeoff and landing capabilities,
3. Aircraft must have the ability to take off and land on rough, unprepared fields, and
4. All aircraft must possess a high degree of all-weather capability.[23]

These priority requirements for each aircraft developed for Vietnam and beyond are in addition to mission-specific requirements approved by the Army at the outset of each new aircraft's development.

The was no eureka moment in the advent of helicopters for the world, but rather, a multitude of inch-stone progressions by free-thinkers, experimenters, and men enraptured with the wonder lust of untethered mechanical flight. It took the amalgamation of their collective efforts to penetrate the mysteries of rotary-wing control, vertical ascent, and transition to intentional vectored motion. The seemingly unbounded complexities of their aviation problems demanded the best efforts and a margin of luck among the undaunted. Mastery of rotary-wing flight was not the end of the journey. It was merely the beginning. It would take a collection of likeminded, unnamed visionaries to determine, now that the capability existed, what is to be done with it and how do we make it commercially or operationally practical. Much work remained before the chapters of America's Helicopter War could be written.

ARMY HELICOPTERS ARE BORN

The Constitution of the United States provides that Congress shall have the power to "… provide for the common defence, to raise and support Armies, and to provide and maintain a Navy."

(Article 1, Section 8)

Inherent in this constitutionally granted responsibility is the authority to procure the equipment necessary for the Army and the Navy to provide for the nation's security. With the creation of the Army Air Corps and, ultimately, the United States Air Force, such powers and responsibilities extended to these services as well. Equipping the armed forces covers a wide array of gear and equipment needs, from the individual to the largest formation of soldiers, marines, sailors, or airmen. The process by which these procurements are made must therefore be sufficiently comprehensive and flexible in considering the variables of the combat environment, enemy threat and capabilities, service member skills and qualifications, companion and complementary weapon systems available, and the size and structure of the employing formation, to name but a few.

Additionally, one must take into consideration the various sources of modern technologies needed to meet military requirements, the underlying research, development, and militarization of those technologies, and the sources of affordable production of the end item within the constraints of a marketplace with a single buyer and limited competition. The relationship among government laboratories, arsenals, academia, and private industry further magnifies the complexities of the defense acquisition process, especially when considering those participants competing for the contract and their often divergent motives.

Noteworthy is the fact that many of the weapons, including the helicopters discussed here, were procured through an acquisition process born of the post-World War II period and modified under successive presidential administrations, each seeking the holy grail—superior technology, enhanced combat capability with overwhelming battlefield advantage, reduction in military manpower requirements, minimal procurement cost, and even lower operating costs.

Further, the specter of the Soviet Union in the post-war period played an influential role over the defense acquisition process. The explosion of an atomic bomb in 1949, and a hydrogen bomb in 1953, by the Soviet Union, its development of long-range strategic bombers and intercontinental ballistic missiles, and the launch of Sputnik in October 1957, gave acquisition a sense of urgency not too dissimilar from that experienced in World War II. These events and developments portended a change in the nature of future conflicts, especially with the Soviet Union. The lead time to prepare for war disappeared. The next war would be a come-as-you-are affair necessitating the availability of sufficient quantities of equipment prior to a conflict. This meant that dispersion and mobility were necessities for victory and survivability. America's new war for national survival helped shape the emerging acquisition process.[1]

For ground operations in such an environment, the Army recognized that it was neither currently equipped nor technologically modernized for such a conflict. It readily concluded that battlefield supremacy is inextricably linked to innovations in research, operational concepts, development, materiel production, and organizational advancement. To accomplish this, Army Combat Developments and Research and Development Systems emerged and offered a coordinated approach for future battlefield solutions.

The Combat Development (CD) System encompassed the Army agencies charged with shaping the future force with regard to new doctrine, new organizations, and new equipment. Further, the direction of the future concept development of the process rested with the United States Continental Army Command (USCONARC). In its initial incarnation, the CD system had broad-ranging responsibility and equally expansive freedom to act in its exploration and evaluation of organization, tactics, and weapons concepts. Later in the lineage of the CD system, the user's representatives and the research and development agents would take on potential solutions to future problems by examining doctrinal, organizational, training, and leadership options. However, not all issues on future battlefields necessitated a material or equipment solution; sometimes modest changes in organization, training, doctrine, etc., could provide an operationally satisfactory answer. Especially during the immediate post-war period when defense budgets were reduced during demobilization, sophisticated material solutions for future warfighting problems could not be afforded. When a material solution was determined to be the best course of action, the first alternative was to see if a product improvement to a weapon system already in the hands of the troops could satisfy the need. Failing that, the Army would set out to initiate a new weapon system development to fulfill the requirement.

When new hardware was determined to be the necessary response to the requirements generated by the concepts for future operations, the Research and Development (R&D) System undertook the efforts to bring such a solution to fruition. Regardless of how superior they might be, Army doctrine, strategy, and tactics are inconsequential if the soldiers do not have the tools to carry them out. Notwithstanding the complex nature of CD, the R&D System required that the Army keep pace with and be aware of advances in science and technology. New weapons for ground forces stem from scientific research and engineering developments that are linked to "… military requirements with the advancing frontier of science and technology."[2] Such an evolution requires a business-like approach to scientific research and the appropriate prioritization for applying vast sums of taxpayer resources to the most promising technologies. The Army's cadre of researchers and their industry partners broach basic, advanced, and applied research as they identify, isolate, and move suitable technologies from their infancy to a level of maturity where they are appropriate for application to systems.

Within USCONARC, the Deputy Chief of Staff for Material Development (MD) exercised staff responsibility for establishing the military characteristics (MC) for systems destined for the field army. As the MD process matured and evolved over time, MC would eventually become known as system requirements, specific performance characteristics that the new weapon system had to be able to perform. The USCONARC Deputy Commanding General supervised the R&D System within the command. In that capacity, he oversaw the service testing of materiel projects by the USCONARC test boards, i.e., Airborne and Electronics, Air Defense, Armor, Artillery, Arctic Testing, Aviation, and Infantry Boards. The Deputy Commanding General also maintained close interaction with his Army staff counterparts, the Deputy Chief of Staff for Combat Developments, and the Chief of Research and Development.

The two-phase processes for Combat Developments, the Combat Development System, and the Research and Development System, represented an ideal approach for moving the Army from the doctrine, concepts, and ideas that had evolved from national policy and national military strategy to service missions and objectives culminating in organizations, techniques, and weapons to meet the resultant warfighting needs. The CD and R&D agencies tailored these ideal systems from concept through hardware development in "practical, useful, reasonable steps."[3]

The key player in the CD process was the Army Ground Forces. The function of the Army Ground Forces in the postwar Army was to develop tactical doctrine, operate much of the service's school system, and conduct field training for units stationed in the United States. In terms of the acquisition process, the Army Ground Forces (renamed the Army Field Forces in 1948) represented the combat arms—infantry, armor, artillery—the "users" of new weapons and other systems. It established the need ("requirement") for the new systems' desired performance characteristics, thus, initiating their development. It also validated requirements for systems under development or already fielded, and carried out extensive testing programs, essentially determining when a new item was ready for standard issue to Army units.

To assist the Army in formalizing its combat development process, the California Institute of Technology received a contract—Project Vista (after the project site, the Vista del Arroyo hotel in Pasadena, California)—which had the objective of identifying tactics, techniques, and equipment, including the use of tactical nuclear weapons that would improve military effectiveness.

The Army implemented Project Vista's recommendation to establish a "combat development group" which, as a result, had long-term consequences for the service's acquisition process. According to the Vista scientists, the Army needed an organization to apply scientific methods of analysis and experimentation in relating new weapons to existing doctrine or tactics or identifying a requirement for a weapon based on new tactical concepts.

The Army's missions and role in the world of aviation, compared with that of the United States Air Force (formerly the Army Air Forces), was decidedly impacted by the post-war separation of the Army Air Forces from the aviation of the ground forces. The internecine rivalry between the independent Air Force and the Army began well before they existed as two distinct services and only intensified afterward. They battled over service roles and missions, the Army's dependence upon the interservice cooperation of the Air Force on the battlefield, and most significantly they fought for scarce dollars for national defense. While all four armed services understood the potential of organic aviation to the war fight, the Air Force and the Army engaged in a prolonged and bitter debate. This dispute would influence the definition of air transportability of troops and, more importantly, the assignment of responsibility for close air support for the Army. The latter aspect would influence the Army's desire for helicopter gunships and aerial rocket artillery.

Through a series of JCS meetings convened by the then Secretary of Defense James Forrestal, the service leaders divided up the national defense functional pie with the Air Force responsible for strategic air warfare and the Navy for control of the seas. The Army became responsible for "land combat and service forces and such aviation and water transport as may be organic therein."[4] With additional functions assigned to each service, the other services were thus dependent upon those with primary responsibility for the related functional support. Once the service responsibilities were delineated, no other service was permitted to develop an organic capability that infringed upon the responsibility of another service. An example was the modification of the Army's intra-theater lift capability wherein later meetings and memoranda of understanding between the Air Force and Army defined Army functional aviation more narrowly to reduce interservice conflict. This set the conditions for Army organic aviation to limit fixed-wing aircraft to fewer than 2,500 pounds and 4,000 pounds or less for helicopters. Such aircraft were intended to provide the Army the ability to improve ground combat capabilities in the forward battle areas. Later modifications eliminated weight constraints, defined functions that organic Army aircraft could and could not perform, and instituted a seventy-mile operational range limit on those aircraft. As the Korean War continued and the Army gained more active operational experience, aircraft weight limits were reinstated with the new fixed-wing limit increased to 5,000 pounds, and the operating range extended to 100 miles. From these machinations emerged the allowable and unallowable Army organic aviation missions. Allowable included missions related to aeromedical evacuation, enemy forward area surveillance, and front line photography. Unallowable included close combat support, assault transport, and reconnaissance, among other missions.

Also embedded in these agreements was the assignment of aircraft procurement responsibilities to the services. The Navy became responsible for procuring aircraft for itself and the Marine Corps. The Air Force, in turn, was assigned the same responsibility for itself and the Army. While the Army Air Forces and the Navy both saw the benefit from helicopters during World War II, the Air Force saw little or no military value in them. As a result, when deciding procurement priorities, Army helicopter procurement actions were either delayed or denied.

The road to the doctrinal considerations of aviation and helicopters, in support of ground forces, was punctuated by numerous fits and starts. One of the earliest known proposals appeared in 1909 from a thesis authored by a Marine Corps Lieutenant Alexander A. Vandergrift entitled "Aviation, The Cavalry of the Future" written to fulfill the Marine School of Application requirements.[5]

General Vandergrift, while the earliest, was not alone among forward-looking Marine Corps leaders to recognize the potential for helicopters within the Corps. In 1946, a distinguished Marine Corps joint force commander and experienced aviator, Lieutenant General Roy A. Geiger, witnessed Operation CROSSROADS, the atomic bomb tests conducted at Bikini Atoll. Considering the devastating power of the explosions he observed and his World War II experiences as an amphibious force commander, General Geiger reflected on the weapon's implications for amphibious warfare. He opined that the World War II-style amphibious landings would not be feasible against a nuclear-armed adversary.[6] He wrote a letter to the commandant, General Alexander Vandergrift, the same 1909 aviation visionary, wherein he states, "It is trusted that Marine Corps Headquarters will consider this a very serious and urgent matter and will use its most competent officers in finding a solution to develop the technique of conducting amphibious operations in the atomic age."[7] The resultant blue-ribbon panel, led by then Major General Lemuel C. Shepherd, Jr. concluded that vehicles such as "carrier-based helicopters presented the only viable possibilities for an amphibious attack in an atomic war,"[8] thus giving rise to the vertical lift concept of assault helicopters for rapid movement of troops ashore.

In 1954, General James M. Gavin, as the Army's Chief of Research and Development, sharply focused the Army needs for aviation assets on a broader scale than the resources used during the Korean War. In an article, "Cavalry, and I Don't Mean Horses," that appeared in the April 1954 issue of *Harpers*, he espoused that the ability to perform the traditional cavalry functions of reconnaissance, screening, and blocking had vanished in modern armies due to reliance on road-bound motor vehicles, which in the rough country could be easily ambushed or taken in the flank by light infantry, as was witnessed during the recently concluded war in Korea. Gavin proposed that the Army consider a modern version of the cavalry whereby aircraft would transport mechanized forces and light armored fighting vehicles. His vision included roles for aircraft or gliders in the ground commander's new three-dimensional battlespace. It was widely held that such a reinvented air cavalry capability should be a high priority for the Army, especially in the environment of the anticipated nuclear battlefield. He cast the end of his article onto the future battlefield, one dominated by tactical nuclear weapons. He concluded that the only countermeasure to such weapons was the significant reduction of troop density in the battlespace yet with the simultaneous capability to rapidly mass those troops at the opportune time over the extended distances involved. He closed his article by noting that all that he espoused is possible and that the essential mobility differential "is within our grasp, fortunately, in the air vehicles now being developed—assault transports, light utility planes, helicopters."[9]

In the mid-fifties, the Army was obsessed with maintaining its military relevance in a global strategic and tactical nuclear weapons environment. Already encouraged by the Project Vista vision that tactical nuclear weapons could bring success on the plains of Central Europe against the armored might of the Warsaw Pact, the Army began considering how to use them. The Eisenhower Administration had already dispatched the Army's 280-mm "Atomic Cannon" to South Korea to encourage China's acceptance of the cease-fire on the Korean peninsula. Soon there were other, less cumbersome, and more flexible tactical nuclear weapons in the Army inventory. The reduced size of these weapons and their launchers and the necessary battlefield dispersion of American ground forces crucial to avoiding the battlefield effects of these weapons opened new opportunities and requirements for Army helicopters.

The Chief of Research and Development initiated a plan to develop Army guidance for aviation for the decade of the 1960s. In October 1959, Army Study Requirements (ASRs) were prepared to describe for industry broad development objectives for light observation, manned surveillance, and tactical transport aircraft which the Army presented to industry on December 1, 1959. In response, on February 1, 1960,[10] forty-five companies submitted 119 design concepts proposing solutions to the ASRs;[11] they were a variety of helicopters, compound helicopters, autogiros, and fixed-wing aircraft representing short takeoff and landing (STOL) and vertical takeoff and landing (VTOL) types.[12]

Between 1960–1962, the political and military realities of South Vietnam necessitated the Army's evaluation of the helicopter requirements and tactics necessary for the burgeoning conflict. In 1960–1961, CONARC began studying and formulating a plan for a single Army airmobile program. On January 15, 1960, Lieutenant General Gordon B. Rogers, deputy commander of CONARC, was appointed by Army Chief of Staff General Lyman L. Lemnitzer, as chair of the Army Aircraft Requirements Review Board, hence its subrogate, the Rogers Board. The board was tasked to consider the Army Aircraft Development Plan and industry proposals. This was the first time that most of the major aircraft companies took official notice of the aviation potential within the Army.

The primary purpose of the requirements review was "to upgrade Army aviation to meet any tactical contingencies like bushfire wars or what would later be referred to as low- to mid-intensity level conflicts."[13] The board's direction was to assess and recommend, as a matter of priority, a program plan to satisfy Army requirements for light observation aircraft (LOA) during the period 1960–1970, and which could be initiated with the research, development, test, and experimentation funds available in the fiscal year 1961.[14] The board further evaluated feasible courses of action to improve the Army's surveillance and tactical transport capabilities. In turn, it offered a program plan including proposed procurement with anticipated costs and quantities by year for current and future aircraft types.[15] Following a month of technical and operational evaluation of the concepts, the Rogers Board reconvened from February 28 to March 6 to evaluate the Army Aircraft Development Plan, assess aircraft types and requirements, procurement, and funding for the same.[16]

The board recommended that the UH-1 *Iroquois* helicopter become the primary helicopter in the active-duty inventory. The Army also moved forward with the CH-47 *Chinook* cargo helicopter procurement instead of the current aircraft and helicopters such as the L-19, H-13, CH-21, and H-23. Both proposed helicopters would perform yeoman's service during their active operational engagement in Southeast Asia. It was further recommended that additional scientific effort be focused on assessing "sensory devices, data link, and intelligence processing."[17] The board also offered two lesser-known recommendations: the first was to replace each aircraft model at least every ten years or sooner if operational requirements or technological advances warranted,[18] and the second called for a joint DA and CONARC study to determine whether the concept of air fighting units was practical and if an experimental unit should be activated to test its feasibility.

Following the above recommendations, Major General Hamilton H. Howze, a member of the Rogers Board, submitted a significant addendum to the board report "The Requirements for Air Fighting Units." He observed that the latest operational studies merely assigned or attached additional aircraft to combat units that substantially benefited unit operational effectiveness only by enhancing the units' ability to carry out their traditional missions. He envisioned and proposed the development of combat units whose tactical employment would maximize the advantages of the mobility and flexibility of light aircraft. These aircraft would transport unit personnel and equipment and provide direct fire support, artillery fire adjustment, command, control and communications, security, reconnaissance, and supply benefits.

General Howze's addendum recommended forming an experimental air cavalry unit within one of the Army's airborne divisions. He acknowledged that while this concept would be costly, he viewed this development as a vital requirement in the evolution of a modern army in the emerging environment of a strategic nuclear strategy of flexible response and guerrilla wars in the Third World. General Howze's addendum recommended forming an experimental air cavalry unit within one of the Army's airborne divisions. The combination of the Army acquisition objectives for aircraft and the existing aircraft inventories were sufficient to permit establishing the proposed experimental unit. The recommendation and the others in the Rogers Board report moved forward and were set into motion. The significance of the recommendation and its subsequent experimentation would significantly impact another effort that was initiated two years later.

On October 18, 1961, a special mission dispatched by President Kennedy arrived in Saigon.[19] It was charged with exploring all options for American involvement in Vietnam, from limited troop deployment to full intervention. The two-man team consisted of the President's Special Military Representative Maxwell Taylor and the Deputy Assistant for National Security Affairs Walt Rostow. In his post-mission final report to the president, Taylor proposed modest troop increases to include intelligence personnel and advisors to reform the ARVN command and control system. He was also critical of the French-style static warfare, arguing for the "deployment of helicopters, seen as the indispensable ingredient for introducing mobility to the battlefield."[20] Upon review and deliberation by the National Security Council (NSC), President Kennedy rejected the mission's full recommendation except for the deployment of helicopters and a modest increase in troops.[21]

On April 19, 1962, Secretary of Defense Robert McNamara sent a memorandum to the Army directing it to conduct a study on the tactical mobility of Army ground forces with specific instruction to include helicopter air mobility and heliborne close air support (CAS). The secretary was so detailed in his directions that in a second memorandum, he designated eight Army officers whom he wanted to be included in the study and six specific areas to take in the study effort. The result was the establishment of the U.S. Army Tactical Mobility Requirements Board, established and chaired by Lieutenant General Hamilton H. Howze, Commanding General of the XVIII Airborne Corps. The defense secretary was decidedly interested in more substantial Army innovation in its consideration of the options and opportunities for the use of helicopters beyond an alternative form of transportation. Secretary McNamara wanted the Army study effort to be a "bold new look at air mobility" and "divorced from traditional viewpoints and past policies."[22]

As it was popularly known, the Howze Board convened at Fort Bragg, North Carolina, that same year. From its studies, analyses, and tests, the Board concluded that helicopters could indeed provide the air mobility assets needed to increase the force effectiveness of ground combat troops.[23] From the Howze Board also emerged recommendations for broad changes in the Army's aviation program and force structure based on air assault formations equipped with armed helicopters, fixed-wing fire support, and other aircraft.[24] Specifically, its recommendation called for a five-year program to transition the Army to a force that was the most responsive to the identified requirements for increased combat effectiveness. The proposal also called for a force structure of eleven Reorganization Objective Army Divisions (ROAD), five air assault divisions, three air cavalry combat brigades, and five air transport brigades in addition to other combat, combat support, and combat service support units by the end of 1967.[25] With the conclusions in hand, the Board further recommended that the Army field an air cavalry brigade "to fight brushfire wars."[26]

While somewhat supportive of the board's latter recommendation, the Department of Defense decided that the Army should field and test an air assault division complete with an organic helicopter battalion. The creation of the 11th Air Assault (Test) Division at Fort Benning, Georgia, in February 1963, followed with the specific intent of testing all aspects of air mobility, and was to undertake a three-phase test program.

As 1964 ended, the 11th Air Assault Division convincingly demonstrated the combat utility of an airmobile division in the Army force structure. In January

1965, the JCS recommended, with the Air Force chief of staff dissenting, cancellation of the Air Force's tests for new concepts for USAF close support of ground forces. In March 1965, the JCS recommended, again with the Air Force dissenting, approval of the Army request to add an airmobile division to its force structure by converting the 11th Air Assault Division (Test).[27] In June 1965, Secretary Robert McNamara authorized the 1st Cavalry Division (Airmobile) organization, which was activated on July 1, 1965, from the resources from the 11th Air Assault and the 2nd Infantry Divisions. It was subsequently alerted for deployment to South Vietnam.[28] Deployment began in August when the division departed from Mobile, Alabama, and Jacksonville, Florida, aboard an aircraft carrier and three transport ships for the twenty-one-day voyage to Vietnam. Before the end of August, the division's advanced party was in Vietnam preparing for the main body's arrival. By October 3, the entire division closed at its base area at An Khe in the Central Highlands and prepared for combat.[29]

With the organization of the airmobile division, the Army completed an almost quarter-century of reviewing and reorganizing its division force structure with each change including, except for the last, an incremental change in the aircraft, both fixed and rotary winged, that were part of the unit. The graph below is a histogram of those divisional structures and the change in aircraft density within each.

Aircraft Density Changes in the Evolving Army Division, 1939–1968[30]

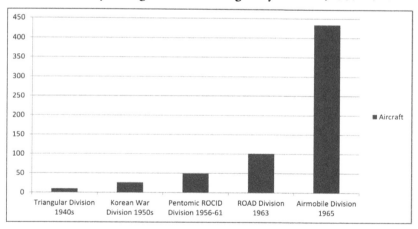

The following table illustrates the then-current and Vietnam War-era Army helicopters that emerged from the studies mentioned above and which saw combat service in Vietnam and are covered here. They were named for Native American Tribes or warrior chiefs and will be included in the chapters that follow. The twelfth Vietnam War Army helicopter, the AH-1 Cobra, is not included in the list because it does not meet the criteria of being named after a Native American tribe or war chief.

The Army's Vietnam War Helicopters
(Those with Native American Names)

Helicopter	Native American Name	First Flight	Production Period	Quantity
OH-13	*Sioux*	12/8/1945	1945–1973	2,407
OH-23	*Raven*	11/11/1947	1948–1965	2,000
UH-19	*Chickasaw*	11/10/1949	1949–1961	1,281
CH-21	*Shawnee*	4/11/1952	1947–1959	707
CH-37	*Mojave*	12/18/1953	1953–1960	153
UH-34	*Choctaw*	3/8/1954	1953–1970	1,820
UH-1	*Iroquois*	10/22/1956	1955–1987	16,000
CH-47	*Chinook*	9/21/1961	1962–Present	1,180
CH-54	*Tarhe*	5/9/1962	1961–1975	92
OH-58	*Kiowa*	12/8/1962	1961–2007	2,200
OH-6	*Cayuse*	2/27/1963	1962–Present	1,420

IDENTIFYING ARMY HELICOPTERS

With the technological, engineering, design, testing, production, and fielding aspects of a new aircraft weapon system well in hand, attention would turn to another part of the weapon—its identity and nomenclature. Accompanying this was the consideration of its common name, the name by which it would be officially referred to in public releases and other documents as a ready reference. The formal terminology by which a military aircraft is known is determined by a specific service or joint policy directive, and after an informal process start, the common naming process would be reduced to a written Army regulation. The evolution of the two different naming conventions are discussed in this chapter.

Aircraft initially acquired by the Army would carry the manufacturer's designation. Before the First World War, some airplanes in the inventory were used for observation purposes. More specialized aircraft were acquired during the war, but although a more precise aircraft designation system was needed, it had to wait until after the War.

In 1919, the Army Air Corps (AAC) introduced an aircraft designation system that assigned a Roman numeral, one through fifteen, for each aircraft type. Each digit was further associated with a two or three-letter abbreviation for the kind of aircraft. With the Naval Appropriations Bill signed on March 3, 1915, President Woodrow Wilson created the National Advisory Committee on Aeronautics (NACA) to research the airplane's military application and seek improvements in airplane technology. NACA instituted a series of letter designations to supplement the type series and, by 1924, it would add eight more letter designations to the AAC aircraft designation system. Those aircraft designations are presented as follows:

1919–1924 Army Air Corps Aircraft Identification System[1]

Type	Identifier	Type Name
I	PW	Pursuit, Water-cooled
II	PN	Pursuit, Night
III	PA	Pursuit, Air-cooled
IV	PG	Pursuit Ground Attack
V	TP	Two-seat Pursuit

(Continued)

11

Type	Identifier	Type Name
VI	GA	Ground Attack
VII	IL	Infantry Liaison
VIII	NO	Night Observation
IX	AO	Artillery Observation
X	CO	Corps Observation
XI	DB	Day Bombardment
XII	NBS	Night Bombardment—Short Range
XIII	NBL	Night Bombardment—Long Short Range
XIV	TA	Trainer, Air-cooled
XV	TW	Trainer, Water-cooled
—	A	Ambulance
—	G	Glider
—	LB	Light Bomber
—	M	Messenger
—	PS	Alert Pursuit (Special)
—	R	Racer
—	S	Seaplane
—	T	Trainer

The revised Engineering Division system was replaced in 1924 by the United States Army Air Service aircraft designation system built around seven specific identifiers: status prefix, mission modifier prefex, mission letter, model number, sub-type, block number, production facility code. This designation system was used by the U.S. Army Air Corps, the U.S. Army Air Forces, and the independent U.S. Air Force, as well as for those aircraft remaining in the U.S. Army after 1947, with some minor changes until 1962, when a unified tri-service designation system for all services came into effect.

Further progress was made in developing an Army aviation identification system with the publication of Army Regulation 705-42 in 1956, whereby the Army, not the Air Force, would be responsible for the designation of all future Army aircraft.[2] This Army system was initially used to designate some of the Army's Vietnam War aircraft until the unified tri-service designation system for all services came into effect.

The Tri-Service Designation System was officially introduced on September 18, 1962. It provided a unified designation for almost all aircraft, whether operated by the United States Air Force, United States Navy, United States Marine Corps, United States Army, or United States Coast Guard and included the following identifiers: status prefix, modified mission, basic mission, vehicle type, designation number, series letter.

Called the Model Design Series (MDS), all military aircraft were given a two-part alpha-numeric symbol or designation based on what was in use by the U.S. Air Force. The first part of the designator was a letter describing the type of aircraft in question. The second component was a number designating the model of the craft. The MDS designations for aircraft types include those below. If a letter followed the model number, it referred to an improved model type.[3]

MDS Aircraft Type Identification

Designator	Aircraft Type	Designator	Aircraft Type
A	Attack	N	Test—Permanent
B	Bomber	O	Observation
C	Cargo	P	Patrol
D	Drone	Q	Drone Target
E	Electronic	R	Reconnaissance
F	Fighter	S	Anti-Submarine
G	Glider	T	Trainer
H	Search and Rescue (SAR)	U	Utility
I	Not Used	V	VIP
J	Test - Temporary	W	Weather
K	Tanker	X	Experimental
L	Polar	Y	Prototype
M	Multi-Mission	Z	Lighter-Than-Air

The system consisted of up to six alpha-numeric characters as designated by the following: status prefix, modified mission, basic mission, vehicle type, designation number, series letter. At present, the system is codified in Department of Defense Publication 4120.15-L, *Designating and Naming Military Aerospace Vehicles.*

In this way, there is a common understanding of what a particular aircraft is intended to do, the missions it can be expected to perform, and its relative newness in terms of modifications and upgrades. While this system has considerable utility among mission planners, aviators, maintainers, logisticians, etc., it is complex, cumbersome, often incomprehensible, and of limited utility in communicating information to other national security constituencies and the American people. Thus, while an aircraft has an official identity, having a common name is highly useful.

The six-digit alphanumeric designation for an aircraft or helicopter is quite cumbersome but of the greatest utility when conversing in technical details or for operational planning. But for informal conversation and routine dialogue, it offers an extraordinary specificity that is unnecessary. Similarly, in the jargon of airmen, sailors, marines, and soldiers, shorthand monikers for their aircraft will always be there. In communications with the media and the taxpaying public, a readily identifiable, easily understandable, and relatable name is extremely beneficial for establishing and maintaining the civil-military relationship. Hence, the armed services determined that common names were desirable.

The procedure for assigning popular or common names to major items of Army equipment is difficult to trace with any precision and certainty. Major General Hamilton H. Howze is credited with starting the convention of naming Army helicopters after Native American tribes because he found the names suggested by the aircraft manufacturers to be without character. The Bell H-13, which had already been in service since 1948, was renamed *Sioux* at his suggestion. Howze perhaps suggested the name as a tribute to his father, Major General Robert Lee Howze, who had been awarded the Medal of Honor while serving as a second lieutenant with the Sixth Cavalry Regiment during an engagement with the Brulé Sioux on January 1, 1891, along the frozen White River in South Dakota.

Retired Army Major General Robert R. Williams, in a letter of October 20, 1988, confirms that "the source and authority for naming Army aircraft after Indian tribes [...] is Hamilton H. Howze. General Williams explains that when he [General Howze] was Director of Army Aviation [1956–1958], a meeting occurred in his office, and the subject of names for Army aircraft came up. The group decided that they should be named after Indian tribes."[4] Others like Bob Mitchell, curator at the Army Aviation Museum in Fort Rucker, Alabama, suggest that General Howze "envisioned the helicopter as a fast, mobile, stealthy machine on the field of battle using terrain and vegetation to an advantage similar to the Warrior Tribes' and thus Native American Tribal names were indeed appropriate."[5]

The Army's helicopters and some fixed-wing aircraft bear names that reflect the courageous warriors who, it must not be forgotten, bravely fought in the United States Army. Further, acceptable names for the Army must promote confidence in the abilities of the helicopter or plane; they cannot sacrifice dignity, and they must foster an aggressive spirit.

Ultimately the Army policy for assigning popular names to significant items of equipment was assembled into Army Regulations (AR), with one of the earliest being AR 705–14, October 31, 1963. That document was superseded on April 4, 1969, by AR 70–28, *Assigning Popular Names to Major Items of Equipment*, which spelled out the policies, responsibilities, criteria, and categories for the selection, coordination, and approval of popular names which may be assigned only to major equipment items. While the Army did not deem it mandatory to give popular names to equipment, it was encouraged; such names were not only meant to reflect "the functional characteristics" of the major equipment item but also the Army's "progress toward modernization of its concepts of warfare."[6]

For all major equipment items, except aircraft, the popular name was to be assigned at the earliest possible time following the Department of the Army's approval of the project for engineering or operational systems development initiation. However, popular names for aircraft were not assigned until "the time the aircraft enter[ed] the production phase or ha[d] immediate prospects of going into production."[7]

The commanding general of the U.S. Army Aviation Missile Command (AMCOM) at Redstone Arsenal, Alabama, was responsible for setting into motion the process of determining a popular name for Army helicopters and fixed-wing aircraft. A list of possible one-word names was maintained from a list provided to AMCOM by the Bureau of Indian Affairs, and at the appropriate time, the commanding general selected five Native American names from it based on "the sound, the history, and the relationship of the name to the mission of the helicopter."[8] When the regulation was changed in 1976, the materiel developer had the responsibility of proposing three common names ranked in priority and submit them to the commander of U.S. Army Materiel Development and Readiness Command.[9]

The chief of Research and Development within the Materiel Development and Readiness Command ensured that the proposed popular names were appropriate and met the criteria of AR 70-28 and that there were no objections from within the Army staff. The chief made the final decision and approved the common name for the helicopter or aircraft. Approved popular names for aircraft were then forwarded to the U.S. Air Force Aeronautical Systems Division of the Engineering Standard Directorate at Wright-Patterson Air Force Base. The Department of Defense unit is responsible for officially registering the names of all aircraft used by the military. It also prints a list of the names in a publication called *Model Designation of Military Aircraft, Rockets and Guided Missiles*.

Certain criteria are followed for popular names and the functional characteristics and their relationship to the modernization of Army concepts of warfare.[10] Proposed names should appeal to the imagination; they should suggest an aggressive spirit and confidence in the system's capabilities without sacrificing dignity. The name should also imply mobility, agility, flexibility, firepower, and endurance when the characteristics are relatable to the system. Common name appropriateness will be judged from the viewpoint of tactical application rather than the source or method of manufacture of the item. When a person's name is proposed for use, it too should connote an association with the qualities and criteria specified elsewhere in AR 70-28. Major equipment items with popular names approved or in common use before the publication of AR 70-28 were not to be changed to conform to the new regulation. Hence, the O-1 popular name *Bird Dog* was not changed to a Native American tribe and chief. In 1988, AR 70-28 was superseded by Army Regulation 70-1, *Army Acquisition Policy*.

Since the selected name for an aircraft will be used throughout the aviation and defense industry, in the public domain, as well as within the service, the Army rightfully also seeks a determination that there are no legal objections or encumbrances to the use of any of the proposed names and to obtain registration of that identity or trademark. For aircraft, the commanding general, U.S. Army Materiel

Command, is responsible for submitting the trademark registration application for the proposed names to the Trademark Division of the United States Patent Office to determine using the name.

The Lanham (Trademark) Act (Public Law 79-489, 60 Stat. 427, as codified at 15 U.S.C. § 1051 et seq. (15 United States Code Chapter 22)) is the primary federal trademark statute in the United States. It defines federal trademark protection and registration rules and grants the United States Patent and Trademark Office (USPTO) administrative authority over trademark registration. The law, named for Representative Fritz G. Lanham of Texas, was passed on July 5, 1946.

To be eligible for trademark protection, a proposed trademark must be used in commerce and be distinctive. The United States uses "common law" trademark rights acquired automatically when a business uses a name or logo in commerce and are enforceable in state courts. Marks registered with the U.S. Patent and Trademark Office are afforded more protection in federal courts than unregistered marks. However, both registered and unregistered trademarks are granted some federal protection under the Lanham Act. In this instance, it would be the trademark registration by the Army of a particular rotary-wing aircraft with its associated Native American name. In filing an application for trademark registration for a specific Native American name for one of its helicopters, the Army is branding the major system as its own; that is, the Army is registering a word, phrase, slogan, symbol, device, or design or a combination of two or more of these identifiers which distinguish the Army as the owner of the goods (helicopter). The trademark differentiates the helicopter's mark from the mark used by another owner.

While probably not as significant to the Army as to an entrepreneur, a primary register trademark registration serves as nationwide constructive notice of ownership, and use of the mark and a registered mark may achieve incontestable status after five years of continuous use, which enhances the owner's rights by eliminating some defenses to claims of infringement. Researching the trademark registration of the eleven Vietnam War Native American-named helicopters was not as straightforward as the process suggests. The Army used an abbreviated methodology to follow a previously approved registration to carry their helicopter marks forward. On September 22, 1958, the Army notified the U.S. Patent Office's assistant commissioner that it, following DoD directives and with DoD approval, named fifteen aircraft, including eight helicopters, with Indian names or terms. It requested that the names be registered and "that registration of names for any product which could be confusingly associated therewith be denied."[11] It asked that the USPTO follow the registration model used for the August 20, 1957, request to register "Medicare" (Serial Number 89000008) made by the Executive Director of the Department of the Army Federal Symbol Office for the Dependent's Medical Care.[12] The Army also requested that notes associated with the registration application request be placed in the Trademark Search Room. The table below summarizes the Patent and Trademark Office's action on the Army's registration request.

Vietnam War Helicopter Trademark Registered[13]

Helicopter	Filing Date	Serial Number	Submitted Mark (TYPED DRAWING)
H-13	9/22/1958	89000012	SIOUX
H-19	9/22/1958	89000013	CHICKASAW
H-21	9/22/1958	89000014	SHAWNEE
H-23	9/22/1958	89000015	RAVEN
H-34	9/22/1958	89000016	CHOCTAW
H-37	9/22/1958	89000017	MOHAVE
HU-1ABF (H-40)	9/22/1958	89000018	IROQUOIS
HC-1	9/22/1958	89000021	CHINOOK

Further research at the U.S. Patent and Trademark Office and the U.S. Army Office of the Staff Judge Advocate failed to produce additional documents to reflect the request to register the remaining three Vietnam War Native American named helicopters, OH-6 *Cayuse*, CH-54 *Tarhe*, and the OH-58 *Kiowa*.

With the exception of these few shortcuts, the Army's naming regimen did not change during the post-Vietnam War helicopter development period. According to former Army acquisition officials, now retired, the Army, Bureau of Indian Affairs, and USPTO jointly coordinated the naming process for the RAH-66 and the UH-60.[14] Although there was no hesitation by the BIA about approving the names *Comanche* or *Black Hawk*, the trademark applications necessitated a thorough review from among the existing "live" trademarks.[15] In the case of the Comanche application, there was the potential for conflict with the variously spelled Piper "Commanche" or "Comanche" aircraft. In the case of *Black Hawk*, which was initially registered as "Blackhawk" by United Aircraft Corporation on March 20, 1973, and, among other marks, the Blackhawk hockey franchise was created in 1926. Then on March 28, 1978, when United Technologies amended the trademark registration to become Black Hawk, there was the matter of "Black Hawk" meat products produced by Rath Packing Company of Blackhawk County, Iowa. Apparently, in neither case was there a sufficient threat to commerce by the helicopter applications for them to be denied.

The Department of Defense worked to standardize and coordinate the designation and naming of aerospace vehicles, including helicopters, and in 1971 the department promulgated the Department of Defense Directive (DODD) 4120.15 *Designating and Naming Military Aerospace Vehicles*. While the military departments are responsible for assigning popular names to their military aerospace vehicles, the Air Force is charged with the responsibility of setting the MDS designator to all military aerospace vehicles, coordinating the assignment of popular names to all aerospace vehicles, and annually publishing a list of approved MDS designators and names for aerospace vehicles in a single DoD-wide source document.[16]

As aircraft manufacturer Eurocopter (now Airbus Helicopters, Inc.) neared completion of the military version of their EC-145 for the U.S. Army, the program manager undertook the designation and naming of the aircraft, and from the joint MDS process, the helicopter officially became the UH-72A in December 2006. Recognizing the non-arms-bearing missions of the aircraft, Army officials sought an appropriately fitting Native American name from a candidate poll of three: Crow, Lakota, and Cherokee. The Lakota, a peaceful, non-aggressive, horseback riding, buffalo-hunting people, was one of the seven tribes in the Sioux Nation, was selected. Upon notification of the selection to the Bureau of Indian Affairs, the Army was instructed that it would require the approval of the majority of the Sioux Nation council members.[17] With the majority vote in favor of the naming, the UH-72A became the *Lakota*.

So significant was the new helicopter to the tribe that they agreed to the naming and participated in the ceremony in Columbus, Mississippi, on December 11, 2006, wherein the Army accepted the first production aircraft. General Richard A. Cody, Vice Chief of Staff of the Army, and Joe Redcloud, Chief of Staff of the Oglala Sioux Tribe, Lakota Nation, officiated at the ceremony.[18] Then again, on February 5, 2006, when the Army marked the inception of the *Lakota* fleet during ceremonies at Redstone Arsenal, key members of the Rosebud Sioux participated, including the tribal council president, Rodney Bordeaux.[19]

This event, and more generally, Native American support for the Army's naming policy, was not unique but rather a continuation of Indigenous backing of the practice through lending their name to U.S. military endeavors. An earlier example is the White Mountain Apache representatives, who have participated in the dedication of every version of the AH-64 *Apache* since its initial delivery on September 9, 1983. When the *Apache* Block III aircraft was dedicated in 2011, a White Mountain Apache official, speaking of the helicopter, said it "is a reminder to the world of Apache history and the Apache's ongoing place in it."[20]

Rosebud Sioux of the Lakota Nation participates in the UH-72 fleet inception ceremony. (Courtesy of the U.S. Army.)

THE NATIVE AMERICAN
WAR EXPERIENCE

"We honor our veterans for their bravery and because by seeing death on the battlefield they truly know the greatness of life."[1]

One cannot reflect upon any period in American history, especially American military history, without crossing paths with Native Americans serving in or alongside the military, though not always in support of those who colonized the United States. Since the arrival of Europeans in North America, the continent's Indigenous peoples have taken up arms in the conflicts on the continent.

Dr. Francis Flavin, a prominent historian of Native American history and culture, as well as a historian of the western American frontier, writes, "It can be argued that no character in the pantheon of American historical figures has been cast and recast, interpreted, reinterpreted, and misinterpreted more frequently than the American Indian."[2] His observation acknowledges that historians and students of American Indians have tended to view them through the lens of their own biases. Thus the view and story are not uniformly the same. An additional complication to Native American history is the absence of substantial written records. Tribal histories and legends are passed from generation to generation by song, dance, and elder narrations. Oral histories perished with time; diseases, wars, forced relocations, and starvation eliminated the population and the historians who were the guardians of their past. As a result, awareness of Native American history was usually through the European perspective of the trappers, traders, missionaries, and explorers who were in contact with the dispersed tribes of North America. And while their writings were about the Native Americans, they were not necessarily recorded from their perspective.

Historians thus face the challenge of assessing whether one historical account is more correct than another due to the absence of any one universally accepted source of truth. However it is collectively accepted that America's Native Indians were a proud people who were aggressive and cunning in their warrior skills and the defense of their land and people. From these warrior traits and experiences, we have gained an appreciation for their battlefield capabilities and grown the desire to emulate them and instill such traits among non-Indian soldiers. Our military has exploited their warrior spirit in the tactics and techniques it uses, their languages resilience, the fear that their appearance inspires, and the fearfulness their very tribal names instill.

Even before they were the United States, the Indigenous peoples of the region of the thirteen colonies participated in conflicts with other nations. In early battles with European interests, tribal nations would often be known to even split their loyalties. From the European viewpoint, the Native American warrior was not a soldier. Despite this perspective he was adept at employing complex tactics and comfortable operating within a quasi-military organization. The warrior was agnostic about waging war for terrain; he was motivated by the imposition of his will upon his enemies. His objective was achieved if his enemy realized that he could not transit the tribe's land with impunity or was obligated to relocate elsewhere.[3]

Native American history is replete with evidence of the warrior's capacity for savagery, but cruelty was not imposed for its own sake. Native Americans were aware of the harsh and unforgiving aspects of the natural world in which their daily lives were entwined, intimately acquainted with nature's law of order. It is the strong who survive, and in following that aspect of natural law, strong Indigenous tribes had the option to follow the warpath or live in peace, while lesser tribes did not enjoy such possibilities.

Russell F. Weigley, in his work on the history of the United States Army, aptly describes the character and nature of combat by Native Americans in his discussion of the arrival of regular European military forces in the new world and their encounters with the local inhabitants: "they were skillful in the ambush and hit-and-run raid in the forest and were hardly sufficiently foolish to abandon their resulting advantages for a mode of combat in which they would not have had a chance. [...] The Indians saw nothing wrong in employing stealth, trickery, and ruthlessness."[4]

The military strategy of America's Indigenous peoples was focused on weakening their adversary's will to engage in combat and upon his economic capabilities.[5] Native Americans achieved such objectives through raids and ambush vice assaults on European forts and settler fortified settlements, which were costly in lives and equipment and often ineffective. The tribal warriors preferred instead to isolate the fort or settlement while making the surrounding environs extremely dangerous for their enemy to venture into. Blockading the encampment allowed the Indians to lay siege to it.

In addition to the sieges and war party engagements, Native Americans predominantly engaged in attacks on relatively weak and minimally defended targets such as farms and small settlements, which today are soft targets. While there was no military significance to such undertakings, the Indian warriors wanted to demonstrate to their adversaries that the region was inhospitable and unwelcoming. If they remained, they would likely not be able to sustain themselves.

The fear spawned among the settlers was frequently sufficient to cause them to abandon their settlement or farm, or made them fearful of working their land and venturing out to hunt for game. While some Europeans dwelt within the confines of their protective fortresses, if they could not harvest their crops or hunt for furs from which to gain income, there was little point for them to remain on the frontier. Therefore, it was often sufficient for the Native American warriors to make the land untenable to attain dominance and victory over European interlopers. The strategic imperative for the Indigenous population was "territorial control [...] rather than capturing ground" whether the enemy was European settlers or other Indian tribes.[6] The desired outcome was the freedom of action and opportunity over any given territory.

During the American Revolution, the Oneida and Tuscarora tribes, unlike the other tribes of the Iroquois Confederacy, supported the American colonists and remained steadfast in their commitments. George Washington noted the potential of Native Americans helping the colonists when he reported to the Continental Congress that they could "be made of excellent use as scouts and light troops."[7] The other tribes of the Iroquois Confederacy, the Seneca, Mohawk, Cayuga, and Onondaga, took up the British cause. In the lead-up to the Revolution, Native American tribes emulated their Bostonian patriot brethren in hosting tea-related events. In March 1774, His Majesty Oknookotunkogog, king of the Narraganset Tribe of Indians, destroyed over a score of tea chests belonging to a New England merchant because they bore the hated tax seal.[8] About the same time, the New York Mohawks discovered a consignment of tea for New York City merchants, which they promptly committed to the saltwater of the harbor. November of the same year, the local tribes burned the tea cargo of the ship *Greyhound* in Greenwich, New Jersey.

With the engagement of the Iroquois Confederacy on one side or another in the American War for Independence, the conflict, at least for them, was not only for the determination of freedom and liberty in the colonies but also as a civil war within their nation. For the Iroquois Confederacy, the American Revolution led to its ultimate disbandment.

By war's end, the Continental Army's Native American warriors comprised 2.2 percent of the force and more than two and three-quarters times the 2,000-man Indigenous force authorized by the Continental Congress in 1775.

With the Treaty of Paris and his inauguration as the first president of the United States, George Washington focused on the new republic's critical issues. Among them was the massive westward surge of American settlers into Indian country, whose flood gates were opened wide by the defeat of the British. With the peace, the Native American population was forced to deal with a nation that "evinced increasing hostility to tribal survival, autonomy, and land rights."[9] Their participation in future continental wars would be motivated as much by "an attempt to retain or even regain tribal autonomy"[10] and to hold on to tribal land.

The newly ratified Constitution created a government that committed itself to a policy which intended "to avoid Indian removal at almost any cost."[11] So significant was the Indian policy that President George Washington, Secretary of State Thomas Jefferson,[12] and Secretary of War Henry Knox personally engaged themselves to address it. The three, from the outset, were resolute in their commitment to treating the Indian question as a matter of foreign policy because "independent tribes of Indians ought to be considered as foreign nations, not as the subjects of any particular states" and "Indians being the prior occupants of the rights of the soil [...]. To dispossess them [...] would be a gross violation of the Fundamental Laws of Nature and of that distributive Justice which is the glory of a nation."[13] While lofty aspirations, the triumvirate recognized that ultimately the resolution, regardless of the moral considerations, intentions, and treaty provisions, was vested with the settlers coursing into Indian Territory.

By the summer of 1789, an Indian policy for the United States emerged whereby the conquest theory was abandoned in favor of a series of treaties between equals to be negotiated "on principles consistent with the national justice and dignity of the United States."[14] Terms of such treaties were to be binding on all signatories "in perpetuity and both the power and honor of the federal government would be pledged to their enforcement."[15] If required, it was also envisioned that Army soldiers would be garrisoned along the boundaries of Indian Territory to oppose migration and expel any settlers who managed to cross the border.

In August 1789, the new administration decided upon the Creek Nation[16] as the initial prospect for these treaties because other regions were on the brink of erupting into open warfare between Indigenous people and trespassing settlers. The Creek Nation was thought optimal because it approximated a pan-Indian confederation that included the Upper and Lower Creeks and Cherokee, Chickasaw, and Choctaw under the titular leadership of a single chieftain, Alexander McGillivray. In May 1790, President Washington conveyed an offer for McGillivray to come to New York, then the nation's capital, to conclude a treaty ratified with the signature of Washington and McGillivray as co-equals.

The Treaty of New York created an Indian protectorate for the Creek Nation that included what are now western Georgia, eastern Tennessee, northern Florida, Alabama, and eastern Mississippi. Of this territory, the United States "pledged to protect Creek Country from all encroachment by state governments and white settlers."[17] The Senate ratified the treaty on August 7, 1790, by 15-4.[18]

In less than two years, all prospects of an enduring peace with the Native Americans disappeared. In July 1792, McGillivray concluded the Treaty of New Orleans with the Spanish governor, which essentially repudiated everything that was the Treaty of New York.[19] The Creek-Spanish alliance would prove incapable of halting settler encroachment, so once again, the country found itself not on a transformative Indian policy but rather on the previously inherited policy, "headed inexorably toward the extermination of Indian Country east of the Mississippi."[20]

The War of 1812, America's second war for independence, similarly saw the split loyalties of the Native American Indian nations. However, the Native Americans saw the war as a desperate struggle for freedom and independence. Native Americans became involved in the conflict to secure British support for their purpose, the war against the United States. In the years leading up to the conflict, the U.S. government's appetite for westward and southern continental expansion placed their tribal homelands at risk. This goal led to the broader invasion of the native lands of the Shawnee, Potawatomi, Ojibwa, Muscogee Creek, Seminole, Choctaw, Cherokee, and Chickasaw.[21] The issue for Native American leadership was the preservation of their tribal lands. Thus, Indian support for the British was a gambit predicated upon the belief that their victory would halt the encroachment upon tribal lands by the newly formed United States.

More than two dozen Indian nations participated in the War of 1812, which expanded the base of tribal warriors and yielded a cohort of leaders capable of forming multi-tribe coalitions marshaling the native strengths decisively. These leaders included Red Jacket, Farmer's Brother of the Seneca, and Chief John Norton, chief of the Mohawks. Tecumseh, a Shawnee chief, and a British general was preeminent among the warrior chiefs. By 1811, they assembled a powerful tribal confederation that expected to use their united strength to end settler intrusion onto their lands. Chief Pushmataha was instrumental in his leadership of Choctaws alongside Andrew Jackson in numerous engagements in the South. Like the Iroquois Confederacy of the Revolutionary War, for the Creek Nation, the War of 1812 became their civil war.

The Indian nations that participated in the war fought in more than forty battles and skirmishes against American soldiers. With the significant exception of the Iroquois, who fought for both the British and the United States, Native Americans fought most engagements alongside the British, meaning that Indian versus Indian actions were limited. Many of the noteworthy British battlefield successes were indeed attributable to the contributions of Indigenous warriors. Detroit, Queenston, Beaver Dams, Horseshoe Bend, Pensacola, and New Orleans are a few such examples of tribes that joined forces with the British.

Despite their fighting strength and woodland skills, the negotiated settlement of the War of 1812 represented a severe loss to the Native American tribes, with over two hundred agreements ceding their tribal lands to the United States. A further ninety-nine additional treaties created Native American reservations west of the Mississippi River.[22]

The tenacity, courage, and ferocity of the Native American warriors were not limited to their participation in the wars of the white man. With increasing frequency, the Indigenous population of America found itself defending its ancestral homelands from encroachment by the burgeoning European population with an insatiable appetite for land for westward expansion. Concerning the settler's plans for the treatment of the Native Indian population and their avarice for the tribal homelands, the watchwords were "... more land, no Indians, and total control."[23]

Even before the United States achieved independence, by the mid-1760s, the colonists had already conceived of setting aside areas of land reserved for Native American tribes and governance.[24] And by 1824, the government had established the Office of Indian Affairs in order to rationalize the complex, quilt-like arrangement of Indian reserves created over the preceding six decades. The plan was that the patchwork of locally concluded agreements would be replaced by treaties between the Federal government and the Indigenous tribes, with the tribes being accorded the status of a sovereign state.[25] Not surprisingly, the pattern of new deals invoked lesser land allotments to the tribes and inadequate assistance for the hardships endured when moving to new homes. All too frequently, it precipitated military intervention to enforce the terms of the latest deals.

Furthermore, over time would emerge a series of systematic pieces of legislation that collectively set into motion the purge of Indigenous peoples from their homelands. The unitary act of systematic genocide was the "act to provide for an exchange of lands with the Indians residing in any of the States or Territories, and for their removal west of the River Mississippi," also known as the "Indian Removal Act of 1830."[26] The act was one of the seminal pieces of legislation enacted during President Andrew Jackson's first term. Four years later, the "Indian Trade and Intercourse Act of 1834" established the Mississippi River as the permanent Indian frontier and consequently relegated the Native Americans to the Indian Territory, which was all lands west of the boundary except Louisiana and Arkansas.[27]

Within two years of assuming the presidency, Jackson purged the office of Indian Affairs of many incumbents from the John Quincy Adams administration. He replaced them with "men who could be relied on to aggressively pursue the expropriation of Indian lands."[28]

Jackson's primary targets for removal were the tribes located in the southeastern United States, of whom almost 60,000 or eighty percent were driven or voluntarily immigrated to the Indian territory.[29] As the American population moved westward across the Mississippi River, Army regulars encountered a population of Indigenous people different than those they met in the East—a population unwilling to relinquish their homes without a fight. In the almost sixty years leading up to 1849, soldiers recorded a mere 122 engagements with Native Americans, whereas 121 combat interactions were recorded in the 1850s alone.[30] The onset of the removal was followed by innumerable wars between the white settlers and the Native Americans which would continue for almost six more decades until 1890.

The preponderance of research on the role of Native American tribes during the Civil War focuses on the "Five Civilized Tribes" of the Southeast: the Cherokees, the Creeks, the Choctaws, the Chickasaws, and the Seminoles. Both the Union and Confederacy realized that a strong alliance with the Five Civilized Tribes would be a prudent relationship to maintain. The Indians could bring men to fight and show support for the state's rights toward the governing system in Washington. Since some Native Americans at the time were living in regions controlled by the states, the abridgment of state's rights by the federal government directly impacted their well-being, so they were amenable to lending their support to the Confederate effort. Additionally, some of the tribal members were slave owners, a cause fully within the agenda of the Confederacy. The larger tribes—the Cherokees and the Creeks—sided with the Confederacy and had significant sway over other tribes. With substantial inducements in hand, over 15,000 Five Tribes warriors joined the cause of the South and waged war against the Union, predominantly in the western regions.

The Indigenous forces that fought alongside the Confederacy included a substantial number of warriors of the 1st Cherokee Brigade under the command of Cherokee General Stand Waite. The brigade had the 1st and 2nd Cherokee Regiments, the 1st and 2nd Creek Regiments, separate Cherokee, Osage, and Seminole Battalions, and a Creek Squadron.[31] The Confederacy also deployed Kiowa and Cherokee formations in Texas and Oklahoma.

The Union enlisted about 4,000 Native Americans into their ranks during the Civil War.[32] Because of their skill as trackers, the North quickly recruited American Indians into their ranks, and established three separate fighting units to secure the Indian territory, in which Indians enlisted as scouts for service throughout the northern states with the war's progression. As scouts, they were adept at locating and reporting enemy troop positions without endangering their comrades.[33] The Confederacy on the other hand, enjoyed the services of almost 25,000 Native American warriors, most from the Cherokee, Creek, Choctaw, Chickasaw, Seminole and Catawba nations. The Confederacy found the same utility from their Native American scouts and guides who were also used to capturing runaway slaves. Unlike the Union, Native Americans in the service of the Confederacy were permitted units comprised of their own members, and were able to include officers.

At the outset of the War Between the States, the War Department opposed inducting Native Americans into the Union Army. The rationale was one of geographic and resource realities. The theater of operations during the Indian Wars was so vast, almost continental in size, and the Army was unable to balance requirements with resources to include sustainable manpower. However, the president and his cabinet remained steadfast in their opposition, and the War Department resolved that loyal Native Americans could be formed into a "Home Guard" for local service.[34] Thus the Department of Kansas created an expeditionary force of white troops and three Home Guard regiments: two Creek and one Cherokee. The force took part in operations intended to "restore the refugee Indians to their homes, neutralize the Confederate Indian force, and establish a base of operations from which to strike at Confederate forces in the West."[35] The success of these operations induced the War Department to relax previous objections to Indian service. However, one should note that Native Americans were still not citizens and thus not eligible to be drafted.

During the quarter century that followed the end of the Civil War, the complexion of American hostilities with the Indigenous population took on a dramatic and severely more punitive nature. By April 9, 1865, the nature of the Indian Territory and the western two-thirds of the country was changing, and the relief that it offered was disappearing quickly. With the war over, large numbers of eastern white men with pent-up energy were now interested in resuming their pursuit of the riches and opportunities of the West, notwithstanding any inconvenience the Native American population might impose. The Indian tribes, without anywhere else to retreat, had two undesirable options: surrender to the white man or fight for what was theirs, as evidenced by the endless trail of tribal nation treaties with the U.S. government. Most would choose to fight.

Believing that many of America's Indian wars could be avoided, Ulysses S. Grant, as General of the Army, was willing to limit Army strikes against Indigenous people in the territory, replace volunteers with Army regulars, and transfer Indian Affairs back to the War Department. In reaction to the above approaches, delegations from the Cheyenne, Arapaho, Kiowa-Apache, Comanche, and Kiowa tribes joined Indian Affairs commissioners in agreeing to "perpetual peace" in the Little Arkansas River treaties of October 1865. At the same time, further north at Fort Sully in South Dakota, the United States Government and nine Lakota and Dakota Sioux tribes made mutual promises to "restore peace, respect reservation boundaries, and provide annual annuities."[36]

While much of our discussion on the Indian War period (1825–1890) will appear in the chapters that follow, noteworthy during this time is the Army Reorganization Act, enacted by Congress on July 28, 1866, which authorized the president to "enlist and employ in the Territories and Indian country a force of Indians not to exceed one thousand to act as scouts, who shall receive the pay and allowances of cavalry soldiers and be discharged [...] at the discretion of the department commander."[37]

Following the conclusion of the Indian Wars, the U.S. Army found itself with a cadre of skilled warrior scouts and police who had proven immensely useful to the Army for their experience and mastery of hunting and warfare techniques. Now, however, with need for a supportable Army requirement greatly reduced, the Army formed the few scouts it required into dedicated Native American troops and companies in Arizona and the Northern Plains. The initiative also permitted the Army to confront the lagging enlistments among the non-Native population. The potential of Native American enlistment in the Regular Army became the discourse of some forward-thinking service members and War Department officials. Among the former was Major William Powell, who added his voice to the discussion through several articles in *United Service*, a monthly periodical on military affairs. In his first article, "Soldier or Granger?" the major argued that the Army should educate the Native Americans in that which is the most acceptable to their instincts and tastes—that is, "make soldiers of them."[38] He further wrote that "the physical endurance of the Indian was unequaled."[39] In his second article, "The Indian as a Soldier," Major Powell proposed enlisting Indians from among graduates of several Indian Schools who were fluent in English. He also judged that any lingering concerns about 'barbarous customs' would be removed over time through Indian contact with civilization.[40] His third and final article, "The Indian Problem," echoes the sentiments of the two preceding articles. Following the *United Service* discussions, government officials began joining the chorus favoring the addition of Native Americans as regular soldiers in the Army.

Badly needing personnel knowledgeable of Indian tactics and of western terrain, in 1866 the Army formed the Indian Scouting Service, which was later expanded by enlisting two 100-man companies to serve under the leadership of seasoned white officers with frontier experience. The newly formed companies were to be stationed at Army posts distant from the reservation homes of the recruits. First Lieutenant Edward Casey, 22nd Infantry, commanded the first of the two companies, Company A, Department of Dakota at Fort Keogh, Montana, made up of Cheyenne, also known as "Casey's Scouts."[41] The core of the second company was made up of Kiowa and Comanche soldiers stationed at Fort Reno, Indian Territory (Oklahoma). It was led by First Lieutenant Homer W. Wheeler, 5th Cavalry. Their success, operating along with the 800 Sioux and Cheyenne scouts in quelling the Messiah Craze of 1890–1891,[42] resoundingly convinced Secretary of War Redfield Proctor and the Army's commanding general, Major General John M. Schofield, that there was a place in the Regular Army for Native American "natural Soldiers."

Reception to the notion of enlisting Native Americans into Regular Army positions beyond merely scouts and police grew and resulted in a broadened call for efforts beyond the mere experimentation stage. Those Native Americans currently serving as scouts welcomed the thought of Regular Army service with a few caveats: long multi-year enlistments were not appealing, and being an infantry soldier was repugnant. The momentum resulted in the promulgation, on March 9, 1891, of the War Department General Order 28.[43]

Broadly summarized, General Order 28 contained provisions which definitively shaped the scope and breadth of the Army's willingness to launch a dramatic policy shift that had the potential for redressing personnel, economic, and certain societal issues associated with the restive male Native American population on the quieting frontier. Those provisions included:[44]

1. The authorization of 1,485 Indian enlistments within the total army manpower cap of 25,000 men;[45]
2. The specification of a total requirement within the Regular Army for eight troops of Indian cavalry, excluding the 9th and 10th Cavalry Regiments, and nineteen companies of the Indian infantry, excluding the 24th and 25th Infantry Regiments;
3. Authorization of the strength of each Regular Army troop and company to be set at fifty-five enlisted soldiers who would be assigned to Army posts near their homes;
4. Abandoning the requirement of English fluency as an enlistment prerequisite;
5. Lowering the ceiling on Army scout personnel to 150 soldiers, a reduction of 850 souls;
6. Allowing Army Department commanders to appoint Indians as non-commissioned officers, sergeants, and corporals;
7. Requiring all new enlistees to be vaccinated against smallpox before induction and;
8. Permitting no more than ten married Indians per troop or company. (This provision could be waived; however, recruiters were strongly encouraged not to reduce their efforts to recruit single male Indians.)

The luster of the regular Indian soldier and his service started to lose its shine in 1893 as Indian disillusionment with the Army experience began to rise. Individual and unit drunkenness plus absenteeism were among the most frequently observed transgressions. When the Army planned to relocate some of the more troublesome units, their members balked and accepted *en masse* discharge as preferential to any other service or disciplinary option. Concomitantly, reenlistment lost its popularity, with Indian soldiers preferring to return home and care for their families. Even the program's earliest advocates for the Regular Army enlistment of Native Americans were forced to conclude by 1895 that the program was a failure. The only markedly successful Regular Army Native American unit was Troop L, 7th Cavalry, whose soldiers served their entire enlistment until discharged in 1895. Their success can be attributed to the strong advocacy for their service and the enlightened leadership of their troop commander, First Lieutenant Hugh L. Scott. However, the initiative was short-lived, lasting less than a decade. Some of life's most significant accomplishments are born of failure, and the experiments of the 1890s set the stage for future successful military and combat service by Native Americans during the great trials of the twentieth century.

Born of the 1890s in Indian Territory were experiences whose benefits would be manifest decades later as America organized for World War I. In 1890, future General John J. Pershing served in the campaign to suppress an uprising among the Sioux in the Dakota Territory. Based on his service on the Pine Ridge Indian Reservation and experience with Indian troopers, he strongly supported the formation of Indian-only units for service during World War I.

As the country marshaled its might in the Spanish-American War, Native Americans were at the head, stepping forward and volunteering their service. Of the regiments authorized by Congress for service in Cuba, Indigenous men and women from the Indian Territory served in, among others, the First Territorial Volunteer Infantry and famously in the First Cavalry Volunteer Regiment, the Rough Riders.[46] The latter 1,000-man regiment included Cherokee, Chickasaw, Choctaw, and Pawnee[47] who had once again proved themselves as men of courage and honor in the nation's service. Also, among the Native Americans serving in Cuba were four Lakota nuns, the first known Native American Army nurses who remained on the island after the war.[48]

When asked about his service in Cuba, one Cherokee soldier, known only by his surname, Holderman, explained that "his people had always fought when there was a war, and he could not feel happy to stay at home when the flag was going into battle."[49] William Pollock, a Pawnee Rough Rider, struck a similar note: "[I]n the memory of our brave fathers I will try and be like one of them, who used to stand single-handed against the foes."[50]

As in America's previous wars, Native American tribal members fought in the Spanish American War with courage and honor even though they were serving a nation that had historically oppressed them. But, as a consequence of the war, newer politics of the Progressive Era emerged and marked the beginning of better relationships between the white man and his Native American counterpart.[51]

The prelude to World War I was punctuated by several political and demographic questions that entwined the status of Native Americans and their place in the military of 1917 and included whether Native Americans should serve in integrated or segregated companies. But before they could serve in numbers greater than those who volunteered, Native Americans had to be admitted into the military, giving rise to their status vis-à-vis the draft. The crux of the issue centered on their status as citizens or non-citizens[52] and the existence of Native American entities as sovereign nations. The latter question had its legal foundation in the Commerce Clause (Article 1, Section 8, Clause 3) of the United States Constitution and Supreme Court decisions of the nineteenth century. Thus as non-citizens, Native Americans could not be drafted but were required to register for the draft, which introduced considerable confusion into raising the wartime force.

The court history of Indian law begins with the Marshall Trilogy: *Johnson v. M'Intosh*, 21 U.S. 543 (1823); *Cherokee Nation v. Georgia*, 30 U.S. 1 (1831); and *Worcester v. Georgia*, 31 U.S. 515 (1832). The trilogy, primarily authored by Chief Justice John Marshall, "established federal primacy in Indian affairs, excluded state law from Indian country, and recognized tribal governance authority. More to the issue here, these cases established the place of Indian nations in the American dual sovereign structure that still governs today."[53] Chief Justice Marshall separately concluded, "You can't get any more sovereign than that."[54]

As America considered its entry into World War I and sought men for Army units on the Western Front, its recruiters focused attention on the Federal Indian boarding schools, especially the Carlisle Indian Industrial School in Carlisle, Pennsylvania. The Carlisle School, as it was commonly known, was the premier federal, off-reservation Indian boarding school charged with immersing its Native American students into mainstream Euro-American culture. Its primary objective was to provide young Native Americans with the opportunity to advance and thrive in the dominant white man's society. The school's graduates were desirable to the military because of its soldierly-focused curriculum and the "assiduous efforts to inculcate patriotism"[55] which gave the students a head start on their wartime military training. When it came time to be counted, nearly all eligible students in the approximately 100[56] on- and off-reservation schools in the federal boarding school system served during the war; almost "ninety percent volunteered, including 205 soldiers from the Carlisle School."[57]

During the Great War, President Woodrow Wilson implemented wartime conscription; however, some Native Americans who were not considered citizens of the United States, were ineligible for the draft. Of those who were, 17,313 registered, and out of that 6,509 registered warriors were inducted.[58] Notwithstanding their lack of citizenship and obligation to serve, between 12,000 and 13,000 Native Americans served during the wartime period in the Army.[59] They represented twenty to thirty percent of all Native American males, compared to the fifteen percent of all American men who served during World War I.[60] Indigenous people also represented approximately 0.4% of the 3,703,273 Americans serving on Armistice Day 1918.[61] Ultimately, among the 2,003,935 Americans who served in France on the Western Front, 0.2% or approximately 4,000 of them were Native Americans.

More specifically, nearly 10,000 served in the Army within the cavalry, medical service, signal, military police, balloon squadrons, and the aviation corps. Another thousand Native Americans served in the Navy, mostly on transport and escort vessels, while others found service on battleships.[62]

Furthermore, Indigenous peoples rallied around the war effort on the home front, including planting victory gardens, making monetary donations to service member support organizations, and buying war stamps and Liberty Bonds, worth more than $25 million.[63] In a uniquely Native American sacrifice, some tribes would lease reservation and tribal lands to non-Indians, which could be used to graze cattle and sheep to provide beef and mutton for soldiers overseas. Approximately four million acres of Native American land were diverted to support the war effort.[64]

Native American tribes that maintained their status as sovereign, independent nations and not as subjects of the United States also participated in the First World War. Tribes such as the Onondaga and Oneida of the Iroquois Confederacy adopted a position supporting American involvement in the war. They declared war on the Triple Alliance (Germany, Austria-Hungary, and Italy) in July 1918 as independent nations and as allies of the United States.[65]

Even after the Indian Wars, warrior traditions were considered an integral part of Indian culture and were an important component in the education of young recruits who were born after this period. As part of the oral tradition passed down from one generation to another, the lore of warrior strength and discipline shaped the expectation that the nature of their service would be in frontline combat and highly hazardous situations. In 1912, an army major observed that the real secret which makes the Indian such an outstanding soldier is his enthusiasm for the fight.[66] Non-Native American combat leaders capitalized on their warrior skills and routinely assigned Native Americans to infantry positions that endangered them and led to disproportionate injury and death.

It was common to find large concentrations of American Indians from one or two tribes in a single military unit. The 36th Texas-Oklahoma National Guard Division had a single Native American unit, the 142nd Infantry Regiment, which included 600 Native Americans of the Choctaw and Cherokee tribes. The regiment was formed and trained at Camp Bowie, Fort Worth, Texas, with the 36th Division, and was assigned to the 71st Brigade, 36th Division, on October 15, 1917. The Regiment later departed Texas and headed for East Coast Ports of Embarkation (POE) to await its shipment to France on July 18, 1918. The 142nd arrived off the coast of St. Nazaine, France, on July 30, 1918,[67] where it first engaged in battle; "its soldiers were widely recognized for their contributions in battle. Four members from this unit were awarded the French Croix de Guerre, while others received the Church War Cross for gallantry."[68] The Regiment proudly served with distinction until returning to the United States in June 1919, where it was demobilized on June 17, 1919, at Fort Bowie, Texas.[69]

One of the distinguishing attributes of the 142nd Infantry Regiment and their Native American soldiers was that no one could understand them when they spoke to one another in their native language. Native soldiers of the regiment conversed in twenty-six different languages or dialects. The origins of the Choctaw Telephone Squad, as they were called, stem from the German attack on American forces at St. Etienne in October 1918. When Colonel Alfred Wainwright Bloor, the regimental commander, overheard two Choctaw Indians in his command speaking with each other and realized that he could not understand them, he also acknowledged that the same would be true for Germans, regardless of their English language skills. Another unique facet of many Native American languages was that they were not written down. With the active cooperation of his Choctaw soldiers, Colonel Bloor tested and deployed a code using the Choctaw language in place of regular military code. Besides the Choctaws, Cherokee, Cheyenne, Comanche, Lakota, Yankton, and Osage speakers transmitted messages during World War I.[70]

The first recorded use of Native American code talkers occurred on October 17, 1918, when the regiment ordered the withdrawal of two companies of the 2nd Battalion from Chufilly to Chardonnay.[71] This was the first time in modern warfare that military messages in an Indigenous language were used to bewilder an enemy. The movement was successful: "The enemy's complete surprise is evidence that he could not decipher the messages," Bloor observed.[72] A captured German officer confirmed they were "completely confused by the Indian language and gained no benefit whatsoever" from their wiretaps.[73] Following a decisive American victory on the Western Front, a captured German general inquired of his captors concerning the telephone message traffic the night before the battle "What nationality was on the phone that night?" The response was, "It was only Americans that were on the phone."[74] Because the Choctaw language used to transmit information was not based upon a European language or mathematical progression, no one could understand it except other native Choctaw speakers.

With Native Americans already serving as messengers and runners between units, by placing Choctaws in each company, messages could be transmitted regardless of whether the radio traffic was overheard or if the telephone lines were tapped. While the success of the Choctaw Code Talkers is undeniable, the language did require some modification to accommodate words and military terminology that were not part of the native Choctaw language. One particular example illustrates their ingenuity for describing a machine gun. They used existing vocabulary for "big gun" to describe "artillery" and "little gun shoot fast" for "machine gun."

The men who made up the United States' first code talkers were either full-blood or mixed-blood Choctaw Indians. All were born in the Choctaw Nation of the Indian Territory, in southeastern Oklahoma, when their nation was a self-governed republic. There were nineteen Choctaw Code Talkers of World War I, and they chose to live in obscurity and never received the acclaim like their Navajo Wind Talker brethren did in World War II.

The Choctaw government awarded the code talkers posthumous Choctaw Medals of Valor at a special ceremony in 1986. Three years later, the French government awarded them the Fifth Republic's *Chevalier de l'Ordre National du Mérite* (Knight of the National Order of Merit).[75]

On October 15, 2008, The Code Talkers Recognition Act of 2008 (Public Law 110-420) was signed into law by President George W. Bush, recognizing every Native American code talker who served in the United States military during World War I or World War II. A Congressional Gold Medal was presented to each tribe in recognition of the service of their tribal members as a code talker in either war. A duplicate silver medal was awarded to each code talker, their next of kin, or personal representative.

According to William C. Meadows of Missouri State University, World War I would mark the first time "American Indians served as regular combat troops, not just auxiliary units attached to non-Indian units."[76] The incredible service of Native Americans on the Western Front prompted the commander of the American Expeditionary Force, General John J. Pershing, to write in 1920, "The North American Indian took his place beside every other American in offering his life in the great cause, whereas a splendid soldier, he fought with the courage and valor of his ancestors."[77] The mutuality of respect among Native American World War I veterans and their non-Native commanders and allied leaders prompted the Crow tribe of Montana in 1920 to honorably induct the wartime Supreme Commander of Allied Forces, French Marshal Ferdinand Foch, into their tribe.[78] Similarly, during World War II, the Blackfeet Indians adopted General Douglas MacArthur into their tribe and bestowed the name Mo-Kahki-Peta, or "Chief Wise Eagle."[79] In his memoir, MacArthur would write that they "made me their Chief of Chiefs, and sent me the war bonnet of the high medicine man. I would not swap it for any medal or decoration I have ever received."[80] That is high esteem from a leader who holds over 100 decorations, including the Medal of Honor, Distinguished Service Cross (3), Distinguished Service Medal (4), Silver Star (7), Distinguished Flying Cross, Bronze Star, Purple Heart (2), and Air Medal among many others.[81]

The year 1917, and later in World War II, marked the military service of Native Americans in the armed forces as well as among the ranks of the Commissioned Corps of the United States Public Health Service (USPHS).[82] As members of the National Oceanic and Atmospheric Administration (NOAA) Commissioned Officer Corps in World War II, they again served their nation.[83] While not considered part of the nation's armed forces, these two branches are part of the nation's uniformed services.

Regarding Native American ability to be drafted, the Selective Service Act of May 18, 1917, required the registration of "all male citizens, or male non-alien enemies who have declared their intention to become citizens between the ages of twenty-one and thirty years, both inclusive."[84] While no data indicates the number of Indigenous males who were citizens or who were "intending" to become citizens at the time of enactment, historians have concluded that substantial numbers of Native Americans were illegally enlisted.

Absent any concrete definition of Indian citizenship, federal Indian agency authorities determined that those Native Americans who held fee patents[85] under the General Allotment Act of 1887 (The Dawes Act) and of the Forced Fee Patenting Act of 1906 (The Burke Act); who had "adopted the habits of civilized life" away from the tribes, and all their children, were U.S. citizens.[86] Furthermore, Native Americans who surrendered their tribal citizenship for a domicile in a state, i.e., Georgia, Alabama, or Mississippi, would be state citizens.[87] Further complicating the citizenship conundrum is the Fourteenth Amendment to the Constitution and the Senate resolution of December 1870, which clarified with certainty that the amendment did not apply to Native Americans and that they were not subject to U.S. jurisdiction because they were already subject to tribal jurisdiction. Although non-citizens, some draft authorities continued to enlist non-draft eligible Indigenous men. Despite familial and tribal complaints to the Bureau of Indian Affairs (BIA) and the courts, no meaningful changes were made to the illegal draft practices.

By World War I, Native Americans were so deeply ingrained in Americana that their symbols, images, and names were frequently used—a practice that would continue into the twenty-first century. At the outset of America's participation in the Great War in 1917, several German vessels were captured in American coastal harbors and interned. They were handed over to the United States Shipping Board and later to the U.S. Navy after being made suitable for wartime use. They included the *Hamburg*, the *Rhein*, the *Prinzess-Irene*, and the *Friedrich-der-Gross*, which were renamed the *Powhatan*, the *Susquehanna*, the *Pocahontas*, and the *Huron*, respectively.[88] Units of the AEF adopted unit insignia that bore the likeness of Native Americans, like the 2nd Infantry Division ("Second to None"), whose shoulder patch was a Plains Indian head on a white star background mounted on a black shield. A Frenchman, attached to a section of the American Ambulance Field Service, designed an Indian head as the emblem for the section's vehicles. The symbol was inspired by the design found on the American five dollar gold piece.[89] The Lafayette Escadrille, a flying unit of American volunteers, adorned the fuselage of their aircraft with "the wild Sioux with a menacing look about him."[90] The use of symbols provided a means to invoke the Native American warrior spirit and signaled the aggression and ferocity that accompanied such an invocation. But it also "shows how strong the Native American image is in the American collective unconscious. It is a complex mixture of feelings of guilt (toward the past treatment of American Indians), feelings of superiority (American Indians have yet to become civilized), admiration of American Indian traditions and proximity to nature (some kind of a lost paradise), memories of childhood (reading dime novels or enjoying Wild West Shows), and many other elements."[91]

The symbolism used extended beyond visual references, and Native American-inspired aphorisms have a long tradition in the lexicon of America's armed forces. A popular one surviving numerous American wars was the reference to the enemy-held territory, which would soon be the target of combat operations as "Indian Country."

In 1964, the remote, sparsely populated Central Highlands became the B3 Front of the North Vietnamese Army (NVA) target to further weaken the South Vietnamese government's influence in the region. One of its objectives was the destruction of the "nettlesome" Special Forces (SF) camps in the Western Highlands. Established at the beginning of 1963, the SF camps were located in remote, largely ungoverned areas in what SF troops satirically called "Indian Country."[92]

American senior government officials involved in directing the nation's role in Vietnam were also not beyond using pejorative terms when discussing the war. Following his second fact-finding mission to Vietnam at the behest of President Lyndon Johnson, Secretary of Defense McNamara, in his report to the president, declared that the Mekong Delta was fast becoming "injun country."[93] In 1968, the marines at Khe Sanh drew parallels between their situation and that confronted by the French fourteen years earlier in the debacle of Dien Bien Phu. While there was an eerie similarity in the geography of both locations, the U.S. Marines referred to their area of operations as "Indian Country," no home for the tender-hearted,[94] where many ventured but fewer returned.

One has witnessed examples of this disparaging tradition during more recent history; as coalition operations against Iraq during Operation Desert Shield/Desert Storm took place, a command spokesman suggested that victory would soon follow once forces were committed to "Indian Country."[95]

And twenty years later, on May 2, 2011, a Navy Seal team would invoke the name of legendary leader and medicine man from the Bedonkohe band of the Apache tribe, Geronimo. The team was engaged in a covert operation, Operation NEPTUNE SPEAR, to capture or kill the founder and first leader of the Islamist group Al-Qaeda, Osama Bin Laden, in Abbottabad, Pakistan. The communications signal to U.S. military command authorities that the operation was successfully completed was, "For God and country—Geronimo, Geronimo, Geronimo."[96]

As recently as February 10, 2022, senior U.S. government officials were still invoking Native American aphorisms when the director of the Center for Disease Control, Dr. Rochelle Walenski, in speaking about the need for covid epidemic guidance said it must "be general enough that it can be applied to New York City and rural Montana and 'Indian country,' which is our responsibility."[97]

While Native Americans served disproportionately in the military during the First World War, they also sacrificed more than their American citizen counterparts. The entire American Expeditionary Force suffered 146,066 killed and wounded, or a one percent casualty rate; Native Americans suffered a five percent casualty rate.[98] Among the various tribal groups, the Pawnee soldiers experienced a fourteen percent casualty rate, and the different Sioux groups had an average casualty rate of ten percent.[99]

One of the paradoxes of the First World War that weighed heavily on the Native American population and especially its veterans was the question of loyalty. For some observers, the whole idea of Native patriotism as expressed by service to the nation was concurrently "perceived as an abandonment of tribalism and acquiescence to being conquered."[100]

Unfortunately there are very few first-person accounts on the return of Native American combat veterans to their homes following the end of the Great War due to the fact that returning soldiers would not speak of their experiences, choosing instead to remain silent; their lives in the trenches and at the front were not relevant to their people at home.

Noteworthy, but only limitedly acknowledged, was that Native Americans who volunteered for military service in World War I were not eligible for U.S. citizenship; however, in 1919, Native American veterans were offered citizenship under the Indian Citizenship Act of November 6, 1919. Citizenship was not automatic under the law; it merely allowed those honorably discharged veterans desiring American citizenship to apply for and be granted citizenship. In 1924, the Indian Citizenship Act, officially known as the Snyder Act, an all-inclusive act, was passed by Congress. The privilege of citizenship was included in the legislation; however, voting rights were intentionally excluded from the statute. Authority was left to the individual states to determine the voting status of their Native American constituents. American Indian voting status was not a significant issue for most states involved, and in turn they granted voting rights to their people along with the passage of the Snyder Act. However, Arizona and New Mexico elected to deny the fundamental right to vote. It was not until 1948 that the Arizona Supreme Court struck down its constitutional provisions and opened the way for all Arizona constituents, including American Indians, to vote. For Native American residents of New Mexico, it would take until 1962 for that state to change its exclusionary laws and enfranchise them.

Thus the Vietnam War would be America's first conflict where its citizens who were twenty-one years old could vote for the individuals who set policy and made decisions ordering them off to war. It would not be until 1971, with the approaching end of the war, when the 26th Amendment to the U.S. Constitution was passed, granting voting rights to eighteen-year-olds, two years older than the youngest soldier killed in Vietnam and four years younger than the average age of the Vietnam War infantryman.[101]

Despite a history of more than a half-century of obstacles to their citizenship and enfranchisement, America's Native Indians never eluded the nation's call to service. Before 1942, they were not eligible to be drafted, so they volunteered their service, yet no other American minority population segment gathered for military service as rapidly as Native Americans. Moreover, they were the largest per capita contributors to the uniformed forces during World War II. More than eleven percent of the population and a third of the eligible and non-disabled men between eighteen and fifty served during the war. Some Native American tribes had as high as seventy percent participation in the war.[102] Notwithstanding the disrespectful treatment levied upon them by the federal government, Native Americans were still ready and willing to serve. On December 7, 1941, more than 5,000 American Indians were serving in the armed forces. By January 1942, ninety-nine percent of all eligible Native American warriors had registered for the draft. The Department of Defense data reported that over 24,521 reservation Natives and another 20,000 non-reservation

Natives served out of a total U.S. Native American population of 350,000, or approximately 12.7 percent of the Native American population saw military service. Each who served overlooked their past relationship with the American government and was willing to take up arms alongside white men to overcome a greater evil in what they considered a white man's war.

While the evidence strongly supports the patriotic fervor of the Indigenous population in the war effort, some used the opportunity of universal military service as an means to emphasize their view of the importance of tribal nation identity. The passage of the Selective Training and Service Act in September 1940 was the instrument by which Native Americans, not wishing the mantel of universal citizenship, chose to challenge the legitimacy of the draft as it applied to them.[103] Not unexpectedly, the Iroquois Confederacy took up the legal challenge in October 1940, citing the 1794 Treaty of Canandaigua, which recognized the Confederacy as a nation coequal with the United States. Thus, the latter did not have the authority to impose U.S. citizenship on the Six Nations people, which meant that they could not involuntarily be drafted. Although the Second Circuit Court of Appeals ruled against the Confederacy in November 1941, its decision afforded the Six Nations another opportunity to assert their sovereignty. In a public event, on June 14, 1942, they independently declared war on the Axis powers (Germany, Italy, and Japan) and committed to defeating them as a national ally of the United States.[104]

Another 40,000 Native Americans, including 12,000 women, left their reservations or homes to take defense industry jobs in airplane factories, ordnance depots, shipyards, railroads, mines, and sawmills. By most reasonable estimates, by 1945 over 150,000 Natives had directly participated in the war effort in the military, industrial, and agricultural sectors. Some Native American historians opine that the response of the Native American population to Pearl Harbor was an awakening of the ancestral warrior spirit among tribal members, who willingly overlooked their familial disappointments and resentments because they understood the importance of defending their land, as it was their particular warrior history and ethos that distinguished them from other World War II service members. It earned them enduring respect and admiration from their brothers-in-arms of all service branches and in the several theaters where they fought. When you include men and women, those in uniform, and the defense industry, approximately twenty percent of the Indian population participated in World War II.[105]

Indigenous men were not alone in their uniformed service to the nation. As many as eight hundred Native women served in the military as Women Accepted for Volunteer Emergency Service (WAVES), Women's Army Corps (WAC), and the Army Nurse Corps (ANC).[106] Those who did not don the uniform took up the yoke of jobs previously held by men now in the military, becoming mechanics, farmers, loggers, transport drivers, and many other essential jobs on the home front.

Once in uniform, commanders found Native Americans to be exceptional soldiers. They excelled in infantry fundamentals, including marksmanship, bayonet drills, and physical endurance. In every way, they were superior to the average non-Native recruit and were universally esteemed for their tenacity and courage. Native Americans fully understood and appreciated the consequences of failure to master combat skills: the loss of life, property, land, and freedom, which were often the penalties of their heritage.

Another Native tradition, particularly among the Great Plains Indians that dates to the 1800s, was counting coup or striking an enemy. As a rite of earning prestige against your enemy and, in turn, garnering status within his tribe, counting coup was the highest honor earned by warriors participating in the intertribal wars of the Great Plains. Native peoples recognized and valued precise systems of graduated war honors, and the key to a man's success in combat was demonstrating his courage by proving superiority over his opponent. While killing was acknowledged as a part of the war, showing courage in the process was more important for individual status. The accomplishment of four specific war deeds would yield the most significant recognition and, with the approbation of the tribal council of elders, the distinction as an Indian war chief. The four war deeds that must be demonstrated included: touch a live enemy in battle, take an enemy's weapons, capture an enemy's horse, and lead a victorious war party.

The four war deeds did not necessitate taking the enemy's life. Counting coup was testament to the skill and daring of one man against another.[107] While all Great Plains warrior exploits are not recorded, there is an illustrative case from World War II that further reflects the warrior prowess of Native Americans in combat. Joe Medicine Crow entered the Army in 1943 and served in Europe near the Siegfried Line. With war paint on his arms and an eagle feather on his helmet, he led successful war parties (demolition teams) behind enemy lines. He stole a German horse and rode it while stampeding the remaining fifty horses used by a Wehrmacht unit. And finally, he engaged an enemy soldier without killing him, a German whom he overcame in hand-to-hand combat before sparing his life. Upon his return from the war, at an elder's council, Joe Medicine Crow was asked to account for his service and bravery, including counting coup. His recounting demonstrated the feasibility of the nineteenth-century warrior tradition in a twentieth-century war. Satisfied, Dr. Joseph Medicine Crow became the last Plains Indian war chief.[108] While his story was not unique, it was representative of the warrior spirit and skills Native Americans brought to the war and for which they were greatly admired.[109]

One of the hallmark chronicles of the Native American warriors' contribution to the Allied triumph in the Second World War is the account of the Navajo Wind Talkers, who continued the legacy of the Choctaw Code Talkers of World War I. The latter's success had aroused great fear among the military and intelligence leaders of 1930s Nazi Germany for the potential use of Native languages for communications in the future, especially as World War II loomed on the horizon. So deep-seated was this apprehension that German agents, posing as anthropologists, writers, and scholars, actually infiltrated some Native tribes in an attempt to learn their languages.[110] These efforts failed, and some historians believe that these attempts served to further stimulate Native American enlistments to fight the Germans.

During the interwar years, Germany was also expending great effort to exploit the potential gulf between Native Americans and the U.S. government. Nazi spies were dispatched to the United States to represent themselves as parties interested in Native culture, assess their support for Nazi policies, document the economic and political conditions prevalent among the Indigenous Tribes, and study Native languages. The Nazi propaganda machine went so far as to grant American Indians 'Aryan' racial characteristics to secure their allegiance.[111] Germany found it unimaginable that Native Americans would wage war against them on behalf of a government that oppressed them. The Nazi propaganda apparatus voiced the problem as a question for all Native Americans, "How could the American Indians think of bearing arms for their exploiters?"[112]

The response of America's first citizens was unambiguous. A representative of the Celilo tribe of Oregon exclaimed, "… the U.S. government defends our rights. We know that under Nazism, we should have no rights at all."[113] The Iroquois Nations urged, "We represent the oldest, though smallest democracy in the world today […]. It is the unanimous sentiment among the Indian people that the atrocities of the Axis nations are violently repulsive to all sense of righteousness of our people."[114] Not to be silent on the matter, the Cheyenne characterized the Axis powers as an "unholy triangle whose purpose is to conquer and enslave the bodies, minds, and souls of all free peoples."[115]

German interest in Native Americans as Wehrmacht soldiers perhaps surfaced from the reports written by members of the Kaiser's army. German records from World War I observed that "The most dangerous of all American soldiers is the Indian […]. He is an Army within himself. He is the one American soldier Germany must fear."[116] Such an army would have been attractive to recruiters and propagandists of the late 1930s, and the Wehrmacht campaign to gain alliances with Native Americans was thus a combination of an appreciation of Indigenous culture and an admiration of their warrior skills and ethos as would apply to a more modern conflict.

Following Pearl Harbor, the U.S. government began calling upon the Comanche Nation to support an Army effort to develop a secret code based upon the Comanche language. In 1942, the Army had recruited approximately fifty Native Americans from the Comanche, Choctaw, Hopi, and Cherokee Indians for certain native language communications and cryptology assignments. In the European Theater of Operations (ETO), seventeen code talkers from the Comanche were employed as part of the Army Signal Corps.[117]

In February 1942, Philip Johnston, recalling his World War I experiences, and reflecting upon his twenty-four years spent with the Navajo people and his fluency in their language, recommended to Marine Corps Major General Clayton P. Vogel, Commanding General Amphibious Corps, Pacific Fleer at Camp Elliott, California, that the Corps could guarantee voice communications security through the use of native-speaking Navajo[118] since the Navajo language was unwritten and unintelligible to anyone except a fellow Navajo. Moreover, it was also a language rich in vocabulary adaptable for specialized military terms.

On February 25, 1942, five Navajo demonstrated to General Vogel and his staff the ability to translate simulated combat messages into their dialect and transmit them to another Navajo, who in turn translated the messages into English in the same form as the original message.[119] With the approval of Lieutenant General John A. Lejeune, commandant of the Marine Corps, recruitment of Navajo code talkers began in May 1942. After an initial recruitment of twenty-nine men, their number grew to nearly 420 Navajo from sixteen tribes by war's end, and who had all participated in the highly classified code talker project using the Diné language as the basis for an unbreakable tactical code. It was used in all Marine Corps operations in the Pacific Theater of Operations (PTO) from Guadalcanal to Okinawa.

The Navajo code talkers became a vital link in the fire support communications and battlefield survivability of soldiers and marines fighting in the Pacific Theater. Based upon Marine Corps experiences during the long and bloody battle for Guadalcanal (August 7, 1942 – February 9, 1943), Joint Assault Signal Companies were created to improve ship-to-shore, air-to-ground communications to coordinate naval gunfire and close air support for ground forces. The First Joint Assault Signal Company (JASCO) was activated at Camp Pendleton, California, on October 20, 1943, to coordinate supporting fires during amphibious operations.[120] It was attached to the 4th Marine Division for the Marshalls operation, and the code talkers were under the command of this battalion-sized unit. The JASCO was broken into thirteen detachment-sized teams provided to Army and Marine divisions, regiments, and battalions. The detachments included a naval gunfire liaison office with a five-man communications team and a marine artillery officer with five forward observers.[121] The Navajo Marines served as radio operators linking the detachment with the Combat Information Center (CIC) aboard the fire support ships at sea. This is where their unintelligible language contributed the most.

Their code combined acronyms and symbolic words that ultimately had 411 terms. It should come as no surprise that the Japanese proved no more adept with the Navajo code than the World War I Germans did with the Choctaw code.

The Navajo story would not be complete without an appreciation for what it took to preserve the tribe's language. Reservation-free schools were established for Native American children, and while they were appealing to Indian parents, students were routinely disciplined and punished for talking in their native tongue. In retrospect, it is ironic that the same language that was so instrumental in the United States' World War II victory was once forbidden.

However, as an unfortunate consequence of the World War II experience, the national emergency opened the opportunity for the federal government to designate tribal lands as essential lands and natural resources, appropriating them for the war effort. During the war, reservation lands were confiscated by the American government to establish internment camps for Japanese Americans, prisoner-of-war camps, and other military operations. Asbestos, coal, copper, gas, gypsum, lead, oil, vanadium, and zinc were among the natural resources acquired and used during the war from Native homelands.[122] Helium, essential in developing the atomic bomb, came from Navajo tribal lands in New Mexico. As in-reservation doctors and nurses were drawn into military service, reservation populations experienced a shortage of medical care for the families, children, and elders left behind. Also, during the war, federal appropriations made by Congress for Indian reservations were diverted to military programs and the war effort.

The Second World War was the event that "caused the greatest disruption of Indian life since the beginning of the reservation era."[123] Indians left the reservations in unprecedented numbers and were exposed to a lifestyle that heretofore was foreign to them. The changes were dramatic for many, individually and collectively, and their habits, views, and economic well-being were all affected in deep and impactful ways. While many veterans chose to remain in the major cities, some rejected the urban lifestyle and elected to return home to the reservation. Those who returned to the reservation did not harbor animus toward those who moved to more cosmopolitan areas. They recognized that the relocation was not a rejection of their Native culture but rather a necessary step for success through the opportunities offered in the white man's world.

Not all Native American World War II veterans left uniform at the end of the war. Some elected to remain in the service and were readily available for the outbreak of the Korean War on June 25, 1950. With the Truman Administration ending segregation in the military, the armed services no longer kept records indicating racial makeup during the Korean War. The Department of Veterans Affairs (VA) estimates that approximately 10,000 Indigenous Americans served during the War.[124] Yet, despite the military's end to segregation, anti-Indian racial discrimination continued within American society without regard to Native American contributions to the War. In a lamentable incident in 1951, the managers of a Sioux City, Iowa cemetery refused the burial of a Winnebago Sergeant who was killed in action in Korea. Because of the notoriety of the incident, Sergeant John Raymond Rice became the first Native American buried at Arlington National Cemetery.[125]

During the Korean War, four American Indians were awarded the Congressional Medal of Honor, the Nation's highest decoration for conspicuous gallantry and intrepidity at the risk of life above and beyond the call of duty. Since the Medal of Honor was established in 1861, thirty-one Native Americans have received the award. The complete Native American Medal of Honor recipients register can be found in Appendix A.

When the country faced another total and global war in less than a quarter of a century, the Native American population responded enthusiastically. The popular media at the time, especially *The Saturday Evening Post*, *Reader's Digest*, and *Colliers*, with equal enthusiasm, reported the unique value of the Indigenous warrior in World War II and the breadth of the support given to the war effort by those tribal people who remained on the home front.[126] Despite the more favorable depiction of First Nation Americans that appeared in the press, on television, and in motion pictures, less than two decades later, the nation gave little or no notice to the American Indians who fought in Vietnam. To the Native American veteran of Vietnam, this mattered little. Unlike their non-Indian veteran comrades who failed to receive a warrior's welcome upon their return home, as was their due, American Indians consistently demonstrated their respect for their returning warrior veterans. Native American people held ceremonies honoring them, organized by relatives, friends, tribal veteran's organizations, and warrior societies.[127]

While the widely recognized estimate of Indigenous service in Vietnam between 1966 and 1973 is more than 42,000, with approximately 37,800 who were volunteers, undeterred by the war's growing unpopularity, this may be an understated estimate for several reasons.[128] One reported issue was that during the period, documentation for military accession contained no option for racial identification as "American Indian."[129] Recruiters, not knowing the correct category to indicate, would assign the category themselves, so Native Americans would find themselves classified as "Caucasian," "Mongolian," "Hispanic," or "Other." The VA likely derived an estimate of 42,000 by accumulating the number of Native Vietnam veterans from each of the BIA Indian Reservations; this most likely did not include Native American veterans from non-reservation domiciles, from tribes that were not federally recognized, nor from those service members who had less than twenty-five percent Native blood.[130] Thus it is probable that the actual Native American Vietnam War military service number is far more significant than 42,000; nevertheless, even with that estimate, one out of four eligible served, compared to one out of twelve in the broader U.S. population.[131]

A demographic and non-inferential study by Robert LaDue, Harold Barse, Frank Montour, and Tom Holm between 1985 and 1988 of 170 American Indian veterans[132] that included representatives from seventy-seven Native Tribes, provides insight into the motivation of the respondents for their service during Vietnam.[133] The prime factors, Family and Tribal Tradition, are consistent with Native American military and Tribal histories over the generations and anecdotal evidence. Speaking of military service, Northern Cheyenne Vietnam War veteran Windy Shoulderblade said, "Most American Indians don't view their military service as something patriotic. It's something deeper than that, passed down from generation to generation. It was our fathers—it was our grandfathers. The warrior status was always an achievement for Indian men. They had always gone to face the enemy when it was their turn."[134]

There has been long-held respect for the warrior ethos of the Indian warrior by his white brothers and comrades-in-arms. Examples of this include the adaptation of the Cherokee word Currahee (quu-wa-hi), meaning "stand-alone," by the para-troopers of the 1st Battalion, 506th Parachute Infantry Regiment of the 101st Airborne Division. They trained near and frequently on Currahee Mountain in Stephens County, Georgia. Before deploying to Europe in World War II, part of their training was a grueling run of "3 miles up, 3 miles down" the mountain. The stamina, endurance, strength, and dogged determination to complete the runs and the rest of their training led to the adoption of "Currahee" as the proud nickname of the regiment and their battle cry. They first used the cry when exiting the aircraft on their first parachute jump, which was made at Fort Benning, Georgia, in August 1940, and on each jump after that.

Among the rituals of other airborne units and soldiers was the cry "Geronimo" by each trooper as he exited the aircraft trusting in his silk canopy. Historians attribute the origin of the practice to World War II Army private Aubrey Eberhardt.[135] The tall, lanky Georgian was stationed at Fort Benning in 1940 and presumably participated as part of the parachute unit test. Following an evening of movie[136] watching at the post theater and later beer-drinking, Eberhardt is reported to have proclaimed to his buddies that he did not fear stepping out of the airplane the next day and declaring: "To prove to you that I'm not scared out of my wits when I jump, I'm gonna yell 'Geronimo' loud as hell when I go out that door tomorrow!"[137] He was true to his word, and the cry caught on, even to the point that the 501st and 509th Parachute Regiments added "Geronimo" to the unit soldier insignia.

As Great Britain stood alone against the might of the German Luftwaffe, she welcomed many international pilots willing to fly with the Royal Air Force (RAF). Three fighter squadrons of American pilots, Eagle Squadrons, volunteered to fly with them. The second of these was the No. 121 (Eagle) Squadron, activated on May 14, 1941, and flew with the RAF until it was transferred to the U.S. Army Air Corps on September 29, 1942, as the 335th Fighter Squadron. As the No. 121 Squadron, the unit emblem bore the head of a Native American Indian with a feathered war bonnet below, which was inscribed "For Liberty."[138] When "the Chiefs," as they were known, transferred to American service, they carried with them the emblem and motto. When reactivated for the Korean War, the 335th even had the warrior emblem emblazoned on the fuselage of the North American F-86 *Sabre* that they flew.

Similarly, many airborne soldiers adopted the Native American persona on the eve of Operation OVERLORD, the Allied invasion of the European continent over the beaches at Normandy. Countless images of the troopers encountering their Supreme Commander, General Dwight D. Eisenhower, were captured on the eve of the Normandy Invasion; he in his classic pressed uniform and they with their Mohawk Indian haircuts and "war paint," actually facial camouflage to prevent betrayal by wayward lights against their pale white skin. This swaggering group belonged to the 506th Parachute Infantry, who had cut their hair in the Mohawk style for the Normandy invasion.[139] These were the same highly trained and motivated paratroopers who volunteered to be "Pathfinders," and who would later jump into the environs of Bastogne and Senonchamps beginning on December 23, 1944, to emplace "Eureka" beacons that transmitted a radio signal to the C-47s equipped with "Rebecca" receivers so that resupply drops could be made to the surrounded and beleaguered "Screaming Eagles" in Bastogne regardless of the weather and visibility.[140] Over 800 "Skytrain" sorties successfully delivered supplies, ammunition, rations, fuel, and essential medical material.[141]

Perhaps the most memorable instance of the haircut and facial war paint was that of the men of the 1st Demolition Section of the Regimental Headquarters Company of the 506th Parachute Infantry Regiment. The Filthy Thirteen, as they were known, were led by Sergeant James Elbert "Jake" McNiece, who was part Choctaw and was the inspiration for the Native American appearance and tenacity of the Section. They flew off to the environs of Normandy, France, on June 5, 1944, to secure or destroy the bridges over the Douve River. Such facial painting clearly served as a manifestation of the aggressive and fearless fighting spirit for which the American Indian warrior was known throughout our history, conjuring their fear-inspiring tenacity and vengeful nature.

There were indeed other instances where America's military and their commanders were less than subtle in evoking the Native American warrior ethos to inspire their subordinates to aggression. During the waning days of the Second World War, the executive officer of the USS *Yorktown* (CV-10), Commander Myron T. Evans, in anticipation of battle on July 10, 1945, admonished the ship's crew to keep a close eye on the sky, as "there is a possibility that a few Indians may be running loose, so it behooves us to keep alert and scalp 'em as soon as they get within gun range. Remember that we have room for more scalps upon our scoreboard."[142]

With the USS *Shangri-La*'s (CV-38) Carrier Air Group 85 aloft over Japan on July 10, 1945, for an airstrike against Japanese airfields and anti-aircraft gun positions around Tokyo, the Air Group commander, Commander W.A. Sherrill, used the signal, "Seminole! Seminole!" for the fighters to commence their strafing runs, and for the fighter bombers, torpedo bombers, and dive bombers to start attacking their assigned targets.[143]

One of the unique organizations in Vietnam was the 12th Infantry Regiment, the only infantry regiment to have five battalions serve during the war. Among them was the 2nd Battalion, 12th Infantry, known as the "White Warriors." To motivate the battalion and to provide a source of organizational pride, soldiers of the battalion had the head of an Indian warrior painted on the butt of their weapons and on the side of the camouflage cover of their helmets.[144] To differentiate the units in the battalion, each company had a different color. Headquarters Company used black, Company A, red; Company B, green; and Company D, blue.

On the other hand, the more informal and familiar language description used to identify military aircraft was, and still is, more casual, a derivative of the parlance of the GI and what they felt about a plane. Thus emerged such endearing monikers as the "beast," "flying banana," "grasshopper," "widow maker," and countless other ingratiating or otherwise unflattering nicknames for some of the American industry's most innovative creations. Almost all of the helicopters covered here benefited from the GI's endearing assignments. Appendix C presents the informal names bestowed upon the Army Vietnam War helicopters included in this volume by the men who flew them, serviced them, or went into battle in them.

When the military reflects upon the Army's policy of naming its helicopters after Native American tribes and leaders, it contemplates much about the Native American history, tradition, and culture. The same culture and virtues that bring the Indian warrior to the military are the same spirit that is embraced by the aluminum, wire, electronics, and many other components that make up the aircraft. The physical and spiritual are inseparable. The Department of Defense commissioned a paper by CEHIP Incorporated of Washington, D.C. in 1996, in partnership with Native American advisors Rodger Bucholz, William Fields, and Ursula P. Roach entitled "20th Century Warriors: Native American Participation in the United States Military," which encapsulates that which is essential to the Native American warrior, and which is a strong and embracing ethos that all warriors can share.

> "Being a warrior in traditional American Indian society gives one a sense of pride and a sense of accomplishment at a time in life when self-esteem is just developing. Becoming a warrior brings status to young men and women in their culture."

> "United States military service provides an outlet for Native Americans to fulfill a cultural purpose rooted in tradition — to fight and defend their homeland."[145]

In the words of Native American Vietnam veteran of the Crow people, James Chastain "Carson Walks Over the Ice," being a warrior means "being out front, taking on challenges, setting the example, and never asking a soldier to do something that you would not do first."[146]

The use of a Native American descriptor for Army helicopters should surprise no one. Regardless of their individual or collective motivation to support the causes of the various "white man's" wars, the Native American contribution to battlefield success was unparalleled. The periods of participating Tribal or Nation ancestry reads like a litany of the mighty Indigenous warrior populations of eighteenth, nineteenth, and twentieth-century America.[147] Their numbers include Iroquois, Choctaw, Huron, Oneida, Shawnee, Cherokee, Sioux, Shawnee, Apache, Chickasaw, Delaware, and countless more.

This Native American tradition and heritage establish the framework from which the Army considers its alternatives for whom it will honor in the naming of each of its new helicopters. The chapters that follow address each of the eleven helicopters the Army used in Vietnam, each which bears a Native American name. The chapters begin with the developmental history of the aircraft and a discussion of the intended military application and missions for which it was fielded. The narrative continues with an examination of how the helicopter was employed in theater during the entire period of its time there. It examines the frequent, routine missions conducted by the aircrews with their ship plus those infrequent, unusual missions they were called upon to perform. The chapters conclude with the tribal or warrior chief's history which commends their name being given to the helicopter highlighted therein.

OH-13 SIOUX

OH-13 of C Troop, 1st Squadron, 9th Cavalry. (Courtesy of Mike Sloniker via VHPA Calendar Program.)

In 1946, the Army began testing Bell Helicopter's YH-13, a modification of the Bell commercial Model 47, as a potential replacement for light, fixed-wing observation aircraft.[1] The Model 47 was an evolutionary version of the Bell Aircraft Company's prototype helicopter development from September 1941, the Model 30. The Model 47 was first flown by the company in September 1945, and the following year it received federal government civilian use certification.[2]

In 1947, the U.S. Air Force designated their military version of the Model 47 as the YR-13. Shortly after the Air Force became a separate branch of the armed services, the Army Aviation community received its first helicopters, thirteen H-13 *Sioux*.[3] And a year later, the Army placed an initial order for an aircraft designated the OH-13B *Sioux*. The Bell H-13 *Sioux* first entered military service in 1948 as a three-seat observation and primary flight training helicopter that also performed observation, reconnaissance, and medevac operations. By June 1949, the Army had fifty-nine OH-13Bs in its inventory.

Despite the immaturity of the U.S. helicopter industry, the Bell Model 47 and the H-13 were quite capable and innovative rotary-winged aircraft for their time. The H-13, in its initial variants, featured an opened cockpit or a sheet metal cabin. The universal model introduced in 1953 had saddle fuel tanks, a welded latticed tube tail boom, and the signature full bubble canopy. It also featured a Bell

Company innovation: the short, weighted gyro-stabilizer bar, which was mounted beneath and at ninety degrees to the main rotor and increased the stability and safety of the helicopter.[4] When the Army began receiving the *Sioux,* its configuration included two blades with a thirty-seven-foot main rotor diameter powered by a Franklin 157 horsepower (hp) piston engine. Later versions mounted a Lycoming 305 horsepower engine. These early aircraft could range to 255 miles at a cruising speed of seventy miles per hour. At its gross weight (loaded), the helicopter could operate at a service ceiling of 12,700 feet.

The Army used this first coming-of-age helicopter in Korea, the Bell H-13B version, which carried a pilot and one passenger. The H-13s were also subsequently modified to change to skid landing gear, the addition of two external medical evacuation panniers with acrylic glass shields, and the upgrade to the Franklin O-335-5 225-horsepower engine. Shortly after the onset of war in Korea, the Army also contemplated the purchase of twenty H-13s from uncommitted funds.

To meet Far East Command (FECOM) requirements, the Department of the Army ordered the 2nd Helicopter Detachment from Fort Bragg, North Carolina, to Korea, where it arrived on November 22, 1950, with its four H-13B helicopters, aviators, and mechanics under the command of Captain Albert C. Sebourn.[5] Sixteen H-13Bs were furnished for early shipment to that theater, and ten more were returned from Alaska to the Sixth Army area to be rehabilitated before onward shipment to FECOM by December 14. Finally, eight H-13D helicopters were airlifted from the manufacturer to the theater. These H-13s proved to be a real asset in the early days of the war in Korea, especially as a means of medical evacuation.

Although the focus here is the service of Army rotary-wing aviation during the Vietnam War, it is essential to consider the experiences of the H-13 and other first-generation helicopters during the Korean War. From Korea's experiences and experiments, Army helicopter aviation doctrine, tactics, and procedures would evolve and enlighten its leadership for the helicopter war that Vietnam would become. At the beginning of the Korean War, the Army had fifty-six H-13s in its inventory—the B Models and four of the older YH-13As. All models were used widely by the helicopter detachments in the country.

Development and procurement of the H-13 continued throughout the Korean conflict and many years later. By June 30, 1954, the Army had acquired 790 H-13s of various models. The majority of these were H-13E and H-13G aircraft obtained between 1952 and 1953. The H-13 was the primary helicopter used during the war for all tasks (e.g., wire laying, liaison, reconnaissance, scouting, and training). Further, the *Sioux* earned its reputation for dependability by scouting for enemy troop movements, rescuing the wounded from the field, and carrying them swiftly to the nearest medical unit. Later, during the Vietnam War, the OH-13 was used primarily for observation.

While the Army was the earliest among the armed services to embrace the helicopter and recognize its potential for revolutionizing warfare, it was the last to introduce its helicopters onto the Korean peninsula. On August 2, 1950, helicopters from Marine Observation Squadron 6 (VMO-6) arrived in Pusan, Korea.[6] At that time, the squadron was flying the Sikorsky HO3S-1, and in December of the same year, they added the Bell HTL-3/4 to their fleet.[7] On November 22, 1950, the Army's 2nd Helicopter Detachment, equipped with four H-13Bs, arrived in Korea. Following some in-country orientation and training, the 2nd was declared operational on New Year's Day 1951. Later that month, the 3rd Helicopter Detachment arrived, and in early March, the 4th Helicopter Detachment arrived. The three Army detachments, adopting evacuation procedures that originated with the Air Force, quickly assumed the majority of the in-theater medical evacuation missions. During the first six months of the war, the three Army Helicopter Detachments and their meager eleven *Sioux* helicopters airlifted 1,985 wounded.[8] They would be the core of the Army's aeromedical evacuation capability during much of the Korean War.

Ultimately defined within the theater guidelines, those patients with head, chest, and abdominal wounds, multiple fractures, and substantial blood loss were candidates for aerial evacuation. Further, evacuation would be made available only if an ambulance could not reach the patient, if a rough ambulance ride would exacerbate his injuries, or if the patient needed immediate treatment at a medical installation. The responsibility of applying the guidelines to determine the need for aerial evacuation rested with the local surgeon, and the decision as to whether the aircraft could reach the casualty fell to the aviation detachment commander. The Eighth Army later stipulated that no helicopters would participate in a medical evacuation that might involve the danger of enemy ground fire.[9]

Those restrictions having been promulgated, pilots were not opposed to evacuating patients from units operating forward of friendly lines or units surrounded by the enemy. Within the community of pilots of the helicopter detachments charged with medical evacuation emerged an unwavering commitment to saving the lives of as many wounded comrades as possible regardless of the personal cost, not unlike the bond between infantrymen sharing the same foxhole. The Army noted that actual medical evacuation operations violated all the general rules and undid the standard operating procedures. But in so doing, the helicopter detachments revealed the broader capabilities of the helicopter. Medical evacuation aviators were not beyond carrying out other equally hazardous missions beyond their remit. It was not uncommon for an evacuation aircraft to be loaded down with ammunition and other critical supplies to venture beyond the lines to aid troops in contact during their hour of greatest need. Tasks clearly not covered in their unit's standard operating procedures. These moonlighting experiences would become the norm for transportation helicopter aviators as those aircraft became more numerous.

By mid-1951, the helicopter detachments were re-designated as Army-level units by the 8th Army to serve behind the Corps under the auspices of the Army Medical Service and further attached to Mobile Army Surgical Hospital (MASH) units. They would later become Medical Detachments, Helicopter Ambulance. The H-13s proudly earned the nickname "Angel of Mercy" for evacuating approximately 18,000 United Nations casualties by the war's end.

In 1950, the Army and the Bell Helicopter Company experimented with mounting a man-portable, recoilless, anti-tank rocket launcher (Bazooka) onto the *Sioux*. Shortly thereafter, the initiative came to an end due to lukewarm support among senior Army officials for arming helicopters. That lack of support notwithstanding, the Korean War witnessed numerous instances of aviators firing their service weapons from the open doors of their helicopters.

A few years later, in 1953, aviators in the 24th Infantry Division stationed in Japan began experimenting with the arming of the *Sioux* by mounting a makeshift grenade launcher onto the fuselage.[10] Successive commandants of the Army Aviation School at Fort Rucker, Alabama, beginning with Brigadier General Carl I. Hutton, called by many the "father of the armed helicopter,"[11] began to seriously experiment with arming helicopters and used the OH-13 *Sioux* as their flying testbed. He instituted a team, initially known as the Armed Helicopter Mobile Task Force, led by Colonel Jay D. Vanderpool to test the concept of an armed, anti-tank helicopter.[12] The Ft. Rucker experiments evolved a standard air cavalry package for troop tests and demonstrations built around a foundation of the *Sioux* armed with four .30 caliber aerial machine guns and four rockets per helicopter.[13] With the primary mission of rotary-wing aircraft being the delivery of ground troops, it was concluded that some defensive or suppressive fire would be beneficial to the safe insertion and extraction of the infantry. Furthermore, weapon ships were needed to protect the entire force, and maximum firepower was essential within the airframe's capabilities.[14]

In 1956, Fort Rucker experimenters persuaded the General Electric Company to build a kit consisting of two 7.62-mm M-60 machine guns and an eight-tube 89-mm rocket launcher to be mounted on the skids of the OH-13. The 89-mm rockets were a Redstone Arsenal experimental aerial anti-tank rocket fabricated in small numbers. The Army's total rocket inventory was exhausted before the General Electric kit could be mounted and tested. The kit was then modified to accommodate the 2.75-inch folding fin aerial rocket (FFAR). Due to machine gun and rocket launcher interference, the final configuration was two machine guns and two rocket launchers.[15]

The rising interest in armed helicopters throughout the Army aviation community and ground commanders' support was insufficient to convince senior Army officials to endorse the development and procurement of strictly armed attack helicopters. The Department of the Army decreed that a single flexible machine gun system from current weapons and on existing aircraft would have to suffice.[16]

Undeterred, ground commanders began their experiments. The commanding general, 8th Infantry Division, was directed on August 9, 1958, to develop the doctrine and tactics for the employment of armed helicopters, while the commanding general, Seventh Army, was instructed to integrate armed helicopter capabilities into specific combat units.[17] The U.S. Army Ordnance Plant in Mainz, Federal Republic of Germany, designed a machine gun system for the OH-13. The plant manufactured thirty kits each for the OH-13G and the OH-13H to be mounted between the skids when installed. Elevation, charging, and rendering safe were accomplished by the pilot manually through three levers that could be manipulated while in flight.

In 1963, the Air Cavalry Troop of the 1st Armored Division (Old Ironsides) experimented with several helicopter weapon systems. Their "Old Ironsides" machine gun kit with twin .30 caliber machine guns was mounted on OH-13 helicopters. While these experiments, evaluations, exercises, and demonstrations highlight what the Army was doing to weaponize the OH-13, concurrent efforts were ongoing with the UH-19, CH-21, CH-34, and UH-1. When the Army ultimately resolved upon the helicopter armament subsystems to standardize for the OH-13, it selected the fixed version of the M37 tank machine gun, the M37C, which was the skid-mounted M1 armament subsystem .30 caliber twin machine gun, and the M60C, fixed mounted, electrically fired, and hydraulically charged 7.62-MM twin machine gun, M-2, helicopter armament subsystem.

The OH-13 *Sioux* in Vietnam

Though the Army introduced more sophisticated helicopters during the Vietnam War, in the early days, the Army used its inventory of 861 OH-13s as observation aircraft for the cavalry, infantry, and air assault divisions. When the 1st Cavalry Division arrived in Vietnam, their Cavalry Squadrons, like the 1st Squadron, 9th Cavalry, were equipped with light *Sioux* scout helicopters, *Iroquois* gunships, and *Iroquois* transports.[18] The scouts located the enemy, the gunships mounted the aerial attack, and the slicks landed the rifle platoon to engage the enemy. The H-13E *Sioux* proved immensely valuable in this role.

In 1965, the concept of helicopter-borne fighting forces was still in its infancy and largely untested, and units in Vietnam developed tactics for their operations literally on the fly. The U.S. Army found the combination of the Bell OH-13 *Sioux* and the Hiller OH-23 *Raven* helicopters, once artillery spotters, initially helpful as precursors for air assault operations. The tandem of these two rotary-winged aircraft preceded the UH-1D *Iroquois* troop transports. They would reconnoiter the designated landing zone for the presence of enemy activity and confirm the terrain's suitability in the final moments before the air assault aircraft commenced the insertion of troops. Unfortunately, the mountainous terrain and Vietnam's temperature and humidity extremes stressed the obsolete and underpowered OH-13 and OH-23 to their limits. So stressed, they could neither fly fast enough to escape the enemy fire nor carry enough weapons to represent a significant threat to enemy forces in and around the landing zone.[19]

In time, units in Vietnam began receiving UH-1Bs which were outfitted with rocket pods and machine guns. These aircraft were designated to orbit at about 600 feet above the scouting *Sioux* and *Raven* helicopters over the landing zone. The armed *Iroquois* attacked anything that might interfere with the imminent troop landing. Just as their scouting brethren, these armed helicopters also had limitations. They were too slow and lacked the agility and responsiveness necessary to be effective against the threats. Thus, the Army found itself simultaneously confronted with the urgent necessity to replace its air assault scouts and the ships designated to protect them.[20]

Ultimately, the OH-13 *Sioux* became one of the most popular and versatile light utility helicopters ever built. It was produced from 1946 to 1976 in twenty different configurations, with models ranging from A to T. The commercial equivalent, the Bell model 47, would eventually be used in forty countries. The Bell OH-13 *Sioux* was replaced by the more advanced OH-6A *Cayuse* light observation helicopter and the OH-58 *Kiowa*.

The Great Sioux Nation

The first helicopter to be named under the Army's policy for assigning names to rotary winged aircraft after Indigenous Indian tribes was the H-13. While the younger Howze may have opted to, in part, honor his father's courage, the name importantly reflected courageous warriors who fought well as part of the United States Army and, when required, against the Army. The choice of name was intended to promote confidence in the abilities of the helicopter without sacrificing the tribal dignity while promoting an aggressive spirit.

Over one hundred years before the Lewis and Clark Expedition encountered the Sioux; their tribal ancestors lived in present-day Minnesota, and were trade partners with the French, British and Spanish. By 1803 the Sioux had lived for nearly two generations near the Missouri River.

The Sioux Nation was a confederacy of several tribes over a broad area that shared the Siouan language family. Besides the Great Plains tribes of the Lakota or Teton Sioux, consisting of seven tribal bands from North and South Dakota, including the Brulé, Hunkpapa, and Teton,[21] there was the smaller group of the Dakota or Santee Sioux of Nebraska and Minnesota, and the final group of the Nakota from tribal lands in Montana and the Dakotas, both North and South. Siouan people were also found in Virginia: Manahoac, Monacan, Occaneechi, and Saponi.

The U.S. efforts to subjugate and exercise control over the Sioux and their northern plains allies were a matter of greater consequence than anticipated. On August 18, 1854, Brevet Lt. John L. Grattan "led a force of twenty-nine soldiers and two cannons into a Brulé and Oglala camp near Fort Laramie, demanding that the alleged thief of a lame cow be turned over." After a forty-five-minute verbal exchange, the lieutenant ordered his men to open fire. With that, "he started the First Sioux War, and the warriors responded by annihilating his entire command."[22]

The Army responded slowly to the Grattan episode with a motley assembly of nine companies of infantry, dragoons, and artillery drawn from five different regiments at Fort Kearney led by Colonel William S. Harney. On September 3, a portion of the force descended upon Chief Little Thunder's Blue Water Creek camp. The regulars drove the Native Americans into the waiting fire of the dismounted dragoons and infantry that Colonel Harney positioned to block their escape. The engagement ended with the destruction of the camp and the loss of eighty Sioux dead and seventy captured compared to losses among the Army soldiers, including four soldiers killed, seven wounded, and one missing. The quick engagement effectively ended the First Sioux War.[23]

By the end of the Civil War, the United States Army was nearing the end of twenty-five years of intermittent warfare with the Indigenous tribes of the Great Plains. These were the tribes who had forcefully defended native lands against the westward expansion of the republic in order to protect their way of life. The Lakota lifestyle was based upon gathering and hunting, but mainly upon the abundant herds of bison that ranged on the plains. The hunting grounds of the Lakota Sioux were, of necessity, vast because of herd migration. The tribe's very existence was threatened by the influx of wagon trains headed west which brought diseases across the plains for which Native people had no immunities. The advent of railroads also brought more settlers to Sioux lands, further increasing their vulnerability. Exacerbating the situation, the U.S. Government, in violation of treaties, encouraged buffalo hunters onto the plains to exterminate the Lakota food source. Despite these encroachments, the Sioux resisted with great fortitude.[24] By this point in American history, more white citizens in the West were manifold than Native Americans, and more would be following.[25] As these new frontier folks moved into the Indian's land, they bared the land and its resources, leaving less suitable land for the Indians.

To calm the strife that permeated the Great Plains, the Army needed a military force capable of adapting to the rugged environment, extreme hardships, and unorthodox war-making nature of the new adversary. Indigenous warriors did not conform to the nineteenth-century norms of the armies of the Civil War. Their dispersal and marauding throughout the region required equally remote and isolated forts and settlements for the soldiers.

Success in the Indian Wars of the post-Civil War nineteenth century necessitated employing innovative and unconventional warfighting techniques. Nevertheless, it also required an equally non-traditional manner of dealing with the Indian tribes, different from the scandalous methods of the broader federal government. To that end, General George R. Crook, based upon his experiences fighting Native Americans in the Pacific Northwest and on the Great Plains, framed four precepts to guide his officers and troops in their interactions with the Indians: "Make no promises that could not be kept, tell the truth always, provide remunerated labor, and be patient, be just, and fear not."[26]

Crook could not widely inoculate the broader Army or the Indian Bureau with these precepts, especially when sharing authority with non-military officials and reporting to superiors who could overrule him. These precepts helped him and his subordinates as long as he could exercise control of the operational environment permitting him to follow them, Often, external governmental interventions prevented their use and limited his success.

Many special conditions that distinguished Indian service would reappear with remarkable similarities to Army assignments in the second half of the twentieth century. Native American combatants usually could not be discretely identified by the frontier soldier and, more disturbingly, could not be distinguished from their non-warring Native American relatives. Indian warriors could rapidly change from enemy to neutral observer to friend without yielding distinguishing attributes that could be used to classify one from the other confidently. Native Americans stimulated differing and often conflicting emotions among Army troopers; the Indian warrior was not the traditional, conventional European soldier. Unconventional in both techniques and military aims, the Native American used cunning, stealth, agility and endurance, weaponry skills, mobility, and exploitation of his natural habitat for military advantage. The Indian warrior engaged on his terms and deferred a fight unless he enjoyed overwhelming odds.

Throughout the pre-and post-Civil War periods, the Army erected over 690 forts in the territories that bordered Indian lands and later along trails that moved into and through their homelands. Ultimately these territorial frontier outposts would be in thirty-five of today's states. The consequences of a conventionally organized and trained Army trying to perform an unconventional mission were a battlefield record populated with more failures than successes and a lack of preparedness for the conventional foreign and domestic wars intermingled with Indian service.[27]

To obtain unimpeded access to the plains highways, including the Bozeman Trail, the shortest route to the goldfields at Virginia City, Montana, the Army and the Indian Bureau needed to bring about a cessation of hostilities with the Plains Indian tribes and get them to relocate to areas beyond the boundaries of the trails, especially after the bloody Indian wars of 1864–65. In 1865, treaties were negotiated with the warring tribes, and peace was restored. In the Northern Plains, treaties were signed with the Teton Sioux—Oglala, Hunkpapa, Miniconjou, Brulé, Two Kettle, Blackfeet, and Sans Arc—along with the Upper and Lower Yanktonai Sioux.[28] The Sioux agreed to leave the warpath and withdraw from the existing overland routes and any established through the Sioux country.

In reality, the Sioux had no intention of withdrawing from the Bozeman Trail, which went straight through their land, and relocating to Montana or allowing the white man to use it. By August 1866, hostilities between the Sioux and the white man had been reignited. The Army dispatched troops to the trail and began constructing Forts Phil Kearny and C.F. Smith. By December 1866, the former was ready to host a contingent of ten officers, three surgeons, and 389 enlisted men under Colonel Henry B. Carrington.[29]

Committed to offensive action against the Sioux, Colonel Carrington began operations along the Bozeman Trail in early December. When the Sioux attacked the wood train, Carrington seized the opportunity to punish the marauding Indians—sending a contingent to lift the wood train's siege and drive the Sioux westward toward another contingent that would fall in behind the Indians. Unfortunately for the blue coats, the Sioux turned on their pursuers, who panicked and stampeded.[30] Another opportunity presented itself on December 21, when the Sioux concealed 1,500 to 2,000 warriors in the ravines on both sides of a narrow ridge by which the Bozeman Trail descended from Lodge Trail Ridge. The Miniconjou warrior High-Back-Bone planned an ambush, and a young Oglala Lakota named Crazy Horse led the Indian decoy party.[31]

Instead of following the plan laid out by Colonel Carrington, the officer charged with leading the relief column, Captain William J. Fetterman, chose to cross Big Piney Creek and ascend Lodge Trail Ridge to attack the Indians from the rear and above their concealed ravine positions instead of relieving and securing the wood train. The cavalry formation under Lieutenant George W. Grummond, the second part of the relief force, charged down the slope of Lodge Trail Ridge into the positions of the concealed Indians who burst forth from both sides of the trail. A third contingent, infantry and dismounted cavalry, under Captain Tendor Ten Eyck was dispatched to support Captain Fetterman after the sounds of the heavy rifle fire beyond Lodge Trail Ridge. Within an hour's combat, Captain Fetterman and his entire unit were killed on what has since been known as Massacre Ridge and what has become known as the Fetterman Fight, as the Fetterman Massacre, or the Battle of the Hundred-in-the-Hands. Meanwhile, the deceptive Sioux lost as little as "a mere handful up to a hundred."[32]

The Fetterman disaster was cause for shock and outrage within the ranks of the Army, leading to a hardening of attitudes and dispositions toward all Indians and demands for retaliation among westerners. Speaking for the Army on the frontier, General William T. Sherman, commander of the Military Division of the Missouri, telegraphed General Grant, General of the Army of the United States: "We must act with vindictive earnestness against the Sioux, even to their extermination, men, women, and children."[33] Further blurred now was the distinction between hostile and peaceful or combatant and noncombatant Indians.

By March of the following year, the Army had planned a punitive strike against the Sioux and Cheyenne, and organized a strike force of 2,000 cavalry and infantry troops under the command of Colonel John Gibbon, who would operate under General Sherman's admonishment that "no mercy should be shown these Indians for they grant no quarter nor ask for it."[34] The arrival in Omaha of a presidential Indian Peace Commission for meetings with the Sioux and Cheyenne forced the postponement of Gibbon's expedition.

Portrait of Jack Red Cloud Prince [Oglala Lakota (Oglala Sioux)] 1899. (Courtesy of the National Museum of the American Indian, Smithsonian Institution P27506.)

The United States government, in its Indian policy, favored an approach of concentration, moving Indians to reservations. Most of present-day South Dakota, north of the Platte River and west of the Missouri River would be set aside for the North Plains Indians, the Sioux. They would further be granted hunting rights on the Republican River and in Nebraska and Wyoming north of the Platte. In deference to the Sioux Chief Red Cloud, the treaty setting aside the North

Plains, the Fort Laramie Treaty, included a provision "reserving the Powder River country as 'unceded Indian territory' on which no white might trespass without Indian consent."[35] The land south of the Arkansas River was set aside by the Medicine Lodge treaties for the South Plains Indians, i.e., Caddo, Comanche, Kiowa, Kiowa-Apache, Lipan Apache, Arapaho, and Southern Cheyenne. The government ceded over 7.2 million acres to the tribes in Oklahoma, Arkansas, portions of Texas, the eastern foothills of New Mexico, and parts of Louisiana.

The Great Plains would thus become the heartland of the Indian problem because they were home to the largest and most powerful tribes that enjoyed better organization and leadership than tribes elsewhere.[36] As the Indian tribes began to take their places on the North and South Plains reservations, tranquility was not uniform. Indian raiding parties began spreading their lust for vengeance and retribution for the government's failure to make good on the several treaties' provisions, including the provision of adequate food and the decision to withhold firearms and ammunition from the Indians for hunting wild game. The warring bands stirred the angst of white settlers and fired the thirst for retribution of Generals Philip H. Sheridan and William Sherman. No longer would they and their men respect the conventions of "civilized" warfare but would instead embrace the doctrine of subjecting the entire enemy population "to the horrors of war and thereby undermine the will to resist," in other words, total war.[37] The Sioux were included among the targets of this new doctrine.

The inauguration of Ulysses Grant as the eighteenth President of the United States marked a change in federal Indian policy. He fostered a climate whereby a 'Peace Policy' could be created and flourish. The policy contemplated "conquest by kindness," whereby civilian authorities had supremacy over the Army in Indian affairs. Management of the Indian reservations focused on pursuing peace, agricultural self-sufficiency, and education. The Indian Bureau had "exclusive control and jurisdiction" of all Indians on their reservation, while Indians off their reservation were the province of the Army, and they would be considered and treated as hostile. Furthermore, the Army had to be invited by the agent or his superior to interfere with any Indian of the reservation.[38]

Sitting Bull was among the greats of Indian warriors and political leaders. Even his name in the tipi language signified all that was great and generous. Although chief of the Hunkpapa Sioux, he markedly influenced the Blackfoot, the Oglala, Brulé, Miniconjou, and Sans Arc Sioux. The Northern Cheyenne and Northern Arapaho who traveled with the Sioux accepted his leadership. He deeply hated the white man and harbored anger over their continued encroachment upon Indian lands. Sitting Bull could not countenance the white man and therefore was unwilling to yield or negotiate.

At issue for the Sioux Nation were the terms in the Treaty of 1868, which ended the war for Red Cloud, chief of the Oglala Sioux. The government's objective was to lure the Sioux to a reservation and further subvert them to the ways of the Indian administration. The Treaty set aside the Great Sioux Reservation, which was located in present-day South Dakota west of the Missouri River and promised free rations and other emoluments for those Native Americans who would affiliate themselves with an Indian agency. The government also wanted the Sioux agencies to be built along the Missouri River to facilitate the delivering supplies to the agencies and enable surveillance by the Army. The Sioux, however, were not inclined to go to the Missouri River. They instead preferred their former haunts—the Powder and Upper Republican country—along with Fort Laramie as their trading post. That was the life they desired.[39]

Dissatisfied with Indian agency alternatives geared toward the civilizing of the Indian, the Sioux, Northern Arapaho, Northern Cheyenne, and Brulé, under the aegis of Red Cloud and Spotted Tail, split their time between the agencies and the hostile camps. The Indians became a constant threat, raiding the agencies, abusing the agents, threatening their lives, killing their cattle, and, in general, doing whatever possible in opposition to the civilizing efforts.[40] The over five years of Indian-sponsored turmoil and desperation for the agencies brought about frequent pleas for protection from the Army.

The Army responded by stationing its troops and establishing patrol routes to protect the westward advance of the Union Pacific railroad. Both did little to dissuade the continuing raids of the Sioux and their Cheyenne and Arapaho allies, who by this time were operating well beyond the hunting limits set by the Treaty of 1868. Concurrently, the Northern Pacific railroad builders were inching their way west beyond the Missouri River toward the Rockies. Both realities alarmed the Sioux as they anticipated the arrival of the iron horse and the hosts of white men that would follow. Sitting Bull and his braves vigorously opposed the Northern Pacific construction crews and the almost 2,000 soldiers and civilians General Sherman dispatched under the command of Colonel David S. Stanley to protect them.[41]

The size of the Stanley expedition was by far the largest dispatched by the Army; it had ventured further west than any of its predecessors, had remained in the field longer than any others, and had aroused the Sioux and their allies to previously unseen tenacity and vengeance. While the financial failure of the Northern Pacific in 1873 gave the Sioux a respite from the white man in the Yellowstone River area, the depression that seized the country following the Panic of 1873 unleashed countless prospectors to seek the purported mineral wealth of the Black Hills. The Black Hills were clearly within the delineated boundaries of the Great Sioux Reservation delimited by the Treaty of 1868.

On July 2, 1874, the Black Hills Expedition of over 1,000 men in ten troops of the Seventh Cavalry and two companies of infantry under the command of Lieutenant Colonel George Custer set out to survey the territory and select a site for a military post. Such a site was found near Bear Butte on the northeastern border of the Black Hills.[42] The expedition was shortly followed by newspaper reports of the verdant potential of the Hills and the "gold among the roots of the grass."[43] The resultant media-hyped gold fever prompted the President to charge the Army with barring prospectors from the Great Sioux Reservation lands. Notwithstanding the

Army's best, but somewhat embarrassing, policing efforts, some 800 gold prospectors were working the streams of the Black Hills during the summer of 1875.

The government, in time, concluded that the best outcome for all would be to purchase the Black Hills from the Sioux. Neither the proffered $6 million purchase price nor the $400,000 per year lease presented by the Great Father appealed to the Sioux, especially the young Sioux hunting tribe members. The negotiations collapsed, and while the Sioux, in every legal and moral sense, owned the Black Hills and the white man had no standing there, the government set out to search for another way to separate the Sioux from their reservation lands.

In the winter of 1875, the Army determined that it would withdraw from the Black Hills, thus allowing prospectors unfettered access to the mineral-rich region of the Great Sioux Reservation. The original 1866 reservation boundary encompassed almost all of present-day South Dakota. By the Fort Laramie Treaty of April 29, 1868, the Great Sioux Reservation, including the Black Hills was "set apart for the absolute and undisturbed use and occupation of the Indians."[44] Due to its size, plentiful availability of buffalo and other food, and the attractiveness of the mineral potential of the region to white men, the Army would, by force of arms, compel the hunting bands to leave the territory outside the boundaries and return to the reservation. This last stroke ended the Sioux raiding. By the latter treaty and the Army's stand, the Sioux lost the right to permanently reside outside the boundaries of the Great Reservation but retained the right to hunt in those regions, Thus their recourse was to settle in the Black Hills. Indian Bureau inspectors laid the blame for the Indian raiding parties at the feet of Sitting Bull and the other chiefs, and demanded that all Indians return to the reservation by January 31, 1876.[45] Unsurprisingly, January 31 passed without sizeable numbers of Sioux braves returning to the reservation. Equally unsurprising, the next day the Interior Department declared all Indians off the reservation hostile the next day and what would follow would become known as "Sitting Bull's War."

General Sheridan and his subordinates, Generals Terry and Crook, devised their plans to strike against the Sioux and Cheyenne quickly and aggressively before the early spring. Once their plans were set into motion, the winter weather intervened, preventing the assembling of forces, the detection and engagement of Indian bands, and the embarrassing setback when tribal lodges were attacked, as in the case of the Battle of Powder Run on March 17, 1876. The battle affirmed the belief of all three generals that there would be no campaign against the tribes until the summer.

The summer campaign plan called for General Crook, with ten troops of the Third Cavalry and five from the Second, plus two companies from the Fourth Infantry and three from the Ninth, to drive northward from Fort Fetterman. Lieutenant Colonel Custer, with twelve troops of the Seventh Cavalry plus two companies of the Seventeenth Infantry, and one company of the Sixth Infantry, would march westward from Fort Abraham Lincoln. With six companies of the Seventh Infantry and four troops of the Second Cavalry, Colonel John Gibbon would move eastward from Fort Ellis, Montana. The moving columns were to search out, locate, and engage the hostile Indians and force their return to the reservation. The commanders hoped that Custer's "Dakota Column" would sweep the Indians toward the Bighorn River while Crook's troops would push them toward Custer. It was also expected that Gibbon's "Montana Column" would intercept any hostile who might attempt to flee toward the north and the Missouri River.

By June 1876, the three approaching columns were converging upon a substantial segment of the Sioux and Cheyenne. They had migrated to the camps of the hunting bands in more significant numbers than the previous annual gatherings. In the six tribal circles, five Sioux and one Cheyenne, on the Rosebud Creek in the Montana Territory, there were nearly 2,000 lodges in the camps with as many as 15,000 people and between 3,000 and 4,000 warriors.[46]

On June 17, 1876, Crook's column, which was marching northward along the south fork of Rosebud Creek, paused for a morning break. Crook's Crow and Shoshoni auxiliaries had taken up screening positions to protect the resting troops when the Sioux and Cheyenne attacked the outposts on the bluffs to the north. Heavily outnumbered, the Crow and Shoshoni fought back toward the Army camp and bought time for Crook to organize and deploy his troopers. The ensuing six-hour battle consisted of separate charges and countercharges by General Crook and Chief Crazy Horse. Both contingents were divided into several smaller formations across the three-mile front, with neither side being decisive. Despite the unity and uncommon tenacity of the Sioux and Cheyenne, General Crook ultimately claimed victory in the Battle of Rosebud Creek because his enemy had withdrawn, and he was left in possession of the battlefield.

Within a week, in response to General Terry's strategy to catch the Sioux thought to be encamped in the direction of the Little Bighorn River, Lieutenant Colonel Custer led his 600- to 700-man regiment of the Seventh Cavalry up Rosebud Creek. When Custer reached the divide between Rosebud Creek and the Little Big Horn River, his scouts, viewing the region from the "Crow's Nest," reported sighting the Sioux encampment some fifteen miles distant. In response, Custer divided his force into three columns. Captain Benteen with three troops headed south, while Major Reno with three troops and Custer with five troops advanced along the Indian trail leading to the Little Big Horn. Sighting a small Indian band, Reno was ordered to attack. Unlike many previous engagements with Indians, the Sioux did not withdraw from battle; instead, they advanced toward the charging troopers.

Reno and his 112 soldiers forded the Little Bighorn and advanced down the valley toward the village. The hostiles swarmed to meet the attack causing Reno to stop short, dismount his force and engage them. The soldiers remounted their horses and, in a formation, became intermixed with the Indians, fled to the bluffs back across the river. Reno's attack, battle, and flight cost almost half of his command in killed, wounded, and missing.[47]

The Hunkpapa Sioux, under Chief Gall, joined by the warriors who forced Major Reno's retreat, swarmed across the river and pressed forward from the south. From the north, Chief Crazy Horse led another warrior band. In a short and violent episode lasting about an hour, the soldiers in uneven terrain fought under conditions favoring the Indians—not a single white man survived the battle. Captain Benteen, responding to Custer's summons, joined his men and the ammunition train with the remnants of Major Reno's troops and established a perimeter defense from which they held off the growing numbers of Sioux and Cheyenne until nightfall, and then twice again, the following day.

In stunned horror, a nation engrossed in celebrating its centennial received word of the tragedy that befell the Army at the hands of the Sioux and Cheyenne at a remote place called Little Bighorn. Custer and half of the Seventh Cavalry, every officer and man in five companies, 262 souls, were dead and another fifty-three wounded.[48] Once again, the unconventional foe defeated the Army's heavy conventional columns burdened with provisioning requirements for man and horse tied to bases distant from the combat action.

In the wake of the Army's humiliation at the Little Big Horn, Colonel Nelson A. Miles and about five hundred infantry soldiers pursued Sitting Bull in a running battle in October 1876. The colonel assessed that the Indians were "in great want of food, their stock is nearly worn down, and they cannot have a large amount of ammunition." Miles continued his pursuit despite the subzero temperature, success-fully repelling Crazy Horse's attack at the Wolf Mountains on January 8, 1877. In May, Miles defeated Lame Deer's Miniconjou at Muddy Creek. Sitting Bull was safely ensconced in Canada at this stage of the campaign, and the remaining Lakota and Cheyenne surrendered themselves to the government. The Great Sioux War was over.[49]

The threat of Sitting Bull remained over the northern plains after the campaign of 1876 and would continue for five more years. Peace for the white man would never materialize while he was free. The U.S. government actively encouraged the overhunting of buffalo as a means to an end: to bring and ensure control of the Native tribes, their confinement on reservations, and their transition to farming.[50] Within a few years, the Great Plains buffalo was all but extinct, and the Sioux were gradually migrating north across the border into Canada. By late 1877, Canada hosted the Hunkpapa, Oglala, Miniconjou, San Arc, Blackfoot Sioux, and Nez Percé warriors in lands still inhabited by sparse populations of buffalo. However, the concern that the remaining buffalo herds were insufficient to sustain the Canadian tribes like the Blackfoot, Cree, and Assinniboine led to the united desire of Canadian and American officials to return the Sioux to their reservation in the United States.

By 1879 and 1880, Sioux camps in Canada dwindled because the buffalo were disappearing. In short succession, one tribal chieftain after another led his starving people across the border to surrender and accept a settlement on the reservation. Finally, on July 20, 1881, Chief Sitting Bull and forty-five warriors plus women and children rode into Fort Buford in present-day North Dakota and surrendered. His surrender marked "the passing of the northern Plains from the Indian to the soldier, the pioneer, and the railroad."[51]

Following the end of the Sioux War in 1881, the Army, as voiced by General Sherman, considered the Indian problem no longer a concern of the Army. Tribes were safely and peacefully corralled on reservations, and cattlemen with their herds now occupied the Powder, Bighorn, and Yellowstone country, the last vestiges of Sioux and Cheyenne hunting grounds. Forever gone were the safe havens to which Indians could flee.

The Dawes Act of 1887 would make matters worse by authorizing the division of reservation land into individual allotments and opening the remaining reservation land to white settlement. Impacted by drought, loss of their lands, inadequate government annuities, weak agents, and government dissembling, the Lakota and Northern Cheyenne residing on the Pine Ridge, Rosebud, Lower Brule, Crow Creek, Cheyenne River, and Standing Rock Reservations sought solace in the *wanagi wacipi*, Ghost Dance.[52] The Ghost Dance was a "spiritual quest for an Indian millennium in which they might rid themselves of white domination."[53]

Dispirited Sioux subsisting on the meager rations provided by the government agents administering the reservations and suffering from the cold of the impending winter found hope in the spiritual Ghost Dance movement. This circle dance prophesied the end of encroachment on tribal lands and the restored prosperity of Indigenous peoples. Numerous mystic prophets appeared on the reservations and in Indian lodges spreading the message. One of these was a Paiute shaman named Wovoka. His Ghost Dance religion set into motion events that would lead to the final confrontation between Indians and soldiers.[54] While Wovoka preached a peaceful doctrine, the Ghost Dance religion took on militant associations for the Teton Sioux, angered by the civilization program and the halving of the Great Sioux Reservation by government agents. The Sioux were ready to hasten the fulfillment of the Wovoka prophesies by killing white men.

As the movement spread, non-Native Americans pleaded for increased bluecoat protection. With more than five thousand men at his disposal, Major General Nelson Miles undertook the breakup of the Ghost Dancers. By November 1890, the Ghost Dance leaders, Short Bull and Kicking Bear had sufficiently agitated the Oglala of Pine Ridge and the Brulé of Rosebud that government employees feared for their safety. By November 20, Army troopers were on the scene, separating the Indians into "friendly" and "hostile" encampments. By December, the Oglala and Brulé hostiles had united on the Pine Ridge Reservation with 600 men and their families. The Army, wanting to head off more significant trouble on other reservations, began negotiating peace. Chief Sitting Bull, still the most respected and revered Sioux warrior chief was residing at Standing Rock Reservation, the last bastion of Indian resistance to the white man's way. Standing Rock agency officials ordered the arrest of Sitting Bull, and on December 15, 1890, agency policemen attempted to affect the arrest. Spurred on by his people, Sitting Bull resisted and was summarily shot in the chest by a policeman. A second policeman shot the chief in the head, killing him instantly.

Also arrested was Chief Big Foot, who had successfully eluded apprehension and headed to Pine Ridge Agency with the assembled Sioux tribes. Four troops of the Seventh Cavalry under Major Samuel M. Whitside encountered Big Foot's Indians on December 28 and persuaded them to accept an escort. The entire assembly encamped that night in the Valley of Wounded Knee Creek,[55] and the following morning the Indians found themselves surrounded by the whole Seventh Cavalry, 500 troopers strong, issuing demands that they surrender their guns.

The Indians resisted and refused to surrender their Winchester repeating rifles, which were hidden in their lodges and in the blankets of both men and women. During the search for the weapons, an altercation ensued between a soldier and an Indian, and a rifle went off. A point-blank melee immediately followed, and when the firing ended, the valley was filled with the carnage: 250 to 300 Sioux, including at least sixty-two women and children, dead, compared to twenty-five officers and soldiers dead and thirty-nine wounded.[56]

The Wounded Knee Massacre was the last in a litany of failed events. "The Ghost Dance was the Indian's last hope. Accommodation had failed. The retreat had failed. War had failed. And now, Wounded Knee made it plain that religion had failed. No choice remained but to submit to the dictates of the government."[57]

With the *Sioux* in its inventory and in the hands of a growing number of Army-trained aviators, the service was on the brink of a new era, exploring the possibilities and potential of vertical lift, albeit for limited tactical missions. A greater potential lay on the horizon awaiting newer and larger aircraft and innovators able to visualize and capitalize on the greater tactical opportunities portended. The Army had also crossed the threshold of reaching out to the broader American populace with the foundation of its helicopter naming convention and tribute to the great Native American tribes and warriors of the past. Both service initiatives were nascent but ripe with the promise of better things to come. Next in line was the Army's first true transport helicopter, the Sikorsky H-19 *Chickasaw*.

CH-19 CHICKASAW

*Army H-19 Chickasaw, shown here in Korea, was used
by the Army in Vietnam during the early advisory period.
(Courtesy of the Army Aviation Museum.)*

The Second World War saw the initial limited but highly successful use of heli-copters in prominent specialized roles. The achievements of early helicopters only whetted the appetite of the armed services for aircraft with more capability and capacity in addition to the more universal requirements developed earlier. There was a growing appreciation by ground commanders of the significantly greater poten-tial for the helicopter's expanded use. To satisfy these potentialities would require rotary-winged aircraft with substantially greater mission flexibility. The core of this conundrum lay in the trade-offs among available airframe space, engine size and placement, and main rotor optimization.

In the vernacular of the day, the armed services were looking for a large cabin utility helicopter. Recognizing the limitations of their R-4 and Bell's H-13 designs, the Sikorsky Aircraft Company undertook a company-funded design effort for a novel helicopter, the S-55, which incorporated the four principal military requirements and the heavy-lift requirement. In less than twelve months, Sikorsky produced a mockup of their unique and revolutionary design. Critical to achieving a large capacity cabin was the unconventional placement of the Wright R-1300-3 seven-cylinder, 700 hp, air-cooled radial piston engine. A large cabin was possible directly under the main rotor head with the engine below and forward of the cockpit.

The cabin permitted transporting ten soldiers or six litter patients and a medic plus the two-man flight crew. The helicopter had a service ceiling of 11,400 feet, a maximum speed of 109 miles per hour, and an operating range of 405 miles.[1] Additionally, the aircraft had a one-ton external lift capability.

In the H-19s, the Army designation for the S-55, the fuselage was constructed primarily of aluminum with weight-saving applications of magnesium. Aluminum was further applied to the three main rotor blades, whose hollow spars were filled with nitrogen under pressure. By the day's standards, at over sixty-two feet in length and almost 13.5 feet in height, the *Chickasaw* was a large helicopter and represented the Army's first actual cargo and troop transport aircraft.

The *Chickasaw* made its maiden flight on November 10, 1949, less than one year after the start of the design. On April 16, 1950, it was first introduced into service use with the U.S. Air Force. Two of the five test aircraft delivered by Sikorsky were sent to South Korea for evaluation under combat conditions in March 1951. The successful assessment of the *Chickasaw* in combat led to production orders from the Air Force, Army, Navy, Coast Guard, and Marine Corps and in total Sikorsky produced 1,281 S-55s.

The H-19 began its military career in the ranks of the air rescue squadrons of the Air Force's Military Air Transport Service (MATS). The Army's 6th Transportation Company tested the H-19C for suitability as an air ambulance, vertical rescue work, external sling cargo movement, and troop transport. User testing paid particular attention to aircraft reliability with measures of merit emphasizing the comparison of maintenance hours per flight hour. Successful testing by the Army Field Forces Board convinced the Army to order ninety-seven *Chickasaws,* which were received by the end of the fiscal year 1954. The versatile helicopter performed yeoman service throughout the Korean War, transporting inspection teams, military assistance officials, mobile training teams, distinguished visitors, and resupplying isolated and widely dispersed troop units. The Army ultimately had two transportation corps helicopter companies, the 6th and the 13th, supporting the Korean theater, each with twenty-one H-19 aircraft.

After introducing the H-13 into Korea and its success as an "Angel of Mercy," the addition of the H-19 *Chickasaw* to the 6th Transportation Company (Helicopter) fleet in July 1952 was a significant event in the lineage of Army rotary-wing aviation. By January 1953, the company was ready to begin operations and was receiving operational missions sixty days later. It participated in Operation TERRY BLUE on March 20, supporting the 3rd Infantry Division by resupplying its units when the division was isolated from its sources of supply and overland supply routes were swamped by floodwaters. Ten *Chickasaws* made thirty round trips to landing spots a mere 300 yards behind the main line of resistance,[2] airlifting 33,925 pounds of desperately needed fuel, ammunition, food, and charcoal during the operation.[3]

When the *Chickasaw* was deployed to Korea in 1952, the Army's need for a suppressive fire system for its helicopters became painfully apparent. Like its predecessor, the H-13 *Sioux*, the *Chickasaw* would play an early role in the quest for armed helicopters. With the end of the Korean War, interest among the Army's hierarchy in arming helicopters began to wane. The concept was not lost, however, among visionary aviators. Colonel Jay D. Vanderpool was charged with forming an experimental armament program at Fort Rucker, Alabama, in June 1956. Included in Vanderpool's coterie was a single H-19 on which his team demonstrated two pods of fifteen two-inch rockets each.

A few years later, the U.S. Army Pacific Operations Chief, Major General Normando Costello, asked an alumnus of "Vanderpool's Fools" to come to Okinawa to arm some helicopters for a pending exercise. In addition to skid-mounted machine guns for the UH-1B, a 2.75-inch folding fin aerial rocket (FFAR) system was added to the UH-19. These formed the beginning of an armament system that would be further developed by the Utility Tactical Transport Helicopter Company (UTTHCO) in Okinawa and was later ordered to Vietnam.[4]

The H-19C was powered by a single Pratt & Whitney R-1340-57 550 hp engine; H-19D by a Curtis-Wright R-1300-3D 700 hp piston engine. It served as a utility, troop carrier, and rescue helicopter with a winch. The Air Force flew the H-19A and H-19B, while the Army used the H-19C and H-19D.

The *Chickasaw* had a very innovative design, leading to many new rotary-winged aircraft capabilities. In the hands of equally creative minds and skilled aviators, the H-19 was a very capable aircraft and achieved many unique firsts in helicopter aviation which included: main rotor blade twist, offshore oil support, anti-submarine warfare, jet assist take off (JATO), transatlantic crossing, and schedule passenger service among others.[5]

Every helicopter has peculiarities that influence the pilot's assessment of its flyability. The *Chickasaw* was no different, especially among aviators who were exposed to it early in their flight training or flying experiences. The H-19 was commonly assessed as "a handful for a beginner; it wasn't an easy machine."[6] Young pilots frequently found themselves compensating for the "pendulum effect" in a hover caused by the flight deck being so far above the center of gravity. The aviators were constantly making RPM adjustments because the aircraft had no throttle coordination like the turbine-powered helicopters did. Moreover, the task was exacerbated when working at higher elevations. A drawback with a lasting impact was the positioning of the Chickasaw's massive engine exhaust, just four feet from the pilot's head. With the exhaust noise and the limited noise attenuation of the helmet, many aviators would suffer permanent hearing loss, especially in the left ear. Still, those who mastered the CH-19 felt they ended up solidly well-qualified pilots.

Following the cessation of hostilities on the Korean Peninsula and with an armistice declared, the Army Field Forces and operations staff of the Department of the Army undertook several studies based upon their helicopter experience during the war with the aim of projecting future requirements. The conclusion was that future Army aviation resources would necessitate more utility rotary-wing aircraft than any other variant.

The Department of the Army urged the Office of the Chief of Army Field Forces (OCAFF) to prepare a development and fielding plan to assure the earliest meeting of the increased aircraft requirements. The new utility helicopter would be used for advanced training for cargo helicopter pilots, special operations by the Transportation, Signal, and Engineer branches, casualty recovery and movement, and anticipated missions for proposed Division, Corps, and Army aviation companies. The assessment of all the proposed missions included determining the optimal helicopter for each task and the designation of missions not suitable for the utility helicopter that could be performed by the reconnaissance or light helicopter. The OCAFF determined the number of utility helicopters needed Army-wide to accomplish those missions designated for the utility helicopter. Similarly, changes to the reconnaissance and light cargo helicopters inventory were assessed for assignments that the utility helicopter was not suitable for but could be performed by the other two model helicopters. By mid-FY1957, the Army determined that with projected future procurements of modified H-13s, its on-hand inventory, and utility helicopter procurement, which totaled 353 Sikorsky H-19s; 72 H-19Cs, and 281 H-19Ds, it had sufficient utility helicopters to meet its force requirements.[7]

As the Army field organization design was emerging for the 1955–1960 period, utility helicopter requirements were substantially expanded to accommodate such missions as "command and staff transportation; liaison and courier, aeromedical evacuation; transportation of small groups of personnel and limited amounts of materiel, supplies, and equipment, and transition instrument training."[8]

In the Korean War, the CH-19 unambiguously demonstrated the role and utility of the unarmed transport helicopter. With the combat record that the helicopter accumulated, it played an instrumental role in the continuing evolution of Army doctrine related to air mobility and the combat employment of troop-carrying helicopters, all of which would come to fruition during the impending American war in Southeast Asia.[9]

Following the Korean War and during the period before the Vietnam War, the Aviation Center at Fort Rucker began experimenting with different configurations of weapons systems on its helicopters and the *Chickasaw* was among those that were tested. The Rocketdyne Division of North American developed a 1.5-inch spin-stabilized research rocket called "NAKA" that the Vertol engineers would subsequently mount on the H-19. The configuration included thirty-two rockets plus machine guns.[10] While the R&D package was of marginal effectiveness and not ultimately selected, the experiments gave the researchers a realistic preview of the effects of forty millimeter armaments that would later be tested.

The CH-19 was included in the Weapons Platoon of the Aerial Combat Reconnaissance Company (Experimental) and participated in the weapons systems demonstrations sponsored by the Association of the United States Army in 1957. For the Army Aviation-Industry Symposium at Fort Rucker on June 6, the CH-19 mounted two pods each of fifteen two-inch rockets.[11] The second incarnation of an armed CH-19 in the Fort Rucker experiments came equipped with 2.75-inch FFAR. This jury-rigged system would represent the embryonic beginning of armaments that would later be used in the Utility Tactical Transport Helicopter Company.[12]

The CH-19 saw its last combat action with the U.S. military in the early days of the Vietnam War. Although deployed in-country, the Army found that the helicopter was not capable of dealing with the operational requirements and the environment in the theater. Some *Chickasaw* helicopters were used in the opening operations of the Vietnam War until being replaced by the H-34 *Choctaw*, which was based on the H-19 and showed an apparent resemblance. Little is known about the service of the CH-19 by U.S. forces in Vietnam other than the fact that at least four are known to have been shipped there for combat service, however, not even their tail numbers are known.

Although the H-19 entered the Army as a true transport helicopter, its versatility unlocked numerous other tactical and operational prospects for its Cold War roles and later those in the counterinsurgency environment. The lessons learned with it helped shape the requirements for subsequent aircraft that expanded their adaptability to yet unimagined roles and missions.

The Chickasaw People

The Chickasaw Nation, one of the so-called Five Civilized Tribes, is among the largest of the federally recognized tribes.[13] Before their first contact with Europeans, they were widely considered "unconquered and unconquerable."[14] They were an agrarian people who were also skilled craftsmen that commonly settled in sizeable towns that were called chiefdoms that possessed their own democratic political system. Their docility placed importance on the formation of alliances with their neighbors for their common security and the expansion of trading opportunities.

The distant origins of the Chickasaw people lay in the territories that are now the states of Mississippi, Kentucky, Alabama, Tennessee, and Missouri, where they remained until 1837, when they became part of the "Great Removal," and were forced to travel along the "Trail of Tears" with the Cherokee, Choctaw, Creek, and Seminole to the Indian Territory. With the passage of the Indian Removal Act signed by President Andrew Jackson on May 28, 1830, the Chickasaw people were displaced to their new homeland in south-central Oklahoma. Their departure included 4,914 of their tribal members plus 1,156 enslaved people, and extended from 1837 to 1851, with the last tribesmen being enrolled in the 1890s.[15]

Even from its earliest times, the history of the Chickasaw tribe was one frequently punctuated by skirmishes with other Indian tribes and, eventually, the Europeans from Great Britain, France, and Spain. The Chickasaw were thus considered to have very few friends but an abundance of enemies, and by some accounts, their enemies included almost every tribe that lived near them.

Chickasaw war parties were phenomenally stealth-like when engaging their opponents, exploiting their familiarity with the terrain. Without the benefit of horses, they traveled on foot and were incredibly swift runners. They were excellent swimmers, and rivers presented no barrier. Large, massed formations of warriors were not typical of the Chickasaw except when needed to defend their towns. Otherwise, their method of warfare was a small war party of thirty to fifty men who could travel quietly and surprise their opponent. Since the "unexpected" was typical of Chickasaw warfare and because of the Chickasaw belief that a dead warrior's ghost would haunt his relatives until avenged, the only question about Chickasaw retaliation was when and where.

In 1540, a Spanish expedition led by Hernando de Soto encountered the Chickasaw, their first contact with Europeans. A century later, the British arrived and established the Carolina colony in 1670. The English engaged in active trading with the Chickasaws, exchanging guns, metal goods, manufactured cloth, and other items for deerskins and Indian captives. The English then sold their captives as slaves to the sugar plantation owners in the Caribbean Islands. Recognizing the benefits of this trading relationship, the Chickasaws used their armed advantage to repeatedly raid the neighboring Choctaws to seize them as captives and sell them to the English.

In time, however, the Chickasaw embraced the advantages of slave labor as they witnessed their white neighbors using it in the production of cotton. The use of slaves for their own purposes aided in the gender role issues within the tribe, as women were relegated to farming tasks while the men were hunters. The advent of slaves allowed the male population to support tribal agrarian pursuits as supervisors of the slave population.

The arrival of the French in 1699 and the establishment of their presence along the Gulf coast altered the Chickasaw-Choctaw military balance. By restricting their trade to the Choctaws and providing them with guns, the French established the latter as their principal allies in the region, forcing some of the Chickasaws to move closer to the English Savannah River settlements.

Twice before the middle of the eighteenth century, specifically the periods of 1720–1725 and 1733–1743, the Chickasaws went to battle with the French and their Choctaw Indian allies. The French were distrustful of the English-Chickasaw relationship because every time France and England were at war, the Chickasaws would harass French ships transiting the Mississippi River. These attacks disrupted the trading relationship between the French Louisiana colony and the French colonies in Canada. In reaction to the killing of a French fur trader in 1720, the French provided even greater numbers of guns and ammunition to the Choctaw and encouraged them to attack the Chickasaw in retaliation. After repulsing all Choctaw raids on their villages, the Chickasaw launched their offensive and cut off all French shipping on the Mississippi.

Throughout their history, the Chickasaw people were recognized as perhaps the fiercest warriors in their region. In 1726, the governor of French Louisiana wrote that they "breathe nothing but war and are unquestionably the bravest of the continent."[16] Decades later, the British Indian Superintendent John Stuart called them "the bravest Indians on the Continent."[17]

Before the American Revolution, the Chickasaw were trading partners and committed British allies. Yet with the outbreak of the War for Independence, the

Chickasaw attempted to remain neutral, favoring neither their former trading partner nor the American colonists. However, in May 1779, the Virginians warned the Chickasaw to stay neutral or risk being invaded. The Indians replied that they were willing to abandon their neutrality, meet the Virginians, and would treat them as they had the French and their Indian allies. They further declared that they feared no foreign nation as long as King George stood by them. Thus like their former Native American rivals, the Choctaw, the Chickasaw sided with the British and sent warrior patrols up and down the Mississippi River protecting British settlements against the American troops often led by Colonel George Rogers Clark. A significant Chickasaw engagement during the Revolutionary War was their attack on Fort Jackson in western Kentucky. Additionally, small bands of Chickasaw warriors participated in defending Mobile and Pensacola against the Spanish, who had by then declared war against the British.[18]

Following the American Revolution, the Chickasaw Nation skillfully maintained peace with the American and Spanish inhabitants. Through capable diplomacy, they kept their sovereignty through a series of three treaties with Spain (1784, 1792, and 1793) and six with the United States (1786, 1801, 1805, 1816, 1818, and 1826). However, with the Treaty of San Lorenzo (Pinckney's Treaty of 1795), Spain ceded all its lands above the 31st parallel which resulted in all Chickasaw land now falling within the territorial boundaries of the United States.

Soon followed the movement of Americans to land along the Mississippi River and through the mid-section of Chickasaw lands. With the influx of new settlers came changes to the Chickasaw way of life and culture. Their chiefs encouraged their people to shift from trading deerskin to growing renewable crops and raising cattle. The tribe began to adopt American or "civilized" values, and because they resided in the south, the economic system would eventually replicate that of the southern states to include a socioeconomic hierarchy influenced by the dependence upon slave labor. By 1817, Mississippi became a state, and by 1829 it enacted a law that relinquished all Indian land claims in the state and subjected those lands to state jurisdiction. With that ended Chickasaw sovereignty over their land. Before their removal, they had controlled the waters of the Mississippi River and were referred to by historians as the "Spartans of the Mississippi."[19]

The impact of the passage of the Removal Act of 1830 fell upon the Five Civilized Tribes, including the Chickasaw, who left their native homeland without resistance. They were educating their children, building homes and churches, and farming in accord with the Mississippi frontier standards.[20] Through treaties, the tribe felt the manifestation of state control beginning in 1832 and progressing to removal to Oklahoma in the winter of 1837–1838.[21] Not until 1837 did the Chickasaw Nation find a suitable homeland west of the Mississippi River in Indian Territory on land leased to them by the Choctaws, with whom they shared a similar language.

The approaching War Between the States demanded political, economic, and military decisions among the southern states. It similarly forced choices on the Native American population who had entered into a treaty partnership with the Union under which obligations and commitments were exchanged. Southern tribes, including the Chickasaw, made pronouncements in response to the "present unhappy political disagreement" between the North and the South that if the Union was dissolved, their "natural affections, education, institutions, and interests: would bind them to the South."[22]

In March 1861, the Confederate government commissioned Albert Pike of Arkansas to negotiate treaties with the Indians to establish the "United Nations of the Indian Territory" to resist the "invading forces of Abolition under Abraham Lincoln."[23] When the War Between the States broke out in the east, federal troops stationed in the vicinity of Chickasaw villages departed and were soon replaced by soldiers of the Confederacy. With the loss of their promised federal protection, the Chickasaw were forced to take a stance. Besides the issue of black slavery, the Chickasaw were still angry with the federal government about their removal, the corruption accompanying the sale of their lands, and the three million dollars still owed them. They also felt threatened by republican support of the Homestead Act, which would open the plains up to white settlement. So, in May 1861, the Chickasaw Nation declared its independence from the United States.[24] On July 12, the Chickasaw signed a treaty with the Confederacy under terms more favorable than those they enjoyed with the United States and formally joined the Confederacy. The Confederacy "assumed the financial obligations of the former treaties, made explicit guarantees against territorial government and allotment, and gave the tribes the privilege of sending delegates to [the Confederate] Congress."[25]

The decision to join the armed ranks of the Confederacy was costly to the Chickasaw and Choctaw people. In order to link up with southern units, their warriors had to leave their tribal homes. This left the tribal homeland unprotected and open to being overrun by refugees from neighboring tribes. Additionally, after the war and the Confederacy's loss, they were forced to forfeit some of their remaining territory.

Few Americans recognize how bitterly contested the Civil War was between the Five Civilized Tribes in Oklahoma. Members fought for the Union and the Confederacy. Europeans introduced tribal nations to racial slavery, which some tribes practiced on a somewhat flexible basis, including opportunities for Negro freedom through marriage to a Native American. Gradually mixed-blood enslavers dominated tribal governments and committed them to the Confederacy with promises to raise three regiments for the Confederates. The first unit formed was the First Choctaw and Chickasaw Mounted Rifles, which left the second two units to be created from the number of the Creek, Seminole, and Cherokee tribes. Later the Chickasaw provided two additional Confederate units: First Chickasaw Infantry (or Hunter's Regiment, Indian Volunteers); and Shecoe's Chickasaw Battalion of Mounted Volunteers (or Chickasaw Battalion, First Battalion of Chickasaw Cavalry). However, the traditional full-blood majority was not always eager to defend black slavery and join the Union Army or leave the Indian Territory. The stage was set for the Civil War in the Indian Territory to become a war of Indian brothers against Indian brothers.

The anguish and deprivation of the Civil War period among Native American Tribes in the Indian Territory produced thousands of suffering refugees, with as many as 190,000 in Kansas and others scattered among the Choctaw and Chickasaw Nations.[26] Among those aligned with the Confederacy, they were "never reduced to the helpless destitution of their relatives in the North."[27] In the words of a Native American survivor of that time, the Choctaw and Chickasaw "were always willing to give us a part of anything they had."[28]

On June 23, 1865, the Cherokee Stand Watie was the last Confederate general to surrender his command to Union forces. On July 14, 1865, the Chickasaw Nation became the last political unit of the Confederacy to capitulate.[29]

The Chickasaw warrior was marked by extraordinary self-discipline, fierceness in battle, and a passion for liberty. They were observed for their meticulous, ritualistic preparation for battle. James Adair, in his 1775 book, *History of American Indians*, noted that "every warrior holds his honour, and the love of his country, in so high esteem, that he prefers it to life, and will suffer the most exquisite tortures rather than renounce it."[30] From this, we understand why in both life and death, warriors would do nothing to sully their warrior forefathers.

When engaging their enemy, the Chickasaw warrior approached by stealth. Once engaged, the battle was bitterly fought with a cacophony of battle sounds but lasted only a minimum amount of time because Chickasaw believed that the shedding of blood made them impure. Additionally, spilling too much blood could result in casualties among their own. Leaders who lost several warriors in battle were thought to be out of divine favor and meriting appropriate punishment.[31]

On March 4, 1856, the Chickasaw Nation was reestablished as a tribal government in Tishomingo, Indian Territory. After the Civil War, the tribe wrote a new constitution which was adopted on August 16, 1867. Like other tribes resettled in Indian Territory, the Chickasaw saw their land exploited and expropriated by the Dawes Act and Oklahoma statehood. By 1920, over 4.7 million acres—over seventy-five percent of Chickasaw lands—passed from the tribal hand through sale or lease.[32] Despite removal and other actions by federal and state governments, the tribe flourished and enjoyed a strong self-governmental infrastructure, including educational, vocational, and social services.

The Chickasaw Nation ardently believes that sometimes war is necessary, including occasions when it is necessary to defend their homeland and country. Therefore, Chickasaw warriors can be counted among the numbers who fought during the American Revolution, the War of 1812, the Civil War, World War I, World War II, the Korean War, Vietnam, Iraq, and Afghanistan.

CH-21 SHAWNEE

CH-21 Shawnee approaches for the recovery of a sister ship. (Courtesy of the Army Aviation Museum.)

The military rotary-winged aircraft industry giants were Bell, Hiller, Sikorsky, and Boeing. Frank N. Piasecki's Piasecki Aircraft Corporation was small and sought its niche by solving some of the most troubling problems of early single-main-rotor helicopters. All single-rotor helicopters, then in service or under development, required a tail rotor to counteract the effects of torque caused by the large main rotor. This tail rotor also consumed considerable horsepower, which reduced the horsepower available for lifting the aircraft and its load. Single main rotor helicopters also had critical "center of gravity" restrictions. Frank Piasecki took a broader, more holistic approach to solving the early power plant and rotor technology problems. Realizing that present helicopter power plants were limited to reciprocating gasoline-driven engines, he looked to develop a tandem rotor helicopter, i.e., oversized rotors in the front and the rear. Piasecki and his company focused on designing and developing tandem rotor helicopters, which ultimately led to some of the most recognizable heavy-lift helicopters: the Boeing Vertol 107, the Navy's CH-46 *Sea Knight,* and the Army's CH-47 *Chinook* helicopters. This approach appeared to have significant advantages if a successful design could be developed. The Piasecki tandem design could overcome the aerodynamic limitations; virtually all power, less that required to drive the power distribution system, would be utilized to lift the load. Besides, and of even greater importance, the "center of gravity" travel of the tandem design would significantly increase the utility of the design.

71

During World War II, the Nazi U-Boat threat reached the Atlantic coast of the United States and into the Gulf of Mexico. From America's beaches, citizens could witness the sinking of countless merchant ships shuttling raw materials and finished military hardware needed to sustain the Allied war effort. The United States Coast Guard desperately needed an at-sea air rescue aircraft to pluck surviving crew members from the torpedoed ships to cope with the carnage. Frank Piasecki proposed a helicopter with a tandem configuration as the optimal design for an aircraft of the necessary size. The Coast Guard was convinced by the Piasecki Aircraft Corporation's engineering proposal and persuaded the Navy, its wartime master, to sign a contract with the company on January 1, 1944, for the XHRP-1 (Experimental, Helicopter, Transport, Piasecki, Model One).[1]

Fourteen months later, on March 7, 1945, Frank Piasecki flew the first XHRP-1 tandem helicopter control demonstrator. The helicopter was forty-eight feet long and made of tubular construction, with the engine located slightly to the rear of the helicopter's center with the fuel and oil tanks. The passenger compartment was situated between the two pilots and the engine. The XHRP-1 demonstrator proved immensely valuable to Piasecki Aircraft as it facilitated the design and development of their first production tandem rotor helicopters.

The improvements spawned by the XHRP-1 were incorporated into the HRP-1, for which the company received a contract for twenty aircraft to supply the U.S. Navy and U.S. Coast Guard. The Marine Corps in turn acquired twelve HRP-1s to develop their Vertical Assault Concept. The Corps concept incorporated helicopters flying off the light carrier *Saipan* (CVL-48) and the escort carrier *Palau* (CVE-122). The sea service retained its Piasecki aircraft until 1953. With time, the Navy was impressed by the success of Piasecki's tandem helicopter design. Subsequently, it issued a compact tandem rotor helicopter requirement to meet the emerging utility and rescue missions while operating from battleships, cruisers, and aircraft carriers. Two contracts were awarded, one to Piasecki for his overlapping tandem rotor design, the XHJP-1, and a second to Sikorsky for his single rotor XHJS-1. As a result of the fly-off between the two test models, the Navy awarded a production contract to Piasecki for the new tandem utility helicopter, the HUP-1.

The small size of the HUP-1 and its versatility were significant advantages for Navy use and its missions. Ultimately a total of 301 helicopters were produced for domestic and international customers, including the U.S. Army, which procured seventy H-25As (*Army Mule*). This would be the first tandem-rotor helicopter purchased by the U.S. Army; however, the Army determined that its size and capability were unsuitable to meet its mission requirements. Despite this, it was proven to be an excellent helicopter for familiarizing Army aviators with the flight characteristics of a tandem-rotor helicopter.

Following World War II, the United States Air Force Air Rescue Service (ARS) developed a requirement for a helicopter to conduct rescue operations in the Arctic due to the anticipation of a potential conflict with the Soviet Union and the fact that the Arctic would figure prominently in the U.S. strategy in such a confrontation. The rationale was that the shortest route to the industrial heart of the Soviet Union was over the Arctic due to the limitation of Strategic Air Command's bomber fleet. As a result this limited them to the Polar route. With SAC's Strategic Bomber Plan, the Air Force needed air bases in Greenland and expanded facilities in Alaska. Thus, a helicopter that could operate in these environs was required.

On June 17, 1949, the ARS issued a request for proposals to American helicopter manufacturers to submit proposals to meet these requirements. Piasecki responded with two proposals: the single-engine PD-22 and the multi-engine PD-23. The USAF accepted Piasecki's PD-22 design and assigned the designation as YH-21, *Arctic Rescuer*.

The Air Force started taking deliveries of YH-21/PD-22 in February 1953. By that time, the Air Force had named the aircraft *Workhorse*. By August 1953, eighteen *Workhorse* utility and rescue versions of the production H-21 were in the Air Force inventory. Twenty-eight "A" model *Workhorse* helicopters were delivered to the United States Air Force and Canadian Armed Forces between November 1953 and December 1954. Between November 1953 and January 1958, both countries received 163 H-21B's. USAF versions of the helicopter were also equipped with rescue hoists and heavy-duty heating sufficient to withstand temperatures of –65°F.[2]

Given the expectation that when needed, the Air Force would provide combat assault transportation within the legal limitations on the size of its aircraft, the Army began with the H-21B since that aircraft was specifically designed and built for the troop transport mission. The "B" model of the H-21 enjoyed an additional 275 horsepower from its Wright engine models, plus self-sealing fuel and oil tanks and provisions for externally mounted fuel tanks.[3] With the end of the Korean War and the relaxation of the limitations on the size and capabilities of Army helicopters, it began outlining increased capabilities for its future helicopter needs.

The Army began with the H-21C/PD-43, ordering 334 "C" models, and took production deliveries between September 1954 and March 1959. Following Army policy, the aircraft was named after an American Indian tribe, *Shawnee*. The *Shawnee* had a higher weight cargo capacity plus a 4,000-pound capacity using the fuselage-mounted sling hook. The Army *Shawnee* was a 52.5 foot long aircraft with a forty-four-foot diameter of the twin main rotors and stood fifteen feet nine inches in height. The almost 9,000-pound helicopter was operated by a standard crew of three, the aircraft commander, pilot, and crew chief. When the *Shawnee* was deployed to Vietnam, one or two aerial gunners were added to the crew. It was powered by a single Wright R-1820-103A air-cooled, radial engine mounted within the fuselage aft of the cargo-passenger compartment. An argument in favor of using the Wright 1820 engine was that so many were available, as it was the same type of engine used in the WW II B-17. The engine generated 1,425 horsepower and 2,700 rpm, which permitted a maximum speed of 127 mph and a cruising speed of 98 mph. Despite these numbers, the CH-21C required more power than the B-17 for takeoff and cruising. This placed additional stress on an engine not built for it. As a result, a *Shawnee* engine had a life expectancy of only around 400 operational hours.[4] The helicopter had an operating range of 265 miles and a service ceiling of almost 9,500 feet. It had a maximum takeoff weight of 15,200 pounds, allowing twenty fully equipped combat soldiers on board or twelve patients on stretchers.

One of the operational advantages of the *Shawnee* was its capability to carry Army units while simultaneously maintaining unity integrity. Under combat conditions, unit commanders strongly opposed splitting up their squads and platoons among multiple aircraft. Under such circumstances, upon closing on the landing zone (LZ), the first task was to find and join up with the other unit members to perform their combat assignment. The H-21 could carry an entire infantry squad with all its equipment, and so when they disembarked the helicopter, the men were ready to fight as a unit. This paid substantial dividends in Vietnam and would create operational voids between the retirement of the CH-21 and the arrival of the new CH-47B in 1967.

The CH-21 was large and roomy, considered by many to be the Douglas C-47 *Skytrain* of the helicopter family. Its tandem rotors permitted smooth flying in crosswind conditions and various cargo load placements. Among the aircrews who routinely flew the *Shawnee,* some described it "as a large collection of moving parts, flying in fairly close formation, in the same general direction."[5] The instrument placement within the cockpit reflected the designers' consideration of MANPRINT factors. The flight and engine instrumentation were logically arranged with easy-to-reach switches and easy-to-read indicators. The flight controls felt comfortable to the user with finger-tip accessory trip switches built into the handgrips. Its sensitive cyclic control allowed precision directional movement, and its collective pitch control seemed to be the only restraint against the power available to the pilot. It had plenty of power to lift and pull out the payload. Moreover, the vibration level was uncharacteristically low for such a large and powerful helicopter.[6]

The Army *Shawnee* was the only helicopter with wooden rotor blades produced in matched sets of three blades. When metal rotor blades became available, the Army opted not to make the changeover due to the probability that the CH-21C inventory would soon be replaced by newer helicopters.

During the design and development of the CH-21 and its early operational life, the services recognized that conventional radial engines would soon be replaced as the power plant for the larger military and commercial helicopters. Exception-ally reliable yet more advanced and powerful, efficient gas-turbine engines were the future for helicopters. Two different gas-turbine installation configurations were designed for the *Shawnee* which prompted the change in the helicopter's designation to CH-21D. The first package was intended to install two Lycoming T53 engines, while the second used two General Electric T58 engines. Both installations were neither complex nor required much modification to the aircraft. Despite successful tests of the CH-21D configuration, the Army discontinued further development of the helicopter, choosing instead to wait for the next generation of turbine-powered helicopters that were already advanced in their development.

The H-21 was the first helicopter specifically designed for missions in a combat environment. The fuselage was made of aluminum rather than instantaneously ignitable magnesium. The large and virtually vacant inverter compartment separated the 300-gallon fuel tank and engine, thus eliminating the potential for a catastrophic fire caused by the hot engine igniting leaking fuel in a crash. The view from the cockpit was superb regardless of the helicopter's flight attitude; however, the Plexiglas afforded limited protection in the event of a crash and provided enemy gunners engaging the ship with an unobstructed view of the commander and pilot. Flak curtains were added to overcome the aircrew's limited frontal and side protection. Aluminum armor plates were also installed to protect the three vital transmissions.[7]

Army Aviation Center and aviation units worldwide were experimenting with options to arm helicopters. By mid-1957, "Vanderpool's Fools" and the Aerial Combat Reconnaissance Company (Experimental) had acquired two CH-21s to experiment with and conduct proof-of-principle demonstrations of armed helicopters. These aircraft mounted a twin caliber .50 machine gun turret as one option and two .30 caliber machine guns, two .50 caliber machine guns, and eight Oerlikon rockets.[8] After expending all available and limited production rockets, they identified two potential rocket solutions: the 2.75-inch folding fin aerial rocket (FFAR) and the 4.5-inch spin-stabilized artillery rocket. The former was an Air Force air-to-air weapon with a limited warhead bursting radius. It was still easy to mount on a helicopter, and, more importantly, there were more than eight million of them in the national inventory. The Army had a useful package when mounted on the CH-21C nose wheel strut and combined with the machine guns for range adjustment. The suitability was aided by the ability of the aircraft's tandem rotor to provide firing platform stability.[9] During the Association of the United States Army (AUSA) sponsored helicopter weapon systems demonstrations, the two *Shawnee* demonstration helicopters were equipped with a twin caliber .50 machine gun turret or two .30 caliber machine guns, two .50 caliber machine guns, and eight Oerlikon rockets.[10] Based upon further experimentation, the Army Aviation Board, in April 1961, tested a CH-21C armed with 2.75 FFAR and concluded that the system was suitable for helicopter armament.

The size of the *Shawnee* opened new possibilities for helicopter-borne armament systems. Experimenters may have let their imaginations run wild when they teamed with the Air Force and General Electric to mount a World War II B-29 Superfortress gun turret under the nose of the aircraft. The package permitted the gunner, who was the pilot, to adjust the twin caliber .50 guns in elevation, depression, and traverse. The system, with ammunition, added a 650-pound weight penalty or more than ten percent of its available cargo weight. The gun turret was frequently troubled by inadequate electrical power malfunctions.[11] Ultimately, weight and power issues eliminated the B-29 turret.

By 1958, the Department of the Army had concluded that there would be no development of a singular purpose attack helicopter, deciding instead to use a combination of existing helicopters and weapons. This followed earlier Army direction that a single machine gun installation system would be developed for the OH-13, CH-21, and CH-34 helicopters. A four-gun installation kit would then be designed for the UH-1.[12] When the *Shawnee* was ultimately deployed to the Vietnam combat zone, its armament packages varied but were usually one or two .50 caliber or

7.62 mm M60 machine guns which provided suppressive or defensive fires.[13] The crew chief operated one machine gun, and the gunner crewed the second, typically a private or private first class, from the authorized manpower of the unit's assigned personnel. There were no gunner positions on the helicopter company's table of organization and equipment (TO&E), so they relied upon volunteers, of which there was never a shortage. The door gunners were usually trained by a company member who had served as an infantryman during the Korean War. Gunner qualification standards were locally set but exacting because the gunners were critical to the aircraft's survival. This practice continued until the Army sent trained door gunners to each helicopter company from the 25th Infantry Division in Hawaii to Vietnam for ninety days of temporary duty.

Previously designated as the 71st Transportation Corps Truck Battalion after World War II, the Army's first helicopter battalion was reactivated at Fort Riley, Kansas, on July 19, 1954, as the 71st Transportation Battalion (Helicopter). It was organized with an authorized strength of seven officers and twenty-nine enlisted. The battalion's primary mission was to activate, supply, and supervise the training of other helicopter companies. Its secondary mission was to prepare those companies as combat-ready units for assignment overseas or within the CONUS. On November 9, 1954, one officer and five warrant officers departed Morton, Pennsylvania, for Fort Riley with the battalion's first three H-21 helicopters. By Christmas, the battalion received instructions to commence H-21 Pilot Transition Courses, and at year's end, it had trained thirteen H-21 aviators and flown 325 hours.[14] The 71st also trained entire aviation units from their activation to unit testing and certification as operational units.[15] The 71st was also charged with pilot transition training for the Army's new fixed-wing utility transport, the U-1A De Havilland short take-off and landing (STOL) aircraft, *Otter*.

Ultimately the Army organized its CH-21C inventory into ten transportation companies. Each had approximately 155 men and was commanded by a major. The headquarters element also had a captain executive officer, a first sergeant, and two clerks/drivers. There were two flight platoons with ten CH-21Cs each, an aircraft maintenance platoon, and a service platoon. The flight platoons were further composed of two sections of five helicopters each. Each company also had two OH-13 *Sioux* reconnaissance helicopters. Additional *Shawnee* helicopters were assigned to Fort Rucker, Alabama, for the Aviation School, Aviation Test Activity, and a detachment of experimentally armed helicopters. Other CH-21Cs were assigned to the Army Air Defense Command to support its Nike missile sites.

The 1960s saw the rise of expansionary communism, which troubled America's allies, who saw the U.S. as a safe harbor because it was "one of a handful of great powers that never violated a treaty."[16] The inauguration of the Kennedy administration brought a revised approach to war-winning, i.e., the fusion of diplomacy and arms, which prompted an authoritative bonding of the policy interests of the White House and the Departments of State and Defense. Besides the modernization of the nuclear triad, the young president also focused on conventional forces because he felt that "the free world's security can be endangered [...] also by being nibbled away at the periphery [...], by forces of subversion, infiltration, intimidation, indirect or non-overt aggression, internal revolution, diplomatic blackmail, guerrilla warfare, or a series of limited objective wars."[17] Kennedy's response was to direct the JCS to resuscitate the exiled Special Forces troops and the newly arrived five hundred soldiers to train foreign indigenous personnel in his "putting out-the-local-fire campaign."[18]

The president was soon confronted with requests from commanders in Saigon for American ground combat troops and increases in aviation support. The administration assessed that the South Vietnamese risked the loss of their country to communism if something was not done to give them a spark to catch fire. So in May 1961, four hundred Army Green Berets were sent to South Vietnam. Shortly afterward, forty Army helicopters and the personnel to fly and maintain them were dispatched.[19] They included one Marine Corps squadron of Sikorsky H-34 helicopters and five Army aviation companies flying the CH-21C *Shawnee*. The latter were earmarked for air mobility support of the Army of the Republic of Vietnam (ARVN) soldiers because it would not be until early 1963 that U.S. ground personnel would begin arriving. By mid-1962, eight thousand advisers served alongside the ARVN.[20] The *Shawnee* units fully embraced their tactical missions of providing air transportation, expediting the tactical operations, and providing logistical support in the forward areas of the combat zone. The CH-21Cs quickly became known as "the packhorses of the Vietnamese mountains and jungles."[21]

The five CH-21C companies going to Vietnam took different journeys to get there. The 509th Transportation Company at Fort Bragg, North Carolina, was initially equipped with the Piasecki H-25A (Army Mule) tandem rotor helicopter, which the Army found underpowered and inadequate for transporting the soldiers. The H-25As of the 509th were transferred to the Navy which was pleased to add them to their others for the rescue mission off aircraft carriers. The 509th became the 8th Transportation Company (Light Helicopter) (H-21). It was temporarily assigned to Fort Riley, Kansas, for transitioning to the CH-21C under the tutelage of the 71st Transportation Helicopter Battalion. The objective of Army aviation helicopter training was the successive and progressive graduation of helicopter aviators from reconnaissance helicopters to utility helicopters and then to cargo rotary-winged aircraft.[22] From their consolidated training site at Fort Riley's Marshall Army Airfield, transitioning aviators underwent three weeks of intensive classroom, field, maintenance, and flight training, including 25 flight hours as the first pilot and eighty hours of maintenance instruction. Upon its return to Fort Bragg, the 8th Transportation Company participated in unit training and was evaluated as combat-ready.

Another *Shawnee* unit was the 57th Transportation Company (Light Helicopter) (H-21), supporting the 4th Infantry Division stationed at Fort Lewis, Washington. It provided divisional support and civil assistance that included search and rescue, flood relief, forest fire assistance by transporting firefighters into the mountains of eastern Oregon, medical evacuation, and numerous other missions suited to their H-21C helicopters.

On November 1, 1961, the 8th and 57th were alerted for deployment. On the morning of November 6, the twenty-two helicopters of the 57th Transportation Company departed Gray Army Airfield at Fort Lewis for Oakland Army Terminal in Stockton, California. After their multi-day flight, including a nocturnal flight over the Sierra Mountains at 10,500 feet, all aircraft arrived safely after darkness had fallen on November 8. Fifteen CH-21C helicopters from the 8th Transportation Company were ferried in a record-breaking cross-country flight from Fort Bragg, North Carolina, to California. Another five CH-21s were provided by the 33rd Transportation Company (Light Helicopter) at Fort Ord, California, and Sharpe Army Depot provided the two OH-13 aircraft. The remaining equipment and supplies belonging to the 8th were airlifted to California aboard the Douglas C-133 *Cargomaster*.[23]

Destination Overseas:
Exercise Area in Excess of Thirty Days

After being prepared and treated at the Alameda Naval Air Station with an opaque white colored vinyl spray-on coating called Spraylat[24] to prevent corrosion and damage from the saltwater spray, all thirty-two helicopters were loaded on the flight deck of a converted World War II "jeep carrier,"[25] the Military Sea Transportation Service (MSTS) ship USNS[26] *Core* (T-AKV-41).[27] Several Air Force T-28s and the equipment needed to make the helicopters flyable were stowed below deck. The 400 men of the two transportation companies and the supporting field maintenance, signal, and medical detachments were squeezed into the remaining small spaces. On November 21, 1961, the USNS *Core* set sail for "destination unknown;"[28] proceeding under Movement Order #3, dated November 8, 1961, dispatching the unit to an Overseas Exercise Area on a "Temporary Change of Station (TCS) for a period in excess of thirty days."[29] Although the overseas destination for the helicopter companies was included in their movement orders, the affected commanders were embargoed from informing their subordinates until the *Core* had passed through the Philippines.[30] The four OH-13s and the remaining eight CH-21Cs of the 8th Transportation Company were boxed, loaded aboard a cargo ship with vehicles, equipment, and company cadre, and departed for Vietnam a week later.

The H-21 was the first helicopter to be assigned to tactical operations in Vietnam as part of a more extensive and accelerated program of support for the forces of South Vietnam. It was anticipated to be the Army's solution "… to the free-ranging movements of the Communists guerrillas who held the advantage […] against the U.S.-supported government of President Ngo Dinh Diem."[31] The new mobility and striking power afforded by the *Shawnee* enabled the ARVN troops to be deployed rapidly against enemy locations regardless of the vagaries of the terrain.

The voyage of the two ships from the U.S. to Vietnam was not without its adventures. Deck-stored helicopters began to show evidence of saltwater spray corrosion on the rotor head areas. Although the *Core* considered diverting to Subic Bay, Philippines to make repairs, actions by members of the Transportation Companies supplemented with frequent inspections resolved the issues, and the *Core* continued to Saigon. The second ship experienced similar difficulties; however, one of the CH-21s broke loose from its tie-downs inside its crate and was severely damaged. The vessel diverted to Pearl Harbor, Hawaii, to replace the damaged aircraft with one from the 81st Transportation Company.[32]

On December 11, 1961[33], the 8th and 57th Transportation Companies arrived aboard the USNS *Core* in Saigon.[34] The vessel bore 33 Vertol CH-21C helicopters and 400 aircrew members, and ground support personnel.[35] The USNS *Core* was one of four escort carriers from World War II reactivated for the Vietnam War and transferred to the MSTS.[36] As MSTS vessels, they were manned by civilian merchant seamen. The *Core's* sister ships were the *Breton*, *Card,* and the *Croatan,* which ferried fixed- and rotary-winged aircraft from U.S. ports of debarkation to the various ports in the Pacific and Vietnam that supported the war effort. Albeit not glamorous or glorious duty, just the routine responsibilities which pleased the merchant seamen, the four transport ships still faced the hazards of the war zone.

The USNS *Card* arrived in Saigon Harbor on May 1, 1964, with a cargo of helicopters and other materials, and was moored in the commercial port district of the city awaiting her scheduled sailing after discharging her cargo and loading a new load of helicopters for return to the United States.[37] Saigon was controlled by the Republic of Vietnam's governmental port authority as a civilian port. Therefore, the loading and unloading of a ship's cargo were performed by civilian Vietnamese stevedores, including Lam Son Nao. He had a far different objective when he learned the day before that the *Card* would be arriving shortly.[38] In 1963 Nao became a commando, and one of his earliest missions was the attempted destruction of the USNS *Core* on December 9, 1963.[39] His demolition charge failed to detonate because of a dead battery,[40] but by 1964 his tradecraft was much improved.

As the *Card* awaited her scheduled sailing, unbeknownst to Captain Borge Langeland[41] and her crew, now twenty-seven-year-old Nao and a second Vietnamese commando of the 65th Special Operation Group were surreptitiously placing two time-delayed charges, one of over 175 pounds of TNT, and a second of about eighteen pounds of plastic explosives (C-4), just above the ship's water line[42] on the starboard side near the bilge and the engine compartment.[43] The charges were set to detonate at 3:00 AM on Saturday, May 2, 1964. The explosions created a twelve-foot by three-foot hole resulting in the loss of power and initial flooding of amidships.[44] Emergency actions and prompt salvage operations would ultimately save the ship, settling stern-first in the forty-eight-foot pier-side mooring.

Immediate post-incident reports stated that all seventy-three civilian members of the *Card* crew were safe;[45] however, later official reports identified five crew members who had succumbed to the injuries they sustained in the explosions.[46]

Within seventeen days of the explosion, the *Card* was refloated with sufficient buoyancy and capability to begin the tow down the Saigon River.[47] One of the twists of fate surrounding the sinking of the carrier was the discovery by one of the five salvage divers of the remains of a U.S.-made demolitions pack, strongly suggesting that the explosives used in the attack may have been stolen American military munitions.[48] The Navy salvage vessel, USS *Reclaimer,* and the fleet ocean tug, USS *Tawakoni,* dispatched to Saigon to respond to the *Card* explosion, undertook the wounded ship in tow to Subic Bay in the Philippines,[49] and then onward to the repair facilities at Yokosuka, Japan.[50]

While officials in North Vietnam celebrated the *Card's* sinking as a propaganda victory and even issued a commemorative postage stamp later that year, the U.S. government did not acknowledge the sinking, only publicly admitting that the vessel sustained damage while operating in the vicinity of South Vietnam.[51] The *Card* would be modified, thoroughly repaired, and reintroduced to service on December 11, 1964, and would continue to serve as a transport ship for the Maritime Service until her retirement in 1970.[52]

When the second vessel ultimately arrived in Saigon with the remaining twelve helicopters, there was insufficient space to reassemble and fly off the helicopters. After significant difficulties, a crane of sufficient capacity was located, and the off-loading was completed. Once all the aircraft were unloaded and prepared for flight, they self-deployed to Tan Son Nhut, the international airport in Saigon. The 8th Transportation Company flew on to Qui Nhon, where they joined another CH-21C company for operations in the mountainous region of the II Corps Tactical Zone (CTZ). The 57th Transportation Company remained at Tan Son Nhut, where it was responsible for airlift across the breadth of the Mekong River Delta in the southern III Corps area. It shared the mission with the Sikorsky UH-34 helicopters of Marine Medium Helicopter Squadron 362 (HMM-362). Twelve days after the aircraft arrived in the country, they were sent into combat in Operation CHOPPER. This first airmobile combat action involved 1,036 Vietnamese paratroopers sent to assault a possible Viet Cong headquarters complex ten miles west of Saigon.[53] The surprised Viet Cong fighters suffered heavy casualties while the American advised ARVN paratroopers achieved a tactical victory. The successful operation netted an underground radio transmitter after encountering only slight resistance from a quite surprised enemy.[54] It also demonstrated the value of air mobility in an active region with poor roads, harsh terrain, and constant danger.

The aircrews and maintenance personnel quickly learned about operating in the hot, humid, and often extreme climate in South Vietnam and making accommo-dating adjustments and modifications to the *Shawnee.* If the experiences of the 81st Transportation Company were typical of the other CH-21C companies in Vietnam, the helicopter was challenging to maintain and required an average of eleven hours of maintenance for every flight hour.[55]

The helicopters of the 8th Transportation Company had the vertical stabilizers on the tail of the aircraft removed, leaving only the protruding stub mounts. This modification reduced the helicopter's weight and helped to eliminate frequent sheet metal repairs due to cracking caused by excessive airframe vibration. Additionally, when repairs were needed, the number of man-hours necessary to repair cracks in the fuselage skin and brackets was substantially reduced. However, it also reduced the maximum permissible airspeed of the *Shawnee* to sixty knots, though crews found that washing the helicopter and rotor blades helped improve performance. One minor modification was made upon arrival in Vietnam: CH-21C crews removed the aircraft's rain shield and the forward and aft aluminum fairings around the transmissions.

Besides airspeed, crews were always concerned about power loss. Recognizing that there was almost no chance of carburetor icing in the Vietnam climate, carburetor heat doors were sealed shut to prevent heat from entering the carburetor and to avoid a power loss source. Another troubling condition was the consequences of the hot and humid conditions, especially in the central highlands. Such weather reduced the lift capability of all helicopters but especially the CH-21C. Coupled with the periodic heavy rains in-country, wooden rotor blade delamination and separation of the leading-edge metal wear strip required higher than routine rotor blade replacement.[56] Some rotor blade sets lasted fewer than ten hours. Ground crews also soon became adept at performing "routine unscheduled maintenance," which was the euphemism for repairing bullet holes and fragment penetrations.[57]

The introduction of the CH-21C into Vietnam quickly exposed the Army to significant mechanical and operational challenges with the aircraft. Besides lack of power and mechanical reliability, crews, maintainers, and maneuver commanders were concerned with part fatigue and parts shortages, especially wooden rotor blades and R-1820-103A engines. Both were major contributors to the reduced availability of operational helicopters. The 8,000-mile supply line was unable to sustain the demand for rebuilt engines. To partially compensate for the engine supply issue, units removed the functional engine from an aircraft scheduled for its 100-hour periodic inspection and placed it in the helicopter that had just completed its inspection.[58] The engine crew of each helicopter company's maintenance detachment typically spent eight days tearing down a worn engine and building up a newly rebuilt engine to get a helicopter back online.[59] Blades for the CH-21, three per rotor head, were issued in a matched set so that when one blade was worn or damaged, the entire set had to be replaced.[60] Both engines and main rotor blades were the pacing items or critical components essential to keeping the *Shawnee* flying. The objective for each of the *Shawnee* companies was to have seventy percent (fourteen CH-21s) of their assigned aircraft available to fly missions each day. However, because of the slowness with which lost aircraft were replaced and the shortage of repair parts which caused helicopters to not be operationally available due to maintenance issues, more and more missions required combining helicopters from multiple companies to meet mission needs.[61] In one instance, to attain the mission requirement of sixteen aircraft, helicopters were brought together from three companies, the 33rd, the 57th, and the 93rd; companies that cumulatively should have had sixty helicopters.[62]

Boeing-Vertol (the name of the *Shawnee* contractor at the time) dispatched a team of their engineers to Vietnam to determine the sources and scope of *Shawnee's* problems. The corporate inspectors determined that the Army helicopter companies in Vietnam would require additional industry technical support. So, while the CH-21C was operational in Vietnam, technical representatives from Vertol were available to assist the Army in maximizing the helicopter's performance.[63]

From the arrival of the CH-21 *Shawnee* in Vietnam in December 1961 until mid-1965, the Army focused its attention on developing and maturing airmobile operations supporting the ARVN soldiers. Over time, the breadth and scope of their operations increased. Initially, U.S. pilots were occupied teaching ARVN commanders and their soldiers how to use airmobile tactics effectively. The next phase of ARVN training and battlefield experience included battalion-size air assaults by rangers, paratroopers, and regular infantry.[64]

The first *Shawnee* and the first helicopter lost to enemy fire occurred on February 4, 1962. The CH-21C was one of fifteen helicopters ferrying ARVN troops to attack the village of Hong My in the Mekong Delta when it was shot down by Viet Cong ground fire.[65] Fortunately, no service members were lost in the shootdown. Four months later, the first CH-21C was lost to enemy fire with casualties.[66] A year later, on February 24–26, 1963, three Army CH-21C helicopters were lost to enemy ground fire while transporting South Vietnamese troops.

Initial provision for door gunners occurred when gun mounts for .30 caliber MGs were added to the aircraft. This, however, did not solve the issue of door gunners. Company personnel were assigned the additional duty of serving as door gunners at the forward door while the aircraft crew chief served as the door gunner at the rear door. The training was yet another issue with each unit adopting its field expedient. For example, the 33rd Transportation Company had an assigned Warrant Officer who had been a combat infantryman during the Korean War and took charge of the gunners.[67] The combat loss of the *Shawnee* helicopters resulted in the Army authorizing helicopters moving ARVN troops to engage enemy combatants upon sight. About six weeks later, one hundred soldiers from the 25th Infantry Division arrived in Saigon to take positions as door gunners on *Shawnee* helicopters.[68]

Air mobility operations were being learned on the fly by the ARVN forces, and the air and ground integration tasks were also becoming known as they went along. Unlike American airmobile forces, the ARVN commanders did not release their transport helicopters following the insertion of their troops in the target LZ. CH-21C units were usually sent to a staging airfield where they would standby to assist in medical evacuation if summoned or, if required, to pick up and deploy the ARVN reserve.[69]

In 1957, the 33rd Transportation Company (Light Helicopter) (H21) completed its transition training to the *Shawnee*. It was assigned to Fort Ord, California, until it was alerted for deployment to South Vietnam on March 6, 1962. Although Fort Ord was a Basic Training installation, the 33rd was a Strategic Army Corps (STRAC) unit, continuously combat-ready and prepared for rapid deployment. It often trained with the 57th Transportation Company from Fort Lewis, Washington, until it deployed to South Vietnam in 1961. With the deployment date set for late March, the helicopters of the 33rd were turned in to Sharpe Army Depot for shipment to Vietnam as replacement aircraft for units already in-country, the 8th, 57th, and the 93rd Transportation Companies. The personnel from the company were directed to New Orleans to meet up with an aircraft carrier already loaded with twenty CH-21Cs earmarked for them. Before shipping out to New Orleans, the deployment orders for the 33rd Transportation Company were canceled, and a Marine Corps CH-34 helicopter unit (Marine Helicopter Squadron HMM-362)[70] was deployed in its place. In the interim, the 33rd Transportation Company personnel were tasked to find twenty additional CH-21Cs. A second deployment alert order was issued on April 18, 1962. By August 1962, the helicopters were assembled at Fort Ord and then flown to the Alameda Naval Air Station Aircraft Rework Facility, which prepared them for overseas shipment. The company's wheeled vehicles were delivered to Oakland Army Base to be loaded aboard the commercial freighter *Ocean Evelyn*.[71] The company's main body personnel departed from California on September 10, 1962, aboard a USAF C-121, a Lockheed-built *Constellation*. The complement of the company's helicopters and those for the 81st Transportation Company, which were picked up at Pearl Harbor, Hawaii, arrived in South Vietnam on September 18, 1962, aboard the USS *Croatan* (CVE-25).[72] The Military Assistance Command, Vietnam (MACV) allocated up to ten weeks for the 33rd to assemble, prepare their equipment and become operational. They were declared operational in slightly more than two weeks.

The operational base for the 33rd Transportation Company was Bien Hoa, a Vietnam Air Force (VNAF) base for covert operations. The USAF "Farm Gate Detachment" of North American T-18 *Trojan* fighter bombers and Douglas RB-26L *Invader* light bombers were also stationed at Bien Hoa. These aircraft flew with VNAF markings and conducted operations in Laos, among other non-disclosable places. The 33rd served in Vietnam from September 1962 until June 1963, when it was inactivated. Its equipment, personnel, and other assets were transferred to its successor unit, the 118th Aviation Company (Airmobile Light).[73] At the time, the United States did not acknowledge that U.S. personnel were participating in combat operations, so operations emanating from the airbase, regardless of units involved, were classified, so very little is known or openly available about the 33rd's operational history.[74] What is known is that because no U.S. troops were serving in Vietnam until early 1963, the 33rd Transportation Company worked extensively with the ARVN 5th and 10th Divisions on airmobile operations during the company's early period in-country.

From its location at Tan Son Nhut, the 57th Transportation Company was ideally situated to train ARVN forces to embark and disembark from the *Shawnee* and then deploy on an air assault training mission. Training efficiency was ideally set with the proximate units, ARVN instructor cadre, and American Army advisors available to supervise and enforce training standards. Each helicopter would carry an entire ten-man ARVN squad when conducting a combat assault. This unit integrity was essential to combat maneuvering and firing by the troops following disembarkation at the landing zone.

The 81st Transportation Helicopter Company (Light Helicopter) (H21) was stationed at Wheeler Army Airfield, Schofield Barracks, Hawaii, when alerted for deployment to the Republic of South Vietnam. It was to be met at Pearl Harbor by the USS *Croatan* (CVE-25), which carried the helicopters and personnel of the 33rd Transportation Company from San Francisco. The unit was temporarily housed at Tan Son Nhut until it assembled its personnel, vehicles, and equipment. The company then proceeded to the Central Highlands and its new base, later becoming Camp Holloway at Pleiku. The base was situated along the travel corridor between Cambodia, Laos, and Vietnam. The personnel and equipment endured the climatological extremes of high heat, high humidity, and seasonal rainstorms. Fortunately for most unit personnel, they deployed to Vietnam from another overseas duty station, so the time at Pleiku was shortened based on their already being on an overseas tour. From Pleiku, the 81st would support four Special Forces teams deployed in Vietnamese villages deep in the interior of South Vietnam.

The last of the five *Shawnee* companies deployed to Vietnam was the 93rd Transportation Company (Light Cargo Helicopter) (H21), whose original home station was Fort Devens, Massachusetts. The unit and its helicopters were deployed to the Republic of South Vietnam on December 15, 1961, aboard the USNS *Card* from Quonset Point, Rhode Island. The unit's transit took them across the Atlantic Ocean through the Mediterranean Sea, down the Suez Canal, across the Indian Ocean, and on to Subic Bay, Philippine Islands, where the personnel and equipment were transferred to the Amphibious Assault Ship (Helicopter) (LPH) USS *Princeton* (LPH-5). They arrived ten miles off Da Nang on the Central Coast of Vietnam on January 25, 1962. Their helicopters were flown off the *Princeton* for their new base at Da Nang. All was in readiness for the first combat support operation from Da Nang on February 1, 1962.[75] By October 1962, all five of the companies were operational.

Likewise, the 93rd Transportation Company was principally assigned support missions for the Vietnamese Army. The company operated in the dense jungle region of I CTZ, which was just below the 17th parallel Demilitarized Zone that separated North and South Vietnam. They supported the ARVN 1st and 2nd Infantry Divisions and, on numerous occasions, the U.S. Special Forces. Of particular importance to the South Vietnamese Army was the resupply capability of the UH-21C. In their area of operations, there were few or no roads through the jungle, and those that existed were hardly passable for cargo trucks. The *Shawnee* crews would bring ammunition and supplies to the remote field locations. Rice was carried in 100-kilogram sacks, and meat came as live animals trussed up in wicker baskets. Small animals like ducks and chickens posed few problems, but the pigs on the hoof were not gracious travelers. Each aircraft that carried live pigs was destined for an extensive cabin cleaning after the delivery.[76]

The 93rd supported numerous Special Forces outposts throughout the heavily populated Central Highlands area that the Viet Cong controlled. Like other Central Highlands *Shawnee* units, they experienced significant rotor blade erosion because of rain and corrosive dust.

CH-21C troop lifts, or combat assaults as they were known, usually began at the company's home station with a departure before daybreak. The helicopters then flew to the designated staging airfield, usually a dirt airstrip. The lift helicopters and crews would arrive about two hours in advance so that the helicopters could be refueled to a standard fuel load of 1,300 pounds. While less than the helicopter's total fuel capacity of 1,800 pounds, the lesser fuel load allowed each aircraft to carry a complete ten-man ARVN squad.[77] The flight crew tried to maintain a fuel load of 1,000 pounds, so they never passed up a gas station.[78] The flight crews also received the mission briefing from the ground commander at the staging airfield. Before each combat assault, the Cessna L-19 *Bird Dog* reconnaissance plane assigned to each company would make a high-altitude flight over the intended LZ to provide current and essential details about its configuration, size, and enemy activity. During the actual mission, the *Bird Dog* would fly overhead the participating CH-21Cs, providing them distance and direction. This was necessary for the helicopters that were flying in a tight formation at treetop level, where map reading was a dangerous diversion. Soon navigation directional support for the low flying, terrain-following CH-21s would be provided by U-1A *Otter* or U-6A *Beaver* fixed-wing aircraft loaned from the Army Military Assistance Advisory Group—Vietnam (MAAG-V), which provided radio directions directly to the CH-21 flight.[79]

The mission briefing permitted all pilots to synchronize their activities, including engine start and takeoff checks. Landing lights were illuminated as each pilot completed his checks, and when the lead pilot saw that all lights were on, he announced, "flights up." This commenced the countdown to lift off. Because of the dust stirred up by the rotor wash, helicopters lifted off two at a time. The flight leader held the designated course, altitude, and sixty knots airspeed while the remaining aircraft lifted off. When the last helicopter lifted off, its pilot announced, "The flight is formed." The leader increased speed to eighty knots, the best formation speed for the CH-21C. For inflight protection against small arms fire, the flight would maintain a 2,500-foot altitude before descending to treetop level for the final fifteen to twenty kilometers to the landing zone. The treetop approach to the landing zone would muffle the sound of the helicopters and contribute to surprising the enemy. During the CH-21C period of the war, it was common practice to prepare the landing zone with an airstrike before the arrival of the lift ships. The *Bird Dog* supervised the strikes conducted by North American T-28 *Trojans* flown by Vietnamese pilots. The L-19 pilot was responsible for ending the airstrike approximately three minutes before the helicopter's landed.[80]

For a multi-lift troop insertion, the helicopters would return to the staging airfield where additional troops were loaded, and once all was in readiness, the subsequent lift would depart for the assault LZ. This sequence was repeated until all the infantry soldiers were delivered to the LZ. As required, the CH-21s would refuel at the staging airfield. Once all the troops were delivered, the helicopters would return to the airfield and remain until the ground force commander released them. They frequently returned to the LZ to resupply the infantry force and evacuate casualties.

Using staging airfields weakened the operation security (OPSEC) of the pending air assault and substantially improved the VC's intelligence on the ARVN's operations. A simple way for the VC to be alerted to the intentions of the ARVN force was to observe the "shipping of high-test aviation fuel by commercial truck to the staging airfield."[81] The transport carrier typically paid a tax to the VC to allow the fuel trucks to travel on the highway. Using their trusty "CH-21 string" set to the length of the *Shawnee's* average estimated operational radius, the VC could circumscribe a circle within which the ARVN objective would be found.[82] The enemy then had the option to either resist the landing or avoid the area. Either choice compromised the planned operation.

Events in Ap Tan Thoi province during the final week of December 1962 and early January 1963 would irrevocably change the geopolitical and military complexion of the war. American vulnerabilities would be highlighted, the combat capabilities of our South Vietnamese allies would be questioned, and the commitment of U.S. combat forces would be considered.

Aircraft flying over portions of Dinh Tuong Province intercepted radio transmissions from a VC transmitter in the hamlet of Ap Tan Thoi.[83] This convinced the U.S. advisory team to the ARVN 7th Infantry Division that the hamlet was a headquarters site. Nearby was the village of Ap Bac, and together they were approximately thirty miles southwest of Saigon in the Mekong Delta and the home to the ARVN 7th Infantry Division.

Intelligence estimates supported the presence of two enemy task forces comprised of six companies and between 120 and 350 soldiers.[84] Task Force A consisted of the 174th, 842nd, and 892nd companies, and Task Force B included the 171st, 172nd, and 839th companies.[85] The friendly order of battle had ~1,500 ARVN troops and civil guards supported by thirteen M113 APCs, ten CH-21 *Shawnee* helicopters, five UH-1C Iroquois gunships, and an L-19 *Bird Dog* C&C aircraft.[86]

When the three-prong multi-directional ARVN attack battle plan, Operation DUC THONG 1, was launched on January 2, 1963, it had been compromised and leaked to the enemy.[87] The enemy was adequately forewarned of a pending operation by using captured ARVN radios, monitoring unsecured radio nets, and listening to unencrypted radio communications within the ARVN force.[88] The arrival in Din Toung of seventy-one trucks of ammunition and other essential supplies from Saigon on the days before the battle was sufficient confirmation of a pending attack.[89]

The plan envisioned an air assault of three ARVN rifle companies of the 11th Infantry Regiment assaulting from the north, the Dinh Tuong Civilian Guards Regiment marching north in separate columns, and an infantry company mounted in APCs approaching from the southwest. The plan further provided for two rifle companies staged at Tan Hiep Airfield, which could be assault landed by the 93rd Transportation Company.[90]

Situated within 1.5 kilometers of each other within the objective area were the 1st Company, 261st Battalion (at Ap Bac), and the 1st Company, 514th Battalion (at Ap Tan Thoi), totaling 320 VC regulars and approximately thirty local force soldiers and auxiliaries from the Chau Thanh District.[91] VC preparation of the battlefield was intricate and deadly for the attacker. Exploiting the terrain, well-concealed positions were established at Ap Tan Thoi in the north, along a tree-lined creek in the southeast, and at Ap Bac in the south. The camouflaged Viet Cong MG positions were adroitly hidden in the banana and coconut groves and were undetectable. South and west of Ap Bac, deep foxholes were dug in the front of irrigation dikes affording open fields of fire into the surrounding rice paddies. Unbeknownst to the ARVN force and their advisers, the communist province chiefs had instructed their forces "not to pull back as usual when the ARVN struck, but instead stand and fight."[92]

Only ten of the required thirty *Shawnee* helicopters were available to support the attack. The 1st Battalion, 11th Infantry Regiment soldiers would assault with only one company at a time. At 7:00 AM, three hours after the initial warning of the pending assault from the VC scouts, the first lift of ARVN soldiers arrived at their LZ, where they awaited the remainder of the battalion follow-on lifts.

The Civil Guards of Task Force A approached within thirty meters of its objective at Ap Bac before coming under withering fire, which stopped the momentum of the attack. The now fully assembled battalion of the 11th Infantry Regiment assaulted on three separate approaches to within twenty meters of the VC soldiers of the 514th Battalion, which unleashed a defensive onslaught that would repel three major ARVN assaults over the next five hours.[93]

Mother Nature now interposed her will to thwart the ARVN further. Socked in by heavy fog, the CH-21s could not land the two reserve companies at Tan Airfield until 9:30 AM. With, at best, an emerging tactical stalemate on the ground, the ARVN and their American advisors sought options to regain the initiative. With ten *Shawnee* from the 93rd Transportation Company loaded with the first reserve company and escorted by five UH-1C gunships in the air toward the planned LZ, a request by the American adviser to the 7th Infantry Division was made to divert them to an LZ 300 meters west and south of the Ap Bac position.[94] But, because of ambiguities in the command relationship between U.S. units and MACV advisers, aircrews frequently deferred to standing operational orders or on-site direction from ARVN unit commanders. Such was the case at Ap Bac, where the *Shawnees* instead landed 200 meters west into the teeth of VC small arms, automatic weapons, and machine gunfire.[95] The immediately available gunship support could not suppress the enemy fire. One severely damaged *Shawnee* failed to get airborne, and a second, sent in to rescue the first crew, was heavily damaged upon touching down. Their downed crews would defend themselves for eight hours as intense enemy fire in the landing zone prevented rescue.

During the day, only two of the remaining helicopters were flyable, and an *Iroquois* attempting to rescue the crews of both downed CH-21s also crashed under hammering enemy fire. A heavily damaged third CH-21 force landed a short distance from the other downed aircraft.[96] The 93rd relocated two of its damaged aircraft to the staging field, where they were repaired with cannibalized parts. They continued resupplying the downed crews with ammunition and evacuating the wounded for the remainder of the day. Eight hours after the loss of the first *Shawnee*, ARVN armored personnel carriers reached the downed aviators and evacuated them through a two-hour running gun battle until they reached a safe extraction point and accomplished a further helicopter evacuation. By battle's end, the 93rd Transportation Company lost one killed and nine wounded, and all ten aircraft sustained damage from enemy fire.[97]

With all ARVN troops on the ground and all units under continuous heavy enemy fire, they sought options. M113s from the 4th Mechanized Rifle Squadron of the 2nd Armored Cavalry Regiment were ordered to the battle site to improve the friendly situation at Ap Bac and to rescue the downed aircrews.[98] The squadron commenced its slow, tortuous 1,500-meter advance. In the interim, a fourth CH-21 attempting the rescue of the aircrews was forced down on a nearby rice field. Its loss marked the first operational loss of five helicopters to the VC within a short period.[99] By 1:30 PM, the M113 column reached the five downed aircraft and commenced the rescue. The Rifle Squadron and its M113s were unsuccessful in contributing to the continuing ARVN battle, disengaged from the fight, and withdrew.[100]

With the deteriorating ground situation, the American adviser appealed to Colonel Huynh Van Cao, Commander of the 7th Infantry Division, for an airborne battalion drop on the east side of Ap Bac, the most likely route of a potential future VC withdrawal. Cao opposed the plan and elected instead to reinforce the failure of the 4th Mechanized Rifle Squadron by dropping the battalion behind and west of the squadron's APCs.[101] The ARVN 8th Airborne Battalion was assigned the mission in conjunction with the second Civil Guards Task Force.

The ARVN parachute drop made that evening from a flight of seven USAF C-123 *Provider* aircraft with approximately three hundred ARVN paratroopers yielded yet another calamity as the troops landed a half-mile distant from their intended drop zone (DZ). This placed the paratroopers on the ground directly in front of the VC positions and well within the range of enemy fire from the VC forces in Tan Thoi[102], which tore through the descending paratroopers, killing nineteen and wounding thirty-three, including two Americans.[103]

At the same time, the VC commander, Colonel Hai Hoang, appreciated that his perimeter was collapsing from three directions, leaving only the eastern flank open. He ordered his exhausted troops to assemble at the southern extreme of Ap Tan Thoi, from whence they would commence their evacuation at 10:00 PM. Destined for their base camp in the Plain of Reeds, the VC safely closed on their base camp at 7:00 AM on January 3.[104]

The VC suffered eighteen men killed and thirty-five wounded by battle's end, principally from artillery fire and airstrikes. At the same time, three Americans died, five others were wounded, and sixty-three ARVN soldiers were killed and 109 wounded.[105] And then there was also the matter of losing five helicopters.

Ap Bac was more than an ARVN-American loss on the battlefield; it was a milestone for the Viet Cong insurgency. They had won one of their first major victories against South Vietnamese troops while American equipment and advisers supported them. Despite having a four-to-one manpower advantage over their VC adversary and the support of artillery, armor, and helicopters, the ARVN troopers suffered heavily.[106] The VC proved they could shoot down a relatively new and intimidating American weapon: helicopters. Ap Bac also demonstrated that ARVN forces remained limited in combat operations despite the experiences of 1961 and were slow to achieve the progress U.S. officials had hoped. The U.S. Army Command Pacific (USARPAC) reported the outcome of the Battle of Ap Bac as "one of the bloodiest and costliest battles of the S. Vietnam war"[107] and noted that the battle "will provide an enemy morale-building victory."[108]

Ap Bac was a significant moment along the road toward direct U.S. ground combat troop involvement in Vietnam. The Viet Cong attributed their battlefield success at Ap Bac "to preparation, motivation, and discipline in the executing of small-unit tactics,"[109] while the American press reported it as a "major defeat" in which "communist guerrillas shot up a fleet of United States helicopters carrying Vietnamese troops into battle."[110] Following the victory at Ap Bac, the Central Office for South Vietnam (COSVN)[111] broadcasted to their pro-communist audience a new slogan and encouragement, "Emulate Bac!"[112]

The largest heliborne operation within the northernmost area of operations in South Vietnam, the I Corps Tactical Zone, took place on August 2, 1963, and included the 93rd Transportation Company. The operational mission was to destroy the Viet Cong (VC) 5th Region Headquarters in the Do Xa area. The air movement of the ARVN troops permitted the rapid capture of the VC radio station and the significant loss of enemy combatants. The 93rd also participated in Operation LAM SON II on August 30, 1962. This was an assault mission against a VC Battalion located deep in the jungles of Quang Ngai Province. Besides the 93rd, the 1st Helicopter Squadron of the VNAF complimented with their ten CH-34 helicopters. Heavy ground fog over the landing zone delayed the assault two hours after the pre-strike instead of immediately after that. Thus alerted, the Viet Cong subjected the inbound helicopters to intense ground fire. The 93rd lost two of the twelve aircraft participating during their mission. Nine of the *Shawnee* aircraft sustained damage from ground fire, and the unit lost six aircrew members and five wounded.[113]

On September 19, 1962, the 1st Marine Aircraft Wing of Soc Trang exchanged locations with the 93rd Transportation Company, and the company moved to the Soc Trang Airfield in the flat Mekong River Delta. After ninety-six flying hours carrying forty-seven loads totaling 855,299 pounds of cargo, the 93rd was ensconced in Soc Trang and flew its first operational mission four days later, on September 23.[114]

The early combat operational experience of the CH-21 *Shawnee* witnessed what became known as the "Eagle Flight." While the exact origin of the designation is uncertain, it is widely held among the Army aviation community that it occurred during the fourth quarter of 1962, when the five U.S. CH-21 companies in-country joined forces with the Utility Tactical Transport Helicopter Company for the armed escorted deployment of ARVN forces.[115] The aircraft mixture for the lift was five CH-21s to transport an ARVN platoon and an escort of two to five armed

UH-1s to complete the flight. The operational concept saw the UH-1s conducting an aerial reconnaissance of the designated landing zone and engaging any located enemy forces on the site with aerial suppressive fires. The South Vietnamese infantry troops were then landed to engage any remaining enemy force. If no forces were found, the ARVN force could be re-embarked and similarly deployed to another suspect location to repeat the same recon-engage-assault cycle. The uncertainty of the following "Eagle Flight" landing zone magnified the uncertainty and confusion for the NVA and VC forces.

From these early successes emerged an airmobile tactic that was feasible under combat conditions that would become core to the expanding air assault force, contributing to the growing momentum for the development and fielding of dedicated single-purpose armed helicopters. The early *Shawnee* experience revealed the Army's need for a larger, heavier lift aircraft to perform the essential heavy cargo movements and recover downed aircraft.[116]

As 1963 arrived, the consequences of the relative proximity of the deployment of the five *Shawnee* companies to Vietnam began to manifest themselves. Everyone in each company would be scheduled to DEROS at the same time. Thus to maintain the operational readiness of all the companies throughout the rotational period, MACV was forced to cross-level the experience of CH-21 pilots of all units through a balancing of newly arrived aviators with the reassignment of original pilots from different companies so that there were more staggered departure dates. The command anticipated that there would be cross-fertilization of lessons learned from the old-timers to the newbies with this process. Human nature being what it is, not all newly reorganized units were willing or prepared to capitalize on the experiences of the pilots with nearly a year's service in-country. The loss of personnel and aircraft during the transition reflected that.

The ARVN battalion air assault operations period was when the UH-1 began to make its mark. Its compact, powerful, and reliable gas turbine engine was the technological breakthrough needed to make airmobile operations a wholesale reality on a broad scale in Vietnam. Army aviation assembled the trifecta of needed essential capabilities from that single innovation: the *Iroquois* for troop lift, the *Chinook* for resupply cargo and medium artillery movement, and a fledgling attack helicopter.[117]

On June 23, 1963, the five *Shawnee* companies were redesignated, and with that change, they initiated their change-over to the UH-1B *Iroquois*.

With the increased number of *Iroquois* helicopters available in-country, the Army converted the helicopter companies to a new airmobile company TO&E. Each of the airmobile companies had one armed platoon of eight UH-1B helicopters and two transport platoons with eight UH-1B helicopters.

The timing was good because the *Shawnee* was beginning to show its age. Metal fatigue was causing cracks, replacement parts were difficult to obtain, and cannibalization was the rule and not the exception.[118] On June 27, 1964, Brigadier General Delk M. Oden, the Acting Commanding General, U.S. Army Support Command, Vietnam, formally retired the last CH-21 in Vietnam,[119] tail number 56-02049, which was also the first CH-21 to land in Vietnam three and a half years earlier.[120]

Lieutenant Colonel Robert Dillard, who also flew 02049 off the aircraft carrier in 1961, was at the controls on this day.[121] With the final entry in the helicopter's logbook, the end of the *Shawnee's* Vietnam career of "heliborne assaults, evacuations of wounded and refugees, and deliveries of rice and pigs" came to a close.[122] The ceremony concluded with a fitting tribute to the helicopter's Vietnam legacy as a formation of nineteen UH-1Bs flew overhead.[123]

Although no longer in service, the remaining *Shawnees* still had to be moved to the ships that would carry them back to CONUS. That last *Shawnee* to make that trip was flown on August 18, 1964, by CWO Charles D. Holbrook of the 120th Aviation Company, who passed the helicopter from Saigon to Vung Tau for transport back to the United States on the same day.[124]

The departure from Vietnam did not mark the end of the *Shawnee* story with the United States Army. It would be another five years before the CH-21's final logbook entries would be made. In 1964, the 19th Aviation Battalion was activated with sixteen CH-21 helicopters and a contingent of U-1A *Otter* geographically divided between Fort Wainwright and Fort Richardson, Alaska.[125] Over time, the old *Shawnee* warrior approached the end of her useful active-duty service life. That end came in 1969 when thirteen of the final sixteen aircraft were transferred to the Post Fire Department at Fort Richardson. Then in August 1969, with much fanfare, the last three helicopters, with an escort of UH-1D *Iroquois* helicopters, were flown to Fort Wainwright, where they were transferred to the 568th General Support Maintenance Company. At day's end, the final entries in the logbook of any CH-21C anywhere in the world were made, and the logbooks were closed out.[126]

The Shawnee Nation

The original Shawnee Nation or Eastern Woodlands Indians lived together throughout the region east of the Mississippi River. They were an Algonquian-speaking Native American tribe of about 10,000 strong whose origins are unclear. By 1600, they lived in the Ohio River Valley in present-day Ohio, Kentucky, Pennsylvania, West Virginia, and Indiana.

The Shawnee are traditionally considered the Lenape (or Delaware) of the East Coast mid-Atlantic region, the "grandfathers," and the source of all Algonquian tribes. They shared an oral tradition with the Kickapoo, with whom they were once members of the same tribe. The identical language of the two tribes supports this oral history and the fact that they were both living in northeast Ohio before European contact. They also had a special friendship with the Wyandot, whom they referred to as their "uncles."

In 1669, the Shawnee separated into numerous bands and scattered to South Carolina, Alabama, Tennessee, Illinois, Virginia, Maryland, and Georgia. They were driven from their territorial home in the central Ohio River valley by the westward expanding Iroquois. Two decades later, both began a protracted conflict with English settlers and southern tribes. The climax witnessed the Tennessee band driven north to the Ohio Valley while the South Carolina band returned to Pennsylvania. Later, the French and Indian War saw the Shawnee of Ohio aligned against the British while their Pennsylvania brethren remained neutral. Both bands united in 1755, and together with other midwestern tribes after the American War for Independence fought to prevent further European-American incursion into the Ohio Valley.[127]

A highly nomadic and wandering tribe, the Shawnee can be traced to three countries—the United States, Canada, and Mexico—and in numerous states, including Alabama, North Carolina, South Carolina, Illinois, Delaware, Kentucky, Indiana, Maryland, Michigan, Pennsylvania, Tennessee, Ohio, Virginia, West Virginia, Texas, Arkansas, Missouri, Kansas, and Oklahoma.[128] Their wanderings were primarily caused by their willingness to move in order to avoid confrontations with other Indian tribes.

CA-TA-HE-CAS-SA-Black Hoof, Principal Chief of the Shawanoes. (Courtesy of the Smithsonian American Art Museum.)

The tribal warriors were well known for their ferocity in combat, in which they were almost continuously engaged from the seventeenth century until their forced departure from Ohio in 1832. Their enemies were known to outnumber their friends and allies vastly. They also fought with the French during the French and Indian War until 1758, when they switched sides and supported the British.

With the outbreak of the Revolutionary War, many of the Shawnee tribe members tried to remain neutral. Nevertheless, before long the issue divided the tribe with internal conflicts as to whom their allegiance should be given. In early 1774, some 170 Shawnee families moved away from their tribal land to avoid being drawn into the war on either side.[129] The American colonists' persistent encroachment onto Shawnee land soon decided the allegiance question, and with the murder of Chief Cornstalk by American militia in 1777, the issue was resolved.

Shawnee villages were a frequent target of the colonists during the Revolutionary War. One, in particular, was Chillicothe, which was situated on the west bank of the Scioto River in Ohio. In May 1779, the village was violently attacked by American troops led by Colonel John Bowan. In that engagement, Shawnee Chief Black Fish was killed. The following summer, the Virginia militia under George Rogers Clark set out to revisit the attack on Chillicothe; however, the Shawnee, not wishing to see the town fall into colonial hands, burned it to the ground.[130] Clark's forces would return to Shawnee territory in 1782 and put five villages to the torch and all the tribal crops.

Walter Blue Jacket was among their greatest warrior chiefs leading the Shawnee during the Revolutionary War. After the Treaty of Paris resolved the War for

Independence, at least between the British and American combatants, the Shawnee would continue their conflict with the Americans for another twelve years. Moreover, the conflict was further stimulated by the expanding encroachment on Shawnee land by more and more white settlers.

The first large-scale retaliatory strike against the Shawnee led by General Josiah Harmar was a poorly trained force of regulars and militia supported by light artillery along the Great Miami River in the Northwest Territories. The local Native tribes were alerted to the Army's movements as they advanced. Under the leadership of Chief Little Turtle of the Miami tribe, successive ambushes were sprung upon the moving force.[131] Induced to give chase to small groups of Indian warriors onto unfavorable terrain, American troops and militia were brought under fire by Native American sharpshooters and vanquished. The fleeting and highly mobile men of Little Turtle were able to concentrate their forces at times and places of their choosing and then, with equal rapidity, vanish. Before the end of October 1790, a large detachment of Hamar's expedition was roundly defeated while the main body remained in defensive dispositions at the Battle of the Pumpkin Fields. Heartened by their victory, Little Turtle and the several tribes of the Western Confederacy increased the intensity and scope of their attacks against settlements throughout the region.[132]

The following year, General Arthur St. Clair was ordered into the Wabash Valley to resume the campaign against the marauding Native Americans. On November 4, 1791, Little Turtle "administered one of the most disastrous defeats in the history of United States Indian fighting."[133] Poorly disposed in a valley camp, St. Clair and his men were quickly overrun with a heavy loss of life in what is known as the Battle of St. Clair's Defeat.[134] After these two striking American defeats, Confederacy leaders began formulating their demands for peace while the Americans constructed forts precisely and determinedly to regain control over the territory. Indecision among Native leaders allowed the conflict to continue into 1793. A new American army force, the Legion of the United States, emerged as a highly trained Army with each of their sub-units containing a combination of infantry, cavalry, and artillery.[135] Little Turtle and Blue Jacket assailed the Legion at the Battle of Fallen Timbers with relatively equal numbers in both forces; however, the skilled and better fighting legion vanquished the Confederation's warriors. Forced to sue for peace, the Native Americans, through the 1795 Treaty of Greenville, would relinquish much of Ohio and surrounding states.[136]

Regarded by many as among the greatest leader of the Shawnee was Chief Tecumseh who was also a spiritualist and warrior. Known as a deft diplomat, he combined his warrior skills, inspirational oratory, and linguistic knowledge to unite a Native American coalition of Southern Great Lakes tribes to oppose the European-American expansion.[137] He combined forces with his brother Tenskwatawa, a tribal prophet who promoted abandoning European influence. Together in 1808, they founded multitribal villages in Greeneville, Ohio, and Prophetstown, Indiana. In 1811, Indiana territorial Governor William Henry Harrison led an attack on Prophetstown in what became the Battle of Tippecanoe, named after Tippecanoe

Creek,[138] where he forced the warriors to withdraw before burning the village. Although not present for the battle, the defeat was a major setback for Tecumseh. Despite this, his coalition of tribes remained joined against the Americans during the War of 1812.

The onset of the War of 1812 provided Chief Tecumseh another opportunity to wage war against the encroaching Americans. However, the Battle of the Thames in October 1813 would claim the life of Chief Tecumseh, thus ending his war against the Americans.[139] Under the terms of the Treaty of Fort Meigs in 1817, the Ohio Shawnee and some Seneca ceded all their land to the government of the United States. They were uprooted and moved to three reservations in Northwest Ohio.

When the Shawnee tribes fought, they fought to protect their families and for the right to remain on their land, whether it was their original tribal land in the Ohio Valley or in what is now Missouri, where they were forced to relocate, or on the lands in the Indian Territory where they were sent under the terms of the Indian Removal Act. Every time the Shawnee and their brothers fought, they lost more land to the advancing tide of the white man's encroachment.

Today, there are three federally recognized Shawnee tribes—the Absentee Shawnee who live near Shawnee, Oklahoma; the Eastern Shawnee in Ottawa County, Oklahoma, near Seneca, Missouri; and the Shawnee Tribe headquartered in Miami, Oklahoma. Originally these three tribes were unified as the Shawnee Nation and lived throughout the region east of the Mississippi River. There are other bands of Shawnee that are not federally recognized who live in Illinois, Kansas, Kentucky, Louisiana, Maryland, Ohio, Virginia, and West Virginia. The Shawnee population today is estimated to be approximately 14,000.

The *Shawnee* represented the Army's foray into medium-lift, tandem-bladed helicopters that it continues today. Besides the ability to move larger quantities of critical equipment and support to locations of vital need on the battlefield, the aircraft validated the tactical imperative of maintaining unit integrity in the movement phase to maximize combat effectiveness at the LZ. These were not insignificant initial steps in the evolution of the air mobility doctrine that would fully play out in Vietnam.

Army records do not always tell the backstory for the naming of its early helicopters, leaving it to the individual to discern the precise factors that commended the tribal or warrior chief name to a particular aircraft. In the present case, the Army selected a people that were swift of foot and could unexpectedly appear prepared for battle at their enemy's encampment. Their prowess in battle also could not be overlooked in the naming decision process. As masters in the enterprise of trade, the Shawnee valued the ability to efficiently move their products throughout the dispersed marketplace. Regardless of the unspecified precise rationale, no one disputed the wisdom of the decision, nor did it diminish the affection with which the helicopter was held by her crews.

OH-23 RAVEN

OH-23 Raven scout at rest. (Courtesy of the Army Aviation Museum.)

Among the early pioneers in rotary-wing aviation was a young California inventor and innovator named Stanley Hiller, Jr. At the age of eight, he built his first transportation device, a racing buggy, using the motor purloined from his mother's washing machine. With his father's technical help and financial backing, he formed a business manufacturing and marketing miniature gasoline engine-powered model racing cars known as the Hiller Comet[1]. Soon his company was producing 4,200 cars and earning $100,000 a year. In 1937, at age thirteen, the precocious Stanley and his father were credited as co-inventors of a die-casting machine based on a cooling process that increased the strength of cast aluminum. It was a boon to the profitability of their toy business, the toy industry overall, and would play a substantial role in his later aircraft business.

By 1941, using his die-cast process, his new business, Hiller Industries, was manufacturing aircraft parts for Army Air Corps combat planes used during World War II under a sizeable federal contract. During the war, Hiller Industries ran two shifts and fully utilized their seven die casting machines.[2] Recognizing that the Second World War was winding down and with it his military aircraft spare parts business, Stanley Hiller began looking for alternative uses for the company's casting machines. Soon he was producing aluminum kitchen utensils and toy water pistols, the Hiller Atom Ray Gun.[3]

In the early 1940s, the American rotary-wing industry was centered along the eastern seaboard with Igor Sikorsky building helicopters in New England; Frank Piasecki was finalizing the second successful American helicopter in Philadelphia, and, in upstate New York, the duo of Arthur Young and Larry Bell were advancing the design for the first commercially produced helicopter. On the west coast, Stanley Hiller Jr. was wading into the world of aircraft capable of vertical flight. Like his east coast counterparts, Stanley Hiller's quest to develop a helicopter was full of challenges. Intrigued with the obstacles to vertical flight and the potential of helicopters from the descriptions of Igor Sikorsky's rotary-winged aircraft experiments, young Hiller began to manifest some of his most important innovations and inventions focused on the design of helicopters. He overcame these challenges and went on to design several successful helicopter models.

Hiller rationalized that a coaxial rotor could at least partially surmount some of the instabilities experienced in Sikorsky's single-rotor design configurations without a tail rotor design. A coaxial rotor design eliminated the power require- ments necessary for a tail rotor, hence freeing up engine power for additional lift. He and the three employees of Hiller Aircraft began on their coaxial design at the end of 1942. Although a University of California at Berkeley dropout, Hiller possessed enough innate engineering acumen to develop sketches of a co-axial helicopter—the first helicopter with a double set of blades spinning in opposite directions on the same shaft.[4] On July 4, 1944, self-taught Hiller flew his experimental helicopter, the XH-44 Hiller-Copter, around the football field at the University of California at Berkeley stadium.[5] Built mainly from scavenged parts and a Franklin air-cooled ninety horsepower civilian aircraft engine that he purchased with the permission of the War Production Board, the innovative design served to stabilize its flight and helped make rotary-wing aircraft less rickety, safer, and more commercially practi- cable. On August 31, 1944, the day before Stanley Hiller was to be inducted into the military, he revealed his experimental helicopter to armed forces members. The Navy considered the craft as a potential rescue vehicle, and with an immediate draft deferment in hand, Hiller set out to mature his design.[6]

Around this time, shipbuilding industrialist Henry J. Kaiser's interest in heli- copters was stimulated by reports of the Berkeley boy genius Stanley Hiller's easy- to-fly gyrocopter. After witnessing one of Hiller's demonstration flights in the San Francisco area, Kaiser invested in the fledgling enterprise and made Hiller Aircraft the Hiller-copter Division of Kaiser Cargo. The investment was not a spurious reaction by Kaiser, as he had long entertained the vision of personal aircraft and a network of airfields with their own hotels, restaurants, repair shops, and traveler conveniences. With the cash influx from Kaiser, Hiller began in October 1944 to build three larger two-seat versions of the XH-44. The X-2-235, as it was called, was powered by a Lycoming 235 horsepower engine with super-rigid rotors and a metal-clad fuselage.[7] There was no stated military requirement for the X-2-235; however, Hiller intended that the helicopter would serve the Navy well for light utility, observation, and training. The Navy did acquire the third but incomplete X-2-235 aircraft to conduct wind tunnel testing by the National Advisory Committee for Aeronautics at Langley, Virginia. While the testing was abbreviated for fear of damage to the tunnel, it substantiated the validity of super-rigid coaxial rotors for very high-speed helicopter flight.[8] With the Langley success, Hiller modified the design of the X-2-235 to incorporate a three-bladed coaxial rotor and added an aft-thrusting rear propeller to enter the range of helicopter speeds beyond that attainable by existing helicopters.

By 1945, the Kaiser-Hiller partnership ended, at least in part, because of a disagreement over the capital to be set aside for the Hiller-copter Division's commencement of full-scale production.[9] That year Stanley Hiller and a group of investors would form United Helicopters, Inc., which was later changed to Hiller Aircraft Company. The Hiller team wanted to capture part of the postwar, low-cost helicopter market for the flying public and what they were offering was an improved version of the XH-44 Hiller-copter; however, the anticipated civilian helicopter boom never materialized. This business setback, coupled with his near-fatal crash, led Hiller to focus his inventive talents on developing a more straightforward and more reliable alternative conventional rotor system. The resultant dormant period allowed for new developments and a breakthrough in helicopter stability—the mounting of a series of small paddles on the main rotor blades, which were operated by the pilot, to control the movement of the main rotor disk. The system reduced the control forces and significantly increased the stability of the aircraft. All of this led to what became arguably the most successful of Stanley Hiller's helicopters, the Hiller 360 or UN-12. His stabilizing paddle system, which he dubbed the "rotormatic control system," was patented and incorporated into the future products of Hiller helicopter companies. The system is also referred to as the "Roto-Matic Control System" and the "Rotormatic cyclic control system." The simplicity of its design made Hiller helicopters, including the Model 360 light-utility helicopter and its variants, including the Army's H-23 *Raven,* considerably easier to fly. Also from this period of development focus, Hiller introduced all-metal rotor blades and the Hiller *Hornet,* powered by ramjets mounted on the tips of the rotor blades. With a price point of less than $5,000 per aircraft, Hiller entertained hopes that it would find a spot in the marketplace.

In 1948, Stanley Hiller introduced the Hiller 360, a single main rotor and tail rotor helicopter certified for production by the Civil Aeronautics Authority. The 360 went into production the following year, which was also the year a Hiller 360 made the first transcontinental commercial helicopter flight with Stanley Hiller flying the final leg into Manhattan at the end of a three-month, 5,200-mile demonstration tour.[10]

The Hiller 360 quickly found many uses, including agricultural, sightseeing, and VIP transport applications. The United States' entry into the Korean War opened numerous military applications, and military operational demands for the helicopter's capabilities quickly outstripped the ability of the existing helicopter fleets. The U.S. Army turned to Hiller's United Helicopters for a military version of the Model 360 for evaluation and designated it the YH-23. Based on the success of the Army trials, an order for one hundred two-seat H-23As was placed with Hiller from the fiscal year 1951 Army budget. It was the Army's largest procurement of helicopters to that point in time. Most of the aircraft delivered from this procurement were in the air ambulance configuration, which included two enclosed, externally mounted panniers affixed to the fuselage sides for stretchers. These initial aircraft, used for aeromedical evacuation, were instrumental in saving many lives early in the Korean War; however, the helicopters had a low availability rate. In 1951, an upgraded H-23B model with a larger engine, a changed undercarriage, and other refinements was introduced, which solved most of the helicopter's initial problems. Two hundred and seventy-three of the new helicopters were delivered to the armed forces in 1951 alone. Between 1952 and 1955, another 453 were built and delivered.[11] The *Raven* was used primarily for battlefield medical evacuations in Korea and Indochina. Subsequently, more than 3,000 of the famed Model 360 light-utility helicopters and numerous variants were sold to commercial and military customers worldwide. Perhaps the most widely recognized version was the U.S. Army H-23, which Stanley Hiller affectionately called "jeeps of the air."

The H-23 was widely assessed as a helicopter adept at reconnaissance, observation, medical evacuation, and training roles. In all these functions, it served the U.S. Army and the armed forces of thirty foreign countries well and helped train many thousands of student aviators with the skills they would later apply in other aircraft and peace and war situations.

The *Raven* could be armed with twin M37C .30 caliber machine guns utilizing the XM-1 armament subsystem or the twin 7.62-mm machine gun helicopter armament subsystem M2, which included two 7.62-mm fixed machine guns M60C and one 7.62-mm machine gun mount. Common to both subsystems was the XM76 sighting system. The M2 armament subsystem was primarily mounted on the "D" and "G" models.

The Hiller H-23 *Raven* light observation helicopter was based on the Hiller-produced U.S. Navy UH-12, first flown in 1948. During the Korean War, the *Raven* performed as a utility, observation, and medical evacuation helicopter. Ultimately the H-23 was produced in A through D and F and G variants—Hiller never produced an E model. Many of the distinctions among the several H-23 models were subtle and indistinguishable to the untrained observer, as in the case of many other multivariant helicopters. The two-seat A-model used in civilian and military applications had a sloping front windshield and wooden rotor blades. The C and subsequent models of the *Raven* featured a molded "goldfish bowl" canopy like that of the early H-13 models, a three-seat configuration, and metal rotor blades. The A-, B- and C-models had either a Franklin 200 or 210 horsepower engine. The D-model was a military C-model, first flown in April 1956, which mounted a Textron Lycoming 250 horsepower engine and a new transmission. All *Ravens* were three-place aircraft with the pilot seated between the two other crew members. The D-model was also equipped with a set of dual flight controls. The H-23F was a four-place helicopter, and because of the twenty-five-inch extension to the cabin, the pilot was seated in front of the three-man row of passengers/crew. Only thirty-three of the F-model version of the *Raven* were manufactured and delivered to the Army.

The most common version of the H-23 *Raven* was the H-23G which replaced the D-model. The more capable G-model was powered by a Lycoming O-540-9A six-cylinder, horizontally opposed, air-cooled 305 hp engine. The H-23G carried two external skid-mounter litters or patient pods when outfitted as an air ambulance. In 1962, when the Army standardized the numerical nomenclature for its rotary-winged aircraft, the H-23s became OH-23s.

The *Raven* at War

The *Raven* saw service as a scout during the early part of the Vietnam War before being replaced by the OH-6A *Cayuse* in early 1968. As discussed in the chapter dedicated to the OH-13 *Sioux*, the OH-23 *Raven* served as a scout and advanced reconnaissance ship preceding the assaulting transport aircraft over the designated landing zone to detect and draw fire from the enemy who would oppose the pending helicopter troop landing. It was a job for which both aircraft were well suited. They were slow-moving, low-flying scout aircraft that could conduct a reconnaissance of the designated landing zone and alert the follow-on aircraft to any enemy danger lurking in the vicinity. The *Sioux* and *Raven* were both used to attract enemy ground and air defense fire. The accompanying armed helicopters could neutralize it before the lift ships arrived and disembarked their infantry cargo. In their role, the *Raven* and *Sioux* were witnesses to many of the most intense combat engagements in the war, with many American and South Vietnamese lives hanging in the balance. An overall assessment the performance of these two early helicopter pioneers was probably best summarized by an Army aviation pioneer, General Hamilton H. Howze: "The little bubble helicopters (H-13 and H-23) have ridden out the earlier suspicion that they were particularly vulnerable and are also doing very well indeed in the scouting mission."[12]

Raven pilots broadly felt the nimble little aircraft was challenging to fly. Among its peculiarities of flight was that whenever the "pilot added power with the collective, the throttle had to be increased to keep rotor and engine RPM constant. When the pilot reduced power, he did the opposite and reduced throttle."[13] The OH-23G also had "low rotor momentum," which meant that if the engine shut down in flight, the pilot must immediately initiate autorotation procedures, depress the collective, and add right pedal. Besides two "poor quality radios," the crew felt intense vulnerability sitting in the Plexiglass fishbowl canopy.[14] Their aluminum padded bench afforded little protection from gunfire coming from below the aircraft unless aircraft maintenance personnel installed a piece of armor-plating under the bench seat.

The OH-23 would also witness one of the darkest chapters of America's involvement in the Vietnam War. On March 16, 1968, an OH-23 from the 123rd Aviation Company with a crew of three was tasked with flying low over the village of My Lai in Quang Ngai Province in the I CTZ to draw ground fire so that accompanying gunships could attack the identified enemy positions. The aircraft was piloted by Warrant Officer Hugh Thompson, Jr. that day. Also, crew chief Specialist Four Glenn Andreotta and door gunner Specialist Four Larry Colburn were part of the crew. There was no enemy fire and no enemy soldiers or insurgents on that day and at that particular village. On that mission, Thompson and his crew saw only mounds of corpses and livestock. Bodies of civilians—women, children, infants, and older men—lined a nearby irrigation ditch. Over 504 Vietnamese non-combatants had been tortured, raped, and murdered during a four-hour American Army rampage.[15]

What the aircrew witnessed in My Lai was the massacre of a Vietnam village by the men of Company C of the 1st Battalion, 20th Infantry Regiment, 11th Brigade of the 23rd (Americal) Infantry Division. The company had been previously alerted that enemy fighters and Viet Cong sympathizers occupied the village of My Lai. Supposedly, this village had recently sprung ambushes, mines, booby traps, and sniper activity, which exacted a heavy toll on the U.S. and allied forces, and the soldiers were under orders to conduct an aggressive search and destroy mission in the village. Lamentably the tactical intelligence was wrong.

Warrant Officer Thompson repeatedly set his helicopter down to save innocents and confront members of the company chain of command and individual soldiers to try to put an end to the slaughter that was going on. At the end of this appalling episode, Thompson would land his helicopter one last time and dispatch Specialist Andreotta to recover a surviving boy from the irrigation ditch. The OH-23 would fly the child to a hospital and then return to the home base of the 123rd Aviation Battalion. Thompson would report what the crew saw at My Lai over the radio throughout the flight. The outraged OH-23 pilot reported the incident to his operational chain of command and related his observations to the division chaplain.[16]

Only one person was tried and convicted of mass murder at courts-martial and ultimately served three years under house arrest.

In 1966 and 1969, the Korean DMZ Conflict, or the Second Korean War as some called it, took place. In that period, one of the last known exploits of the *Raven* occurred in August 1969. On August 17, a *Raven* from the 59th Aviation Company at Ui Jong Bu with a three-man crew strayed north of the Demilitarized Zone (DMZ) into North Korean airspace.[17] Kim Cheol-man, First Deputy Chief of the Korean People's Army General Staff, reported to authorities "… that at 11:15 AM, anti-aircraft artillery of the Korean People's Army shot down an American military helicopter, which intruded into the airspace of DPRK."[18] The crew included David Hodges Crawford, Herman Hofstatter, and Malcolm "Buck" Loepke.[19] They survived the shootdown, but were held as prisoners for 108 days, during which they were beaten and tortured daily until negotiations by General John H. "Iron Mike" Michaelis, Commander in Chief, United Nations Command/Commander, United States Forces Korea/Commanding General, Eighth United States Army, affected their release on December 3, 1969.[20]

It was amazing that the *Raven* survived enough to protect the crew from the North Korean air defense shootdown, though it was not atypical of the "strong, rugged machine."[21] To the aviator and non-aviator alike, the *Raven* looked like a simple aircraft, yet it proved to be reasonably reliable even under wartime conditions in both Korea and Vietnam. Additionally, the small helicopter was subjected to and expected to withstand all the abuse intended for it when the Army decided to use 216 of the initial H-23Bs as training aircraft at the Primary Helicopter School and Center at Fort Wolters, Texas, affectionately referred to as "Miserable Gulch" by the student pilots.[22] When the school was activated on July 1, 1956, it had a training fleet of 125 OH-23 helicopters.[23] The training fleet was primarily the OH-23 until the demand for rotary-winged aviators in Vietnam and the diversion of some of its number to Vietnam meant that the training aircraft fleet was increased with the addition of the Bell OH-13 and the Hughes TH-55A. By September 1967, the training fleet would ultimately reach over 1,300 helicopters, including the OH-23 (D and G); the OH-13 (E, G, and H), and the TH-55A.[24] Once a would-be aviator began the actual flying portion of the curriculum, he would do so in one of those three helicopters He would complete 110 hours of flying in the same model helicopter from that point forward.[25]

While the *Raven* was procured before the Army tradition of naming rotary-winged aircraft after Native American tribes, chiefs, or terms was established, it is nevertheless reasonable to assume that the aircraft's name *Raven* is linked to America's first residents. However, among the many resources concerning Army rotary-wing aircraft of the Vietnam War, only one mentions that the *Raven*, like the *Bird Dog*, was not given an Indian name. That source is a journal summarization of a resolution text. Of interest, though, is the fact that the OH-13 *Sioux* and the OH-23, both Korean War veterans, made their first flights in the mid- to late-1940s, and the former was given a Native American tribal name which was before the publication of Army Regulation 705-14, dated October 31, 1963. Moreover, the Army Aviation Center officials agree that the OH-23 bears a Native American name. Operating under that evidence, the more significant question becomes which of several possible and feasible Native American-related alternatives is the *Raven* linked to the H-23?

Which *Raven*, and the Arapahoe Chief

Few, if any, records remain that illuminate the nomination, rationale, and *Raven* name selection process. There are many uses of the term raven in the lifestyle, culture, religion, mythology, and language of the Indigenous people of North America, which can offer a potential justification for the Army adopting it for the H-23. Reference to raven is most prevalent among the tribes of the Pacific Northwest, Canada, and Alaska, but not exclusively.

Because of the non-secretive character of the raven and its familiarity among the Indigenous peoples, each tribe had its own name for the bird. Notable among the traits ascribed to the raven by Native Americans is that the bird is the bearer of magic and the herald of messages from the cosmos. The midnight-colored wing of the Raven is believed to be the repository of messages from beyond space and time that will only be revealed to those within the tribe deemed worthy of the knowledge. Other Native Americans maintained that the raven was a keeper of secrets and revealed the meaning of one's inner, hidden thoughts—those things in a Native American's life that he was unwilling to face. The raven was believed to be capable of assisting the Indian to expose the truth behind the secrets and then wing him back to health and harmony.[26]

The raven was frequently honored among Native American Holy and Medicine Men for its shape-changing attributes. Also believed is that the raven is all-seeing. Native Indian Holy Men understood that what the physical human eye sees is not necessarily the truth. When the Holy Man sought clarity, he would call upon the raven to provide it. The raven was summoned in rituals so that visions could be clarified. Thus during tribal rituals, the raven would be beckoned to explain the conflicts between the versions of the truth. Although often used in rituals, there is no evidence that Native Americans worshiped the raven.

Among other possibilities is that the raven in Native American tradition is linked in their lore as the symbol of death. Yet another alternative is that in some tribes, especially in the Pacific Northwest, the raven is a creature of metamorphosis because it is endowed with a transformative attribute, thus symbolizing change or transformation.

Finally, there is one last possibility stemming from among the nomadic Arapaho people who were hunters who followed the buffalo herds and the changing seasons through present-day Colorado, Nebraska, and Oklahoma. Among them was a Chief named Little Raven, a noted peacemaker between the Indians and the White Man. Since the Army's preference was for one-word names for their helicopters, it would not be unexpected that Little Raven would be compressed to Raven. In a conversation with Robert D. Mitchell, curator of the Army Aviation Museum at Fort Rucker, he confirmed that the namesake of the OH-23 *Raven* was a Southern Arapahoe priest named Little Raven.

Little Raven, also known as Hosa, or "Young Crow," at age thirty-three, was made head chief, not by the people of his tribe but rather by the U.S. government. Little Raven was born in 1810 in the central Great Plains along the Platte River in present-day Nebraska. He was a warrior, a diplomat, and an orator in life. As an intelligent leader, Little Raven brought peace in 1840[27] among the warring Plains Indian tribes, the Cheyenne, Comanche, Kiowa, and Plains Apache.[28]

His life's work was the struggle to protect the lands and the rights of his people from the swelling encroachment of the white settlers and gold seekers who burst upon the scene in the mid-nineteenth century. Efforts to set aside land for the Native population, provide them protection, and ensure unhindered passage of settlers through Indian territory were at least temporarily achieved with the Fort Laramie Treaty of 1851. The Cheyenne, Sioux, Arapaho, Crow, Assiniboine, Mandan, Hidatsa, and Arikara Nations were granted territory with no U.S. claim to any portion of it. The tribes pledged safe passage through their territory along the Oregon Trail and would permit the forts and roads to be built on their land.

The eight tribal nations were also granted an annual annuity of $50,000 for fifty years.

In short order, the U.S. failed to prevent the mass migration of whites into the demarcated Indian territory. The settlers soon established homes, farms, and roads, quickly followed by towns. Matters were made worse by the Pike's Peak Gold Rush and the miners who swarmed into the territory and claimed the land for their mining enterprise.

Little Raven and his Cheyenne counterparts were committed to finding a diplomatic way to peacefully coexist with the interlopers and become a part of the new frontier economy. In 1859, he hosted a council in Denver with local American leaders where both sides indicated their desire to live in harmony and on good terms. He explained to the settlers that they "could take the gold but not the land."[29] He spent time after the council learning about the federal government, American society, the Great Father, mining, and "civilization wonders."[30]

The federal government chose to ignore the mass influx of Americans into the Indian territory in violation of the Treaty of 1851. It was unprepared and unwilling to evict the transgressors and preferred to make the problem disappear by obtaining legal title to the land.

The plan was to dispatch Congressionally authorized Commissioner Alfred B. Greenwood to a council meeting at Fort Wise with the Cheyenne and Arapaho to obtain the cession of most of their Treaty of 1851 land.[31] With the territorial violence of 1856–57 fresh on the minds of the Native participants, the Cheyenne were reluctant to enter the fort, and only a few southern leaders participated. Little Raven and the others stressed that the meeting did not represent a treaty because the northern bands and the essential representatives of the southern bands were not present. The government went ahead with another treaty meeting with a new commissioner and Indian agent, an unreliable interpreter, and without the northern Arapaho and Cheyenne leaders in attendance. The treaty made "over their heads" provided for the cession of the 1851 lands except for a reservation on the Arkansas River west of Fort Wise.[32] The Indian representative may have thought they were merely making their marks on documents to receive trade goods, a tactic often used by other Indian officials. Little Raven commented that the tribes had not been paid for the gold that the trespassing miners took from the treaty lands: the president "must give a good price as they are digging gold on our land. We know it was, but never troubled the whites thinking the government would make it up."[33] They had been deceived, and the Cheyenne and Arapaho regarded the treaty of 1861 as invalid. The tribes pressed for permission to present their grievances about the violations of the 1851 treaty by the settlers and their fears about the intentions of the soldiers directly to the Great Father, President Abraham Lincoln. The less than satisfactory meeting with the Great Father, who was otherwise preoccupied with the Civil War, took place on March 27, 1863.[34] Lincoln was dismissive of the Indian representatives, stating when confronted with the allegations that "white children" were attacking the Indians, "We are not, as a race, so much disposed to fight and kill one another as our red brethren."[35] As to the treaty violations by the settlers, he remarked, "If our children should sometimes behave badly, and violate these treaties, it is against our wish. You know it is not always possible for any father to have his children do precisely as he wished them to do."[36]

The Fort Wise Treaty of February 8, 1861, forced the Arapaho away from their homes in the Cherry Creek and the South Platte valleys. The Indians secured a 600-square-mile reservation and annuity payments from the government through the treaty. The nine chiefs who led the Indian negotiating delegations reasoned that continued hostilities would jeopardize their bargaining power. Although many Arapaho chiefs did not sign the treaty, Little Raven did; envisioning peace would be maintained. John Evans, governor of the Colorado territory, invited non-hostile Indian tribes to settle near military posts, and they could continue to hunt and receive provisions and protection from the military.

In August 1864, Governor Evans met with Black Kettle, Chief of the Cheyenne, and several other chiefs to forge a new peace. Black Kettle moved the Cheyenne and Arapahoe to Fort Lyon, Colorado, where the commanding officer encouraged him to hunt near Sand Creek. In what many historians consider an ultimate act of treachery, Colonel John Milton Chivington moved his force of Colorado volunteers to the plains. On November 29, he attacked the unsuspecting Native Americans, scattering men, women, and children and hunting them down. While only nine of Chivington's men were killed, 148 Indian followers were slaughtered, and more than half were women and children.[37] The volunteers then returned and killed the wounded, mutilated their bodies, and set fire to the village. Little Raven and his band of Arapahoe survived the massacre only because they had chosen to camp away from the other Arapahoe and Cheyenne.

Despite the atrocities visited upon the Arapahoe and Cheyenne by the Colorado volunteer militia and their commander, Colonel Chivington, and the collaboration of Governor John Evans, Little Raven, and Black Kettle would not abandon their pursuit of peace for their people.

With the conclusion of the Civil War, the Army turned its attention to the west and the southern plains, where previously displaced Native American tribes were an impediment to expansion. By March 1867, several tribal chiefs figured prominently among their contemporaries in the eyes of Army officers. They included Little Raven of the Arapahoe; Tall Bull, White Horse, Bull Bear, Roman Nose, and Black Kettle of the Cheyenne; and Satanta and Kicking Bird of the Kiowa. With an unsuccessful peace ultimatum delivered by General Hancock at Fort Larned, the assembled tribes faded into the sunset, a perceived insult by the general. What followed became a season of violence on the plains of Kansas, with no fewer than nine battles, fought between the tribes and the Army and increased raiding along the Santa Fe Trail. By early autumn General Philip Sheridan had replaced General Hancock, and diplomacy and negotiations were on the agenda.

Some 5,000 southern Plains tribal members and leaders assembled at the natural basin formed by the confluence of the Medicine Lodge River and Elm

Portrait of Chief HO-HOCA-GE (Little Raven). (Courtesy of the National Anthropological Archives.)

Creek. They participated in "several days of feasting, oratory, and distribution of presents" as a prelude to discussions.[38] Ultimately peace treaties were signed. On October 21, the Kiowa and Comanche signed their treaty, and the Kiowa-Apache theirs. The Southern Cheyenne and the Arapaho signed treaties on October 28.[39] By the Medicine Lodge Treaty, the participating tribes agreed to move onto two large reservations in western Indian Territory. One was for the Kiowa, Comanche, and Kiowa-Apache, and the second was reserved for the Cheyenne and Arapaho.[40] No whites were permitted on the reservations. Seed and farm implements were provided along with agricultural instruction in their use. The Native Americans relinquished all rights to territory beyond the reservation limits, although they could hunt below the Arkansas River as long as there were buffalo. With a mark of the pen, the warrior-huntsmen of the Plains became farmers and "inculcated with Anglo-Saxon values."[41]

Ultimately, by the Medicine Lodge Treaty of October 27, 1867, the Southern Arapahoe and Cheyenne accepted assigned tribal lands between the Arkansas and Cimarron Rivers in present-day Oklahoma's Indian Territory. Chief Little Raven would lead his people there.

Following the Battle of the Washita on November 27, 1868, Little Raven led the Southern Arapaho to Fort Sill for protection. Then the Southern Arapaho and Southern Cheyenne were granted a reservation in western Indian Territory. Eventually, Little Raven settled at Cantonment in present-day Blaine County, Oklahoma, where the old military hospital served as his home. Little Raven died at Cantonment in 1889.

The H-23 *Raven* might have been small in stature compared to the newer and larger helicopters being added to the Army inventory, but its role was no less significant. And as its story unfolded, the little helicopter was also a brave eyewitness to history, military, tactical, and geopolitical. The Hiller product is a fitting bearer of the name of a man of peace, intelligence, and leadership of his people.

CH-34 CHOCTAW

CH-34 Choctaw *delivers ARVN troops to the battlefield. (Courtesy of the Army Aviation Museum.)*

Shortly after the H-19 *Chickasaw* (Sikorsky S-55) was introduced into service, the U.S. Navy initiated a search for an improved aircraft. The Navy wanted a new helicopter with an increased operating range and a greater payload capacity to satisfy the requirements of its Anti-Submarine Warfare (ASW) mission: detect, identify, track, or destroy enemy submarines.

The competition between Bell Helicopter and Sikorsky began in 1952 with Bell offering the Navy the HSL-1, a twin-rotor helicopter along the design lines of the Piasecki H-21 *Shawnee*. The Sikorsky offering would follow the precedent of the S-55 design process in that it would be funded with the company's internal research and development funds. Their S-58 design, which was a product improvement to their S-55, had a tail-dragger rear fuselage with landing gear instead of the S-55's high tail and four-post pattern wheel arrangement. It retained the nose-mounted, radial reciprocating piston engine with the drive shaft passing through the cockpit placed high above the cargo compartment. The S-58 family of aircraft was the last piston-engine powered helicopter in production by Sikorsky. The new helicopter was twice as powerful as its S-55 predecessor, with a more streamlined, aerodynamic configuration.

The Navy selected the Bell aircraft, and the Marine Corps chose the Sikorsky aircraft from the naval services competition. However, both helicopters developed problems resulting in the Navy and the Marine Corps reverting to the SH-34J and

UH-34D. On June 30, 1952, a prototype contract for four helicopters was awarded to Sikorsky by the Navy. The prototype's first flight was less than two years later, on March 8, 1954, and the Navy's first production aircraft flew six months later, on September 20, 1954. In August 1955, the anti-submarine configured HSS-1 *Seabat* (SH-34J) and the utility transport configuration HUS-1 *Sea Horse* entered service with the Navy.[1]

The U.S. Army and Marine Corps followed suit and ordered the aircraft in 1955 and 1957. The Marine Corps initially ordered forty-five of the Sikorsky aircraft, however, when their planned procurement of the HR2S-1 encountered difficulties, they increased their procurement to 572.[2] The Army procurement ultimately reached 359 aircraft. Under the United States Army's aircraft designation system, also used by the Air Force, the helicopter was designated H-34. In 1962, under the new unified Department of Defense aircraft designation system, the *Seabat* was redesignated SH-34, the *Sea Horse* as the UH-34, and the *Choctaw* as the CH-34. These were utility and cargo helicopters that were readily adaptable to the transport, anti-submarine, search and rescue, executive transportation, and aeromedical evacuation roles. As configured off the production line, the UH-34 could carry twelve to sixteen troops or eight stretcher patients and a medical attendant in the medical evacuation configuration.

The CH-34 *Choctaw* had the same engine and cockpit configuration as the H-19. Beyond these inherited features, Sikorsky completely redesigned the remainder of the helicopter, extending the length of the S-55 fuselage and installing both a four-bladed main rotor and tail rotor, in contrast to the H-19's three-bladed main rotor and two-bladed tail rotor. The aerodynamic fuselage and low tail boom design that emerged from early wind tunnel testing enabled increased speed and reduced aircraft vibration. The *Choctaw* also had an all-metal fuselage with weight-saving magnesium in specific locations such as the skin; however, saltwater corrosion and fire hazards eliminated the latter metal in later models. The new helicopter also adopted a tricycle wheel landing gear which improved its ground handling due to its shortened turning radius. The rear tail wheel also improved safety by making it the first thing to hit the ground in a quick stop landing rather than the tail rotor blades. Additionally, a manually folded main rotor and a folding pylon were provided to allow the helicopter to fit on aircraft carrier elevators. The H-34 was also the first helicopter equipped with a stability augmentation system. The "automatic stabilization equipment" (ASE) was a rudimentary autopilot that assisted in-flight and directional control without multitudinous inputs that would overtax the mental and visual capabilities of the pilot.[3]

The D model of the *Sea Horse* was powered by a Wright R-1820 Cyclone radial engine which had a protracted aviation history. The engine was previously used in the Navy's last biplanes to the Army Air Corps' B-17s and the commercial DC-3s introduced during the years between the world wars.[4] The Marines and Coast Guard later acquired a version with floatation gear (pontoons) designated the UH-34E and UH-34F, respectively. Additionally, the Marines obtained four LH-34D models for use in Arctic operations. Several *Choctaw* and *Sea Horse* models were outfitted for executive and presidential transport in the Executive Flight Detachment. These were the VH-34A, VH-34B, VH-34C, and the VH-34D. Both the Army and the Marine Corps operated the aircraft to transport government officials, including Presidents Dwight Eisenhower and John Kennedy.[5]

The Marine Corps took the D model H-34 to Vietnam in large numbers. They served the Corps well, proving to be rugged and reliable in considerable measure due to the existence of a dependable support infrastructure to sustain them at the availability rates demanded by the operational tempo (OPTEMPO) established by Marine commanders.

During the armed helicopter experimentation period, the Army CH-34 was one of three helicopters that the Army's Deputy Chief of Staff for Operations wanted armed. He directed the development of a single, multi-aircraft machine-gun installation that could be used on the OH-13, CH-21, and UH-34. The YU-40 (later designated the UH-1) was to have a four-gun kit developed. The directed effort began in 1958 when the Townsend Company and the Springfield Armory undertook the task while the General Electric Company installed a 40-mm grenade launcher on the CH-34.

In July 1957, the commandant of the Army Infantry School and Center directed that a helicopter be integrated with weapons to provide airborne suppressive fire during assault landings. The CH-34 was selected to be the demonstration aircraft, and, as a result, became the "world's most heavily armed helicopter."[6] With the assistance of Sikorsky Aircraft personnel, the helicopter was armed with two 20-mm machine guns, two .50 caliber aerial machine guns, four .30 caliber aerial machine guns, two pods of twenty 2.75-inch FFAR each, two 5-inch high-velocity aerial rockets (HVAR), two additional .30 caliber machine guns in the left side aft windows, and one .50 caliber machine gun in the cargo door.[7]

After modifications at Sikorsky's facilities, the CH-34 was taken to Fort Benning for test firings. Following corrections to the sighting system and the HVAR launcher, successful test firings were conducted two days later. Unfortunately, the muzzle blast from the 20-mm cannon damaged the helicopter's air intake duct, and the engine firewall was severely cracked from the cumulative vibrations experienced. Following the testing at Fort Benning, the *Choctaw* was transferred to Fort Rucker for further experimentation.[8]

Six years later, under the auspices of the Committee for Aerial Artillery Test and Evaluation, the CH-34 underwent further testing at Fort Sill, Oklahoma, as a possible aerial fire support candidate. The platform-mounted one ten-tube 4.5-inch rocket launcher on each side of the fuselage. During one of Fort Sill's famous firepower demonstrations, the CH-34 demonstrated the ability to deliver the equivalent of one volley from a battalion of 105-mm howitzers. Rock Island Arsenal later tested the CH-34 with a 105-mm howitzer in the cargo bay for firing out of the cargo doors. Two months after the Fort Sill demonstration, the modified *Choctaw* was introduced as part of the Aerial Artillery Battery (Provisional).[9]

The CH-34 found greater favor with the Marine Corps, which began experimenting with the helicopter armed with the Navy's *Bullpup* missile on one side and a twin 20-mm cannon pod on the other. When the *Bullpup* missile testing took place, it became the first time in aviation history that a radio-controlled missile was launched from a helicopter. Despite its success, it took the Corps four years, until December 31, 1964, to issue the authorization of armed helicopters. In April 1965, the Marines deployed the armed variants to the Republic of Vietnam.[10] The Corps used USMC H-34s fitted with the Temporary Kit-1 (TK-1), comprising two M-60C machine guns and two 19-shot 2.75-inch rocket pods as armed helicopters. Operations with them were met with mixed enthusiasm, and the armed H-34 were quickly phased out. The TK-1 kit would form the basis of the TK-2 kit, which would be used on the UH-1E helicopters of the USMC.

Operational Use of the CH-34

While the *Choctaw* enjoyed a favorable reputation with its aircrews in terms of combat experience, the CH-34 illuminated several design flaws: the high cockpit presented an attractive target for enemy gunners. A partition created by the positioning of the drive shaft made it difficult for the crew chief to move from the cabin to the cockpit to assist a member of the cockpit crew during an in-flight emergency, and the magnesium metal components burned with such intensity that a fire endangered the entire aircraft and crew. Furthermore, weight reduction techniques employed in the CH-34 so weakened the airframe that it could not support many of the weapons that would later make the UH-1 *Iroquois* an effective flying gun platform.

The French Army Light Aviation experience in the Algerian War in the mid-1950s helped solidify the demand for helicopter-borne fire suppression weapons. However, during that war, their experience with the CH-34 brought its vulnerability to ground fire to the fore. There are indications that these shortcomings may have influenced the U.S. Army to deploy the CH-21 *Shawnee* to Vietnam. At the same time, it awaited the production and introduction of the ubiquitous UH-1 *Iroquois*. The Army CH-34s that served in Vietnam were transferred to the ARVN forces, who made little use of them because of maintenance issues and the availability of replacement parts. The U.S. Navy and Marine Corps, on the other hand, had the infrastructure and support systems to sustain the helicopter adequately and, therefore, requested its procurement for their purposes.

The helicopter's simple design, reliability, and high availability rates added to its attractiveness to the Navy and Marine Corps. The *Seabat's* folding main rotor blades and hinged tail section simplified its stowage and shipment aboard the ship. The Navy used the initial versions of the aircraft in the ASW role as it carried a dipping sonar plus a homing torpedo or depth charge externally on each side of the fuselage. These helicopters were later converted to utility duties by removing all the onboard ASW gear.

The UH-34 was most widely used in Vietnam by the Marine Corps, the Vietnamese Air Force, and in a limited capacity by the Army. The marines claimed the bulk of the Sikorsky production of the *"Seahorse,"* as they called it, including the entire 150-unit production of the UH-34D, of which almost all were lost. The Marine Corps and Army versions of the H-34 were rugged and straightforward but vulnerable because of their size and slowness, with less than 100-knot airspeed.[11] Despite this drawback, the marines armed the aircraft and called it the *"Stinger."*[12]

The Marine Corps took their UH-34D helicopters to Vietnam in large quantities, where they proved their worth as rugged and reliable machines. Between 1962 and 1964, the Marine Corps made extensive use of the *Sea Horse* in combat, principally as a troop transport and utility helicopter, but rarely as an armed gunship. They carried "troops, cargo, crates of ammunition, [...] paperwork on admin runs, chaplains (holy helo trips) [...] the wounded."[13] They would have a Browning 7.62-mm machine gun on a door or window mount when armed. The lighter 7.62-mm M-60 machine gun later replaced the Browning. The Marines also added armor plating to protect the crew and the engine.[14]

While the Army brought the CH-34 to Vietnam, it was in smaller numbers and, more importantly, not for use by U.S. Army ground forces. Late in the year 1960, the Army's Military Assistance Advisory Group in Vietnam (MAAG-Vietnam) sought and received approval for eleven CH-34C *Choctaw* helicopters from the U.S. Army to support the combat operations of the ARVN Rangers. These aircraft replaced the aging and worn-out H-19s of the Vietnam Air Force's (VNAF) 1st Helicopter Squadron. The combat story of the CH-34 in Vietnam is mainly one of the Marine Corps and the soldiers of the Army of the Republic of Vietnam.

The Marine Corps initially used the H-34 helicopter in Vietnam, bestowing the less than complimentary moniker the *"Ugly Angel"* because they found it rather bizarre looking, ungainly and awkward.[15] In August 1965, Marine Lieutenant General Lewis Walt launched a 5,500 Marine assault against the 1st Viet Cong Regiment.[16] The force rode into battle aboard the Marines' *Sea Horse* fleet. As it was known, Operation STARLITE was the first major regimental size offensive combat operation conducted by a purely American military unit in the war.

The operation revealed many inadequacies in the equipment and weapons employed by the U.S. troops. With the AK-47 assault rifle, a superior weapon to the M-14 rifle carried by the Marines, the Viet Cong unleashed a torrent of well-aimed fire.[17] The same gun in the hands of trained North Vietnamese forces also neutralized five Landing Vehicle Tracks and three flame tanks. The Marines also learned that "hydration was paramount [...], a more rapid-firing assault rifle was needed, and conventional vehicles such as personnel carriers, tanks, and other types of tracked vehicles were rendered useless in the thick jungle. Most of all, the Marines would need a rotary aircraft superior to the H-34."[18]

The enemy's operational sanctuary of the dense jungle demanded an allied response. The U.S. looked to its technology tool kit for a solution, resorting to something, in the eyes of many, akin to the chemical warfare of World War I. Four herbicides were used: orange, white, blue, and purple, identified by the band's color painted on the containers.[19] In early 1962 Operation RANCH HAND commenced with aerial delivery of the herbicides by the 12th Air Command Squadron and the 12th Special Operations Squadron.[20] To avoid a U.S. linkage to modern chemical warfare, President Kennedy authorized the first RANCH HAND mission on August 10, 1961, to be flown by South Vietnamese H-34 helicopters.[21] Presidential authorization was necessary for all defoliation missions for the next twelve months. Subsequently, authority was delegated to the U.S. ambassador and the MACV commander. Operation RANCH HAND ultimately dispensed 18,850,000 gallons of herbicides, of which over fifty-eight percent were the controversial Agent Orange.[22]

The UH-34 was a workhorse performing yeoman service in the war's early engagements for the marines positioned along the DMZ in the I Corps. In 1966 the UH-34 lineage of combat included Khe Sanh, Hue, Dong Ha, Quang Tri, and Song Ngan Valley, which the marines called "helicopter valley." Operations VIRGINIA and HASTINGS required over 10,000 helicopter and 1,677 tactical fighter sorties. The former allowed the marines to maintain the tactical advantage and sustain unrelenting pressure on their adversaries.[23]

The deficiencies of the "*Ugly Angel*" inconveniently and almost disastrously became more apparent to the Corps early in 1966. During March 9–12, 1966, a Civilian Irregular Defense Group (CIDG) encampment, Special Forces Camp A Shau, came under siege by the NVA's 235B Division forces.[24] After losing a Marine A-4 *Skyhawk*, an Air Force AC-47 *Spooky* gunship, and an Army UH-1E *Iroquois* in earlier relief and rescue attempts, Marine H-34s from HMM-163 "Super Chiefs" responded.

The "Super Chiefs" flew into the cauldron of violence to aid the surrounded troops and attempt a rescue.[25] Upon landing, the helicopters were swarmed by the surge of "panic-stricken ARVN soldiers, indigenous friendly personnel, and U.S. troops."[26] The human wave quickly exceeded the weight capacity of the venerable H-34s, making them unable to lift off. A single H-34 had twenty-four soldiers in the cabin or hanging on the landing struts, with aircrew members franticly trying to force some of the ARVN troops off while attempting to gain altitude. The VC and NVA forces focused their small arms, mortar, and anti-aircraft fire on the struggling helicopters.

Twenty–four hours later, the "Super Chiefs" were dispatched to rescue a downed Air Force pilot. The pilot's location and the inability to put the helicopter on the ground forced an attempt at a cable extraction. The crew had to jettison all non-essential cargo and equipment to attain sufficient lift. In contrast, the flight deck crew increased their altitude to avoid a repeat of the melee of the previous day, enemy ground fire, and burn off fuel and its associated weight. The maneuver consequently caused severe damage to the aircraft's radial piston engine. With the weight reduction accomplished, the pilot was safely extracted, but the Marine

Corps was belatedly convinced that the H-34 could not measure up to the combat demands of Vietnam. The following day, a high-altitude rescue attempt presented another opportunity for disaster for the aged H-34.

Both the UH-19 and UH-34 were at the obsolescence stage of their service life when the industry abandoned reciprocating engines in favor of compact, higher power density turbine engines. The *Choctaw*, more so than the *Chickasaw*, enjoyed the benefit of a service life extension through the installation of a turbine engine retrofit kit.[27] The UH-34, even with a new engine, was not a real competitor to the newer helicopters designed from the outset to capitalize on the turbine engine's design advantages. The turbine engine solved the engine placement problems in the more modern, smaller aircraft allowing the engine to be placed near the rotor or directly above the cabin in single rotor helicopters.[28]

The Choctaw Indians

The ancestral home of the today's Choctaw tribe is believed to be in the southeastern United States and from east-central Mississippi to just west of the Mississippi River and is thought to be more than 2,000 years old. The Choctaw are of Mississippian descent and share a Muskogean language with the Chickasaw. Their first encounter with European visitors was with Spanish explorer Hernando de Soto in 1540.[29]

When the Europeans began settling in America during the sixteenth century, the Choctaw resided in the southeastern United States in an area that would later become western Alabama, eastern Mississippi, and the panhandle of Florida. The arrival of Europeans in the Choctaw homelands was a mixed blessing, as while it brought many new opportunities, it also presented hardships, suffering, and death. Diseases common in Europe but unknown in the new world were visited upon the Choctaw with the arrival of shipwrecked Spanish sailors in the 1520s. Soon half the Indigenous population of many of the Choctaw settlements was claimed by disease.

The arrival of Europeans brought to light their insatiable appetite for land and labor—slave labor. This created a demand for slave traders and slave raiders among the Native tribes who were equally willing to satisfy the market created by the Spanish, French, and English by providing laborers for the European settlements on the continent and in the West Indies. These enslaved people, including women and children, came from among the populations of the rival tribes of the Choctaw. The Shawnees became a particularly important slave-raiding and trading power as they built their trading network to obtain firearms, munitions, and other desirable trading goods.[30] This gave rise to numerous iterations of inter-tribal conflict during the centuries following first contact, especially among the tribes in the south and southeast. The tribes of the region, aligned with their respective European trading partners, sought to protect and expand their markets, resulting in conflict with other Europeans and their different tribal allies.

The Choctaw frequently found themselves allied with the French in their running battles with the Natchez and Chickasaw and in turn the English supporters of these tribes. By 1740, a civil war engulfed the Choctaw Nation with internal strife between pro-French and pro-British factions. By 1750, with a pro-French victory, the Treaty of Grandpré was concluded and the Choctaw Nation was "reduced to a French protectorate."[31]

The Choctaw tribe of Mississippi primarily lived off agriculture and hunting. During the French and Indian War (1754–1763), they sided with the French, and with the British victory, some of the Choctaw tribal lands were confiscated. Tribal members were also forced into a westward migration in search of new land.

During the period of the Revolutionary War, the Choctaw were a tribe numbering about 15,000 souls residing in some fifty villages along the Mississippi River. British and American adversaries desired the Choctaws as an ally during the fighting. The presence of an ally along the Mississippi would aid in the denial of access to and use of the river by their adversary. It was the Redcoats, however, who prevailed and engaged the Native warriors as patrolling parties that guarded the Mississippi against the attacking American frontiersmen.

American colonials under the command of Captain James Willing, led an expedition to attack British settlements along the Mississippi River, hoping to reach New Orleans ultimately. To counter their excursion, a band of 155 Choctaw under British leadership headed to Natchez, one of the villages under threat by the Americans. To British advantage, upon learning of the advancing Choctaws, the Americans withdrew from Natchez.

On June 21, 1779, Spain entered America's Revolutionary War and declared war on the British. In response to the needs of their British allies, the Choctaw marshaled hundreds of their warriors to aid in the defense of Mobile in 1780 and Pensacola in 1780–81. However, with the loss of the war by the British, the southern tribes, including the Choctaw, were forced to enter into trading partnerships with the Americans and the Spanish.

In 1784, the Spanish successfully negotiated a series of treaties with the Choctaw, Chickasaw, and Creek people that in exchange for Spanish protection, the tribes agreed to "exclude all traders without a Spanish license."[32]

The creation of the United States brought increased pressure on tribal lands as the new government sought outlets for the growing European population. The Choctaw, along with other southeastern tribes, were forced to negotiate with the federal government for their lands. The formation of the Mississippi Territory in 1798 and the election of Thomas Jefferson as president in 1800 made it clear how critical the Choctaw lands were to the security of the new country. Jefferson's military strategy was to protect the United States against France, Spain, and England, which in turn depended on the government to acquire all lands on the eastern side of the Mississippi River.

In 1786, the U.S. government initiated a series of three agreements with Native American tribes. Each was called the Treaty of Hopewell and was to be negotiated between the U.S. Congress and representatives of the Cherokee, Choctaw, and

Chickasaw, respectively. They began with the Cherokee who were outside the Spanish trading sphere of influence.[33] The Choctaw and Chickasaw were also invited to the council meeting in Hopewell, South Carolina. Both tribes would sign their version of the Treaty of Hopewell which was similar in content to that signed by the Cherokee. The tribes were motivated to reach an agreement because the Spanish had not fulfilled their promise to provide trade goods. The agreement would eventually devoid them of all their land east of the Mississippi River.[34] In 1801, the Treaty of Fort Adams was signed with the Choctaw, wherein the tribe ceded to the United States 2,641,920 acres of land from Mississippi's Yazoo River to the thirty-first parallel.[35] Eventually, seven treaties would be consummated between the government and the Native tribes through which the Choctaws ceded more than twenty-three million acres of their tribal lands. Other treaties included the Treaty of Hoe Buckintoopa, the Treaty on Mount Dexter, the Treaty of Fort Stephens, the Treaty of Doak's Stand, and ultimately the Treaty of Dancing Rabbit Creek.[36]

As Shawnee Chief Tecumseh traveled among the Native American tribes seeking to unite all Indian Nations during the period before the War of 1812, he visited the Chickasaw Nation. A great council of chiefs and warriors was convened

to consider Tecumseh's proposal that all the tribes of the Northwest and the South unite and collectively resist the growing encroachment of the white man. Among the participants was Pushmataha, the most influential chief of the Choctaw. The evenly divided council resolved that they had "had enough of civil war," so left the decision to a medicine man, who interpreted the omens as supporting Pushmataha's position of supporting continued friendship with the United States.[37]

In 1826, the Choctaw people formed a constitutional government with written laws that included the delineation of political districts to prescribed punishments for various crimes.[38] A national government was viewed as an effective counter to the federal government and those outside the Choctaw sphere so that the Nation was able to speak with one coordinated voice

PUSH-MA-TA-HA, the "Indian General," one of three regional chiefs of the major divisions of the Choctaw in the 19th century. (Courtesy of the Smithsonian American Art Museum, Museum purchase ca. 1837–1844.)

against the "bitter and endless persecution" of their people and the sovereignty of their nation.[39]

Over time, following the American Revolution, many Native American tribes were slowly assimilating into the new United States. Farmsteads and mule-and-plow agriculture increasingly became the norm. Male members of the tribe found employment working the land or herding cattle on horseback while women spun and wove clothing.[40] Additionally, Christian settlers brought a different form of education which encouraged men to work in agriculture and pushed for a tribal shift from patrilineality. However, by May 28, 1830, the Indian Removal Act had become law, and President Andrew Jackson's initiative for all Native American tribes east of the Mississippi River to be removed west of the river to the Indian Territory became a reality. As enacted, it called for the voluntary relocation of the Indigenous people and allowed for their forced resettlement if necessary. The Choctaw were one of the Five Civilized Tribes, along with the Cherokee, Chickasaw, Muskogee, and Seminole, and were the first of the five tribes to be relocated to the territory granted to them west of the Mississippi under the terms of the Treaty of Dancing Rabbit Creek, which was signed, under threat of unprovoked destruction, in Noxubee County, Mississippi on September 27, 1830.[41]

Implementation of the Removal Act happened in three waves: between 1831–1833, 1845–1854, and 1902–1903. The years of the Choctaw removal, the 1830s and 1840s, are without question tragic periods in their history. Approximately 20,000 Choctaws were forced to leave their homes in Mississippi, for which they were to receive land and provisions for their journey. Under the terms of the removal, the Choctaw were given three years to leave Mississippi. Although, those Choctaw wishing to remain in Mississippi were allowed to stay with dual citizenship. During the first wave of emigration, the Choctaws faced some of the worst winters in recorded history. Coupled with either insufficient provisions for the numbers or non-existent provisions and inadequate clothing and shelter, an estimated 2,500 Choctaw men, women, and children perished while making the journey.[42] Due to the extreme hardship endured by the Choctaws, their march to the Indian Territory became widely known as the "trail of tears and death."[43] Eventually, all of the Civilized Tribes would be removed from their ancestral homes. The descendants of those tribal members who survived the arduous removal are today's Choctaw Nation of Oklahoma.

In the early years following the negotiated removal of the Five Tribes, they successfully adapted to life in the Indian Territory and became economically sufficient. The Chickasaw and Choctaw established cotton plantations, while the Cherokee, Creek, and Seminole engaged in subsistence farming, ranching, and cattle raising. The Native American tribes had a decidedly southern orientation with their open market connections with New Orleans. This gave them access to markets for the sale of their products beyond the continent. Also, the strong ties to the slavery traditions of the South would continue these outlets during the approaching Civil War. With their tribal governments in place, land that was demarcated and recognized specifically for their people, and a United States government representative charged with fulfilling the federal government's obligations of the removal treaties, the tribes began the slow process of healing from the dislocation.

Influenced by their geographic proximity to the Confederacy and their demographic surroundings, the Choctaw were predisposed to support the South during the Civil War. They were also more willing to accept the notion that "the dissolution of the Union as an accomplished fact."[44] With that, the Union would no longer be able to satisfy its treaty commitments to the Native Americans, and by July 1861, the Creek, Choctaw, and Chickasaw signed treaties with the Confederate government.

Descendants of the Choctaw people who stayed in Mississippi make up today's Mississippi Band of Choctaw Indians, and those members of the Jena Band of Choctaw Indians are descended from Choctaw people who remained in Louisiana.

The Sikorsky Model 58 was a case of being at the right place at the right time. The S-58 was a product improvement of the S-55, which meant that much of the new helicopter was flight proven at a time when the uniformed services need a robust ship to meet a variety of critical missions. At the same time, other helicopters were falling on hard times in their design maturation stages. In time, the Army, Navy, Marine Corps, Air Force, and Coast Guard would use the workhorse that the H-34 became. That was especially true for the Marines, for whom the helicopter was vital in Vietnam until the arrival of the UH-1. The Army had a limited number of *Choctaws* in country, but they used them extensively for medevac, cargo transport, and offensive gunships. When the fabled UH-1 began displacing the H-34s, the latter were turned over to the South Vietnamese.

For the Army, the CH-34 bore the proud name of the Choctaw tribe. They were an agrarian and hunting society that became dependent upon their trading network and, to some extent, the benefits of slave labor and trading. Early in the nineteenth century, they suffered from the U.S. government's removal policy which made them among the first southern tribes forced to the distant lands west of the Mississippi River into Indian Territory. True to their ancestral heritage, the removed Choctaws prospered in their new home with their cotton plantations and trading practices.

CH-37 MOJAVE

CH-37 Mojave *is recovering a downed de Havilland L-20* Beaver. *(Courtesy of the Army Aviation Museum.)*

On September 15, 1950, the Navy released a contract solicitation for a Class HR (Assault) transport helicopter capable of airlifting twenty-six combat troops and their equipment. In response, Sikorsky submitted a design on December 31, 1950, based on their S-56 design work. The company offered two different yet similar airframes. One was a basic helicopter identified as XHRS-A, and the other was a compound aircraft with folding wings identified as XHRS-B.[1] Both proposals were powered with two Pratt and Whitney eighteen-cylinder R-2800 reciprocating engines. Sikorsky, however, offered the Navy the option of replacing the piston engines with Allison XT-38-A2 gas turbine engines.[2]

The Navy selected the more conservative and risk-averse approach and awarded a contract to Sikorsky in early 1951 to develop and deliver four prototypes for the basic helicopter with the piston engines designated XHR2S-1.[3] On December 18, 1953, the prototype's first flight took place, with the Sikorsky S-56 being the company's first multi-engine helicopter and the largest piston-engine helicopter ever built.[4] Following successful testing of the prototypes, the Marine Corps issued a production contract to Sikorsky, and the first flight of a production aircraft took place on October 29, 1955. Deliveries of the Marine Corps' fifty-five helicopters began less than a year later.[5] Their final procurement was only thirty-one percent of the planned acquisition (180 helicopters) because of the Marine Corps' experience with the HR2S-1's development, testing, and deliveries.[6]

The Army obtained one Marine helicopter in 1954 for testing, and after a successful test program, it ordered nine aircraft in the tested configuration. Subsequently, the Army purchased ninety-four of the H-37A in 1956. The first H-37A was delivered to the Army Aviation Board at Fort Rucker for further service testing and the definition of suitable operational missions for the Army's fleet of new heavy-lift helicopters. The first unit equipped (FUE) with the *Mojave*, as the Army named it, was the 4th Transportation Company at Fort Benning, Georgia, in July 1957. Two years later, the first H-37As were deployed to Germany.[7] The H-37 was the first heavy-lift helicopter in the Army inventory and the last powered by piston engines. It would later give way to even larger and more powerful helicopters, the CH-54 *Tarhe* and the CH-47 *Chinook*, both turbine-powered.

The CH-37 would open the doors to many firsts in the Army. One such first was its maiden subjection to the rigors of testing by the Army Transportation Aircraft Test and Support Activity (TATSA) at Fort Rucker. Activated on July 1, 1956, TATSA's mission was to improve the maintainability and supportability of Army aircraft through improvements to procedures and maintenance publications due to strenuous testing through accumulated flight hours.[8] The TATSA regimen included the accelerated accumulation of 1,000 hours on the aircraft by flying it at every moment that it was not in maintenance without regard to weekends or holidays. The first helicopter to undergo such intentional abuse of both man and machine, the *Mojave* completed the test program in 128 calendar days.[9] As a result of its accomplishments during the test flights of the H-37, the TATSA was awarded the prestigious William J. Kossler Award in 1958 from the American Helicopter Society for "the greatest achievement in the practical application or operation of a vertical flight aircraft."[10]

While the *Mojave* would eventually be shipped to Vietnam, its initial duty stations were in CONUS, West Germany, and Korea. The H-37s would play a role in developing the Army's airmobile concept and operational organization, including assignment to units of the 11th Air Assault Division (Test) at Fort Benning, Georgia.

Production of the *Mojave* ended in May 1960; however, after all of the production models were delivered, ninety aircraft were returned to Sikorsky to be upgraded to the H-37B configuration, with conversions being completed by the end of 1962. The B model conversion included the addition of Automatic Stabilization Equipment (ASE), the standardization of radio and electronic components, installation of crash-resistant fuel cells, relocating the stabilizer from both sides of the rear fuselage to the top of the tail rotor pylon, increasing the size of the engine oil tank from 13.3 to 30 gallons per engine, replacing the rear split cargo door with a sliding door, and modification of the clamshell nose doors.[11]

The S-56 fuselage was fabricated around an aluminum structure with aluminum and magnesium skin and removable access panels made of reinforced plastic or fiberglass. The initial production of a two-row radial engine could produce 1,900 horsepower to drive the seventy-two-foot diameter five-bladed main rotor and four-bladed tail rotor. With the five-bladed configuration, the aircraft was designed to maintain sustained flight even after losing one blade.[12] Each engine nacelle was fixed at the end of a short shoulder-mounted stub wing mounted on each side of the bulbous fuselage. Later models were outfitted with Pratt and Whitney R-2800-54 engines that generated 2,100 hp each. The engine nacelles were large enough to retract the main landing gear into them for flight, and the *Mojave* was the first production helicopter to have retractable main landing gear. The cabin was 1,900 cubic feet and accessible through two clamshell doors located beneath the cockpit and was manned by three crew members and could carry twenty-three combat troops, twenty-four stretcher patients, or three jeeps. An available ramp accessed through the sizeable frontal clamshell doors permitted the loading of vehicles by driving directly into the cargo bay. Thus loaded, the *Mojave* could internally carry three M-38 jeeps, a light M-37 three-quarter ton cargo truck, an M101A1, or later the M102, 105-mm towed howitzer.[13]

Besides its 6,000 pounds internal cargo-carrying capacity, the CH-37A helicopters were equipped with a 10,000-pound external cargo hook. The aircraft also hosted a 2,000-pound capacity electric cargo hoist that could slide out the side cargo door to permit the self-loading of the helicopter. Through a hatch in the cargo cabin floor, the crew could conduct rescue hoist operations with a limit of 600 pounds.[14]

The CH-37 was the largest and fastest helicopter built in the West during its service life.[15] In November 1956, the Marine Corps would set three world records for helicopters with their HR2S-1: a speed record of 162.7 miles per hour without payload (November 9, 1956); an altitude record of 12,100 feet with an 11,023-pound cargo load (November 9, 1956), and a load-carrying record of 13, 277 pounds to 6,561.7 feet (November 10, 1956).[16]

The Army would use the CH-37 extensively in the Federal Republic of Germany beginning in July 1959. Both the Army and Marine Corps would employ

Volkswagen "Beetle" awaits loading into the belly of the beast. (Courtesy of Jerome "Jerry" Riggs via Ray Wilhite.)

them in Korea and Vietnam, where they would be used for aircraft recovery, cargo and artillery transport, and medical evacuation. Soldiers serving with the *Mojave* in West Germany spoke highly of their experiences with the "Beast" and their missions, including the periodic stockpile transport of cannon and surface-to-surface missile munitions. High on the crew hit parade of excursions were those where the crew would secret away in the belly of the Beast someone's Volkswagen (VW) Beetle so that they would have their ground transportation at their destination, thus ensuring themselves comfortable overnight quarters and sumptuous dining at a local German restaurant or *biergarten*. A beetle could be nestled securely in the cargo cabin by driving it through the nose-clamshell doors.

Door Gunners for the *Mojave*

During the nascent period of Army rotary-wing aviation in Vietnam, an issue plagued all of the Army's aviation units: the need for defensive and suppressive fire support. It was a problem complicated by the absence of a standardized weapons system for helicopters. The differences among helicopter configurations required either a helicopter unique or a universal installation configuration kit. Further complicating the prospect of armed helicopters in Vietnam was the absence of standardized doctrine and tactics for such helicopters. Because the Table of Organization and Equipment for aviation units at the time did not include armed helicopters no aerial door gunner manpower authorizations were included in the unit's personnel strength. A final challenge was the existence of a national military policy and the international agreement governing the employment of American troops in offensive combat operations in Indo-China.

While the arming of helicopters was the subject of intense investigation and experimentation at command levels at Fort Rucker and elsewhere in the United States Army materiel community, specific aircraft and unique point solutions were to a certain extent the result of the early deployment of helicopters to Vietnam. The 11th Air Assault Division (Test) was still maturing doctrine and tactics that would become the bedrock of the first deployed airmobile division. Additionally, the Table of Organization and Equipment for each transportation company sent to Vietnam during the advisory period had no allocation for men to be assigned as aerial gunners for the helicopters used to transport and support the ARVN combat forces.

Under terms of the Geneva Conference on Indochina (April 26–July 20, 1954), members of the MAAG-V, established in November 1955, and later personnel from MACV founded on February 2, 1962, held the status of military forces designation as advisors.[17] As such, U.S. military advisory personnel were precluded from accompanying their ARVN advisee units and commanders on combat operations.[18] While this restriction remained in effect until conventional American combat forces arrived in Vietnam and began conducting combat operations against the VC and NVA, the constraint was relaxed in 1961, when the insurgency expanded in ferocity and strength.

Military commanders searched for a creative solution without personnel in Vietnam authorized to engage in offensive combat operations. MACV, in late 1962, spawned a highly classified (Top Secret) plan that solicited volunteers from the only combat authorized unit in the Asia-Pacific Theater, the 25th Infantry Division (Tropic Lightning) at Schofield Barracks, Hawaii, to train and perform combat missions as aerial door gunners. Operation SHOTGUN[19] was the plan that, at the end of its three-year run in 1965, would provide almost 2,200 volunteer aerial machine gunners organized into Provisional Machine Gun Platoons, or "Shot Gun Platoons," shipped to Vietnam for ninety-day periods of Temporary Duty (TDY) to protect such aircraft as the CH-21 *Shawnee*, CH-37 *Mojave*, and the UH-1 *Iroquois*. Reminiscent of the armed stagecoach guard of wild west television shows popular at the time, the new breed of "shotgunners" evoked memories of that colorful past as their Indian named steed carried them into battle. The volunteers were drawn from the full range of Military Occupation Specialties (MOS) available within the 25th Division: Infantry, Mechanized Infantry, Military Police, Field Artillery, Cavalry, Armor, and Aviation.[20]

Officer and enlisted volunteers who passed a Class III flight physical were subjected to three weeks (112 hours) of intense training, including aircraft introduction, aerial observation techniques, and firing various weapons from assorted aircraft altitudes and attitudes. Their primary weapon was the M-60 machine gun, though shotgunners were versed in others, including the .50 caliber machine gun, M79 grenade launcher, .30 caliber M2 carbine, and the M16 and M14 rifles, plus vintage weapons like the Korean War Browning Automatic Rifle (BAR) and the World War II .30 caliber machine gun.[21]

Once temporarily assigned for ninety-day stints in South Vietnam, these professional aerial gunners became the most experienced U.S. combat soldiers among American forces because they were the only ones actively and routinely engaging the enemy. While three months was the standard TDY tour, at least one known instance exists where a "Shot Gun" platoon extended for an additional ninety days.[22] It is a tribute to the distinguished "Shot Gunners" community that throughout the total commitment of CH-37 *Mojave* helicopters in Vietnam, which they vigorously protected on numerous dangerous missions transporting their ARVN brethren, only one *Mojave* was lost to enemy action. This was in part attributed to the fact that they did not wait until they were fired upon because their job was to protect their aircraft and crew and ensure the safe delivery of the cargo, personnel, equipment, or supplies.[23]

The seeming ad hoc nature of the "Shot Gunner" assignment and rotation changed in March 1965, when the Aerial Door Gunner Detachments, as they were then formally called, were augmented by seven different Security Detachments, which started by performing the airfield security mission before rotating through door gunner duties.[24]

After 2,145 Operation SHOTGUN volunteers served through eleven in-country rotations over two-and-a-half years between 1963–1965, the program was ended in November 1965. As Shotgun 12 was preparing for their training, the 25th Infantry Division received word to discontinue the program. The concern in Washington and Saigon was that continued training would deprive the 25th Infantry Division of door gunners if it were ordered into combat.[25] In December 1965, the first combat elements of the division began arriving in Vietnam.

Army officials say that the honor roll of the Shot Gunners or "hired guns," as some of their supported units affectionately called them, may never be entirely known due to the classified nature of the entire effort. They amassed almost 2,300 individual awards with reasonable accuracy, including the Silver Star, Soldier's Medal, Bronze Star, Purple Heart, and the Army Commendation Medal. Of their number, 125 were wounded, and twenty-eight gave their last full measure of devotion.[26]

The CH-37 in Vietnam

In mid-1963, the Army began shipping nine CH-37B helicopters to Vietnam to recover downed American aircraft. The A Flight, 1st Platoon, 19th Transportation Company (CH-37) was transferred from its base in South Korea to Vietnam in May 1963.[27] The unit, including eight pilots and sixteen enlisted men, was accompanied by its four CH-37B helicopters. They flew to the port of Pusan Harbor, where the helicopters were loaded onto a railroad locomotive and railcar transport ship, the USNS *Private Leonard C. Bronstrom* (T-AK-255).[28] As additional helicopters arrived, they were further distributed to A Flight, 1st Platoon, 19th Transportation Company; 56th Transportation Company (ADS); 339th Transportation Company (ADS), and the 611th Transportation Company (ADS). The *Mojave* would continue combat service through April 1964.[29] In the summer and autumn of 1963, the Army *Mojave* employed in Vietnam were credited with recovering an estimated $7.5 million of aircraft and equipment, most of which were in inaccessible terrain controlled by NVA and VC forces.[30] Included in those recovery statistics were 139 downed aircraft, including 54 CH-21s and 43 UH-1s.[31]

The *Mojave* was a durable and survivable aircraft despite its continuous exposure to intense enemy ground fire as it performed its airlift and recovery missions. During the CH-37's combat tour of duty, only one aircraft was lost to enemy fire, and that incident was on its third encounter with the enemy. On December 12, 1963, a CH-37B ("Don Juan," tail number #55-0627) assigned to the 61st Transportation Company participated in a helicopter recovery mission in Tuong Dinh Province. While attempting to sling load the downed aircraft, it was hit by enemy ground fire. The *Mojave* was struck on the fuselage's port side, causing it to crash and subsequently burn. Four members of the five-man crew did not survive the crash, including one whose body was not recovered.[32] Three other CH-37s were lost during their three years of service in America's helicopter war for reasons other than enemy fire and with no additional loss of crew lives.

Twenty-seven months later, in September 1965, the Marine Corps deployed eight of their CH-37C helicopters for general support duties with Marine Air Group 16 based at Marble Mountain. With only ten pilots, the Group logged 5,400 accident-free hours and 1,500 missions during which they transported 12.5 million pounds of cargo and 31,000 passengers.[33] During its Vietnam War service, the *Mojave* and the H2RS were used by the Army to recover downed aircraft, including those of the Marine Corps, and by the Marines almost exclusively to haul heavy cargo.[34] But by that time, designers had stretched the radial engine envelope to as much capability as it could provide. In addition to suffering from high maintenance costs per flight hour, the CH-37 could not approach the efficiency of the newer turboshaft-powered helicopters of comparable size.

The *Mojave* and its crew members would participate in some of the armed forces' most covert operations during the war. Beginning in 1964, the Strategic Air Command's 4080th Strategic Reconnaissance Wing (SRW) was ordered to Southeast Asia to support the reconnaissance effort in the theater. On March 5, 1964, three of its U-2E aircraft from the 4028th Strategic Reconnaissance Squadron (SRS) were bedded down at Bien Hoa Air Base to supplement the tactical reconnaissance flights by the F-101s. This portion of the operation was code-named LUCKY DRAGON in deference to the U-2E's moniker, *Dragon Lady*. The second component of the 4080th SRW mission was code-named Operation BLUE SPRINGS.[35]

BLUE SPRINGS was a program to send unmanned reconnaissance drones over the Hanoi area of North Vietnam. The drones were various versions of the Ryan Corporation *Firebee*, *Firefly*, and *Lightning Bug*. The improved Model 147D version had a 1,200 nautical mile range (1,381 miles), a 60,00-foot ceiling, and a maximum Mach 0.74 (563.3 mph) speed.[36] With such performance capability, the remotely piloted drone could fly missions over North Vietnam and Southern China. During the BLUE SPRINGS missions of the Vietnam War, more than 3,000 unmanned aerial missions were flown.[37]

Each BLUE SPRINGS mission comprised four discrete elements: an Air Force DC-130A aircraft for launch and control, the drone and its onboard reconnaissance package, a ground control station for drone recovery, and a helicopter for drone retrieval.[38] The DC-130A "mother ship" carried up to four drones to an altitude from which it launched the drone that proceeded to the designated reconnaissance area on autopilot. The "mother ship" monitored the drone's track to ensure that each designated target was covered before the drone turned toward the recovery area.[39] The ground control station for the BLUE SPRING missions was located at Marble Mountain near Da Nang. Once over the recovery area, the engines shut down, and a parachute emerged from the top of the fuselage. After the drone settled in its jungle recovery site, it would be picked up by the crew of a CH-37s assigned to the 339th Transportation Company (ADS) tasked for the mission.[40] The 339th participated in Operation BLUE SPRINGS missions out of Da Nang Air Base from September through December 1964.[41] Later in the war, after the Air Force had their CH-3 helicopters in Vietnam, they used a modified CH-3 to capture the drone in mid-air using a trapeze-type apparatus to snag the inflated parachute as it floated earthward.[42]

As a unit priority, BLUE SPRINGS missions were frequently a case of watchful waiting for the designated crews. The crew would stand by their aircraft awaiting the recovery order or their release to carry out missions transporting ARVN troops, or resupplying remote special forces camps, some frequently along the Laotian frontier.[43]

The lore of aeromedical evacuation during the Vietnam War is that of legends and heroes, undaunted pilots, and crews willing to sacrifice all for their wounded and fallen comrades. *Mojave* crews had their own take on the medical missions of the war. The pilots of the 339th Transportation Company took medical personnel to remote villages to make house calls in February 1964. Called upon to aid a village experiencing a combined outbreak of malaria, tuberculosis, and rheumatic fever, the crew transported Special Forces medical personnel to help the uncooperative village witch doctor treat the 500 villagers.[44] After a week of treatment, the epidemic subsided.

The CH-37's first venture into a combat operation was on May 31, 1965. It participated in the largest air assault to that point in the war and, in doing so, demonstrated the flexibility in the aerial deployment of cannon artillery in support of ground forces. The 3rd Battalion, 319th Artillery, plus a cavalry troop, an engineer platoon, and a volunteer composite platoon of support troops (Task Force SURUT) secured a landing zone (LZ) into which CH-37s delivered the battalion's howitzers into the hasty position. From that position, the howitzers, within three hours of landing, provided preparatory fires on another LZ for Task Force DEXTER, which was an infantry force from the 173rd Airborne Brigade.[45] This was the first such operation ever conducted in actual combat by an American Army unit, and more specifically in Vietnam in less than thirty days.

With the advent of the CH-47 and the CH-54 in the Southeast Asian theater, the utility of the *Mojave* quickly diminished. The Army began the transition, and the old yet reliable CH-37s were shipped back to the United States, with some finding homes with units of the Army National Guard. The retrograde of the Army *Mojave* helicopters was completed in March 1966. While the CH-47 replaced the *Mojave,* it did not have the heavy-lift capability of the former helicopter. While the CH-54 weighed less than the CH-37, it could carry more than five times the cargo and, when outfitted with the pod, could carry nearly four times the number of combat soldiers.[46]

Numerous vignettes in the annals of Army Aviation history document and support the animate—inanimate relationship between crew and aircraft. One acclamation regarding the *Mojave* is that the aircraft had a "soul." Crewmembers believed the *Mojave* "had a life inside of them that they shared with those of us who worked on and flew them."[47] It was a hardy aircraft, and its crews were confident of one thing, the *Mojave* would always bring you back. During the war, the Army lost only one of its nine CH-37Bs. As Specialist Five Scott Drew would write years after the war, "… I feel blessed that I was able to serve on these aircraft during that war. She was truly the last of her breed."[48] Former crew members universally agree that the "Beast," as she was often referred to, was noisy. Countless email exchanges from these men read by the author all report applying for veterans' disability benefits for their hearing loss.

It took a lot of tender loving care to keep the *Mojave* in the air. Some maintainers report that the Army CH-37s in Vietnam required thirty hours of maintenance for each flight hour. The early days of the *Mojave* were particularly challenging because the density of aircraft in the theater was so small and would never be measured in significant numbers. There being so few supported aircraft, the inventory of authorized spare parts and their quantity made it exceptionally difficult to procure and stock them. Keeping the Equipment Deadlined for Parts (EDP) rate low was a never-ending test of resolve.[49] Considering that it had two eighteen-cylinder radial piston engines with two spark plugs per cylinder per engine, as well as auxiliary power units with four plugs, a change of the seventy-six spark plugs when required, was an all-day activity as the maintainers tried to ferret out each plug, often in some of the most inaccessible places. There were also well over one hundred grease fittings on the ship, and each required the regular application of grease.[50] The oil consumption of the *Mojave* was another matter; it was measured in gallons per flight hour per engine, so the crew had to replenish the thirty-gallon oil reservoir for each engine, of which almost two-thirds were consumed on each mission. The combination of AeroShell 50W oil and the 115/145 aviation fuel turned engine start-up into a nearly all-encompassing blue oil smoke cloud.[51] Indeed, the *Mojave* helicopter was a challenge to keep operationally ready, and its extreme maintenance-to-flight hour time ratio was a significant determinant for the Army as it developed mission requirements for the next generation of heavy-lift helicopters and transitioned to turbine-powered aircraft.

The first Sikorsky CH-53A *Sea Stallions* began arriving in Vietnam in 1966, and with their arrival, the Marine Corps started to ship the ten-year war veterans back to the United States to be placed in storage. The Marines completed the retrograde shipment of their H2RS helicopters in May 1967.

The operational life of every major piece of military equipment must eventually end. There is a point beyond which product improvements cannot be made, as technologies would have moved far beyond the useful life of the chassis or airframe. In 1971, the retirement of the *Mojave* was underway in earnest, with much being written about the process within the Army in Europe.

Within the VII Corps Support Command, the mission was given to the 48th Transportation Company (Aircraft Maintenance) of the 87th Maintenance Battalion in Goeppingen, Federal Republic of Germany. By performing the disassembly in Germany, the Army would save substantially on transportation costs, as most of the salvageable components would be directed to Army units in Europe. A portion of the helicopters assigned to the Seventh Army's 15th Aviation Group which had flown with the 4th Aviation Company in Schwaebisch Hall was consigned to the 48th for retirement. Those six helicopters represented the last *Mojave* in service with the active Army, although National Guard units were still flying others in the CONUS.[52] The last Army National Guard CH-37B was retired from service in November 1969.[53]

After service in the Army and National Guard, some *Mojave* helicopters performed similar roles in civilian commercial companies like Keystone Helicopters, with forty FAA-certified *Mojaves* on the payroll.[54] However, one of the most unusual post-retirement missions for a helicopter was the suspension of a CH-37 to seventy-five feet inside the 100-foot-deep Dutch Springs Quarry in Bethlehem, Pennsylvania. The *Mojave*, Keystone Helicopters' N14463, a World War II Curtiss SB2C dive bomber, an Army 2.5 ton, 4x4 truck, and thirteen other large objects populate the deep waters of the fifty acres of this freshwater scuba diving facility.[55]

The People of the River

The Mojave Indians are a semi-nomadic tribe of Native Americans from the Southwest region of the United States. Their homeland includes portions of today's states of Arizona, California, New Mexico, and Utah, with tribal life primarily centered along the Colorado River and the Mohave Valley. They were farming along the lower Colorado River since before recorded history, hence their native name, Pipa Aha Macay, "The People of the River."[56] The Mojave belonged to the River Yuman tribal community, and like the other tribes in the community, they were warlike and often hostile toward other tribes in the same area.

With the arrival of the Spanish in the sixteenth Century, the Mojave was the largest concentration of people in the Southwest territory. However, early Mojave history remains unknown or, at least, not reliably known due to the absence of any written precolonial Mojave language. Tribal members relied upon oral storytelling to communicate their history and culture to subsequent generations. The cultural and language upheavals that befell succeeding generations complicated the original meaning of their stories and songs, rendering contemporary translation for the following generations potentially impossible or at least imprecise.

Unlike many of their Indigenous neighbors, the Mojave traced their heritage and ancestry through the male members of the tribe. The tribe was highly hierarchical, and although scattered in settlements throughout their territory, it was efficiently organized to wage war. The tribes had designated war Chiefs determined by heredity and warriors with specific individual fighting skills; for example, some warriors specialized as archers while others wielded war clubs as hand-to-hand combatants.

The first known Spanish contact with the Mojave came in 1604 with the arrival of explorer Juan de Oñate.[57] Father Francisco Garces appeared in the valley more than a century-and-a-half later. The Spaniards made no effort to establish religious missions or settlements among the Mojave people allowing them to remain religiously independent.

During the nineteenth century, peace in the Colorado River Valley changed with the arrival of settlers and gold prospectors. The discovery of gold in California and the ensuing gold rush in 1849 brought thousands of prospectors and settlers through Mojave territory on their journey to the goldfields in the California territory. The influx of non-Indians into the Mojave homeland ultimately led to confrontations and misunderstandings that prompted the U.S. government to erect Fort Mojave on the Arizona side of the Colorado River, which served as a base for military operations against the belligerent Indians.

The arrival and transit of white men in the Colorado River Valley did not end the existing animosity among Native American tribes, One of these enmities was between the Quechan or Yuma and Maricopas. The Mojave, Yavapi, and Apache were allied with the former, while the Pima sided with Maricopa. The Quechan and their allies, attacked the Maricopa at Pima Butte on August 31 and September 1, 1857. The combined strength of the Maricopa and Pima was sufficient to administer a devasting loss to the aggressors.[58] The Battle of Pima Butte is significant not only for the Mojave participation and losses but also because it was the last major battle fought in North America solely between Native Americans. Despite their diminished warrior strength, the Mojave continued to remain hostile toward the Americans in their midst and the imposed changing lifestyle. In the late 1850s, the Army assembled the Mojave people and pronounced its peace terms, submission or extermination. The Mojave elected the former. As years passed, the BIA began an extensive assimilation program where Mohave and other reservation native children were forced into boarding schools in which they learned to speak, write, and read English. As at other Indian schools across the country, native students were taught American culture and customs. They were also required to adopt European-American hairstyles, habits of eating, sleeping, toiletry, and manners. Ultimately, assimilation helped to break up tribal culture and governments.

President James Buchanan commissioned the survey and construction of a 1,000-mile road from Fort Defiance in Northern New Mexico Territory to the Colorado River under the supervision of Edward Fitzgerald Beale in 1857. The road, known as the Beale's Wagon Road, traversed the 35th parallel route from Zuni Pueblo, New Mexico, to the Colorado River near present-day Needles, California. This migratory route, intended to facilitate the movement of non-Indians to California, crossed the Colorado River at a shallow ford, Beale's Crossing, located within the Mojave homelands.

The explosion of westward transiting of non-Native people through Mojave territory precipitated what became known as the Mohave War, a series of armed exchanges between the Mojave people, the emigrants, and the U.S. Army in 1858 and 1859.

The passage of the Rose–Baley Party, who were originally from Iowa, and were the first European American emigrant party to make the passage along Beale's Wagon Road, remained peaceable until they arrived at the river crossing. The party immediately established an encampment and created a dock to build large rafts to ferry their heavy wagons and equipment across the Colorado River. In a subsequent meeting among the party's leader, Leonard John Rose, and the Mojave chiefs, Irataba, Cairook, and Sickahot, the settlers reassured the tribal leaders that their stay on Mojave lands was temporary and that they would soon be on their way to California. Like other Native American tribes, the Mojave were concerned about the sanctity of their homelands and what was their own, and were anxious not to have any long-term or permanent non-Indian encroachment.

In short order, it became apparent that the trailing Baley Company, led by a forty-four-year-old veteran of the Black Hawk War, Gillum Baley, would soon be following the Rose Company through Mojave lands. With aroused tensions, the Mojave began stealing cattle from the Americans to feed their people. At the same time, the Americans began harvesting valuable Mojave cottonwood trees to use in building their rafts. The tribe and some of its Walapai allies responded by attacking the Rose Party, and the Battle of Beale's Crossing resulted in the loss of seventeen warriors and one American; however, the migrants lost most of their cattle and other livestock. Instead of continuing to California, they returned to Albuquerque, New Mexico.

When word of the Beale's Crossing engagement reached War Department officials in Los Angeles, General Newman S. Clarke ordered an expedition of the 6th Cavalry under Lieutenant Colonel William Hoffman to set out for Beale's Crossing, where they were to build a military post for the protection of migrants crossing the Colorado River. They departed on December 28, 1858, and while they were encamped near Beaver Lake, the fifty-man contingent was set upon by nearly 300 warriors led by Chief Cairook. The skirmish, known as the Battle of Beaver Lake, resulted in the loss of twelve warriors when the Native warriors could not contend with the volume and accuracy of the Army's musket fire. Colonel Hoffman and his expedition returned to their California base without establishing the Colorado River crossing outpost following the engagement.

In March 1859, the Army sent a resupply caravan of wagons and camels to northern Arizona to deliver provisions to Lieutenant Edward Beale and his road survey and building detachment. Upon reaching Cave Canyon in the Mohave Desert, the fifty-eight-man detachment was attacked by 1,500 Mojave warriors. The ensuing engagement again saw the effectiveness of Army musketry and left one warrior killed and another wounded with no reported losses among the soldiers. The caravan's wagons returned to California while the camels and troopers completed their journey to Beale's encampment.

Using the Battle of Beaver Lake as justification for more soldiers to launch a second expedition against the Mojave, Colonel Hoffman returned to Colorado with a force of about 600 infantry, cavalry, and artillery troopers in April 1859. Hoffman and his men reached Beale's Crossing and established Camp Gaston on April 19. On April 28, Captain Lewis Addison Armistead renamed the camp Fort Mohave. Lieutenant Colonel Hoffman traveled to the Mojave villages and offered a commitment to peace with the Mojave in exchange for their promise not to molest immigrants traveling through Mojave land and not to oppose the Army building of roads and forts in Mojave homelands. The Mojave agreed, though Chief Cairook surrendered to the Army with great reluctance. With fifty troopers from the 6th Cavalry and a few artillery pieces, Captain Armistead remained at Fort Yuma while Colonel Hoffman returned to California.

In the interim, Chief Cairook and eight Mojave warriors arrested with him were taken to and incarcerated at Fort Yuma, where they endured hellish conditions under the Arizona summer sun. In June 1859, the nine Mojave warriors attempted their escape, with Chief Cairook being bayoneted and shot and a second warrior killed. In time, three surviving Mojave escapees reached their villages and reported the circumstances and events ensuing at Fort Yuma to the tribal High Chief,

Espaniole. The Mojave breached the peace and attacked the mail station near Fort Mohave. In the only pitched battle of the Mohave War, Captain Armistead and his fifty–man force attacked over 200 Mojave warriors at a site on the Colorado River twelve miles south of the fort. The warriors were quickly routed, leaving twenty-three at the battle site.

Ultimately, American troops' advanced weapons and tactics forced the Mojave and other Native American allies to sue for peace. The treaty ending the Mojave War also drew to a close the long-running guerrilla war between the Mojave and their ancient enemies, the Maricopa Indians of south-central Arizona. The 1859 treaty also marked the last instance of armed conflict between the United States and the Mojave. Confronted with two unacceptable options—submit to the white man's authority or engage them in a war that the tribe had no possibility of winning—the Mojave resigned themselves to accepting the violation of their native lands and eventually relinquishing them to the white man.

The years of the American Civil War brought further change to the lives of the Mojave. The constraints of the war forced the Union to abandon Fort Mojave in 1861. By executive order signed by President Abraham Lincoln on March 3, 1865, the federal government created the Colorado River Indian Reservation and set it aside for the Mojave people and "all tribes of the Colorado River drainage"[59] which was conducive to agriculture. The tribe was split, with many wishing to remain at the ancestral homeland near Fort Mojave, and others willing to relocate to the designated reservation. Great Chief Irrateba (or Yara tav) led approximately 800 tribal members onto the poor farmland after the U.S. government agreed to make the irrigation changes necessary to improve the sandy, alkaline soil, which the Mojave believe made it unfit for cultivation. The government never dug the irrigation canal. In 1867 Chief Irrateba completed a canal almost nine miles in length, which brought water to a mere forty acres of the reservation. While Chief Irrateba led the Mojave who moved onto the Colorado River Indian Reservation, Chief Homoseh awahot ("orator of the stars") assumed the leadership of those tribe members who elected not to leave the fertile Mojave Valley. The Mojave people were now split into two tribes. Similar executive orders in 1872, 1873, and 1876 brought the Chemehuevi people onto the reservation.

In time the fort was completed and became a school for the children of the tribe. The federal government forced the Mojave to send their children to school with the strictly enforced admonishment that they were forbidden to use their native language or follow their tribal customs; harsh punishment would be imposed for disobedience. And to further strip them of their identity, English names were assigned to all the children. Further, all tribal children and non-reservation children between ages six and eighteen were compelled to live at the school. Such practices of the white man, as were imposed at other schools for Indian children, led to the gradual but inevitable extinction of the Mojave culture and the potential destruction of their tribe. Ultimately the boarding school was closed in 1931, and the Native Indian children began attending school in Needles.

Over time, additional land was added to the Colorado River Reservation so that it extended onto both sides of the Colorado River, in California and Nevada. However, during World War II, the federal government appropriated 25,000 acres of the Reservation for the internment of U.S. citizens of Japanese heritage. In 1945, the Mojave people invited former citizens of the Hopi Tribe and the Navajo Nation to join their community, resulting in what is now known as the Colorado River Tribes.

A pioneer in Army rotary-wing aviation, the *Mojave* made its mark in the early years of air mobility and the question of arming medium transport helicopters. It also proved the value and long-term efficacy of TATSA. The versatility of the helicopter and crew added to the growing portfolio of missions for vertical lift aircraft. Its capabilities were proven globally wherever the Army's footprint was found, extending the proud legacy of its namesake, the people of the river, the Mojave.

As this book was being prepared for typesetting, President Joseph Biden was hosting the White House Tribal Nations Summit, wherein he committed to setting aside and protecting 450,000 acres of land in southern Nevada, including Spirit Mountain, which is sacred to the Mojave and other tribes. Of this tract of land, he said, "I'm committed to protecting this sacred place that is central to the creation story of so many tribes that are here today."[60] The land is considered the source of life and place of origin for ten Yuman-speaking tribes, the Mojave, Hualapai, Yavapai, Havasupai, Quechan, Maricopa, Pai Pai, Halchidhoma, Cocopah, and Kumeyaay, as well as the Hopi and Chemehuevi Paiute. Included in the designated region to be protected is Spirit Mountain, which was enrolled in 1999 on the National Register of Historic Places as a Traditional Cultural Property in recognition of its religious and cultural importance. For the Yuma people, the area is tied to their creation, cosmology, and well-being. This announcement is not the final achievement for the ten tribes as they are continuing to press for either passage of legislation (H.R. 6751) to create the Avi Kwa Ame National Monument or the invocation by President Biden of the 1906 Antiquities Act to proclaim this protected area as the Avi Kwa Ame National Monument. With the approaching expiration of the term of the 117th Congress, the legislative tract will have to be renewed with the new Congress. However, either result will be a significant achievement toward the reclaiming of sacred Mojave tribal lands.

UH-1 IROQUOIS

Iroquois *Med Evac DUSTOFF mission. (Courtesy of the Army Aviation Museum.)*

Among the missions it performed during the Korean War, the H-13 *Sioux* is universally recognized for its role in the medical evacuation of United Nations forces, being credited with rescuing approximately 25,000 wounded troops and injured civilians, a role memorialized by the 1970s television comedy M*A*S*H. Despite the heroics of their crews, the H-13 began to manifest problems, and over time the operational demands of combat in Korea and the topographic and climatological extremes stressed the *Sioux* and its support infrastructure. The Franklin 200 hp engine was insufficient to carry the helicopter and its loads to the required altitude. Poorly located and capacity-limited fuel tanks presented center of gravity issues and operating range limitations. There were spark plug fouling problems and other maintenance issues exacerbated by the shortage of spare parts in the theater.

So strong was the legacy of the H-13 as an "Angel of Mercy" that shortly after the war's end, the Army began developing requirements for a purpose-built medical evacuation helicopter, one which a gas turbine engine would power. As the larger Army discussed its need for a new multi-purpose helicopter, the Army's Surgeon General recommended that "… all aircraft designed, developed, or accepted for the Army (regardless of its intended primary use) be chosen with a view toward potential use as air ambulances to accommodate a maximum number of standard litters."[1]

When specifically addressing a dedicated air ambulance, the Medical Department and the surgeon general specified that an air ambulance needed to be "... highly maneuverable, of low profile, and capable of landing in a small area. It was to carry a crew of four and at least four litters, yet easily loaded with litters by just two people. It had to be able to hover with a full patient load even in high altitude areas and cruise at least ninety knots per hour fully loaded."[2] Mobility and flexibility also became the touchstones for the Army's next helicopter. The ship would be destined to transport personnel, equipment, and supplies, perform utility and liaison missions and serve as an instrument trainer.

The Army also stipulated that the new aircraft would have to meet additional performance requirements that included:

- Being lightweight with a gross weight of 8,000 pounds,
- Able to lift an 800-pound payload and transport to a distance of 227 miles,
- An operational range of 100 nautical miles (115.1 miles),
- A cruising speed of 100 knots (115 mph),
- A climb rate of 1,500 feet per minute, and
- A service ceiling of 6,000 feet with the temperature at 95°F.[3]

The Army wanted a helicopter supportable by the crew and organic maintenance personnel with a minimum set of special tools in austere conditions. Aircraft maintainers envisioned unit-level replacement of major components in the field. It must also be strategically deployable by ship or aircraft, with minimal time required to prepare it for shipment and restore it to the flying configuration at the destination. Compared to today's rotary-wing aircraft, these requirements are modest; however, in 1955, they were on the cutting edge of technology and aircraft performance.

The competition for the Army's new helicopter evolved into a contest between the Kaman H-43 turbine-powered helicopter with inter-meshing twin rotors and without a counter-torque tail rotor and the Bell Helicopter Company HU-1 derivative of the company's XH-40 model. By the onset of the competition, Bell was already gaining experience flying the H-13D with a French-designed, American-made Continental XT-51 gas turbine engine. Based upon the success of the turbine-powered H-13, Bell partnered with the Lycoming Company to develop an engine specifically for the Bell ambulance helicopter specifications, the XT-53.[4] The air ambulance competitors were evaluated for the Army by the Air Force, which determined that both offerings could meet the service's requirements and were so close in evaluation scoring that differences were without distinction. The Air Force procurement community deferred to the Army for the ultimate decision because of the potential scale of the procurement and the decision's impact on future Army doctrine and force structure. In the end, then-Secretary of the Army William M. Brucher, satisfied that the testing validated the selection of either helicopter, pronounced, "Well then, I'm going with the company that did something for our boys in Korea."[5] His remarks acknowledged the role of the H-13 in Korea and the absence of any Kaman helicopter in use during that war. The selection of the Bell Helicopter Company for the aircraft was ratified in June 1955.

Using a new configuration powered by a turbine-powered engine in an aircraft "designed for the pilot,"[6] the Army received one of the earliest and premier examples of its design and procurement philosophy of "equipping the man; not manning the equipment."[7] The design team integrated human factors considerations from the very beginning of the design through demonstration, prototyping, testing, production, fielding, and support phases. The design was adjusted to accommodate the man instead of forcing the crew, maintainers, and combat cargoes to change to the design.

The industry testing regimen included operational, functional, static, and fatigue testing. The *Iroquois*, as the Army named it, would be one of the most exhaustively tested new aircraft in the Army's history to that time. The first XH-40 prototype was ready for its first flight a mere sixteen months after the commencement of the design effort, yet, as they were taking helicopters into a new realm, they were also challenging the testing communities to devise exhaustive and comprehensive tests that would assure the Army that the aircraft would perform as expected under all the conditions and environments that it envisioned the helicopter being used. The XH-40 would make its maiden flight on October 20, 1956, sadly the same day that Bell founder Lawrence Dale "Larry" Bell passed away.

Military historians have opined that distinct icons have emerged from America's twentieth centuries conflicts that evoke the sights, sounds, and memories of the war they appeared in. World War I witnessed the biplane as fixed-winged aviation came to the fore, while World War II and Korea embraced and claimed the jeep as their hallmark. Vietnam hosts the ubiquitous UH-1 *Iroquois*, more commonly called the Huey, for its image. It was the first, longest-serving, most recognized turbine-powered helicopter of the era and the one aircraft used in every major battle of "America's helicopter war."[8]

In 1956, the Army obtained the first Bell YH-40 pre-production aircraft for evaluation. Its extended cabin, greater ground clearance, and more powerful 770 hp Lycoming T53-L-1A engine over the XH-40 proved its versatility and operational utility. Six aircraft were ordered before it made its first flight during Bell's development program.[9] They were destined for service testing with Bell retaining one, and Eglin Air Force Base in Florida receiving one for climatic and cold-weather testing; the Air Force would conduct service testing with the single helicopter sent to Edwards Air Force Base in California, and three were delivered to Fort Rucker for Army trials.[10] The Army would begin its flight testing of the XH-40 in 1958, when Army aviator Frank Jones flew the aircraft, now upgraded to the YH-40 standards, to Fort Rucker. Designated the HU-1A *Iroquois* in 1958, the Army accepted the first nine pre-production aircraft on June 30, 1959. In March 1959, the Army placed an order for one hundred production aircraft. From this production lot, aircraft were delivered to the 57th Medical Detachment and the Army's two airborne divisions, the 82nd and the 101st[11], with deliveries completed in June 1961.[12] By August 16,

1961, Bell had already made the first flight of the next iteration of the helicopter, the HU-1D. By late 1961, the Army ordered 247 HU-1Bs. The initial military designation of the Bell helicopter, HU-1A (Helicopter, Utility, Model 1A), was retained until the advent of the tri-service aircraft designation system on September 18, 1962, which was the basis of the *Iroquois*' most common nickname, *Huey*.

One of the participants told the story of when the aviators in the UTTHCO were enjoying a beer or two or more, contemplating the proper pronunciation of the aircraft they had on the flight line, the HU-1A, and the HU-1B. As the evening and the beer consumption progressed, the pilots successively offered "ho-we-ah," "hu-we-ah," "h-unoe-aaa," "hu-wi-aah," "hu-ie-ah," "hu-ie-ah," "huey," "huey," "huey." From that night forward to the pilots and crews in the UTTHCO, their UH-1As were henceforward known as the *Huey*.[13] Ultimately, the name became so popular that Bell began casting *Huey* on the helicopter's anti-torque pedals.

The UH-1 *Iroquois* was a multi-purpose aircraft; it carried warriors to the battle, and once troops were engaged, it would repeatedly weather the storm of action to keep her comrades resupplied. When the designated LZ was contested, it was flown as a gunship to support troops in contact or suppress enemy fire. Numerous UH-1s were used at all levels as command and control aircraft offering the senior force commander a bird's eye view of the action on the ground. Similarly, a trained observer aboard the aircraft could direct artillery, naval gunfire, or close air strikes on the enemy from its overhead position. The *Iroquois* took several sundry missions, including defoliant spraying, VIP transport, aerial smoke generation, and psychological operations.

The *Huey*'s enduring place in the annals of America's helicopter war stems from another critical type of mission. The helicopter's uniquely recognizable shape and the distinctive sound of the main rotor blades slicing through the hot, humid air were the sights and sounds of deliverance to countless soldiers and marines on the worst day of their young lives. Yet, because of the *Iroquois* aeromedical ambulance, eventually known by the call sign "Dustoff," hope descended from the clouds on the rotary wings of those battlefield angels of mercy. True to the words of the father of Dustoff, Major Charles Kelly, medical evacuation pilots would remain on station, recovering the wounded, dying, and dead, ultimately leaving their station only "... when I have your wounded."[14]

Before discussing the use of the helicopter's role for medical evacuation during combat, stepping back into the aviation annals of World War II, one finds what is reported as the first use of a helicopter to perform a combat rescue behind enemy lines.

The situation involved a multi-purpose liaison aircraft, the Stinson L-1 Vigilant of the 1st Air Commando Group, which supported the British "Chindits" expeditions in the China-Burma-India theater of operations. Some Vigilants were converted into ambulance aircraft, as was the one forced down west of Mawlu, Burma, in April 1944. Technical Sergeant Ed "Murphy" Hladovcak, the pilot of a Stinson with three wounded British soldiers on board, went down over one hundred miles behind Japanese lines. The rugged terrain and dense jungle negated any prospect for the injured soldiers to attempt to evade and escape to friendly lines. The men were forced into hiding close to Japanese forces and spent days away from the nearest ground-rescue force.[15]

The 1st Air Commando Group had recently taken delivery of a Sikorsky YR-4B, a two-seat helicopter designed by Igor Sikorsky with a single, three-bladed main rotor and powered by a 185-hp radial engine. On April 21, 1944, Army Lieutenant Carter Harman flew from Lalaghat, India, with the YR-4B (tail number 43–28247) 600 miles, to Taro, Burma, in twenty-four hours.

After a brief rest, he continued 125 miles to a jungle airstrip called "Aberdeen," well behind Japanese lines. Guided by another liaison aircraft, Lieutenant Harmon located the downed plane and its survivors. By Harmon's first visual surveillance of the crash site, the Japanese had already discovered it and searched for survivors they did not find.

Harman planned to lift one survivor at a time out of the jungle clearing and fly him to a nearby sandbank where a liaison airplane would fly them back to "Aberdeen." This process would be repeated until all four men were rescued. It took the rest of the day to airlift the two most seriously wounded and sick soldiers. During the second flight, the helicopter's engine overheated and, upon landing, seized. Unable to restart the engine, Lieutenant Harman was stranded on the riverbank, and Sergeant Hladovcak and the remaining soldier were still in the jungle.

On the morning of April 25, Lieutenant Harman was again airborne and completed the rescue of the two remaining survivors. A liaison plane flew out the wounded soldier while Hladovcak rode with Harman back to "Aberdeen." Lieutenant Harman was awarded the Distinguished Flying Cross for his actions, and by year's end, the YH-4B had been condemned.

However, the first aeromedical evacuation of the size and scale that would become the norm during later conflicts, especially the Vietnam War, would occur in June of 1945 in the Pacific theater of operations. It involved the 112th Cavalry Regimental Combat Team (RCT) under the command of Lieutenant Colonel Clyde Grant while operating in the Philippine jungles.

At the time, Sikorsky R-4B and R-6A helicopters were conducting flight operations off the Operation IVORY SOAP fleet, which included six Liberty ships in Manilla Bay configured as Army Transportation Service aircraft repair ships complete with machine shops and an almost 3,000 square-foot landing pad, sufficient to accommodate two helicopters. Lieutenant Colonel Grant suspected these helicopters could recover and transport his wounded soldiers from the battlefield. Ultimately prevailing in his bid to gain their use, five Army pilots, First Lieutenants James H. Brown, Robert W. Cowgill, and John R. Noll, plus Second Lieutenants Louis A. Carle and Harold Green, would evacuate a total of seventy wounded from the battlefield to Manilla hospitals during the period June 16 through 29, 1945.[16] This evacuation of American and Philippine wounded marked the first concentrated aeromedical recovery operation on a large scale. The success of these rescue missions encouraged helicopter advocates and sufficiently proved the concept of MEDEVAC that it would be used in Korea and Vietnam.

An Illustrious History in War

During America's advisory period, the advent of aeromedical helicopter evacuation arrived in Vietnam. Along with the Army's two airborne divisions, the 57th Medical Detachment (HA) received some of the initial production UH-1 units, and, on April 26, 1962, the detachment would become the first *Iroquois* unit deployed to Vietnam, where it would remain until deactivated at Tan Son Nhut Air Base on March 14, 1973.[17]

The Detachment was part of the first Army medical unit to be shipped to Vietnam to support the American force buildup. The Army medical package deploying to Vietnam in April 1962, in addition to the 57th Medical Detachment, included the 8th Field Hospital and medical detachments for dental, thoracic, orthopedic, and neurological treatment.[18] Upon arrival, the detachment commander, Captain John Tempereilli, Jr., established the unit and its five UH-1 helicopters with the remainder of the medical package in Nha Trang, which was almost 200 miles from Saigon and the Mekong Delta region, where most of the American forces then in Vietnam were located and operating. For a unit dedicated to the rapid recovery and evacuation of American and ARVN wounded, the 57th Detachment was a long distance away from where it would be needed.

The 57th would conduct its first aeromedical evacuation on May 12, 1962, when an Army Captain advisor to ARVN forces in Tuy Hoa became seriously ill.[19] The detachment made the over eighty-mile round trip flight and delivered their patient to the 8th Field Hospital. By the end of the second month of their Vietnam tour, the 57th had only evacuated twenty-six patients: twelve Americans and fourteen ARVN. For a unit dedicated to evacuating wounded soldiers from the battlefield, this level of effort, to many of the ground commanders and staff in Saigon, did not support the dedication of the mission and the limited usage of valuable aviation assets. Many would covet the only five UH-1s in South Vietnam. As the inventory of armed UH-1s grew, aviation unit commanders would claim aircraft parts that kept the detachment's helicopters flyable, only to be cannibalized so non-operationally ready gunships could be restored.

It would take a regrettable and probably unnecessary loss of life to awaken Army commanders to the contribution potential of air ambulances if they were in locations where fighting was taking place. Tactical South Vietnamese intelligence alerted commanders to an enemy radio station operating from the village of Ap Bac in the Plain of Reeds in January 1963. The ARVN commander planned an assault into the delta with 400 men from the ARVN 7th Infantry Division and fifty American advisers. Ten CH-21 *Shawnee* helicopters escorted by five armed UH-1s were assigned to lift the force. The first three lifts were accomplished without incident. On the fourth wave, the Viet Cong attacked and shot down four CH-21s. One of the American UH-1B gunships assaulted the landing zone, attempting to rescue one of the *Shawnee* crews when it was shot down. With the fire support from the remaining gunships, the surviving CH-21s would leave without further loss of aircraft. The result was the escape of the Viet Cong under cover of darkness and the loss of three American advisers and 63 ARVN soldiers who were killed. The 57th Detachment, still stationed at Nha Trang and Qui Nhon, was too distant to the north and could not help evacuate the wounded.[20] The losses at Ap Bac were enough to convince ground commanders that air ambulances could best serve the foot soldier when they were close to the action. So, on January 16, the 57th Detachment was ordered to relocate to Saigon, where it closed station on January 30, 1963. There it awaited the arrival of five of the new UH-1B helicopters. The U.S. Army Support Group, Vietnam (USASGV) issued the new helicopters still aboard a ship in Saigon Harbor on March 11. The 57th Medical Detachment returned to full operational status in its new location and with its new aircraft on March 23.[21]

The 57th Medical Detachment's first medical evacuation marked the beginning of the long and proud legacy of the *Iroquois* as an air ambulance and angel of mercy for the military, civilian, allied, and enemy souls it safely recovered from the South Vietnam battlefields.

During the 57th Medical Detachment's service in Vietnam, the unit's dedicated, unhesitating service to the fighting forces, combined with an excellent medical support system, contributed to the lowest mortality rate for the United States armed forces of any conflict in military history to that point in time. When the 57th Medical Detachment (RA) was sent to Vietnam, it became the first unit to use the UH-1 helicopter for MEDEVAC in actual combat operations, evacuating more than 100,000 patients within the combat zone.

During the 57th Medical Detachment's first year in Vietnam, it operated without a tactical call sign. Instead, it used "Army" plus tail number digits less the two designating the aircraft's production year. On the tactical radio net, helicopter #62-6789 became "Army 6789." Furthermore, for internal communications the 57th operated on any radio frequency that was vacant at the time. The unit's second commander, Major Lloyd E. Spencer, did not find this a workable solution and was determined to change it. The Navy Support Activity in Saigon controlled all the radio call words used in South Vietnam, and Major Spencer found the call words not assigned to any user by reviewing the Activity's Signal Operating Instructions. Excluding those words that suggested assault units vice medical evacuation units, Spencer found the phrase "Dust Off." He quickly equated them to the reality of the detachment's operational environment wherein pick-up zones were dry and dusty, and the hovering air ambulance would "blow dust, dirt, blankets, and shelter halves all over the men on the ground."[22] The unit call sign would thus forever be equated to medical evacuation and recovery. While the call sign lived throughout the Vietnam War, its life continued in the military lexicon for future wars in which the United States would be involved. Whenever a wounded American soldier needs help, the singular expression "DUSTOFF" is instantaneously understood as the summoning of help.

Many successful evacuations were also conducted during the Korean Conflict; however, the term "DUSTOFF" became synonymous with Army aeromedical evacuation during the Vietnam conflict. While statistics cannot describe the contribution made by DUSTOFF crews, they put into perspective the enormity of their accomplishments. From 1962 to 1973, 496,573 missions were flown, with more than 900,000 patients from all sources airlifted to various medical facilities by air ambulances.[23] Vietnamese patients, military and civilian, and VC and NVA personnel represented approximately fifty percent of the total. Americans made up about forty-five percent (390,000), including approximately one-third (120,000) of combat casualties. The balance was non-Vietnamese allied military.[24] The average time between wounding to hospitalization was less than one hour.[25] This sense of urgency drove the DUSTOFF crews, and often they paid a high price for their dedication.

The Effect of Air Ambulances in American Wars

	Time to Treatment Facility after Wounding[26]	Percent of Wounded Who Later Died[27]	Medevac Wounded Who Died After Admission to Treatment Facility[28]
World War II	12–18 Hours	29.3%	4.5%
Korea	2–6 Hours	26.3%	2.5%
Vietnam	30–35 Minutes	19.0%	2.6%

The DUSTOFF success story is attributed to the ground combat medic or unit leader's evacuation prioritization of the wounded soldier. Typical priorities, such as those used by the 237th Medical Detachment, were urgent, intermediate, or routine.[29] An urgent case was to be evacuated within sixty minutes; intermediate case evacuations were within six hours, and routine would be sometime during the initial twenty-four hours.

The doctors and surgeons who staffed the in-country hospitals were most able to assess crucial nature of the evacuation helicopter during Vietnam. In 1968 surgeon Dr. Al Levin observed, "[T]he soldiers looked at me like I was God like I could put this mess back together. But a lot of times, there was nothing I could do. I remember the sense of timelessness. Except for the helicopters, I might as well have been in the mud in Gettysburg or Valley Forge—that's how much I could do for those guys."[30] Dr. Ben Eiseman, a World War II and Korean War veteran and consultant to Navy medicine in Vietnam put the aeromedical evacuation helicopter in perspective. He opined that speed set the pace, and speed saved lives: "The speed with which the injured are taken to a forward hospital is the unique feature of this war."[31] Based upon his wartime experiences and observations, Eiseman concluded: "Wounded in the remote jungle or rice paddy of Vietnam, an American citizen has a better chance for quick, definitive surgical care by board-certified specialists than were he hit on a highway near his hometown in the continental United States."[32]

The DUSTOFF community included approximately 1,400 commissioned and warrant officer pilots during the Vietnam War. The average pilot availability during the war was ninety percent, and the average patient load was two patients. Only about seventy-five percent of the air ambulance helicopters dedicated to the DUSTOFF mission were flyable at any given time. The universality of the *Iroquois'* capabilities and the ability of other aircraft to perform medical evacuations increased the availability of an aircraft to complete a patient pick-up when called.

During the eleven-year conflict, the UH-1, UH-1B, UH-1D, and UH-1H were used as aeromedical ambulances. There were 6,020 of those four aircraft flown in Vietnam, of which 2,691 were lost. Of those numbers, not all were medevac birds. At the peak of aeromedical evacuations, there were a total of 116 *Iroquois* helicopters dedicated to lifesaving missions.[33] Aeromedical evacuation would cost the loss of 199 aircraft.[34] The war would claim 211 DUSTOFF crewmen, including about forty pilot aviators who were killed, and many more were wounded.[35] Flying DUSTOFF was three times more dangerous than any other helicopter mission. For that reason, many of those who were beneficiaries of the courage of DUSTOFF crews would reverently refer to them as the "Lunatics of God."[36] The lack of regard for the red cross painted on the air ambulance fuselage was demonstrated by the statistic that an ambulance was hit by ground fire once in every 311 sorties. At the same time, that number rose to one in every forty-four sorties when the mission involved hoisting the patient into the aircraft.[37]

By early 1972, military officials in-country became increasingly concerned about the rising loss of air ambulances to enemy ground fire. Reasoning that the red crosses painted on each medevac ship were not conspicuous enough for enemy gunners to discern, the decision was made to paint the air ambulances in Vietnam in a design similar to those back at Fort Rucker and Fort Sam Houston that were participating in the Military Assistance to Safety and Traffic (MAST).[38] Painted white, the crews gave them the less than affectionate moniker, "White Elephants."[39] The logic for the decision was that the white painted helicopters would be readily visible and better identifiable as a non-combatant and demonstrate more clearly the U.S. commitment to the Geneva Conventions. The hope was that the enemy would thus not fire upon them.[40] The crosses were wryly visible, and, as some would say, they were "bullet magnets." When making their decision, Army authorities did not fully recognize that the Liberation Armed Forces (LAF) did not find itself particularly bound by the Geneva Conventions or any other international accord governing the laws of war.

The DUSTOFF experiences and traditions are carried on today by Army aeromedical evacuation pilots and crews as they perfect lifesaving techniques in support of civilian populations during disasters and accidents. To someone lying injured on the ground, the large red cross on the bottom of an Army helicopter is still one of the most beautiful sights in the world. The importance of and the impact on morale that the DUSTOFF had is best expressed in the words of one of its beneficiaries. Wounded when his APC struck a VC mine, Private Nathaniel Walker exclaimed, "When you heard the rotors of the *Huey* coming, you knew that you were alright. To see it was a sigh of relief. Hell was over; you were going home."[41]

It was not long after the arrival of the UH-1A and UH-1B *Iroquois* in Vietnam that their limitations became evident. The density altitude and temperature extremes of the two northern corps zones, I and II Corps Tactical Zones, where U.S. troops were most engaged, placed severe limitations on the lift capability of these utility, gunship, and air ambulance aircraft. Even with its longer body, larger capacity, and increased lift from its longer rotor blades, the UH-1D could not fully utilize its carrying capacity in the north. In July 1967, the UH-1H arrived in Long Binh, and with its more powerful Lycoming T53-L-13 engine, *Huey*'s propulsion and lift problems ended.[42] By late January 1968, the UH-1D helicopters were distributed to assault helicopter companies, and the UH-1H became the Army's standard air ambulance in Vietnam. With the success of the Lycoming T53-L-13 engine, some of the UH-1Ds were modified to H-models and received the newer engine.

As recorded earlier, the journey to the ultimate armed helicopter was long and sometimes tortuously punctuated by numerous false starts, and the *Iroquois* was not exempt from this journey. It should not have been unexpected that the aircraft in the vanguard of the Army's transition to turbine power and the great enabler of America's helicopter war should also play a pivotal role in searching for an armed helicopter.

Armed helicopters made their appearance in Vietnam by mid-1962, with H-21 *Shawnees* from the 8th and 57th Transportation companies outfitted with .30 caliber machine guns.[43] And while these ad hoc configurations were functional, they were not optimal. These Korean War vintage weapons were not optimized with aircraft-specific mounts nor did they use the standard infantry machine gun and ammunition, the 7.62mm M60. The Army's ability to provide armed helicopters was further thwarted by the Air Force's objections to the Army obtaining close air support capabilities, i.e., armed helicopters. In the Defense Department's division of labor, roles, and missions, close air support to the Army was an Air Force task. To circumvent this internecine opposition, the Army began experimenting with armed helicopters in the United States, Germany, and Okinawa, to assess the feasibility and create evidence to support its case. The Army would create and operate a tactical helicopter company, the Utility Tactical Transport Helicopter Company, that would eventually see combat in Vietnam.

The company was destined to become the first armed helicopter company in Army aviation history. It was activated as a Table of Distribution and Allowances (TDA) unit in Okinawa on July 25, 1961.[44] The Army formed TDA units to accomplish a specific purpose and have a temporary organizational life with the anticipation that they would either be deactivated upon completion of that purpose or reorganized as a TOE unit. This revolutionary organization, designated the Utility Tactical Transport Helicopter Company, was composed of fifteen UH-1A *Iroquois* helicopters armed with a weapons system consisting of two .30 caliber machine guns and sixteen 2.75 inch rockets mounted on the aircraft with locally fabricated mounting systems, and was created to test armed helicopter concepts and tactics. On October 7, 1962, a direct field maintenance unit, the 517th Transportation Detachment (Aircraft Maintenance), was attached to the company.[45] The detachment was also assigned maintenance responsibility for the 57th Medical Detachment (DUST OFF). From its inauspicious beginnings, the unit, its aircraft, and its crews were destined for greatness in their combat role in Vietnam.

When it came to committing an armed helicopter unit to combat in Vietnam, the UTTHCO arrived in Vietnam on October 9, 1962, from its home station on Okinawa by way of ninety days of combat training in Thailand.[46] The company and its aviators were engaged in their first in-country combat mission on October 16, 1962. Being the only gunship unit in-country, the entire country soon became their area of operations, flying combat missions from the DMZ near the 17th parallel to the region far south of Saigon.[47]

Its mission was to provide armed escort for troop-carrying aircraft with the company's UH-1A helicopters carrying the skid-mounted AN-M2 aerial machine gun system. Other weapon combinations would also soon become options for arming UTTHCO *Iroquois* helicopters following added in-country weapon system experimentation. By June 1963, four other helicopter companies in Vietnam were armed.

With duty in Vietnam, the UTTHCO was based at Tan Son Nhut, from where it provided close-in battlefield support to the dual-rotor H-21 *Shawnee* helicopters of the 33rd, 57th, and 93rd Helicopter Companies.[48] By November 1963, the company received the first eleven UH-1B helicopters. With its more powerful engine, it could carry more armament, and it had a factory-installed pack of four M-60 machine guns and a different set of mounts for the sixteen 2.75-inch rockets.

The UTTHCO helicopter's quad M-60C mounted machine guns remained the effectiveness standard until 1966 when they were replaced by the M-21 mini-gun system, which would become the most commonly mounted weapons system configuration on armed helicopters during the balance of the war.[49]

Legendary Army aviation units stood out for their courage and élan, the innovation of how they flew, and the selflessness with which they supported the soldiers on the ground without whom they had no purpose. The UTTHCO was such a unit. And as true leaders, they bequeathed a set of Twelve Cardinal Rules to their successor gunship aviators. Considering their groundbreaking role, a great benefit was gained from their hard-learned lessons. A thirteenth rule was later added; however, it goes without saying that it is equally a pillar of the warrior ethos.

1. Do not fly in the dead man zone without reason.
2. Always do a high reconnaissance first.
3. Never fly behind another aircraft.
4. Never fly parallel to any feature.
5. Never over-fly the target.
6. Always assume the area is hot.

7. Never fire until you have friendly force identified.
8. Avoid firing over the heads of friendly troops.
9. Fire only when you have a worthwhile target.
10. Always know the situation.
11. Brief your elements to a man.
12. Take your time.
13. Never leave anyone behind.[50]

With the growing number of *Iroquois* armed helicopters (UH-1B) in theater following their October 1962 introduction, five discrete and standardized missions were institutionalized. Those missions included:

1. "armed escort of other aircraft, surface vehicles and vessels, and personnel on the ground,
2. security for an observation helicopter performing low-level reconnaissance,
3. direct fire support against targets assigned by a commander of a ground maneuver element,
4. aerial rocket artillery functions against targets assigned by a fire support coordination center, forward observer, or airborne commander, and
5. hunter-killer tactics to provide security for an observation helicopter performing low-level reconnaissance."[51]

The *Iroquois* was also called upon to perform several specialized airborne missions, including signals intelligence, psychological warfare, aerial smoke generation, defoliant spraying, electronic warfare, an aerial sensor platform, and search and rescue.[52]

Early *Iroquois* armament experimentation saw the attachment of an Emerson Electric Company helicopter fire suppression kit, later designated XM-153, with four M-73 7.62-mm MG to the UH-1A in 1958.[53] By replacing the M-73 with the M-60C, the kit became the XM-6. In the late 1950s, the Aerial Combat Reconnaissance Company (ACRC) at Fort Rucker also experimented with mounting one to twelve 4.5-inch rocket tubes on the UH-1.[54]

The Army, the Army Aviation Center, and aviation unit experimentation began to bear fruit and the service started a formal development program for armament systems and kits for mounting on the various *Iroquois* models that found themselves in combat in Vietnam and forward-deployed units in the Federal Republic of Germany and South Korea and stateside units.

Besides looking for a helicopter fire support and defensive suppression capability from the outset of its efforts to arm helicopters, the Army also wanted a weapons system suitable to attack hard point targets like bunkers and armored vehicles. In turn, the Army Aviation Board experimented with the French SS-11 Manual Control to Line of Sight (MCLOS) wire-guided missile mounted on the *Iroquois*. A combination of three wing-mounted SS-11 missiles on each side of the *Iroquois* fuselage became the M-22 system.[55]

While the Army's original inclination was to procure the turbine helicopter as a dedicated aerial ambulance, the rapidly evolving air mobility concept expanded the mission envelope of the *Iroquois* to include encompassing combat assaulting troops into hostile territory. One of the most militarily significant and immortalized combat assaults in Vietnam occurred on November 14, 1965, when the UH-1D helicopters of the 1st Cavalry Division lifted the troops of the 1st Battalion, 7th Cavalry Regiment into Landing Zone X-Ray. Into the Ia Drang Valley, near the base of the Chu Pong Massif, the troop insertion began at 10:48 AM. It thus triggered an engagement against the PAVN's 33rd Regiment, the first significant battle between North Vietnamese soldiers and American troops in Vietnam.[56]

Standing up UH-1 units in Vietnam often meant standing down in-country aviation units already in Vietnam, deactivating them, and turning in their aircraft and associated unique equipment. The unit was then issued their new aircraft and equipment particular to the new aircraft and their new roles and missions and subsequently activated by a General Order (GO).

An illustrative example of this transition process occurred in June 1963 when the 33rd Transportation Company (Light Helicopter), in Vietnam since the fall of 1962, flew the CH-21C *Shawnee*.[57] It was deactivated and reconstituted as the 118th Aviation Company (Airmobile Light) (AML) on June 7, 1963.[58] The company was then activated on June 25 and declared operational the following month[59] with the *Iroquois* as the majority of their aircraft. Although operational as a UH-1 company, it was still flying some *Shawnee* helicopters and would continue to do so until the last UH-1Bs arrived and were issued to the company's gun platoon in September 1963.[60]

A challenge with the in-country transition from one aircraft to a successor aircraft generation—from the CH-21 to UH-1—was training all the unit's personnel: aviators, flight engineers, crew chiefs, maintainers, supply specialists, etc. It was neither practical nor operationally efficient to rotate everyone back to Bell's Fort Worth facility and the Army training base at Fort Rucker to complete the transition. Alternatively, a New Equipment Training Team (NETT) was formed, which involved taking the required training to the soldiers on the battlefield. The CH-21 to UH-1 transition was the first test proving that "… the combination of the training base in the United States, an aerial line of communications, superb logistics, and the know-how of American industry" made it possible.[61] The NETT personnel traveled from unit to unit, standardizing procedures, recording early problems, and immediately relaying them to CONUS. The conversion to a modern fleet of thousands of turbine-powered, technologically sophisticated aircraft was thus routinely accomplished after that throughout the war.

The 118th Aviation Company (AML) men were an operational mainstay known as the "First of the Assault Helicopter Companies" that participated in every major battle and operation in III CTZ.[62] The AHC unit concept model would be widespread in Vietnam by the end of 1965. On December 1, 1965, the company was redesignated as the 118th Assault Helicopter Company (AHC) and would join with the 117th AHC and 120th AHC as part of the 45th Combat Aviation Battalion (CAB).[63]

One of the genuinely intriguing capabilities of the companies within the battalion was the "Smoke Ship" which was spawned by the need to protect the "slicks" from enemy small arms fire. "Slick" refers to the fact that it lacked any fixed forward-firing external armament. The primary terrain features in the III CTZ were its network of canals and rice paddies, which in the otherwise flat landscape were outlined by man-made dikes and tree lines that afforded enemy combatants cover and concealment from visual detection, as well as an unobstructed line of fire to engage incoming helicopters with small arms fire.

Such a combination of tactical situation and terrain confronted the men of the 145th CAB. Necessity was the mother of invention in the 145th CAB, which employed its UH-1B "Smoke Ship" in 1966.[64] The "Smoke Ship" or ships would accompany any troop insertion of platoon, company, or larger unit size, and the 145th CAB was the first aviation unit in Vietnam to use airborne smoke generators in combat. The conversion to smoke generation capability entailed the addition of the XM-52 integral smoke generator to the *Iroquois*. It consisted of either a sixty-gallon storage tank or two fifty-five-gallon bladders placed in the aircraft's cargo area and pumps to transfer the stored "Fog Oil" (FO)[65] to a ring of nozzles encircling the turbine engine's exhaust.[66] The atomized oil was injected into the heated engine exhaust, which vaporized immediately, producing a billowing smoke trail to the rear along the helicopter's flight path. The configuration would generate about eight minutes of dense smoke that would last four to five minutes before dissipating.[67] Integral smoke generation was successfully used to screen landing zones for combat assaults or medical evacuations, screen helicopter movements by dispensing smoke along the flight path, or as a tactical deception by smoking an unintended landing zone.[68] The system's success led to the Army procuring 121 of the XM-52 systems.[69] Then in February 1968, the 118th AHC acquired an additional UH-1H to use as a company "Smoke Ship," which was named "Pollution IV."[70]

The typical "Smoke Ship" crew included the aircraft commander (AC), pilot, crew chief, and two gunners. One of the gunners was charged with controlling the oil tank, the dispersal of the cloud, and the post-mission cleaning of the aircraft's tail boom. The FO was quite corrosive and destroyed rivets and hard points of the tail boom, requiring its frequent replacement.[71] The employment technique for the "Smoke Ship" was to precede the "slick" formation by about a minute, then drop down onto the deck and fly at eighty knots parallel to the feature to be obscured, trailing a wall of dense smoke. The troop carriers would land in the LZ with a wall of smoke between them and the enemy force. Once the soldiers were disembarked, the helicopters left the LZ unseen by the enemy troops.

Information gathering was another area where aircraft proved their mettle in Vietnam. One of the key resources for information gathering and intelligence dissemination was the Army Security Agency (ASA). Its role in Vietnam was three-fold. The first was the introduction of fixed-wing aircraft like the U-6 *Beaver*, U-1 *Otter*, U-8 *Seminole*, CV-2B *Caribou*, and P-2E *Neptune* as airborne radio direction finding (ARDF) platforms. The ASA also modified aircraft for the airborne signals intelligence (SIGINT) collection mission—the interception and collection of enemy communications and non-communications (radar) signal emissions. The third was an aerial intelligence capability using an imagery platform, the OV-1 *Mohawk,* which supported combat operations with day and night visual and photographic surveillance and targeting, imagery intelligence (IMINT).[72]

In mid-1967, the ASA expanded its aircraft usage to include the abundant UH-1 *Iroquois* in Project LEFT BANK, a highly classified and unique airborne SIGINT role. The specially modified helicopters were assigned to the 1st Cavalry and 4th Infantry Divisions. ASA used two Radio Research (RR) Direct Support Units (DSU): the 371st RR Company, which supported the 1st Cavalry Division, and the 374th RR Company, which supported the 4th Infantry Division. Additionally, the 11th General Support Company supported the 1st Cavalry Division by providing the aircrews and maintaining the specially configured aircraft. The RR DSU in turn provided the radio operators. The *Iroquois* aircraft was also equipped with the AN/ARQ-27 Direction Finding (DF) system, which included two external systems: the DF array under the helicopter's nose and a black cable antenna that was run under the aircraft. The system operator's consoles were inside the aircraft for monitoring and recording NVA radio traffic. These DSUs were also tasked with locating the enemy's radio antennas. Once thus equipped, the aircraft was designated EH-1 LEFT BANK.[73]

LEFT BANK was successful because it combined the ASA direction-finding platform with the firepower and mobility of airborne and airmobile warfare. If the LEFT BANK team located a "fix" in the jungle, the pilot hovered over the area at canopy level, looking for evidence of troop movement or enemy installations. If enemy personnel were spotted, the pilot called in an ARCLIGHT mission (B-52s), gunships, or troops. During January 1969 alone, LEFT BANK was responsible for six B-52 strikes, multiple artillery rounds, and troop insertions that resulted in over 300 enemy soldiers KIA.[74]

In the fullness of time, the helicopter war in Vietnam would devolve into a late-twentieth-century war of attrition. The metric of merit for all engaged allied forces was the enemy body count. Such a standard necessitated every effort humanly and technologically possible to deny the enemy any tactical advantage he might garner. One such early advantage arose from his relative impunity when operating at night. Many war observers claim that the VC and PAVN forces initially "ruled the night."[75] Flares, mortar, and cannon artillery delivered illumination, plus early generation Night Observation Devices (NOD) would initially shift the tide and change the combat calculus. Yet, they were not without their disadvantages to the Army aviator. In the usual cycle of a problem–field expedient–solution, the Army and its aviators seized the night flight operations challenge and experimented with several heliborne lighting systems.

The Army's thrusts to gain the night followed two vectors, one through the aviation industry and a second in-house effort capitalizing on soldier-aviator ingenuity. The Army contracted the Hughes Aircraft Corporation to design a night-fighting kit for the UH-1 *Iroquois*. As conceived, the entire kit—helicopter, weapon system, and night vision subsystems—became the INFANT, *Iroquois* Night Fighter, and Night Tracker.[76]

The complex INFANT system was housed in a nose-mounted turret that included an image intensifier, an infrared video camera, and cockpit and cabin displays. The host aircraft also carried the M-21 armament subsystem in the twin miniguns and dual rocket pod configuration. Field testing of the INFANT revealed some shortcomings, including the muzzle flash of the miniguns, which overwhelmed the cameras and the electronics and permanently damaged the electronic and image processing subsystems.

In November 1969, three INFANT-equipped UH-1Ms arrived in Vietnam to solve the early problems and were ready for operational use. The UH-1M was an upgraded UH-1C with a Lycoming T53-L-13 engine. The UH-1M helicopters, with flash reducers mounted on the muzzles of each of the miniguns barrels, and a new formulation for the tracer bullets resolved these early issues. Although found to be operationally capable, problems nonetheless persisted, and their early combat experience with the 1st Cavalry and 25th Infantry Divisions would prove the system to be complicated to operate and maintain and hardly a cost-effective solution for nighttime operations.[77] The reliability and durability of the night vision equipment were less than desired, and the flight characteristics of the UH-1M with the system mounted caused the imposition of some flight restrictions.

To evaluate and mature helicopter systems of all types emerging in response to urgent aviation requirements in-country, the Army maintained a flight detachment of the Army Concept Team in Vietnam (ACTIV) at Tan Son Nhut Army Heliport.[78] One of their earliest efforts was helicopter night-vision systems known as the Helicopter Illumination System (HIS). The Lightning Bug and Firefly were characterized by a "fixed bank of C-123 landing lights mounted in a gunship."[79] Using the same seven bulb configuration, landing lights from the C-130 *Hercules* and the Lockheed C-121 *Constellation* were also used for the HIS. There and elsewhere, combat aviators were developing and testing rudimentary and bargain-basement intense spotlight systems, which consisted of a frame-mounted cluster arrangement of seven aircraft landing lights[80] called "Firefly."[81] When configured with the seven C-130 *Hercules* lights, the Firefly aircraft provide the equivalent of 1.2 million candle power of light.[82] The original light array was retrograded to Fort Rucker to be modified by the team at Page Aviation Maintenance, who fixed the center light to the frame and hinged the perimeter lights to the same structure so that the beam width could be adjusted.[83] At sixty-six pounds and a power requirement of 150 amperes, this HIS version was well within the capabilities and capacity of the *Iroquois*. The illumination system, part of the HIS initiative, was strapped into UH-1 transports or gunships, connected to the host aircraft's power supply system, and manually operated by a crew member in the cabin. Married to the HIS was an M-2 .50 caliber MG mounted on the XM-23 or mounted on the floor inside the cabin. ACTIV evaluated the system in September 1965.

The penultimate of the HIS was the "Night Hawk," another field-expedient created and used while the aviation community awaited INFANT's arrival. Innovators from the 25th Infantry Division working on the "Nighthawk" system installed an AN/VSS-3 xenon searchlight developed for the M551 Sheridan Armored Reconnaissance/Airborne Assault Vehicle (AR/AAV) in the cabin of a specialized *Iroquois* "H" model, which in this configuration would conduct "FireFly" and "Lightning Bug" missions. The VSS-3 offered both infra-red and visible light options plus the AN/TVS-4 Night Observation Device (NOD), frequently referred to as the "Starlight scope," which added ambient light intensification capabilities to those provided by the VSS-3. The aircraft included a six-man crew (two pilots and four gunners). It had an illumination package, an M134 7.62-mm minigun armament, or other armaments option like the twin M60D 7.62-mm machine guns or an M2HB .50 caliber heavy machine gun. In the "Nighthawk" configuration, an M-134 7.62-mm minigun was installed on a floor-mounted pintle. The UH-1H troop transport, thus configured, became a devastating weapon system. Compared to the expensive and problem-plagued Hughes rig, this option led Army leaders to prefer the "Night Hawk" and invest in the maturation of some of the Hughes' components for future use on the *Iroquois* or other aircraft. It should be recognized that the Firefly and Nighthawk aircraft were pretty much ad hoc and unique to each unit that flew them, so experienced *Iroquois* pilots will report that they have never seen two aircraft of the species laid out the same.

The operational employment of assets during a Nighthawk mission, as exemplified by the techniques employed by the men of the 191st Assault Helicopter Company (AHC), consisted of a three-aircraft team led by a UH-1H Command and Control (C&C) aircraft equipped with two flare pods.[84] The second aircraft of the group was a well-equipped *Iroquois* H-model that carried a .50-caliber machine gun on the starboard side, and a xenon searchlight mounted on a handheld minigun on the port side. A gunner armed with a pintle-mounted 40-mm grenade launcher was in the back on the helicopter's right side. Armed with an M60 machine gun, the fourth crewman would freely shift from side to side in response to the tactical situation. The final helicopter of the team was a UH-1C gunship with the usual package of rocket pods and miniguns. This ship was the heavy reinforcing fire support to reply to enemy ground fire.

Time and experience, reinforced by survival, taught "Nighthawk" and "Firefly" aviators the optimal technique for engaging the enemy with their aircraft. They learned that combat effectiveness increased when the illuminating ship preceded the accompanying gunships. This allowed target engagement without the gunship crew losing its night vision. However, it greatly endangered the illuminating crew, whose lights created bright spot targets for enemy ground fire. Soon followed the arrival of the AH-1G *Cobra*, which often flew on "Firefly" missions using the

UH-1H "Nighthawk" to locate and illuminate targets. This combination provided maximum capability and flexibility in advancing allied force mastery of the night. After the experience with these missions, senior aviation leaders would pronounce, "The Nighthawk mission substantially slowed night movement by the NVA and VC because the enemy was afraid of the threat it posed."[85]

The utility of Army helicopters was as varied as the human mind could conjure, and science could create. In particular, the "Snoopy" and "Red Haze" missions illustrated unique capabilities. These were flights flown in significant numbers by OH-6 *Cayuse*, OH-58 *Kiowa*, and UH-I *Iroquois* helicopters whose purpose was to detect enemy soldiers under the dense, triple canopy jungle by sensing the effluents, ammonia particles, unique to humans, such as those found in sweat and urine, as well the condensation nuclei from campfires.[86] The airborne version of this personnel detector was the XM-3 Olfactronic Personnel Detector (OPD).[87] The U.S. Army Vietnam (USARV) standard employment approach for XM-3 missions was a three-ship flight. The sniffer aircraft and the protector gunship flew at fifty feet above the treetops, with the latter aircraft trailing no more than fifty feet behind. A second gunship flew 500 feet above the jungle and ahead of the formation for navigation and protection.[88]

Several divisions employing the XM-3 and the XM-2 backpack-mounted senor were positive in assessing the sniffer capability. While commanding the 9th Infantry Division, Major General Ewell claimed that "over thirty-three percent of all readings [from the XM-3 OPD] were confirmed by operational contacts."[89] A 1967 report of the 101st Airborne Division's experience with the detectors reported they "effectively produced intelligence in areas of heavy vegetation where visual reconnaissance was ineffective."[90]

As a utility and transport aircraft, the *Iroquois* supplanted the World War II C-47 *Skytrain* and the Korean War-era C-119 *Flying Boxcar*, and surpassed airborne operations such as NEPTUNE, MARKET, and VARSITY in the Second World War,[91] and SUNCHON and MUNSON[92] during the Korean War. The 173rd Airborne Brigade conducted the Vietnam War's only airborne operation, Operation JUNCTION CITY, on February 11, 1967. During the war, large and small troop movements were frequently carried out as airmobile assaults using the CH-47 *Chinook* and the "slick" version of the UH-1 *Iroquois.* The UH-1 enjoyed an unprecedented speed, flexibility, capacity, and responsiveness compared to its Word War II and Korean War predecessors.

The lift ships or slicks carried infantry soldiers and other combatants and, on numerous occasions, brought along combat photographers (CP). "Shooters," as combat photographers were referred to, belonged to the Department of the Army Special Photographic Office (DASPO). Authorized in 1962 by President Kennedy, DASPO cameramen were charged with documenting the war, capturing images for the historical record, and recording their fellow soldiers' lives in a sort of self-initiated public relations effort.[93] Combat photographers would "see the elephant"[94] through their viewfinder and capture on film—both still, and motion—"everyday activities in and out of combat, the struggles to cope with conditions in the field, the battles with a mostly unseen enemy, booby traps, helicopter evacuations of the wounded and dead, anything and everything that went on in the war"[95] Collectively the government and the military wanted to document the war, bolster home support, and propagandize the noble effort being made in an effort to halt the spread of communism in Southeast Asia.[96]

CP accompanied air assault and infantry missions of American, Australian, New Zealander, and South Korean forces. Unit commanders were directed "to extend all necessary cooperation to the CP to enable him to carry out his duties as an official Army Photographer."[97] With the latitude afforded them by these instructions, CPs were at liberty to travel throughout South Vietnam, accompany any unit on a combat operation, and take pictures of anything consistent with the DASPO mission.

While most CP actively sought opportunities to observe, record, and, frequently, due to exigencies, participate in combat operations, eventually assault troops lost their enthusiasm for having CP among their number. Soldiers began to realize that CP were harbingers of intense fights. "Shooters" frequently received operational briefings from major commands before selecting the assaults they would record. By personal choice or encouragement from commanders who wanted to see media coverage of their unit's operations, the accompanied units were slated for significant enemy contact—not the most sought-after prospect for 11B soldiers.

Combat assaults in Vietnam were flown without pathfinders or sophisticated navigational aids. Flying at comparatively high altitudes between the pickup zone and the vicinity of the landing zone, aircrews navigated their route using roads, trails, or natural terrain features until reaching their intended hole in the jungle, when they rapidly and directly spiraled into the designated landing zone. Disembarking their assault troops in seconds, the aircraft speedily departed the area to make room for slicks following in subsequent waves and to escape any ground fire intended to destroy their ship. If the landing zone was hot, that is, contested by enemy troops in the vicinity, lift helicopters could anticipate receiving fire once their descent cleared 1,000 feet in altitude. The standard assault lift was accompanied by armed gunships flying on the flanks in their trail formation to protect the slicks en route and in their descent into and ascending exit from the landing zone. Once the troopships began their flare close to the ground, the gunship ceased firing or shifted their fire to avoid the slicks being hit by ricocheting bullets.

During the air mobility concept testing with the 11th Air Assault Division at Fort Benning, the Army concluded that a substitute was needed to offset the lack of helicopter mobile medium indirect fire support in the division. The alternative was a concept of aerial rocket artillery (ARA), which consisted of two XM-3 armament subsystems externally mounted on each side of the "B" and "C" models of the UH-1 *Iroquois*. Each subsystem carried twenty-four of the 2.75-inch FFARs. For self-defense, each aircraft was armed with two M60 machine guns mounted in the aircraft's cargo doors, operated by the crew chief and a door gunner.

ARA organizations were employed in Vietnam in much the same way as conventional cannon artillery units were, except with the advantage of achieving greater ranges. Their reach was limited only by the operational radius of the aircraft. The ARA units were called upon to support ground forces, landing zone preparation and security, route interdiction, and counter-battery fires. They could also provide escort support for medical evacuation and re-supply helicopters. When teamed up with an observation helicopter, the OH-6A or OH-58A, they performed tactical reconnaissance.

On July 1, 1965, the 11th Air Assault Division was re-designated as the 1st Cavalry Division; its medium support artillery battalion was designated as the 2nd Battalion Aerial Artillery, 20th Artillery. The 20th Artillery became the first unit organized as an ARA battalion with a headquarters and three firing batteries of twelve *Iroquois* gunships each. In 1969, the Army fielded a second ARA battalion, the 4th Battalion Aerial Rocket, 77th Field Artillery, assigned to the 101st Airmobile Division. Following the Stand Down Ceremony for the 1st Cavalry Division at Bien Hoa on March 26, 1971, and the assumption of the Division's remaining mission by the 3rd Brigade, 1st Cavalry Division (Separate) on April 30, 1971, Battery F, 79th Artillery was formed to provide aerial rocket artillery support for the brigade.[98] As the unit name suggests, the division artillery commander controlled these specialized aviation units and was charged with integrating the fires of the indirect fire battalions and the aerial rocket battalions. While attack helicopters were in the division artillery, they were also assigned to the airmobile division cavalry squadrons and the lift helicopter battalions. The ARA concept and organizations remained in the Army until the mid-1970s when general attack helicopter aviation units replaced it.

Notwithstanding the success of the armed *Iroquois,* the Army continued its search for a true, single-purpose rotary-winged gunship. On August 29, 1967, the first helicopter gunships, the Bell AH-1G *Cobra*, although still experimental, arrived in Vietnam.[99] Outfitted with 7.62-mm miniguns and rocket pods, able to fly at speeds almost twice as fast as the UH-1s, they would ultimately supplant, and expand the envelope of potential missions. They also played an anti-armor role when on April 13, 1972, a *Cobra* from Battery F, 79th Artillery, engaged and destroyed an enemy tank during the battle of An Loc.[100]

Unlike other helicopters, this aircraft was not named after an Indian chief or tribe. The *Cobra* was initially and informally named by its manufacturer, Bell Helicopter. As a division of Bell Aircraft Corporation, Bell Helicopter shared the lineage of the parent company, which had a distinguished reputation for the fighter aircraft they made during World War II, including the P-39 *Aircobra* and the P-63 *Kingcobra*. The AH-1 *Cobra* thus enjoys part of its *nom de plume* from Bell Aircraft's World War II history. The story continues, and in April 1963, the 114th Airmobile Company deployed to Vietnam directly from its home station at Fort Knox, Kentucky. The gun platoon of the company was known as the Vinh Long Cobras. Thus when Bell Helicopter officials briefed Army officials about their scout helicopter design program, they referred to it as the UH-1 *Cobra*, based upon the Cobra platoon of the 114th Airmobile Company.[101] As the story continues, General Hamilton Howze, who worked for Bell Helicopter after retirement, suggested to a colleague, Cliff Kalista, that the helicopter not be called the AH-1 *Cobra* but instead be given an official company name *HueyCobra*.[102] The Huey portion of the name, of course, coming from the field vernacular for the original *Iroquois*; the Huey. However, due to the already wide acceptance of *Cobra*, the Army decided not to replace *Cobra* with a Native American name. Despite its singularly distinguished war record, for that reason, it is not included among the Vietnam War helicopters chronicled in this volume.

The Army began its initial interest in the *Iroquois* as an air-to-ground missile firing platform in 1963. The Army bailed two NUH-1Bs (tail numbers 62-12553 and 62-12554) directly from the Bell production line to Hughes for development work on the XM-26 armament system. The XM-26 was being designed for the American-made Tube-launched, Optically tracked, Wire-guided (TOW) missile. The 155th Aviation Company undertook preparations to conduct experiments to assess the efficacy of helicopter-mounted, anti-tank missiles.

On March 30, 1972, the People's Army of Vietnam (PAVN) swept across the DMZ in a massive offensive against the armed forces, people, and infrastructure of South Vietnam in what became known as the Easter Offensive of 1972.[103] The offensive was not limited to targets in Military Region I, south of the DMZ, but elsewhere in the country with a combined strength of twenty-four NVA Divisions. The North Vietnamese force was supported by Soviet-provided armored vehicles and several U.S. M-41 *Walker Bulldog* light tanks which they had recovered after being abandoned on the battlefield by ARVN troops.

While the ground combat situation in Vietnam, being conducted almost totally by ARVN forces, deteriorated, a group of Army aviators was participating in experiments sponsored by the Army Combat Developments Experimentation Command (CDEC) in order to evaluate the effectiveness of an AH team operating as part of a combined arms organization engaged against an attacking armor-heavy force. These flight crews were flying overaged NUH-1B *Iroquois* helicopters armed with the XM-26 TOW subsystem as part of CDEC Experiment 43.6 (Attack Helicopter, Daylight Defense) at Fort Lewis, Washington. On April 14, the experimental unit received a Warning Order from the Joint Chiefs of Staff (JCS) to prepare for a sixty-day TDY assignment in Vietnam,[104] while at the same time, the Army alerted the Missile Command (MICOM) at Redstone Arsenal, Alabama, to rush XM-26 subsystems and a load of 144 BGM-71A TOW missiles to Southeast Asia.[105] TOW missiles were also taken from production lots held at the Hughes Aircraft Company manufacturing facility in Tucson, Arizona. An Air Force C-141 *Starlifter* was dispatched to Davis Monthan Air Force Base to pick up the missiles and continue to McChord Air Force Base in Washington.[106] There the inter-theater transport aircraft rendezvoused with two other C-141s carrying the personnel and equipment of the 1st Combat Aerial TOW Team from Fort Lewis.

The 1st Combat Aerial TOW Team (known as Hawk's Claw) deployed to Vietnam on April 22, 1972.[107] The team's core consisted of six highly experienced Vietnam aviator veterans, nine support personnel, two TOW-equipped NUH-1B aircraft (SN 62-12552 and 62-12554)[108], a single UH-1H command and control (C&C) helicopter, and two AH-1G helicopter gunships.[109] Upon arrival in-country, the aircraft and weapons systems were reassembled at an initial base at Ton Son Nhut. After moving to Sanford Army Airfield, Long Binh, and assignment to the 1st Aviation Brigade, the flight crews underwent additional TOW gunner tracker training. They gained proficiency in handling the heavily weighted UH-1B in the RVN high-density altitude environment. Completing system checkout and installation of armored seat modifications at their new home at Camp Holloway near Pleiku in the Central Highlands, the entire TOW Team was considered operationally ready.[110]

By May 1, the 1st Combat Aerial TOW Team, OPCON to the 17th Aviation Group, had already completed its first missile firings.[111] On May 2, and for the next forty days, the team was engaged in combat in the Kontum area contributing to the fight against the two NVA divisions attacking the central highlands targeting Kontum as part of the 1972 "Easter" or "Spring Offensive." The evolved operational tactics for the team saw mission initiation by the 17th Group Operations Center, followed by an in-flight operational briefing from the C&C UH-1H while the team was on the way to the target area. The target engagement was designed to take place at a standoff range of three kilometers, the TOW's maximum range, and an altitude sufficient to preclude hazarding the aircraft to small arms fire, usually 3,000 feet, and at an airspeed of fifty to eighty knots (fifty-eight to ninety-two mph).[112]

On May 2, the Combat Aerial TOW Team engaged and destroyed their first enemy armored vehicles: three Soviet-built PT-76 amphibious light (17.7 tons) tanks near Ben Het Ranger Camp.[113] The team followed that success by destroying two 39.7-ton Soviet T-54 main battle tanks (MBT) on May 14.[114] Ten more T-54 MBTs were destroyed during the 2.5 hours of the Battle of Kontum on May 26.[115] On the following day, the last two MBTs of the twenty-four tanks destroyed by the 1st Combat Aerial TOW Team were claimed. Two team aviators, CW2 Danny G. Rowe and CW2 Douglas Hixon were credited with twenty-one of the twenty-four tanks destroyed: Rowe with twelve and Hixon with nine.[116] With the absence of suitable TOW targets and the onset of the monsoon season's adverse flying weather, the TOW team thoroughly trained the in-country replacement crews who would fly the team's aircraft after it returned to the United States on June 22, 1972.[117]

The following observations emerged from the after-action reports: the PAVN did not aggressively respond to or engage the Hawk's Claw aircraft with their AA systems; they did not recognize or appreciate the threat posed by the older model *Iroquois*. The reports show that even tanks did not return fire or attempt to evade the helicopter; most of the twenty-four tanks destroyed by the Hawk's Claw aviators were stationary when decisively engaged.[118]

Helicopters, including the Iroquois, *Chickasaw*, *Choctaw*, and *Cayuse*, found themselves engaged in unique missions capitalizing on their low and slow capabilities, missions that did not envision the lethal engagement of enemy combatants. Regardless of the air vehicle used, the outcome of the aircraft flights was equally effective. They reduced the number of enemy combatants and junior leaders confronting the U.S. and their allies, the support provided by peasant villagers to opposition forces, and accurate awareness of the ebb and flow of the war. Helicopters became dispensers of targeted audio messages and paper leaflet drops for those opposed to the South Vietnamese government and American and allied forces. Expectations were that enemy combatants would remove themselves from the battlefield by voluntarily abandoning their weapons and returning to their villages or electing to fight for the ARVN.

Throughout the war, the United States engaged in an extensive psychological operations program targeting combatants and civilians. The program was carried out under the aegis of the almost 1,100-person 4th Psychological Operations (PSYOP) Group from their Cruz Compound headquarters in central Saigon and its four geographically dispersed battalions - the 7th at Da Nang supporting I Corps, the 8th at Pleiku and Nha Trang supporting II Corps, the 6th at Bien Hoa supporting III Corps, and the 10th at Can Tho supporting IV Corps.[119] The group's direction for white activities came from MACV and the Joint U.S. Public Affairs Office (JUSPAO), also located in Saigon. The PSYOP and Civil Affairs (CA) campaign of MACV and the JUSPAO was aimed at the enemies' psychological, emotional, and religious vulnerabilities. The campaign included researching, producing, and distributing PSYOP and CA products, including newspapers, magazines, pamphlets, flyers, posters, placards, and audiotapes. The PSYOP battalions could produce and drop one billion paper products per month.

One audio operation of the campaign was Operation WANDERING SOUL, which targeted the enemy's mind, fears, and religious beliefs. In the Buddhist tradition, an individual is destined for a bad or good death. The former occurs when the remains of a believer are not recovered, returned to his home, and interred in an ancestral burial ground. Such a soul is fated to wander aimlessly through eternity. Most PAVN and VC combatants understood that their remains were likely never to be found, recovered, and properly buried. They would be numbered among approximately 300,000 North Vietnamese and Viet Cong soldiers missing at the war's end.[120] To reinforce this emotional vulnerability, the 4th PSYOP Group delivered aerial broadcasts of "eerie sounds intended to represent the souls of enemy dead who have not found peace,"[121] admonishing the listener to avoid the same fate by ceasing fighting or defecting. The last remaining known tape of the Operation WANDERING SOUL[122] effort is "Ghost Tape Number 10."[123]

For these tasks, the PSYOP unit's personnel would report to the supported maneuver unit, which provided the aircraft from its available assets. Single or multiple high-powered loudspeakers like the 1000-watt Westerner Electric Beachmaster loudspeaker, also known as the Navy Public Address Set (PAB-1) or the

AN/AIQ-2 900-watt airborne speaker were mounted to the aircraft structure with the audio system including controls and cassette or reel-to-reel tape deck and microphone set-up in the cabin.

For broadcast flights, the transmission of scripted messages is broadcast from a pre-recorded tape or, in some cases, by an onboard interpreter. The flights were flown at fifteen hundred feet and almost always drew hostile fire, exposing the enemy position for the benefit of accompanying gunships. MACV was zealous for conducting loudspeaker missions. In 1969 alone, the 4th Psychological Operations Group pre-recorded 13,146 messages,[124] typically in three dialects of Vietnamese and thirty to forty seconds in length.

A helicopter broadcast mission was usually six hours with two hours of broadcasting. Aerial PSYOP missions included planned flights with a known target and tailored message. Quick reaction missions were flown to support ongoing combat operations that a pre-recorded or live broadcast could further exploit.

Another aspect of the PSYOP offensive was preparing and distributing paper products for such efforts as the *Chieu Hoi* (open arms) Amnesty Program, a combination of leaflet and audio message deliveries. For paper product delivery, helicopters were equipped with interior or exterior chutes from which stacks of *Chieu Hoi* flyers were dropped onto areas with a known enemy presence. In other cases, a crewmember merely threw the leaflets overboard and into the slipstream. Although the number of defectors stemming from the *Chieu Hoi* effort is disputed in various publications, it is estimated that the amnesty program resulted in "the pacification and neutralization of over 193,000 enemy adherents and personnel."[125]

There were many other helicopter-delivered leaflet programs. One was the *Dai Doan Ket* program, specifically targeted to middle and higher-level VC cadre members, individuals with more significant influence over individual VC members, and potentially greater awareness of enemy plans within South Vietnam. There were also the post-strike follow-up programs like that following a B-52 Arc Light, when in the words of an American infantry officer who found himself perilously close to the strike, "the effect was absolutely terrifying. I thought the world was going to end."[126] Such leaflets were dropped within four hours of the bombardment, informing the surviving combatants that B-52s had just bombed them and they would not be able to hide from them in the future. Helicopters delivered similar leaflets with the same cautionary note following a shore bombardment by the sixteen-inch guns of the U.S.S. *New Jersey*.

With the arrival of advanced utility helicopters in the Army inventory, including the UH-60 *Black Hawk*, the days of the venerable UH-1 *Iroquois* were numbered. Following transfer to the National Guard and years of service there, the *Huey* would soon be set for retirement. As the Army divested them, some were transferred to the Air Force, where they were modified as primary helicopter trainers. The Army's last UH-1 *Iroquois*, tail number 74-22478, stationed at the Army's White Sands Missile Range, made its final flight as a U.S. Army-operated aircraft on December 15, 2016. Following the last flight on the missile range, it was transferred through the Army's Law Enforcement Support Office to the Louisiana State Police, where it was placed into service.[127]

During America's helicopter war, the UH-1 was the most prolific helicopter and found itself in the inventory of the Army, Marine Corps, Air Force, and Navy. Bell Helicopter built 10,005 *Hueys* between 1957 and 1975, and of that number, 7,013 would ultimately be shipped to and serve in Vietnam. Of the *Iroquois* flown in Vietnam, 3,042 were lost. The final *Huey* version to be deployed in Vietnam was the twin-engine UH-1N that saw service with the USAF 20th Special Operations Squadron (SOS). During their time in Vietnam, from October 1966 through December 1975, the Army *Iroquois* fleet accumulated a remarkable 10,693,902 flight hours.

The graphic below illustrates the family tree of the UH-1 family of helicopters used during America's helicopter war in combat in Vietnam, Cambodia, and Laos by all services that flew them during the conflict.

UH-1 "Huey" in Vietnam Family Tree
(Courtesy of Ray Wilhite. Helicopter silhouettes used with permission from Textron Innovations Inc.)

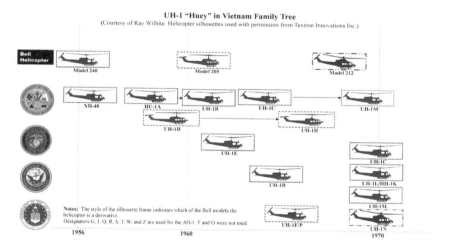

People of the Longhouse

As prolific as the *Iroquois* was during America's helicopter war, as much can be said regarding the deeds and dedication of the tribes of the Iroquois Confederacy throughout the history of America's white-man wars, beginning with the tribes of the Six Nations who allied with the colonists and the Americans. In particular, the Oneida, a member tribe, can be acknowledged as our Nation's first ally. As the exploits of the *Iroquois* in Vietnam abound, so too do the numerous deeds of the Iroquois during battle, aiding America since the War for Independence.

The Iroquoian tribes, the second largest of the three mother groups of the Northeast, maintained a sophisticated matrilineal clan system, where the women of the clan had a high degree of political empowerment, and even had "veto power over war decisions, appointed male chiefs, and maintained separate councils."[128]

The Iroquois Confederacy, also known as the Iroquois League, or the Six Nations, was a powerful Native American community in the eastern regions of the Ohio Valley. Some historians believe that among the Native American tribes and communities north of Mexico, they were unequaled in military might, statecraft, and political organization. According to historical tradition, the Confederacy was founded in 1390.[129] The Confederacy was initially made up of five east coast tribes that included the Seneca ("people of the big hill"), Cayuga ("where they land the big boats"), Onondaga ("people of the hills"), Oneida ("people of the standing stone"), and Mohawk ("people of the flint country"). They collectively referred to themselves as "Haudenosaunee" ("people of the Longhouse").[130] Of the tribes, the Seneca were the Western Doorkeepers, controlling trade and traffic of the Iroquois territory, while the Mohawk, residing near the Hudson River, were the Eastern Doorkeepers. The Onondaga were the keepers of the central fire.[131]

Around 1540, the Iroquois organized a sophisticated cultural and ceremonial institution, the Iroquois League, with fifty chiefs from among the original five-member tribes, meeting in a joint council. The political and military body of the Haudenosaunee was the Iroquois Confederacy, through which they dominated an extensive territory. By 1600, the Confederacy reached the apex of its military and political power.[132]

After the British began trading for cultivated crops and game with the Tuscarora ("people of the shirt") in North Carolina in the late 1600s, they began kidnapping Native men, women, and children and selling them into slavery; the British also started seizing Native lands without payment. Over time the Northern Tuscarora would attain greater benefits from the trade than their Southern Tuscarora counterparts, who were forced further south by a greater influx of settlers. Additionally, conflict arose over shared hunting grounds, cultural differences, and the attractiveness of the more fertile land to the west that the Native Americans held. A tenuous peace existed between the North Carolina colonists and the Tuscarora until 1711 when the former "drove the [Native Americans] off a tract of land without payment."[133] The Tuscarora responded by raiding settlements during three days of carnage. As the colonists sought revenge, war ensued. It would rage from September 10, 1711, until February 11, 1715, between the Tuscarora and their allies against the European settlers or the Yamassee and their allies. It ended in defeat for the Native Americans as they did not possess an arsenal of artillery and explosives as the colonists did. In addition to the casualties they suffered, approximately 400 Tuscarora were sold into slavery in the New England colonies and the Caribbean.

By 1710, the Tuscarora appealed to the commissioners of the governor of Pennsylvania for a new home, freedom from slavery, serenity and sanctuary from violence, and lasting peace. The Pennsylvania Quakers, who controlled the Pennsylvania government, were not welcoming. They had gone so far as to encourage frontier Native Americans to wage war on other tribes and provided them with money to do so. The Seneca, who were present at the appeal of the Tuscarora to the Pennsylvania Council, took up the tribe's cause before the Iroquois Confederacy, which decided to accept them for membership.

On September 25, 1714, the Confederacy chiefs notified the governor of New York of their decision, "They were of us and went from us long ago, and now are returned and promise to live peaceably among us."[134] The English colonists officially recognized the Tuscarora membership by treaty in 1722.[135]

The Iroquois "balanced their warrior tradition with an equally stout tradition of peacemaking and diplomacy."[136] At the core of the Iroquois Confederacy was a "social, political, and spiritual structure" that was the message of peace brought to them by Denanawida, the Great Peacemaker.[137] The Peacemaker, a Huron, lived during the dark period of the Confederacy when the five initial Nations were at war with each other. When he arrived in the lands of the Confederacy with his message of peace and unity, the first to greet him and accept his message was a Seneca woman, Jigonsaseh. According to tradition, since she was the first "to accept his message of peace," she became known as "The Mother of Nations," and "women were given an important role in the new Confederacy."[138]

Over the years, the Five Nations tribes came to accept the Peacemaker's message of harmony and united to become a peaceful league. He instituted for the Iroquois Confederation a constitution known as The Great Law, which combined the Iroquois into a union protective of the cultural differences of the individual member tribes but joined them in common political purpose and, ultimately, military action. During the formative years of the American republic, it was reported that Benjamin Franklin met "on many occasions with the Haudenosaunee,"[139] and as a result portions of the The Great Law found their way into the U.S. Constitution. In 1754, as a Pennsylvania delegate to the Albany Congress, Franklin first proposed a unified government for the thirteen colonies. The plan submitted to Congress by Franklin was based upon his observations of the governance of the Iroquois Nation and its constitution. While not enacted by the Albany Congress, his Albany Plan of Union of 1754 became the "blueprint for the Articles of Confederation and later the federalism embodied in the American Constitution."[140]

Democratic governance, following The Great Law of Peace, should not be misconstrued as a weakness within the tribes of the Confederacy. The Iroquois, of necessity, were intimidating warriors who, before the Confederacy, fought amongst themselves and, after its formation, fought against neighboring tribes. Canassatego, the leader of the Onondaga in 1744, also encouraged the colonists to unite, for it would make them stronger. The tribal leaders' union and amity between the Six Nations made them formidable and gave them great weight and authority with their neighboring Indian Nations. Canassatego, encouraging the thirteen colonies, stated that "… observing the same [M]ethods our wise forefathers have taken, you will acquire fresh Strength and Power; therefore, whatever befalls you, never fall out one with another."[141]

As in many locales in the coastal United States and later into the continent's interior, the arrival of European settlers soon upset the equilibrium within the Indigenous populations. Such was the case for the Iroquois when the Europeans arrived and began trading firearms with the neighboring Mohican and Huron tribes which they, in turn, began using in their skirmishes with Confederacy tribes.

The strength of the Confederacy and the war-making skills of the individual and collective membership of the Iroquois League were sufficient to overcome any perceived advantage of other tribes; their warfighting skills dominated enemy Indians throughout their history. They scattered the Huron in 1649, the Tobacco and the Neutral Nation in 1650, the Erie in 1656, the Conestoga in 1675, and the Illinois by the turn of the century. By then, the Confederacy numbered approximately 16,000 members and dominated the region bounded by the Kennebec, Ottawa, Illinois, and Tennessee Rivers.

Throughout the history of the League, there is evidence of intermittent conflict between the Iroquois, its tribal neighbors, and the Europeans. The earliest evidence of the warrior prowess of the Iroquois and their dominance in the northeastern woodland region was the conflicts that took place in the latter half of the seventeenth century. Collectively known as the Beaver Wars, they saw the Iroquois engaged against other tribes and the French. The Beaver Wars began in the 1640s with the Confederacy campaigning against the Huron people along the Saint Lawrence River. These were large-scale affairs that ultimately drove other tribes onto the Great Plains or north into Canada, with other tribes being eliminated or absorbed by the Iroquois.

These wars, precipitated by the expanding French interest in the fur trade, especially beaver pelts, increased pressure on the Iroquois, who wanted to command the fur trade and were dubious about their Native adversaries' growing power. The rival tribes were also obtaining firearms by trading with the French. The armed tribes and the Frenchmen rapidly depleted the beaver population, causing the Iroquois to make war against the neighboring Huron to gain access to their hunting grounds and improve their control of the fur trade with the Europeans. The Iroquois raids drove the Huron northward, so in turn, the French began trading with the Ottawa. These factors led to the expansion and escalation of the fur trading wars. Concurrently, the Iroquois moved westward into the Great Lakes region and toward the Mississippi, which displaced the regional tribes there.

The French responded by launching punitive campaigns against the Iroquois, who avoided major defeats but could not prevent the destruction of their homes and crops. With their homes and crops gone, many Iroquois died of exposure and starvation with the onset of winter. The Iroquois sued for peace which only lasted for a generation. Once again, a dispute over the control of the fur trade arose, ending the peace in 1683. This time things were different with the French petitioning for terms. They were willing to use the Iroquois land as a buffer between themselves and their English neighbors. The Grande Paix, or Great Peace treaty was signed in Montreal in 1701, with English and French representatives and thirty-nine Indian chiefs as signatories. As part of the treaty, the Iroquois allowed Great Lakes refugees to go back to the East. However, the English now took up the musket against the Iroquois, quickly reducing the strength of the tribe. After the treaty of 1701, the English allowed some of the tribes they had displaced to return to their homelands.

During the French and Indian War of 1754–63, tribes on both sides of the Appalachian Mountains and southern Canada became involved in the conflict. This

North American war preceded the European global conflict known as the Seven Years' War of 1756–63 by two years. The British and the French, each with strong Native American allies, became embroiled in a conflagration that crossed the Atlantic Ocean and engulfed two continents. Although there were Indigenous participants, the conflict was essentially a war between the two nations. The war ended with the Treaty of Paris, which in North America saw the British gain control of Canada and the lower continent east of the Mississippi. Spain acquired the former French territory west of the Mississippi, and the French were relegated to a few islands in the Caribbean. Although Indian tribes participated in the war, they neither participated in the negotiations nor were consulted before it was finalized, with much of their land being parceled out by the peace treaty. To the Native Americans, the Treaty of Paris merely substituted one oppressor nation and their settlers for another equally despotic one.

The treaty ending the French and Indian War was short-lived as the British colonists migrated further and further into Indian territory. To staunch the flow of colonial and Indian blood, the English colonies and the Six Nations leaders met at Fort Stanwix, New York, in 1768 to negotiate a treaty that would establish firm boundary lines. The Boundary Line Treaty set a clear demarcation between Indian and colonial lands. Despite its good intentions, the treaty did little to stem the colonial settlement on Indian land.

In 1775, the Continental Congress sent a message to the Iroquois Nation informing them of the colonial war against the British, which said in part, "This is a family quarrel between us and old England […] we desire you to remain at home, and not join on either side, but keep the hatchet buried deep."[142] The Oneida and Tuscarora tribes attempted to remain neutral while the other four member tribes took up arms alongside the British. Eventually, the Oneida and Tuscarora succumbed to the pressure and supported the colonial cause.

The American Revolution spelled the end of the Iroquois Confederacy. The Revolution would set tribe against tribe, differing coalitions of Confederation tribes against each other, and even warriors within one tribe taking opposing sides. The most prominent warrior chief among the Six Nations was the Mohawk Chief Thayendanegea or Joseph Brant, as he was known among the colonists and the British. Using his influence and the Native American hope that a British victory would end colonial expansion into Indian homelands, Brant persuaded Red Jacket, Chief of the Seneca, the Cayuga, and the Onondaga to join the Mohawks as allies of the British. The Oneida and Tuscarora tribes took up arms alongside the

THAYENDANEGEA, The Great Captain of the Six Nations (Captain Joseph Brant). (Courtesy of the Smithsonian American Art Museum.)

colonists in opposition to the British and the Tory loyalists. The American War for Independence, as a consequence, became a civil war that broke the peace among the Confederacy Nations that had existed for hundreds of years. In contrast, they provided valuable service to the Americans as scouts and guides, and some tribal members even joined the Continental Army for a while.

At General Washington's direction, the Continental Army and the militia, and Native American allies waged a devastating campaign into the heart of the Confederacy homeland against the tribes allied with the British. As Washington instructed Major General John Sullivan by letter on May 31, 1779, the objectives of the campaign were "… the destruction and devastation of their settlement and the capture of as many prisoners of every age and sex as possible. It will be essential to ruin their crops now in the ground and prevent their planting more."[143] The resulting "Sullivan Expedition" laid waste to forty towns along with 160,000 bushels of corn and vegetables.

During the early years of the war, the American colonists and their militia found themselves ill-prepared for a conflict against the British. They lacked almost every necessity of war and the essentials for sustaining the Continental Army and militia. Every American was aware of the shortages of gun powder, cannons, lead, uniforms, blankets, etc., that General Washington's army endured. An extremely close second to the lack of gun powder was the *unum necessarium,* salt. Besides being a preservative for meats, salt was also used to "tan leather, fix the dyes in military uniforms, churn butter, and supplement livestock feed."[144] In response to the crucial need, the colonies made an all-out effort to produce salt or seek it from the Iroquois tribes, who possessed impressive salt works. The colony of New York paid four dollars for each fifty-pound bushel they produced.[145]

As was the case in the Treaty of Paris, which ended the French and Indian Wars, the contribution of the Native Americans to both sides during the American Revolution counted for little when the conclusion of the war was negotiated, principally among the European warring parties. The British ceded the land between the Appalachian Mountains and the Mississippi River, unsettled by Europeans in North America and inhabited mainly by Native Americans, to the new American republic. On October 22, 1784, the Confederacy was forced to sign a treaty with the United States that resulted in the Confederacy tribes allying with the English and forfeiting significant portions of their tribal lands. Even the colonist-friendly tribes, like the Oneida and Tuscarora, were forced to surrender their tribal homelands.

On December 2, 1794, Congress enacted the Treaty of Canandaigua, which was signed by President George Washington, officially recognizing the wartime service of the Oneida. It also affirmed the tribe's authority to "oversee their affairs and lands without interference from other governments."[146]

After the war, the new republic felt no need to treat the Native Americans fairly. By virtue of their victory and the terms of the peace treaty, the Americans claimed ownership of Indigenous land. The cohesion of the Confederation was shattered, and the tribes themselves suffered egregiously during the immediate post-war period and ultimately never recovered their pre-revolution strength and status. Many

Iroquois, especially those allied with the British, resettled in Canada. Those who remained in New York soon lost most of their land to colonists who resented that certain members of the Iroquois Nation fought for the British.

Following the peace, Native Americans realized they could no longer depend upon trade with the Europeans. Their destiny was now dependent upon their relationship with the new government, terms of treaties in exchange for Native land, and the marauding of encroaching settlers. In an effort to thwart the influx of Europeans into their territories, the unification of North American tribes began in 1786 with an alliance called the Western Confederacy, which included the Iroquois and the Seven Nations of Canada, the Illinois Confederacy of the Mississippi Valley, and the Wabash Confederacy.[147] The Western Confederacy engaged in sporadic raids against the settlements of land-encroaching Americans who retaliated with assaults against Native American villages, especially the Shawnee. The cycle of strike, counterstrike, and retaliation escalated the violence and became known as the Northwest Indian War or Little Turtle's War. In late 1790, large-scale American expeditions under General Josiah Harmar were assembled and dispatched with cavalry and infantry regulars supported by artillery.[148] Engagements were fought on Indian Territory, which gave the advantage to the Indigenous warriors whose ambush and hit-and-run tactics overwhelmed the overly-cautious American regulars. The superior mobility of the Native warriors permitted their massing at critical points and times of their choosing. General Harmar and his expedition were soundly defeated at the Battle of Pumpkin Fields, which emboldened the tribes of the Western Confederacy to undertake a broader scope and more intense attacks on settlements throughout the Northwest Territory.[149]

The American campaign resumed the following year under the leadership of General Arthur St Clair with similar weaknesses in senior leadership and raw troops plus untrained militia on battlefields that were home to the Western Confederacy's warriors. The result was the same, but this time called St Clair's Defeat.[150] Divergent opinions among the chiefs of the Western Confederacy failed to produce a unified set of peace demands to be imposed upon the United States, so the conflict continued into 1793. The circumstances were, however, different for the Americans.

The American army would form the Legion of the United States, organized into fighting units, each consisting of a combination of infantry, cavalry, and artillery, and trained to fight as a combined arms team.[151] The Legion built fortified positions as it advanced against Western Confederacy attacks. In 1794, two of the Confederation's greatest war chiefs, Sagamore Chief Little Turtle of the Miami people and War Chief Blue Jacket of the Shawnee, with their 1,500 to 2,000 warriors, confronted approximately 2,000 troops at the Battle of Fallen Timbers on the Maumee River in present-day northwest Ohio.[152] The unexpectedly more capable American fighting force surpassed the effort shown by the ill-trained, poorly motivated, and nervous soldiers of the St Clair expedition. The Confederacy force was driven from the battlefield and compelled to sue for peace. The resulting 1795 Treaty of Greenville exacted more land from the Confederacy, including much of Ohio today and some in surrounding states. Many of the warrior chiefs now discouraged further conflict by their warriors.

The federal government held that the future prosperity of the United States was, in considerable measure, linked ultimately to the possession of the Northwest Territory. It provided land for expansion, access to trade routes, and gateways to the west. Now land, where white man's settlements were previously prohibited, was opened up for settlement. So while the Northwest Indian War swirled around them, the Iroquois people, under the leadership of Seneca Chief Cornplanter, worked to maintain neutrality during the years of fighting; however, the consequences of the peace did not escape them. Tribes, under Huron leadership, joined in declaring lands north and west of the Ohio River as Indian territory, united in resistance to encroachment by the white man. The Northwest Indian War would prove that the government was stronger by calling for a centralized consolidation of Indian Affairs and a federal Army for the national defense. This combination facilitated America's ultimate victory during that war, a success that convinced citizens, Indigenous, and European nations that the fledging republic indeed merited "the respect of the World."[153]

As the War of 1812 opened, the Iroquois Nation adopted an initial neutral position concerning the combatants. However, the Nation's leaders allowed tribal warriors to choose with whom to ally if they were disposed to enter the war. Viewing it as another white man's war, the six tribal chiefs confirmed internal neutrality and a most potent provision which declared that no Iroquois warrior would meet his brothers in battle. Nevertheless, just as the U.S.-Canadian border divided the warring parties, American versus British, it also divided the Iroquois Nation.

Those warriors wanting to fight alongside the British followed the Mohawks under Chief John Norton as they were free to do. Their opposite number, American allied warriors, followed Seneca Chiefs Red Jacket (Sagoyewatha) and Farmers Brother (Ho-na-ye-was). By 1813, the former was in his sixties, and the latter in his eighties, yet both willingly led their Iroquois warriors with a youthful warrior spirit and concomitant vitality. With the Iroquois tribal alignment in place, British allied Canadian Iroquois supported the victory at the Battle of Detroit on August 16, 1812. The response of the defeated Americans and their American Iroquois allies was to reengage the British to the east along the Niagara Frontier.

Setting their military objective as the Canadian Queenston Heights and a nearby village, the Americans under Major General Stephen Van Rensselear intended to establish a beachhead in Canada on the north side of the Niagara River. With his force of approximately 3,000, the river was rapidly crossed, and the Heights and village were captured with equal celerity in October 1812. British Major General Sir Isaac Brock, charged with the defense of Upper Canada and the civil administration of Ontario, marshaled forces to thwart the Americans using in addition to the militia and Canadian Iroquois warriors led by their chief, John Norton and John Brant, son of war Chief Joseph Brant. Those 150 warriors included eighty Cayuga braves, who attacked the rear guard of American Lieutenant Colonel Winfield Scott using traditional ambush, cover, and maneuver tactics. Once engaged, the British regulars, militia, formerly enslaved people, plus Iroquois and Chippewa warriors regained the Heights and the village in less than an hour, inflicting nearly 500 casualties and more than 900 captured. Among the Canadian losses was the death of General Brock on October 13.

With further military setbacks in Canada in mid-1813, the U.S. Army approached the American Iroquois tribes to help secure the Americans ensconced at Fort George, which was used as a base for the further invasion of Upper Canada. Oneida, Seneca, and other Iroquois warriors responded and assembled along the Niagara River over the next two months. After seven months of occupation of the fort, the Americans were forced from the fort and Canada during the Battles of Stoney Creek and Beaver Dams, with the latter engagement forcing the capitulation of 484 American troops. Once retaken by the British in December, Fort George remained in British hands until the war's end. Having time to rebuild their forces for further battle, the British and their allies crossed into the United States in July 1813 to assault Black Rock, the headquarters of the U.S. Navy force charged with defending Lake Erie and the Buffalo region. The British quickly overwhelmed Black Rock while the American ground force partially withdrew from Buffalo. The American reaction included Chief Farmers Brother and thirty-seven Seneca warriors, joined by regulars, militia, and Plains and Cold Springs volunteers. They forced a British withdrawal after a fifteen-minute engagement. The violence and desecration visited upon the Americans, especially the American Iroquois, was sufficient to cause the latter to abandon their Six Nation Neutrality Agreement and declare war on the British, including their Iroquois brethren allied with the British.

Major General Jacob Brown commanded America's foremost Army on the Niagara Frontier in strength and preparedness. It included 500 Seneca, Onondaga, Tuscarora, and Oneida warriors, led by Seneca Chief Red Jacket. They crossed into Canada and quickly seized Fort Erie on July 3, 1814. On July 5, the bloodiest battle on the Niagara Frontier commenced with Iroquois brothers facing each other at the Battle of Chippewa. The ensuing struggle inflicted the heaviest native casualties of the entire war. Chief Norton's Grand River Iroquois left eighty-seven dead on the field. Red Jacket's American Iroquois lost twenty-five and many more wounded. Many Iroquois casualties were inflicted by their relatives. A battlefield strewn with the pain-stricken and lifeless remains of Iroquois warriors was beyond the ability of Chief Red Jacket to behold, so he proposed that the Iroquois Nation withdraw from the war, which they did, along with stating their decision to remain neutral henceforth.

For many Native American tribes, the American Civil War was the last hope. It drew close to 25,000 Native Americans into the services of the warring parties of the Union and Confederate armies. A majority took up arms with the Confederacy, in part because many of their tribal homelands were in regions of the Confederacy. For some the bitter and painful memories still lingered from the Indian removals presided over by the government in Washington during the 1830s, others could not forget or forgive the federal government for the violations of treaties the tribes negotiated in good faith. So as participants alongside the white man, the Indigenous people hoped that their service would be reciprocated with favor from the prevailing government and end discrimination and relocation from ancestral lands to the western territories. Native warriors saw action in such engagements as Pea Ridge, Second Manassas, Antietam, Spotsylvania, Cold Harbor, and federal assaults on Petersburg. Yet despite their service, courage, and sacrifice, the Civil War failed to meet the meager expectations of the Native peoples. The Civil War "… proved to be the Native American's last effort to stop the tidal wave of American expansion. While the war raged and African Americans were proclaimed free, the U.S. government continued its policies of pacification and removal of Native Americans."[154]

The Iroquois Nation was committed to the fight against the South. They appreciated the North's sympathy for their people and held the President [Abraham Lincoln] in veneration and confidence.[155] The Iroquois had few complaints about the Great Father's leadership during the war. Members of the Iroquois Nation joined Union volunteer units not as tribal contingents but as individual soldiers or sailors. In an ironic twist familiar in Army service, twenty-five Iroquois from the Alleghany, Cattaraugus, Onandoga, Tonawanda, and Tuscarora Reservations joined "D" Company of the 132nd New York State Volunteer Infantry alongside the company's core of naturalized Germans who hailed from Buffalo, Brooklyn, Lewiston, Manhattan, and Syracuse. The Tuscarora Company, later so named in respect for its commander, Lieutenant Cornelius C. Cusick, a Tuscarora sachem, was dispatched to New Bern, North Carolina, on December 25, 1863, a territory from which the Tuscarora had been expelled 140 years earlier by the ancestors of the adversaries they now faced.

In New Bern, the Tuscarora Company was assigned to guard the Union railway, the provisions, and supplies stored there and to prevent Confederate General Robert E. Lee's Army of Northern Virginia from being resupplied by sea. In January 1864, Lee's forces, commanded by General George E. Pickett, assailed New Bern in the second attempt by the Confederacy to recapture the second-largest town in North Carolina and an important railroad and river trade center. Since its capture by the Union in March 1862, New Bern became a base for Union raids against railroads and communications in the interior. With approximately 13,000 troops and fourteen Confederate cutters, Pickett's three columns attempted to converge on the city. Despite this strength, they were plagued by inept leadership, a poor intelligence assessment of enemy capabilities, and withering Union musket and artillery fire. The Confederates never captured the Union railhead or the urgently needed supplies stored there.

The portion of the *Union Official Record of the War of the Rebellion* for the period and the units involved in the New Bern engagement contains substantial citations illustrating the courage of Lieutenant Cusick and his warriors of Company D of the 132nd New York State Volunteer Infantry when denying the Confederates a river crossing, stalling their advance, and ultimately protecting the Union's stores. Early in the summer of the same year, Lieutenant Cusick marched his men on a reconnaissance of Jackson's Mills at Kinston, North Carolina. Again, the *Union Official Record* recorded his courage and that of his men when capturing

107 rebels, including the commandant of Kinston, and inflicting nearly forty rebel casualties.

By whatever measure used, the twenty-five Haudenosaunee in Company D and their brethren in Company K, 5th Pennsylvania Volunteer Infantry, distinguished themselves in the War of Rebellion, not for states' rights or against slavery, but for reasons of their culture, traditions of military service, economic and social survival, and the hope that by their service federal and state officials would end the white man's encroachment upon their lands.

As the United States edged its way toward involvement in the Great War, Native Americans, including the Iroquois Nations, did not sit idly on the sidelines. Leading up to World War I, there was great debate among the tribes of the Six Nations regarding the manner in which Native Americans would participate. Most of the 5,000 potential Iroquois volunteers ardently preferred segregated, all-Indian companies.

Cognizant of their right to act as a Nation, the tribes of the Iroquois Confederacy took it upon themselves to state their position vis-à-vis the war against the "Austrian and German Empires." Encouraged by Arthur C. Parker, a Seneca, who drafted a declaration of war, the Onondaga Nation declared war in July 1918. He urged his tribal leaders to follow suit, and in September 1918, the Oneidas, in addition to other tribal nation members of the Confederacy, declared war on Germany.

Tracing Native American tribal participation in World War I is difficult because they served in integrated units. However, if one traces tribal records of members who served in the Great War and the units to which they were assigned, one can find their campaign and battle participation. However, most of these records indicate the tribal members who perished during the war while overseas. Members of the Iroquois Confederacy who fell did so at some of the bloodiest sites of the war. Native American Marines of the 15th Company, 6th Machine Gun Battalion, died at Belleau Woods. Their Army brethren of the 108th Infantry Regiment fell at the Somme and along the Hindenburg Line. Other Iroquois warriors in the 306th Infantry Regiment succumbed to the wounds sustained at the Meuse-Argonne and Lorraine. 325th Infantry Regiment warriors fell at St. Mihiel. Even with this small sample, it is quite obvious that Iroquois Confederacy warriors served with distinction in the most fiercely fought battles alongside the finest units.

As discussed earlier, the Army's premier aerial ambulance in Vietnam was the UH-1 *Iroquois*. While researching this volume, there was uncertainty about an Iroquois medical linkage to support the Iroquois name, not that it was essential given the Iroquois Confederacy's culture and warrior legacy and its role in fighting alongside colonial and American soldiers. However, at the outset of America's participation in the Great War, the Army had only 403 nurses on active duty. The War Department brought 21,000 additional nurses into the ranks, fourteen Native Americans with two Iroquois in the last number.

Cora Elm, a Wisconsin Oneida, and (Charlotte) Edith Anderson, a Mohawk from the Grand Reserve in Ontario, Canada, responded and later volunteered for overseas service. Cora Elm came to nursing through the Episcopal Hospital of Nursing, graduating in 1916. Assigned to Base Hospital 34, The Episcopal Nursing Unit, Nurse Elm sailed with contemporaries of the New York Division of the U.S. Transport Force aboard the S.S. *Leviathan* bound for Liverpool. By April 1918, the Episcopal Unit treated casualties in the base hospital at Nantes, Brittany. During her nine months serving at the hospital, the unit cared for more than 9,000 patients.

(Charlotte) Edith Anderson, or "Andy" as she was known to her colleagues, became part of the Winchester County Unit B of the AEF. Following further training at Fort Slocum on David's Island, the unit joined nurses from the Buffalo General Hospital who had completed their training and mobilization. The combined unit sailed for Liverpool, where they arrived in March 1918. A ship from Southampton ferried the nursing team to La Havre and then onward by train to Vittel, a resort, vacation, and spa venue in the northeast region of France. The twenty-one-building hospital complex accommodated 1,800 patients at a time, and by the time the hospital completed its wartime mission in February 1919, it had treated more than 11,000 allied and enemy patients.

Throughout their service, both Cora and "Andy" experienced all the horrors and human depravity of the war through the anguish and suffering of the patients that passed through their wards and their care and the devastation to towns and villages they knew were no longer there. They each overcame their fears, the anxiety compounded by what they witnessed, and brought honor and recognition to their people through their distinguished service.

Following the First World War, Congress enacted two measures. The first was the 1919 American Indian Citizenship Act, and the second was the 1924 Indian Citizenship Act. The former merely opened the way to citizenship for those honorably discharged war veterans wishing to apply for American citizenship. The latter granted citizenship to "non-citizen Indians." By 1928, most Iroquois could vote, but many refused, seeing the act of voting as a loss of sovereignty of their Nation and the status of a co-equal partner to the United States. Not all Native Americans embraced these provisions of the law. Among those who refused citizenship were the Iroquois, who felt that their "participation in non-Indian society would be a denial of their separate status, this status being guaranteed by treaties."[156] The Iroquois refusal represented the Confederacy's internal conflict between the status of citizenship and the status of their sovereignty. The tribes felt that citizenship was "another pretext found by the United States government to deny its treaty obligations."[157] The Iroquois entered the war as a sovereign nation, and they intended to remain one in its aftermath. However, among numerous tribes of the Sioux Nation, those who did not vote were stripped of the privilege of ever becoming a chief or clan mother in their nation.[158]

The Iroquois Confederacy's battle with the federal government did not end with the Armistice or the Indian Citizenship Acts of 1919 and 1924. Confederacy members, the Tuscarora, the St. Regis Mohawk, and the Seneca resumed the challenge to their warriors being drafted in 1941; arguing that the Selective Training and Service Act passed on September 16, 1940, and amended on December 20, 1941, did not apply to them since they had refused citizenship in 1924. The compulsion to serve was an insult to the Iroquois, so they enacted their own conscription act and sent their warriors to join National Guard units.[159] At trial, they argued that the Indian Citizenship Act of 1924 was unconstitutional, that the Iroquois were sovereign foreign nations, and that Congress could not enact laws affecting them without their consent.[160] The Second Circuit of the U.S. Court of Appeals would later reject the case, and the Iroquois would continue challenging the jurisdiction of the Selective Service until the Vietnam War.[161]

The Iroquois Confederacy declared war on the Triple Alliance during World War I and never concluded a separate peace treaty with the Alliance. They were also not included in the Treaty of Versailles at the war's end. Thus, the Confederacy was automatically a party to the Second World War. On June 14, 1942, on the steps of the U.S. Capitol, in Washington, D.C., a representative of the Six Nations declared war on the Axis Powers. The Chippewa and Sioux later followed suit and declared war on the Axis.[162] The declaration concluded, "Now we do resolve that it is the sentiment of this council that the Six Nations of Indians declare that a state of war exists between our Confederacy of Six Nations on the one part and Germany, Italy, Japan, and their allies against whom the United States has declared war, on the other part."[163] In so doing, the Six Nations reaffirmed their status as a sovereign Nation, notwithstanding recent legal setbacks in the fight against the Nationality Act of 1940. Yet, they demonstratively asserted their willingness to serve in the Armed Forces of the United States in the fight against the Axis Powers.

There is not a Vietnam War veteran, friend, or foe, alive today who does not instantly respond to the rhythmic thumping of the *Huey*. It transports him back five decades or more to a time of anticipation, fear, promise, or hope. Each would not be wrong if they proclaimed that what they heard was the "sound of our war." The iconic and ubiquitous Iroquois was everywhere over the battlefields of South Vietnam, Laos, and Cambodia. The UH-1 opened the age of the turbine, which no modern helicopter flies without.

As the democratic governance of the Iroquois Nation helped guide our forefathers to nationhood, so to were their ways of warfare, especially the Oneida, advantageous to the colonists in bringing independence. The Iroquois Confederacy provided a great model and example for our young nation, becoming a fitting namesake for one of the Army's most respected helicopters.

OH-6 CAYUSE

11th Armored Cavalry Regiment OH-6A Cayuse *at the Pho Loi POL point. (Courtesy of Donivan Earhart via Ray Wilhite.)*

The previously discussed Roger's Board had strongly endorsed the early development of a light observation helicopter (LOH) as a potential replacement for the Cessna L-19 *Bird Dog*, the Bell OH-13 *Sioux*, and the Hiller OH-23 *Raven*. The Board laid out the Army's priorities for new aircraft and a general improvement plan for Army aviation from 1960 to 1970. By the end of the 1950s, the Army was particularly growing weary of these two piston-powered engine helicopters. While they provided yeoman service in everything they were called upon to do, the Army's aviation visionaries determined that the future would require a fleet of three new helicopters that relied upon powerful and space-efficient gas turbine engines. By the end of 1959, two of the three aircraft were already on order by the Army. The first was the Bell UH-1 *Iroquois,* and the second was the Boeing-Vertol CH-47 *Chinook.* The third piece of the helicopter triumvirate would be a new LOH.

Also emanating from the Roger's Board was a clear vision of the performance expected from the LOH. Primary among all considerations was the necessity for the aircraft to "live well" in the field with ground troops.[1] The new helicopter needed improved air mobility, reconnaissance capability, command and control performance, and target acquisition ability for the commander at battalion level and below to replace the already named aircraft. Such combinations necessitated better speed, payload, range, and low gross weight.[2] The Army would thus be looking for a helicopter that would provide a thirty percent improvement in the overall existing U.S. light observation helicopters.

In Vietnam, few light observation helicopters survived combat operations long enough to reach the accumulated 300 hours needed for the aircraft's first scheduled maintenance. Because of the scout's short life expectancy, high among the requirements for a replacement of the OH-13 *Sioux* was a low initial procurement cost—it had to be cheap. Not unexpectedly, the Army's request for proposal (RFP) prioritized the new aircraft's characteristics for the potential bidders. Those priorities included: 1) cost and gross weight, 2) reliability, 3) ease of maintenance, 4) specific capability for overload items, and 5) performance.[3]

The procurement of the LOH was also a new step forward for the Army in that it marked the first aircraft acquisition that the Army was permitted to manage since the Army and the Army Air Force separated in 1947. For that privilege, the Army had to ensure that the LOH they ultimately selected would meet the FAA's Civil Air Regulation which meant that the helicopter could consequently be considered an off-the-shelf helicopter ready for both civil and military service. What would follow was probably one of the most confusing acquisitions in Army aviation acquisition history. The solicitation and competition for the new LOH were opened industry-wide in the winter of 1959–60. The LOH competition was critical to the helicopter industry because it held out a potential Army procurement of 4,000 aircraft, meaning that the winner with Bell and Boeing-Vertol would have the power of incumbency for the military helicopter market for the next decade. Furthermore, a modified LOH, developed mainly at government expense, would be a prospective player in the still undefined civilian market.

On October 14, 1960, the United States Navy issued an RFP on behalf of the Army to 25 helicopter manufacturers for a gas turbine-powered LOH and liaison helicopter with a potential production quantity of over 3,600 units for the single winning design. The competition winner would benefit by holding a multi-decade-long position of leadership in the industrial market segment.

As expected, the Army's premier small helicopter builders, Bell and Hiller, offered LOH proposals, hoping to capitalize on their incumbency, experience, and performance record in supplying aircraft to the Army. However, 42 other companies submitted bids that included 119 design concepts overall.[4] Hopeful bidders submitted designs for the helicopter, light aircraft, and vertical-takeoff aircraft. A year later, in January 1961, the Army officially excluded all competitor design proposals save those for the helicopter. Subsequently, the Army received proposals from Bell, Hiller, Kaman, Sikorsky, Boeing-Vertol, Cessna, McDonnell, Republic, Doman, Gyrodyne, Lockheed, and Hughes Tool's Aircraft Division.[5]

The Navy chaired a source selection review of the qualified proposals submitted in May 1961, with the Army inviting Hiller and Bell to advance their designs to the next phase of the competition. The Army later awarded three contracts for test articles (prototype aircraft) for the LOH competitive fly-off. Bell and Hiller each received a contract for the OH-4A and the OH-5A, respectively, but surprisingly,

Hughes Tool–Aircraft Division was also granted a contract for their previously rejected OH-6A design.

Each of the three companies received approximately $6 million to build five FAA-certified prototypes of their respective design utilizing an Allison turbine engine provided as government-furnished equipment (GFE) and deliver them to the Army by year's end 1963.[6] The companies would each spend $2 million or more of their own research funding to finalize their design and their prototypes before delivering them to the Army in the winter of 1963–64 for competitive testing. The LOH competition was the first post-war military program whose selection process included the competitive flight testing of the prototypes. Each test article sample underwent six months of testing ending in June 1964 with an average flight time of ten hours a day, seven days a week, for the entire test period accumulating almost 2,000 flight hours each. Each company operated another aircraft for at least 1,000 hours for reliability, maintainability, and critical part durability information.[7]

After extensive deliberations within the Army acquisition community and senior Army leadership over the testing results, the Bell helicopter prototype was eliminated from further consideration. The Army declared that the Hughes and Hiller proposals would be further assessed, and a winner determined solely based on price.

In the LOH solicitation, the Army stipulated that it did not intend to further increase the capabilities and performance of the successful bidder through modifications, as had been the Army standard practice with all earlier helicopter selection decisions. The Hiller team assessed that the Army would ultimately fall back on their historic norms and offered a prototype with sufficient excess structural capability to allow the Army to modify the aircraft to achieve additional performance without necessitating airframe modification. In contrast, Hughes chose to offer a prototype that satisfied the Army's request. It offered the Army a light aircraft optimized for performance as built without performance growth through future modification. The Hughes decision to deliver stripped-down, smaller aircraft resulted in a faster and 400-pounds lighter prototype than its competitor.[8] With a pilot and five passengers, the *Cayuse*, as the Army named the helicopter, could reach 130 miles per hour and, with a lighter load, up to 170 miles per hour.[9]

Following the field testing, Hiller and Hughes were given from October 1964 to May 1965 to prepare their firm-fixed-price proposals for the Army's production contract. Anticipating and budgeting for a $50,000 airframe and another $13,000 for the GFE Allison engine, the Army was prepared to invest $63,000 for each production aircraft, or approximately $45 million for the 714 aircraft production run. With both surviving competitors anxious to win the production contract, they were willing to buy into the contract at unit prices below their costs and investments. Hiller, calculating a production cost of $35,000 per airframe plus the GFE engine and electronics gear, bid a unit price of $29,415 or about a $5.6 million loss on the contract plus the approximately $2 million in development costs which would not be recouped. Hughes was even more aggressive in its pricing to the government. They offered their production helicopter to the Army at $19,860 per airframe or an additional $6.8 million less than the Hiller bid.[10] While external observers questioned the cost realism of the Hughes bid versus that of Hiller, Army experience indicated that airframe costs for a light helicopter were expected to range from $30 to $40 per pound. Thus the 400-pound lighter Hughes airframe would easily translate into a $10,000 unit price difference with some profit potential for the company.[11] As stipulated in the down-select to the final two prototypes, the Army's final selection was priced based.

One of the concerns emerging from the technical evaluation of the Bell, Hiller, and Hughes test article aircraft was the weight discrepancy between the Hughes model and the other two competitors. Against an Army specification of 2,450 pounds gross weight, Hughes delivered an aircraft at approximately twenty percent less, or 2,050 pounds. The Bell and Hiller test articles grossed out closer to the Army specification. The helicopter comparison became more startling when the three were assessed based on empty weight. Hughes came in at 1,050 pounds, about thirty percent less than its competitors who were at approximately 1,500 pounds. According to Hughes, such weight advantages translated into lower acquisition costs and higher speeds with the same engine.[12] At 142 miles per hour at sea level, the Hughes OH-6A enjoyed a 19% and 10.5% airspeed advantage over Bell and Hiller, respectively.[13]

In 1965, while the LOH source selection and competition continued, helicopters and the concept of helicopter-borne fighting forces in Vietnam were still new and fundamentally untested. Aviation units in-country were, in many cases, developing their tactics on the fly and in response to their crews' operational experiences. During the early days of the Vietnam War, the Army employed the Bell OH-13 *Sioux* and the Hiller OH-23 *Raven* helicopters as a scouting combination in advance of the UH-1 *Iroquois* troop-carrying formations. The *Sioux* and *Raven* would reconnoiter the designated air assault landing zone to gather information about enemy locations, dispositions, and terrain conditions moments before the troop insertion commenced. Neither helicopter was ideally suited for the mountainous terrain and the hot and humid days in Vietnam. These three factors would severely stress these obsolete and underpowered helicopters. Likewise, they could not fly fast enough to escape enemy ground fire nor carry an adequate armament load to represent a significant threat to the enemy.

To in part redress these weaknesses, Army units began sending UH-1B helicopters armed with rocket pods and machine guns to orbit around 600 feet above the scout helicopters, poised to attack anything identified by the scouts that might interfere with the troop landings which would immediately follow. The additional *Iroquois* helicopters did little to shift the balance of combat capabilities since their slow speed precluded the effectiveness needed on the ground. The Army thus found itself in need of replacements for both the helicopter scouts and the presumed protector helicopters.

Notwithstanding the questionable source selection process with its allegations of political favoritism and even industrial espionage, the Army resolved upon the

Hughes Light Observation Helicopter, the OH-6A *Cayuse*. The new helicopter would begin arriving in Vietnam in December 1967 and with it began preparations for the departure of the OH-13.

The Aerial Scouts Find Their Aircraft

For the old OH-13 and OH-23 drivers, the arrival of the *Cayuse* was a giant leap into a new age. It was "jet-powered, fast, maneuverable, and supposedly quite survivable in a crash."[14] Besides the "new car smell," it had four radios and flight and navigation instruments, including an automatic direction-finder (ADF), a radar transponder, and a larger artificial horizon for each flight crew member.[15]

The OH-6A, and later the OH-58A *Kiowa*, was deployed to Vietnam to primarily perform the scout mission, which was one of observation, not engagement. The only problem with this distribution of mission tasks was that the enemy voted on the mission outcome.

The dynamics of the scout, high-low, and hunter-killer aerial combat ballet would dramatically change with the introduction of the nimble *Cayuse*. Army troops did not refer to the OH-6A as the *Cayuse*, as it was named, but rather colloquially as the "Loach," a contraction of "light observation helicopter." The combat aviators who depended upon the OH-6 for their lives characterized the ship as "unusually light and had plenty of power, perfect for flying nap-of-the-earth missions. Its 26-foot-diameter main rotor made getting into tight landing zones a snap. It had no hydraulic system, and its electrical setup was used primarily to start up the helicopter. For practical purposes, it was easier to maintain and harder to shoot down."[16] On the coin's obverse side was the reality that small arms bullets easily pierced its light aluminum skin. In a crash, the skin crumpled and absorbed energy while its strong structural truss arrangement protected critical systems and the people inside. *Cayuse* crews routinely survived crashes that in other aircraft would doom their crews.

The initial phase of the Vietnam War witnessed the cat and mouse interactions between the Viet Cong and their ARVN adversaries. Straight-leg infantry formations would seek engagements by clandestine movement through enemy terrain searching for combatants. These search and clear operations were often preceded by days of foot march only to culminate with a brief small arms exchange or the fleeing of the VC alerted by the ARVN approach march. The absence of timely, actionable intelligence, insufficient mobility, and the loss of tactical surprise in execution resulted in command exasperation and the search for a better alternative.

The arrival in Vietnam in September 1965 of the airmobile/air cavalry concept exemplified in the 1st Cavalry Division represented a solution designed for the challenge. Combining an aerial observation aircraft or scout with a helicopter gunship was the tandem needed to address the identified tactical shortcomings. The airborne scout of the Vietnam War was the twentieth-century embodiment of the eighteenth and nineteenth-century Indian warrior scout requiring that both displayed exceptional skill at reading and interpreting signs made and left behind by their respective adversary.

The early deliveries of the Loach in Vietnam were flown by the 7th Squadron, 17th Cavalry Regiment. The crews that flew it highly praised the *Cayuse,* which had two and half hours of flight endurance. The typical choreography of the Loach–*Cobra* team was performed during their transit to an assigned area of observation, typically at 1,500 feet in altitude. Upon reaching the designated area, the LOH would descend in an unpredictable flight path to an observation flight level of typically ten to forty feet above the jungle canopy. The gunship usually remained at the higher altitude providing armed overwatch of the nimble scout helicopter. The scout would then commence flying in overlapping circular or racetrack patterns. They were capable of flying down trails under the jungle canopy and tracking enemy combatants.[17] Scouts frequently flew close enough to enemy combatants that the aircrew could see them and identify their weapons, uniforms, and even their faces. The practice of the hunter-killer team relied upon the scout pilot/observer to watch and note any evidence of the enemy in the team's assigned area of observation. All noteworthy sightings were reported to the gunship crew orbiting above. In the case of the *Cobra* gunship, the front seat crew member recorded all the scout's reported sightings on his map, which the team would later use to support their debriefing by the supported maneuver commander's intelligence staff. The *Cayuse* crew's detection of enemy activity usually meant engagement and death dealt by the accompanying gunship. The LOH crew would report their sighting and often mark it with a colored smoke grenade. With gunship confirmation of the location, the scout aircraft would depart the immediate target area for a higher altitude to permit the unobstructed engagement by the gunship.

After an enemy target had been successfully engaged or on those occasions when the target warranted boots on the ground to neutralize the situation, the team would often request the insertion of the air cavalry troop's aero rifle platoon. The platoon, always on alert when hunter-killer teams were working, would immediately respond aboard their organic *Iroquois* lift ships. Depending upon the significance of the enemy threat, other options for the team were to request additional hunter-killer teams, artillery fire, or available close air support from the Air Force, Navy, or Marine Corps.

Despite the excellent, real-time target information, the standard *Cayuse* configuration limited the aircraft to a defensive response if engaged. With a door gunner and an M-60 machine gun situated in the starboard side cabin door, and the automatic small arms of the pilot and observer being the only weapons the scout could bring to bear on a direct threat, and only when the *Cayuse* was circling in a clockwise direction, the aircraft all too often returned to base (RTB) with combat damage.

Unwilling to accept the scout vulnerability status quo, aviators sought armament and crew configurations to enhance the offensive capability of the OH-6A. Many scout pilots wanted to remain engaged with the enemy as long as possible rather than withdrawing or seeking the safety of altitude upon an encounter with an enemy determined to harm the scout;[18] seeking cover and relinquishing the engagement to the gunship did not sit well with some scout crews. One such scout pilot was Lieutenant Colonel (then Lieutenant) Hugh L. Mills, who was assigned to the Scout Platoon of Delta Troop (Air), 1st Squadron, 4th Cavalry, 1st Infantry Division in 1969.[19] Mills' response to the challenge was to forego the left-seat observer for weight savings and then install the XM-27E1 minigun shipped to Vietnam with the helicopter, but it was not installed as a standard practice. The argument among some within the Cavalry command structure was that the installation of armament on the scout aircraft would divert the focus and attention of the scout helicopter crew from their primary mission: scouting. It was not the scout's job to try to kill the enemy—just to find him for the *Cobras*.[20]

The efficacy of the XM-27E1 minigun and OH-6A combination would be proven in early post-installation missions. On one of those missions, Mills spotted an enemy bunker complex and directed its engagement by his *Cobra* teammate. Following the *Cobra's* first rocket run, green tracers from a second location followed the gunship. Responding to the attack, Mills returned to the target and engaged the complex to protect the *Cobra*. The two helicopters continued their engagement and ultimate neutralization of the target, marking what was undoubtedly the first target attack by a scout aircraft and a scout's protection of its accompanying gunship.[21]

The enemy responded by creatively embedding countermeasures to the penetrating eye of the Loach. Low-hanging wires stretched between hillsides, and explosively rigged booby traps were common. Large shells attached to a VC flag flying from a pole were among the latter. The objective was for the shells to detonate when a crewmember grabbed the flag for a war trophy.[22]

Highly prized NVA flag at Hien Luong Bridge. (Courtesy of the author.)

In 1969, the author frequently flew around an enormous North Vietnamese flag waving in the wind from a pole near the southern terminus of the remnants of the Hien Luong Bridge, or the "Peace Bridge" as it was also known, over the Ben Hai River in the ten-kilometer wide Demilitarized Zone dividing North and South Vietnam along the seventeenth parallel. The flag was a highly coveted war trophy among some military officials in I Corps, with a $1,000 bounty purportedly offered for its retrieval. Despite the lucrative reward being offered and the visible nearby bomb craters, the flag was still flying from the same pole by the tour's end.[23]

The *Cayuse*, as the replacement for the *Sioux* and *Raven*, was routinely paired with the *Cobra* for the scouting missions following the arrival of the first AH-1G *Cobra* in Vietnam on August 29, 1967.[24] The *Cobra* came on the scene as a fast and deadly machine. While most aerial missions in Vietnam reached altitude and speed to promote aircraft and crew survivability, OH-6A *Cayuse* scout pilots flew low to attract enemy fire and identify targets for the *Cobra* gunships flying well above the scout. These hunter-killer missions, considered among the most hazardous for rotary-wing aircraft and crews during the war, quickly measured the mettle of the OH-6 pilots, aerial observers, and occasional door gunner flying onboard.

The paired helicopters operated out of fixed facilities to accommodate and support the aircraft and crews. Crews were accustomed to operating in the same operational area repeatedly, which enabled them to detect even the most subtle differences in the area from one mission to the next. Over time, the teams focused more on information gathering than landing zone reconnaissance and prepara-tion. Both flight crews, hunter and killer, lived together and were scheduled as a paired team for missions as often as possible. Just as the habitual area of operations assignment enriched the information from the reconnaissance over-flights, the customary crew pairings increased the team's combat effectiveness. The partnered crews were in constant radio communications and jointly experienced some of Vietnam's most intense combat. It was not long before each crew could anticipate the other's moves or recognize unspoken cues merely by the tenor of someone's voice in such a setting.[25]

The flying teams were deployed as a Pink Team, one scouting *Cayuse* and an aerial fire supporting *Cobra* or, as the troopers of the 101st Airborne Division referred to them, the Tadpole and the Snake.[26] The color was derived from a White Team scout and a Red Team *Cobra* combination. Also common was a Purple Team made up of two *Cobras* and a single *Cayuse*.

The gunship pilot locked his eyes onto the small aircraft as the *Cayuse* recon-noitered in and among the trees and jungle canopy. The front-seat pilot/gunner had his ears closely tuned to the radio transmissions of the scout below and recorded whatever was reported by the scout's observers. Upon detecting enemy activity or receiving enemy fire, Loaches would drop smoke grenades to mark the area and leave the site without further delay. If possible, the crew would attack the target as they fled with their personal small arms, M60 machine gun, grenades, or the occasional homemade explosive device.[27] The gunship would respond within seconds to the visual and aural cue, delivering either long-range rockets or machine guns and grenade fire. Commonly, a Blue Team of four *Iroquois* troopships was orbiting or resting nearby, prepared to insert troops if the nature of the target warranted or to rescue crew members from downed aircraft. The troopships or "slicks" were considered chase birds or troubleshooters in these missions.

For such a daunting mission, it is safe to assume that Army aviators selected to be scout pilots had been exhaustively trained and tested before strapping themselves into the OH-6. Most aviator accounts report no formal Army training to prepare scout pilots and observers. Instead, the doctrine, tactics, and techniques were developed in the field, and each unit in-country did things that worked for their portion of the Vietnam War, which meant that no two units engaged in scout hunter-killer missions the same way.[28] The gunship crews were familiar with the *Cobra* because they received training before deploying to Vietnam. On the other hand, a scout pilot did not take control of his OH-6 until arriving in Vietnam.

Many veterans assert that after around ten hours at the controls of the OH-6, they were deemed ready to fly in combat.[29] Other units reported that prospective scout pilots would spend up to 50 hours flying in combat in the observer's seat before they were given their check ride from the unit platoon leader and cleared to be a scout pilot in combat.[30] Scout pilots routinely flew at low-level executing maneuvers at or below tree-top level interspersed with frequent quick stops, fast starts, flying backward, sideways, constant pedal turns, and prompt and accurate firing passes.[31] Their observers and gunners who flew in the Loaches were even less experienced in the flying role, though gunners may have been the more fortunate since many transitioned to door gunners after serving with infantry or armor troops. They were knowledgeable and experienced with the M60 machine gun installed in the *Cayuse*. Observers might come from the ranks of artillery or mortar observers or reconnaissance sergeants. Their Military Occupational Specialty (MOS) training and area orientation flights earned them a seat aboard the scout helicopter.

In 1964, the Soviet Union began developing heat-seeking missiles with their 9K31 Strela-1 and 9K32 Strela-2. The latter progressed smoothly and entered service four years later. It was a man-portable, shoulder-fired, infrared-homing missile (MANPADS) known within NATO as the SA-7 *Grail*. Wanting to assess its performance in actual combat against western aircraft, the Russians shipped them to Vietnam, where it was successfully used in the later stages of the war, 1971–1975.

As the American troop withdrawal program began, the PAVN increased their man-portable air defense capabilities, which posed a significant new threat to the hunter-killer teams. In turn, it necessitated a countervailing response by Army aviation units and crews. In March 1972, the anticipated NVA attacks into South Vietnam were launched with unexpected size and ferocity. The 1972 Spring-Summer Offensive, one name among others by which it was named, included the first significant use of the SA-7 *Grail*. The *Grail*, a heat-seeking missile, could bring down the *Cayuse* without warning. Even the gunships were potential targets, although their higher altitude afforded some notice as the crew watched the missile's exhaust plume rise. The *Cobras* were also easier to spot because of their flight level. As the NVA deployed more and more of the missiles, both the hunter and killer searched for spaces into which they could remain well hidden.

The presence of a man-portable aid defense system (MANPADS) threat in theater necessitated modifications to aircraft and procedures. One such aircraft was the OH-6, where the engine exhaust outlets were altered to dissipate the heat upward and away from the fuselage.

Accompanying this structural change was a modified engine shutdown procedure. The crew had to idle the engine for two minutes to stabilize the temperature within the turbine before shutting it down. This offered an opportunity to heat the field ration meals directly from the exhaust or to enjoy a freshly popped batch of Jiffy Pop® popcorn in its familiar aluminum frying pan and foil dome that inflated as the kernels opened. Fresh, buttery popcorn right out of the turbine's exhaust.

The Army invested substantially in reliability, maintainability, and availability when it bought the *Cayuse*. Because of that, the Army maintenance policy for the aircraft required a significant inspection after 300 flight hours. In practical experience, these three hundred-hour inspections were rarely accomplished—few of the aircraft flew long enough to reach the threshold.[32] A sobering reality pursued the *Cayuse* in its Vietnam combat experience: "Out of 1,419 OH-6s built, 842 (59%) were destroyed in Vietnam ..." and out "of nearly 1,100 Cobras, 300 (~27%) were lost."[33] Of the OH-6s lost, most were shot down while others succumbed to high-speed, low-level flying hazards. With these kinds of statistics, it was not uncommon for Loach crews to have their aircraft succumb to enemy fire on more than one occasion. Despite the high aircraft loss rate, each ship lost claimed less than one crew member's life. This fact was, in large measure, attributable to the absence of flammable hydraulic fluids and that the fuselage was supported by a truss A-frame which maintained structural integrity in a crash. Though injured and banged up, many a crew member walked away from a downed OH-6. One former scout pilot, Clyde Romero, summarizes the typical scout pilot's experience, "I was wounded three times and shot down nine times. The shelf life of a scout pilot was probably six months. You were killed, shot down, or got scared and quit.[34]

While the price for the initial order of the *Cayuse* was reasonable and affordable, the Hughes price for replacing aircraft lost in combat was unrealistic, so the Army reopened the LOH competition from which the Bell OH-58 *Kiowa*, an off-the-shelf aircraft based on the Bell Jet Ranger, was selected.[35]

The replacement for the OH-6 *Cayuse* was in development as the new LOH was on its way to Vietnam. Thirteen months before the first units flew the OH-6 in Vietnam, the Bell OH-58A *Kiowa* underwent its first flight on January 10, 1966.[36] *Kiowa* deliveries continued notwithstanding the objections from scout crews in Vietnam who argued that the OH-58A *Kiowa*, powered by the same Allison T-63 engine as the OH-6, was inferior to the agile *Cayuse*. The Army's rationale was that helicopters in Vietnam were now flying uniform-altitude missions with all participating aircraft flying nap of the earth. It assessed that the *Kiowa* was suitable for the low-threat cargo and liaison missions routinely assigned in Vietnam.[37]

Army aviation leaders envisioned the helicopter as a fast, mobile, stealthy machine on the field of battle. The helicopter would be capable of imitating the skills and fieldcraft of the Native American tribes, such as they used terrain and vegetation to a tactical advantage. Considering the stories and exploits of the OH-6 *Cayuse* in the environs of Vietnam, it cannot be any more symbolic of America's first Indigenous inhabitants, and the tribe for which the aircraft is named could not be more precisely the embodiment of the attributes the Army sought and received in that little bird.

People of the Rye Grass

The Indigenous people who ultimately became known as the Cayuse were identified by various names over time. The French-Canadian fur traders who often encountered them called these Native Americans Calloux, "Rock People," due to the rocky landscape of their homeland. The "Rock People" referred to themselves as Liksiyu, while their neighbors, the Nez Percé Indians, knew them as the "People of the Rye Grass," Weyiiletpuu or Waiilatpus. To the early immigrants arriving in their region, they became known as Cai-uses, Cayouses, Skyuse, Kaus, and other forms of the name.

The Cayuse Indians were among the greatest and noblest of the Indigenous tribes of the Pacific Northwest, the present-day states of Washington and Oregon. These few but much-feared masters of a homeland that once exceeded six million acres of verdant land survived by their guile, cunning, and bargaining acumen. The Cayuse were also noted for their bravery and constant battles with the Snake and other weaker tribes. They were the first of their brethren to acquire horses and exploit their advantages in tribal life.

Long Hair, Cayuse warrior, 1900.
(Courtesy of the National Anthropological Archives.)

The Cayuse were originally river people, living along tributary streams in the Columbia Plateau, which is defined on its northern border by the Columbia River and the mouth of the Okanagon River. The southern side of the Plateau includes the Oregon drainage of the Deschutes River. The eastern boundary consists of the Camas Prairie of central Idaho, and the western side hosts the foothills of the Cascade Mountains. The Plateau people, including the Cayuses, were governed by the "seasonal round." Seasonal round meant that the Native American tribes' nomadic treks were based upon the availability of the food supply, which sequentially followed the seasons. The salmon began running in the spring, forcing the tribes to move toward the Columbia River with bounteous salmon runs. They followed the ripened berries or camas roots to other locales. The mountains beckoned the hunters for the deer, antelope, bear, and other game in the autumn. Finally, the Cayuse and their Columbia Plateau cousins migrated to the river valley villages where shelter and firewood were abundant in the winter. They remained in their rectangular longhouses until spring, when they were replaced by flat-roofed structures built on raised bases, providing the protection the tribe needed to survive the runoff from the melting high country snow. Interspersed among the villages were the Cayuses' neighbors, allies, and, in many cases, relatives: the Nez Percé, the Walla Walla, and the Umatilla. They also formed joint war parties, especially against their common adversary, the Shosonen tribes who lived and encamped to the south.

One of the keys to the territorial dominance of the Cayuse tribe was their acquisition of horses. According to Cayuse oral tradition, the trade occurred between a Cayuse war party and the Shoshone in the early eighteenth century.

Bewildered by the strange-looking animals with solid, round hooves that bore the Shoshone warriors, the Cayuse chief arranged for a trade of almost all the war party's possessions for a stallion and a mare. The advent of the horse opened their world; the Great Plains and California were no longer beyond their horizons or opportunity to hunt, fish, trade, fight, and capture slaves. The Cayuse expanded their homeland with abundant horses and maintained their dominance over their neighbors. By increasing their geographic reach, they assimilated the culture, traditions, and warrior skills of the tribes they encountered, especially those on the Great Plains.

Over decades and generations, the Cayuse horses were developed to be durable animals, enabling them to move unimpeded by physical limitations across the terrain at high speeds, not unlike the helicopter that would bear the same name nearly two centuries later. The history of the Cayuse Indian pony has been lost over time; however, several theories have been hypothesized, including that the pony is a descendant of a seventeenth-century Spanish barb or a cross with a French Percheron draft horse. The Cayuse pony is a distinct, unique breed regardless of its origins.

Cayuse's exposure to the outside world was not limited to other Indigenous peoples. Their first non-Indian contact came in October 1805, when Meriwether Lewis and William Clark crossed Cayuse territory on the trail to the Pacific Ocean. Eight months later, the Lewis and Clark Expedition would re-cross the Cayuse homeland on their return journey. During the passage of the white man through their land, the Cayuse were impressed by the manifestation of the power of their visitors. Power was significant in the Cayuse culture, and they seemed to be perpetually looking for it. The white man's guns, technological advancement, and metallurgy were particularly impressive to the Indigenous people. But there was another way this new power was essential to the Cayuse. At this early juncture of the nineteenth century, the Cayuse were a small tribe with barely 500 members. Notwithstanding their overwhelming herd of horses, the tribe did not possess sufficient power to maintain their supremacy on the Columbia Plateau. However, with the magic of the weapons possessed by their visitors, the tribe would overwhelm the bow and arrow, and their place on the Plateau would not be further threatened.

After the departure of Lewis and Clark, Canadian fur traders descended upon the Columbia Plateau. Twelve years later, the Montreal-based North West Company began building a trading post at the mouth of the Walla Walla River. The traders brought a wide array of commodities, essentials, and novelties to the shelves of the trading post. Thus, the tribal members were exposed to another white man's power source, the "spiritual power." The Natives rationalized that if power originated from the Creator, it was the source that enabled the white man to make and do many powerful things. The tribal interest in the Euro-American faith opened the Plateau to an onslaught of Christian missionaries in the 1830s. Multi-denominational missionaries from the eastern regions of the United States made the over seven-month journey to the Pacific Northwest and the tribal homelands of the Cayuse.

Among the missionaries making the trek were husband and wife, Marcus and Narcissa Whitman, from the Burned Oven District of upstate New York. The Whitman's established their Presbyterian mission among the Cayuse at Waiilatpu in 1836.[38] By 1847, the once amicable relationship between the Whitmans and the Walla Walla band of the Cayuse began to deteriorate seriously. The missionaries believed that the Indians must be civilized before their eternal souls could be saved. This meant that the Cayuse must forsake all aspects of their native culture, which was considered evil and satanic, and live in the American fashion. The missionaries began forcing the Cayuse to dress in American clothing styles, live in white man's design homes, and eat European-style food. Furthermore, Marcus Whitman was a physician. He tried to impose European medical practices upon the Indians to discredit Indian medicine people and ingratiate himself with the Indian people.[39]

By 1847, the Columbia Plateau experienced an influx of more than 4,000 settlers and various strains of Anglo-American communicable disease. According to Cayuse culture, should a patient succumb while under the treatment and care of the medicine man, the deceased's relatives had the right to seek revenge by taking the life of the medicine man.[40] In 1847, an outbreak of measles occurred among the Cayuse children enrolled in Whitman's mission school and eventually became an epidemic that killed half of the enrolled students with either measles or the accompanying dysentery within two months. Infected white children with their natural immunity did not experience the same fatal results. A troublesome, half-blooded Maine Indian, Joe Lewis, was booted off a passing wagon train at the Whitman mission. He led the Cayuse to believe that Dr. Whitman was poisoning their children so he could take their land. He pointed to the recovery of the white children as proof of his claim.[41] As a result, this instilled nefarious suspicions among the Cayuse as to different standards of medical treatment for whites and Indigenous. Some Indians thought that Dr. Whitman was a sorcerer and contributed to their deaths. Not surprisingly, the Cayuse affixed the blame upon the missionaries, including Dr. Whitman and his wife. The Indians accused them of poisoning 200 Cayuse whom the doctor was inoculating for measles.[42] Cayuse Chief Tilokaikt, who lost a child to measles, and a warrior named Chief Tomahas[43] exacted their revenge by killing Marcus Whitman and eleven other American settlers at the mission on November 29, 1847.[44] In addition to the slayings, the Indians took fifty-one women and children captive for eventual ransom by the Hudson's Bay Company.[45] The rationale for the killings was that measles was a white man's disease, and as a white man healer, Whitman would have known how to cure the disease, but he did not, at least not among the Cayuse.

This singular event set into motion the seven-year Cayuse War (1847–1855) between the Cayuse and the federal government. The Cayuse War would set a precedent for the course of Indian-white man relations in the Inland Northwest that would remain unchanged for the next fifty years. The war, the first Indian war in the Pacific Northwest, amounted to a series of skirmishes that took place primarily between January and March 1848. A 500-man volunteer army was raised by Reverend Cornelius Gilliam, a fire-and-brimstone, bigoted Baptist minister. The self-appointed militia colonel despised the Indians and believed that they should be exterminated. With Army support, Gilliam and his force marched against the Cayuse and the other tribes in central Oregon, seeking the surrender of the five warriors responsible for the Whitman Massacre. The Cayuse refused peace overtures and began raiding isolated settlements.

On February 24, 1848, the Battle of Sand Hollows which was also known as the Battle of Dry Plains began when a group of soldiers led by Captain Lawrence Hall pressed out on the old emigrant road towards Whitman's Station and were attacked by Umatilla, Cayuse, Palouse, and a few Walla Walla braves as they approached the Umatilla River. The Native Americans fought not so much to protect the Whitman murderers but to defend their country from a further white man's invasion. Despite their efforts, after three hours, the battle ended inconclusively as the Cayuse withdrew.

In 1850, twenty-nine months after the Whitman Massacre, Oregon Territory Governor Joseph Lane secured the surrender of five members of the Cayuse tribe. It was unknown whether the five Cayuse warriors who were arrested—the Cayuse Five—were the actual perpetrators of the crime or just five Cayuse volunteers. They were indicted and tried according to American frontier justice and, after four days, condemned. The five defendants, Telokite, Tomahas, Clokomas, Isiaasheluckas, and Kiamasumkin, were publicly executed on June 3, 1850.[46] This egregious act, however, did not end the Cayuse War. The bloodshed continued until the Cayuse were ultimately defeated in 1855. As the war with the white man diminished the Cayuse population, they were, by the Treaty of Walla Walla with the federal government, forced along with the Umatilla and Walla Walla to a reservation in Oregon, the 510,000 acre Umatilla Indian Reservation.[47] The tribes ceded 6.4 million acres of their homeland to the U.S. government and received $200,000; however, when government surveyors marked out the reservation, it included only 245,000 acres.

The nearby grassland would become the range for their horses; however, within two weeks of June 9, 1855, the date the treaty was signed, Territorial Governor Isaac Stevens declared all Indian lands, including that set aside by the new treaty, open to white settlers. During the late 19th century, settlers began herding the tribal horses from the grasslands for a source of food or for pulling trolleys in eastern cities. Partially stemming from this runaway encroachment, Congress enacted the Slater Act of 185, which reduced the acreage of the reservation but allotted limited land to the Native people.[48] By the end of the nineteenth century, federal legislation reduced the Umatilla Reservation to 172,000 acres. The three tribes became the Confederated Tribes of the Umatilla Indian Reservation. Their tribal homelands were confiscated, and the Cayuse territories were opened to white settlements. The relationship between the tribes and the white settlers was never the same. It led to wars between them for forty more years. Since 1855, the Cayuse have officially resided within the reservation's limits.

The legacy of the Cayuse people has been deeply overshadowed by the events surrounding the Whitman Massacre. History "has dealt harshly with the tribe and its leaders.[49] The appeal of the Whitmans and their tragic fate obscured the legitimate grievances of the tribe.

The end of the Cayuse War did not mark the end of hostilities in the Pacific Northwest; they merely melded into and continued as the Yakima War (1855–1858) and the other bloody outbreaks that followed. The territorial governor's attempts to get the tribe to cede their land and establish a reservation only intensified ongoing hostilities. The discovery of gold near Fort Colville in Washington Territory only made matters worse as prospectors and settlers in even greater numbers trespassed on Yakima lands through the Naches Pass.[50] As the conflict escalated, the Army could not conclude it before it spread to the region west of the Cascades and to the Puget Sound. The spillover from the Yakima War and the government's efforts to compel the Native tribes to agree to treaties ceding their land continued the enflamed relationships in the Pacific Northwest.

The Puget Sound War (1855–1856) followed the Yakima imbroglio. It was further inflamed by the continued intimidation of the Northwest tribes to sign treaties that included the cession of their land, including that of the Puyallup and the Nisqually tribes. The second phase of the Yakima War followed the closing of the Puget Sound War when violence erupted into the Coeur d'Alene War (1858) involving the Yakima, Palouse, Spokane, and Coeur d'Alene tribes. Later that same year, the four tribes were defeated at the Battle of Four Lakes.

The discovery of gold added impetus to increased land encroachment by the white man and the shedding of more blood. The California Gold Rush witnessed increased prospector travel through the Rogue River Valley and the outbreak of the Rogue River War (1855–1856). The discovery of gold in British Columbia drew 30 to 40,000 gold seekers from Washington, Oregon, and California into the Fraser Canyon War (1858), which took place in Canada. Regardless, the involved militia emanated principally from the U.S.[51] Then, with gold unearthed in Idaho and Oregon, similar conflicts occurred, including the Bear River Massacre (1863) and the Snake War (1864–1868).

Another series of violent encounters occurred in the late 1870s that engulfed Oregon, Idaho, Montana, and Wyoming, including the Nez Percé War of 1877. It was instigated by "the large influx of settlers, the appropriation of Indian lands, and a gold rush […] in Idaho."[52] The Bannock War, spurred by the same grievances, erupted in 1878 and was followed by the last Indian war in the Pacific Northwest in 1879, the Sheepeater Indian War.[53]

While the *Iroquois* may be the poster child of the Vietnam War, the *Cayuse* was one of the ships that many aviators aspired to command. It was the ship that was in an almost constant battle of wits and daring with the enemy, a real *mano e mano* test of skill and courage. There was pride in the ability to walk away from it at the end of the day, whether it safely landed or crashed. Others unceasingly depended upon this single aviator's ability. As their Native American namesake, these twentieth-century warriors mounted their stead. They charged into the lair of the enemy, defying their clutches so others might live and carry on the fight.

CH-47 CHINOOK

Army CH-47 Chinook inbound to the Pho Loi POL point. (Courtesy of Donivan Earhart via the VHPA Calendar Program.)

Following the end of the Korean War, the United States Army was fighting for relevance in the American national security establishment. This was an era where the potential of nuclear weapons dominated strategic defense thinking, force organization and structure, and, most importantly, the allocation of Defense Department resources. Manpower organized into divisions paled in comparison to the utility and efficiency of nuclear weapons. In a strategy dominated by the nuclear triad—manned bombers, land-based intercontinental ballistic missiles, and ballistic missile-carrying submarines—a conventionally armed Army was an expensive, blunt instrument in a time enamored by the prospect of disarming precision nuclear strikes. Part of the relevancy debate was the vision within Army Aviation that it could support the atomic environment by transporting tactical and intermediate-range nuclear-armed missiles around the battlefield. To haul the MGM-31A Pershing 1 and Pershing 1a field artillery missile systems, the Army required a heavy-lift helicopter which would also have as its primary role the ability to move troops and emplace artillery and for battlefield resupply.

The CONARC Combat Developments Objective Guide of February 1956 outlined the service's requirements for a heavy transport helicopter.[1] The aircraft was to carry a five-ton payload to an operating radius of one hundred nautical miles (~115 miles) or a heavier cargo to shorter distances. The resultant helicopter was destined for use as a "basic transport of troops, supplies, and equipment in the combat zone, including aeromedical evacuation, and heavy lift in the field army area."[2] These requirements and progress on the aircraft's development lay dormant as the Army focused on light and medium cargo aircraft.

Late in 1956, the Department of the Army announced its intention to replace the piston-driven H-37 helicopter with a new, turbine-powered aircraft. A design competition was held, and, in September 1958, a joint Army-Air Force source selection board recommended that the Army procure the Boeing-Vertol medium transport helicopter. However, the project languished with uncertainty about the aircraft's design requirements and without the funds necessary to proceed with full-scale development. Some Army leaders felt that this new helicopter should be a light tactical transport targeted for the old H-21s and H-34s mission. Such a specification would consequently restrict the helicopter's size to what was necessary to carry approximately fifteen combat troops onboard. Others in the Army argued for a much larger aircraft to serve as an artillery prime mover with minimum interior cabin dimensions compatible with the Pershing missile system. This "sizing" problem was a critical decision.[3] The Army's relevance on the tactical nuclear battlefield necessitated it being able to move its theater missiles to where they could be effectively employed. The *Chinook* was the instrument to accomplish that for the Pershing system, so it had to be sized so that the missile and transport would fit.

There was a helicopter engineering and manufacturing company located in Philadelphia, Pennsylvania, with considerable expertise in tandem rotor helicopters. The P-V Engineering Forum was founded by Frank Piasecki and his New York University Guggenheim School of Aeronautics undergraduate classmate, Harold Venzie.[4] Piasecki's work attracted attention from the U.S. Navy, which in 1945 awarded a contract to Piasecki's company to design a large tandem rotor helicopter capable of carrying heavy loads. That year the first tandem-rotor helicopter, and the first helicopter designed specifically for the U.S. Navy was rolled out. The new aircraft was popularly called the "Flying Banana." The company grew into the Piasecki Helicopter Corporation, which Frank Piasecki left in 1955, to form the Piasecki Aircraft Corporation to develop advanced vertical takeoff and landing systems. The former company was renamed Vertol Aircraft Company in 1956 and was acquired by Boeing in 1960 to make it their helicopter division. The company then worked on three tandem-rotor helicopters: the *Chinook* for the Army, the *Sea Knight* for the Navy and Marine Corps, and the commercial 107–11 for air carriers.[5]

On October 9, 1958, CONARC prioritized its cargo lift needs in order, as a light three-ton STOL aircraft, a light transport helicopter, and the Vertol *Chinook* helicopter. CONARC further stipulated that if budgetary constraints precluded purchasing the *Chinook*, then the three-ton STOL and the new light transport helicopter would be needed to be placed into active service as soon as feasible.

Finally, by May 1959, the specifications for what would be designated as the CH-47A *Chinook* were approved, and a contract was issued to Boeing-Vertol.[6] The Army tested the first Vertol prototype, the YHC-1A, to derive engineering and operational data. Three aircraft were built with a maximum troop capacity of twenty. This model eventually became Vertol's commercial 107. However, the ship was considered by most Army users to be too heavy for the assault role and too light for the transport role. The decision was made to procure a heavier transport helicopter and, at the same time, upgrade the UH-1 as a tactical troop transport, thereby giving the Army both a transport aircraft and a troop lift helicopter. This decision ultimately would determine the pattern of airmobile operations for the next decade. The sizing of the *Chinook* was related to the growth of the *Iroquois* and the insistence by Army tacticians that initial air assaults should be built around the rifle squad.

A Medium Lift Helicopter for the Helicopter War

The UH-1 program reached a critical stage when the technicians insisted that the Army should not go beyond the UH-IB model with Bell; there should be a new intermediary tactical transport between the Huey and a medium transport helicopter. The proper *Chinook* size became apparent with the creation of the UH-ID. By resolutely pushing for the *Iroquois* and the *Chinook*, the Army accelerated its air mobility program by several years. The Army finally settled on the larger *Chinook* as its standard medium transport helicopter, and by February 1966, 161 aircraft had been delivered to the Army. The first unit equipped (FUE) with the CH-47A came into active service in August 1962, and the aircraft made its first combat appearance in Vietnam when the "Hillclimbers" of the 147th Transportation Company (Medium Helicopter) arrived in Vietnam on November 29, 1965.[7] As a separate medium helicopter company, the 147th was initially placed in support of the U.S. 1st Infantry Division. The 1st Cavalry Division had brought their organic *Chinook* battalion with them when they arrived in 1965.

Boeing introduced an improved *Chinook*, the CH-47B, in 1966, which was followed a year later by the CH-47C. The improvements for the "C" model were driven by specific requirements forced by Army experiences in Vietnam. The Army needed a medium-lift helicopter that could carry loads under extreme temperatures, precisely 15,000 pounds, thirty nautical miles (~thirty-five miles), on a 90°F day, at an altitude of four thousand feet.[8] The helicopter was a twin-turbine, tandem-rotor transport capable of moving an infantry assault platoon of forty-four combat-equipped soldiers.

As it was created and applied in Vietnam, air mobility became a narrative of the men and their flying machines. If the UH-1 *Iroquois* helicopter became the cornerstone of air mobility, the *Chinook* was considered one of the main building blocks.[9]

The defining mission of the *Chinook* was as a pack mule, capable of placing cannon artillery batteries in perilous mountain positions that were inaccessible by any other means and then keeping them resupplied with the large quantities of ammunition they demanded. The *Chinook* of the 1st Cavalry Division was limited to 7,000 pounds of payload when they operated at the higher altitudes in the mountains. In comparison, operations near the coastline permitted them to carry an additional 1,000 pounds. The early *Chinook* was limited by its rotor system, which did not use all of its installed power. Pilots and ground commanders were anxious for an improved version that would upgrade the rotor system.

New equipment training and early customer experience with the aircraft exposed a severe problem for the platform. The cavernous cargo compartment was so inviting that soldiers frequently overloaded the aircraft. Crew members and supported commanders had to be constantly vigilant that soldiers did not try to stuff too much gear into the helicopter. Similarly, soldiers had to be diligent when preparing external sling loads. Improperly placed heavy cargo straps or ancillary howitzer equipment not properly stowed could cause damage to the slung load—many a howitzer gunner's sights failed to complete the journey in the early experience with the *Chinook*. The *Chinook* rapidly proved to be the mainstay aircraft for artillery movement and heavy logistics transport, so it was rarely used as an assault troop carrier.[10]

The 1st Cavalry Division became adept at improvising landing zones in the dense jungle terrain of their area of operations. One example came during Operation MASHER/WHITE WING. The division employed carpet bombing to clear sufficient space for its *Chinooks* to hover overhead while soldiers repelled into the blasted areas.[11] During MASHER, helicopters performed miraculous deeds lifting battalion after battalion. While this was impressive enough, they also conducted fifty-seven artillery battery lifts, including the division artillery's medium 155-mm howitzers.[12] It is worth noting that a battery lift required twelve CH-47 sorties to move both howitzers and ammunition.[13]

With the *Chinook* as his prime mover, the airmobile artilleryman learned to fire in all directions with minimal confusion, and he became accustomed to rapid and frequent moves. The supporting artillery even developed a unique tactic, known as "the artillery raid," whereby an artillery battery would be moved deep into enemy territory, rapidly fire prepared concentrations on targets developed by intelligence, and then be extracted before the enemy could react. Such raids could be planned and executed in a few short hours by experienced artillery and aviation units.[14] While most artillery raids were conducted with light, direct support artillery units (105-mm), the first known tactical lift of a medium artillery piece, a 155-mm howitzer, by a CH-47 *Chinook* in Vietnam was performed by the 147th Assault Support Helicopter Company which was supporting elements of the 9th Infantry Division at the time.[15]

Artillery raids supported by air cavalry units included fires from both tubes and aerial rockets, delivered into areas where the enemy thought he was immune to such fire. During a tube artillery raid, the air cavalry troop would reconnoiter the selected landing zone and secure it with a rifle platoon before the CH-47 landed light artillery and the CH-54 for medium artillery. Pink teams consisting of observation and gunship helicopters conducted visual reconnaissance to develop targets of opportunity. They would adjust the cannon fire onto the target and then perform an immediate post-attack battle damage assessment. At other times, the rifle platoon was used to exploit significant target sightings. The air cavalry units performed the same missions in aerial rocket artillery raids, except that no landing zone had to be selected and developed.[16]

Unusual battlefield circumstances required unique solutions. One such situation placed the *Chinook* in the role of an "ad hoc bomber." With the vast enemy underground tunnel networks throughout the battle zone, the battlefield commander faced the challenge of driving the enemy from his tunnel system and into the open, where he could be engaged. Like the legendary "Tunnel Rats," sending specially trained soldiers into tunnels to drive the enemy out was extraordinarily hazardous and time-consuming. Alternatively, riot agents were an effective way of inducing the enemy to leave his tunnel haven. The 1st Cavalry Division and the 3rd Brigade of the 25th Infantry Division, the ARVN 22nd Division, and the Republic of Korea Capital Division conducted an eleven-month operation, Operation PERSHING, in Binh Dinh Province to clear North Vietnamese Army and Viet Cong activity from the province.[17] On February 12, 1967, and January 19, 1968, *Chinook* units dropped 29,600 pounds of riot agents from their helicopters using an ingenious, locally fabricated fusing system integrated into a standard fifty-five-gallon drum. The drum was rolled off the back-ramp door of the aircraft, and the fusing system was armed by a static line that armed the drum after it left the helicopter. This allowed the accurate placement of large concentrations of tear gas in short order.[18] Also, during Operation PERSHING, when tactical aircraft could not be used effectively, the CH-47 similarly dropped 5,000 pounds of napalm on an enemy installation using the same rigging and fusing system.[19]

In June 1965, the Army hastily placed an order with the Vertol Division of the Boeing Company for a helicopter capable of providing helicopter-borne aerial fire suppression. The June 30 order was for four armed Chinook helicopters to be delivered by the end of the calendar year. The resultant aircraft would be designated the A/ACH-47A.

During the week of October 24, 1965, the Boeing Company revealed the details of a new, heavily armed, modified CH-47A.[20] The modified *Chinook* was outfitted with 2,681 pounds of armor plating for increased survivability from enemy ground fire. Additionally, Boeing equipped the helicopter with three forward-firing gun mounts and five manned gun positions located in the cargo cabin. The aircraft was further provisioned to carry other weapons like the M-5 40-mm grenade launcher, a 20-mm cannon, a rocket pod with nineteen 2.75-in rockets, and a 7.62-mm and a .50 caliber machine guns.[21] The armament placement enabled the crew to engage targets a full 360 degrees around the aircraft. The concept was to use this newly armed and armored helicopter to protect troop-carrying helicopters and provide suppressive fires during disembarkation operations in a contested landing zone. The up-armored helicopter with its eight-man crew had the flight performance of the standard CH-47A because of its more powerful turbine engines. With a speed of 132 mph, it had two hours of endurance for its operational missions. The few aircraft made were assembled at the Boeing Morton, Pennsylvania, facility and shipped to the Army's Aberdeen Proving Ground in Maryland for testing.

Three of the new aircraft were shipped to Vietnam in May 1966 and uniquely supplied to the 1st Cavalry Division, whom the Army had asked to introduce the helicopters into combat. They formed the 53rd Aviation Detachment, Field

Evaluation (Provisional) to undergo combat evaluation for six months of testing under combat conditions.[22] The fourth aircraft remained at Edwards Air Force Base (AFB) in California to undergo weapons systems testing. All four helicopters ultimately became part of the 53rd Aviation Detachment and spent three months operating out of Vung Tau, while the second half of their tour was spent at An Khe.

The Detachment's aircraft, "Go-Go Birds," as they were affectionately referred to by the Infantry, were the "Co$t of Living" (#64-13145), "Easy Money" (#64-13149), "Stump Jumper" (#64-13151), and "Birth Control" (#64-13154). The test models delivered to the division were armed with five M60D 7.62-mm machine guns or M2HB .50 caliber machine guns, two M24A1 20-mm cannons, two XM159B/ XM159C 19-tube 2.75-in rocket launchers, or, at other times, two M18/M18A1 7.62-mm gun pods, and a single M75 40-mm grenade launcher in the nose.[23] Except for a 105-mm howitzer recoiling mass[24], the "Go-Go Birds" could be likened to a much smaller-sized AC-130 *Spectre* or C-47 *Spooky* Air Force gunship. Though not particularly graceful in flight, these special helicopters had a tremendous positive morale effect on the friendly troops they supported. The "Go-Go Birds" were among the most requested fire support assets in the 1st Cavalry Division.[25]

During their evaluation period, the ACH-47As destroyed every assigned target they engaged. Although the 1st Cavalry commonly employed these helicopters in pairs as was the standard technique for heliborne aerial fire support within the division, the practice revealed some inadequacies for the giant aircraft. The "Stump Jumper" was lost in a ground taxing accident with another CH-47 at Vung Tau Airfield on August 5, 1966.[26] Moved to Vietnam following the destruction of "Stump Jumper," "Co$t of Living" was lost in a 20-mm gun accident on May 7, 1967, at Bong Son,[27] when one of its M-24A 20-mm cannon mounting pins vibrated loose, allowing the cannon to fire upward through the fuselage and into the rotating forward rotor system causing it to crash.[28] "Birth Control" was lost to enemy fire during the Tet Offensive on February 22, 1968, in the fight to recapture Hue.[29] After successfully and safely autorotating, it was destroyed by enemy mortar fire. Fortunately, "Easy Money" rescued the crew of "Birth Control." "Co$t of Living" was lost in a 20-mm gun accident on May 7, 1967, at Bong Son,[30] when one of its M-24A 20-mm cannon mounting pins vibrated loose, allowing the cannon to fire upward through the fuselage and into the rotating forward rotor system.[31] "Birth Control" was lost to enemy fire on February 22, 1968, in the fight to recapture Hue during the Tet Offensive.[32] With only a single helicopter left in the detachment and the Army's unwillingness to let it fly on a single aircraft mission, "Easy Money" was taken out of fire support action in 1968, used in recurring roles, and restored as a maintenance trainer. It is now preserved at the Cargo Helicopter Program Executive Office in Redstone Arsenal, Alabama.[33] With the arrival of the AH-1 *Cobra* gunship, the A/ACH-47A testing project was concluded.[34]

Chinook companies and crews of the 173rd Airborne Brigade shared the concern that friendly mortar rounds, fired conventionally from elevated tubes, could not penetrate the heavy jungle canopy that dominated the brigade's area of operations. Inventive crew members constructed wooden chutes mounted to the helicopter's door. While flying over the target area, the cabin crew would send the mortar rounds sliding down the chute toward the enemy soldiers below.[35] The air warriors claimed 200 enemy combatants killed or wounded using this practice.

During this same period, armed helicopters experienced a rapid increase in use. In October 1962, the UTTHCO (the Army's first armed helicopter unit) equipped with UH-1As replaced B-26s and T-28s as escorts for CH-21 (*Shawnee*) troop helicopters, and as a result, losses decreased significantly. By May 1964, "B" model Hueys (UH-1B) had replaced the CH-21 for carrying troops, and ten light airmobile aviation companies, with one to three armed platoons each, were in Vietnam. In 1965 the 1st Cavalry Division (Airmobile) brought the first air cavalry squadron and aerial artillery battalion to the Republic of Vietnam.[36]

The versatility of the *Chinook* in Vietnam spread beyond the missions previously described. The aircraft and its crew were called upon to recover downed or disabled aircraft on many occasions. This was a daily task performed by aircraft maintenance units like the 56th Aircraft Direct Support Maintenance Company, which recovered over 350 downed aircraft in 1968 alone.[37] Between 1965 and 1971, the CH-47 *Chinook* rescued downed aircraft worth approximately $2.7 billion.[38]

The U.S. Consolidated Improvement and Modernization Program for the RVNAF included a proposal to transfer *Chinook* helicopters to them. The modernization plan gained added impetus from the 1970 campaign in Cambodia. In August 1970, the first fifty-five RVNAF pilots started their transition training from CH-34s to CH-47s at Tan Son Nhut Air Base. The trained cadre, including maintenance personnel and flight crews, formed the basis of the first RVNAF CH-47 squadron that was activated on September 30, 1970. At the same time, preparations were underway to stand up a second CH-47 squadron.

The Chinook People

A ribbon of land extends from the Alaskan peninsula to beyond the southern border of present-day Oregon. Bordering on the east are the Cascade Mountains and the northern extension of the Rocky Mountains, and on the west is the Pacific Ocean. The region, what is now Oregon and Washington, represents the ancestral homeland of the Chinook people.[39] The tribal name is derived from the warm Rocky Mountain winds that blow toward the Great Plains and induce rapid temperature increases in a noticeably short period. The Chinook people lived predominantly along the banks of the Columbia River and the coastal lands of the Pacific Ocean on a tract of land encompassing more than two million acres. There they lived contently as nomadic hunters and masterful traders with the other Indigenous tribes of the region. Their homeland marked the center of an expansive trading network that stretched from Alaska to California and east to the Great Plains. Among those with whom they traded were the Nez Percé, who shared the lands of present-day Washington and Oregon, and into parts of Idaho and Montana. The Chinook enjoyed the presence of the Columbia River and its tributaries on their land, which enabled their

HEE-DOH'GE-ATS Chinook youth,
1837–1839. (Courtesy of the Smithsonian
American Art Museum.)

trading expeditions and provided a bountiful harvest of salmon, an integral part of their diet. Not surprisingly, the Chinook people were skilled craftsmen in canoe building and were knowledgeable navigators. They traveled thousands of miles to conduct their trading enterprise, exposing them to many Indian and non-Indian people.

From the 1740s, the sea otters along Oregon's coast were widely hunted for the commercial fur trade by Europeans who first encountered the Chinook people along the lower Columbia River.[40] The once plentiful sea otters were so overhunted that by 1800, their vanishing population paralleled the other nineteenth-century calamities that befell the Native Americans of the Pacific Northwest, which included wars, disease, the loss of land, native boarding schools, and the loss of life.

The British and American traders sought new sources of wealth by trading for beaver pelts and other furs from the regional tribes. The traders built forts along the coast and numerous tribes settled near them, including the Chinook. To facilitate their trading, the Chinook created a pidgin language by combining English phrases with their own terms, forming a unique Chinook jargon.[41] The Chinook language, which was shared among many tribes along the Columbia as a trade language, became the primary language among northwest reservation tribes.[42]

The Chinook Indians were by nature a people who did not savor participation in war, preferring to resolve conflicts through rituals and ceremonies. However, they were skilled with the bow and arrow as their primary weapon to harass their enemies when needed. At the same time, combat was traditionally carried out hand-to-hand in close quarters or with spears and harpoons as the enemy drew near. Skilled spear fishers, the Chinook often turned their spears against their human enemies. Benefitting from their extensive trading enterprise, the Chinook were among the wealthier tribes of the region, so they were able to hire warriors from other tribes as mercenaries to fight for them. The combat objective of the Chinook was not always to kill their enemies but rather, in many cases, to incapacitate them so they could be disarmed and captured to become enslaved to serve the tribe or to be traded.

The Chinook Nation encompassed five tribes: the Clatsop, the Kathalmet, the Lower Chinook, the Wahkiakum, and the Willapa. The closely knit tribes of the nation who shared the Chinookan language each signed the five Anson Dart treaties with the U.S. government at Tansy Point in 1851, securing the right to remain on their historical land, keep their rights to natural resources, and continue to live near the bones of their ancestors. However, those treaties were never formally ratified by the U.S. government.

Among the notable leaders of the Chinook people was Chief Comomly, a trader and navigator. Accounts of the chief are found in the ship's journal of the British merchant ship *Ruby*, which sailed in September 1794, from Bristol, England, under the command of Charles Bishop. In May 1795, the *Ruby* reached the Columbia River as a destination for her journey to procure otter furs from the American Indians to be sold in Canton, England, as part of merchantman Sidenham Teast's trading business. As guests of Chief Comcomly, Bishop and his crew wintered over in Baker's Bay from December 1795 to January 1796 before sailing on to Hawaii with plans to return in time to be the first ship off the coast later in the year—a return journey they did not make.

Under Chief Comcomly's leadership, the Chinook also cordially received the Lewis and Clark expedition, the Corps of Discovery,[43] when it arrived at the source of the Columbia River in 1805.[44] Later that year, after crossing the Rocky Mountains, the Corps of Discover made its way to where the Columbia River reached the Pacific Ocean. The first encounter between the Chinook people and the expedition took place on October 26, 1805. Since the Chinook were experienced in trading with white men, the initial meeting was peaceful despite the ominous warning the expedition had received earlier from the Nez Percé Indians.[45]

The second of the Chinook Nation Chiefs to welcome Lewis and Clark was Chief Coboway, leader of the Clatsop Tribe, whose people the explorers found more friendly and decent than those led by Chief Comcomly. So cordial was the time spent with the Clatsop that when Lewis and Clark departed in March 1806, they relinquished Fort Clatsop to Chief Coboway. The two Chinook chiefs gifted the corps with deer meat and root bread cakes which were reciprocated with medals and trinkets. Similar receptions followed in other Chinook settlements as the expedition moved toward the Pacific Ocean.

The tranquility of the Corps of Discovery's stay in Chinook territory was neither universal nor indefinite. The corps encamped during the brutal winter of 1805–1806 on the southern shore of the Columbia River among the Clatsop Indians. Here the expedition experienced the theft of their supplies, presumably by the Chinook, and the unreasonable charges demanded by the two tribes for replacement food and provisions. Tensions ran high among the soldiers, and Lewis and Clark worked mightily to restrain their men who "… seem[ed] well disposed to kill a few of them [Chinook]."[46] However, the Chinook people extended great friendship to the expedition. They helped the expedition survive the harsh winter before returning to Nez Percé county without firing a single shot at their hosts and benefactors.

In June 1810, John Jacob Astor's Pacific Fur Company was established as a New York—London—China trading enterprise. In September of that year, company partners led an expedition from New York aboard the ship *Tonquin* destined for the Pacific coast to establish a western terminus of their China trade. Upon reaching the Columbia River, they erected at Point George the first permanent U.S. settlement on the Pacific seaboard, Fort Astoria. After several days of successful and profitable meetings with the Chinook people on the north shore of the Columbia River, on the morning of April 7, 1811, the expedition leader, despite a warning from Chief Comcomly of the hazardous waters and fresh winds on the bay, set out for the *Tonquin's* anchorage. After less than a mile of rowing, their boat was swamped, and the passengers, including non-swimmer Duncan McDougal, were in danger of drowning. Fearing potential disaster for his visitors on the open bay, Chief Comcomly trailed McDougall's boat in his light canoe and was on hand to rescue the soaked foreigners.

Despite the centuries of their North American history, today, there is no official Chinook territory—at least not according to the federal government, which refuses to recognize the approximately 2,500-member nation which resides on the Quinault Reservation in Washington State as a sovereign entity despite legal battles stretching over 164 years.[47] The modern Quinault Nation includes the Quinault people and the descendants of five other coastal tribes: Hoh, Quileute, Chehalis, Chinook, and Cowlitz.

The first contact with the Quinault people was in 1775 when a Spanish vessel under Bruno de Hezeta arrived off Port Grenville. Twelve years later, British citizen Charles William Barkley arrived, followed a year later by American Robert Gray. While initially peaceful encounters, they quickly turned violent with the Quinault killing members of both the Spanish and British parties. For eighty years, the Quinault Nation tribes tried unsuccessfully to segregate themselves from the burgeoning white settlements. Under government pressure, the Quinault River Treaty was signed on July 1, 1855. The 1877 General Allotment Act divided the Nation's Reservation into individual allotments until by 1933 virtually no commonly held tribal lands remained.[48]

In 1981, the Chinook tribe again applied for federal recognition for their members, who, upon approval, would be eligible for additional government funding as well as the opportunity to apply for reservation lands close to the traditional homelands. The federal government considered their application for sixteen years before declining approval. The tribe appealed this preliminary ruling. On January 3, 2001, his final day as the head of the Bureau of Indian Affairs, Kevin Gover acknowledged that the Chinook people had suffered at the hands of the U.S. government for too long and granted them federal recognition as a tribe and Indian nation. The Chinook became the 562nd federally recognized Native American tribe.

Eighteen months later, on July 5, 2002, Assistant Secretary of the Interior for Indian Affairs under President George W. Bush, Neal A. McCaleb, signed a reconsidered final determination which rescinded the federal recognition of the Chinook Indian Tribe and Chinook Nation. The Bureau of Indian Affairs' position was that eight of the claims made in the Chinook petition for Federal recognition were improperly considered and given credence.

In August 2017, the Chinook Tribe filed a lawsuit in the U.S. District Court in Tacoma against the U.S. Department of the Interior, arguing for federal status for the tribe. The Interior Department subsequently filed a motion to dismiss the suit. On June 21, 2018, U.S. District Court Judge Ronald B. Leighton denied seven of the claims by the government to dismiss the case, thus allowing the Chinook suit for Federal status to continue. As of early 2022, the Chinook people are still fighting for federal recognition and the benefits their people would derive from it.

Including its Vietnam War service, the *Chinook* has become the Army's most versatile heavy-lift, tandem rotor blade helicopter. It continues the proud Native American tradition of the tribe for which it is named of carrying essential supplies, equipment, and warriors when they are needed on the diverse and rugged battlefield.

CH-54 TARHE

September 1969, the Tarhe *is on the ramp at Da Nang Air Force Base, ready for the first bombing mission with the M-121 10,000-pound "daisy-cutter" bomb. (Courtesy of Jim Oden via the VHPA Calendar Program.)*

With the S-56 (Army H-37A) in the Sikorsky lineage, the company had a testbed for further evolutions in the heavy-lift cargo/passenger cabin helicopters. In early 1955, Igor Sikorsky launched discussions for his vision of a new helicopter capable of carrying heavy cargo loads externally rather than internally loaded in the aircraft cabin, which appeared feasible given his idea was for a stick-like structure aircraft without a cargo cabin. The structure would carry all the mechanical systems, and the reduced fuselage weight would be translated into additional carrying capacity. Additionally, Igor envisioned a rear-facing pilot's station with an unrestricted view of the cargo, facilitating precise aircraft maneuvering for attachment/detachment operations.

By harvesting the two Pratt & Whitney R-2800-50 piston engines, rotors, and the dynamic systems of the H-37A, they were then integrated with the fuselage and landing gear of the crane. The re-use of previously proven engines, main rotors, and transmission would allow Sikorsky to accelerate development and minimize actual flight testing of his heavy lift concept aircraft. With company go-ahead and shared U.S. Navy and corporate funding, work on the S-60 Heavy Lift Crane began on May 1, 1958,[1] was completed on March 18, 1959, and made its first flight on

197

March 25, 1959.[2] The Navy accepted one of Sikorsky's S-60 models for its evaluation and found that the aircraft was underpowered for its intended missions. Over the next two years, the S-60, before it was destroyed in April 1961,[3] would accumulate 335 flight hours during which it would demonstrate its advantages: "unobstructed visibility of the cargo, larger cargo size not limited by cabin dimensions, greater payloads, and lower production costs than cabin helicopters."[4] Thus began the development of the series of Sikorsky "sky cranes."

On August 27, 1958, CONARC approved and sent to the Department of the Army a Qualitative Materiel Requirement for a flying crane capable of lifting twelve tons.[5] However, with the high development and production expense and the limited application of the aircraft, the incremental development process was held in abeyance. Renewed Army acquisition interest began in 1960, and by May 1962, Sikorsky began flying a twin turboshaft engine aircraft, the S-64 *Skycrane*. The new heavy-lift helicopter was terrific. Sikorsky found it possible to land and release one load, move to a second lift, hook up, and take off with the latter within one minute with its aft-facing pilot's position.

In October 1961, the Army requested a CONARC review "covering operational and organizational concepts, essentiality, and priority of the aerial crane development."[6] A DA proposed five-year development program emerged following the review for a twenty-ton payload aerial crane for the fiscal year 1962–1967 period. CONARC responded by challenging the Army program, indicating that it believed the *Chinook* could fulfill the heavy equipment lift requirement and that crane development would jeopardize other critical development requirements. CONARC counter-proposed that DA monitor the West German *Bundeswehr* evaluation of the Sikorsky S-64. After that assessment, if the U.S. required additional testing aircraft, it could acquire no more than two helicopters through a rental or loan agreement with Sikorsky. CONARC objections notwithstanding, the Army continued to develop the CH-54.

Buoyed by the success of the S-60, Sikorsky was willing to commit additional internal research and development funds to develop a turbine engine version of the S-60, the S-64 *Skycrane*, that would ultimately become the Army's CH-54. The company envisioned the helicopter as a "heavy cargo transport with quick, safe, and efficient turn-around time due to its external cargo configuration."[7] It differed from the S-60 in that it had a pair of Pratt & Whitney T73-P-1 4500 turbine engines mounted side-by-side on top of the fuselage boom, each producing 4,050 shaft horsepower (shp) while turning the six-blade main rotor. Weighing 20,700 pounds, it could lift 20,000 pounds while cruising at one hundred nautical miles per hour (115 mph). (The CH-54B with two Pratt & Whitney T73-P-700 turbine engines could lift over 40,000 pounds.) Sikorsky delivered the first CH-54A prototype to the Army for testing at Fort Benning, which first flew on May 9, 1962[8], while the remaining two prototypes were destined for testing by the U.S. Army in Europe. The following year, the Army ordered six production models of the *Tarhe* and accepted the first aircraft on June 30, 1963.[9]

Like the UH-1A, the CH-54 enjoyed the logistical and operational advantages derived from the advent of turbine power. Turbine engines required less maintenance, and because they ran at a constant speed, they allowed the aircrew to focus on mission performance versus continuous engine speed monitoring.

Since its mission was cargo carrying, the Army did not prioritize speed among its top requirements for the aircraft. The aft-facing pilot, one of three onboard, was able to maneuver the helicopter for attaching and detaching its load and fly the aircraft in search of a suitable landing zone for their load. The landing gear on the helicopter could be hydraulically lengthened or shortened, allowing the craft to crouch onto its load, lift it off the ground, and, if necessary, taxi without a suitable take-off site.

As the development of the CH-54 neared its conclusion and production was anticipated, the Army considered the helicopter's common usage name, and ultimately settled upon "Tarhe" (pronounced, Tar-Hay) in honor of a noted Wyandotte Indian Chief of the Porcupine Clan in Ohio.

On November 7, 1968, Sikorsky announced that it had received a contract from the Army to improve the CH-54A. The Army wanted to increase the aircraft's payload capacity to 12.5 tons and improve the engine, gearbox, rotor head, and structure. For the CH-54B, the Army also sought improvement in altitude performance and operating capability in hot weather. The first two CH-54Bs were accepted by the Army the following year.

The Army ultimately purchased ninety-two production *Tarhe* helicopters for heavy-lift aviation units in the United States, the Republic of Vietnam, and the Federal Republic of Germany. That number included sixty-seven CH-54A and twenty-five improved CH-54B models, which went into Army service in 1969. Five of the original version pre-production aircraft were sent to Vietnam for service and evaluation with the 1st Cavalry Division. After their thorough in-country field evaluation, the Army placed orders for fifty-four of the CH-54A aircraft. The first production CH-54s began arriving in Vietnam in 1965. Only the CH-54A models were deployed and flown in Vietnam. The forty-two *Tarhes* that went to Vietnam were assigned to the 273rd, 295th, 343rd, 355th, and 478th Aviation Companies (Heavy Helicopter).[10] The Aviation Companies also had the *Tarhe*'s universal cargo pods to carry up to eighty-seven battle-ready soldiers or serve as mobile hospitals, command posts, or quarters for troops. During the first two years of the *Tarhe*'s operations in-country, it recovered 357 downed allied aircraft valued at more than one hundred times the cost of a single CH-54 helicopter.[11] The CH-54A also served as an ersatz bomber on a few occasions. The aircraft was distinctive in that it was among the few that could pick up, carry, and drop the M-121 10,000-pound 'daisy-cutter' bomb from an altitude of 6,000 feet. The bomb was used when the ground forces needed to create and clear a helicopter landing zone,[12] and would detonate at about three feet above the ground and clear an area of one hundred feet in diameter.[13]

With the deployment of the 1st Cavalry Division to Vietnam, a fuller understanding and appreciation of air mobility came to light. Rather than just the utility of moving men and equipment from one place to another by rotary-wing aircraft, air mobility was the reality of a balance of both maneuver and firepower. However, with the introduction of the 1st Cavalry Division and its fleet of turbine-powered utility helicopters, the prospect of infantry soldiers outrunning their supporting firepower, especially their supporting artillery, became a genuine possibility. What was especially needed was supportive weapons that could achieve the same mobility as the supported infantry.[14] Ultimately, the Army needed a heavy-lift helicopter that would replace the CH-37 *Mojave*.

Infantry and field artillery soldiers have long enjoyed a symbiotic relationship in battle. The infantryman expects and receives continuous cannon fire support regardless of where he maneuvers or when he needs it. On the other hand, the artilleryman depends upon the infantry to secure his firebases and ensure the uninterrupted availability of his resupply routes. The terrain and rapid infantry mobility in Vietnam threatened this long-held relationship. With the advent of the airmobile division, organizational designers recognized that the traditional general support 155-mm howitzers would have to be abandoned. A greater dependency was placed upon the direct support of 105-mm howitzers, which could be airlifted by the CH-47 *Chinook* helicopter. However, once in-country, the 1st Cavalry Division was continuously augmented with a non-organic 155-mm howitzer battalion with sufficient CH-54s to provide it with extended range, medium fire support.

The *Tarhe* was a dramatic collection of aviation innovations when it appeared on the scene. Its turbine engines were lighter due to the elimination of one stage of gearing; the lost weight could in turn be translated into additional lift potential. The aircraft also had an automatic flight control system and altitude hold, a boon to the helicopter while flying under instrument flight conditions. In 1962, it had the first fly-by-wire controls. Since the fuselage was a unique skeletal frame design, the airframe had a minimal weight, and there was full access for inspection and maintenance operations.

The *Tarhe* Finds Its Place in Vietnam Airmobility

The Army's expectation for high-volume, sea-based logistics led to the acquisition of the CH-54 *Tarhe*. Anticipating that a greater quantity of in-theater equipment and supplies would arrive by sea rather than by air, the Army intended to use the CH-54 to unload ships anchored offshore. The feasibility of ship-to-shore transfer by helicopter would eliminate the need to construct extensive port facilities and substantially speed up offloading. Ultimately, little of this kind of transfer work was performed by the *Tarhe*. The 478th Heavy Helicopter Company, 44th Air Transportation Battalion, received the first CH-54s and after training with the new aircraft, deployed to Vietnam to support the 1st Cavalry Division (Airmobile). New equipment training (NET) on the operation and maintenance of *Tarhe* was conducted at the Sikorsky plant in Stratford, Connecticut, for the pilots and crew members before taking charge of their new aircraft. A thirty-day school supplemented the factory training at Nha Trang after the crews arrived in-country.[15] *Tarhe* instructors and aviators had immense confidence in their aircraft, claiming that "the *Tarhe* could lift the world if it could only find a place to fasten the hook."[16]

During the period of January-February 1966, the 1st Cavalry Division and the 22nd ARVN Division participated in Operation MASHER-WHITE WING with an initial air assault into the Cay Giep Mountains. Subsequently, they moved to the Bong Son Plains, the An Lao Valley, the Kim Song Valley, and ultimately Cay Giep Mountains. The joint allied force was able to drive the 3rd North Vietnamese Army regulars out of the area. This operation was the first time the CH-54 airlifted 155-mm howitzers in a combat operation.[17]

An early problem during the CH-54's tour in Vietnam was the ingestion of dust stirred up by the rotation of its mammoth blades into the twin turbines. Sikorsky adapted engine air particle separators from giant earthmoving equipment to address the problem. With the extra power available from the engines, the separators did not negatively impact the helicopter's performance.[18]

On April 19, 1968, the 1st Cavalry Division was called upon to deploy to the I Corps Tactical Zone in the northernmost region of South Vietnam to participate in Operation DELAWARE/LAM SON 216 in the A Shau Valley. Operation DELAWARE was a coordinated airmobile and ground attack by elements of four divisions—the 1st Cavalry, the 25th Infantry, the 101st Airborne, and the ARVN 1st Infantry Division. The 1st Brigade of the 1st Cavalry Division built up the A Luoi airfield on the Valley floor. It did this by flying in heavy engineer equipment, sectionalized into loads that could be lifted by *Tarhe* helicopters. These lifts were possible by providing the aircraft with only enough JP-4 fuel to make the round trip. Thus each helicopter had sufficient lift capability to sling load this heavy engineer equipment over the ridgelines.[19]

During his tour of duty in Vietnam, the author, in April 1969, while traveling in Thua Thien Province west on Route 547 from Hue near the Perfume River,

CH-54 Tarhe *is warming up. (Courtesy of the author.)*

witnessed a CH-45A[20] working with an engineer bridging load. The helicopter lifted off the ground and maneuvered to a fifty-nine-foot, 15,000-pound girder bridge section. A ground guide standing inside the bridging section attached the bridge rigging to the helicopter's lowered cargo hoist. The guide did not need a static electricity discharge pole—he merely held the clevis until it was secure in the hoist. After the guide's work was completed, he left the area while the pilot raised the aircraft to the height of the combined hoist cable and bridge rigging. With

CH-54 Tarhe *is hovering to connect with the engineer bridge load. (Courtesy of the author.)*

the bridging entirely off the ground, a second ground guide played out a stabilizing drogue chute attached to the rear of the bridge section. The aircraft hesitated while the pilot confirmed the stability of the load and the absence of any swinging pendulum motion. The rotor downdraft created a small dust cloud and fully inflated the parachute. The helicopter continued its ascent and departed to the northwest to deliver its load.

Not much has been recorded about the Army's experience with the universal mobile pods included in the CH-54's equipment. The pods were intended to carry up to eighty-seven troops, a basic unit of a hospital, troop quarters, or a mobile command post. The "people pod," as it was called, initially received mixed reviews from passengers who feared that the pod might detach while in flight; the installation of positive-locking bolts overcame this trepidation. Army records also indicate that the 1st Cavalry Division experimented with the pods for its forward command post. Based at Landing Zone Two Bits, the division practiced a movement of its forward headquarters to An Khe for twenty-four hours and then returned to Two Bits. The first pod was set aside for the G-2 and G-3 Operations Center, while the second pod contained the Fire Support Coordination Center and other control elements. With a complete, integrated communications system, the forward command post could take up operational control of the division as soon as it was emplaced. Although logically and efficiently laid out as a command center, the division concluded that the two pods "were really a headache to emplace in Vietnam and terribly immobile once emplaced."[21] After returning to the original divisional base, the 1st Cavalry Division discontinued using the impractical command center pods.

The *Tarhe* helicopters were again called upon to support the Division during its participation in the Cambodian campaign, Operation TOAN THANG 43, TOAN THANG 5, and TOAN THANG 46, from May 1, 1970, to June 30, 1970. The division's organic CH-54s were augmented by the 273rd Aviation Company (Heavy Helicopter) for the campaign's duration. The 273rd flew 2,486 sorties during the campaign and lifted essential pieces of engineering equipment (272 bulldozers, 54 backhoes, and 41 road graders).[22] This was in addition to the standard mission of airlifting 155-mm howitzers within the combat zone. The company also recovered numerous downed aircraft.

Further to its outstanding operational performance in Vietnam, the CH-54 achieved some notable firsts among rotary-winged aircraft. When equipped with the auxiliary equipment pod, it became the first helicopter to lift ninety people—three-man crew and eighty-seven combat troops—and achieve a world record on April 29, 1965.[23] The *Tarhe* also held four National Aeronautic Association altitude records. Most notably, on December 30, 1968, a CH-54A climbed to an altitude of over 31,280 feet[24], and when it passed through 30,000 feet, it was still climbing at 995 feet per minute.[25] The ultimate altitude record of the *Tarhe* would never be known, given the darkness that forced the termination of the flight. The CH-54A also held records for the speed climb: 3,000 meters in 96.8 seconds, 6,000 meters in 211.5 seconds, and 9,000 meters in 454.4 seconds.[26]

During the Vietnam War, nine CH-54s were lost, primarily to accidents and, in one case, to hurricane weather conditions. One aircraft was lost to enemy 37-mm cannon fire while delivering a howitzer to a fire support base in the A Shau Valley in 1968. Among these downed aircraft, five pilots and seven crewmen were lost.

In the late 1960s and early 1970s, the CH-54 was gradually withdrawn from front-line service and transferred to CONUS-based units of the Army National Guard and Reserve. They were supplanted by the CH-47B and C, the Army replacement tandem rotor heavy-lift helicopter with both internal and external load capabilities. On January 10, 1993, the CH-54 flew its last mission with a Nevada National Guard unit,[27] D Company, 113th Aviation, the last *Tarhe*-equipped unit to relinquish its CH-54s.[28]

After its military service, the CH-54 continued to be quite productive in its second career. In 1993, the nation watched as a *Tarhe*, owned and operated by Erickson Air-Crane Company of Central Point, Oregon, was used to remove and replace Thomas Crawford's bronze statue of *Freedom* from the dome of the U.S. Capitol building in Washington, D.C., where it had stood since 1863, to undergo a complete facelift and refurbishment. Even today, civilian contractors employ the CH-54 to support the U.S. Forest Service in fighting forest fires, who take advantage of its lift capacity which allows the helicopter to bring large quantities of water for precision drops on fire sites.

A Chief of the Wyandotte[29] Nation

Chief Tarhe was born in 1742 near present-day Detroit. He is variously referred to as Tarhee, Takee, or the Crane and the French called him Le Grue, Le Chef Grue, or Monsieur Grue.[30] The English knew him by the Anglo-American exonym "Chief Crane." The Wyandotte elders referred to his name as "at him" or "at the tree." They may have chosen the latter as a reflection of his height, for, at six feet four inches tall, he towered over his brethren, who rarely achieved six feet.

Chief Tarhe remained consistent and constant in his faithfulness to the American cause. A possible rationale for bestowing the Wyandotte name on the CH-54 requires a brief look back into American colonial history and the Northwest Indian Wars.

Wyandot Chief Tarhe. (By Unknown author - Taylor, William Alexander (1909) Centennial history of Columbus and Franklin County, Ohio, 1, Chicago: S J Clarke Publishing Company, p. 71, Public Domain, https://commons.wikimedia.org/w/index. php?curid=14526238)

The people of the Wyandotte Nation are the descendants of the Wendat (Huron) Confederacy, the Attignwantan Nation, and the Khionontateronon (Petun) Nation. They had their territorial home near Georgian Bay of Ontario, Canada, and Lake Huron. Many of the original twelve tribes of the Nation no longer exist. Pressured by the Iroquois, with whom they were fierce enemies, the European settlers, especially the French whom they encountered in the early sixteenth century, the Wyandotte left their traditional home and migrated southward. Finally, the U.S. government and its various land treaties forced the Wyandotte to move into Michigan, Ohio, Kansas, and, ultimately, Oklahoma.

Initial encounters between Europeans and the Wyandotte Nation came in the 17th Century with French trappers and missionaries, at which time the Native Americans subsisted on the fruits of their hunting and fishing. They shifted to an agrarian lifestyle when they migrated from their traditional home. They and their Huron allies fell to the Iroquois Confederacy in 1649,[31] and fled to present-day Mackinac Island, Michigan. The Nation would continue to flee the advance of the Iroquois Confederacy until 1700. A year later, the tribe settled at the French outpost in Detroit.[32]

During the years before the American Revolution, the eyes of the colonists along the Atlantic seaboard and the surrounding environs turned westward, looking for new lands to occupy and cultivate. Like most American Indians living in the region, Chief Tarhe opposed the increasingly invasive white settlement of the Ohio region and fought to prevent the encroachment of new settlers onto Indian land. In the Proclamation of 1763, the British declared to the colonists that the lands west of the Appalachian Mountains belonged to the American Indian tribes, and that they were not to attempt to move into these tribal areas. However, the proclamation was largely ignored, and a significant westward migration soon ensued. As the encroachers arrived, more frequent combative encounters followed.

In 1774, the governor of Virginia, John Murray, the Fourth Earl of Dunmore, sent troops to attack members of the Shawnee and Mingo Nations, who were led by the Shawnee leader Chief Cornstalk with assistance from Chief Tarhe. While Chief Tarhe was not considered a genuinely great warrior within his tribe, this was most likely due to the fact that excellence was commonplace in a nation of warriors. The

Treaty of Camp Charlotte concluded the war, which ceded Shawnee land south of the Ohio River to the colonists. With the treaty and the exchange of pledges between the parties, Tarhe honored the peace between white settlers and the region's Indian inhabitants.

As a provision of the 1783 Treaty of Paris that ended the American Revolution, the Northwest Territory was ceded to the United States. The territory included the land west of Pennsylvania, north of the Ohio River, east of the Mississippi River, and south of the Canadian border, and encompasses the present-day states of Ohio, Indiana, Illinois, Michigan, Wisconsin, and the eastern portions of Minnesota. However, neither party included in the negotiations the resident Native American Indians that claimed the region as their tribal homes or any other spokesperson for their interests. Such an oversight would eventually contribute to two of the young American Army's most significant battlefield defeats up to that time.

In 1790, President Washington dispatched a punitive expedition of the First American Regiment and 1,500 militiamen from Kentucky and Pennsylvania under Brigadier General Josiah Hamar to the Northwest Territory in order to deal with the marauding Indians attacking American settlers. Little Turtle masterfully led his forces, inflicting heavy casualties on Harmar's troops during the battle of October 19 and 22. The victory and ensuing rout served to further embolden Little Turtle's warriors against the encroaching Americans.

On September 17, 1791, another expedition, again comprised of the First American Regiment, one other infantry regiment, Kentucky militiamen, and a few cavalry troopers under Major General Arthur St. Clair headed for the Northwest Territory with the same objectives that President Washington had initially put forth. On November 4, after advancing a mere ninety miles, the St. Clair force was surprised and viciously attacked by Little Turtle along the Wabash River. Over 600 members were killed, and countless others who were abandoned or wounded were scalped by the Indians. St. Clair and his remaining forces retreated to Fort Washington.

Dismayed by the humiliation at the hands of the Native American warriors, Congress agreed to the reorganization of the Army as the Legion of the United States on March 5, 1792. The Legion comprised 5,120 infantry, riflemen, artillery, and dragoons. For its commander, Washington and Secretary of War Henry Knox decided upon a distinguished Revolutionary War leader, Major General "Mad Anthony" Wayne. While General Wayne was building and training his force during the two years that followed, the Federal Government was in peace negotiations with the Indians.

By the spring of 1794, Wayne's Legion was ready to deploy, and, by August, it reached northwestern Ohio and the Maumee River. Shawnee Chief Little Turtle and his warriors were set to ambush Wayne's force at a place called Fallen Timbers, named thus due to a tornado having previously toppled hundreds of trees there. However, Wayne quickly assessed the situation and ordered a bayonet charge which flushed the defenders from their hidden positions among the fallen timbers and exposed them to musket fire. The battle was over in less than an hour, and the victory was decisive.

During the Battle of Fallen Timbers, Chief Tarhe bravely led the Wyandotte against General Anthony Wayne. Recognizing the magnitude of the defeat and the consequences for his people, Tarhe once again supported making peace with the settlers and signed the Treaty of Greenville on August 3, 1795.[33] Then and afterward, his objectives in negotiations were always the same: "to hold his tribe together, to serve the other tribes in the area, and to relinquish each parcel of land only after the pressure had become unbearable."[34] Other signatories from the Western Confederacy were representatives of the Delaware, Shawanee, Ottawa, Chippewa, Pattawatima, Miami, Eel River, Wea, Kickapoo, Piankeshaw, and Kaskaskia. Even after the Treaty of Greenville, other American Indian leaders, including Tecumseh, attempted to establish a united American Indian confederation in the Ohio Country to unite against the settlers. Tarhe, however, advised the Wyandotte to honor the treaty that they had signed. Twice after the Treaty of Greenville went into effect, Tarhe and his fellow tribal leaders signed reaffirmations of peaceful intentions and renewed treaties of friendship with the government of the United States. The first was by letter to President James Madison on September 26, 1810.[35] The second was a Treaty of Peace and Friendship on December 21, 1814, between the Northwestern tribal leaders and the United States Commissioners William Henry Harrison and Lewis Cass.[36]

In 1812, the British and the Americans were at war again. Although Tarhe was in his seventies, he joined in the conflict as an ally of the United States and was present at the Battle of the Thames in 1813. After the war, Tarhe settled in Cranetown, Ohio, and remained there until his death at age seventy-six in November 1818.

In its determination to name the CH-54 helicopter "*Tarhe*," the Army determined that he was a noted Wyandotte Indian Chief of the Porcupine Clan in Ohio, who had fought alongside the United States Army during the formative conflicts in the late eighteenth century. Settlers throughout Ohio knew him "as a venerable, intelligent and upright man."[37] Peace Treaty Commissioner William H. Harrison cited Chief Tarhe as "the noblest of all Indian Chiefs in the region."[38]

Among the helicopters used during the Vietnam War, the CH-54 was one which the Army identified its rationale for the name selection. That rationale included:

- The CH-54 was the helicopter with the largest payload in the Army inventory.
- Chief Tarhe was renowned for his outstanding leadership and endurance.
- The helicopter was a flying crane honoring the name of the Indian Chief.
- Chief Tarhe held the Indian tribes together through negotiation with their adversaries rather than engaging in battles.

- The crane bird has long legs and a passive disposition rather than an aggressive nature.
- The CH-54's mission was logistic support rather than an aggressive attack.[39]

Some other accounts attribute the naming honor partly to Chief Tarhe's tall, slender build. Regardless of which rationale was more accurate, the choice was perfect.

While the distinctive sound of the *Iroquois* was unforgettable, the ungainly silhouette of the *Tarhe* was so distinguishable that no veteran of the Vietnam War who ever saw one would forget the experience. It served the Army and the National Guard for less than three decades but continues today with some of the most unimaginable heavy lifts that the civilian sector can conceive of. Similarly, it is hard to imagine that Chief Tarhe would not be justifiably proud of the helicopter that bears his great name.

OH-58 KIOWA

OH-58A Kiowa *at the Pho Loi POL point. (Courtesy of Donovan Earhart via VHPA Calendar Program.)*

When Bell Helicopter's YOH-4A was not selected in the original LOH competition in 1960 because it was too heavy and did not satisfy the Army's performance requirements, the company began working on a civilian version of the helicopter—one which would offer a sales potential for a market expected to average one hundred units per year for the next five years. Bell also sought to correct issues surrounding the marketing of the aircraft. The aircraft earned the moniker Ugly Duckling because of its lack of sex appeal due to its bulbous bubble nose and traditional boom and tail design. Its "utilitarian appearance made it a hard sell."[1] The fuselage was redesigned to be more aesthetically appealing, and sixteen cubic feet of additional cargo space was added.[2] The result was the Model 206A JetRanger, which received FAA certification in October 1966 and rolled off the production line to commercial sales in January 1967.[3]

As Hughes Tool Company Aircraft Division struggled to fulfill their contractual obligations for *Cayuse* production levels and to replace combat losses, the unit price of the OH-6 escalated to almost twice its original price. At the same time, the Army's role in Vietnam was expanding with a greater demand for aviation assets, including the LOH. The Army decided to reopen the competition in order to prompt the creation of a capable platform at a more affordable price.[4] In turn, Bell offered its remodeled Model 206A and the incumbent Hughes presented the OH-6.

209

Fairchild-Hiller, a competitor in the original competition with its YOH-5A design, did not participate. To reopen the LOH procurement, the Army had to confront the possibility that research and development of the new aircraft might be governed by the terms of early inter-service agreements, which, for cost savings purposes, stipulated that either the Air Force or the Navy would lead the process. However, an additional provision of the agreements permitted the Army to lead and procure for itself an off-the-shelf civilian helicopter if it could demonstrate that the platform would meet Army requirements. In turn, the Army solicited for an aircraft already commercially available and thus avoided most of the helicopter's development costs being added to the service's price tag. It also declared its intent to award a multi-year, fixed-priced production contract to preclude another case of rapid price escalation.

In March 1968, the Army selected the Bell Model 206A, designated it the OH-58A, and named it *Kiowa*. With the selection of Bell, the company received a multi-year production contract for the delivery of 2,200 aircraft. At the time of the *Kiowa* contract award, Bell's production facilities were fully committed to their contracted production runs of the UH-1 helicopter series. To satisfy the *Kiowa* requirements, Bell signed a five-year agreement with Beech Aircraft to supply Bell's airframes and other accessories for the OH-58A.[5] Over time, Bell transferred the *Kiowa* and civilian JetRanger production to the company's facility in Mirabel, Quebec, Canada.

The Army Aviation Materiel Command (AMCOM) commander, Major General John Norton, accepted the first production unit of the OH-58A in May 1969,[6] and almost sixty days later, on August 17, 1969, quantities of the *Kiowa* began arriving in Vietnam along with a NETT made up of Army and Bell Helicopter personnel. All of the NETT's officers were Vietnam veterans and highly experienced Army helicopter pilots. The team was charged with thoroughly indoctrinating the "Vietnam-based helicopter units in every aspect of the aircraft's operation and maintenance."[7] Although the new Bell production contract replaced the Hughes LOH contract, the OH-58A was not an automatic operational replacement for the *Cayuse*. The two aircraft, OH-6A and the OH-58A, would continue operating simultaneously in Vietnam until the war's end.

The redesigned Bell Helicopter aircraft had a low silhouette and a single two-bladed main rotor powered by an Allison 250-C18 gas turbine engine. The turbine produced 317 shp and a maximum airspeed of 132 mph. In addition to a limited self-deployment capability, the *Kiowa* was air transportable aboard inter-theater and intra-theater USAF aircraft like the C-141, C-5, and the C-130. Bell went on to produce 2,038 OH-58A helicopters from 1968 through 1973.

The *Kiowa* in Vietnam

Once in the country, the OH-58A operated with air cavalry, field artillery, and attack helicopter units. Additionally, it was configured for medical evacuation, troop transport, and external lift tasks with its external hook. Like the *Cayuse*, the *Kiowa* served as a light observation and scout helicopter and was frequently paired with a UH-1 gunship or the AH-1G *Cobra* to draw enemy fire by flying low and slow, then would mark the target for gunship attack, and finally control the engagement. The *Kiowa* crew conducted the mission's bomb damage assessment (BDA) in a post-strike role.[8] Used in this role, the *Kiowa* could be armed with the M27 armament subsystem and a port side-mounted gun mount for the M134 Gatling machine gun (7.62-mm "Mini-gun"). However, the vibration from the mini-gun proved too great for the initial *Kiowa* airframe, so it was not reintroduced until the frame was rebuilt for the OH-58D configuration. The OH-58A could also be armed with the XM8 armament subsystem, a single M129 40-mm grenade launcher interchangeable with the port side mounted M27 mini-gun.[9]

Ten months after the first OH-58A helicopters arrived in Vietnam, troopers of the 3rd Squadron, 17th Air Cavalry ("Silver Spurs") began receiving the *Kiowa* helicopters to replace their OH-6A *Cayuse* scout helicopters. The *Kiowa* also took up the *Cayuse's* aero-scout missions, emphasizing the slow speed, low altitude, aircrew tenacity, and sheet metal and combat damage repair skills of the unit's maintenance personnel. The squadron's troopers did not universally acclaim the squadron's transition to the *Kiowa*. For some, the OH-58A was considered "less agile, under-powered, but slightly faster" than its *Cayuse* predecessor.[10] The *Kiowa* was also assessed as requiring more maintenance and revision of the aero-scout tactics than in use with the *Cayuse*.[11]

The "Silver Spurs" would go on to take their OH-58A scouts (Aero-Scouts), AH-1 gunships (Aero-Weapons), and UH-1 lift (Aero-Rifle) aircraft into Cambodia during the period from May 6 to June 29, 1970. The squadron conducted daily visual reconnaissance (VR) missions to locate "enemy units, base camps, caches, lines of communication, and infiltration routes; and [...] inflicted heavy casualties against a numerically superior force."[12] For this period and these actions, the squadron and its attached units were awarded the Valorous Unit Award, considered the equivalent of the individual degree of heroism required for the Silver Star, the Army's third-highest award for valor.[13]

In the 1970s, the Army began evaluating its need for a more capable scout aircraft to partner with the new AH-64 *Apache* attack helicopter, which replaced the AH-1 *Cobra*. Forgoing the development of a brand new scout helicopter, the Army turned to improving the *Kiowa*. By 1978, in its life after Vietnam, the Army began to convert some of its OH-58A aircraft to the OH-58C configuration, using the latter's more powerful engine and its dynamic flight components. Besides avionics upgrades, the aircraft was equipped with a radar detector to warn the crew when they were in proximity to an anti-aircraft radar. Some of the C models were also equipped with the AIM-92 Stinger missiles. In 1983 the Army began receiving deliveries of the OH-58D *Kiowa Warrior* helicopter with its Mast Mounted Sight system that expanded its scout role with the addition of a target designation capability for artillery engagement. In 1992, seventy-six of the Army's OH-58A *Kiowa* helicopters received yet another engine upgrade, a thermal imaging system, a law enforcement communications package, and upgraded navigation equipment. Also, because of the size of the imaging system, the original skid gear was replaced with a high-landing-gear skid package for the necessary ground clearance to accommodate the belly-mounted FLIR system. The OH-58A+, as the helicopter was designated, was assigned to Army National Guard (ARNG) Reconnaissance and Aerial Interdiction Detachment (RAID) units as part of the ARNG Counterdrug Program.[14] After forty-two years of faithful service, the venerable Vietnam War veteran OH-58A left service in 2011. As these *Kiowa* aircraft exited, they were replaced by the UH-72A *Lakota* helicopter.

The Native American Kiowa People

Little is known about the prehistoric origins of the Kiowa, with ongoing scholarly debate as to whether they migrated south to the Montana mountains or moved north in more recent times. There is, however, agreement with Spanish sources that the horse-mounted Kiowa were on the Plains in 1732.[15] It is believed that the Kiowa people originated in the northern basin of the headwaters of the Missouri and Yellowstone Rivers that form part of present-day western Montana. By the seventeenth century, the Kiowa had split into two distinct bands. One band, known as the Azatanhop or "angry travelers," moved to the northwest, while the second band of approximately 3,000 members, the Kiowa and Kiowa-Apache, migrated

Three Kiowa delegates at the U. S. Indian Congress of the Trans-Mississippi and International Exposition in Omaha, 1898. From left: Jim Ah-Keah-Boat (Two Hatchet); Frank Tobah (To Bah) or his brother Doyebi, and Jimmy Hummingbird. (Courtesy of the National Museum of the American Indian, Smithsonian Institute P27503A.)

southward to the Black Hills around 1640, where they took up peaceful residence with the neighboring Cheyenne, Arapaho, and Crow Indians. All records of the fate of the Azatanhop were lost after the divide. The Kiowa migration followed the introduction to the tribe of the Spanish horses from the Taos Indians, who, in 1639, had fled their New Mexico pueblos to the lands of the Kiowa, Comanche, and Wichita.[16] The tranquility of the Black Hills was violently ruptured around the mid-seventeenth century when the Ojibwe, through their friendship with the French traders, obtained guns, began to use European goods, and dominated their traditional enemies. They drove the Cheyenne, Arapaho, and Sioux from the Upper Mississippi-Great Lakes region to the present-day Dakotas. This movement forced the Kiowa to move down the Platte River basin and emerge onto the Arkansas, Cimarron, Canadian, and Red River headwaters. There they encountered the Comanche, who occupied the territory after being forced from their former home by the Sioux territorial expansion. The Kiowa eventually settled in New Mexico and Texas, and in 1790 allied themselves with the Comanche.

Among the lore of Native American tribes throughout the United States' history, singular among them is the aggressiveness and tenacity of the Kiowa warriors. The Kiowa and the Kiowa-Apache fought battles against untold Native Americans, including tribal members of the Caddo, Navajo, Ute, Apache, Arapaho, Cheyenne, Sioux, and Osage, as well as non-Native Americans, including Spaniards, Mexicans, and European-Americans.

From the 1830s to the 1860s, Little Mountain was the principal Kiowa Chief. He also recorded much of the tribe's history on buffalo hides. By the 1870s, the Comanche-Kiowa Wars ended, and during that period, several highly influential Kiowa chiefs emerged. Sitting Bear (Satank) was the elder among their leaders who headed the Principal Dogs, a well-known society of the bravest Kiowa warriors dedicated to fighting and warfare. He led the Kiowa against their neighbors, the Cheyenne, Sacs, and the Fox. When the white man appeared, Sitting Bear led raids on settlements, wagon trains, and Army outposts, while the more belligerent of the chiefs was White Bear (Satanta), who led those warriors who were disposed to a prolonged war with the white man. "The Orator of the Plains," as Satanta was also known, spent much of his life fighting U.S. government efforts to force the Kiowa and Comanche Nations onto reservations.[17] He would lead the Kiowa and other plains tribes' warriors on the growing raids of white settlements. Included among them was Kicking Bird, a prominent youthful warrior of Kiowa and Crow descent who would go on to become a principal chief and be instrumental in protecting his people from the hardships accompanying the Red River War of 1874–75. He led the more peaceful faction of the Kiowa and promoted life on the reservation. In 1866, when Chief Little Mountain died of old age, the tribe was torn between the two extremes in their search for a new chief: White Bear on the one side and Kicking Bird on the other. Lone Wolf emerged as the compromise choice, although he, in time, came to support White Bear and the more militant warriors. Lone Wolf and other tribal leaders lost their patience with the white man who failed to fulfill their commitments to the Kiowa while the tribe remained peaceful and on the reservation. Conflict would soon follow.

For almost 200 years, Europeans and Euro-Americans traded with local tribes. Their trading consisted of the exchange of products of the hunt and agricultural fare for cloth, metal goods, and European industrial products. They interacted with the Comanche, Kiowa, Southern Cheyenne, and Arapaho, usually on amicable terms, until the early nineteenth century, when the burgeoning westward migration of the white man descended almost without interruption onto the native lands of the American Indians. During the reservation period, 1868–1906, these tribes found reservation life difficult, as whiskey peddlers, shoddy government annuities, ineffective agents, and buffalo hunters imperiled their economic and cultural existence.[18] White settlers and commercial buffalo hunters encroached on the land of Southern Plains Indians while wagon trains carrying settlers and California-bound gold prospectors traveled the Santa Fe Trail westward. However, as Civil War demands increased, the U.S. Army abandoned the frontier forts previously established to protect the westward migration, leaving settlers vulnerable to Native Americans who increased their attacks in an effort to drive them from their homelands. As a result, the white man was relentlessly subjected to intensified raids during his transit through Native lands.

The conclusion of the War Between the States saw the consummation of the Medicine Lodge Treaty of 1867 between the federal government and some of the Southern Plains tribes. The agreement stipulated that the Native tribes would cease their raiding and relocate to reservations in Indian Territory while the government would provide provisions and guns to the tribes. The government also agreed to allow the tribes to continue their seasonal buffalo hunts on the land south of the Arkansas River, which was a state-owned territory and not federal property.[19] When the Indian migration did not take place as rapidly as the government anticipated, Satanta was seized by General George Custer and detained until the relocation of the Indians took place. In short order, the U.S. government defaulted on the provisions articles of the treaty, and numerous tribal members, starving and exasperated, deserted the Indian Territory reservations only to resume their forays into Texas. By 1871, Satanta was again leading attacks on wagon trains crossing the Texas Panhandle until he was captured, tried for murder, and sentenced to death. His sentence was later changed to life imprisonment, and in 1873 he was released.

For two years, the Army unsuccessfully pursued the Native tribes in the Texas Panhandle, trying to drive them from their encampments and to get them to return to their Indian Territory reservations. At the same time, commercial buffalo hunters, having depleted the buffalo herds in the north, established a trading post at Adobe Walls, Texas, and began depleting the bison herds in the south, which outraged the Comanche and Kiowa warriors led by Quanah Parker. Between 1872 and 1874, white hunters slaughtered almost four million buffalo for their hides and left the unused carcasses rotting on the Plains.[20] On June 27, 1874, Satanta, Lone Wolf, and Quanah Parker led a band of seven hundred Southern Comanche, Kiowa, Kiowa Apache, Cheyenne, and Arapaho. It attacked a buffalo hunters' base at Adobe Walls, triggering the Red River War, which opened on August 30.[21] The twenty-eight hunters held off the superior force of Indians during four days of continuous battle until about one hundred men reinforced the post causing the Indians to retreat.[22] As a result, the tribes split into small bands and began assailing stagecoaches, cattle ranches, and other soft targets in Texas.[23]

The migratory growth and the commercial plundering of buffalo was followed by a further intensification of clashes between the two cultures. Later the U.S. government charged the U.S. Army with the task of forcing all Indigenous tribes from the Texas Panhandle onto the reservations set aside for them in the Indian Territory, present-day Oklahoma. The turbulent Red River War of 1874–1875 saw the U.S. government battling against the Comanche and their allies, the Arapaho,

Cheyenne, and Kiowa. The Army adopted the strategy of burning Indian encampments, killing their horses, and starving their families into submission. The strategy for the Army campaign was to assemble columns of troopers and their supplies to converge on the Indian camps along the headwaters of the Red River from five directions. Elements of the 4th, 6th, 8th, 9th, and 10th Cavalry, as well as the 5th, 10th, and 11th Infantry, or approximately 3,000 federal troops, participated in the campaign, which experienced its first victory at the Battle of Red River on August 30, 1874, where a large band of the Southern Cheyenne was pursued across the lower Palo Duro Canyon.

Two weeks later, Chiefs Lone Wolf, Big Tree, and Satanta led a war party of nearly 400 Comanche and Kiowa warriors against the resupply trains of the 6th Cavalry and 5th Infantry under the command of Captain Wyllys Lyman. During the Battle of Lyman's Wagon Train, the Army suffered its first casualties, one soldier and two civilians. On September 12, 1874, the Native warriors engaged other Army troopers in the Battle of Buffalo Wallow and again at the Battle of Sweetwater Creek before fleeing to join other Indian bands at Palo Duro Canyon for their winter encampment. By September 28, soldiers from the 4th Cavalry and the 10th and 11th Infantry discovered the winter camp and descended into the canyon, attacking the warriors and their families. The Battle of Palo Duro Canyon ended with the camp's destruction, the loss of the entire winter food supply, and the slaughter of more than 1,000 Indian horses.[24] Many of the Palo Duro Canyon survivors began the slow trek back to the reservations in the face of the approaching winter. The canyon battle was the last attempt at armed resistance by the Southern Plains Indians against the white man's encroaching westward migration. In October 1874, Satanta was recaptured and imprisoned until his suicide death on October 11, 1878.

The Army maintained its pressure on the impoverished and demoralized Indians throughout the fall and winter months. Throughout the period, the Army continued to force more and more warriors back into Indian Territory and onto the reservations there. One of the largest single-day Indian surrenders took place at the Darlington Agency when 320 Cheyenne laid down their arms.[25] The last marauding Comanche and free-roaming Southern Plains Indians under Chief Quanah Parker surrendered at Fort Sill in the Indian Territory on June 2, 1875. With the conclusion of the Red River War, although only a year in length, the Texas Panhandle was opened up to the immense cattle business with the vast ranches there and the crisscrossing trails leading to the railheads in Kansas. Farmers soon followed, transforming the prairie land into vast acreages of cotton and wheat.

Many of the great Native American chiefs who led their tribes in war and peace found their final resting place on Chiefs' Knoll in the Post Cemetery at Fort Sill, Oklahoma. Due to this distinction, the cemetery is frequently referred to as the "Indian Arlington" in solemn reference to Arlington National Cemetery, where many of America's great military leaders and private soldiers are interred. Among those buried on Chiefs' Knoll are Chiefs Satan, Stumbling Bear, Big bow, Kicking

Bird, Satanta, and Pacer of the Kiowa tribe; Chiefs Little Raven, Yellow Bear, and Spotted Wolf of the Comanche; Chiefs Quanah Parker and Ten Bears of the Arapahoe tribe.

While the acknowledgment of the great chiefs of the American west is fitting, this chapter addresses a helicopter whose role in combat would mark it among the prominent scout aircraft flown and available to America's Army; a reputation that would not be fully realized until years after the conclusion of the helicopter war. So, what should be appreciated from its reading is an understanding of that which warrants bestowing the name Kiowa on this aircraft?

As previously recorded, especially during the Indian Wars, the Army depended heavily on Indigenous Americans to serve as scouts. Native scouts from the Apache, Sioux, Kiowa, Cheyenne, and other tribes served faithfully for more than a quarter century. Among those was a Kiowa Sergeant named I-See-O (Tahbone-mah), meaning "Plenty Fires," born circa 1849, and served continuously as an Indian scout from his enlistment in 1889 until he died in 1927.[26] During the final campaigns of the Indian Wars, he served alongside First Lieutenant Hugh L. Scott, who in 1892 organized Troop L of the 7th Cavalry Regiment, and whose enlisted members were all Indian Scouts. The troop served until 1897, when the enlistments of the scouts expired, and was thus disbanded. Scott would later rise to the rank of major general and served as Chief of Staff of the United States Army from 1914 to 1917.

I-See-O was the last member of Troop L and was famously known as one of the greatest Indian peacemakers in the early history of the Oklahoma Territory. He is recognized for his efforts in quieting the members of the Apache and Kiowa tribes that went on the warpath in 1890 during the ghost dance craze, which needlessly claimed the lives of hundreds of Native Americans and white men. His efforts are credited with saving innumerable lives among the soldiers, settlers, and Native Americans. I-See-O and Scott developed a solid and lasting relationship and communicated mainly through Native American sign language, which the scout taught the young officer.[27] Scott also learned the techniques of frontier warfare at the side of the Kiowa scout. Later General Scott, recognized for his success in peacefully handling the issues of the Plains Indians, credited much of his success in the late eighties and nineties to his close friend, I-See-O.

In 1915, General Scott persuaded Congress, by a special act, to grant I-See-O a permanent rank of sergeant for life and allow him to serve on active duty for the remainder of his life; he would be stationed at Fort Sill with quarters provided. According to Scott, I-See-O "has simply been stunned by civilization;"[28] and as a result he chose to live in a teepee in a remote part of the post where he prepared his daily meals over an open fire. Before passing, he was welcomed at the White House in 1925 as a guest of President Calvin Coolidge. On March 11, 1927, he succumbed, following a thirty-day battle with pneumonia, and upon his death, was granted his earnest request to be buried in his Army uniform. Sergeant I-See-O would also receive a sendoff with full military honors as his casket was borne upon an artillery caisson from the Old Post Chapel to the Fort Sill Cemetery. He forever lies among the other honored dead at the Oklahoma post.[29] Furthermore, he was credited with being the oldest soldier on duty with the United States Army at his death.

No soldier or marine with a field artillery MOS will conclude their training without taking time to reflect upon the experiences of instruction conducted in I-See-O Hall. The confluence of an honorable warrior and Native scout, a proud and faithful tribal Nation, and the Army's needs for scouting and reconnaissance capabilities are perfectly merged in the OH-58 *Kiowa*.

Among the Native American tribes, the Kiowa are prominent in their tribe-wide esteem for their veterans, living and deceased. The tribe has a long and distinguished heritage and a culture devoted to honoring the warrior legacy of its members. That reverence for the warrior culture is ingrained among their people, acknowledging undying respect for the "courage it takes to charge into battle in the name of protecting your people and your land."[30] Warriors are without equal and have a uniquely revered standing within the society and culture of the Kiowa Tribe of Oklahoma.

Within the Kiowa, there were six warrior societies, one for young boys and five for adults. The former was the Po-Lanh-Yope (Little Rabbits), whose membership included all young Kiowa boys and served social and educational purposes not involving violence or combat. The Adle-Tdow-Yope (Young Sheep), Tsain-Tanmo (Horse Headdresses), Tdien-Pei-Gah (Gourd Society), and Ton-Kon-Gah (Black Legs or Leggings) were the Kiowa adult warrior societies. The sixth warrior society was that of the Koitsenko (Qkoie-Tsain-Gah, Principal Dogs, or Real Dogs), with just ten members elected by the membership of the four other adult warrior societies and considered the ten most elite warriors of all the Kiowa.

The pinnacle of the tribal warrior hierarchy is the Black Leggings Warrior Society. The Black Leggings Society Ceremonial is the penultimate manifestation of the tribe's reverence toward its warriors within the Society. The Ton-Kon-Gah began centuries ago and has been kept vital through oral histories.

Warrior veneration in Kiowa culture is not an occasional or annual event like the American Memorial Day and Veterans' Day observances. One can rather characterize it like the Marine Corps mystique—"Once a Marine, always a Marine"—except among the Kiowa, once you are a veteran, regardless of which war you fought in or if you fought with your tribe, in a tribal unit of the U.S. military, or as an individual unit member, "… that respect is always given to you."[31]

To the Kiowa warrior, the accolade bestowed by American society and its armed forces pales in comparison to the honor a tribal member receives when granted membership to the Warrior Society. The daughter of a Warrior Society member, Dorothy Whitehorse-Deluane, a Kiowa elder and War Mothers member, observes of the revived Black Leggings Society ceremonial after World War II, "Oh goodness, that arena used to be full of hollering. When I think about it now, we're just the dregs of all that, but still, we're going to keep on. It just fills you with pride."[32] The light that shines on the Kiowa warrior casts its shadow on the family as well. Warriors openly welcome society membership less for themselves but more for their families and future generations so that they can understand the legacy of the tribal and warrior culture and where they, as a family of a warrior, fit into that society.

While the Black Leggings Society had its genesis over three centuries ago, its timeline has been intermittent. From 1890 until 1912, the warriors did not dance, and again they stopped shortly after World War I and returned to the arena in 1958. The rebirth of the warrior societies revitalized the importance of veterans to the Kiowa society, strengthened by the number of veterans from World War II and Korea.

Everything involved in the Black Leggings Society has its roots in ancient traditions. Even down to the Society dress, that lineage has remained unchanged since the 1870s, and the clothing accouterments are all made in the same traditional manner. When it came to their turn to enter the ranks of the society's membership and relate their war stories, Vietnam War veterans were enshrined just as the forebearers were. For centuries, a warrior's war record was preeminent in establishing his status within the tribe; it was the source of the great rewards of the tribe's culture. Most significant among these is membership in the Gourd Clan, reserved for the "strongest, most able-bodied men of the tribe."[33] Elders entrust the sacred duty of protecting the tribe to these warriors. The clan emerged in the eighteenth century as a society for "… warriors and rough riders whose duty it was to police and protect their camps."[34] Over the time of tribal history, the clan added veterans, doctors, lawyers, and other Kiowa men. The only membership requirement is the expectation of bringing honor to the Kiowa people.

The principal ceremony of the Gourd Clan is the Gourd Dance which, through Kiowa oral histories, is said to have emanated from instructions given by a red wolf spirit creature that also, by oral tradition, saved a hungry and dehydrated warrior from starvation. The dance is a prideful and respectful dance honoring male warriors. Over time the Gourd Dance has spread to other tribes and Native American societies; however, most do not enjoy the imprimatur of the Kiowa elders. Only the Kiowa Gourd Clan is known to enforce the traditional tenets of the dance strictly.[35]

The long tale of the OH-58 *Kiowa* and its tortuous journey onto the battlefields of Vietnam is less than glorious. Challenged with becoming the operational equal of the *Cayuse*, the OH-58A *Kiowa* fell short in the eyes of many who flew it. The vernacular monikers bestowed on it by GIs, especially "5.8," i.e., almost "6," reflect the aviator's lack of appreciation for it compared to their preferred nimble scouting aircraft. It would have to wait until decades after the Southeast Asia conflict to reach its fuller capabilities and potential as a warbird and reflective of the Kiowa warrior traditions and Army scout.

WHOM SHALL I SEND?

Then I heard the voice of the Lord saying, Whom shall I send? And who will go for us? And I said, Here am I. Send me!

Isaiah 6:8

With the waning of the 20th century, fewer American service-aged males had military experience, and fewer civilian family members knew someone in the military. Although during significant portions of this period, the military was ranked as the most or one of the most highly respected institutions in the country.

From the early days of the founding of the republic, American colonists and the Founding Fathers challenged the concept of a standing army. Embittered by British regulars in the colonies and even quartered in colonists' homes, there was no affinity for a similar norm in the new nation. The source of manpower needed to win independence and later to confront the Indians on the frontier would be a combination of both the state militia and continental regulars; however, the abhorrence of a standing army led to token enlistments frequently interrupted by desertions, family priorities, or the need to care for crops. The expiration of a term of enlistment was a matter of finality in that when it arrived, the soldier departed the field no matter what the Army was engaged in at the time. And making matters more complicated, those of sufficient wealth were even able to hire a substitute. Frequently, the Continental Army was manned by quotas levied upon the individual colonial militias, which meant a force of mixed and uncertain quality if the quota was numerically satisfied.

Separation of the military—militia, Continental Army, or Regular Army—from the civilian population was a distant, estranged relationship throughout the republic's early history, a popular reality that had survived for many decades. It would take a significant internal conflagration and two global conflicts for that relationship to change. But that estrangement would return and intensify during the Cold War and America's later foreign military adventures. As American abandoned conscription, embraced an all-volunteer force, and increased its reliance upon its uniformed services as an instrument of foreign policy, the experience of military service fell upon a smaller percentage of the nation's population. The vocal majority now resonated with a growing anti-military adventurism sentiment and myopic view of the war and the warrior.

During the twentieth century's global wars "National preparedness mean[t]s [...] first of all, the moral organization of the people, an organization which creates in the heart of every citizen a sense of his obligation for service to the nation in time of war...."[1]

Subsequently national policy was and continues to be confronted with the challenge of marshalling the nation's will to accept proclaimed national security interests, accept the costs in treasure, and endure the human sacrifices needed to persevere.

However, in one particular ethnic segment of the population, respect for the military and the warrior's ethos was never an issue. Native Americans have a history of military service in all of America's wars and conflicts. They were never begrudgingly forced into service despite the less than amicable relationship between the U.S. government and the Native American tribes. As an ethnic population group in American society, Native Americans, as a percentage of their population, have consistently served in the armed forces in more significant numbers than any other ethnic group. One has to wonder why American Indians, Alaska Natives, and Pacific Islanders would willingly serve a government that despoiled their homelands, suppressed their culture and traditions, and incarcerated many of them on reservations in alien territory. However, General MacArthur summed it up best: "In these troublesome times of confuse international sophistication, let no man misunderstand why they do that which they must do. These men will fight and perchance die, for one reason only—for their country—for America."[2] While the rationale is complex, Native Americans have protected their lands, people, and communities for centuries. The warrior's lot in life was to care for his people and help in difficult times. Warriors could be counted upon to do all that was required to ensure the survival of their people, including the sacrifice of one's own life. Many Native Americans thus viewed military service as an extension or continuation of the culturally assigned role of the Native warrior.[3] Those who served were not only burdened with the honor held for such service by their family and tribe, they were also challenged with meeting the expectations of the Indian warrior stereotypes harbored by their non-Native battle buddies, many of whom had never seen a Native American.

More than twenty-seven million American men attained draft age during the Vietnam War—more than half avoided military service through exemptions and deferments. Of the remainder, more than 8,615,000 draft-aged men would serve in all the uniformed services. Of that number, most were volunteers or draft-inspired volunteers, in other words, men who volunteered for service with other than the Army or Marine Corps to avoid being drafted into one of them and serve in combat as an infantryman. Those drafted during the war numbered 2,215,000, of whom only about twenty-five percent would go on to serve in Vietnam. More than 42,000 Native Americans would step forward and serve in Vietnam, the highest per capita service rate of any ethnic group in the United States.

With this preliminary understanding of the Native American motivation for again fighting another white man's war, this chapter presents a few of the individual stories of the warrior's experiences and reminiscences of the Vietnam War. The stories are those of a small number of men of Native American heritage who served as aviators or crew members of the previously presented Army helicopters that bore the names of their ancestral tribes or warrior chiefs. The stories are few not because of the number who served in those capacities but for a variety of other reasons. One is the challenge of identifying from the war's surviving veteran population those who were of Native American heritage (and with the task of deciding which acceptable measure would be used to determine their heritage). Within that population one must then locate those who held and served in positions on Army aircrews. Among the latter the numbers further diminish, as only those who were willing to relate and share their own wartime experiences came forth. Native American veterans of Vietnam were very humble and self-deprecating about their combat service. Those who are willing to share their experiences did so only in the blandest of terms, even if records attest to events of immense courage and sacrifice. Even after sharing their stories, some veterans had second thoughts about allowing their stories to be published, fearing that they would stand out among their peers beyond what their service merited in their minds. History conditioned the warrior's response to his war, so it is my hope that the previous discussions of tribal history and the observations regarding the Vietnam veteran's experience will better frame the perspective on the individual vignettes that conclude this chapter.

One of the challenges for the author is the identification of Native Americans as a racial category. As Dr. Tom Holm, professor of Native American Studies at the University of Arizona observes, there are at least four means of determining Native identity: membership in a federally recognized tribe, self-identification, cultural identification, blood quantum, or a combination of the four.[4] For the narrative that follows in this current chapter and the one that follows, I have relied heavily upon self-identification because that was the basis of the DoD's determination, and it was how individual aviators and crew members identified themselves in response to the quest for their numbers.

A brief discussion of ancestral traditions of the Native warrior will help in the understanding of the expectations and experiences of the Vietnam War Native warrior as he prepared for, experienced, and attempted re-entry into Native society following his combat tour of duty. Historically, a war for the Native American warrior was both a physical and spiritual experience; therefore, he was "ritually prepared for and ceremonially returned from the battlefield."[5] Tribes across the continent conducted military ceremonies for their departing warriors. Zuni medicine men, for example, bestowed a protective blessing upon their war-bound warriors. At the same time, the Navajo used corn pollen and holy water to perform the blessing ceremony for their new soldiers, while the Wisconsin Chippewa honored their enlistees with "going away" and "chief" dances, evoking the guardian spirit to aid and protect them while fighting overseas.[6]

The Native American heritage of arms is long, punctuated by periods of violent war. Unlike their white man counterpart, peace was not the absence of conflict but rather the re-establishment of order. So those who engaged in combat experienced the often violent and tragic disruption of order that was not automatically restored by the cessation of battlefield hostilities. Warriors witnessed and performed extraordinary feats in war from which they were benefactors of great wisdom and yet also burdened with significant needs and unique problems.[7]

Among the twist of fate that stunned the Native warrior was the irony of the treaty rationale of American military involvement in Southeast Asia. American foreign policy in the region was partially predicated on the country's perceived collective defense treaty commitment to the eleven nation signatories to the treaty establishing the Southeast Asia Treaty Organization (SEATO).[8] The nations pledged to act in unity against a common danger. The treaty provided only for consultations in case of aggression against a signatory or protocol state before any combined actions were taken. Thus written, the agreement failed to compel a combined military response to communist aggression in the region against a treaty member. Yet the United States interpreted the treaty's terms as the legal basis for U.S. military involvement in South Vietnam. As chronicled by Paul Eckel, "The United States came to the aid of South Vietnam not because it had to, but because it wanted to and did so with the fullest support of the Congress."[9] For the Native American warrior, whose collective peoples were signatories to more than 400 treaties with the United States government, it was almost unfathomable that they were fighting for a treaty obligation when their country had readily and with impunity violated their treaties with them.

When the Second Indo-China War came to America, Native Americans embraced the war through enlistment and induction because of their tribal patriotism. For them, as members of honorable tribal families and adherents to tribal traditions, service was part and parcel of their ancestral heritage. Native American wartime service in Vietnam followed in the footsteps of the fathers and grandfathers who fought in all of America's earlier wars. As their fathers expected them to serve, they would have the same expectation of their progeny. The net result of such commitment was that while Native Americans during the period of the Vietnam War represented approximately .6 percent of the U.S. population, they comprised nearly 1.2 percent of all the military members who served in the theater.[10] These data translate to one in every four eligible Native Americans who served in Vietnam, compared to one in twelve within the broader American population.

Native Americans endured the rights of passage as they transitioned from civilian to soldier, marine, sailor, or airman. The demands of basic training and future specialized training were well within the capabilities of each warrior recruit. However, for many, the ritualized breaking of traditional familial bonds was difficult to understand and endure, particularly when considering the essentiality of family bonds in the Native American culture.

Stirred by the warrior ethos, many Native Americans sought a training regimen that would ultimately lead to direct combat with the enemy. Being a warrior meant engaging with the enemy *mano a mano*. The predominant military specialties they entered reflected that same spirit with approximately eighty percent, based upon the extrapolation of the Readjustment Counseling Service (RCS) data, serving in traditional combat arms military specialties, i.e., infantry, armor, artillery, combat aviation, etc. They were exposed to the terrors of combat which repeatedly confirmed the disruption of the natural order. Many tribal warriors voluntarily found themselves among the Army and Marine Corps elite, the Long-Range Reconnaissance Patrol (LRRP), and Force Recon. The former was among the "Studies and Observations Group," the euphemism for the Special Operations Group, which undertook the war's most sensitive and covert operations.[11]

Regardless of where or with whom they served, the Native American Vietnam War veterans served with distinction in combat and were faithful to the ancestral traditions of arms. However, when their war ended, the warrior tradition imposed by the U.S. military establishment collapsed. Historically, tribal warriors returned to their heritage homes as a warrior band reflective of the united effort manifest by the collective victory. Only defeat would give cause for warriors to steal back into their villages, usually in the dark of night.[12] With the war in Vietnam, military personnel journeyed to battle, in almost all but a unit's initial deployment, as individual replacements. That is, when major combat units shipped out to Vietnam, they went as an entire unit. Once its members' one-year tour of duty was over, replacements began arriving as individuals. A year later, with their war over and no longer bound by a shared experience, the warrior returned home alone.

Some warriors of Vietnam participated in ceremonies when they returned, just as they had before their departure, which were designed "to either honor a combat survivor and/or heal a returning warrior of his battlefield trauma."[13] Ceremonies were held within Native communities to help bring the returned warrior back into harmony with the natural order, returning to peace. Nearly every Indian society in the United States and Canada has rituals with identifiable functions, including the renewal and the restoration of the tribal bond. Specific examples include the Sun Dance, the Green Corn Dance, the Blessing Way of the Navajo, and the Stomp Dance of the Creeks, Seminoles, and Cherokee.[14]

The tribal elders are the key to maintaining the historical traditions and their linkage to the ceremonies practiced today. They tie the identity of the tribe, different generations, customs, and traditions together. The tribal elders, by their longevity, maturity, and experience, represent wisdom in the tribal society. The returning Vietnam Veterans were thus vested with knowledge and respect from their experiences which very few endured. As a Winnebago elder summarized best, "we honor our veterans for their bravery and because by seeing death on the battlefield, they truly know the greatness of life."[15]

The narratives that follow are those of Native American veterans who experienced the violence and carnage of war up close and personal. They were, in many cases, eye-to-eye with the enemy combatant, determined to end their life. They also witnessed the final moments of their comrades' lives. Each day they mounted up and prepared to carry the fight to the enemy. Their courageous stories are presented on the pages that follow.

Sam Bendickson[16]

Life on an Indian reservation in South Dakota in the 1960s offered little prospect for a prosperous or good life for young Native American men. The lot in life for a reservation native was filled with hopelessness. Even the expectation of high school graduation for most residents was a very distant prospect. One such Sioux male continuously looked above and beyond the horizon, searching for his future. Sam Bendickson, who lived on the Lake Traverse Reservation of the Sisseton Wahpeton Sioux Tribe and frequently stood near the border between North and South Dakota, was mesmerized by the frequent appearance of civilian and military aircraft that overflew the Dakota plains. Seeing those airplanes inspired him with the desire to see what his native land looked like from above and he resolved that one day he would fly.

As his twentieth birthday approached, Sam left his father's cattle ranch and enlisted in the Army at the enlistment station in Sioux Falls to become a helicopter crewman; the realization of his dream and the beginning of an experience that he would oft acclaim as most rewarding. Sam reported to Fort Polk, Louisiana, where he underwent basic infantry training following his induction. In recognition of his qualifications and desire to serve in an aviation MOS, following graduation from basic, he was sent to Fort Rucker for training to become an aircraft crew chief. Like his fellow Native Americans training to be a helicopter crewman, Sam was the only Indian in his class.

As an individual replacement, Specialist Fifth Class Sam Bendickson went to Vietnam in August 1969. After processing, he was assigned to C Troop, 1st Squadron, 9th Cavalry of the 1st Cavalry Division in the III CTZ. He served as a crew chief aboard the premier scout helicopter, the OH-6A *Cayuse*, and, on occasion, as a door gunner on an *Iroquois* troop transport ("slick"). Although trained at Fort Rucker to be a crew chief, the squadron trained their soldiers for door gunner duties, including Sam, who doubled as a gunner when flying in his *Cayuse*. Assigned to Charlie Troop, he spent two weeks with an experienced pilot and the latter's crew to become familiar with the unit's AO and learn the skills, intricacies, and nuances of being a door gunner aboard a fast-moving, agile, and gyrating aircraft. Specialist Bendickson was also given training in emergency flight procedures. Placed in the left-hand seat, he was taught to regain control of the aircraft, fly it, and safely land if the AC was incapacitated.[17] The *Cayuse* was a great ship and named after a fierce and honorable tribe, but that lineage "did not alter my feelings about the missions we flew nor instill any unusual motivation to excel. I just did my job as best as I could each day,"[18] said Sam.

Like his other scout crew comrades, Sam characterized his daily missions as "crazy and dangerous, regardless of his assigned unit." Preparation and missions always began before daylight. "We flew hunter-killer flights. The scouts found them, and the gunships smoked 'em. We got our fair share of the body counts each day. We would fly low and slow, getting the VC to reveal their positions so we could mark their positions with smoke grenades so the grunts could be landed and maneuver to annihilate them."[19] The days were long—eight to ten hours in the air each day.

With great emotion, even now, over fifty years later, Specialist Bendickson recalls the most disheartening mission of his combat tour. A long-range reconnaissance patrol came under heavy enemy attack and suffered casualties that required aeromedical evacuation. Sam's scout and its *Cobra* teammate flew support for the DUSTOFF mission that was forced down by enemy fire at the pickup zone (PZ) and was in jeopardy of being overrun by enemy forces attacking the wreckage and surviving personnel. Recognizing the imminent danger, the mission commander ordered the *Cobra* and the scout door gunners to take the swarming enemy and the downed aircraft under machine gunfire. Despite initial hesitancy, but recognizing the exigency of the situation, all fired upon the crash site, including Sam, who painfully witnessed one of his rounds hit the shoulder and wound a friendly trooper. Although the soldier was not seriously wounded and survived, nightmares of that day and event tormented Specialist Bendickson for many years. On the day following the action, the *Cayuse* scout and *Cobra* returned to the crash site to ensure the destruction of the *Iroquois* and all the sensitive and cryptological equipment onboard.

Near the midpoint of his combat tour, ARVN and U.S. forces launched an operation into Cambodia. According to the United States National Command Authority, the military objectives were to eliminate the cross-border sanctuaries and the NVA and Viet Cong soldiers who were defending and using these depots as safe havens. Their targets were the eleven access points from the 12,500 mile Ho Chi Minh Trail and the Sihanoukville Port Route.[20] There were eight entry points from Laos and Cambodia into South Vietnam. Five emerged from Laos and three from Cambodia. The main attack, Operation TOAN THANG ("Total Victory"), included a more than 5,000-man ARVN force operating in Cambodia from April 29 through July 22, while the 10,000 American troops from the 1st Cavalry Division, 25th Infantry Division, and the 11th Armored Cavalry Regiment were there from May 1 through June 30. Specialist Bendickson and his fellow troopers from the 9th Cavalry flew into Cambodia on the first day of the ARVN operation and supported them throughout.

In addition to the large number of helicopters lost during the operation, Sam vividly recalls the discovery of a large logistics base south of Snuol along Route 7 near Base Area 352.[21] After the discovery, troopers from the 1st Battalion, 5th Cavalry were sent into the area to exploit the site, the main base for the NVA 7th Division. Dubbed "the City" by the American soldiers, they discovered large quantities of military supplies and a cavernous ammunition and arms depot concealing over 140 tons of material.[22]

Besides the TOAN THANG operation, the Cambodian incursion included operations BINH TAY ("Tame the West") and CUU LONG ("Mekong"). At the incursion's conclusion and the withdrawal of American and ARVN troops, General Creighton Abrams, Jr., Commanding General, USMACV, reported that the force "seized 23,000 individual weapons, 2,500 crew-served weapons, nearly seventeen million rounds of anti-tank shells, 70,000 mortar shells, 143,000 rockets, 62,000 grenades, 435 vehicles, six tons of medical supplies, and 700 tons of rice."[23] Reaping the rewards of the buried caches all began with the initial discovery by a 1st Squadron, 9th Cavalry scout aircraft.

Recapping his tour in Vietnam, Sam recalled that the survivability prognosis for an OH-6 scout crew was a mere five days. At tour's end, he had greatly surpassed that morose metric. He would also walk away from three aircraft crashes or "controlled crash landings," as he preferred to call them, a number which was not uncommon for scout crews. Either unbeknownst to or at least minimized by Specialist Bendickson is his reputation within Charlie Troop that endured beyond his combat tour. Sam was "one of the brave and legendary crew chiefs of Charlie Troop, 1st Squadron, 9th Cavalry."[24]

So, after three winters away from the reservation, his Army service came to an end at Fort Hood, Texas, and there he and Jennifer were married seven days after his return. Sam returned home, proud of his service and mindful of the obligation that all Americans have to serve their country. He relates to his grandsons and other young tribal members that "if you volunteer, you are protecting your country, the country you live in. It makes you a better man. Gives you self-esteem, integrity; helps you be a good family man."[25] Sam and Jennifer returned to South Dakota and the warm embrace of family, friends, and tribe, where he spent his civilian career as a carpenter for twenty-seven years and owned and operated the Bendickson Remodeling and Construction business in North and South Dakota.

It took many years before members of his tribe fully appreciated and believed that when Sam went to war in Vietnam, he flew helicopters. Forty-four years after his return home, he experienced the tribal hand wiping ceremony where his hands were painted red by the warrior elders, and they collectively prayed with him—the ceremony took all the bad memories of war away. Fittingly, the Dakota name Canku Kinyan Wicasta was bestowed upon Sam the following year, which means "Flying Road Man."

Others in Sam's family served, with his wife Jennifer's father who was a veteran and hero of the Korean War. Her father's cousin, Master Sergeant Woodrow Wilson Keeble, was also a member of Company G, 2nd Battalion, 19th Infantry, 24th Infantry Division, and a Sisseton Wahpeton Oyate of the Lake Traverse Reservation Sioux. The latter was awarded the Medal of Honor for actions on Hill 765, near Sangsan-Ni, Korea, on October 20, 1951.[26] Initially awarded the Army's Distinguished Service Cross, after an Army review of awards for valor made during America's wars, President George W. Bush presented the Medal of Honor for Master Sergeant Keeble posthumously on March 3, 2008, to his family, twenty-six years after his death.[27]

In addition to comrades, Sam's relative, Theodore Magnus Hatle, an infantryman and Sisseton Wahpeton Sioux, who died in combat in Quang Tin Province on June 20, 1969, is memorialized on the Vietnam Veterans Memorial on the Mall in Washington D.C. His name appears on panel 22 west, line 120.

Sam is now retired, and he and his bride of over fifty years currently reside in Minneapolis with their children and grandchildren nearby, allowing him to enjoy one of his favorite foods, oatmeal cookies, which his granddaughter prepares for him.

Russell Cooata, Jr.[28]

Russell Cooata, Jr. (Courtesy of Russell Cooata, Jr.)

Regardless of the circumstances, it was neither surprising nor unexpected to his family and friends that Russell Cooata, Jr., whose Hopi name is Standing Bear, would find himself in uniform in a time of his country's need. Like many other members of the Hopi Tribe, he was reared in an extended family that honored military service and those who served.[29] His father had served in the 158th Infantry Regiment of the Arizona National Guard, formerly the 1st Arizona Volunteer Infantry. As a member of the regiment, Russell, Sr. served under the command of then Brigadier General John J. Pershing in 1916, during the Punitive Expedition.

In addition to his father, Russell had two uncles in the service. His Uncle Guy Maktima served in the Army in Europe during World War I. As a talented musician and a trombone player, Guy found himself among the select chosen to fulfill General Pershing's desire for a band within the American Expeditionary Forces (AEF) to emulate the European military bands of the period. Guy and his bandmates proudly marched during the Armistice Parade along the Avenue des Champs-Elysées in Paris on July 14, 1919, playing, among other selections, "Over There." Russell's Uncle Bennett Cooata also served as a printer in the Navy in 1916.[30]

Brothers James and Cooper and nephew Joe Ayze would later serve in the Marine Corps. James served with the 1st Marine Division in the Battle of the Chosin Reservoir (November 27–December 13, 1950). Throughout the Korean War, Russell would track the movements of his brothers up and down the Korean Peninsula with the ebb and flow of the combat action from news reports and scant information in his letters home. Joe Ayze served and spent thirty years in the Corps, 1962–1992, retiring as a Master Gunnery Sergeant.

In October 1965, after withdrawing from his college studies, Russell lost his college student deferment, entered the Army, and was sent to Fort Polk, Louisiana, for basic training. At age twenty-five, he was the elder of his basic training platoon by at least seven years and was respected among his much younger counterparts. After six weeks of basic training, Russell went to Aberdeen Proving Ground, Maryland, for eight weeks of Advanced Individual Training (AIT) as a helicopter armament/electronics repairman. Following AIT, Russell was assigned to the 608th Transportation Company (Aircraft Direct Support) at Fort Bragg, North Carolina. Although the company had been alerted for overseas deployment on July 1, 1966, their deployment was delayed by twelve months. Starting in April 1967, with the receipt of its Movement Permanent Change of Station Organization/Unit orders, the unit was brought up to its authorized strength and completed its training and preparations for overseas movement. Its equipment readiness date was set for May 13, 1967, and the personnel readiness date for June 16, 1967.[31]

The unit would make its deployment to Vietnam by three separate ships and one chartered flight. The unit's equipment sailed aboard the World War II Victory Ship USS *Lakewood Victory* (AK-236) out of Charleston, South Carolina, on June 17, 1967, and arrived in Vietnam on July 21. The company's inventory of aircraft repair parts sailed from Oakland, California, aboard the S.S. *Rappahannock*, arriving in Vietnam on July 19. The main body of the company's personnel, including Russell Cooata, sailed from the Port of Tacoma, Washington, on June 30 aboard the USNS *Geiger* (T-AP 197), which arrived at Cam Ranh Bay twenty-three days later after stops in Guam, the Philippines, and Vung Tau. The final contingent of men from the company flew from Fort Bragg on July 16 and disembarked in Saigon on July 19. The company was declared operationally ready on August 15, 1967, twenty-three days after its arrival in-country.

After the entire company closed on Vietnam, it was stationed at Dong Ba Thin Air Base, from where it provided aircraft support maintenance, technical supply support, and aircraft recovery to Army aviation units at Cam Ranh Bay, Dong Ba Thin, Nha Trang, Ninh Hoa, Ban Me Thout and Phu Hiep. The company also provided similar support to the 11th Logistics Command (ROK) and the 11th Aviation Company of the Republic of Korea Army (ROKA).[32] Their area of geographic responsibility extended from Pham Thut to Phu Heip along the South Vietnamese eastern coast westward to the Cambodian border. The 608th was assigned to the 14th Transportation Battalion (AM&S) (GS) and attached to the 34th General Support Group.

In addition to his primary MOS as a helicopter armament/electronics repairman, Specialist Four Cooata frequently served as a truck driver and as part of a convoy from his company to the port of Cam Ranh Bay to pick up supplies and repair parts essential to the company's mission.[33] These were not routine assignments but rather ad hoc arrangements when one of the company's sergeants determined a need and selected volunteers to make the run to the port.

As a direct support aircraft maintenance company, the 608th Transportation Company and its personnel were accustomed to working on and flying aboard Army helicopters, including their assigned UH-1B *Iroquois* aircraft. The company was not a combat aviation unit and had no assigned door gunners for its small fleet of aircraft. So, when the company traveled by air to make an in-the-field helicopter repair or recovery, they used their aircraft and company personnel as door gunners. The unit did not have a special training program for personnel like Russell, who performed door gunner and self-protection services while transiting enemy-occupied terrain. The company relied upon the basic training that its men received for using the standard M-60 infantry machine gun. Russell and his comrades would draw an M-60 from the unit arms room and sufficient linked ammunition to support the anticipated mission when assigned.

For the most part, and decidedly in comparison to fire suppression and self-defense missions flown by gunships, Russell believes that his door gunner missions were tame, with the majority of the time spent keeping a watchful eye to the side of the aircraft, searching for any activity or troops that might threaten the continuation of their flight and achievement of their purpose. It was neither bravado nor heroics that colored his perspective of the benign nature of his cumulative flights, but rather an assurance of his readiness to do what was expected of him and confidence in the capabilities of the aircraft and the other members of the flight crew.

When asked about the relationship between his aircraft, the *Iroquois*, and his Native American heritage, Russell observed that the helicopter was and always will be the *Huey* to him and his fellow soldiers. They did not know, nor appreciate, that the helicopters they were repairing and servicing bore the names of Native American tribes and chiefs, and if they had known, it probably would not have made a difference to them. Not familiar with the Army's naming tradition for helicopters, there was no special motivational bond between him and the *Iroquois*. The helicopter would have had to honor his people, the Hopi, for him to possibly experience an ancestral or emotional link. He was not in Vietnam when the OH-58 *Kiowa* started arriving, so he did not have the opportunity to test that theory, and thus felt no special bond to the aircraft he flew because of their Native American name.

Following the war, Standing Bear returned home to his people and, as a warrior, enjoyed the respect of his tribe and his father. The returning veterans were honored at a tribal dinner in a traditional ceremony, where each newly returned veteran would answer the roll call and receive a letter of appreciation on behalf of the entire Hopi Nation. The Hopi fete their veteran warriors annually on Veterans Day, beginning with a roll call of all their veterans and acknowledging the wars in which they served.

Russell's distinguished combat service merited his selection for induction into the Kiowa Gourd Warrior Society, a distinct and unique honor from the tribe and its veterans. The Kiowa recognize their returning warriors with a cleansing ceremony, and during the short tribute, a smoking fire of either cedar or sage is lit and used to generate a dense column of smoke. With the smoke billowing, dancers circle the honoree and direct the smoke onto him, waving an eagle's feather. In particularly special tributes to their Gourd Warrior Society members, dancers lay dollar bills at the feet of the warrior and continue dancing and smoking the warrior until the song has concluded. At that point, the money is collected from the floor and given to the honoree.

When Russell returned from Vietnam, he resumed his employment with the Arizona Highway Department. He also capitalized on his G.I. Bill benefit and completed his civil engineering studies at the University of Arizona. His twenty-six-year employment with Morrison Knudsen Company took him throughout the continental United States, Alaska, and Saudi Arabia until his retirement in 1996. That retirement was short-lived, as he responded to the needs of his tribe and returned to his civil engineering talents as a project manager for his Hopi tribe, overseeing highway paving contracts.

Russell is also a regular attendee of Native American Pow Wow gatherings dedicated to honoring warrior veterans of all tribes and nations. The Pow Wow is a tribute unique to the First Americans and their respect for their warriors.

Today in retirement, Standing Bear resides in Cornville, Arizona, where he continues to enjoy playing softball. Having played for twenty-five years, Russell plays for a Menifee, California, team for eighty-year-olds, the Got-R-Done 80. In November 2022, he began playing for the Arizona Prospectors 85 from Phoenix, Arizona. As their name indicates, the team is composed of players that are at least eighty-five years old.

Warrant Officer Class 58–9. WO Gatewood is the last man on the right. (Courtesy of the Army Aviation Museum.)

Clarence Nelson "Cal" Gatewood

Clarence Nelson "Cal" Gatewood was among the Native American Army aviators who experienced combat in Vietnam. On April 17, 1930, Clarence was born on the Indian reservation at Fort Defiance in Apache County, Arizona, to George Washington Gatewood (1903–1938) and Eleanor Mitchell Gatewood (1907–1933). Young Gatewood attended the Ganado Presbyterian mission school, where he met his future wife, Esther Candelaria, who was attending nurse's training school on the reservation. The couple married on June 14, 1951, at the Second Presbyterian Church by her father, Reverend J.I. Candelaria. At age seventeen, Clarence would enter the Army as a paratrooper. He would later become a warrant officer aviator upon graduation from Warrant Officer Candidate Class '58–9 and flight school.

Upon graduation, Gatewood became the Navajo Nation's first Army helicopter pilot, and would go on to become a rated pilot in the OH-13 (*Sioux*), UH-19 (*Chickasaw*), H-34 (*Choctaw*), H-37 (*Mojave*), CH-47 (*Chinook*), and CH-54B (*Tarhe*). His Army service took him to Holloman Air Force Base, White Sands Missile Range, New Mexico, from 1962 to 1964, where he flew the CH-37. The *Mojave* was rigged with extension hooks projecting from the helicopter's open front doors, and it was this configuration that was used to support Army missile test flights from White Sands. As the expended missile descended by parachute, the helicopter crews would position their aircraft to retrieve the missile by catching it by the parachute from which it was suspended in mid-air.

CW4 Gatewood served in several overseas locations as an Army aviator, which included the Republic of Korea and the Federal Republic of Germany. In West Germany, he served at both Illeshiem and Hanau Army Bases. Gatewood also served two tours in-country during the Vietnam War. In 1966–1967, his first tour was assigned to A Company, 228th Aviation Support Helicopter Battalion of the 1st Cavalry Division as a CH-47 Chinook pilot. It was during this tour that Gatewood was awarded the Distinguished Flying Cross for a nighttime rescue of fourteen Air Force personnel whose plane had crashed into the side of a mountain.

From 1967 to December 1968, he flew the CH-37 with the 90th Transportation Company at Illeshiem Army Airfield, Germany, where he and fellow pilot Dan DeStefano took great pleasure in flying the *Mojave,* including those occasions when they would secret Dan's Volkswagen Beetle into the cargo compartment so that they would have a way for the crew to get to a nearby town for a better room and food compared to the accommodation and fare at the local Army base.[34]

Gatewood would return to Vietnam in 1970–1971 to fly the CH-54A *Tarhe* with the 355th Aviation Company (Heavy Helicopter) of the 268th Combat Aviation Battalion.

His Army career also took him to aviation duty assignments at Ft. Rucker, Alabama, and Hanau Army Airfield on Fliegerhorst Kaserne, Germany, Ft. Eustis, Virginia., and Fort Wainwright, Alaska, before he retired after thirty years of service in 1977 as a Master Army Aviator and Master Parachutist. He was the recipient of, in addition to the Distinguished Flying Cross, the Bronze Star, the Air Medal with eight Oak Leaf Clusters, and the Army Commendation Medal.[35]

Clarence Gatewood died on September 13, 2004, in Albuquerque, New Mexico, and was laid to rest in Sunset Memorial Park, also in Albuquerque.

Leslie Hines[36]

Leslie Hines. (Courtesy of Leslie Hines.)

Among the Native American veterans of Vietnam, many were determined to serve their country from the outset. One such Chippewa/Cherokee warrior was Specialist Five Leslie Hines, who hails from Nebraska, the Cornhusker state. So resolute was he to serve that he competed for and received an appointment to the United States Military Academy at West Point, where he was looking forward to a college education, playing football for the Black Knights, and serving as an Army officer in Vietnam. Unfortunately, during the Academy's extensive medical examination process, Leslie was found to be color blind, a condition that could not be remedied and which would require a waiver for admission.

Still determined, young Hines volunteered for Army service as an enlisted man with a three-year service commitment. He was inducted in July 1967 and shipped off to Fort Benning, Georgia, for basic training, the school of the soldier. Earning high Armed Services Vocational Aptitude Battery (ASVAB) scores, Leslie, following his Fort Benning training, was assigned to the U.S. Army Aviation Center and School at Fort Rucker, Alabama, where he underwent fifteen weeks of MOS training to become a UH-1 Helicopter Mechanic (MOS: 67N20). Since Specialist Hines and his classmates were ultimately destined for *Iroquois* units in Vietnam, it was highly probable that they would be required to perform the duties of a door gunner during the combat tour. Accordingly, the faculty at Fort Rucker included in the flight portions of the curriculum the opportunity, as Leslie reports, "to shoot down trees."[37] While imitating Paul Bunyan might have been amusing in southern Alabama's southern longleaf pine acreages, the serious portion of their gunnery training came at the elbows of the old hats, the long-experienced gunners within their unit of assignment.

After completing training at Fort Rucker and a period of leave before heading to Vietnam, Specialist Hines and classmates from two of the 67N20 courses met at McChord Air Force Base in Washington state for the flight which took them to Yokota Air Base in Japan and finally to Cam Ranh Bay, Vietnam. Arriving at Cam Ranh Bay, the new *Iroquois* mechanics were designated for their unit of assignment and subsequently transported to the respective base of each unit. As he did, many of the passengers on Leslie's flight from the states would remain at Chu Lai Combat Base in the southern portion of I CTZ. At the time, Chu Lai was a Marine Corps Air Base and the home of the 23rd Infantry Division (Americal) and its subordinate units. The Marine Corps departed the base in October 1970 and the division in November 1971.

Following his arrival in-country in February 1968, Leslie's initial assignment was with the 406th Transportation Company (Aircraft Maintenance). Specialist

Hines would remain there throughout his twenty-four months assigned to combat duty in Vietnam. While with the 406th TC, he and his colleagues on the helicopter maintenance team would perform regularly scheduled and unscheduled maintenance. The former were time-based services and overhauls like the one hundred-hour inspections, while the latter were maintenance actions necessary because of flight operations (accidents, part failure, or battle damage).

In the narrative that follows, the reader should appreciate the harrowing experiences that Leslie's extended tour entailed. The last person who seeks war is a soldier, for he faces death daily and the ever-present fear that a personal failing might endanger his battle buddies. Specialist Hines accepted his role in aircraft maintenance and as a crew chief with trepidation. That alone, facing one's fears, speaks volumes about his courage. Most air missions were mundane, even dull, but they were also periodically punctuated by low-level flights filled with sheer terror. There was the ever-menacing enemy anti-aircraft fire, the snatch and grab flights to capture enemy combatants fleeing the field of battle where their unit was devastated, and the solemn duty of recovering dead and wounded comrades. The nightmares from these experiences afflicted the mind then, and the memories never go away, even over fifty years later.

Initially, Specialist Hines served for a couple of months as a mechanic on the OH-23G *Raven*. While with the 406th TC, Specialist Hines violated one of the first principles of being a soldier: never volunteer. He stepped forward and volunteered to be a crew chief for a *Raven* with the Warlords of B Company, 123rd Aviation Battalion. But alas, that was not to pass because, unfortunately, Leslie was too tall to be accommodated in the space set aside for the crew chief in the *Raven*. He was later moved to a maintenance team for UH-1 helicopters as the *Ravens* were being phased out. After a couple of months of honing his maintenance skills on the aircraft, an opening for a UH-1 crew chief occurred in the battalion, and he volunteered again.

The opening was on a UH-1 *Iroquois* belonging to A Company, 123rd Combat Aviation Battalion. Once he got his first aircraft, Specialist Hines remained a crew chief of either a UH-1D or UH-1H until his last combat mission in July 1969. He accompanied his aircraft through the gamut of *Iroquois* missions: command and control, courier, combat assault, flare, medevac, downed aircraft crew recovery, and even a snatch mission (capturing an enemy combatant fleeing across the rice paddies following a significant engagement that had not gone well for the fleeing soldier's unit).

As the aircraft crew chief, Specialist Hines continuously monitored the health of his aircraft and ensured its continuous mission readiness, documenting its health and readiness in the aircraft logbook. The crew chief was empowered to deadline the aircraft with a red X if he discovered a deficiency that warranted it. When his helicopter was assigned a mission, Leslie would often serve as a door gunner. The standard weapon for the UH-1D/-H slicks was the M60D pintle-mounted machine gun with butterfly grips (sometimes called spade grips) and the trigger itself being the two rings inside the grips. The machine gun configuration took some getting used to for the inexperienced gunner, especially one that did not benefit from hands-on training alongside a unit veteran door gunner. During engagements, it was not unusual for the pilot or aircraft commander to put the *Iroquois* through violent pitching and yawing to protect the aircraft or to position its gunners so they could optimally engage the enemy.

Even the most intrepid members of a flight crew hold in the recesses of their memory that one unusual or hair-raising mission that they will never forget. Specialist Hines has many memories of missions flown at night, at low levels, constantly within range of AAA fire, in bad weather, and bearing the bone tiring fatigue, boredom, and high anxiety from combat action.

Beginning May 1969, massed units of PAVN forces attacked throughout Vietnam, including the Americal Division AO. On May 11, 1969, Leslie had flown a flare mission supporting LZ Dottie, twelve miles south of Chu Lai. He and his crewmates illuminated the battlefield below the aircraft to aid the U.S. infantry in seeing the enemy. On that mission near LZ Dottie, the crew observed under the light of their first flares enemy RPGs slamming into seven or eight friendly bunkers on the LZs perimeter. Within four seconds, the VC instantaneously destroyed the bunkers and their occupants, leaving only large clouds of sand above where the bunkers once stood. The entire aircrew, especially Specialist Hines, was severely shaken from witnessing their comrades' sudden and traumatic loss. The mind can barely process such a cataclysm in the time that it took.

That same evening, the PAVN V-16 Sapper Battalion launched a similar attack on Fire Support Base Professional, located thirty-two kilometers northwest of Chu Lai. It was the home of the 1st Battalion, 46th Infantry of the 23rd Infantry Division. An intense battle raged there during the period May 12–16. Within seventy-two hours, the intensity of the battle rose to emergency levels causing the Americal Division to request assistance from the 101st Airmobile Division. The entire 1st brigade of the 101st Airmobile Division arrived in the AO within twenty-four hours.

During the daylight hours of May 12, Specialist Hines and his flight crewmates were to bring replacements into the battalion headquarters on FSB Professional. Mortar fire was a concern as intermittent indirect fire was being taken during the day, but the accurate direct fire of the recoilless rifle (RR) was a genuine threat. The helipad of the FSB was situated 322 meters (~1,100 feet) below a hilltop from which the PAVN had a direct field of fire with their RR.[38] Dramatic and unusual orders were given to the crew—they were to immediately evacuate their helicopter if it was hit by RR fire on the helipad, as any disabled helicopter was to be bulldozed off the side of the hill. The scenario seemed unreal, except there was already one helicopter pushed over the side before the helicopter assault began.

Besides the omnipresent RR overwatching the helipad for arriving targets, the enemy ringed the FSB with nineteen .51 caliber heavy machine gun AAA weapons.[39] During the period of action around FSB Professional, the DShK, in a single twenty-four-hour period three days later, would disable fifty-eight American helicopters out of sixty-two that were sent into action. The men of FSB Professional found forty-eight deceased PAVN soldiers in their wire after the initial attack of May 11–12, 1969.

A company reinforced with elements of the reconnaissance company of the 1st Battalion, 46th Infantry deployed four kilometers west of LZ Professional was swarmed over by large numbers of NVA troops advancing in the general direction of LZ Professional. They were pinned down and became engaged in a subsequent two-day battle. The unit staved off the immense forces of the enemy to survive and be rescued. For his actions in the battle, Captain Kern W. Dunagan, Commander of Company A, 1st Battalion, 46th Infantry, was awarded the Medal of Honor.

On another occasion, the crew received an emergency call for a medevac mission. The VC had executed an elaborate plan which resulted in a massive explosion, the death of seventeen infantrymen, and the wounding of countless more. One of the seriously wounded was a staff sergeant who lost both of his legs below the waist from the explosion. When Specialist Hines and the helicopter reached him, the NCO was already ashen in color, signifying his imminent death. Within a few minutes, the soldier was aboard an offshore hospital ship[40] which could treat him and perform the necessary lifesaving surgery; however, the flight crew was convinced that he did not survive. Years later, Hines discovered that this soldier had miraculously survived. He was an inspiration to other Vietnam War survivors throughout his ordeal and afterward because of his remarkable attitude, despite his grievous wounds.

Specialist Hines and the crew were once called upon to fly a flare mission that rivaled the stress felt on any of the other missions that they had flown. First, the crew chief evaluated the aircraft as "X" (a red X = deadlined) for three consecutive night flights because of excessive iron filings in the forty-two-degree gearbox.[41] Each time an oil sample test was conducted by the technical inspectors to verify that the gearbox was OK. When Hines marked the aircraft with an "X" a fourth time, the assessment was overruled, and the helicopter was cleared for a night flare mission. During the flight, the foty-two-degree gearbox failed and caught on fire. Without a tail rotor, the cockpit crew must maintain sixty-five knots of airspeed, otherwise the helicopter will go into a fatal spin. The centrifugal force from such a spin would crush everyone on board before the aircraft hits the ground. The aircraft went from 3,000 to 300 feet before flight control was regained. During the descent, the fire was extinguished, which left the sky dark and gave the VC nothing to shoot at with their .51 caliber AAA except the sound trailing from the injured helicopter. A successful emergency running landing[42] was made at the Chu Lai East runway.

Specialist Hines observed a U.S. M-48 Patton tank hit a 500-pound bomb during a command and control mission. In amazement, the helicopter crew watched as the tank's seventeen-ton turret was blown so high that Leslie and the crew lost sight of it. Then, like a baseball, it reappeared as it tumbled down and hit the ground—the entire tank crew was lost.

On October 11, 1968, with their assigned mission completed, Specialist Hines and the aircrew were returning to Chu Lai through the Hoi An River area when they heard the distinctive sound of AK-47 fire. The last round they heard was the one that hit the gunner's side machine gun mount. As the cockpit crew swung the helicopter around for a firing pass, more rounds were heard, and again, the last round hit the helicopter cabin piercing the floor and nicking the legs of a jump seat passenger. In one of the ordinary but inexplicable tragedies of war, the soldier behind the AK-47 was a young girl intent on downing the helicopter and killing the crew. In the exchange that followed with the door gunner, she tragically lost. This was warfare in Vietnam, and it needed to be done. For all aboard the aircraft, especially the door gunner, it was hard not to feel bad about the death of a young girl.

The standard combat tour in Vietnam for Army personnel was twelve months. Leslie Hines spent twenty-four months in Vietnam, from February 1968 to April 1970, plus two months of CONUS leave before his tour extensions. After his last tour extension leave, when he returned to Vietnam, Specialist Hines was assigned to E Company, 723rd Maintenance Battalion, the reorganized version of his original Vietnam unit of assignment, the 406th Transportation Company.

Since Specialist Hines was serving a three-year enlistment and because he volunteered for service rather than awaiting being drafted, he took advantage of the combat tour extensions so that at the end of his final extension, he would be concurrently eligible for both his DEROS and ETS when he left Vietnam, and therefore would not receive another assignment in the United States.

Like many fellow Native American Vietnam warriors, Leslie knew that his aircraft was named after a great Native American Nation. For him, it was a source of personal and professional pride. But it was something that he neither dwelled upon nor made an issue of among his non-Native American comrades; there was too much to do for him and others, and "there were bigger things at stake."[43]

By 1970, American public support for the Vietnam War was plummeting with increasingly vocal and violent demands for the drawdown of American forces in the country. In those tumultuous times, some Americans were more inclined to direct their contempt for the government's Southeast Asia policy not at the politicians but rather toward veterans as they were returning home and traveling through the country's airports. Like so many veterans, Specialist Hine experienced hostility and animosity while making flight connections at Stapleton International Airport in Denver, Colorado, when he returned home for his second extension leave. Leslie chooses not to dwell on the incident but rather to focus on the more positive aspects of his return from America's helicopter war. One such experience was a ceremony conducted and performed in Oklahoma City by the Cherokee Tribe inducting honorees into the Oklahoma Military Hall of Fame.

Comprehensive and continuing family genealogical research strongly suggests that Leslie Hines is the great-great-grandson of principal Cherokee war chief Tsiyu Gansini ("he is dragging his canoe").[44] Chief Dragging Canoe, as he is more commonly known, is considered by many to have been one of the most noteworthy Native American warrior leaders in the southeast United States, having made his mark during the American Revolutionary War.[45] Born of a prominent

Cherokee family, Dragging Canoe's birth is estimated to be around 1740 in Eastern Tennessee.

Dragging Canoe was an outspoken force against the settler encroachment onto Native tribal lands. He stood his ground in vigorous opposition to the Treaty of Sycamore Shoals, which his father had accepted as a trading rights treaty, but which in reality ceded 20,000,000 acres of Cherokee land that today comprise Kentucky, Central Tennessee, and parts of Northeastern Tennessee to Judge Richard Henderson's North Carolina-based Transylvania Company.[46] Although the territory was governed by British law, which prohibited land transactions between British subjects (Richard Henderson) and Indian tribes, the onset of the American Revolution prevented the British authorities from evicting the colonists who flooded the new territory as petitioned for by the Cherokee. Henderson and company, now declaring themselves Americans because of the revolution, had a ready-made excuse for permanently retaining possession of the tribal lands.[47]

This turn of events gave the Cherokee common cause with the British throughout the revolution, which led them to abandon the remaining land and continue their war against the colonists rather than rebuild the destroyed homes and entertain submission to the Americans. Dragging Canoe continued to lead Cherokee expeditions against colonial settlements in East Tennessee, Kentucky, and south to the Georgia and South Carolina frontiers to help the British suppress the rebellion. The success of his force caused the governors of Georgia and North Carolina to dispatch a combined force against Dragging Canoes' new settlements and towns. Colonel Evan Shelby's force destroyed eleven Cherokee towns, facing little to no opposition.

In response, Chief Dragging Canoe relocated his people and devised a complete and rolling blockade of the Little Tennessee River whereby canoes of Cherokee warriors were situated at various points along the length of the Little Tennessee River from which they would pounce upon any white men who dared navigate the river. Successive assaults greeted anyone who managed to survive an initial assault. The Little Tennessee experienced no large-scale colonial migration along its length, as was the case along the Ohio River and its tributaries.[48]

Thirteen years later, on August 22, 1788, War Chief Dragging Canoe led a force of Cherokee warriors near present-day Chattanooga. At that point, he violently engaged and repeatedly ambushed from concealed positions a militia force of 500 under the command of Brigadier General Joseph Martin.[49] The fleeing militiamen were harassed throughout their retreat by the Cherokee. The devastation of General Martin's force conclusively ended the Battle of Lookout Mountain, marking the only and last time white men attempted a military invasion of the Cherokee stronghold.[50]

As stated in previous chapters, the warrior tradition runs deep among Native Americans. It is instilled with pride from one generation to the next in an unending lineage. The warrior spirit of Chief Dragging Canoe still flows and resides well within the heart of his kinsman, Leslie Hines. Today, in retirement, Leslie Hines resides in Des Moines, Iowa.

Clifford Claude "Cliff" Mosier[51]

Clifford Claude "Cliff" Mosier.
(Courtesy of Clifford Mosier.)

Much of the story of the Osage Tribe can be garnered by tracing the family tree of Clifford Mosier's family. He is the grandson of one of the original Osage Indian allottees created by the Dawes Act of 1887. His grandfather Bismark from Osage County, Oklahoma, was allottee #1583, while his two sisters, Clara and Thelma, allottees #1584 and 1585, respectively. The act permitted the federal government to break up tribal lands by partitioning them into individual plots and granting them to registered tribal members who, in turn, were allowed to become U.S. citizens. Bismark also shared in the division of tribal mineral resources. Those members born after 1906, like Cliff's father, were referred to as "too lates" because they were not beneficiaries of the Dawes Act land distribution.

In his teens, Bismark Mosier was forced to attend the Carlisle Indian Industrial School, where he received taxidermy instruction before leaving the school. During the period when William Hale was attempting to obtain Osage wealth by murdering as many as twenty-four county residents, Bismark had the U.S. Marshal escort him and his family to Siloam Springs, Arkansas, for their protection. Unfortunately, an uncle and a neighbor were murdered before the family could make their way to Arkansas.

The family was of the utmost importance to the Osage people, with special pride being felt for those who served in the armed forces or achieved prominence. Cliff had cousins who served in the Air Force and Navy as well as during World War II and Korea. A special member of the family was America's first prima ballerina Elizabeth Marie Tallchief who was also the first Native American to be so ranked.

Clifford spent his early years in Pawnee, Oklahoma, where he was reared in the tribal ways, including participation in traditional Osage dances and community feasts. Along with his father, Cliff was a Fancy Dancer where they danced according to the beat and must strike a pose whenever the drum beat stopped. Such dancing required strength and stamina. The male dancers wore brightly colored regalia and were flashy and highly energetic in their movements. Even today, Cliff still remembers the haunting sounds of the drummers and singers that led the dance.

The pathway to becoming an Army aviator can be pretty circuitous at times, and not for the faint of heart. Clifford Mosier's route was certainly one of the most roundabout. Clifford's journey to Army flight school began with his enlistment in the Navy. Upon graduation from high school in Oklahoma and almost a year shy of his eighteenth birthday, Clifford sought his opportunity for military service through a special Navy program called the "Cradle Cruise"[52] program. The program offered enlistment to a recruit who was less than eighteen years old when joining for a period of service that extended to the recruit's twenty-first birthday. In Cliff's case, he would serve three years, ten months, and twenty-six days. After active-duty service, the "Cradle Cruise" graduate incurred a four-year reserve duty service obligation during which he trained as an electrician's mate. On his twenty-first birthday he left the Navy as a Petty Officer Second Class (PO2/E5).

Should there be another war in America's future, Cliff was determined that he did not want to serve in it as a shipboard sailor. He was sure that whatever he did, "he wanted a gun in his hand to protect himself."[53] Cliff thus sought a home in the Arkansas ARNG, which he entered in the grade as Sergeant, commensurate with the highest rank from his Navy service. While attending training in his Fort Smith ARNG unit, he was encouraged to consider attending Officer Candidate School (OCS) at Camp Robinson in Little Rock, which he did. The twelve-month officer candidate program was a challenge for all candidates, and doubly so for Cliff since his prior Navy service did not provide him with adequate preparation and was dissimilar to the Army training he was undergoing at OCS. Additionally, he was only a high school graduate during a period when college graduates were serving in the National Guard as an alternative to active service and duty in Vietnam. Despite this, from among the seventy-five candidates who began the class and the fifty-one who ultimately graduated as second lieutenants, Lieutenant Clifford C. Mosier was Honor Graduate, the top graduate based upon his academic standing, tactical officer assessments, and peer ranking.

As commissioning approached, Clifford contemplated volunteering for combat duty in Vietnam. However, he was cautioned against appearing too gung-ho for combat duty, lest he be considered unfit for such an assignment. His counselors recommended that he proffer the Army and National Guard a *quid pro quo* for his possible service in Vietnam. So, Mosier would volunteer for combat duty in exchange for further education, specifically rotary-wing aviation training.

He was subsequently assigned to flight school at Fort Wolters, Texas, and then to Hunter Army Airfield, Savanah, Georgia, to complete his training. Flight school was a challenge for Cliff, being the last of the three pilots-in-training under his instructor pilot to solo. Cliff readily admits that he was not an excellent undergraduate pilot and feared being recycled to a later class or washed out. What he was, was slow and steady, attributes that got him through flight school. He squeaked through and graduated in 1968 as an Army aviator. Upon graduation, his most ardent wish was fulfilled when he was assigned to A Company, 25th Aviation Battalion of the 25th Infantry Division at Cu Chi in III CTZ of Vietnam.

Cliff served in Vietnam from 1968 to 1970, primarily as a UH-1 *Iroquois* pilot. With the 25th, he accumulated many more flight hours, and with them, he became a good pilot. He would participate in many of the sundry missions flown by the battalion, including troop insertion and extraction, resupply, courier, convoy escort and overwatch, command and control, smoke generation, mortar air delivery system (MADS) flights, agent orange spraying, psychological operations, and Nighthawk, among others. During his tour, Division Commander, Major General

Ellis W. Williamson, needed a new command pilot for his aircraft. The commander of A Company was tasked with finding skilled and qualified candidates for the general's selection, and at the end of the screening process, First Lieutenant Mosier was selected. After he was chosen, General Williamson would ask Cliff if he knew why he was selected. The general went on to explain that he wanted the best aviator he had in the left seat.

After that assignment, Cliff served on the battalion staff as the standardization instructor pilot (SIP). As the SIP, it was Cliff's responsibility to ensure that all the designated IPs in the battalion were qualified to perform the duties and certify that each of the battalion's aviators was sufficiently experienced and qualified to pilot the aircraft for which he was being tested.[54] As the battalion SIP, Cliff performed the IP duties for all other IPs and some pilots. With the departure of the former commander, the incoming commander Colonel Gosney briefed the battalion staff on his expectations, announcing that "no incoming pilot will fly one of my helicopters without a proficiency ride with Cliff."[55] Lieutenant Mosier thus dutifully set out with the new commander at the controls of his UH-1 helicopter. In short order, the colonel had crashed the aircraft, rolled it on its port side, rendered himself unconscious, and inflicted a head wound upon the SIP. According to SOP, Cliff promptly announced mayday and code 6 over the radio, indicating that aboard the downed aircraft was a full colonel, O-6. The world descended upon the crash site to recover and protect the colonel, who emerged no worse for wear from the helicopter—such was the life of a SIP.

Cliff's aviation unit assignment was not dissimilar to others. And like other units, it was essential to have a good time when you could and to decompress from the rigors of the day, even if that meant doing so at one another's expense. Within its compound, the battalion was fortunate to have a small space set aside for an officer's club, which was cooled by a small temperamental window air conditioner which Cliff had amply demonstrated a capacity to restore to life with some gentle persuasion—imagine a hammer in hand. First Lieutenant Mosier completed his second year of commissioned service during that time. On one sweltering day, the air conditioner chose to lapse into one of its periods of ill-temperament. Since the battalion commander was attempting to enjoy a cool beverage at the time, the emergency call went out to find Cliff. The latter was by happenstance enjoying an equally refreshing shower. Admonished by the executive officer that there was no time to complete his shower, Cliff was instructed to grab his towel and hasten to the club. Upon arriving there, he was greeted by an assembly of the battalion's officers. At that point, the commander promoted him to captain by affixing his new insignia of rank to his towel. The air conditioner was working fine.

Captain Mosier felt that the most incredible honor bestowed on a citizen of the United States was to serve his country in combat. While he was older than almost all of his peers in Vietnam, he cherished the many opportunities offered him to fly for his country, even those that demanded fourteen hours in the cockpit. For him, no mission was unimportant; he always felt that the most important thing at any particular moment in time was the mission to which he was assigned and was flying—even it was delivering ice cream to grunts in the bush or transporting Bob Hope and his United Service Organization (USO) troupe to their show sites.

Captain Mosier would end his flying service in Vietnam with an award of the Distinguished Flying Cross and the Air Medal with numeral "31."

When the Vietnam War was over, the Army found itself with too many captains and too many Army aviators, so to restore balance, a reduction in force (RIF) was conducted. Based upon an inverse order of merit for Army captains by year group, a portion of them were released from active duty. The most common rationale for the release of commissioned officers was the lack of a college degree. And thus, with only a high school diploma to his credit, Cliff left active duty during the drawdown.

After spending a couple of years in civilian life without a link to the military, Cliff returned to service by re-entering the Arkansas ARNG. However, in order to do so, he was forced to resign his commission and return to uniform as a sergeant, the last grade he served in before attending OCS. In this rank, he was assigned to the unit's logistic and supply function, where he served as the driver for the S-4, logistics officer.

In time, war clouds once again began to gather over Cliff and his ARNG comrades. This time it was Operation Desert Shield/Desert Storm. Cliff and his unit deployed and fought throughout the one hundred hours of Desert Storm and safely returned home when the guns fell silent—at least for a period. With his military service concluded, Captain Clifford Mosier entered military retirement with a fitting ceremony worthy of his long and distinguished service to the nation.

Following the tragedy of 9/11, Cliff opened a business that manufactured and installed flag poles so that his community could regularly show its pride for the United States and the strength of her armed forces and first responders here at home. By doing so, Cliff recalled that it made him "feel like he contributed."[56]

Now in his eighties, and after a successful career in real estate, Cliff is retired and resides in Fayetteville, Arkansas.

WO Melvin Sheldon, his LOACH, and air-conditioned helmet courtesy of NVA ground fire while flying in Cambodia. (Courtesy of Melvin Sheldon, Jr.)

Melvin Robert Sheldon, Jr.[57]

Among the Army aviators who flew in Vietnam, one particular group merited acknowledgment even among their peers. Often flying "on the edge," testing their skills and, yes, daring against the cunning and tenacity of their opponents, these were the scout pilots and their crew—a crew chief and door gunner—who engaged in a cat and mouse, life or death ballet often mere tens of feet above the battlefield floor or jungle canopy. In chronological order, they flew the *Sioux*, *Raven*, *Cayuse*, and *Kiowa*.

Among their number was a Native American of the Tulalip Tribes, Melvin Robert Sheldon, Jr. A teenager at the time, Melvin volunteered for service in the Army and, armed with the commensurate Armed Forces Qualification Test (AFQT)[58] battery of aptitude scores, was inducted in August 1969, and destined for flight school. Following infantry basic and school of the soldier training at Fort Polk, Louisiana, Melvin reported to Fort Wolters, Texas, to commence initial flight training and his pathway to becoming an Army aviation warrant officer. During his training at Fort Wolters, he accumulated one hundred hours of flight time in the Army's piston-powered, light training helicopter, the Hughes TH-55 *Osage*. Of the sixty aviation candidates in Melvin's class (4th WOC 70-27), he was the only Native American and one of the twenty-one who graduated Primary Flight School.[59] Upon completing this phase of flight training, Sheldon continued his advanced training at Fort Rucker, Alabama, gaining an additional one hundred or more flight hours in the *Iroquois*. Noteworthy in his flight training was that he was only eighteen when he accumulated one hundred hours of flight time and soloed. By age nineteen he had also accumulated one hundred hours in the turbine-powered *Iroquois*. When questioned about what it took to become an Army aviator, his response was "attention to detail." Advanced flight training also granted him his "tactical ticket" at graduation and an appointment as a warrant officer (WO). The "tactical ticket" meant that the aviator was sufficiently trained and skilled to fly his aircraft in basic combat operations. WO Sheldon graduated from Fort Rucker with his classmates in Class 70-29. More experience and time in combat would follow from the training he received in his assignment unit.

Sheldon would be somewhat victimized by the adage that first impressions are lasting impressions. As the commercial aircraft taking him to Da Nang, South Vietnam, was descending toward the airbase there, he unexpectedly witnessed an American stationed in-country enjoying some downtime water skiing off Cam Ranh Bay. Man, how strenuous was service in Vietnam going to be? Like every other soldier shipped to Vietnam as an individual replacement, Warrant Officer Sheldon arrived at the replacement center at Bien Hoa Air Force Base, not knowing where in-country or in which unit he would be assigned—in October 1970, individual pilot replacements were assigned to any unit that needed a pilot. Given the opportunity to express his assignment preference, with absolutely no assurance that it meant anything in the personnel system, Sheldon stated that he wanted to fly with the troopers of the 1st Cavalry Division and that he would like to pilot slicks. The sun must have been shining that day because he was directed to Charlie Troop, 1st Squadron, 9th Cavalry Regiment of the 1st Cavalry Division, located at Phuoc Vinh, due north of Bien Hoa in III CTZ. The 9th Cavalry is one of the most distinguished of the Army's Cavalry Regiments, with an extensive history and impressive lineage and honors extending back to the Indian Wars. Warrant Officer Sheldon took up his duties as an aviator and cavalryman among the Army's elite.

When he got to his new unit, it wasn't long before the young warrant officer volunteered to be a scout pilot flying the OH-6A *Cayuse* paired with an AH-1G *Cobra*, a hunter-killer team as they were referred to in the 9th Cavalry. Mel was a *Cayuse* scout pilot after aircraft transition training with the Squadron IP and the obligatory check ride. The skillset necessary for the daring life of a scout pilot did not miraculously materialize once one nestled into the pilot's seat of the *Cayuse*. Sure, the newbie accumulated some added hours in the new aircraft and completed his AO orientation flights; however, the most valuable training came from the "old hands," the experienced scout pilots, who willingly shared the hard knocks lessons they learned and some of the experiences painfully acquired by pilots who paid for them with their lives. Once the *Cayuse* left the ground, there was no rank among the flight crew; Mel relied upon his experienced crew who helped him learn the various ways scouts on the deck would conduct visual reconnaissance. The combat that Warrant Officer Sheldon experienced over the jungles of Vietnam and the occasional adventure across the border into Cambodia would indelibly change the once carefree life he previously enjoyed.

The pilot in command of the aircraft worries not only about the accomplishment of the mission supporting the troops on the ground but also about the safety of his crew—the flight and hostile fire pay they each received were well earned each day. While, the Loach was among the most damaged aircraft of the war, victimized by enemy fire and the aerial tactics survival demanded, WO Sheldon was one of the few scout pilots who brought each aircraft that he flew back to base after the mission was accomplished. That does not mean that the helicopter did not experience some battle damage, but it was sufficiently flyable to bring the crew home safe. As he is prone to saying, "we were shot up, but never shot down." Sheldon's crew members were equally resilient. His crew always survived during his scouting tour, although two of his crew chiefs were wounded-in-action (WIA).

In early 1971, WO1 Sheldon and the squadron participated in Operation LAM SON 719, which took them across the border into Laos and Cambodia as the ARVN conducted operations to disrupt the flow of NVA logistical support that moved through the Kingdom of Laos along the Ho Chi Minh Trail[60] (the Truong Son Road from North Vietnam). Sheldon and the troopers of Charlie Troop supported the operation by conducting missions in Cambodia.

When asked about some of his most exciting missions, Melvin recalls a deep penetration into Cambodia during LAN SON to conduct a BDA of the results of a B-52 strike that was part of Operation ARCLIGHT.[61] With barely twenty minutes of fuel remaining, he made a low-level assessment of the destruction wrought by the massive bombers on an NVA staging compound and training center. The smell of the tritonal filler of those bombs still lingers with him today.

While flying an aerial reconnaissance mission over Cambodia, they spotted new firing positions in the typical design used by the PAVN for .51 caliber and .30 caliber crew-served weapons. Unusually the new works were unoccupied and showed no evidence of their intended forthcoming occupation. As instinct would have scouts do upon the discovery of something out of place in their AO, WO Sheldon took his aircraft lower for a closer investigation, which brought the aircraft within range of enemy small arms fire from soldiers hidden in the jungle undergrowth below. As a result, Sheldon's crew chief was wounded while they tried to evade the ground fire.

When transferred to Bravo Troop of the 3rd Squadron, 17th Cavalry of the 1st Aviation Brigade, Warrant Officer Sheldon would continue flying scout missions and accumulate more hours in command of the OH-6A.

The key to success in combat—mission accomplishment and survival—is inextricably linked to confidence: confidence in your training, your equipment, your senior leadership, and your crew. No one can dispute the caliber of the training that aerial scout crews received or the capabilities and ruggedness of the *Cayuse*. The crews that flew with Mel attested to the capability of their pilot in command, "Mel was unflappable in the face of fire."[62]

During the final two months of his time in Vietnam, the young, but mature aviator, found himself stationed in Vung Tau with the NETT. For the average soldier, Vung Tau was a beach resort on the South China Sea and a place of respite from the rigors of war where, with the approval of your unit commander, you could spend three days of in-country rest and recuperation (R&R). Such was not the assignment for Mel, as he spent his final sixty days in-country teaching emergency and evasive maneuvers to inexperienced OH-6 pilots.[63]

Warrant Officer Sheldon's Native American heritage weighed on him during his tour and upon returning home. He observed that there were not many Native Americans in Army aviation during the war years; therefore, the only exposure that his comrades probably ever had to Indigenous people was their service with him. And so, it was from him they formed their lasting impression of his people and his race—and a good impression that was. WO Sheldon also became an inspiration to the people of his tribe and hoped this would be the case to members of other tribes to which his service and sacrifice were exposed.

At the end of his war in October 1971, Warrant Officer Sheldon returned home to an uncertain environment, not knowing what to expect from his fellow countrymen, a populace increasingly disenchanted with the continuing war in

Southeast Asia, and a government seemingly unable to win it or incapable of ending it. He came home to a citizenry harboring animus toward its government and willing to vent it against its veterans; the nation was not ready to separate the warrior from the war. Upon reaching American soil, any expectation of a warrior's welcome from the non-Native population was immediately dispelled. While to Melvin, his military service, including his combat tour in Vietnam, was a source of personal and professional pride, he found that he had to suppress those feelings and, as he says, "put them on the shelf." However, such was not the case among the people of his tribe. Vietnam veterans such as himself were genuinely welcomed home and honored for what they had done. The tribe made it a point of ensuring that all of their numbers were aware of their veterans' service and their place of respect within the tribe. While unpopular off the reservation, veterans were made to feel the well-deserved pride of accomplishment and honor that was justifiably theirs from their fellow tribe members—accompanying these positive feelings came the healing and returning to harmony with nature that is lost with going to war.

Each year the Tulalip people renew their respect for their veterans by conducting a Pow Wow dedicated to them, in addition to their annual gatherings to celebrate Memorial Day and Veteran's Day. No Tulalip veteran, regardless of the war in which they served, suffers remorse or despondency because of the warmth and welcoming of the people of the tribe and their collective pride for the service of their sons and daughters.

For Melvin, the challenge he faced after returning was what to do with the education that he acquired during his military service. Following his return home and armed with his GI Bill benefits, he saw education as a route to transition back into civilian life. He thus enrolled in undergraduate studies at Skagit Valley College, a community college in Mount Vernon, Washgington, and even participated in collegiate sports, baseball. He would also attend the University of Washington, where he received a Bachelor of Arts degree in political science. Still young, and drawn by the call of the sea, in 1973, Sheldon embarked upon a twenty-five-year career as a commercial fisherman harvesting Bristol Bay and the Puget Sound.

Despite his new adventures, Melvin never lost the desire to serve, but this time his efforts were in support of his Native American people, the Tulalip tribe. Beginning in 1999, he served on the Tulalip's board of directors' tribal council successively as secretary, treasurer, and chairman. He also served in several national Native American organizations, including the National Congress of the American Indian (NCAI).

A visionary and advocate for tribal treaty rights as a sovereign people, Mel worked tirelessly for the social, political, and economic wellbeing of the Tulalip people. He and the Tulalip board members accomplished the construction of the Tulalip Resort Casino and the shared economic benefits for the tribe and the first federally recognized chartered tribal city in the country, Quil Ceda village. Mel helped lead the tribe as a sovereign entity to achieve its goals in infrastructure improvement projects, creating a revitalized, effective police department and tribal court, and establishing a series of strong tribal and community partnerships. He still serves as Northwest Vice President of the Affiliated Tribes of Northwest Indians (ATNI), an association of nearly fifty tribes.

Native American veteran issues are still high among Mel's service priorities and volunteer activities. He serves as co-chairman of the Veteran's Committee, ensuring that veteran issues are surfaced within the ATNI and then, when appropriate, advocates for them at the national level, the NCAI, of which Mel is the Northwest delegate. The operating imperative of Mel's work is making sure that veteran initiatives include the Native American veteran's voice. Whenever the VA develops policies affecting Indian country, Mel and his Native American colleagues work to ensure consultation with Indigenous people occurs and that their respective cultures are honored in the emerging policy.

Melvin Sheldon is enjoying his retirement in Tulalip, Washington, with his significant other of over twenty-five years, Wendy Church, Jackson the dog, Jet the cat, and, oh yes, his substitute *Cayuse*, a bright green Harley-Davidson. Mel is a highly regarded and respected member of his tribe, serving as an example for its young people.

The men who shared their stories here are a very small sample of Native American veterans of Vietnam and all of America's wars. They represent an even smaller fraction of the nation's living 19 million veterans whom we should every day, not just on Veterans' day, offer our thoughtful thanks for their heroic service and sacrifice.

"Whenever we encounter veterans, we should be mindful of the great gifts they offer and express our heartfelt gratitude for all they have done and for the outstanding contributions they continue to make. We acknowledge the considerable sacrifices they offered in service to our country and in protection of our fundamental freedoms. So ... we ask God to watch over all our ... veterans. May He bless them with His love and hope in these ever-challenging times. It is because of them we are afforded the privilege of being Americans who can praise and follow God without fear and enjoy the freedoms safeguarded in the United States Constitution. Thank you, veterans, for everything you do. May God bless you today, tomorrow and always."[64]

SOME GAVE ALL

Only the dead are safe; only the dead have seen the end of the war.
George Santayana[1]

America's history has been troubled with armed conflict, whether at home in the quest for independence, for the nation's preservation, on far-reaching shores at the behest of allies, or against threats to America's national security interests. The nation and its armed forces recently completed a twenty-year war against terrorism and the regimes that sponsor and support terrorism. When people converse about the costs incurred in the most recent or prior wars, a broad litany of items is recited, including economic, political, social, foreign policy, and opportunity costs. Academic institutions, government agencies, think tanks, and individuals have toiled mightily over the decades to calculate and report on their interpretations of the monetary costs of America's wars. The components of wartime costs include military, war debt interest, homeland security, and veteran care expenses.

Regardless of how one considers the magnitude, it is beyond the realm of comprehension for most citizens. To ordinary voting citizens, spending over sixteen million dollars in a lifetime is unimaginable; therefore, how much more incomprehensible is spending that amount of money in an hour. So, if these numbers do not resonate with American citizens, what war-related numerical metrics do? To most Americans, the loss of human life, especially American lives, registers deeply within the heart of the family, relatives, neighbors, and friends. Primarily when the nation was engaged in a total war where every country was mobilized, and there was no single neighborhood where someone's son, father, brother, uncle, or neighbor did not go off to war, and many did not return—World Wars I and II were like that for hometown America.

Wars like Korea, Vietnam, the Persian Gulf, and the War on Terrorism did not have the same disastrous impact as the great wars. With voluntary military service instead of a draft-supported universal military conscription, a majority of citizens today do not know a single person in active or reserve military service. Less than one percent of the service-eligible population of the United States serves their country today. It must thus be recognized that even the staggering casualty figures presented below may not move the reader to value deeply the sacrifice of service made by each soul represented in the numbers.[2] But each number was a life, a life of promise and potential unfulfilled and never realized. In some instances, male citizens of the U.S. during these warring periods may wish to reflect that, "there, but for the grace of God, go I."

Whether you hold that the phrase "all gave some; some gave all" is attributed to the Korean War veteran and Purple Heart recipient Howard William Osterkamp from Dent, Ohio, or is from the lyrics of the 1992 Billy Ray Cyrus song, "Some Gave All," the meaning of those six words is no less poignant and heart-rending. Here they bring us face-to-face with the enormity and finality of the human cost of war. From the Vietnam War, there are 58,281 names memorialized on the Vietnam Veterans Memorial in the Constitution Gardens on the National Mall in Washington, D.C. Each represents a life cut short, a bright promise, and a future unfulfilled. All foregone in selfless service and sacrifice for this great nation and a cause greater than self. They now rest in timeless sleep, never to grow older, but still alive as long as someone remembers them.

Casualties of America's Wars[3]

War	Period	Casualties
American Revolution	1775–83	4,435
War of 1812	1812–15	2,260
Indian Wars	~1817–98	1,000
Mexican Wars	1846–48	13,283
Civil War (Union and Confederacy)	1861–65	498,332
Spanish American War	1898–1902	2,446
World War I	1917–18	116,516
World War II	1941–45	405,399
Korean War	1950–53	36,574
Vietnam War	1964–75	58,281
Persian Gulf War (Desert Shield/Storm)	1990–91	487
Operation Iraqi Freedom	2001–14	4,418
Operation Enduring Freedom	2001–14	2,349
Operation New Dawn	2007–10	74
Operation Inherent Resolve	2014–21	106
Operation Freedom's Sentinel	2014–21	107

From this solemn register of loss, each armed service is represented among the men and women who answered America's call and traveled to the distant shores in Southeast Asia. At the outset of the writing of this book, the VVMF assembled from the DoD casualty records the names of 234 Native American casualties of the war. Since then, three more names were added from information provided by the families of the fallen. One wonders if the true number of Native American fallen will be fully known.

Of the 237, there were 154 soldiers and 76 marines of Native American origin, the vast majority served in combat specialties of infantry, armor, and artillery. This distribution is not surprising, for the greatest manpower needs during the Southeast

Asian war were in the Army and the Marine Corps and among the combat arms within each. Seven found their service calling in either the Navy or the Air Force. These Native American sons hailed from thirty-one states, plus a solitary soul who left Canada to join the fight as a United States Marine. All but forty-four of these warriors were single. A momentary pause brings rushing to consciousness the precious moments and memories these men sacrificed and the nurturing and love that so many children and grandchildren would never witness or experience because of their sacrifice.

The home of record states for each service member is shown in the accompanying map, and most, even today, have significant Native American populations. Examining the data more closely reveals a not unfamiliar trend that has distinguished the Native American population throughout American history. Native Americans have served and sacrificed for their nation in percentages disproportionate to their representation in the total population, whether from the national perspective, or in terms of their home state population.

In the 1960 United States Census, the 551,669 Native Americans and Native Alaskans were a mere 0.3% of the total U.S. population. Yet, their casualty percentage from all the casualties within the states they called home represented twice that number. In some states, the rates are many times greater.

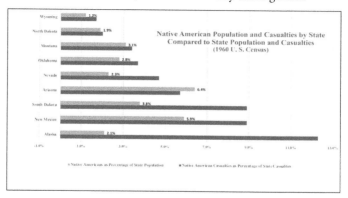

The average age of those Native Americans memorialized on the Vietnam Veterans Memorial was twenty-two years and ten months. The youngest of their number was eighteen years old and the oldest forty-five. The latter was First Sergeant Pascal Poolaw, Sr., a Kiowa Indian veteran of World War II, Korea, and Vietnam. He retired from the Army in 1962 after achieving the rank of first lieutenant. Although retired, First Sergeant Poolaw reentered the Army hopeful that by his service in Vietnam, his four sons, also in the military, might not have to fight in Vietnam. He was killed in Binh Long Province during the Battle of Loc Ninh on November 7, 1967. During his distinguished career of service, he was decorated thirteen times for valor earning the Distinguished Service Cross, three Silver Star medals, five awards of the Bronze Star, three Purple Heart medals, and three awards of the Army Commendation Medal for valor. While First Sergeant Poolaw was the most decorated Native American to serve and sacrifice in Vietnam, many of his brothers-in-arms were decorated for their bravery. From among the fallen Native American warriors, there were over 240 awards of the seven decorations presented. No less so than at Iwo Jima, where courage inspired Admiral Nimitz to write, "Uncommon valor was a common virtue."[4] The universal gallantry of these 237 souls stirred the spirit and encouraged others on the line and in the foxholes.

Native American soldiers, marines, sailors, and airmen experienced combat throughout the length and breadth of South Vietnam and in regions of Cambodia and Laos, and they fell in equal measure across the reaches of the forbidding terrain and weather they found there. As casualties of war, their bodies fell in twenty-eight out of forty-four of South Vietnam's provinces. Military Region One or I Corps Tactical Zone (CTZ) claimed the lives of 120; Military Region Two claimed forty; Military Region Three or III Corps claimed forty-six; the IV Corps area of operations claimed seventeen, and the casualty location for ten service members was not reported. Two warriors were lost in Cambodia, one in Laos and one in Hong Kong.

During the war in Vietnam, 237 service members who identified themselves as American Indian or Alaska Native by checking the Native American box on their induction papers were killed[5] and are now forever memorialized in the letters on the solemn black granite memorial that stands in the shadows of the Lincoln Memorial. While of that number, nineteen were reported as having perished while engaged in aerial flight. Each has a unique story of their final flight, a mission fulfilled or not, or a journey never completed. From the limited records available from the agencies responsible for accounting for aircraft losses and battlefield casualties, from tributes made by battle buddies or high school friends, eyewitness accounts of participants in the same mission, from newspaper articles reporting the tragic events of the last day in each man's life, or from unit histories, their stories are told with the best and most complete information available.

The linkage between Native Americans and the rotary-wing aircraft flown in Vietnam is the focus of this work. Therefore, any discussion of the Native Americans fallen from the Vietnam War should be expected to include the details of the circumstances of those who perished while performing their duties as aviators, crew members, or passengers. What follows are the individual stories of the last mission or last flight of each of the nineteen Native American warriors who perished while engaged in flight operations.

Each story describes what happened, as best as can be reconstructed, on that fateful day and under what conditions the souls aboard and the aircraft were lost. The Vietnam Helicopter Pilots Association (VHPA) has painstakingly worked over the years to gather information from official records and eyewitness stories about many of the incidents reported here, and their generosity in sharing those records with America is acknowledged. Additional supplemental information came from the Coffelt Database of Vietnam War Casualties. In some cases, the loss occurred aboard an Air Force, Marine Corps, or chartered fixed-wing aircraft for which

VHPA records do not exist. In those cases, national aviation accident records were researched for casualty-producing accidents at locations and on dates corresponding to the dates of loss reported by the Department of Defense. This led in some cases to manifest records that confirmed the service member's presence aboard and subsequent loss. Local, national, and international newspaper reporting provided the missing link to complete the casualty loss narrative. Fortunately, two stories are more complete thanks to the invaluable efforts of a VVMF friend, Lisa Lark, who undertook the collection of photographs of the fallen memorialized on the Wall. Specialist Fifth Class Johnny Arthur and Lance Corporal Winford McCosar are included in her book, *All They Left Behind*. Her research broadens their stories beyond their last flight.

The accounts are presented in alphabetical order without regard to the individual's military rank, flight status, or role on the doomed aircraft. Besides the details of the incident, the account includes a photograph of the fallen, which was generously provided by the Vietnam Veterans Memorial Fund from its campaign to obtain pictures of all the 58,281 souls memorialized on the Wall. Each entry is accompanied by a charcoal rubbing of the fallen's name made from the memorial's engravings by the National Park Service volunteers of the Vietnam Veterans Memorial who honor the war's fallen by daily caring for their memorial, enabling the greater appreciation of the Wall and its meaning by its over four million annual visitors.

Trying to capture in a single statement the purpose or rationale for the sacrifice of each Native American fallen seemed almost impossible until a statement by a wife in part eulogizing her husband was discovered. In it, Irene Chalepah Poolaw captured the essence of the ancestral warrior spirit and the importance of tribal respect and obligation when she spoke of her husband, First Sergeant Pascal Poolaw, Sr.: "He has followed the trail of the great chiefs. His people hold him in honor and highest esteem. He has given his life for his people and the country he loved so much."[6]

The Vietnam Veterans Memorial[7]

With the end of the Vietnam War in May 1975, there was a sentiment within the United States that a fitting tribute was needed after twenty years of American participation in the wars in Indochina. The concept was to create a memorial to remember those Americans who fought and served in that theater, those who died there, and those missing in action from the conflict. By the war's end, Vietnam had become so divisive that the country was tormented by internal strife and despondency. The hope was that a memorial would begin the healing of the nation.

On April 30, 1980, the U.S. Senate passed legislation authorizing the Vietnam Veterans Memorial on two acres of land, Constitution Gardens, on the National Mall in Washington, D.C. Less than a month later, on May 20, the House of Representatives likewise approved the legislation. On July 2, President

Jimmy Carter signed the measure into law in a special White House Rose Garden ceremony.

An open competition to Americans over age eighteen was held for a design which must "be reflective and contemplative; harmonious with the site, as well as with the Washington Monument and the Lincoln Memorial; contain the names of all who died or remain missing and make no political statement about war."[8] Over 1,400 designs were submitted and the unanimously selected design was that of a young Yale architecture student, Maya Ying Lin. Her design was considered to be "… a place of quiet reflection and a tribute to those who served their nation in difficult times. All who come here can find it a place of healing. This will be a quiet memorial […]. This is very much a memorial of our times, one that could not have been achieved in another time or place."[9] On November 11, 1982, seven-and-a-half years after the last American casualty fell in Vietnam, the memorial was dedicated and opened to the public.

Made of granite from Bangalore, India, cut and fabricated in Barre, Vermont, each of the Vietnam Veterans Memorial's two wings is 246 feet, 9 inches long, meeting at the apex at an angle of 125 degrees, 12 minutes. The east end of the chevron leads to the Washington Monument and the west to the Lincoln Memorial. The height of the Wall is ten feet, three inches at the center, and moves out in either direction to a terminal height of eight inches. Set into the earth, the memorial acts as a scar in the landscape. Each wall consists of seventy numbered panels inscribed with names. Each panel is three inches thick and forty inches wide and contains anywhere from one to 137 lines with five to six names per line. The names are .53 inches high and .015 inches deep. Names, which are the memorial's focal point, are aesthetic themselves. Here the cut letters emulate a gravestone and act as visual scars on an otherwise perfectly smooth surface. The name's significance is self-evident: it is a label and method of identification. On the Wall, the name also serves as a historical marker. The largest panels tend to correspond to the heaviest years of casualties as if to emphasize the volume of death during that year of fighting. The journey through the names is that of the journey through the war. For the survivors, the name is a point of recognition and acknowledgment. But even for those with no association to a specific name, the collection of all the names creates recognition and acknowledgment of the great loss. The viewer is confronted with the magnitude of the names on the Wall as a collective loss. One name adds up to many, which adds up to a tragedy regardless of how one views the Vietnam War or the idea of war itself. The names begin and end at the apex of the Wall and are listed chronologically by the date of death.[10] A reader who would like to view the story of the Wall can find an informative forty-eight-minute video prepared by the Vietnam Veterans Memorial Fund.[11]

In words of understanding and profound respect for the Vietnam Veterans Memorial, those who served, and those who paid the ultimate sacrifice during an exceedingly difficult period in our nation's history, the words of the National Park Service volunteers at the Wall are most reflective: "most walls keep people apart; this wall has brought a nation together."[12]

The men and women who died in Vietnam all had names and faces, as well as families and friends who loved and cared for them. They had futures that would never be realized. Each would never grow older than their age on the day of their untimely death or disappearance. The potential of each was cut short, and the litany of significant life events that we all anticipate and cherish for ourselves would never be theirs to behold. As a nation and a society, we will never witness the contributions and benefits that their intellect and creativity might have shared with the world. They sacrificed all their tomorrows without expectation of return. Their memory and their deeds must live on forever, and we must never forget!

The following pages contain the stories and tragedies of the nineteen courageous Native Americans who perished because they participated in aerial flight, combat or transport, operations in the Southeast Asia theater of operations, or areas adjacent to it. The final moments and events of that last flight are recorded on their last day on this earth.

Johnny Arthur[13]
Specialist Five
Army of the United States
Fruitland, New Mexico
Born: September 6, 1949
Died: June 10, 1971
Casualty Location: Pleiku Province
Memorial Panel: 3W, Line 71

Johnny Arthur.
(Courtesy of the Vietnam
Veterans Memorial Fund.)

Specialist Johnny Arthur was one of seven youngsters, five siblings, and two cousins raised on the family farm on the Navajo Reservation in Fruitland, New Mexico.[14] Both intelligent and athletic, young Arthur excelled in high school and played football, and was an occasional jockey. After graduation, he worked for the Department of Economic Opportunity, during which time he met and married Judith Bekise.[15]

In September 1969, Johnny enlisted in the Army and underwent basic training at Fort Ord, California, before being stationed at Fort Bragg, North Carolina. A year after enlisting, Johnny Arthur was in Vietnam serving with the 192nd Assault Helicopter Company of 10th Aviation Battalion, 17th Aviation Group, of the 1st Aviation Brigade out of Phan Rang in II Corps Tactical Zone. He was serving where he wanted and doing what he liked best, hoping that he could work as an airline mechanic once back home.

On Saturday, June 10, 1971, helicopters from the 192nd Assault Helicopter Company were performing a landing zone reconnaissance. One of the UH-1C's (#66-00597) was commanded by Warrant Officer Steve A. Watson and piloted by 1LT Robert E. Goolsby. The crew chief and gunner on the mission were Specialist Five Johnny Arthur and Specialist Four Louie G. Montoya, respectively. WO1 Watson and his crew were flying protective air cover for a sniffer aircraft attempting to determine if enemy forces were in proximity of the proposed LZ by flying low and slow enough to attract enemy small arms fire with each pass. Watson and crew would respond with fire to any enemy action.

As WO1 Watson initiated a descent from altitude over the landing zone, an explosion occurred in the engine area when the gunship was at 400 feet. Immediate actions to recover flight control failed, the helicopter plummeted nose down steeply and to the right, into the heavy jungle canopy and exploded and burned upon ground impact. The crew recognized their plight, and 1LT Goolsby transmitted a mayday call as they descended earthward. The crash site was thirty-three kilometers south-southwest of Phu Nhon airfield.

A UH-1H that was also part of the mission package was flying low over the scene, low enough for its crew chief to jump from the aircraft into a tree and begin descending to the burning wreckage. However, the rotor wash of the helicopter from which he jumped blew him from the tree, causing him to break his arm in the fall.

After an intense struggle, the crew chief of the second helicopter was able to extract WO1 Watson and 1LT Goolsby from the burning helicopter. They were airlifted by medevac to Pleiku. Unfortunately, Specialists Arthur and Montoya perished in the burning wreckage.

Specialist Five Arthur is interred at Navajo Methodist Mission Chapel in Farmington, New Mexico. He and Specialist Four Montoya are remembered on Panel 3W and Lines 71 and 72, respectively, on the Vietnam Veterans Memorial.

(Courtesy of the Vietnam Veterans Memorial Fund.)

Elliott Crook[16]
Specialist Five
Army of the United States
Phoenix, Arizona
Born: June 12, 1948
Died: May 17, 1971
Casualty Location: Thua Thien Province
Memorial Panel: 1W, Line 26

In 1971, Specialist Five Elliott Crook served as a crew chief on a UH-1H *Iroquois* with Company A, 101st Aviation Battalion, 101st Aviation Group of the 101st Airborne Division. On Sunday, May 16, 1971, the crew of #68-15491, Chief Warrant Officer Craig Farlow, aircraft commander; Lieutenant Joseph Nolan, pilot; Specialist Timothy Jacobsen, gunner; and Specialist Elliott Crook, crew chief, participated in a combat assault mission.

Their UH-1H would be conducting a combat assault insertion of Army of Vietnam (ARVN) Marines into LZ White not far from the Imperial City of Hue in Thua Thin Province. During the insertion, pilots from the fifth and sixth helicopters in the landing stream preceding CWO Farlow's reported taking fire from around the LZ. Lieutenant Nolan reported upon landing that his ship was under fire and that his crew chief, Specialist Crook was wounded.

Once the ARVN Marines were on the ground, #68-15491 immediately departed and achieved an altitude of 250 feet. At that point, the main rotor began to lose revolutions very quickly. The *Iroquois* crashed into the trees and burst into flames with no survivors.

On Monday, May 24, a search and recovery team was deployed to attempt to find and recover the bodies of the four deceased crew members. While two severely burned incomplete skulls and one partial right foot were recovered, and four possible sets of remains were sighted under the wreckage, the bodies of LT Nolan, CWO Farlow, and Specialists Crook and Jacobsen were never recovered. The recovered remains were those of ARVN Marines. LT Nolan was posthumously promoted to captain and Specialist Jacobsen to sergeant.

The four crewmen of UH-1H #68-15491 were initially carried by the Department of Defense (DoD) as "Missing in Action" status. Subsequently, a defense review board found that all available evidence supported a determination that the crew had indeed died in the crash. So, one year after the aircraft's loss (May 17, 1972), DoD issued findings of Dead, Body Not Recovered for Captain Nolan,

CWO Farlow, SP5 Crook, and SGT Jacobsen. As yet, their remains have not been recovered and repatriated.

These fallen Americans are now reverently memorialized on Panel 1W of the Vietnam Veterans Memorial on Lines 26 and 27.

*(Courtesy of the Vietnam
Veterans Memorial Fund.)*

Warren Leigh Dempsey[17]
Corporal
United States Marine Corps
Church Rock, New Mexico
Born: March 3, 1940
Died: December 3, 1965
Casualty Location: Quang Tin Province
Memorial Panel: 3E, Line 122

The vertical airlift capabilities of the U.S. forces in Vietnam were also used to support the men of the Army of Vietnam (ARVN). The Marine Medium Helicopter Squadron 364 (HMM-364)—Purple Fox—of Marine Aircraft Group 36 (MAG-36) and the 1st Marine Aircraft Wing (1st MAW) provided assault, medical evacuation, logistical, and later aircraft refueling support.

On Friday, December 3, 1965, a flight of eight Purple Fox UH-34D aircraft was conducting a logistics support mission from Quang Ngai to Nui Dao. Two additional aircraft were carrying twelve VC prisoners from Binh Son to Quan Ngai. After their missions were completed, the flight returned to Ky Na. Eight aircraft were immediately launched on an unscheduled ARVN resupply mission from Quang Tin to Hiep Duc, an ARVN outpost in I Corps Tactical Zone, just west of Tam Ky.

Captain Kirk Riley piloted the lead aircraft (#148762) with First Lieutenant Stanley Johnson as co-pilot. Corporals Robert White and Warren Dempsey completed the crew as crew chief and gunner, respectively. The CH-34D *Seahorse* (Army name was *Choctaw*) also carried nine ARVN soldiers to the valley outpost.

Due to the low ceiling at the time of the mission, the aircraft were obliged to fly at 2,000 feet, below the preferred flight level. Traveling over Quang Tin province, they encountered a Viet Cong ground force that engaged them with small arms and automatic weapons fire, including 14.5 mm and mortar rounds with time-delayed fusing. Captain Riley's ship was the first to be engaged and sustained numerous direct hits, including its fuel tanks in the lowest portion of the airframe. The helicopter burst into flames. Captain Riley attempted to get the aircraft safely on the ground, but it lost flight control, rolled inverted, and crashed. The fire engulfed the wreckage, and no one on board survived the fire and crash. The bodies of the crew were recovered save that of the co-pilot, who is still carried as "Body not Recovered."

Corporal Dempsey lays in eternal rest in the Navajo Veterans Cemetery at Fort Defiance, Arizona. He and his fellow members of the crew of #148762 are venerated for their service and sacrifice on Panel 3E Lines 121 through 123.

Ralph Fredenberg[18]
Specialist Four
Army of the United States
Shawano, Wisconsin
Born: October 13, 1947
Died: April 24, 1968
Casualty Location: Thua Thien Province
Memorial Panel: 51E, Line 45

*(Courtesy of the Vietnam
Veterans Memorial Fund.)*

One of the most fiercely contested pieces of real estate in all of Vietnam and by all who served there was the A Shau Valley—the Valley of Death. The valley parallels the Laotian border and runs approximately twenty-five miles northwest to southeast. Its northernmost terminus is twenty-five miles southeast of Khe Sanh and the southern terminus about twenty-seven miles southwest of Hue. The valley is the predominant geographic feature of Quang Tri Province, with the valley floor to the top of its ridgeline spanning over 5,000 feet with double canopy jungle, deep ravines, and protruding cliffs. Besides offering ready access to critical South Vietnamese cities, the valley provided major off-ramps from the North's resupply superhighway, the Ho Chi Minh Trail. Therefore, it is easy to understand why both sides spent nine years fighting for dominance of the valley.

One such day of combat in and over the valley was Wednesday, April 24, 1968, which marked the sixth day of Operation DELAWARE/Operation LAM SON 216, the joint United States and Army of the Republic of Vietnam (ARVN) operation in the A Shau. The objective was to destroy the People's Army of Vietnam forces massing in the valley for an attack against Hue and elsewhere in Quang Tri Province. Participating U.S. forces included the 3rd Brigade, 1st Cavalry Division, the 1st Brigade, 101st Airborne Division, the 196th Light Infantry Brigade, the 23rd Infantry Division, the ARVN 1st Division, and the 6th ARVN Airborne. The operation ended on May 17 with 142 Americans killed and 731 wounded.

During the thirty days of intense air and ground operations, Operation DELAWARE, the U.S. would lose over twenty-four aircraft: one C-130 *Hercules*, one CH-54 *Tarhe*, two CH-47 *Chinooks*, and over twenty UH-1 *Iroquois*. One of those was a UH-1D, #66-16490, belonging to A Company, 101st Aviation Battalion, 101st Airborne Division which was lost to enemy fire on April 24. On her final mission, #66-16490 was commanded by Warrant Officer Brian H. Philibert and piloted by Warrant Officer Stuart A. Werner. The crew chief was Specialist Five Buford G. Johnson, and Specialist Four Ralph Fredenberg flew as the gunner. A passenger on board that day was Specialist Five Dale L. Lambert. Everyone on board that day was killed in action. The *Iroquois* was engaged by hostile ground fire about one and a half miles west of FSB Veghel and about seventeen miles southwest of Hue shortly after departure. The aircraft burst into flames upon impact killing all on board.

Specialist Four Fredenberg was laid to rest in Woodlawn Cemetery in Shawano, Wisconsin. He and his comrades-in-arms of April 24, 1968, are perpetually memorialized on the black granite walls of the Vietnam Veterans Memorial on Panels 51E and 52E, Lines 45 thru 49 and 2, respectively.

(Courtesy of the Vietnam Veterans Memorial Fund.)

Charles F. Gamble, Jr.[19]
Specialist Four
Army of the United States
Juneau, Alaska
Born: November 16, 1948
Died: October 28, 1969
Casualty Location: Kontum Province
Memorial Panel: 17W, Line 127

Not all helicopters lost during the Vietnam War resulted from a combat incident. Some were claimed by mechanical failure, weather-related incidents, and pilot error, among other causes.

On Tuesday, October 28, 1969, a UH-1C *Iroquois* gunship (#66-15129) from the 57th Assault Helicopter Company based out of Kontum conducted a convoy cover mission out of Dak To. The aircraft with WO1 John H. Whittington as commander and WO1 T. L. Morris as the pilot and five passengers on board, including Specialist Four Charles F. Gamble, Jr., a heavy vehicle driver (MOS 64B20) of the 64th Transportation Company, 124th Transportation Battalion, 8th Transportation Group. Gamble and three fellow passengers, Specialist Five Gary A. Best, Specialist Five Donald L. Neely, and Specialist Five Barrent O. Torgerson were the crew of a gun truck called Might Minny.

The helicopter departed Dak To at approximately 6:00 PM toward the west, below 150 feet flight altitude, to avoid artillery fire landing northeast of the airstrip. The aircraft lost lift and plummeted to the ground as it maneuvered to gain altitude, airspeed, and flight heading. After the initial ground strike, the main rotor blades struck the tail boom severing the vertical stabilizer. The aircraft rebounded about fifty feet into the air spinning through three complete revolutions while doing so.

Upon a second impact with the ground, #66-15129 immediately burst into flames. Four souls, including Specialist Gamble, were killed in the crash, and three others were injured. Twenty-seven days after the accident, on Monday, November 24, aircraft commander Warrant Officer Whittington succumbed to his injuries and burns. The pilot and gunner ultimately survived the crash and their injuries.

Specialist Four Charles F. Gamble's remains are interred in the Evergreen Cemetery, Juneau, Alaska. His life, service, and sacrifice are memorialized on Panel 17 W, Line 127 of the Vietnam Veterans Memorial. Three other casualties of that flight are also honored on Panel 17W, Lines 126 and 129. WO Whittington's name is located on Panel 16W, Line 119.

(Courtesy of the Vietnam Veterans Memorial Fund.)

Gene Hawthorne[20]
Staff Sergeant
Army of the United States
Lupton, Arizona
Born: September 27, 1933
Died: May 4, 1966
Casualty Location: Quang Duc Province
Memorial Panel: 7E, Line 25

One of the truisms on the use of larger, more lift-capable helicopters in Vietnam was that when you lost one to an accident or enemy activity, the casualty total would be substantially larger and have a more significant impact upon the operational capability of the parent unit of those lost.

Such was the case on Wednesday, May 4, 1966, when a CH-47A *Chinook* (#64-13138) of the 147th Assault Support Helicopter Company (ASHC) of the 12th Combat Aviation Battalion crashed while on a combat resupply and troop lift mission in support of troops from the 101st Airborne Division. The incident site was approximately fifteen miles northwest of Nhon Co in Quang Duc Province of II Corps Tactical Zone. The *Chinook* carried twenty souls that day, including a five-person flight crew and fourteen men from the 101st Airborne Division's 2nd Battalion, 502nd Infantry, including Staff Sergeant Gene Hawthorne. The twentieth soul was Father (MAJ) William J. Barragy, the division's First Brigade Roman Catholic Chaplain.

The statements of eyewitnesses to the accident and crash report that the helicopter appeared to have lost all forward airspeed and was spinning. It fell straight to the ground and had smoke and flames coming from its rear. The fire was caused by excessive heat in the aircraft's transmission, and it, in turn, caused the drive shaft of the number two engine to separate. It is possible that the other engine ingested the fire, causing a loss of power, stability, and electrical systems. The pilot attempted to flare the ship before impact but failed, and the helicopter crashed on its port side and erupted into all-consuming flames. The *Chinook* was destroyed, and all aboard #64-13138 perished.

Staff Sergeant Hawthorne's remains were buried with military honors in the Santa Fe National Cemetery, Santa Fe, New Mexico. The crew and passengers of *Chinook* #64-13138 are forever memorialized together, as they died, on the same panel of the Vietnam Veterans Memorial, Panel 7E, Lines 22 through 28.

(Courtesy of the Vietnam Veterans Memorial Fund.)

Thomas Hayes[21]
Sergeant
Army of the United States
Shiprock, New Mexico
Born: May 28, 1947
Died: December 27, 1968
Casualty Location: Binh Dinh Province
Memorial Panel: 36W, Line 81

Ground fire attacks on helicopters in service by the allies in Vietnam never took a holiday, and their lower flight altitudes and slower speeds made each one an attractive target. So, whether it was a single helicopter, a flight of two, or a more significant multi-ship troop lift in the air, it was never difficult to find one or a few North Vietnamese Army (NVA) or Viet Cong (VC) soldiers willing to take the lead on one of them regardless of the potential personal consequences.

On Friday, December 27, 1968, such was the case when a UH-1C Iroquois (#66-00640) from the 187th Assault Helicopter Company was overflying Binh Dinh Provence of II Corps Tactical Zone. The helicopter, while returning to its base camp, came under small arms fire by non-explosive ballistic 7.62 mm projectiles. Sergeant Hayes was hit by hostile sniper fire and perished from his wounds.

The helicopter subsequently crashed with Specialist Thomas Hayes found in the wreckage. Hayes, posthumously promoted to sergeant, serving as an infantryman with Company A, 4th Battalion, 503rd Infantry, 173rd Airborne Brigade, was a passenger, not an aircrew member aboard the ill-fated *Iroquois* that day.

Sergeant Thomas Hayes is buried at Memory Gardens in Farmington, New Mexico. He is memorialized for his sacrifice in service to the nation he loved on Panel 36W and Line 81 of the Vietnam Veterans Memorial.

*(Courtesy of the Vietnam
Veterans Memorial Fund.)*

Clifford Curtis Johnson[22]
Chief Warrant Officer
Army of the United States
Fairfax, Oklahoma
Born: November 11, 1938
Died: January 29, 1966
Casualty Location: Binh Dinh Province
Memorial Panel: 4E, Line 110

On Saturday, January 29, 1966, a UH-1D helicopter from Charlie Troop, 227th Assault Helicopter Battalion of the 1st Cavalry Division, was conducting a combat assault as part of Operation MASHER/WHITEWING in the II Corps Tactical Zone of South Vietnam. Onboard were Aircraft Commander CW2 Clifford C. Johnson of Fairfax, Oklahoma; Pilot Captain Robert E. St. Peter of Gilman, Illinois; Crew Chief Specialist Five Melvin J. Stockdale of Moorhead, Minnesota, and Gunner Bob C. Hunt, Jr. of Tucson, Arizona. Also, on board the aircraft that day was a passenger, Specialist Four R. Harris.

UH-1D tail number 63-08750 had an experienced flight crew that January day. The three aviation specialty members had over thirty-six years of combined military service, and the entire crew was within two weeks of the halfway point of their year-long Vietnam combat tour.

During the flight, the aircraft came under heavy ground fire which was sufficient to bring it down. In the attack and subsequent crash into the side of a mountain about two and a half miles west of Phung Du, the *Iroquois* was destroyed, and all four flight crew members were killed. Specialist Harris survived the attack and crash and eventually returned home.

CW2 Johnson was returned home to his family in Fairfax, Oklahoma, and is interred in the Fairfax Cemetery. Captain St. Peter was posthumously promoted to major. He and the other crew members for the final flight of #63-08750 are eternally memorialized on Panel 4E, Lines 110 and 115 of the Vietnam Veterans Memorial.

Oscar Maloney[23]
Specialist Five
Army of the United States
Tuba City, Arizona
Born: August 6, 1945
Died: November 2, 1970
Casualty Location: Kien Gang Province
Memorial Panel: 6W, Line 35

*(Courtesy of the Vietnam
Veterans Memorial Fund.)*

Almost fifty-nine percent of the UH-1C *Iroquois* gunships used in Vietnam were lost to enemy action or accidents at the cost of 362 lives.[24] One of those accidents occurred on the morning of Monday, November 2, 1970.

At 6:50 AM that morning, a UH-1C belonging to the Armored Platoon (3rd) of the 191st Assault Helicopter Company, 13th Aviation Battalion out of Can Tho departed Rach Gia airstrip in Kien Giang Province, IV Corps Tactical Zone. The aircraft was commanded by Chief Warrant Officer John Thomas Orrico and piloted by Warrant Officer Douglas John Campbell. The other crew members onboard were Specialists Five Kenneth Lavern Brown and Oscar Maloney, crew chief and gunner, respectively. Specialist Maloney was a flight-qualified helicopter repairer (MOS: 67N2F)

UH-1C #66-15219 was destined for the Rach Soi airfield to refuel, an otherwise routine flight. The helicopter departed the traffic pattern at Rach Gia and climbed to 500 feet. At that time, the main rotor suddenly separated from the mast, which caused the *Iroquois* to nose down and crash into a fireball explosion when it impacted the ground. The incident was so violent that there was no chance for crew survival.

Seconds behind the doomed aircraft, the trail gunship circled the crash site to determine if there were any survivors. The aircraft was destroyed, and, unfortunately, there were no survivors; the crew's death was instant.

Specialist Maloney left behind his wife Emma and his good buddy Sammy with whom he played football at the Intermountain Navajo Indian Boarding School.[25] He was laid to rest in the Tuba City Cemetery in Tuba City, Arizona.

Today you will find the aircraft crew lost that day in the Mekong Delta on Panel 6W and Lines 34 and 35 on the Vietnam Veterans Memorial.

*(Courtesy of the Vietnam
Veterans Memorial Fund.)*

Winford McCosar
Lance Corporal
United States Marine Corps
Bell, California
Born: November 22, 1947
Died: March 6, 1968
Casualty Location: Quang Tri Province
Memorial Panel: 43E, Line 28

Lance Corporal Winford "Win" McCosar was the eighth of twelve children born to Matthew and Nellie McCosar.[26] He grew up in Holdenville, Oklahoma, and the environs of Oklahoma City before the family relocated to Bell, California. Like most teenagers of the 1960s, Win enjoyed sports and cars, but when he graduated from high school, job opportunities in Southern California were limited. So in 1966 he enlisted in the Marine Corps, following his brother Bunnie, even though three siblings were in the Air Force, and one was in the Naval Reserve.[27]

Following boot camp at Marine Corps Recruit Depot San Diego in October 1966, Winford received further training as an administrative man (MOS 0141) at Camp Pendleton. From there, he was transferred to Naval Base Norfolk, Virginia. Anxious to participate in the war in Vietnam, he volunteered for combat duty, arriving in Vietnam in November 1967.[28]

South Vietnam was a country of over 67,000 square miles, with innumerable military installations, bases, camps, outposts, etc., each needing supplies for their very existence and survival, dispersed throughout it. While helicopters played a vital role in moving supplies, ammunition, and rations forward, the Air Force fleets of C-130, C-123, and C-7 aircraft were the logistics workhorses of the war.

There was no more explicit demonstration of the role of these airlifters and the aerial lifeline they provided than the support of Marine forces at the Khe Sanh Combat Base (KSCB), located sixty-seven miles northwest of Hue-Phu Bai. During the siege of Khe Sanh, these aircraft and the airmen who flew them conducted 1,100 missions and delivered 12,400 tons of critical supplies. KSCB was home to 1st Battalion, 26th Marines of the 3rd Marine Division to which Lance Corporal McCosar was assigned. His arrival coincided with the commencement of Operation SCOTLAND I, the defense of Khe Sanh.

On Wednesday, March 6, 1968, a C-123K (#54-0590) of the 311th Air Commando Squadron, 3125th Air Commando Wing at Phan Rang Air Base and crewed by Air Force Lieutenant Colonel Frederick J. Hampton, First Lieutenant Ellis E. Helgeson, and Sergeant Jeffrey F. Conlin departed Da Nang with cargo destined for Hue-Phu Bai.[29] Mission #702, call sign Bookie 762, proceeded normally. After off-loading in Phu Bai, it was reloaded with forty-three Marines, a Navy corpsman, and a *Newsweek* magazine photographer, plus pallets of repair parts, personal gear, weapons, and beverages.[30] The Marines were to be replacements for those fighting at KSCB. The C-123K, its crew, and passengers were destined for Khe Sanh. Included among the Marine passengers was Lance Corporal Winford McCosar of Company B, 1st Battalion, 26th Marines, 3rd Marine Division.[31]

As Colonel Hampton was cleared to land at KSCB, he was forced to abort the landing due to a Vietnamese Air Force light plane without tower communications was obstructing the runway. During the second approach, Mission #702 took hits in its engines from heavy AA ground fire emanating from outside the KSCB perimeter. Colonel Hampton immediately sought to gain altitude and reported that he was returning to Da Nang with battle damage. Suddenly the aircraft, having lost three of its four engines, began to spiral earthward, impacting in a giant fireball into a rugged jungle-covered mountain outside the perimeter about a mile southeast of the end of the runway.

Due to the combat situation in and around KSCB, recovery efforts could not be launched until after Khe Sanh was relieved overland by Army forces. The first search teams did not reach the crash site until April 26, 1968, fifty-five days after the deadly crash. Additional search missions were made on June 24 and July 3, 1968. All human remains recovered were respectfully transferred to the Army mortuary in Da Nang. Fewer than half the remains were positively identified, and they were returned to their respective families for burial. So devastating was the crash and fire that the only salvageable piece of the aircraft was a tachometer.

The remains of those not positively identified were returned to Jefferson Barracks National Military Cemetery in St. Louis for group internment in Section 81 and grave sites 327–329 on Saturday, November 23, 1968. Lance Corporal Winford McCosar was one of these thirty-seven individually unidentifiable recovered remains buried together. Included in that common grave are thirty marines, one sailor, five airmen, and a single civilian.

Everyone onboard Mission #702 perished together in a single fiery crash, and now they live in hallowed memory on the black panels of the Vietnam Veterans Memorial. They all appear on Panel 43 E in Lines 13 through 39, with Lance Corporal McCosar among them in Line 28.

(Courtesy of the Vietnam Veterans Memorial Fund.)

Eddie Molino, Jr.[32]
Captain
Army of the United States
Fallon, Nevada
Born: June 25, 1949
Died: May 10, 1970
Casualty Location: Cambodia
Memorial Panel: 10W, Line 14

Not all fatal helicopter incidents during the Vietnam War resulted from combat action or extreme weather. A rotary winged aircraft is a highly complex system of systems with innumerable moving parts, not all seeming to be natural. A manufacture and maintenance error of a fraction of an inch can have tragic consequences. Such may well have been the case for the last flight of UH-1H tail number 68-16599.

The helicopter in question was assigned to the Headquarters Section of Charlie Troop, 7th Squadron, 1st Cavalry Regiment of the 1st Aviation Brigade operating out of Vinh Long in IV Corps Tactical Zone. On Sunday, May 10, 1970, Captain Eddie Molino, an armored reconnaissance unit commander (pilot), (MOS: 61204), was piloting the Command-and-Control Huey with Major Allen L. Smith as the Aircraft Commander. The other crewmembers included Specialist Four Gary A. Turnbull as Crew Chief and Specialist Four John W. Merschman as Gunner.

At approximately 1:30 PM, while the helicopter was flying over Cambodia, the 7th Squadron comrades watched in horror as it threw the main rotor blade and, losing lift, plummeted to the ground about twenty-seven miles north-northeast of Phu Hiep Special Forces Camp. Everyone on board perished.

Within a short period, a second *Iroquois* helicopter operating in the delta region threw the main rotor blade and crashed. Within three months of Captain Molino's fatal crash, all helicopters with rotor blades from a particular lot number were grounded until all rotor blades were replaced. Six aircraft had thrown a rotor blade and crashed, each having at least one blade from the recalled lot. The cause was ultimately isolated to a hole over drilled by 1/16 inch, which, when in use, caused the loss of the mounted balancing bolt throwing the rotor out of balance and leading to its loss.

Captain Molino has gravesite markers in the Churchill County Cemetery near his family home in Fallon, Nevada, and in the Lakeview Cemetery in Brundidge, Alabama, near his widow's home. He and the others on board the final flight of #68-16599 are forever memorialized on Panel 10W, Lines 14 and 16 of the Vietnam Veterans Memorial.

(Courtesy of the Vietnam Veterans Memorial Fund.)

Frederick Charles Schmidt[33]
Private First Class
Army of the United States
Parkville, Missouri
Born: May 11, 1945
Died: April 23, 1967
Casualty Location: Khanh Hoa Province
Memorial Panel: 18E, Line 76

Private First Class Frederick Schmidt served as an infantryman (MOS: 11B10) with Company C, 2nd Battalion, 327th Infantry of the 101st Airborne Division. On Sunday, April 23, 1967, PFC Schmidt and three other members of Charlie Company would come to the 129th Assault Helicopter Company, 10th Combat Aviation Battalion, for support.

The mission of the 129th was the tactical movement of U.S. and allied troops within the company's area of operations, and secondly, the tactical movement of supplies and equipment in the same area. This Sunday, Warrant Officers William Wells and Harold Sauer would serve as aircraft commander and pilot, respectively, for UH-1D *Iroquois* #64-13525, a relatively old aircraft with a problematic engine. Specialist Four Michael D. Walker served as crew chief and Specialist Four W.D. James as the gunner. The mission was to carry the four passengers and additional supplies to a division position south of Ban M'Drak in Khanh Hoa Province.

The flight crew was attempting their take-off from a rather confined landing zone. As the aircraft went into a hover, a passenger ran and jumped onto the skids and was eventually pulled into the ship by the gunner. The additional passenger overloaded the *Iroquois,* causing it to fly into the surrounding trees. With that, the main rotor revolutions dropped precipitously, and the ship crashed and ignited. WO Wells, pinned between his seat and the control panel, was mortally burned. Crew Chief Walker was severely burned and died seventeen days later in a stateside burn hospital. The remainder of the aircrew survived the crash and was medically evacuated.

PFC Schmidt and First Sergeant Raymond E. Benson, two of the passengers, were also killed in the crash. The two other soldiers from Charlie Company were rescued and survived their injuries. PFC Schmidt's remains were returned to his family and interred with military honors in the Council House Cemetery, Wyandotte, Oklahoma. WO Wells, FSG Benson, and PFC Schmidt are memorialized on the Vietnam Veterans Memorial Panel 18E and Lines 77, 74, and 76, respectively. Because of his later death, Specialist Walker is found on Panel 19E, Line 88.

FREDERICK C SCHMIDT

(Courtesy of the Vietnam Veterans Memorial Fund.)

Gale Robert Siow
Avionics Electronics Technician Third Class
United States Navy
Huntington Park, California
Born: December 8, 1940
Died: January 11, 1968
Casualty Location: Laos
Memorial Panel: 34E, Line 31

Not all the Native American casualties of Vietnam were soldiers or marines. Six were sailors. One of them was Avionics Electronics Technician (Radio) Third Class Gale Siow, who served with the Navy Observation Squadron 67 (VO-67) out of Nakhon Phanom Royal Thai Air Force Base in Thailand.

During the French Indochina War and the American Vietnam War, western combatants and their allies recognized the dependence of the NVA and VC forces fighting within the borders of South Vietnam on the steady, uninterrupted flow of reinforcements, weapons, munitions, materiel, and food down the Ho Chi Minh Trail in Laos. An element of the Allied strategy was the interdiction of the Trail to deny personnel, supplies, and sustenance to enemy combatants. A significant component of the interdiction campaign was seeding the Trail's length with acoustic and seismic sensors, which generated alerting signals with nearby activity. These signals were radioed to a signals processing center in Nakon Phanom, where their analysis yielded strike missions for the attack of the Trail and its enemy traffic. In January 1968, this effort was called Operation MUSCLE SHOALS.[34]

VO-67 was specifically stood up in November 1967 to accurately seed the Trail with Acoubuoy sensors dropped from their highly modified Lockheed OP-2E *Neptune* aircraft, a mission which was not declassified until 1998. On Thursday, January 11, 1968, OP-2E #131436 and two other *Neptunes* departed Nakon Phanon, each with its crew of nine. They were on a Trail seeding mission in Laos. OP-2A #131436 failed to return. The weather for the mission was inclement with heavy cloud cover. As the *Neptune* prepared to commence its sensor drop run, it began its descent through the cloud layer. The last message the aircraft's mission commander heard was, "I'm going down through this hole in the clouds." At 9:57 AM, all radio and radar contact was lost with the aircraft.

An extensive search was conducted using visual, electronic, and photographic means to find the lost aircraft. Twelve days after the disappearance of the Navy plane, an Air Force A-1 *Skyraider* pilot located aircraft wreckage on the side of a mountain near Ban Napoung, Laos. Later, the pilot of an O-2 Skymaster from the

23rd Tactical Air Support Squadron brought back photographs of the crash site on the northern side of a sheer cliff, 150 feet below the 4,583-foot summit of Phou Louang mountain. The crash site was nine miles northeast of Ban Nalouangnua in Khammouane Province. The crash was so severe and the wreckage so total that it was unsurvivable. The lost crewmen included LTJG Denis L. Anderson, LTJG Arthur C. Buck, AE2 Richard M. Mancini, CRD Delbert A. Olson, AOS Michael L. Roberts, ATN3 Gale R. Siow, LTJG Philip P. Stevens, ADJ2 Donald N. Thoreson, and PH2 Kenneth H. Widon. Also onboard and lost was the crew's mascot, a bull terrier, named Snoopy. Enemy activity, irregular topography, and heavy jungle canopy made a ground search impractical.

The crew was initially listed as Missing in Action because all signs indicated that there were no survivors and no identifiable remains. On February 23, 1968, 43 days after the crash, the crew's status was changed to Killed in Action, Body not Recovered.

Between 1993 and 2003, six U.S.-Lao investigation teams led by the Joint Task Force Full Accounting interviewed villagers in the area surrounding the crash site, gathered aircraft debris, and surveyed the purported crash site.[35] In 1993, Joint Task Force-Full Accounting teams attempted to locate and excavate the wreckage. Finally, in 1996, after three failed attempts, the wreckage was found in an operation using U. S. Army mountaineers, and human remains, two dog tags, and a military identification card were recovered. Later additional remains were recovered. They included identifiable remains from each crew member, which were repatriated on July 10, 2001, and given to respective families for burial. Gale Robert Siow was buried in section 60, gravesite 8140 of Arlington National Cemetery on June 19, 2003. The identifiable remains of seven of his crewmates were also individually buried at Arlington. The commingled remains of the casualties of the MUSCLE SHOALS mission of January 11, 1968, which could not be individually identified, were buried together in a group grave on July 8, 2003, in Arlington's section 60, gravesite 8142. The relatives of Kenneth Mancini elected to have his remains interred at another cemetery. The recovered remains of Snoopy were buried elsewhere because animals are not permitted to be buried at Arlington.

Avionics Electronics Technician Third Class Siow and his Navy crewmates are memorialized on Panel 34E and Lines 27, 28, 31, 32, and 33 of the Vietnam Veterans Memorial.

In the unforgiving Laotian jungle rests another memorial, a bronze plaque bearing the names of the nine crewmen, and "on this sacred Laotian mountain, these VO-67 heroes were not forgotten by their country."[36]

Preston Lee Smith[37]
First Lieutenant
Army of the United States
Essexville, Michigan
Born: September 23, 1947
Died: September 5, 1970
Casualty Location: Binh Dinh Province
Memorial Panel: 7W, Line 40

(Courtesy of the Vietnam Veterans Memorial Fund.)

Flying fixed- and rotary-wing aircraft in Vietnam were confounded with uncertainties that tested the skill and courage of their flight crews each and every day. In addition to the hazards of enemy actions, weather, topography, communications, and mechanical issues threatened the safety of aircrews and their passengers.

On Saturday, September 5, 1970, First Lieutenant Preston Smith of Company A, 4th Aviation Battalion, 4th Infantry Division, was piloting OH-6A *Cayuse* #68-17145 from the Second Brigade pad at An Khe, II Corps Tactical Zone. His passenger was Captain William Huling, 2nd Brigade Artillery Liaison Officer, who was being transported to Landing Zone Uplift. While flying to LZ Uplift, air traffic control alerted the flight to turbulent air conditions along 1LT Smith's planned route with an accompanying recommendation for an alternate course.

Approximately twenty-one minutes after departing An Khe, LT Smith broadcasted a mayday call and reported his position south of his destination. In actuality, the *Cayuse* was an additional sixteen miles west of where it was reported. The flight monitoring station did not pick up the cause of the mayday, but, during the transit, the engine seized, and 1LT Smith was forced to bring the helicopter down by autorotation. The landing in Binh Dinh Province was safe but hard, breaking the skid on the pilot's side, with the aircraft not fully upright when it settled.

Following the landing, CPT Huling managed to exit the aircraft but was knocked unconscious by the continuing rotation of the main rotor. 1LT Smith attempted the same but was decapitated instead. After regaining consciousness some hours later, CPT Huling found the pilot's body in the darkness. Because of the inaccurate location report, the crash site was not discovered until eight hours later, when both servicemen were recovered.

First Lieutenant Preston Smith is now honored for his service and sacrifice on Panel 7W, Line 40 on the Vietnam Veterans Memorial.

(Courtesy of the Vietnam Veterans Memorial Fund.)

Gus Smith, Jr.[38]
Specialist Four
Army of the United States
Oso, Washington
Born: November 13, 1949
Died: April 25, 1970
Casualty Location: Kontum Province
Memorial Panel: 11W, Line 53

The performance of the ubiquitous UH-1 *Iroquois* and its crews to support ground forces, especially during periods of intense enemy contact, are legendary. On each occasion, the success or failure of the assigned mission depended on the flight crew's unity, cohesion, and coordination.

On Saturday, April 25, 1970, the 189th Assault Helicopter Company, 52nd Aviation Battalion, was called upon to deliver ammunition and food to a regiment that was in heavy contact with the enemy south of Dak Seang in Kontum Province. A UH-1C gunship #66-15158 commanded by Warrant Officer Robert L. Pierce and piloted by Captain William R. McKibben flew on the mission. Serving as crew chief was Specialist Four Gus Smith, Jr., along with Private First-Class Norman D. Adkins as the gunner.

The aircraft received heavy automatic weapons fire during the first two gun runs. Still, the crew responded effectively with a combination of the minigun, aerial rocket, and machine-gun fire. However, on their third pass over the landing zone, the gunship received debilitating hits to its control mechanisms. The aircraft commander and pilot struggled to regain and maintain flight control, but the *Iroquois* began losing altitude due to the severity of the damage. Ultimately, the aircraft impacted nearby trees and burst into flames. All four crewmen perished in the crash and fire.

The service, courage, and sacrifice of Specialist Gus Smith, Jr. and his comrades on that April day are eternally memorialized on Panel 11W of the Vietnam Veterans Memorial. Their names can be found in Lines 48 and 51 through 53.

Otha Theander Thompson
Corporal
United States Marine Corps
Fort Worth, Texas
Born: April 26, 1942
Died: August 24, 1965
Casualty Location: Hong Kong
Memorial Panel: 4E, Line 42

(Courtesy of the Vietnam Veterans Memorial Fund.)

One of the provisions of a one-year combat tour in Vietnam was the opportunity to take a one-week rest and recuperation (R&R) leave at some point during the twelve-month tour.[39] Service members were permitted to select a destination from among Hawaii, Sydney, Bangkok, Hong Kong, Kuala Lumpur, Manila, Singapore, Taipei, and Tokyo.

Corporal Otha Thompson, a construction surveyor (MOS: 1441) of H&S Company, 1st Battalion, 3rd Marines was almost four months into his thirteen-month combat tour and elected to take his R&R leave in Hong Kong. While most R&R trips were made on chartered civilian aircraft, the Marines frequently used their C-130 fleet to make round-trip flights to Hong Kong. On August 24, 1965, Corporal Thompson and sixty-four fellow Marines were returning to Vietnam after a relaxing and highly spirited visit to Hong Kong.

Their return trip was to be aboard a USMC Lockheed KC-130F, a dual-purpose aircraft used for assault transport and aerial refueling for fighter and attack aircraft. That Tuesday, there were seventy-one souls on board the airplane: a crew of six and sixty-five returning Marine passengers. The planned flight route was from Kai Tak International Airport, 584 miles to Da Nang Air Base, and 375 miles to the final destination of Tan Son Nhut Air Base in Saigon. Da Nang was to be Corporal Thompson's destination.

Shortly after 10:00 AM on a clear morning, KC-130F #149802 began its take-off roll, and moments after the wheels left the ground, it began to veer left and struck a seawall before settling about forty feet off an industrial suburb on Hong Kong Island in the waters of Kowloon Bay and exploded. The cause of the accident was the partial failure of the plane's No. 1 engine with indications of fire before it hit the water.

By 1:00 PM the survivors were rescued and taken to Queen Elizabeth Hospital in Kowloon City. By nightfall, the aircraft was raised. Of those on board, fifty-nine perished, fifty-seven passengers, and two crew members. Corporal Thompson was among them. His remains are interred at Cedar Hill Memorial Park in Arlington, Texas.

Corporal Otha Thompson and his comrades were not eligible to have their names and sacrifice memorialized on the Vietnam Veterans Memorial at the time of their death, for eligibility was limited to those who died in the Vietnam combat zone. At 583 miles from the in-country destination of Da Nang, Hong Kong, was a considerable distance beyond the defined Vietnam combat zone. Over time, family members worked and petitioned to have an exception made to the combat zone restriction so that the casualties could be added to the Wall, including that of Corporal Thompson. Eventually, the petition reached the White House, and the circumstances of the loss were reviewed. A determination was made that because the plane had orders to return to the combat zone, the names of the casualties qualified to be on the Wall. President Ronald Reagan, in 1983, instructed that the names of the Marines who died in the C-130 plane crash should be honored on the Memorial.[40]

Corporal Otha Thompson is memorialized on Panel 4E, Line 42. His comrades from mission #149802 appear elsewhere before and after his name.

Harold Eugene Willis
Private First Class
Army of the United States
Bishop, California
Born: June 27, 1944
Died: January 25, 1966
Casualty Location: Binh Dinh Province
Memorial Panel: 4E, Line 96

*(Courtesy of the Vietnam
Veterans Memorial Fund.)*

Throughout the Vietnam War, there were numerous instances where large numbers of Army and Marine personnel were killed in a single aircraft accident or lost to enemy action. The incident on January 25, 1966, is one of those tragic losses that claimed many souls.

In late January 1966, soldiers of the 1st Cavalry Division were preparing for Operation MASHER, a division-sized search and destroy sweep operation set to start on January 28. On January 25, the division began redeploying its troops from Camp Radcliff to the area in and around Bong Son. Part of the pre-operation deployment plan was to move cavalrymen from Colonel Harold (Hal) Moore's 3rd Brigade, including from the 2nd Battalion, 7th Cavalry by Air Force C-123K *Provider* #54-0702 from the 311th Air Commando Squadron, 315th Air Commando Group, 13th Air Force. The movement was from An Khe Air Base to the Special Forces Camp Bong Son Landing Zone.

The *Provider* had a crew of four and forty-two soldiers with their weapons, ammunition, and grenades, including Private First-Class Harold E. Willis of Company A, 2nd Battalion, 7th Cavalry, 1st Cavalry Division.[41] It was raining at take-off with the ceiling at a mere 300 feet. The aircraft encountered some trouble as it was attempting to return to An Khe within ten minutes of departure. With one of its two engines on fire it slammed, inverted into a forested hillside along QL-19 at the west end of Deo Mang Pass and about six miles east of An Khe, according to soldiers from the 1st Battalion, 8th Cavalry who were guarding the pass at the time of the incident. At the wreckage site, it was evident that the *Provider* experienced a fire in its number two engine. The aircraft was a total loss, and all forty-six people on board were killed.[42] One-third of the soldiers of Company A lost in the crash were combat leaders—commissioned and non-commissioned officers. That is a tremendous loss, especially for a unit within three days of beginning a major combat operation. It would be the worst air crash in Vietnam to that point involving U.S. troops.

Private First Class Harold Willis was laid to rest at the West Line Street Cemetery in Bishop, Inyo Country, California. He is eternally remembered on Line 96 on Panel 4E of the Vietnam Veterans Memorial in Washington, D.C. The crew and fellow passengers on the January 25, 1966, flight can be found on Panel 4E, Lines 86 through 96, and 110.

*(Courtesy of the Vietnam
Veterans Memorial Fund.)*

Adam Wilson[43]
Warrant Officer
Army of the United States
San Diego, California
Born: May 1, 1948
Died: November 15, 1969
Casualty Location: Quang Ngai Province
Memorial Panel: 16W, Line 82

The helicopter became the workhorse of almost everything the Army did during the Vietnam War, where airmobile operations were the norm. Ground forces and infantry soldiers were frequently lifted by helicopters and transported to landing zones from which they would conduct operations against the enemy to include reconnaissance, combat assault, raids, etc. Such missions would emanate from the landing zone, which also became the infantry unit's command post, with the troops periodically returning there to refit and recover before resuming operations. Such was the case of Bravo Company, 3rd Battalion, 1st Infantry Regiment of the 11th Infantry Brigade of the 23rd Infantry Division (American) which was conducting ground operations in the I Corps Tactical Zone in November 1969.

On Saturday, November 15, 1969, aircraft from the 174th Assault Helicopter Company of the 14th Combat Aviation Battalion were making resupply runs into the Bravo Company's LZ. One aircraft was a UH-1H *Iroquois* (tail number 68-15661) commanded by Warrant Officer Adam Wilson and piloted by Warrant Officer Ricardo W. Regalado. Other crew members included Crew Chief, Specialist Four Forest C. Hodgkin, and Gunner, Specialist Four Ronald L. Ducommun. The entire crew averaged just six months in-country, with Warrant Officer Adams having the most time with seven months. Also on board that day was Specialist Four James J. Gunderson from the 11th Light Infantry Brigade, who had caught a ride on the resupply ship to visit with troopers from Bravo Company, his previous unit.

The aircrew experienced high winds when attempting to land on the hill that was being used as the company landing zone, and as a result they had to follow the same approach for each attempt. Alerted to the helicopter's flight path from previous attempts, the enemy subjected it to intense small arms fire on its fifth approach. The aircraft caught fire, crashed, and was consumed in flames. The infantrymen in the immediate area rushed to the crash site to secure the place and assist the crew, but four perished in the aircraft and the fifth body was found over fifty feet from the wreckage. Bravo Company maintained watch over their fallen comrades until they could be evacuated the next day.

Specialist Gunderson was posthumously promoted to Sergeant. He and the others on board the final flight of #68-15661 are eternally memorialized on Panel 16W, Lines 78 and 80 thru 82 of the Vietnam Veterans Memorial. Warrant Officer Wilson was buried with military honors at the Fort Rosecrans National Cemetery in San Diego, California.

Strather Franklin Wood.
(Courtesy of the Vietnam
Veterans Memorial Fund.)

Strather Franklin Wood[44]
First Lieutenant
United States Marine Corps
Eugene, Oregon
Born: April 26, 1944
Died: February 18, 1971
Casualty Location: Thua Tin Province
Memorial Panel: 5W, Line 119

The first four helicopters of Heavy Helicopter Squadron 463 (HMH-463), the first CH-53 squadron in the Marine Corps, were deployed to Vietnam in December 1966. The Squadron was sited at the Marble Mountain Air Facility. The squadron became part of Marine Air Group 16, 1st Marine Air Wing of the III Marine Amphibious Force flying the Sikorsky CH-53 *Sea Stallion*. The balance of the squadron deployed to South Vietnam in May 1967, joining the early arriving detachment on Marble Mountain. The men of the "Pegasus" squadron would spend the next four years participating in combat operations during the War. As a heavy helicopter squadron, HMH-463 provided assault support transport of combat troops, supplies, and equipment to support ground combat operations.

According to its unit history, during their time in South Vietnam, the squadron was called upon to perform some rather unique, even unusual, missions. In 1968, the squadron was assigned to take part in Operation BAHROOM, which required the transport and delivery of an elephant via helicopter from Chu Lai Air Base to the Special Forces camp at Tra Bong.[45] The elephant was destined to spend its days working for a local sawmill.

The following year, the squadron began experimenting with bombing missions for what would become known as "barrel bombing." The concept was for a two to four-ship flight to make low-altitude passes over enemy positions to draw their fire. Once the helicopters received ground fire, they would overfly the area again, dropping fifty-five-gallon drums of a gasoline and napalm mixture slung below the aircraft. The ground impact was usually sufficient to ignite the mixture; however, occasionally, machine gun fire from the helicopter door guns or white phosphorous rockets (WP) from an OV-10 *Bronco* or AH-1 *Cobra* were necessary to start the conflagration. The biggest "barrel bombing" mission was a twelve-ship attack over "Charlie Ridge" just west of Da Nang. That day the squadron dropped over 400 tons of the fuel mixture against entrenched North Vietnamese Army positions.[46] The following day, Marines mounted a ground assault and found no resistance. The enemy occupants of the ridge were found dead, either from burns or from oxygen starvation for those who took refuge in the deep bunkers found throughout the area.

Marine First Lieutenant Strather Wood arrived in Vietnam on January 11, 1971, and was assigned to HMH-463. On February 18, 1971, one of the CH-53D helicopters (#156667) from the squadron was flying in Thua Thien Province (I Corps Tactical Zone) about six miles northeast of the Imperial City of Hue with a crew of five and four passengers, including an Army Sergeant First Class from the Army's Military Assistance Command. The *Sea Stallion*, returning to its base at Marble Mountain, experienced a mechanical flight control failure and crashed at Doi Dian, which caused the helicopter to explode in mid-air. The crash site was located six miles northeast of Phu Bai Airfield, and the lost crew members included pilot Major Wayne Ruben Hyatt, co-pilot First Lieutenant Strather Franklin Wood, crew chief Sergeant Allen Keith McElfresh, and gunners Sergeant William Clinton Odom, Jr., and Corporal Larry Richard Hatter. The passengers consisted of three Marines: Staff Sergeant Richard Thomas Baker, Sergeant Richard Arthur Lillie, Sergeant Gregory Alec Sloat, and Army Sergeant First Class James Arthur Long.

The service and sacrifice of Lieutenant Wood and his comrades on that February day are eternally memorialized on Panel 5W of the Vietnam Veterans Memorial. The names of the nine men who perished can be found in Lines 114 and 116 through 119. Lieutenant Wood was laid to rest at Eternal Hill Cemetery in Klamath Falls, Oregon.

Three months after that fatal crash, HMH-463 was relocated to Marine Corps Air Station Kaneohe Bay, Hawaii, and there was reassigned to Marine Aircraft Group 24 (MAG-24), 1st Marine Brigade. However, the 463rd was not yet relieved of its Vietnam War duties and returned to Vietnam in 1973. From February through July of that year, it participated in Operation END SWEEP, a minesweeping operation in the Haiphong/Hon Gai area of North Vietnam.

Less than two years later, the squadron embarked on the USS *Hancock,* ultimately taking up station in the Gulf of Thailand. On April 12, 1975, the squadron participated in the helicopter evacuation of Phnom Penh, Cambodia, Operation EAGLE PULL. By the end of that month, the "Pegasus" crews took part in Operation FREQUENT WIND on April 29–30, 1975, the final phase in evacuating American civilians and "at-risk" Vietnamese from Saigon. The operation closely followed the takeover of the former South Vietnamese capital by the North Vietnamese People's Army of Vietnam (PAVN). With the conclusion of these missions, so ended the support by HMH-463 in operations in Southeast Asia and the exclamation point to "America's Helicopter War."

While the above narrative highlights the nineteen Native Americans who died in aerial missions or flights, it would be disrespectful not to mention the non-aviation Native American sons, brothers, uncles, husbands, fathers, and grandfathers who also made the ultimate sacrifice for their country. In the pages that follow, one will find the names of all 237 of these sons of America and information about their lives, service, and sacrifice. Each entry displays the name, branch of service, and the final rank that each service member achieved; in some cases, that rank represents a posthumous promotion. Also included for each entry is the veteran's home of record, which is usually the place they entered the service.

As previously described, tribal affiliation was not captured in the casualty records maintained by the Department of Defense and subsequently reported in the data used to inscribe the Vietnam Veterans Memorial Wall.

"They shall not grow as we that are left grow old. Age shall not weary them, nor the years condemn them. By the going down of the sun and in the morning, we will remember them, less we forget."[47]

John Michael Acosta
Private First Class
Army of the United States
Sacramento, California
Born: August 14, 1947
Died: January 21, 1968
Casualty Location: Pleiku Province
Memorial Panel: 35E, Line 2

John Ira Aleck
Private First Class
United States Marine Corps
Reno, Nevada
Born: December 10, 1947
Died: March 7, 1969
Casualty Location: Quang Nam Province
Memorial Panel: 30W, Line 62

Alvin Adikai, Jr.
Private First Class
Army of the United States
Window Rock, Arizona
Born: January 21, 1949
Died: March 14, 1971
Casualty Location: Quang Tri Province
Memorial Panel: 4W, Line 45

Dennis William Anderson
Staff Sergeant
Army of the United States
Norfolk, Nebraska
Born: September 19, 1936
Died: December 11, 1966
Casualty Location: Not Reported
Memorial Location: Panel 13E, Line 31

Roger Duane Alberts
Private First Class
Army of the United States
Fort Totten, North Dakota
Born: July 11, 1947
Died: February 5, 1968
Casualty Location: Gia Dinh Province
Memorial Panel: 37E, Line 30

Johnnie Antonio, Jr.
Lance Corporal
United States Marine Corps
Crownpoint, New Mexico
Born: December 22, 1946
Died: December 27, 1967
Casualty Location: Quang Tri Province
Memorial Panel: 32E, Line 67

Vallance Galen Arkie
Corporal
United States Marine Corps
Parker, Arizona
Born: September 7, 1947
Died: September 3, 1967
Casualty Location: Quang Tri Province
Memorial Panel: 25E, Line 91

Dudney Nelson Arlentino
Specialist Four
Army of the United States
Coolidge, Arizona
Born: April 29, 1945
Died: December 7, 1967
Casualty Location: Binh Dinh Province
Memorial Panel: 31E, Line 58

Dean Edward Armstrong
Gunnery Sergeant
United States Marine Corps
Atoka, Oklahoma
Born: February 4, 1931
Died: May 13, 1967
Casualty Location: Quang Tin Province
Memorial Panel: 19E, Line 103

Johnny Arthur
Specialist Five
Army of the United States
Fruitland, New Mexico
Born: September 6, 1949
Died: June 10, 1971
Casualty Location: Pleiku Province
Memorial Panel: 3W, Line 71

Herbert Arviso
Sergeant
Army of the United States
Farmington, New Mexico
Born: October 13, 1948
Died: October 29, 1969
Casualty Location: Binh Dinh Province
Memorial Panel: 17W, Line 119

Floyd Samuel Atole
Sergeant
Army of the United States
Dulce, New Mexico
Born: November 7, 1945
Died: February 21, 1969
Casualty Location: Long An Province
Memorial Panel: 32W, Line 69

William Eugene Austin
Sergeant
Army of the United States
Lenoir, North Carolina
Born: August 13, 1949
Died: July 31, 1970
Casualty Location: Tay Ninh Province
Memorial Panel: 8W, Line 72

Elwood Baker
Lance Corporal
United States Marine Corps
Battiest, Oklahoma
Born: January 8, 1947
Died: June 24, 1967
Casualty Location: Thua Thien Province
Memorial Panel: 22E, Line 57

Paul Wayne Barnett
Specialist Four
Army of the United States
Dustin, Oklahoma
Born: July 4, 1949
Died: January 3, 1969
Casualty Location: Binh Duong Province
Memorial Panel: 35W, Line 23

Luther Barney
Specialist Five
Army of the United States
Mexican Spring, New Mexico
Born: November 27, 1950
Died: December 21, 1971
Casualty Location: Bien Hoa Province
Memorial Panel: 2W, Line 90

Edward Nasuesak Barr
Seaman
United States Navy
Brevig Mission, Alaska
Born: October 22, 1949
Died: May 3, 1969
Casualty Location: Dinh Tuong Province
Memorial Panel: 26W, Line 105

Thomas M. Barr
Specialist Five
Army of the United States
Anchorage, Alaska
Born: July 1, 1945
Died: May 12, 1969
Casualty Location: Quang Nam Province
Memorial Panel: 25W, Line 60

James Patrick Barrios
Specialist Four
Army of the United States
Lemoore, California
Born: December 21, 1947
Died: January 12, 1969
Casualty Location: Dinh Tuong Province
Memorial Panel: 35W, Line 74

Andrew Battiest
Corporal
Army of the United States
Calipatria, California
Born: October 9, 1946
Died: June 25, 1968
Casualty Location: Kontum Province
Memorial Panel: 55W, Line 32

Donald Earl Bear
Sergeant First Class
Army of the United States
Mountain View, Oklahoma
Born: April 21, 1942
Died: July 8, 1968
Casualty Location: Hua Nghia Province
Memorial Panel: 53W, Line 42

Leo Vernon Beaulieu
Private First Class
United States Marine Corps
Lengby, Minnesota
Born: September 2, 1944
Died: May 16, 1966
Casualty Location: Quang Tin Province
Memorial Panel: 7E, Line 64

Eddie Charles Begaye
Corporal
United States Marine Corps
Ramah, New Mexico
Born: February 19, 1943
Died: May 25, 1967
Casualty Location: Quang Nam Province
Memorial Panel: 20E, Line 100

Felix Dohaltahe Begaye
Private First Class
United States Marine Corps
Little Water, New Mexico
Born: September 4, 1948
Died: December 10, 1967
Casualty Location: Quang Nam Province
Memorial Panel: 31E, Line 70

Harold L. Begody
Specialist Four
Army of the United States
Tuba City, Arizona
Born: November 12, 1941
Died: February 14, 1968
Casualty Location: Thua Thien Province
Memorial Panel: 39E, Line 28

John George Bellanger
Lance Corporal
United States Marine Corps
Minneapolis, Minnesota
Born: September 1, 1948
Died: February 14, 1968
Casualty Location: Quang Tri Province
Memorial Panel: 39E, Line 29

Dale Earle Benson
Private First Class
Army of the United States
Tama, Iowa
Born: March 19, 1947
Died: January 15, 1967
Casualty Location: Binh Duong Province
Memorial Panel: 14E, Line 31

Vincent Bernard
Lance Corporal
United States Marine Corps
Dorchester, Massachusetts
Born: September 7, 1945
Died: September 21, 1968
Casualty Location: Quang Ngai Province
Memorial Panel: 43W, Line 51

James Victor Bigtree
Corporal
United States Marine Corps
Syracuse, New York
Born: October 9, 1940
Died: January 11, 1966
Casualty Location: Quang Nam Province
Memorial Panel: 4E, Line 63

Larry Rogers Billie
Private First Class
United States Marine Corps
Chinle, Arizona
Born: September 13, 1943
Died: October 11, 1966
Casualty Location: Quang Nam Province
Memorial Panel: 11E, Line 66

Robert Lee Blackfox
Private First Class
United States Marine Corps
Tahlequah, Oklahoma
Born: May 25, 1948
Died: February 17, 1970
Casualty Location: Quang Nam Province
Memorial Panel: 13W, Line 22

Dwight Thomas Blackwater
First Lieutenant
Army of the United States
Phoenix, Arizona
Born: December 28, 1945
Died: June 19, 1971
Casualty Location: Quang Tin Province
Memorial Panel: 3W, Line 82

David Henry Boswell
Hospitalman
United States Navy
Buffalo, New York
Born: December 6, 1945
Died: March 6, 1968
Casualty Location: Quang Nam Province
Memorial Panel: 43E, Line 14

Johnny Charles Briseno
Private First Class
United States Marine Corps
Waynoka, Oklahoma
Born: June 26, 1949
Died: June 18, 1970
Casualty Location: Quang Nam Province
Memorial Panel: 9W, Line 62

Randolph Brown, Jr.
Lance Corporal
United States Marine Corps
North Highlands, California
Born: June 29, 1947
Died: February 12, 1969
Casualty Location: Quang Nam Province
Memorial Panel: 32W, Line 19

Lawrence Dean Brownotter
Corporal
Army of the United States
Bullhead, South Dakota
Born: December 12, 1944
Died: November 18, 1967
Casualty Location: Dinh Tuong Province
Memorial Panel: 30E, Line 13

David Bruner
Specialist Four
Army of the United States
Sapulpa, Oklahoma
Born: October 16, 1946
Died: May 14, 1969
Casualty Location: Quang Nam Province
Memorial Panel: 24W, Line 2

Lawrence Joseph Butler
Specialist Four
Army of the United States
Hayward, Wisconsin
Born: May 4, 1948
Died: April 4, 1969
Casualty Location: Gia Dinh Province
Memorial Panel: 27W, Line 8

Eugene Charles Campbell
Lance Corporal
United States Marine Corps
Redwood Valley, California
Born: July 1, 1947
Died: August 27, 1967
Casualty Location: Quang Nam Province
Memorial Panel: 25E, Line 49

Jose Ramon Cano
Specialist Four
Army of the United States
Austin, Texas
Born: May 22, 1948
Died: January 15, 1969
Casualty Location: Binh Duong Province
Memorial Panel: 34W, Line 4

Joshua Eli Carney
Staff Sergeant
Army of the United States
Mc Alester, Oklahoma
Born: August 23, 1944
Died: February 12, 1971
Casualty Location: Quang Tin Province
Memorial Panel: 5W, Line 98

Peter Charlie
Lance Corporal
United States Marine Corps
Farmington, New Mexico
Born: July 21, 1949
Died: August 8, 1970
Casualty Location: Quang Nam Province
Memorial Panel: 8W, Line 93

Alvin Chester
Lance Corporal
United States Marine Corps
Window Rock, Arizona
Born: December 7, 1943
Died: July 5, 1965
Casualty Location: Binh Dinh Province
Memorial Location: 2E, Line 27

Gerald Gregory Chino
Specialist Four
Army of the United States
Cubero, New Mexico
Born: November 17, 1947
Died: March 24, 1968
Casualty Location: Hau Nghia Province
Memorial Panel: 46E, Line 3

Franklin Delano Chopper
Private First Class
Army of the United States
Brockton, Montana
Born: February 24, 1945
Died: June 13, 1967
Casualty Location: Binh Duong Province
Memorial Panel: 21E, Line 96

Paul Emerson Christjohn
Private First Class
Army of the United States
Oneida, Wisconsin
Born: September 15, 1945
Died: September 9, 1968
Casualty Location: Not Reported
Memorial Panel: 44W, Line 8

Gilmore Wilson Christy
Specialist Four
Army of the United States
Tulsa, Oklahoma
Born: July 23, 1945
Died: February 6, 1967
Casualty Location: Bien Hoa Province
Memorial Panel: 14E, Line 127

Peter Yazzie Claw
Private First Class
Army of the United States
Kayenta, Arizona
Born: November 18, 1945
Died: April 5, 1968
Casualty Location: Kontum Province
Memorial Panel: 48E, Line 18

Ronald Myron Cloud
Sergeant
Army of the United States
Ponemah, Minnesota
Born: June 12, 1945
Died: July 4, 1968
Casualty Location: Thua Thien Province
Memorial Panel: 53W, Line 8

Austin Morris Corbiere
Lance Corporal
United States Marine Corps
Little Current, Ontario, Canada
Born: February 19, 1943
Died: May 9, 1966
Casualty Location: Quang Nam Province
Memorial Panel: 7E, Line 42

Elliott Crook
Specialist Five
Army of the United States
Phoenix, Arizona
Born: June 12, 1948
Died: May 17, 1971
Casualty Location: Thua Thien Province
Memorial Panel: 1W, Line 26

Frank Bryan Cruz
Private First Class
Army of the United States
Detroit, Michigan
Born: November 19, 1947
Died: July 27, 1967
Casualty Location: Military Region II
Memorial Panel: 24E, Line 5

Wilbert Wayne Cuch
Lance Corporal
United States Marine Corps
Springville, Utah
Born: January 8, 1949
Died: May 26, 1968
Casualty Location: Quang Tri Province
Memorial Panel: 66W, Line 4

Albert Allen Curley
Private First Class
United States Marine Corps
Cubero, New Mexico
Born: April 12, 1947
Died: March 30, 1970
Casualty Location: Quang Ngai Province
Memorial Panel: 17E, Line 70

Bennie Dale
Specialist Four
Army of the United States
Wide Ruins, Arizona
Born: June 3, 1945
Died: May 12, 1968
Casualty Location: Quang Tri Province
Memorial Panel: 59E, Line 3

Christopher Wilmer Davis
Specialist Four
Army of the United States
Belcourt, North Dakota
Born: June 1, 1942
Died: March 18, 1967
Casualty Location: Gia Dinh Providence
Memorial Panel: 16E, Line 104

Jerry Lorenzo Daw
Corporal
Army of the United States
Tonalea, Arizona
Born: December 10, 1945
Died: June 8, 1967
Casualty Location: Quang Ngai Province
Memorial Panel: 21E, Line 73

Terry Louis Deer
Private First Class
Army of the United States
Wewoka, Oklahoma
Born: November 5, 1948
Died: October 5, 1970
Casualty Location: Binh Dinh Province
Memorial Panel: 7W, Line 113

Charles Kenneth Deere
Private First Class
Army of the United States
Okemah, Oklahoma
Born: September 16, 1947
Died: May 5, 1968
Casualty Location: Binh Duong Province
Memorial Panel: 55E, Line 8

Bruce Edward Deerinwater
Staff Sergeant
Army of the United States
Mc Alester, Oklahoma
Born: January 30, 1947
Died: January 25, 1969
Casualty Location: Quang Ngai Province
Memorial Panel: 34W, Line 74

Warren Leigh Dempsey
Corporal
United States Marine Corps
Church Rock, New Mexico
Born: March 3, 1940
Died: December 3, 1965
Casualty Location: Quang Tin Province
Memorial Panel: 3E, Line 122

Daniel Dee Denipah
Lance Corporal
United States Marine Corps
Tuba City, Arizona
Born: March 31, 1947
Died: December 28, 1967
Casualty Location: Thua Thein Province
Memorial Panel: 32E, Line 86

James Price DeVaney
Corporal
Army of the United States
Goldsboro, North Carolina
Born: October 29, 1949
Died: February 28, 1970
Casualty Location: Binh Duong Province
Memorial Panel: 13W, Line 68

Eric Melvin Dewey
Private First Class
United States Marine Corps
Bishop, California
Born: December 27, 1946
Died: July 29, 1967
Casualty Location: Quang Tin Province
Memorial Panel: 24E, Line 20

Gary Dean Doctor
United States Marine Corps
Lance Corporal
Basom, New York
Born: December 12, 1946
Died: October 7, 1966
Casualty Location: Quang Tri Province
Memorial Panel: 11E, Line 56

Dennis Paul Dunsing
Private First Class
Army of the United States
Ukiah, California
Born: April 13, 1943
Died: May 6, 1968
Casualty Location: Binh Duong Province
Memorial Panel:56E, Line 5

Forbis Pipkin Durant, Jr.
Lance Corporal
United States Marine Corps
Atoka, Oklahoma
Born: May 17, 1945
Died: March 10, 1968
Casualty Location: Quang Nam Province
Memorial Panel: 44E, Line 6

George Joe Bucky Eisenberger
Sergeant
Army of the United States
Pawhuska, Oklahoma
Born: March 2, 1940
Died: December 5, 1965
Casualty Location: Binh Duong Province
Memorial Panel: 3E, Line 126

David Henry Elisovsky
Sergeant
Army of the United States
Cordova, Alaska
Born: July 24, 1947
Died: January 23, 1966
Casualty Location: Phu Yen Province
Memorial Panel: 4E, Line 83

Van Etsitty
Corporal
Army of the United States
Gallup, New Mexico
Born: November 17, 1941
Died: June 1, 1968
Casualty Location: Kien Tuong Province
Memorial Panel: 61W, Line 3

William John Fisher
Lance Corporal
United States Marine Corps
Arlee, Montana
Born: October 12, 1941
Died: September 22, 1966
Casualty Location: Quang Tin Province
Memorial Panel: 10E, Line 132

Robert Lee Flores
Sergeant
Army of the United States
Parker, Arizona
Born: December 24, 1947
Died: December 15, 1967
Casualty Location: Binh Dinh Province
Memorial Panel: 31E, Line 98

Conrad Lee Flying Horse
Lance Corporal
United States Marine Corps
Mc Intosh, South Dakota
Born: August 29, 1951
Died: August 31, 1970
Casualty Location: Quang Nam Province
Memorial Panel: 7W, Lane 26

George Leonard Fragua
Private First Class
Army of the United States
Jemez Pueblo, New Mexico
Born: November 18, 1947
Died: December 25, 1966
Casualty Location: Binh Dinh Province
Memorial Panel: 13E, Line 78

Patrick Phillip Francisco
Lance Corporal
United States Marine Corps
Stanfield, Arizona
Born: April 15, 1945
Died: April 26, 1967
Casualty Location: Quang Tri Province
Memorial Panel: 18E, Line 93

Thomas Edwin Fraser
Private
United States Marine Corps
Detroit, Michigan
Born: June 16, 1951
Died: April 4, 1970
Casualty Location: Quang Nam Province
Memorial Panel: 12W, Line 92

Ralph Fredenberg
Specialist Four
Army of the United States
Shawano, Wisconsin
Born: October 13, 1947
Died: April 24, 1968
Casualty Location: Thua Thien Province
Memorial Panel: 51E, Line 45

Charles F. Gamble, Jr.
Specialist Four
Army of the United States
Juneau, Alaska
Born: November 16, 1948
Died: October 28, 1969
Casualty Location: Kontum Province
Memorial Panel: 17W, Line 127

Leslie Neil General
Corporal
United States Marine Corps
Niagara Falls, New York
Born: June 26, 1946
Died: May 1, 1968
Casualty Location: Quang Tri Province
Memorial Panel: 53E, Line 31

Luther Anderson Ghahate
Specialist Four
Army of the United States
Zuni, New Mexico
Born: September 2, 1946
Died: October 21, 1968
Casualty Location: Darlac Province
Memorial Panel: 40W, Line 12

Wallace Going
Petty Officer Second Class
United States Navy
Watson, Oklahoma
Born: May 16, 1932
Died: December 23, 1968
Casualty Location: Bien Hoa Province
Memorial Panel: 36W, Line 69

Ronald Christy Goodiron
Private First Class
United States Marine Corps
Shields, North Dakota
Born: December 23, 1947
Died: February 28, 1968
Casualty Location: Thua Thien Province
Memorial Panel: 41E, Line 66

Larry Green
Private First Class
United States Marine Corps
Niagara Falls, New York
Born: June 15, 1945
Died: January 9, 1969
Casualty Location: Quang Tri Province
Memorial Panel: 35W, Line 60

William Archie Gritts
Corporal
Army of the United States
Hulbert, Oklahoma
Born: April 1, 1948
Died: June 13, 1968
Casualty Location: Gia Dinh Province
Memorial Panel: 57W, Line 9

Victor Hale
Lance Corporal
United States Marine Corps
Topeka, Kansas
Born: October 27, 1942
Died: December 8, 1968
Casualty Location: Quang Nam Province
Memorial Panel: 37W, Line 65

Kenneth Dewayne Harjo
Specialist Four
Army of the United States
Seminole, Oklahoma
Born: May 27, 1950
Died: November 18, 1969
Casualty Location: Tay Ninh Province
Memorial Panel: 16W, Line 91

Carl E. Harris
Sergeant
Army of the United States
Rock Hill, South Carolina
Born: February 23, 1937
Died: November 15, 1965
Casualty Location: Pleiku Province
Memorial Panel: 3E, Line 57

Theodore Magnus Hatle
Corporal
Army of the United States
Sisseton, South Dakota
Born: November 24, 1946
Died: June 23, 1969
Casualty Location: Quang Tin Province
Memorial Panel: 22W, Line 120

Gene Hawthorne
Staff Sergeant
Army of the United States
Lupton, Arizona
Born: September 27, 1933
Died: May 4, 1966
Casualty Location: Quang Duc Province
Memorial Panel: 7E, Line 25

Thomas Hayes
Sergeant
Army of the United States
Shiprock, New Mexico
Born: May 28, 1947
Died: December 27, 1968
Casualty Location: Binh Dinh Province
Memorial Panel: 36W, Line 81

Louis Glenn Healy
Private
United States Marine Corps
Dodson, Montana
Born: July 11, 1949
Died: July 5, 1968
Casualty Location: Quang Tri Province
Memorial Panel: 53W, Line 19

Robert Gregory Henry
Private
Army of the United States
San Diego, California
Born: January 7, 1947
Died: June 25, 1968
Casualty Location: Quang Ngai Province
Memorial Panel: 55W, Line 35

Larry Roy Henshaw
Sergeant
Army of the United States
Sapulpa, Oklahoma
Born: March 22, 1950
Died: May 1, 1970
Casualty Location: Thua Thien Province
Memorial Panel: 11W, Line 79

Donald Hicks
Specialist Four
Army of the United States
Tonalea, Arizona
Born: February 10, 1945
Died: June 30, 1968
Casualty Location: Tay Ninh Province
Memorial Panel: 54W, Line 24

Leonard Martin Hickson
Sergeant
Army of the United States
Fort Defiance, Arizona
Dorn: August 22, 1946
Died: May 18, 1969
Casualty Location: Thua Thien Province
Memorial Panel: 24W, Line 42

Charles Vincent Howard
Sergeant
Army of the United States
Brimley, Michigan
Born: March 24, 1943
Died: July 2, 1966
Casualty Location: Binh Long Province
Memorial Panel: 8E, Line 120

Ferrell Hummingbird
Lance Corporal
United States Marine Corps
Oakland, California
Born: August 13, 1946
Died: January 14, 1967
Casualty Location: Thua Thien Province
Memorial Panel: 14E, Line 27

Benny Leo Huskon
Specialist Four
Army of the United States
Leupp, Arizona
Born: May 20, 1947
Died: June 7, 1968
Casualty Location: Gia Dinh Province
Memorial Panel: 59W, Line 23

Jean Baptiste Incashola
Private First Class
Army of the United States
Saint Ignatius, Montana
Born: August 10, 1937
Died: November 23, 1966
Casualty Location: Not Reported
Memorial Panel: 12E, Line 112

John Lee Ingram
Private First Class
United States Marine Corps
Weleetka, Oklahoma
Born: May 15, 1949
Died: April 7, 1968
Casualty Location: Thua Thien Province
Memorial Panel: 48E, Line 41

Sam Ivey
Private First Class
Army of the United States
Mc Grath, Alaska
Born: March 21, 1942
Died: September 16, 1965
Casualty Location: Not Reported
Memorial Panel: 2E, Line 84

Lloyd Wilner Jackson
Sergeant
Army of the United States
Austin, Nevada
Born: April 12, 1948
Died: May 7, 1970
Casualty Location: Thua Thien Province
Memorial Panel: 11W, Line124

Michael Meredith Jackson
Private First Class
Army of the United States
Waubay, South Dakota
Born: August 29, 1944
Died: March 24, 1966
Casualty Location: Not Reported
Memorial Panel: 6E, Line 44

Ralford John Jackson
Private First Class
United States Marine Corps
Tuba City, Arizona
Born: July 15, 1948
Died: May 22, 1969
Casualty Location: Quang Tri Province
Memorial Panel: 24W, Line 76

Kenneth Robert Jamerson
Lance Corporal
United States Marine Corps
Little Eagle, South Dakota
Born: August 3, 1946
Died: April 5, 1967
Casualty Location: Quang Ngai Province
Memorial Panel: 17E, Line 104

Billie James
Specialist Four
Army of the United States
Farmington, New Mexico
Born: May 12, 1945
Died: April 15, 1968
Casualty Location: Ninh Duong Province
Memorial Panel: 50E, Line 3

Frank W. Jealous-Of-Him
Specialist Four
Army of the United States
Wounded Knee, South Dakota
Born: May 5, 1947
Died: June 9, 1969
Casualty Location: Quang Tin Province
Memorial Panel: 22W, Line 2

Clifford Curtis Johnson
Chief Warrant Officer
Army of the United States
Fairfax, Oklahoma
Born: November 11, 1938
Died: January 29, 1966
Casualty Location: Binh Dinh Province
Memorial Panel: 4E, Line 110

Zane Everett Johnson
Lance Corporal
United States Marine Corps
Fruitland, New Mexico
Born: April 1, 1949
Died: March 27, 1969
Casualty Location: Quang Nam Province
Memorial Panel: 28W, Line 61

Michael Bruce Jones
Private First Class
Army of the United States
Mohave, Arizona
Born: June 15, 1947
Died: May 12, 1968
Casualty Location: Gia Dinh Province
Memorial Panel: 59E, Line 5

Wilbert Dwayne Kanosh
Corporal
United States Marine Corps
Vernal, Utah
Born: January 11, 1948
Died: January 30, 1969
Casualty Location: Quang Nam Province
Memorial Panel: 33W, Line 20

Wilson Begay Kee
Specialist Four
Army of the United States
Chinle, Arizona
Born: April 2, 1948
Died: June 17, 1970
Casualty Location: Quang Ngai Province
Memorial Panel: 9W, Line 60

George Gregory Kilbuck
Private First Class
Army of the United States
Bethel, Alaska
Born: August 20, 1943
Died: August 27, 1965
Casualty Location: Not Reported
Memorial Panel: 2E, Line 68

Raymond Sidney Kipp
Specialist Four
Army of the United States
Oklahoma City, Oklahoma
Born: June 2, 1948
Died: March 17, 1970
Casualty Location: Quang Ngai Province
Memorial Panel: 12W, Line 13

Chevo Garcia Lara
Specialist Four
Army of the United States
North Sacramento, California
Born: August 14, 1943
Died: August 10, 1966
Casualty Location: Hau Nghia Province
Memorial Panel: 9E, Line 123

Calvin David Largo
Specialist Four
Army of the United States
Shiprock, New Mexico
Born: April 13, 1945
Died September 19, 1969
Casualty Location: Hau Nghia Province
Memorial Panel: 43W, Line 39

Andrew Ernest Le Beau, Jr.
Staff Sergeant
United States Air Force
Sparks, Nevada
Born: April 30, 1936
Died: February 11, 1968
Casualty Location: Bien Hoa Province
Memorial Panel: 38E, Line 78

Prentice Dale Le Clair
Specialist Four
Army of the United States
Tulsa, Oklahoma
Born: October 27, 1941
Died: August 9, 11967
Casualty Location: Quang Ngai Province
Memorial Panel: 24E, Line 96

James M. Levings
Sergeant
Army of the United States
New Town, North Dakota
Born: October 18, 1948
Died: May 23, 1968
Casualty Location: Binh Dinh Province
Memorial Panel: 66E, Line 10

Thomas Lee Little Sun
Private First Class
United States Marine Corps
Pawnee, Oklahoma
Born: August 20, 1947
Died: February 16, 1968
Casualty Location: Quang Tri Province
Memorial Panel: 39E, Line 63

Walter Norvel Locher
Private First Class
Army of the United States
Lame Deer, Montana
Born: October 23, 1945
Died: June 28, 1967
Casualty Location: Kontum Province
Memorial Panel: 22E, Line 79

Jimmy Locklear
Specialist Four
Army of the United States
Maxton, North Carolina
Born: November 20, 1949
Died: September 4, 1968
Casualty Location: Hua Nghia Province
Memorial Panel: 45W, Line 38

William John Lyons
First Lieutenant
Army of the United States
Banning, California
Born: July 27, 1940
Died: November 4, 1965
Casualty Location: Binh Dinh Province
Memorial Panel: 3E, Line 19

Talton Lee Mackey
Sergeant
Army of the United States
Red Oak, Oklahoma
Born: June 27, 1948
Died: December 9, 1968
Casualty Location: Phuoc Long Province
Memorial Panel: 37W, Line 75

Robert Gary Malone
Corporal
United States Marine Corps
Wichita, Kansas
Born: August 30, 1943
Died: July 28, 1966
Casualty Location: Quang Nam Province
Memorial Panel: 9E, Line 83

Oscar Maloney
Specialist Five
Army of the United States
Tuba City, Arizona
Born: August 6, 1945
Died: November 2, 1970
Casualty Location: Kien Giang Province
Memorial Panel: 6W, Line 35

Eugene L. Manselle, III
Private
Army of the United States
Hartford, Connecticut
Born: May 19, 1947
Died: June 19, 1968
Casualty Location: Gia Dinh Province
Memorial Panel: 56W, Line 36

Harold Joseph Marrietta
Sergeant
Army of the United States
Sacaton, Arizona
Born: April 20, 1933
Died: February 7, 1966
Casualty Location: Phu Yen Province
Memorial Panel: 5E, Line 12

Rodney Elmer Marrufo, Jr.
Specialist Four
Army of the United States
Stewarts Point, California
Born: August 18, 1947
Died: May 23, 1968
Casualty Location: Hua Nghia Province
Memorial Panel: 66E, Line 11

Emerson Martin
Private First Class
United States Marine Corps
Church Rock, New Mexico
Born: December 18, 1947
Died: May 29, 1969
Casualty Location: Quang Nam Province
Memorial Panel: 23W, Line 16

Bobby Joe Martinez
Sergeant
Army of the United States
Fort Wingate, New Mexico
Born: March 27, 1946
Died: May 11, 1968
Casualty Location: Quang Tin Province
Memorial Panel: 58E, Line 23

Manuel Martinez
Petty Officer First Class
United States Navy
Taos Pueblo, New Mexico
Born: February 11, 1932
Died: February 27, 1969
Casualty Location: Quang Nam Province
Memorial Panel: 31W, Line 82

Gilbert Lewis Matthews, Jr.
Captain
Army of the United States
Pine Ridge, South Dakota
Born: June 3, 1941
Died: June 4, 1971
Casualty Location: Hua Nghia Province
Memorial Panel: 3W, Line 87

Myron Mc Clelland
Private First Class
Army of the United States
Downieville, California
Born: June 19, 1941
Died: February 20, 1966
Casualty Location: Not Reported
Memorial Panel: 5E, Line 55

Winford McCosar
Lance Corporal
United States Marine Corps
Bell, California
Born: November 22, 1947
Died: March 6, 1968
Casualty Location: Quang Tri Province
Memorial Panel: 43E, Line 28

John Clark Mc Dowell
Corporal
Army of the United States
Corsica, South Dakota
Born: April 29, 1944
Died: January 9, 1968
Casualty Location: Long Khanh Province
Memorial Panel: 43E, Line 9

Joseph Michael Mermejo
Private First Class
United States Marine Corps
Stockton, Utah
Born: April 26, 1949
Died: March 29, 1969
Casualty Location: Quang Nam Province
Memorial Panel: 28W, Line 83

James Gregory Mesa
Private First Class
Army of the United States
Jamul, California
Born: September 24, 1948
Died: September 30, 1968
Casualty Location: Quang Duc Province
Memorial Panel: 42W, Line 48

Andrew Henry Meshigaud
Staff Sergeant
Army of the United States
Dallas, Texas
Born: December 22, 1938
Died: December 17, 1971
Casualty Location: Darlac Province
Memorial Panel: 2W, Line 89

Steven Mike
Private First Class
Army of the United States
Gallup, New Mexico
Born: October 5, 1950
Died: January 6, 1971
Casualty Location: Binh Dinh Province
Memorial Panel: 5W, Line 29

Charles Daniel Miller
Lance Corporal
United States Marine Corps
Wewoka, Oklahoma
Born: November 22, 1947
Died: March 31, 1968
Casualty Location: Thua Thien Province
Memorial Panel: 47E, Line 24

Arthur Lee Mills
Lance Corporal
United States Marin Corps
Rapid City, South Dakota
Born: June 25, 1949
Died: April 12, 1968
Casualty Location: Quang Tri Province
Memorial Panel: 49E, Line 34

Eddie Molino, Jr.
Captain
Army of the United States
Fallon, Nevada
Born: April 21, 1945
Died: May 10, 1970
Casualty Location: Cambodia
Memorial Panel: 10W, Line 14

Joe Ned Montoya
Corporal
Army of the United States
San Juan Pueblo, New Mexico
Born: December 19, 1939
Died: August 1, 1967
Casualty Location: Binh Duong Province
Memorial Panel: 24E, Line 62

Duane Lee Morningstar
Private First Class
United States Marine Corps
Maple Lake, Minnesota
Born: May 14, 1947
Died: September 7, 1967
Casualty Location: Quang Tri Province
Memorial Panel: 26E, Line 29

Weldon Dale Moss
Private First Class
United States Marine Corps
Ethete, Wyoming
Born: December 23, 1943
Died: April 2, 1966
Casualty Location: Quang Nam Province
Memorial Panel: 6E, Line 76

Harold Bradley Muller
Sergeant
Army of the United States
Mc Kinleyville, California
Born: April 4, 1947
Died: March 13, 1968
Casualty Location: Kontum Province
Memorial Panel: 44E, Line 39

Jay Allan Muncey
Specialist Four
Army of the United States
Battle Mountain, Nevada
Born: December 27, 1947
Died: August 28, 1970
Casualty Location: Thua Thien Province
Memorial Panel: 7W, Line 19

Daniel Harold Muniz
Private
Army of the United States
Dulce, New Mexico
Born: May 17, 1949
Died: May 17, 1970
Casualty Location: Quang Tri Province
Memorial Panel: 10W, Line 58

Wayne Muskett
Lance Corporal
United States Marine Corps
Shiprock, New Mexico
Born: August 11, 1947
Died: August 26, 1969
Casualty Location: Quang Nam Province
Memorial Panel: 19W, Line 120

Baldomero Arturo Nadal
Corporal
Army of the United States
Delano, California
Born: January 26, 1946
Died: April 15, 1967
Casualty Location: Gia Dinh Province
Memorial Panel: 18E, Line 31

Josh Cain Noah
Sergeant
Army of the United States
Hugo, Oklahoma
Born: November 22, 1943
Died: November 20, 1967
Casualty Location: Kontum Province
Memorial Panel: 30E, Line 46

Marvin Tidwell Noah
Lance Corporal
United States Marine Corps
Broken Bow, Oklahoma
Born: February 1, 1944
Died: March 24, 1967
Casualty Location: Quang Tri Province
Memorial Panel: 17E, Line 38

John Okemah
Sergeant First Class
Army of the United States
Harrah, Oklahoma
Born: May 10, 1930
Died: April 13, 1968
Casualty Location: Binh Duong Province
Memorial Panel: 49E, Line 41

Randall Issac-Jed Ortiz
Lance Corporal
Marine Corps United States
Denver, Colorado
Born: March 13, 1949
Died: August 20, 1969
Casualty Location: Quang Tri Province
Memorial Panel: 19W, Line 81

Robert Carlos Pahcheka
Private First Class
United States Marine Corps
Indiahoma, Oklahoma
Born: September 23, 1946
Died: October 22, 1968
Casualty Location: Quang Nam Province
Memorial Panel: 40W, Line 22

Martin James Pamonicutt
Private First Class
United States Marine Corps
Neopit, Wisconsin
Born: January 3, 1949
Died: June 23, 1969
Casualty Location: Quang Tri Province
Memorial Panel: 22W, Line 123

John Patrick Pappin
Equipment Operator Construction Recruit
United States Navy
Pawhuska, Oklahoma
Born: November 9, 1949
Died: March 12, 1970
Casualty Location: Quang Nam Province
Memorial Panel: 13W, Line1 20

Larry Parker
Staff Sergeant
Army of the United States
Winnemucca, Nevada
Born: March 16, 1940
Died: March 21, 1970
Casualty Location: Binh Dinh Province
Memorial Panel: 12W, Line 31

Vincent Bertram Parkhurst
Sergeant First Class
Army of the United States
Chicago, Illinois
Born: January 17, 1934
Died: February 20, 1968
Casualty Location: Binh Thuan Province
Memorial Panel: 40E, Line 46

Jack Poola Pashano
Specialist Four
Army of the United States
Polacca, Arizona
Born: February 2, 1934
Died: August 19, 1968
Casualty Location: Tay Ninh Province
Memorial Panel: 47W, Line 2

Jimmie Patten
Sergeant
Army of the United States
San Carlos, Arizona
Born: March 17, 1941
Died: January 31, 1968
Casualty Location: Bien Hoa Province
Memorial Panel: 36E, Line 29

Warren Paulsen
Boatswain's Mate Third Class
United States Navy
Valdes, Alaska
Born: August 10, 1944
Died: June 23, 1969
Casualty Location Binh Duong Province
Memorial Panel: 21W, Line 1

Ernest Delbert Peina
Specialist Four
Army of the United States
Zuni, New Mexico
Born: March 28, 1947
Died: September 13, 1968
Casualty Location: Binh Long Province
Memorial Panel: 44W, Line 52

David Drake Perkins
Private First Class
Army of the United States
Coolidge, Arizona
Born: August 20, 1943
Died: October 11, 1966
Casualty Location: Binh Dinh Province
Memorial Panel: 11E, Line 67

Russell Eugene Pesewonit
Private First Class
United States Marine Corps
Lawton, Oklahoma
Born: March 28, 1947
Died: July 22, 1966
Casualty Location: Quang Tri Province
Memorial Panel: 9E, Line 59

Franklin Danny Pete, Jr.
Specialist Four
Army of the United States
Sacaton, Arizona
Born: October 18, 1946
Died: May 27, 1968
Casualty Location: Thua Thien Province
Memorial Panel: 65W, Line 13

Joseph Patrick Pink
Specialist Four
Army of the United States
San Jacinto, California
Born: October 17, 1947
Died: October 23, 1967
Casualty Location: Quang Tin Province
Memorial Panel: 28E, Line 56

Babe Pinola
Lance Corporal
United States Marine Corps
Santa Rosa, California
Born: December 20, 1944
Died: December 7, 1968
Casualty Location: Quang Nam Province
Memorial Panel: 37W, Line 58

Raymond Platero
Private First Class
Army of the United States
Canoncito, New Mexico
Born: March 10, 1944
Died: January 26, 1970
Casualty Location: Thua Thien Province
Memorial Panel: 14W, Line 69

Joseph Louis Pokerjim
Private
Army of the United States
Saint Ignatius, Montana
Born: August 20, 1946
Died: October 12, 1967
Casualty Location: Quang Ngai Province
Memorial Panel: 27E, Line 97

Pascal Cleatus Poolaw, Sr.
First Sergeant
Army of the United States
Apache, Oklahoma
Born: January 29, 1922
Died: November 7, 1967
Casualty Location: Binh Long Province
Memorial Panel: 29E, Line 43

Gary Philip Rader
Specialist Four
Army of the United States
Sacramento, California
Born: September 30, 1949
Died: May 7, 1970
Casualty Location: Quang Ngai Province
Memorial Panel: 11W, Line 128

Jewel Lee Rainwater
Private First Class
Army of the United States
Van Buren, Arkansas
Born: January 10, 1949
Died: April 2, 1968
Casualty Location: Thua Thien Province
Memorial Panel: 47E, Line 42

Darwin Esker Ray
Corporal
Army of the United States
East Highlands, California
Born: January 31, 1947
Died: January 3, 1968
Casualty Location: Quang Nam Province
Memorial Panel: 33E, Line 31

Jesse Milton Red Hawk
Private
Army of the United States
Pine Ridge, South Dakota
Born: April 9, 1948
Died: November 10, 1968
Casualty Location: Ninh Thuan Province
Memorial Panel: 39W, Line 45

Albert Tsosie
Lance Corporal
United States Marine Corps
Chinle, Arizona
Born: June 8, 1949
Died: July 10, 1970
Casualty Location: Quang Nam Province
Memorial Panel: 8W, Line 9

Lee Dino Tsosie
Corporal
Army of the United States
Cross Canyon, Arizona
Born: October 1, 1947
Died: July 25, 1968
Casualty Location: Kontum Province
Memorial Panel: 50W, Line 11

Blair William Two Crow
Private First Class
Army of the United States
Kyle, South Dakota
Born: November 12, 1948
Died: December 4, 1968
Casualty Location: Quang Ngai Province
Memorial Panel: 37W, Line 43

Gabriel Lawrence Two Eagle
Private
Army of the United States
Parmelee, South Dakota
Born: October 7, 1950
Died: April 18, 1971
Casualty Location: Hua Nghia Province
Memorial Panel: 4W, Line 133

Edward Tyler
Private First Class
Army of the United States
Oklahoma City, Oklahoma
Born: May 25, 1946
Died: May 9, 1968
Casualty Location: Hua Nghia Province
Memorial Panel: 58E, Line 1

Ernest Vetter, Jr.
Private First Class
Army of the United States
Oklahoma City, Oklahoma
Born: January 30, 1943
Died: April 18, 1968
Casualty Location: Bien Hoa Province
Memorial Panel: 50E, Line 43

Truman J. Walsh
Specialist Four
Army of the United States
Dodson, Montana
Born: August 11, 1948
Died: February 25, 1969
Casualty Location: Thua Thien Province
Memorial Panel: 31W, Line 61

Joseph Lewis White Mouse
Private First Class
Army of the United States
Fort Thompson, South Dakota
Born: September 30, 1951
Died: April 8, 1971
Casualty Location: Quang Nam Province
Memorial Panel: 4W, Line 113

James Alec Williams
Lance Corporal
United States Marine Corps
Bishop, California
Born: December 8, 1947
Died: July 1, 1968
Casualty Location: Quang Tri Province
Memorial Panel: 54W, Line 34

Harold Eugene Willis
Private First Class
Army of the United States
Bishop, California
Born: June 27, 1944
Died: January 25, 1966
Casualty Location: Binh Dinh Province
Memorial Panel: 4E, Line 96

Adam Wilson
Warrant Officer
Army of the United States
San Diego, California
Born: May 1, 1948
Died: November 15, 1969
Casualty Location: Quang Ngai Province
Memorial Panel: 16W, Line 82

Juan Jay Wilson
Lance Corporal
United States Marine Corps
Thoreau, New Mexico
Born: January 10, 1947
Died: February 14, 1969
Casualty Location: Quang Tri Province
Memorial Panel: 32W, Line 35

George Harold Winkempleck
Private First Class
Army of the United States
Porterville, California
Born: June 4, 1947
Died: October 10, 1967
Casualty Location: Quang Tin Province
Memorial Panel: 27E, Line 87

Mathew Wolfe
Private First Class
Army of the United States
Macy, Nebraska
Born: January 7, 1942
Died: February 1, 1968
Casualty Location: Gia Dinh Province
Memorial Panel: 36E, Line 63

Strather Franklin Wood
First Lieutenant
United States Marine Corps
Eugene, Oregon
Born: April 26, 1944
Died: February 18, 1971
Casualty Location: Thua Thien Province
Memorial Panel: 5W, Line 119

Dan Yazzie
Specialist Four
Army of the United States
Continental Divide, New Mexico
Born: December 11, 1948
Died: May 15, 1969
Casualty Location: Long Dong Province
Memorial Panel: 24W, Line 24

Jones Lee Yazzie
Lance Corporal
United States Marine Corps
Tohatchi, New Mexico
Born: July 6, 1947
Died: August 4, 1968
Casualty Location: Quang Nam Province
Memorial Panel: 49W, Line 11

Leonard Lee Yazzie
Private First Class
United States Marine Corps
Pinon, Arizona
Born: February 10, 1945
Died: May 28, 1968
Casualty Location: Quang Nam Province
Memorial Panel: 63W, Line 2

Raymond Yazzie
Lance Corporal
United States Marine Corps
Church Rock, New Mexico
Born: June 1, 1947
Died: February 26, 1969
Casualty Location: Quang Tri Province
Memorial Panel: 31W, Line 70

Carlos Nichol Yellow Elk
Private First Class
Army of the United States
Milesville, South Dakota
Born: May 19, 1950
Died: August 29, 1968
Casualty Location: Gia Dinh Province
Memorial Panel: 45W, Line 2

Richard Clive Youngbear
Sergeant
Army of the United States
Tama, Iowa
Born: August 10, 1939
Died: February 3, 1966
Casualty Location: Phu Yen Province
Memorial Panel: 4E, Line 134

EPILOGUE

The end of America's helicopter war did not sound the death knell of the Army's reliance upon Army aviation and the ubiquitous helicopter. The success of the rotary-winged aircraft in Vietnam was undeniable. However, its utility and combat effectiveness in other than a low-intensity conflict or guerilla war remained uncertain. As initially envisioned, Army strategists, planners, and materiel developers believed that the air mobility concepts were exploitable in the mid- to high-intensity environment of central Europe. Yet, it had only proven itself in and above the jungles of Southeast Asia. So, with American forces back in the continental United States and on bases in Europe and the Pacific regions, Army aviation attention turned to the doctrine, tactics, aircraft, and organization structure that would be necessary to fight and survive in a combat environment populated by opposing armored forces and sophisticated, integrated air defense systems.

Thus in the 1980s, the Army and its aviation community focused once again on the prospect of Army aviation becoming a separate branch, taking into consideration the conflicting assessments of ground force support provided by the Air Force and Army Aviation during the recently ended war. The demonstrated commitment of Army fixed- and rotary-winged aviation units to American and allied forces during Vietnam eased the internal opposition to aviation becoming a separate branch of the Army.

Furthermore, at the same time, Army aviation was expanding in size and technological sophistication, which also presented similar problems associated with other branches of the Army, e.g., training, doctrine and tactics development, proponent responsibilities, procurement, and personnel management. Ultimately the Army's leadership coalesced and established Army Aviation as a separate branch, effective April 12, 1983.[1]

Rotary-winged aviation research and development and modernization continued in the Army even as the Vietnam War was winding down, long afterward as the service came to grips with the potential of helicopters and growing aviation requirements derived from its evolving warfighting doctrine in response to the changing threat and combat environment. Throughout the 1980s, the Army would begin divesting its older aircraft and start investing in more modern and capable systems. From its modernization plan emerged several successful helicopter acquisitions and a few research and development stillbirths. For each, the Army would not abandon its practice of naming its helicopters after great Native American tribes or warrior chiefs.

Beyond the aircraft already highlighted in this volume, the Army initiated six development programs for new helicopters for attack, utility, or reconnaissance missions. Those helicopters included the Lockheed AH-56 *Cheyenne*—attack helicopter, the Sikorsky UH-60 *Black Hawk*—utility helicopter, the Boeing AH-64 *Apache*—attack helicopter, the Boeing-Sikorsky RAH-66 *Comanche*—reconnaissance and attack helicopter, the Eurocopter UH-72 *Lakota*—utility helicopter, and the Bell ARH-70 *Arapaho*—armed reconnaissance helicopter. Some were successful and went from development to production and active service. Others encountered developmental and technological obstacles, and while they may have never gone into production, some of their technological advances would ultimately mature and make their way into fielded aircraft.

AH-56 *Cheyenne*—Attack Helicopter

AH-56 Cheyenne *flight test. (Courtesy of the Army Aviation Museum.)*

The Lockheed AH-56 *Cheyenne* was an attack helicopter developed by Lockheed as a potential solution for the Army's Advanced Aerial Fire Support System (AAFSS) program to field a dedicated attack helicopter. The service wanted an aircraft capable of a top speed of 220 knots (253 mph), hovering at 6,000 feet on a 95°F day, and a range of 2,415 miles.[2] The aircraft used a four-blade rigid-rotor system, the standard tail rotor, and a tail-mounted thrusting propeller. Lockheed Aircraft received a contract for ten prototypes in 1966, while at the same time, the Army ordered production quantities of the Bell AH-1G for the attack mission in Vietnam.

The first flight of the AH-56 prototype took place on September 21, 1967. Satisfied with early flight test results, the Army placed a production contract with Lockheed in January 1968. At 54 feet in length, the *Cheyenne* was an impressive helicopter capable of speeds not yet achieved in helicopters. With aerodynamic wings on each fuselage side, the faster the aircraft flew, the rotor experienced less loading.[3] The *Cheyenne* was capable of cruising at 195 knots (224 mph) and had a maximum speed of 212 knots (244 mph), exceeding the AH-64 Apache's cruising and top speeds of 158 (182 mph) and 197 (227 mph) knots, respectively. Unfortunately, the Department of Defense imposed a commercial pricing and contracting approach—Total Package Procurement (TTP)—which all but guaranteed cost overruns when applied to a cutting-edge technology development program.[4] Some accidents, including a fatal crash, technical problems affecting performance, and mounting costs, delayed the *Cheyenne* development schedule causing the Army to cancel Lockheed's production contract on May 19, 1969.

While the *Cheyenne* never entered Army service, the development results produced numerous new aviation technologies and capabilities available to be incorporated in more recent generations of helicopters. Also, because of the close-air support potential of the helicopter and the reality that the Army had come extremely close to satisfying that mission on its own, some would argue that because of the *Cheyenne*, the Air Force undertook the development of a dedicated close-support aircraft for the Army, the A-10 *Thunderbolt*.

The Cheyenne people, for whom the AH-56 was named, are among the most well-known Native American tribes of the Great Plains. The first evidence of the Cheyenne is a 1680 letter from French explorer Robert Cavalier de La Salle from his visits to their homelands at the headwaters of the Mississippi River.[5] The Tsethaseta, as the Cheyenne referred to themselves, began moving to the plains in search of buffalo by the close of the 17th century, eventually reaching the North Platte River headwaters in Wyoming. By 1833, many Cheyenne settled along the Arkansas River in southeast Colorado, while others remained in Wyoming. During the pre-reservation period, they were often allied with the Lakota Sioux and the Arapaho tribes. Pressured by foreigners, including French fur traders and other Indigenous tribes, the Cheyenne moved onto the plains in present-day Minnesota, North Dakota, South Dakota, Wyoming, Colorado, and Northern New Mexico. By 1840, the perennial enemies Cheyenne and Sioux made peace, established a permanent alliance, and became a formidable adversary for anyone when joined by the Arapaho. The three tribes were allied during Red Cloud's War of 1866 against the U.S. government.

Stimulated by the increased influx of migrants through the Great Plains that followed the beginning of the California Gold Rush starting in 1848, the U.S. government wanted to ensure the protected right-of-way for the transiting population. The solution was the Fort Laramie Treaty of 1851 granted the Cheyenne territory for a reservation encompassing almost half of Colorado and parts of Wyoming, Kansas, and Nebraska.[6] However, the Colorado gold rush brought an onslaught of settlers onto the lands set aside for Native Americans by the federal government. The encroachment led to conflict between the Indigenous peoples and the militia-supported immigrants, and by 1864 open warfare escalated into the

Colorado War. Under the leadership of Chief Black Kettle, the Southern Cheyenne, along with their Arapaho allies, were victims of the Sand Creek Massacre. Despite flying the American flag and a white flag above his tipi, the encampment was attacked by the 1,200-man Colorado militia who savagely killed 150 men, women, and children. During the same turbulent period, the Northern Cheyenne participated in the Battle of Little Bighorn on June 25, 1876.[7]

After the defeat of the 7th Cavalry at Little Big Horn, the Army intensified its efforts to capture the Cheyenne and eventually relocated some 972 Cheyenne to the Indian Territory in Oklahoma in 1877.[8] The following year, 353 Cheyenne left the Territory and returned north, pursued by over 13,000 soldiers and volunteers. The Cheyenne split into two parties, with Chief Little Wolf leading one group to Montana and Chief Morning Star leading the second to Fort Robinson, Nebraska.[9] Living under almost inhuman conditions, Chief Morning Star and his people attempted escape preferring flight and possible death rather than being returned into Army custody—only fifty escapees survived the breakout. The Northern Cheyenne under Little Wolf were more fortunate. They settled near Fort Keogh, Montana, and some began working as scouts for the Army, even aiding it in finding Chief Joseph and the Nez Percé in Northern Montana. In 1884, the U.S. government recognized that a reservation was needed in the north, and by executive order, the Cheyenne finally had a permanent home on the Tongue River in Montana. The Cheyenne, Lakota, and Apache nations were the last tribes to be placed on reservations.[10]

UH-60 *Black Hawk*—Utility Helicopter

Army UH-60 Black Hawk. (Courtesy of the Army Aviation Museum.)

In the 1970s, the Army launched the Utility Tactical Transport Aircraft System (UTTAS) program to find a new helicopter to replace the venerable UH-1 *Iroquois* family of aircraft for troop transport, command and control, aeromedical evacuation, and reconnaissance roles. The acquisition community released a request for proposal (RFP) in January 1972, seeking two contractors for the UTTAS helicopter. On August 30 of the same year, Boeing Vertol and Sikorsky were selected to design and build prototypes for a competitive fly-off to choose a single producer of the winning UTTAS design.[11]

Twenty-six months after the contract award, on October 17, 1974, the Sikorsky YUH-60A prototype made its maiden flight. After the development effort, Sikorsky delivered three matured prototypes to compete head-to-head against three Boeing Vertol YUH-61A prototypes. The competitive testing was completed in November 1976, and on December 23, 1976, the Army awarded Sikorsky a sole source production contract. The service evaluation assessed "… that the Sikorsky YUH-60A was more fully developed, offered less production risk, and provided better value to the government."[12]

In keeping with Army policy, the UH-60A was named in honor of a great Native American war leader, Chief Black Hawk of the Sauk Tribe, with a reputation as a fierce and courageous fighter earned primarily during his youth. He fought on the side of the British during the War of 1812 under the Shawnee warrior and chief, Tecumseh. Noted as being "a captain of his actions," Black Hawk, at age sixty-five, participated in the brief Black Hawk War from April to August 1832, when he led 1,000 Sauk, Fox, and Kickapoo, across the Mississippi River in April 1831, to reclaim tribal land in Illinois which was being sold to white settlers as the result of an 1805 treaty.[13] Under threat of military action against his band, Black Hawk met with the commander of the Western Department, Brigadier General Gaines, but refused to leave Illinois and return west of the Mississippi River. Gaines responded by requesting militia support from Illinois governor John Reynolds, and on June 25, Gaines' regulars and state militia moved against the Sac-Fox village at Rock River. Encouraged by the peace faction within his band, Black Hawk signed an agreement to return westward across the Mississippi on June 30.[14]

Prompted by false promises of British support and anticipated aid from the Winnebago Indians, Black Hawk returned to Illinois on April 6, 1832, with a band of almost 600 warriors, and 1,500 women, children, and elderly, again to reclaim their land.[15] He refused the invitation to meet with the Army commander, Brigadier General Henry Atkinson who, like his predecessor, requested Illinois militias reinforcements from the governor who sent troops under Brigadier General Samuel Whiteside that included an infantry company commanded by Abraham Lincoln.

On May 14, Black Hawk's camp which was located at Sycamore Creek, Illinois, was approached by mounted troops under militia Major Isaiah Stillman.[16] While several Indians appeared under a white truce flag, other Native American scouts were spotted by Stillman's troops. Suspecting a trap, the militia opened fire on the truce party. Black Hawk and his warriors hastily prepared an ambush into which the militia followed. While most of the surprised militia fled to Dixon's Ferry, a small detachment remained to attempt a rear-guard delaying action. The ensuing clash claimed the lives of all twelve men in the detachment.[17]

The Sac-Fox band fled northward into the Michigan Territory, present-day Wisconsin, while the militia's term of service expired and all but 300 returned to their homesteads. Manned with over 3,400 fresh militia and 700 regulars Atkinson resumed pursuit of Black Hawk. Dissatisfied with the performance of some of his field generals, President Andrew Jackson sent Brigadier General Winfield Scott to take charge of the war and provided him with nine regular infantry companies and nine artillery batteries. By July, members of the mounted militia under Colonel Henry Dodge located the trail of Black Hawk's bands moving west toward the Wisconsin River. Skillfully, the militia was kept at bay and the Indians escaped across the river at night. On July 28 the Army force crossed the river and continued their pursuit to the banks of the Mississippi River.[18]

On August 1, 1832, Black Hawk's band was crossing the Mississippi River when the steamboat *Warrior* appeared, loaded with troops. Dubious of Black Hawk's white flag and offer to surrender, the troops afloat were ordered to fire on the Indians. The exchange left twenty-three Indians dead by the time the *Warrior* departed. Colonel Zachery Taylor's regulars and most of the militia assaulted the Sac-Fox camp the next morning, an attack that sent Black Hawk into flight and destroyed his band.

On August 25, the Winnebago Indians captured Black Hawk and turned him over to the military, and Lieutenant Jefferson David was charged with escorting the warrior chief and other Sac-Fox prisoners to Jefferson Barracks. Black Hawk was later transferred to and incarcerated in Fortress Monroe. The brief duration of Black Hawk's War claimed the lives of a single militia officer, five regular enlisted soldiers, sixteen enlisted militiamen, and a total of thirty-six wounded. In contrast, almost 600 Native Americans perished.[19] Following his federal imprisonment, Chief Black Hawk settled in Iowa until his death in 1838.

The war ended on August 3, 1832, with the massacre of Black Hawk's people at Bad Axe, Wisconsin.

While the *Black Hawk* is designed to transport eleven combat-equipped air assault soldiers or a 105-mm howitzer and thirty complete rounds of ammunition, the UH-60 *Black Hawk* performed a variety of missions since it entered service with the 101st Airborne Division in June 1979, including air assault, air cavalry, and aeromedical evacuation. It also served as a command and control, electronic warfare, and special operations platform when properly outfitted.[20] As a DUSTOFF aircraft, the *Black Hawk* would operate differently from other MEDEVAC helicopters used during Vietnam. The large, more powerful, and faster helicopter did not follow the UH-1 *Iroquois* procedure of going to the patient at the drop-off LZ, for the Army was unwilling to send the more valuable *Black Hawk* into harm's way. The revised procedure has the wounded soldier brought off the LZ by the helicopter that had carried him into battele and then take him to a staging area from which a UH-60 MEDEVAC transports him onward to a field hospital.[21] The Army UH-60 *Black Hawk* and its flight crews distinguished themselves in combat in Grenada in 1983, in Panama in 1989, in the Gulf War in 1991, in Mogadishu, Somalia in 1993, and in operations in Iraq and Afghanistan from 2003 to 2021.[22]

AH-64 *Apache*—Attack Helicopter

AH-65 Apache. *(Courtesy of the Army Aviation Museum.)*

With the termination of the *Cheyenne* program, the Army was left without a solution to its anti-armor attack mission. The optimal solution would need to exceed the capabilities of the AH-1 *Cobra* in performance, range, and lethality. It also had to have the inherent maneuverability to permit the crew to fly nap-of-the-earth (NOE) even under limited visibility conditions. Such requirements emerged from the experiences of attack helicopter pilots during the Vietnam War. On August 17, 1972, the Army Advanced Attack Helicopter (AAH) program was initiated, and during the following months, additional requirements were decided upon, and the request for proposal was finalized. Among the requirements, the Army reduced the aircraft's top speed to 145 knots (167 mph) with the government-specified use of twin General Electric T700 1,500 shp turboshaft engines. The redundant engines were an acknowledgment of the need for increased survivability. The AAH reliability, survivability, and life cycle cost requirements mirrored the UTTAS. The required combat load for the helicopter included a 30-millimeter cannon main armament, plus sixteen TOW anti-tank missiles.

The RFP was released to the industry on November 15, 1972, and when bids were due, Bell, Boeing-Vertol, Hughes Aircraft, Lockheed, and Sikorsky responded. Following proposal evaluations, the Army narrowed the competitors to Bell and Hughes Aircraft's Toolco Aircraft Division. Each competitor received a contract calling for each company to deliver two prototype aircraft for competitive fly-off evaluation.

Bell's YAH-63A prototype made its maiden flight on October 1, 1975, and Hughes' YAH-64A made its first flight on September 30, 1975, followed by an exhausting and demanding flight evaluation which began in June 1976. Evaluations were completed by the end of the year, and the Army awarded a phase two pre-production contract to Hughes on December 10. Indicators were that the Army favored the YAH-64's survivability.

The new contract required the delivery of three preproduction AH-64s and the upgrade of the two-phase-one prototypes to the preproduction standard. The latter helicopter first flew on November 28, 1977, while the former aircraft made its first flight on October 31, 1979. Two of the helicopters were outfitted with sensors and targeting equipment. One ship was outfitted with a package provided by Martin Marietta, and Northrop provided the package for the other aircraft. After a head-to-head competition, the Army selected the aircraft equipped with the Martin Marietta package in April 1980, and the vendors received a production contract for 11 AH-64A helicopters 11 months later, on March 26, 1982.[23] The AH-64A *Apache* entered active service with the Army in 1984.

When it came time to name the YAH-64A, the Army resolved on the name "Apache," the fiercest warriors in the Southwest. The Apache people are a group of Southern Athabascan-speaking people who, throughout their history, occupied parts of Arizona, Colorado, New Mexico, Oklahoma, Texas, and northern Mexico.[24] For centuries, the Apache warriors distinguished themselves through their dedication to protect their homeland against encroaching white men and other Indigenous tribes. Further, the tribe recognized that the measure of a warrior leader was his leadership acumen and the record of his exploits in battle with the tribe's enemies.

The first recorded description of the Apache comes from observations of Spanish conquistador Francisco Vásquez de Coronado's expedition to the High Plains of the Texas Panhandle, including their buffalo hunting skills on foot with bows and arrows. The Spaniards pursued the Apache with callous hostility, forcing them to seek refuge in the mountains, where they were forced to subsist by raiding neighboring tribes and settlements, to escape when pursued, but pausing, when possible, to grow corn and harvest editable plant life.[25] The fierceness of the Apache marked their quest for self-preservation from the Spanish and the tribes they enlisted against the Apache such as the Pueblo, Navajo, and Comanche.[26] By 1784, the Spaniards ordered that all Apache except children seven years or younger were to be killed; older than that, they were "implacable, cruel, and in no manner reducible."[27]

By 1848, America's westward expansion brought New Mexico into the republic and, in turn, precipitated wars between the Apache and the Army, which continued until the Indians were moved onto reservations. Among the warrior chiefs of the Apache people were three men of the Chiricahua Apache tribe. The first was Mangas Colorado, who led tribal warriors against the Spanish and the early American miners who flooded onto Apache lands. In 1861 he was joined by his son-in-law Cochise. Together they fought U.S. soldiers sent to the west to support Union efforts against the Confederacy there, but because they arrived too late, they engaged in controlling the Indian problem. Mangas Colorado died at the hands of the Army in 1863, while Cochise continued fighting. In 1872, Chief Cochise requested and received a reservation encompassing Chiricahua Mountain, the longtime home of his people. However, when federal and state authorities consolidated[28] the Apache people at the San Carlos Reservation, known as "Hell's Forty Acres," conflict was renewed.[29] Reservation conditions were intolerable, giving rise to a new generation of Apache leaders, including the third of the Apache great war leaders, Geronimo, who was also a Chiricahua, a spiritual leader and medicine man.[30] He led the last marauding Apache band of 100 warriors, women, and children who fled the San Carlos Reservation for the last time in May 1885.[31] He was notoriously cruel and cunning; he and his band often plundered and killed settlers until they surrendered to Brigadier General Nelson Miles and federal troops in 1886.[32] Successively, their captors relocated Geronimo and his people, first to a prison in Florida, then to a prison camp in Alabama, and finally to Fort Sill, Oklahoma, where he died in 1909.

RAH-66 *Comanche*—Reconnaissance and Attack Helicopter

RAH-66 Comanche *prototype. (Courtesy of the Army Aviation Museum.)*

In early 1981, the Army started investigating what aviation capabilities it would need to counter the expected advanced technological threats in the twenty-first century. The Army's fleet modernization vision called for a new armed reconnaissance/attack helicopter to replace those in the UH-1 *Iroquois* fleet, AH-1 family of *Cobra* light attack helicopters, the OH-6 *Cayuse* scout helicopter, and the OH-58A/OH58C *Kiowa* light observation helicopter. The primary role of the new helicopter was to find and identify enemy targets and then designate them under night, adverse weather, and obscurant conditions for engagement by the AH-64 *Apache* attack helicopter. The Army was looking for an all-composite, low-observable airframe married to a highly sophisticated electronics and communication suite.[33] The aircraft named *Comanche* was destined to replace the helicopters in all air cavalry troops and light division attack helicopter battalions, and supplement the attack helicopters in heavy division and corps attack helicopter battalions.[34] The initial Army aviation force modernization plan set a target of 5,023 stealthy helicopters at an acquisition cost of $12.1 million a copy. Boeing and the Sikorsky Aircraft Corporation teamed to develop and build the *Comanche* in 1991. During the program's demonstration, validation, and prototype phase, 1991–2000, the contractors created and flew two flight-test prototype aircraft. The engineering and manufacturing development phase, begun in mid-2000, was slated to deliver thirteen aircraft for additional flight tests, operational tests and evaluation, and training. The first deliveries of pre-production helicopters were scheduled for 2006, with full-rate production targeted for 2010.

During the twenty-two years of development, six major program restructurings, and approximately $8 billion in development costs, the *Comanche* was the target of program reviews by the Department of Defense, the Department of the Army, the General Accounting Office, and others.[35] The Army faced aircraft capability and affordability challenges with escalating costs, technology maturation, and repeated schedule delays. To bring the *Comanche* to fruition, the Army faced the prospect of mortgaging the balance of its fixed- and rotary-winged fleets for decades. Its study concluded that by terminating the *Comanche,* it could recoup the $14.6 billion earmarked for the 121 *Comanche* helicopters to be purchased between 2004 and 2011, and in turn, procure 796 more *Black Hawk* and other helicopters as well as modernize 1,400 helicopters already in service.[36] On February 23, 2004, the Army officially announced the cancellation of the RAH-66 reconnaissance and attack helicopter program.

With the termination of the *Comanche* program, the Army was thus faced with how to replace the needed combat capabilities that the *Comanche* was to provide. The Army was allowed to retain the future years' funding programmed for the *Comanche* and apply it to other hardware solutions. It was in turn decided that the *Comanche* would be replaced by other programs to include the fielding of three new aircraft, which were to be militarized versions of existing commercial aircraft currently in production for civilian customers. The three aircraft were to be the Armed Reconnaissance Helicopter (ARH), the Light Utility Helicopter (LUH), and the Future Cargo Aircraft (FCA), which was later renamed Joint Cargo Aircraft (JCA).

The developmental reconnaissance and attack helicopter was given the name "*Comanche*," after the Native American horsemen who dominated the Southwest Plains and were prominent players in the history of Texas during the eighteenth and nineteenth centuries.

The observation of General William T. Sherman shortly after the end of the Civil War most typically represents the fate of the Comanche tribe: "The poor Indian finds himself hemmed in."[37] Senator Lot Morrill of Maine amplified Sherman's statement: "As population has approached the Indian we have removed him beyond population. But population now encounters him on both sides of the continent, and there is no place on the continent to which he can be removed beyond the progress of the population."[38]

The Comanche, an offshoot tribe of the Shoshone, came from the Great Plains and migrated from southwestern Kansas through western Texas and eastern New Mexico, and raided as far as Durango in Mexico. They first appeared on the New Mexican frontier at the beginning of the 18th century. They battled the Spaniards, the Pueblo, and the Apache, with the latter encouraged and facilitated by the Spanish. Despite Spanish support, the Comanche were quite efficient in their pursuit and killing of the Apache.[39]

When Texas entered the Union in 1845, it maintained its public domain, which meant the federal government could not set aside tracts of land for Native Americans. With the westward movement of the white frontier, Indigenous tribes were crowded out of their land. What followed were raids and reprisals between the settlers and the Kiowa and Comanches of the Plain.[40] There were negative consequences felt by the tribes because of the white man's hunting in Texas. As a result they and the other regional tribes resorted to cattle rustling and raids, which exacerbated the volatility of the existing tensions between cattle ranchers and farmers, known as "sodbusters."[41] Quick to respond, Texas lawmen, Texas Ranger militia, vigilante groups, and soldiers escalated the initially isolated incidents into a full-scale frontier war. Tragically for both sides, the war continued in varying degrees of carnage for the remainder of the century.

The Native Americans of the region quickly perceived from what they saw and heard that they were being abandoned by the United States. The favorable disposition of white Texans toward the Confederacy influenced the tribal leaders. Additionally, some of the tribal leaders shared with their white counterparts a plantation based economy supported by Negro slaves. So on the eve of the Civil War, Confederate-appointed commissioner Albert Pike was dispatched to negotiate treaties with Native American tribes. On August 12, 1861, he concluded two treaties that included the Penateka Comanche and the Plains Comanche.[42] The treaties included Texas in the peace regimen and promised "livestock, agricultural implements, and training in farming."[43] Following the proceedings, Pike observed that the Comanche "seemed very anxious to be allowed to settle on lands of their own, and to live in peace."[44]

There were multiple attempts to negotiate treaties among the warring parties, but one renegade band, led by the Quahada Comanche, never signed a treaty. Considered the wildest of all Comanche bands, their warrior chief was Quanah Parker, the son of a Quahada war chief and a white woman.[45] While they continued to attack frontier white men until 1875, in 1874, after an unsuccessful foray by Quanah's warriors near Adobe Walls, 5,000 Kiowa, Cheyenne, and Comanche people, fearful of retaliation, fled their reservation home.[46] They followed the westward flow of the Red River to the sanctuary of the river's deep canyons. In September of that year, Army troopers led by Colonel Ranald Mackenzie found them and destroyed their encampment at Palo Duro Canyon. The remaining survivors were driven back onto the reservation by the spring of the following year, while individual leaders were banished to a military prison in Florida.

UH-72 *Lakota*—Light Utility Helicopter

UH-72 Lakota *Light Utility Helicopter. (Courtesy of the Army
Aviation Museum.)*

The LUH program began in 2004 with a stated requirement for a helicopter to conduct domestic missions for homeland defense and security, assistance to border patrol operations, counterdrug operations, terrorist incident response, and disaster response.[47] Worldwide missions for the helicopter in permissive environments would include general support, reconnaissance, command and control, search and rescue, and support to Army test and training centers.[48] For those missions, an initial procurement objective was set at 322 helicopters, but by the fiscal year 2018, it was increased to 462 aircraft.[49] While U.S. new helicopter program initiatives were faltering and failing to reach full-rate production, European aircraft manufacturers were improving helicopter design and technologies which produced enhanced performance results. New rotors, engines with greater power densities, and new superior materials yielded European dominance in the American commercial market space and to a certain extent into U.S. military needs.[50] It thus came as a surprise when in July 2005, the Army contract solicitation was released to the industry with five competing aircraft offered, including the American Eurocopter UH-145. The UH-145 was selected for the LUH program on June 30, 2006, when the military version made its first flight. In October 2006, American Eurocopter was awarded a production contract for 345 aircraft to replace aging UH-1H/V medium transport helicopters and OH-58A/C light observation helicopters in the Army and Army National Guard fleets.[51] Full-rate production approval was received on August 23, 2007. The Army chose to name their new utility helicopter after the legendary warriors of the Lakota band of the Sioux Nation. The Army also introduced the UH-72 into its pilot training program and replaced the venerable Bell TH-67.[52] By selecting a commercial-off-the-shelf (COTS) aircraft, the Army could leverage the existing production base and, more importantly, the commercially operational and proven logistical support and spare parts system whose costs would be capitalized over both the military and civilian inventory. The Army introduced the helicopter into active service in 2007.

The aircraft has a flight crew of two and a passenger capacity for up to eight or two standard litters and a crew chief or medical attendant in a medical evacuation role. Its twin Turbomeca Arriel 1E2 turboshaft engines drive a four-blade main rotor and a two-blade tail rotor to produce a maximum speed of 167 miles per hour and a cruising approximating 155 miles per hour. The UH-72 has an operational range of 425 miles.

In May 2013, Congress challenged the Army on why the UH-72 *Lakota* was not considered for the armed scout role. The Army advised Congress that the aircraft had been developed for homeland operations, not battlefield conditions. The utility version of the UH-72 was envisioned for use by the National Guard in the continental United States, while the UH-60 *Black Hawk* would take on the combat role. Modification of the UH-72 fleet for combat was estimated to cost $780 million and add 774 pounds to the aircraft's weight.[53]

The first *Lakota* was accepted by the Army on December 12, 2006, in a ceremony officiated by Army Vice Chief of Staff General Richard A. Cody and Chief Joe Red Cloud, a chief of the Oglala Sioux Tribe Lakota Nation.[54] The Army Air Ambulance Detachment at the National Training Center (NTC), Fort Irwin, California, became the first operational unit equipped with the UH-72A on June 20, 2007.[55]

Among the great Native American tribes, the Lakota, which means "friends" or "allies," is a tremendously solid and fierce tribe with a long history of legendary warriors of war and treaties with the federal government. The Crow Creek Sioux are members of the Great Sioux Nation who preferably refer to themselves as Lakota.[56] They speak the Nakota dialect of the Siouan language. Their homelands were in Minnesota, Wisconsin, Iowa, and North Dakota.

Lakota oral history maintains that after their 17th-century encounter with European explorers, the tribe left their north-central Minnesota home in continued pursuit of buffalo. It was not until the settlers began to decimate the buffalo herds that the Lakota began resisting the immigration of the white man. In the 1700s, the tribe began acquiring horses which facilitated their buffalo hunting as well as warrior preeminence in the Missouri River basin.

Militarily the Lakota were the most powerful tribe among those residing on the Great Plains. They would demonstrate that prowess in conflict with the American army over land rights. The Red Cloud Wars of the 1860s established the fame of the Nation and distinguished them as the only Native American victors in a war against the government.[57]

The Great Sioux Nation is the traditional political structure for the Sioux language-speaking tribes in North America. These tribes are members of the Seven Council Fires or Oceti Sakowin, which includes three regional or dialect sub-groupings. Those groups are the Lakota (North, Central, and Southern Lakota), the Western Dakota (Yankton and Yanktonai), and the Eastern Dakota (Santee and Sisseton). The Lakota band (Teton) is the largest group.

Although a signatory to the Fort Laramie Treaty of 1851 and the grantor of safe passage for westward-bound settlers along the Oregon Trail, the Lakota and other tribes struck out against the immigrants. The Indian raids soon attracted the attention of the Army, which in 1855, under the command of General William Harney, pursued the warriors and killed over 100 Lakota. A series of short wars against the Indians followed. More settlers fled the region and established settlements deemed illegal by the treaty's terms, which incited even more frontier violence.

The Lakota conflict with the white man's government did not end with the violence along the Oregon Trail. To the Indigenous residents of the Dakotas, the Black Hills were sacred, and tribes fiercely opposed intruders. This did not deter further encroachments, and in violation of the Fort Laramie Treaty, George Custer and the 7th Cavalry penetrated the Black Hills where gold had been discovered. The Sioux resisted the ensuing rush of settlers and miners and even refused government overtures to buy or rent the sacred Black Hills. The Army responded by attacking the Lakota along the Bozeman Trail and engaged a force of Lakota warriors led by Oglala Chief Red Cloud in what became known as Red Cloud's War or the Bozeman War. In response to orders to round up all warring Native Americans and place them on reservations, the Battle of the Little Big Horn took place on June 25, 1876, at Greasy Grass, Montana.

The war resulted in another treaty, the Fort Laramie Treaty of 1868, that prohibited white settlements in the Black Hills. Despite the treaty, a series of engagements and battles followed over the next nine years, known as the Great Sioux War. In the end, in 1889, the Great Sioux Nation was broken up into smaller reservations, and on March 2 of that year, the Crow Creek Reservation was formally established and became home to the Lakota people.[58]

ARH-70 *Arapaho*—Armed Reconnaissance Helicopter

ARH-70 Arapaho *Armed Reconnaissance Helicopter.*
(Courtesy of the Army Aviation Museum.)

In the wake of the Army's faltering *Comanche* helicopter program, a study revealed that by canceling the program, an estimated $14 billion could be released from the overall Army aviation budget to update and replace its aging helicopter fleet.

Targeting the OH-58D *Kiowa Warrior*, on December 9, 2004, the Army solicited proposals for the Armed Reconnaissance Helicopter (ARH) program to replace the aircraft. The Army did not intend for a lengthy research and development program and instead requested proposals capitalizing on commercial off-the-shelf technology that would yield a 30-aircraft operational unit in less than four years, by September 2008.

Bell Helicopter and Boeing responded to the proposal, and the former offered an updated version of the OH-58D utilizing a military version of the Bell 407, using a Honeywell HTS900 engine, an all-composite main rotor from the Bell 430, and the tail assembly from the Bell 427. Boeing offered an upgraded version of MD Helicopter's MH-6 Little Bird that was currently in use with the 160th Special Operations Aviation Regiment. To allay Army fears about the industry being able to meet the production demands if the MH-6 offering won the competition, Boeing purchased the production rights for the design and proposed being the prime contractor.

Seven months later, the Army awarded Bell a contract for 368 *Arapaho* helicopters with prototypes and preproduction aircraft to be delivered to the Army for Limited User Test (LUT). Bell successfully achieved delivery of the first unit equipped by September 30, 2008.

The ARH-70's first flight took place at Bell's Arlington, Texas, facility on July 20, 2006. However, a setback occurred in February of the following year when prototype #4 crashed and was deemed beyond repair during a test flight. No one in the test crew was injured; however, as a result, the Army issued a "Stop Work" notice on March 22, 2007, giving Bell 30 days to submit a plan to return the program to the contract schedule. Bell appealed the notice and received permission to continue its development work using company funding while the notice was resolved, and on May 18, the program continuation was approved.

Despite the approval, while deliberating on the 2008 Defense Budget, the House Appropriations Committee eliminated all production funding for the ARH-70 *Arapaho* production while continuing funding for the development work. In the meantime, while assessing total program costs, including export sales, the Army determined that the program was forty percent over baseline costs and woefully behind schedule, resulting in the requirement to notify Congress of a Nunn-McCurdy program cost and schedule breech. The Bell ARH contract was terminated for the convenience of the government (T for C) on October 16, 2008.

The Arapaho are a Native American tribe that has historically resided in the Great Plains on tribal territory that included portions of present-day Colorado, Nebraska, Oklahoma, and Wyoming, although there is evidence that their sixteenth-century homeland was in present-day Minnesota. Around 1700 the tribe, concerned about its growing size and the pressure on the available food supply, split into two groups: the A'aninin (Gros Ventre) who migrated to present-day Canada, and a second main group, the Inunaina (Arapaho), who moved westward.[59] This latter group divided again with a northern group settling in the mountains near the Platte River in Colorado, and the southern branch near the Arkansas River. With long-term peace achieved with the Kiowa and Comanche, the Southern Arapaho still shared animosity with the Pawnee, Ute, and Shoshone.

Both the Northern and Southern Arapaho found themselves on or near the westward route of white settlers, and as their land was occupied and buffalo herds thinned, the frequency of violent encounters increased. After years of battling with the encroaching civilians and federal troops who were sent to protect them, in addition to privation and hunger, the Arapaho sought a treaty to bring them peace and a secure home. It came in the form and substance of the Fort Laramie Treaty of 1851, which provided them and the Cheyenne much of present-day Colorado, to the foothills of the Rockies and land in Kansas, Nebraska, and Wyoming. Nevertheless, the Northern Arapaho and the Cheyenne were soon pressed by the influx of settlers and gold prospectors. And while they and their Cheyenne and Sioux allies fiercely resisted the white man's encroachment, the Arapaho migrated further north to find land for themselves in Wyoming.

Included in the history of the Arapaho people is one of the darkest episodes in the annals of the Army and its citizen soldiery, the Sand Creek Massacre. It was the massacre of Cheyenne and Arapaho people during the Indian Wars by a 675-man contingent of the Third Colorado Cavalry under the command of Colonel John M. Chivington. "Attacks at dawn against sleepy Native American villages stood as the tactic of choice."[60] Hence the egregious acts of Colonel Chivington and the Colorado militia on the morning of November 29, 1864, against the village of Native American men, women, and children at Sand Creek merely drew celebratory editorials of the valor of the Army perpetrators.

A Methodist minister turned volunteer combat soldier, Chivington was driven by advancement in the military and viewed this as a steppingstone to achieving a seat in Congress. Advancing in rank but falling short of the coveted star of brigadier general, he saw command of a unit tasked "to punish the Indians and to put a stop to their hostile operations in the [Colorado] territory as a means to demonstrate his military genius, and thus reinvigorate his campaign for promotion and political advancement."[61]

At daybreak on November 29, 1864, the 1st and 3rd Colorado Volunteers, a small contingent of New Mexico Cavalry, and a section of two 12-pound howitzers descended upon the peace-seeking Cheyenne and Arapaho, which was comprised of more women and children than warriors, led by Chiefs Black Kettle and Left Hand at the protective encampment outside Fort Lyon along Sand Creek. White surrender flags and attempts to defuse the situation were ignored, and the indiscriminate slaughter ensued. During the over six hours of the attack, all who lived in the village lay dead or dying, slaughtered and mutilated by brutality beyond the pale. The crazed violence was incited by their commander, who admonished his subordinates to kill every person found in the camp and to take no prisoners.[62] The soldiers' acts of depravity resulted in their killing and butchering of everyone they came upon. Over 150 Native American corpses littered the village when the carnage ended while only ten soldiers had fallen.

The Congressional Joint Committee on the Conduct of War began its investigations of the events at Sand Creek on March 13, 1865, parallel to the broader inquiry of the Special Joint Committee on the Conditions of the Indian Tribes on Native American policy, which included an examination of the actions of the 1st and 3rd Colorado Cavalry. The Committee concluded that Chivington was responsible for "deliberately plann[ing] and execut[ing] a foul and dastardly massacre ... having full knowledge of their friendly intent."[63] "Chivington orchestrated the slaughter of hundreds of surrender-seeking Native Americans, destabilized the frontier for many years to follow, and incited tense and prolonged controversy throughout Colorado and the nation."[64] His ignominious and criminal behavior failed to garner him the promotion he sought nor to win him the seat in Congress, ranking him high among the worst commanders in military history, American or otherwise.

The southern kinsmen of the Arapaho in the meantime, were assigned to a reservation in parts of Kansas and Oklahoma by the Treaty of the Little Arkansas signed in 1865. Two years later, a series of three preeminent treaty agreements that affected the Comanche, Kiowa, Plains Apache, Southern Arapaho, and Southern Cheyenne were signed. The Medicine Lodge Treaty of 1867 removed the tribes from the westward routes of the white man's expansion, put them on reservations, and specified certain provisions for tribal support.[65] The land set aside for them was reduced to half of their prior home, but they were allowed to hunt buffalo while the herds continued to exist.

Before the U.S. Supreme Court ruling that gave Congress the "power to abrogate the provisions of an Indian treaty," the Northern Arapaho were placed on the 2.3-million-acre Wind River Reservation in west-central Wyoming in 1867, along with their traditional enemies, the Eastern Shoshone.[66]

In 1847, the Southern Arapaho and the Southern Cheyenne were settled on the North Canadian River at the Darlington Agency. Forty-four years later, their land was confiscated, and each tribal member was granted a 160-acre allotment. The balance of the 3.5 million acres was opened to non-Indians. The Cheyenne and Arapaho Tribes are both federally recognized today and are based in Concho, Oklahoma.

The Pace of Army Aviation Modernization Does Not Relent

Army Aviation of the 2020s operates an enduring fleet of over 4,000 manned aircraft, the UH-60 *Black Hawk*, the AH-64 *Apache*, the CH-47 *Chinook*, and more than 17,000 unmanned aircraft.[67] Concurrently, the Army recognizes that its enduring fleets will lose their battlefield supremacy and relevance without capitalizing on new and emerging technologies. This will be critical while the future aircraft fleet to support the future force makes its way through the research, development, and acquisition cycle. Among the modernization steps intended to create a fleet that will endure and ensure a place for the future fleet is the Improved Turbine Engine Program, which is developing a 3,000 shp engine for the *Apache* and *Black Hawk,* and will also power the Future Attack Reconnaissance Aircraft.

As a matter of priority, the Army intends to employ Future Vertical Lift capabilities in the operational force in 2028.[68] By the start of the next decade, it will begin fielding two platforms to support the future force. These two initial aircraft include the Future Attack Reconnaissance Aircraft (FARA), whose "increased range, speed, lethality, endurance, and survivability will replace the AH-64 in the reconnaissance squadrons and serve as an advanced scout aircraft."[69] The FARA is intended to increase the reach of the Army and Joint forces, enabling the delivery of lethal effects beyond the range of enemy sensors and weapons. The second modern aircraft in the Army modernization plan will be the Future Long-Range Assault Aircraft (FLRAA) with enhanced power projection capabilities derived from increased speed, range, survivability, and payload capacity over existing Army and U.S. Special Operations Command (SOCOM) assault aircraft.[70] The FLRAA will augment the capabilities of the *Black Hawk* fleet. Its development has been a high Army aviation priority. On December 5, 2022, a $1.3 billion contract was awarded to Bell-Textron for the further development of their hybrid tilt-rotor V-280 *Valor* system for the replacement of about 2,800 *Black Hawk* utility helicopters.[70] In less than three weeks following the announcement, the Sikorsky-Boeing team filed a protest of the contract award with the General Accountability Office (GAO), asserting that the "proposals were not consistently evaluated to deliver the best value in the interest of the Army, our soldiers, and American taxpayers."[71] On April 10, 2023, the GAO concluded that "the Army reasonably evaluated as technically unacceptable because Sikorsky failed to provide the level of architectural detail requested by the [Request for Proposal]."[72] The remaining priorities of the Army's efforts are the Air-Launched Effects and Future Tactical Unmanned Aircraft Systems. The former is "envisioned as small, optionally recoverable, air-or-ground-launched loitering aircraft ... [that] detect, identify, locate, and report threats."[73] These will be target acquisition and lethal and non-lethal target engagement systems. The final piece of the aviation system-of-systems will be the Future Tactical Unmanned Aircraft Systems which will replace the *Shadow* in brigade combat teams.

The Education Center at the Wall

During the years between the 2003 Congressional authorization for establishing the Education Center at the Wall and October 2018, when the project was officially terminated, many twists and turns in the road took place.

Tens of thousands of Vietnam veterans who survived the war came home with hearts and minds burdened by their experiences during the war. They felt a profound loss for each name they knew, now memorialized on the Wall, and were excoriated by their fellow citizens for responding to the nation's call and fighting in the war.

They rejoiced at the prospect of an edifice being erected to tell their stories, those of their comrades-in-arms, and those of their fallen buddies.

Abandoned by the Vietnam Veterans Memorial Fund (VVMF) Board of Directors, who turned their backs on the purpose of the Center and lost their zeal and motivation to make the Center at The Wall a reality, the project meandered with unguided direction. The forsaken Vietnam veterans, who returned from an unpopular war to the disparagement and indignant reproach by those for whom they thought they were serving and now by the less than entirely motivated VVMF leadership, was yet another deep and unkind cut visited upon those war veterans. Few Fund leaders at the time acknowledged any shared responsibility to raise funds for the center, even from among their many philanthropic colleagues and associates.

Over the same period, the purpose for which the Education Center was authorized was subverted from the purpose enacted under the Commemorative Works Act, which governs the establishment of American War Memorials on the National Mall.[74] When VVMF leaders embraced the inclusion on the Wall of Faces exhibit within the Education Center, the fallen warriors of America's wars in Iraq, Afghanistan, Syria, and the Global War on Terror, they reached beyond the authorizing legislation. Their actions resulted in confusion among potential donors, large and small, as to the real intent of their donations to the center.

Simultaneously, the organization's founder began lending his name to the active promotion and solicitation of donations for a Global War on Terror (GWOT) Memorial commemorating the fallen of the wars in Iraq and Afghanistan. This redirection of that focus and priorities to a GWOT Memorial diminished the center campaign. VVMF leadership further abandoned the center by calling for ceasing all efforts toward it in April 2016.

Fundraising did not keep pace with the progress of design maturation, the war's historical timeline development, artifacts inventory and curation, and the escalating costs for construction. During this confusion about the center, the Army Historical Foundation was actively fundraising for their capital project, The National Museum of the United States Army, at Fort Belvoir, Virginia. Unlike projects on the National Mall, construction of the Army Museum could begin before having collected eighty-five percent of the total project costs. Mall projects must accumulate seventy-five percent of the project costs plus another ten percent for the National Parks Service maintenance and operation expenses before beginning the site excavation. Consequently, the Army Museum would start construction before its required $200 million was amassed. Such a luxury represented a tremendous advantage to its fundraising ability. Additionally, as VVMF requested and received yet another Congressionally approved multi-year extension to its fundraising window, current and potential corporate donors and large foundations became concerned about whether the center would ever be built. The ceremonial groundbreaking for the center in 2012 did not allay those fears.

Ultimately, the same people who promoted the authorization for the Education Center with media fanfare proclaimed a great accomplishment of their collective failure by terminating it. The Education Center at The Wall officially perished on September 21, 2018.[75]

Notwithstanding the demise of the Education Center, the new leadership of the Vietnam Veterans Memorial Fund continues the work begun over four decades ago in keeping alive the stories and memories of courage and sacrifice of Americans who served during the Vietnam Era. The Fund maintains and keeps watch over the Memorial with countless volunteers who regularly clean the black panels and greet and assist the four million visitors who trek to the Wall annually. The VVMF remains one of the most comprehensive and authentic sources on the Vietnam War for educators, especially those of middle and high school students. For those who cannot travel to Washington, D.C., the Fund has a three-quarter scale Wall and mobile education center that visits cities and towns throughout the country, bringing the Memorial to as many Americans as possible.

The VVMF continues to carry on their remembrance programs. New names are added each year to increase awareness of the entire Vietnam War experience and bring recognition to those who died, served, and are still experiencing the pain and suffering born of their service in Vietnam. Whether it is Memorial Day or Veterans' Day observances, the In-Memory induction, Agent Orange, Post-Traumatic Stress Disorder (PTSD), or National Vietnam War Veterans Day observances, the work of the VVMF continues. As this volume approaches publication, the organization hosted the celebration of the fortieth anniversary of the Memorial.

On August 12, 2022, current VVMF President and Chief Executive Officer Jim Knotts announced a major accomplishment and milestone. "After more than two decades of effort, we [VVMF] are ecstatic to announce that at least one photo has been found for each of the 58,281 service members whose names are inscribed on the Vietnam Veterans Memorial."[76] The goal of the Wall of Faces project is to ensure that the faces and stories of those honored on The Wall are never forgotten for generations to come. The work continues to "… seek better quality photographs and adding remembrances to show the full story behind each name."[77]

National Native American Veterans Memorial

During the writing of this book, the efforts of the American Indian Veterans Memorial Initiative (AIVMI) began raising funds in fulfillment of an agreement with the VVMF, which, when fully satisfied, would result in a tribute to Native Americans who over the nation's history had faithfully served in her armed forces, and would be placed within of The Education Center. The collapse of the campaign for The Education Center at the Wall foreclosed on the prospect of that opportunity to honor Native American veterans.

A meaningful outcome of the Native American campaign to attain recognition on the National Mall of the selfless and courageous service of Indigenous Americans in the country's armed forces would also come to pass during the writing of this book. It would culminate in more than two decades of campaigning, petitioning, and fundraising. The United States Congress, by the Native American Veterans' Memorial Establishment Act of 1994 (Public Law 103-384) and the Native American Veterans' Memorial Amendments Act of 2013, authorized the Smithsonian's National Museum of the American Indian (NMAI) to construct and maintain a National Native American Veterans' Memorial dedicated to memorializing the "long, proud and distinguished tradition of service in the Armed Forces of the United States"[78] by Native Americans, Native Alaskans, and Native Hawaiians. Since no federal funds were authorized and appropriated for the Memorial's construction, the National Congress of American Indians and the National Museum of the American Indians were charged by the same legislation with accepting donations for the Memorial.

In 2017, the NMAI issued a nationwide call for design proposals for the Memorial. In March 2019, NMAI officials announced that a $15 million memorial would be built to honor the veterans and active-duty service members of Native American, Native Alaskan, and Native Hawaiian ancestry.[79]

Following extensive meetings and dialogue with Native American tribal leaders and veterans, the advisory committee for the Memorial established their guidance for the design competition. They directed that the Memorial's design must:

- "Be inclusive of all tribes and traditions,
- Not leave out women.
- Remember the sacrifice of family members,
- Include an element of spirituality, and
- Be broad enough to encompass the vast array of tribes yet specific enough that veterans and their families will recognize themselves and their stories."[80]

The National Native Americans Veterans Memorial was built on the National Mall in Washington, D.C., outside the Smithsonian's National Museum of the American Indian. One day when the sun shone gloriously, Native American veterans, tribal leaders, members of Congress, and officials from the Smithsonian National Museum of the American Indian assembled on the museum grounds. The day was September 21, 2019, and all had come to ceremonially begin the construction of the National Native Americans Veterans Memorial. The first shovels of dirt were turned. Representative Deb Haaland (D-NM 1st District), the keynote speaker[81], intoned, "Native American veterans and their contributions to our country have gone unrecognized throughout history. Today, we broke ground on a memorial that will be a place of healing for our warriors and a place to recognize their sacrifices …"[82]

In response to the request for design proposals for the memorial, officials of the Smithsonian's NMAI selected five finalists from the designs of more than 120 artists and architects. At the end of the eight-member jury selection process, a simple, primarily abstract work entitled "Warriors' Circle of Honor," created by artist Harvey Pratt was unanimously selected. Harvey Pratt is a Cheyenne and Arapaho tribal member and a veteran of the Vietnam War, having served in the Marine Corps in Air Rescue and Security at Da Nang Air Base.

*The National Native Americans Veterans Memorial is the
first on the National Mall to recognize the service of American
Indian, Alaska Native, and Native Hawaiian people in the
United States Armed Forces. The Memorial was designed
by Harvey Pratt, Butzer Architects, and Urbanism. (Photograph
by Alan Karchmer for the National Museum of the
American Indian.)*

The Memorial is situated in the living landscape on the east side of the NMAI at the edge of an upland hardwood forest overlooking the freshwater wetland. The Path of Life meanders through this setting, providing ample time for visitors to prepare themselves for the quiet and reflective experience of the memorial as the pathway's ends. The hardwoods and nearby water separate the memorial and visitors from the noise of the city that surrounds it.

The focus of the memorial is a large, vertical stainless-steel circle that is central to Native American storytelling and symbolic of the universality of the cycle of life and death, the continuity of all things,[83] and the movement of the stars and planets. The circle rests atop a drum-shaped carved stone which together are at the center of the gathering space. Water courses continuously outward from the drum's center. The circular stone is representative of the drum that calls people to gather, while the water which flows rhythmically from the center of the drum denotes purity, cleaning, prayer, and reflection. Circumscribing the memorial is the Path of Harmony, which reflects the respect for the different cultural practices of America's Indigenous peoples. From the Path of Harmony, visitors encounter a circular seating area with access to it and the central space from each of the four cardinal directions. The four arched benches offer seating for visitors wishing to gather, reflect, heal, and remember in the serenity and harmony of the memorial and its surroundings honoring the sacrifices and service of generations of Native American veterans. Equally spaced around the inner circle are four lances with eagle feathers pointing skyward. Visitors are invited to attach prayer cloths to the rings so that they might float heavenward with the wind.

For ceremonial events, a flame at the base of the steel circle will be ignited. The fire represents strength, courage, comfort, and endurance. An acoustic element completes the immersive setting of the memorial with a continuous loop of thirteen Native American veterans' songs from the Ojibwe, Menominee, Blackfeet, Ho-Chunk, Kiowa, and Lakota Nations.[84]

Constrained by the restriction stemming from the Center for Disease Control's response to the coronavirus, the memorial opened to the public on Veterans Day 2020, with a virtual, online program that included remarks from an array of distinguished speakers.

The National Native American Veterans Memorial Dedication Ceremony was rescheduled for Veterans Day, November 11, 2022, and will honor American Indian, Alaska Native, and Native Hawaiian veterans and their families. Over 1,500 Native American veterans from across the length and breadth of American preceded the dedication with a grand procession along the National Mall from the NMAI to the ceremony stage in front of the U.S. Capitol. Punctuated by a light rain, memorial designer Vietnam War veteran Harvey Pratt observed "I want to look at the heavens today, the Creator gave us a nice gentle rain, to water Mother Earth, and for us to start a new day."[85]

Later during the dedication ceremony a rainbow broke out through the clouds above the U.S. Capitol meaning to many in attendance a sign to honor the warriors who had served.

With the memorial's opening and dedication, the Indigenous people and warriors of America have at last realized the honor and gratitude they earned over the centuries but were, until now, denied.

APPENDIX A: NATIVE AMERICAN MEDAL OF HONOR RECIPIENTS

Thirty-one Native Americans so distinguished themselves "for conspicuous gallantry and intrepidity at the risk of life, above and beyond the call of duty, in actual combat against an armed enemy force," that they were awarded the Medal of Honor. The Medal was established on December 21, 1861, by the U.S. Navy; on July 12, 1862, by the U.S. Army; and on April 14, 1965, by the U.S. Air Force, and is presented by the President of the United States in the name of Congress.

The Medal of Honor was first awarded on March 25, 1863, to an Army recipient during the American Civil War. The table below identifies each of the thirty-two Native American recipients, their tribal affiliation, service and rank, and the date and place of the action for which the award was made as they were at the time of the action.[1] There was an additional three Native Hawaiian recipients.[2] The seven individuals with an asterisk (*) following their names received the Medal of Honor posthumously.

Name	Tribe/ Nation[3,4]	Service	Rank	Conflict	Place of Action	Date of Action
Co-Rux-Te-Chod-Ish, (Mad Bear)	Pawnee	Army	Sergeant	Indian War Campaigns	Republican River, Kansas	July 8, 1869
Chiquito, N/A	White Mountain Apache	Army	Scout	Indian War Campaigns	Arizona Territory	Winter of 1871–1873
Bow-os-loh Jim "The Giant"	White Mountain Apache	Army	Sergeant	Indian War Campaigns	Arizona Territory	Winter of 1871–1873
Machol, N/A	Apache	Army	Private	Indian War Campaigns	Arizona Territory	1872–1873
Nannasaddie, N/A	White Mountain Apache	Army	Scout	Indian War Campaigns	Arizona Territory	1872–1873

(*Continued*)

Name	Tribe/ Nation[3,4]	Service	Rank	Conflict	Place of Action	Date of Action
Nantaje Nantahe	White Mountain Apache	Army	Scout	Indian War Campaigns	Arizona Territory	1872–1873
William Alchesay	White Mountain Apache	Army	Sergeant	Indian War Campaigns	Arizona Territory	Winter of 1872–1873
Blanquet, N/A	Apache	Army	Scout	Indian War Campaigns	Arizona Territory	Winter of 1872–1873
Elsatsoosu, N/A	Apache	Army	Corporal	Indian War Campaigns	Arizona Territory	Winter of 1872–1873
Kelsay, N/A	White Mountain Apache	Army	Scout	Indian War Campaigns	Arizona Territory	Winter of 1872–1873
Kosoha, N/A	White Mountain Apache	Army	Scout	Indian War Campaigns	Arizona Territory	Winter of 1872–1873
Adam Paine	Black Seminole	Army	Private	Indian War Campaigns	Canyon Blanco tributary of the Red River, Texas	September 26–27, 1874
Pompey Factor	Black Seminole	Army	Principal Musician	Indian War Campaigns	Pecos River, Texas	April 25, 1875
Isaac Payne	Black Seminole	Army	Trumpeter	Indian War Campaigns	Pecos River, Texas	April 25, 1875
John Ward	Black Seminole	Army	Sergeant	Indian War Campaigns	Pecos River, Texas	April 25, 1875
Y. B. Rowdy	Yavapai	Army	Sergeant	Indian War Campaigns	Arizona Territory	March 7, 1890
Gregory (Pappy) Boyington	Sioux	Marine Corps	Major	World War II	Central Solomons Area, Pacific Ocean	September 12, 1943 – January 3, 1944
Ernest Childers	Muscogee	Army	Second Lieutenant	World War II	Oliveto, Italy	September 22, 1943
Jack C. Montgomery	Cherokee	Army	First Lieutenant	World War II	Near Padigilone, Italy	February 22, 1944
Van T. Barfoot	Choctaw	Army	Technical Sergeant	World War II	Carano, Italy	May 23, 1944

(Continued)

Name	Tribe/ Nation[3,4]	Service	Rank	Conflict	Place of Action	Date of Action
Roy W. Harmon*	Cherokee	Army	Sergeant	World War II	Casaglia, Italy	July 12, 1944
Ernest E. Evans*	Cherokee/ Creek	Navy	Commander	World War II	Off Samar, Philippines	October 25, 1944
John N. Reese, Jr.*	Cherokee	Army	Private First Class	World War II	Paco Railroad Station, Manila, Philippines	February 9, 1945
Mitchell Red Cloud, Jr.*	Ho-Chunk	Army	Corporal	Korean War	Choghyon, Korea	November 5, 1950
Raymond Harvey	Chickasaw	Army	Captain	Korean War	Taemi-Dong, Korea	March 9, 1951
Tony Kenneth Burris*	Choctaw	Army	Sergeant First Class	Korean War	Mundung-ni, Korea	October 8–9, 1951
Woodrow Wilson Keeble*	Sisseton Wahpeton Oyate of Lake Traverse Reservation Sioux	Army	Master Sergeant	Korean War	Sangsan-ni, Korea	October 20, 1951
Charles George*	Cherokee	Army	Private First Class	Korean War	Near Songnae-dong, Korea	November 20, 1952
James Elliott Williams	Cherokee	Navy	Boatswain's Mate 1st Class	Vietnam War	Mekong River, South Vietnam	October 31, 1966
Roy Perez Benavidez	Yaqui	Army	Staff Sergeant	Vietnam War	West of Loc Ninh, South Vietnam	May 2, 1968
Michael E. Thornton	Cherokee	Navy	Petty Officer	Vietnam War	Republic of Vietnam	October 31, 1972

APPENDIX B: WHERE ARE THEY NOW—RESERVATION HOMES OF NAMESAKE TRIBES[1]

Reservation	Tribe(s)	Location	Area (acres)	Enrollment
Absentee Shawnee	Absentee-Shawnee Tribe of Indians	Oklahoma	11,680	3,029
Allegany	Seneca Nation of New York	New York	30,189	1,272
Cayuga Nation	Cayuga Nation of New York	New York	0	475
Chickasaw Nation	Chickasaw Nation	Oklahoma	73,079	38,740
Choctaw Nation of Oklahoma	Choctaw Nation of Oklahoma	Oklahoma	135,745	174,861
Colorado River Indian	Colorado River Indian Tribes (Chemehuevi, Hopi, Mohave, and Navajo)	Arizona California	269,620	3,705
Crow Creek	Crow Creek Sioux Tribe of the Crow Creek	South Dakota	151,512	3,507
Eastern Shawnee	Eastern Shawnee Tribe of Oklahoma	Oklahoma	1,195	2,367
Jena Band of Choctaw	Jena Band of Choctaw Indians	Louisiana	62	243
Lake Traverse	Sisseton-Wahpeton Oyate of the Lake Traverse (Sioux)	North Dakota South Dakota	107,902	11,763
Lower Brule	Lower Brule Sioux Tribe of Lower Brule	South Dakota	144,588	3,036

(Continued)

Reservation	Tribe(s)	Location	Area (acres)	Enrollment
Mississippi Band of Choctaw Indians	Mississippi Band of Choctaw Indians	Mississippi	28,402	9,483
Oneida	Oneida Nation of New York	New York	13,731	1,000
Oneida	Oneida Tribe of Indians of Wisconsin	Wisconsin	6,645	14,745
Onondaga	Onondaga Nation of New York	New York	7,300	1,600
Quinault	Quinault Tribe of the Quinault Reservation (Hoh, Quileute, Chehalis, Chinook, and Cowlitz)	Washington	208,105	2,454
Shakopee Mdewakanton Sioux Community	Shakopee Mdewakanton Sioux	Minnesota	661	391
St. Regis Mohawk	Saint Regis Mohawk Tribe	New York	22,160	11,703
Tuscarora	Tuscarora Nation of New York	New York	5,700	1,138
Umatilla	Confederated Tribes of the Umatilla Reservation (Cayuse, Umatilla, and Walla Walla)	Oregon	86,784	2,542
Wind River	Arapaho Tribe of the Wind River Reservation Shoshone Tribe of the Wind River Reservation	Wyoming	2,268,008	7,417 3,724
Wyandotte	Wyandotte Nation	Oklahoma	218	4,279

APPENDIX C: OFFICIAL AND UNOFFICIAL NAMES OF ARMY VIETNAM WAR HELICOPTERS

True to form and the literary imagination of the American GI, there is nothing sacred about the decisions the Army leadership makes about how things are identified among the men and women in the ranks. The soldier in the field will always have the penchant to come up with a better idea, a more appealing name, or a moniker that expresses a more authentic identity as seen through the eyes and the mind of field soldiers. There can be no exhaustive list of these foxhole names because there are almost as many vernacular names as there are foxholes, but the table below appreciates some of them.[1]

Army aviators in training were not beyond their contributions to the litany with their subrogate for the Hughes TH-55A *Osage*, a training helicopter that they affectionately regarded as the "Mattel Messerschmitt."[2]

Joint Name	Official Common Name	Other "Unofficial" Common Names[3]	
UH-1	*Iroquois*	"Huey" "Hog" "Frog"	"Slick" "School Bus" "Cadillac" of helicopters
OH-6	*Cayuse*	"Loach" "Egg" "Olive on a Toothpick" "Low Bird"	"Flying Egg" "Killer Egg" "Little Bird"
OH-13	*Sioux*	"Bell(s)" "Angel of Mercy"	"Sioux Scout"
CH-19	*Chickasaw*	"Hogs" "Horse"	"Pregnant Guppies"

(Continued)

Joint Name	Official Common Name	Other "Unofficial" Common Names[3]	
CH-21	*Shawnee*	"Flying Banana"	"21"
		"Work Horse"	"The Big 21"
		"Hog Two-One"	"The Flying Coffin"
		"Piasecki's Puzzle"	"Angle Worms"
		"The Beast"	"Sagging Sausage"
OH-23	*Raven*	"Hiller Killer"	
CH-34	*Choctaw*	"HUS"	"Dog"
		"Ugly Angel"	"King Bee"
CH-37	*Mojave*	"Deuce"	"Cross-eye"
		"Beast"	"Cross-eyed Monster"
		"BUF"[4]	
CH-47	*Chinook*	"47"	"Guns A-Go-Go"
		"Shithook"	"Pipe Smoke"
		"Go-Go Bird"	"Hook"
		"Fat Lady"	
CH-54	*Tarhe*	"Flying Crane"	"Grasshopper"
		"Crane"	"Skycrane"
OH-58	*Kiowa*	"58"	"5.8"[5]
		"Scout"	"Scooter"

APPENDIX D: HELICOPTER LOSSES DURING THE VIETNAM WAR

The Vietnam Helicopter Pilots Association (VHPA) maintains tail number records for 11,835 helicopters that saw service in Vietnam from all the military services. The table below summarizes their data and the records of 5,607 helicopters lost. The data is not perfect, and some discrepancies do exist. For example, their information records 16 lost CH-3Cs; however, they only have tail numbers for eleven aircraft. The VHPA also knows that UH-19s saw service in Vietnam, but they do not have tail numbers for any of them. The Association continues to search for more records, and over time, they expect to learn more and discover other tail numbers to add to their database.

Helicopter Model	Total	Lost	KIAs Pilot	KIAs Crewmembers
AH-1G	824	303	235	12
AH-1J	3	3		
HH-1K	1			
UH-1	53	75	19	12
UH-1A	8	1		
UH-1B	711	378	151	157
UH-1C	712	417	180	182
UH-1D	1,856	1,021	252	275
UH-1E	155	100	39	44
UH-1F	32	18	4	5
UH-1H	3,445	1,291	494	544
UH-1L	5		1	2
UH-1M	7	1	6	5
UH-1N	1	2		1
UH-1P	2		3	1
UH-2A	9	6		

(Continued)

Helicopter Model	Total	Lost	KIAs Pilot	KIAs Crewmembers
UH-2B	6	6	3	2
CH-3C	11	16	1	1
CH-3E	11	4	6	7
HH-3E	43	20	8	9
SH-3A	13	9	6	9
OH-6A	1,422	964	233	251
OH-13S	275	173	21	16
UH-19				
CH-21C	148	18	9	11
OH-23G	231	97	12	14
SH-34G	3	4		1
UH-34D	360	211	67	78
CH-37B	10	3	2	2
CH-37C	9	1		
HH-43B	11	8	6	6
HH-43F	11	6		1
CH-46A	187	109	46	66
CH-46D	186	87	41	67
AN-47A	4	2	2	6
CH-47A	327	91	33	87
CH-47B	96	27	17	32
CH-47C	165	37	25	42
CH-53A	79	19	15	18
CH-53C	2	2	2	
CH-53D	20	6	2	7
HH-53B	6	2	2	3
HH-53C	14	7	10	12
HH-53E			2	3
CH-54A	42	9	5	7
OH-58A	312	48	19	22
204B	3	1	1	1
205	4	1	1	2

APPENDIX E: CHARACTERISTICS AND PERFORMANCE OF ARMY VIETNAM WAR HELICOPTERS

OH-13S Sioux. *(Courtesy of Ray Wilhite.)*

OH-13S *Sioux*[1]

Manufacturer	Bell Helicopter Company, Fort Worth, Texas
Crew	Pilot and up to three passengers
Engine	One Lycoming TVO-435-25 turbo-supercharged piston engine of 260 horsepower (hp)
Main Dimensions	
Length	43 feet, 3 inches
Height	9 feet, 6 inches

Main Rotor

- • Rotor Systems   Single two-bladed main, two-bladed tail
- • Diameter   36 feet

Weight (empty)   1,936 pounds

Gross Weight   2,855 pounds

Performance

Maximum Speed   105 mph

Cruising Speed   93 mph

Rate of Climb   1,190 feet-per-minute (fpm)[2]

Service Ceiling   18,000 feet

Hover Ceiling   15,000 feet[3]

Range   324 miles

UH-19 Chickasaw. *(Courtesy of Ray Wilhite.)*

UH-19D *Chickasaw*[4]

Manufacturer	Sikorsky Aircraft Division, Stratford, Connecticut
Crew	Two plus ten passengers
Engine	One Curtiss-Wright R-1300-3 Cyclone radial piston engine of 700 hp

Main Dimensions

Length	42 feet, 3 inches
Height	13 feet, 4 inches
Main Rotor	
• Rotor Systems	Three-bladed main rotor; two-bladed 8 feet diameter tail
• Diameter	53 feet
Weight (empty)	5,250 pounds
Gross Weight	7,900 pounds

Performance

Maximum Speed	112 mph
Cruising Speed	91 mph
Rate of Climb	1,020 fpm
Service Ceiling	12,500 feet
Hover Ceiling	2,300 feet[5]
Range	385 miles

CH-21C Shawnee. *(Courtesy of Ray Wilhite.)*

CH-21C *Shawnee*[6]

Manufacturer	Boeing-Vertol Division, Morton, PA
Crew	Three plus 20 troops or 12 litters
Engine	One Curtiss-Wright R-1820-103 Cyclone radial piston engine of 1,425 hp

Main Dimensions

Length:	52 feet, 6 inches
Height:	15 feet, 9 inches
Main Rotor	
• Rotor System	Tandem, three bladed
• Diameter	44 feet
Weight (empty)	8,950 pounds
Gross Weight	15,200 pounds

Performance[7]

Maximum Speed	127 mph
Cruising Speed	98 mph
Rate of Climb	960 fpm
Service Ceiling	9,450 feet
Range	265 miles

OH-23G Raven. *(Courtesy of Ray Wilhite.)*

OH-23G *Raven*[9]

Manufacturer	Hiller Aircraft Company, Palo Alto, California
Crew	One pilot plus two passengers
Engine	One Lycoming VO-540-A1B piston engine of 305 hp
Main Dimensions	
Fuselage Length:	28 feet, 6 inches
Height:	10 feet, 2 inches
Main Rotor	
• Rotor System	Single two-bladed rotor, single two-bladed tail rotor
• Diameter	35 feet, 5 inches
Weight (empty)	1,759 pounds
Gross Weight	2,800 pounds
Performance	
Maximum Speed	96 mph
Cruising Speed	90 mph
Rate of Climb	1,050 fpm[10]
Service Ceiling	15,200 feet
Hover Ceiling	5,200 feet[11]
Range	225 miles

CH-34 Choctaw. *(Courtesy of Jim Fox via Ray Wilhite.)*

CH-34 *Choctaw*[12]

Manufacturer	Sikorsky Aircraft Division, Stratford, Connecticut
Crew	Two or three crew plus up to 18 passengers or eight litters and two attendants
Engine	One Curtiss-Wright R-1820-84 piston engine of 1,525 hp
Main Dimensions	
Length	46 feet 9 inches
Height	14 feet 3.5 inches
Main Rotor	
• Rotor Systems	Four-bladed main, four-bladed tail
• Diameter	56 feet
Weight (empty)	7,675 pounds
Gross Weight	13,000 pounds
Performance	
Maximum Speed	122 mph
Cruising Speed	97 mph
Rate of Climb	1,100 fpm[13]
Service Ceiling	9,500 feet
Hover Ceiling	2,400 feet[14]
Range	210 miles

CH-37B Mojave. *(Courtesy of Jerome "Jerry" Riggs via Ray Wilhite.)*

CH-37B *Mojave*[15]

Manufacturer	Sikorsky Aircraft Division, Stratford, Connecticut
Crew	Two to three crew plus up to 26 troops or 24 litters
Engines	Two Pratt & Whitney R-2800-54 radial piston engines of 2,100 hp each

Main Dimensions

Fuselage Length	64 feet 3 inches
Height	22 feet
Main Rotor	
• Rotor Systems	Five-blades main rotor, four-bladed tail rotor
• Diameter	72 feet
Weight (empty)	21,450 pounds
Gross Weight	30,000 pounds

Performance

Maximum Speed	125 mph
Cruising Speed	110mph
Rate of Climb	910 fpm[16]
Service Ceiling	8,700 feet
Hover Ceiling	1,100 feet[17]
Range	145 miles

UH-1A Iroquois. *(Courtesy of Ray Wilhite.)*

UH-1A *Iroquois*[18]

Manufacturer	Bell Helicopter Company, Fort Worth, Texas
Crew	Two to three plus 6 passengers or two stretchers
Engine	Single Lycoming T53-L-1A turbine of 700 shp or Lycoming T53-L-11 turbine of 960 shp
Main Dimensions	
Length	30 feet, 4 inches
Height	12 feet, 8 inches
Main Rotor	
• Rotor Systems	Single two-bladed main, two-bladed tail
• Diameter	44 feet
Weight (empty)	4,523 pounds
Maximum Weight	8,500 pounds
Performance	
Maximum Speed	125 mph
Cruising Speed	110 mph
Rate of Climb	2,350 fpm[19]
Service Ceiling	16,900 feet
Hover Ceiling	12,700 feet[20]
Range	220 miles

UH-1B Iroquois. *(Courtesy of Ray Wilhite.)*

UH-1B *Iroquois*[21]

Manufacturer	Bell Helicopter Company, Fort Worth, Texas
Crew	Two to three plus 8 passengers or three stretchers
Engine	Single Lycoming T53-L-5 turbine of 960shp or Lycoming T53-L-11 turbine of 1,100 shp
Main Dimensions	
Fuselage Length	42 feet, 7 inches
Height	14 feet, 7 inches
Main Rotor	
• Rotor Systems	Single two-bladed main, two-bladed tail
• Diameter	44 feet
Weight (empty)	4,523 pounds
Maximum Weight	8,500 pounds
Performance	
Maximum Speed	125 mph
Cruising Speed	110 mph
Rate of Climb	2,350 fpm[22]
Service Ceiling	16,900 feet
Hover Ceiling	12,700 feet[23]
Range	220 miles

UH-1C Iroquois. *(Courtesy of Ray Wilhite.)*

UH-1C *Iroquois*[24]

Manufacturer	Bell Helicopter Company, Fort Worth, Texas
Crew	Two plus 9 passengers or three stretchers
Engine	Single Lycoming T53-L-11 turbine of 1,100 shp
Main Dimensions	
Fuselage Length	42 feet, 7 inches
Height	14 feet, 7 inches
Main Rotor	
• Rotor Systems	Single two-bladed main, two-bladed tail
• Diameter	44 feet
Weight (empty)	5,827 pounds
Maximum Weight	9,500 pounds
Performance	
Maximum Speed	135 mph
Cruising Speed	128 mph
Rate of Climb	2,350 fpm[25]
Service Ceiling	18,500 feet
Hover Ceiling	12,700 feet
Range	315 miles

UH-1D Iroquois. *(Courtesy of Tommy Thornton via Ray Wilhite.)*

UH-1D *Iroquois*[26]

Manufacturer	Bell Helicopter Company, Fort Worth, Texas
Crew	Two plus 12 to 15 passengers or six litters and a medical attendant
Engine	Single Lycoming T53-L-11 turbine of 1,100 shp
Main Dimensions	
Fuselage Length	48 feet
Height	14 feet, 7 inches
Main Rotor	
• Rotor Systems	Single two-bladed main, two-bladed tail
• Diameter	44 feet
Weight (empty)	4,717 pounds
Maximum Weight	9,500 pounds
Performance	
Maximum Speed	145 mph
Cruising Speed	127 mph
Rate of Climb	2,350 fpm
Service Ceiling	18,500 feet
Hover Ceiling	12,700 feet
Range	289 miles

UH-1H Iroquois. (Courtesy of Ray Wilhite.)

UH-1H *Iroquois*[27]

Manufacturer	Bell Helicopter Company, Fort Worth, Texas
Crew	Two plus 11–14 passengers
Engine	Single Lycoming T53-L-13 turbine of 1,400 shp
Main Dimensions	
Length (Overall)	57 feet, 1 inch
Height	14 feet, 6 inches
Main Rotor	
• Rotor Systems	Single two-bladed main, two-bladed tail
• Diameter	48 feet
Weight (empty)	4,667 pounds
Maximum Weight	9,500 pounds
Performance	
Maximum Speed	127 mph
Cruising Speed	127 mph
Rate of Climb	1,600 fpm
Service Ceiling	12,600 feet
Hover Ceiling	13,600 feet
Range	318 miles

UH-1M Iroquois *at Duc Pho 1971. (Courtesy of Robert Brackenhoff via Ray Wilhite.)*

UH-1M *Iroquois*[28]

Manufacturer   Bell Helicopter Company, Fort Worth, Texas

Crew   Four (Pilot, co-pilot and two gunners)

Engine   Single Lycoming T53-L-13 turbine of 1,400 shp

Main Dimensions

   Length (Overall)   53 feet

   Height   14 feet, 7 inches

   Main Rotor

     • Rotor Systems   Single two-bladed main, two-bladed tail

     • Diameter   44 feet

   Weight (empty)   5,110 pounds

   Maximum Weight   9,500 pounds

Performance[29]

   Maximum Speed   144 mph

   Cruising Speed   128 mph

   Rate of Climb   1,600 fpm

   Service Ceiling   18,500 feet

   Hover Ceiling   13,600 feet

   Range   332 miles

OH-6A Cayuse *at Quang Tri 1971. (Courtesy of Robert Brackenhoff via Ray Wilhite.)*

OH-6A *Cayuse*[30]

Manufacturer	Hughes Tool Company, Aircraft Division, Culver City, California
Crew	Two plus two in rear cargo compartment
Engine	Single Allison T63-A-5A turbine of 317 shp
Main Dimensions	
Length	30 feet, 3 3/4 inches
Height	8 feet, 1 1/2 inches
Main Rotor	
• Rotor Systems	Four-bladed main, two-bladed tail
• Diameter	26 feet, 4 inches
Weight (empty)	1,229 pounds
Maximum Weight	2,700 pounds
Performance	
Maximum Speed	150 mph
Cruising Speed	134 mph
Rate of Climb	1,840 fpm
Service Ceiling	15,800 feet
Hover Ceiling	7,300 feet
Range	380 miles

CH-47A Chinook. *(Courtesy of Ray Wilhite.)*

CH-47A *Chinook*[31]

Manufacturer	Boeing Vertol Division, Morton, Pennsylvania
Crew	Two to three plus 22 to 50 troops
Engines	Two Lycoming T55-L-5 turboshafts of 2,200 shp each or two T55-L-7 turboshafts of 2,650 shp each

Main Dimensions

Fuselage Length	51 feet
Height	18 feet 6 inches
Main Rotor	
• Rotor Systems	Two tandem three-bladed rotors
• Diameter	59 feet, 1 inch
Weight (empty)	17,913 pounds
Gross Weight	33,000 pounds

Performance

Maximum Speed	178 mph
Cruising Speed	164 mph
Rate of Climb	1,750 fpm[32]
Service Ceiling	9,500 feet
Hover Ceiling	7,750 feet[33]
Range	115 miles

CH-47B Chinook *180th Aviation Company - Big Windy - at Tuy Hoa 1968. (Courtesy of Richard Dickey Packard via Ray Wilhite.)*

CH-47B *Chinook*[34]

Manufacturer	Boeing Vertol Division, Morton, Pennsylvania
Crew	Two to three plus 22 to 50 troops
Engines	Two Lycoming T55-L-7C turbines of 2,850 shaft horsepower (shp) each

Main Dimensions

Fuselage Length	51 feet
Height	18 feet 6 inches
Main Rotor	
• Rotor Systems	Two tandem three-bladed rotors
• Diameter	60 feet
Weight (empty)	19,375 pounds
Gross Weight	40,000 pounds

Performance

Maximum Speed	196 mph
Cruising Speed	177 mph
Rate of Climb	1,990 fpm
Service Ceiling	16,300 feet
Hover Ceiling	14,200 feet
Range	351 miles

CH-47C Chinook. *(Courtesy of Ray Wilhite.)*

CH-47C *Chinook*[35]

Manufacturer	Boeing Vertol Division, Morton, Pennsylvania
Crew	Two to three plus 22 to 50 troops or 24 litters and 2 attendants
Engines	Two Lycoming T55-L-11A turbines of 3,750 shp each

Main Dimensions

Fuselage Length	51 feet
Height	18 feet 6 inches
Main Rotor	
• Rotor Systems	Two tandem three-bladed rotors
• Diameter	60 feet
Weight (empty)	20,547 pounds
Gross Weight	46,000 pounds

Performance

Maximum Speed	190 mph
Cruising Speed	165 mph
Rate of Climb	2,045 fpm
Service Ceiling	19,000 feet
Hover Ceiling	9,600 feet
Range	245 miles

A/ACH-47A Chinook. *(Courtesy of Ray Wilhite.)*

A/ACH-47A *Chinook*[36]

Manufacturer	Boeing Vertol Division, Morton, Pennsylvania
Crew	Seven to nine
Engines	Two Lycoming T55-L-5C turbines of 2,200 shp or two Lycoming T-55-L-7C turbines of 2,650 shp each

Main Dimensions

Fuselage Length	51 feet
Height	18 feet 6 inches
Main Rotor	
• Rotor Systems	Tandem three-bladed rotors
• Diameter	59 feet 1 inch
Weight (empty)	22,000 pounds
Gross Weight	31,000 pounds

Performance

Maximum Speed	168 mph
Cruising Speed	155 mph
Rate of Climb	1,990 fpm
Service Ceiling	16,300 feet
Hover Ceiling	14,200 feet
Range	351 miles

CH-54A Tarhe. *(Courtesy of Ray Wilhite.)*

CH-54A *Tarhe*[37]

Manufacturer	Sikorsky Aircraft Division, Stratford, Connecticut
Crew	Three plus 2 passengers in cockpit, plus 67 troops or 48 litters in pod
Engines	Two Pratt & Whitney JFTD-12A-1 turbines of 4,500 shp each
Main Dimensions	
Length	88 feet, 6 inches
Height	25 feet, 5 inches
Main Rotor	
• Rotor Systems	Single six-bladed main rotor, four-bladed tail
• Diameter	72 feet
Weight (empty)	19,234 pounds
Maximum Weight	42,000 pounds
Performance	
Maximum Speed	126 mph
Cruising Speed	105 mph
Rate of Climb	1,330 fpm
Service Ceiling	9,000 feet
Hover Ceiling	6,900 feet
Range	230 miles

OH-58 Kiowa. *(Courtesy of Ray Wilhite.)*

OH-58A *Kiowa*[38]

Manufacturer	Bell Helicopter, Fort Worth, Texas
Crew	Two and two passengers
Engine	Single Allison T63-A-700 turbine of 317 shp
Main Dimensions	
Length	40 feet, 11 3/4 inches
Height	9 feet, 7 inches
Main Rotor	
• Rotor Systems	Two-bladed main, two-bladed tail
• Diameter	35 feet, 4 inches
Weight (empty)	1,464 pounds
Maximum Weight	3,000 pounds
Performance	
Maximum Speed	138 mph
Cruising Speed	117 mph
Rate of Climb	1,780 fpm
Service Ceiling	18,900 feet
Hover Ceiling	13,600 feet
Range	299 miles

APPENDIX F: ACRONYMS AND ABBREVIATIONS

A

AA	Anti-Aircraft
AAA	Anti-Aircraft Artillery
AAC	Army Air Corps
AAF	Army Airfield
AC	Aircraft Commander; Airplane, Cargo
ACR	Aerial Combat Reconnaissance
ACRC	Aerial Combat Reconnaissance Company
ACTIV	Army Concept Team in Vietnam
ADF	Automatic Direction Finder
ADS	Aircraft Direct Support
AEF	American Expeditionary Force
AFB	Air Force Base
AFQT	Armed Forces Qualification Test
AGM	Anti-tank Guided Missile
AH	Attack Helicopter; United States Navy hull classification code: Hospital Ship
AHC	Assault Helicopter Company
AIT	Advanced Individual Training
AK	Cargo Ship
AMCOM	Army Aviation Materiel Command; U.S. Army Aviation Missile Command
AML	Airmobile Light
AMS	Aircraft Maintenance and Supply
ANC	Army Nurse Corps
AO	Airplane, Observation; Area of Operations
AP	Troop Transport
APC	Armored Personnel Carrier

AR	Army Regulation
AR/AAV	Armored Reconnaissance/Airborne Assault Vehicle
ARA	Aerial Rocket Artillery
ARDF	Airborne Radio-Direction Finding
ARNG	Army National Guard
ARS	Air Rescue Service (USAF)
ARVN	Army of the Republic of Vietnam
ASA	Army Security Agency
ASE	Automatic Stabilization Equipment
ASH	Assault Helicopter
ASR	Army Study Requirements
ASVAB	Armed Services Vocational Aptitude Battery
ASW	Anti-Submarine Warfare
ATNI	Affiliated Tribes of Northwest Indians
AU	Airplane, Utility
AUSA	Association of the United States Army

B

BAR	Browning Automatic Rifle
BDA	Bomb Damage/Battle Damage Assessment
BDA	Bomb Damage Assessment
BGM	Department of Defense Aerospace Vehicle Designation:
	B - Missile can be launched from various environments
	G - Missile is launched directly from the ground surface
	M - Missile is launched from a mobile ground vehicle
BIA	Bureau of Indian Affairs
BLU	Bomb Live Unit

C

C&C	Command and Control
CA	Civil Affairs
CAB	Combat Aviation Battalion
CAS	Close Air Support
CBI	China-Burma-India
C-Day	"Conversion Day"
CD	Combat Development
CDEC	Combat Developments Experimentation Command
CG	Commanding General
CIA	Central Intelligence Agency
CIC	Combat Information Center

COMUSMACV	Commander U.S. Military Assistance Command, Vietnam
CONUS	Continental United States
COSVN	Central Office for South Vietnam
CP	Combat Photographer
CTZ	Corps Tactical Zone
CV	Aircraft Carrier
CVE	Escort Aircraft Carrier
CVL	Light Aircraft Carrier

D

DA	Department of the Army
DASPO	Department of the Army Special Photographic Office
DEROS	Date Eligible/Estimated to Return from Overseas.
DEW	Distant Early Warning
DF	Direction Finding
DMZ	Demilitarized Zone
DOD	Department of Defense
DODD	Department of Defense Directive
DPRK	Democratic People's Republic of Korea
DS	Direct Support
DSU	Direct Support Unit
DZ	Drop Zone

E

EDP	Equipment Deadlined for Parts
ETO	European Theater of Operations
ETS	Expiration Term of Service

F

FAA	Federal Aviation Administration
FADAC	Field Artillery Digital Automatic Computer
FARA	Future Attack Reconnaissance Aircraft
FECOM	Far East Command
FFAR	Folding Fin Aerial Rocket
FLIR	Forward-Looking Infrared
FLOT	Front Line of Own Troops
FLRAA	Future Long-Range Assault Aircraft
FO	Fog Oil
FSB	Fire Support Base

FUE	First Unit Equipped

G

GAU	Gatling Automatic Cannon
GAO	Government Accounting Office
	Government Accountability Office
GFE	Government Furnished Equipment
GO	General Order
GS	General Support
GSX	Gelled Slurry Explosive
GWOT	Global War on Terror

H

HA	Helicopter Ambulance
HC	Helicopter, Cargo
HIS	Helicopter Illumination System
HMH	Marine Heavy Helicopter
HO	Helicopter, Observation
HP	Horsepower
HU	Helicopter, Utility
HVAR	High-Velocity Aerial Rockets

I

IMINT	Imagery Intelligence
INFANT	Iroquois Night Fighter and Night Tracker
IP	Instructor Pilot
IRBM	Intermediate Range Ballistic Missile

J

JASCO	Joint Assault Signal Company
JATO	Jet Assisted Take-off
JCS	Joint Chiefs of Staff
JTFFA	Joint Task Force Full Accounting

K

KIA	Killed In Action
KP	Kitchen Police
KSCB	Khe Sanh Combat Base

L

LAF	Liberation Armed Forces (Official Communist designation for the Viet Cong)
LOA	Light Observation Aircraft
LOC	Library of Congress
LOH	Light Observation Helicopter
LPH	Landing Platform Helicopter
LRRP	Long Range Reconnaissance Patrol(s)
LZ	Landing Zone

M

MAAG-V	Army Military Assistance Advisory Group – Vietnam
MACV	Military Assistance Command, Vietnam
MADS	Mortar Air Delivery System
MANPADS	Man-Portable Air Defense System
MANPRINT	Manpower and Personnel Integration
MARS	Mid-Air Retrieval System
MASH	Mobile Army Surgical Hospital
MATS	Military Air Transport Service
MBT	Main Battle Tank
MC	Military Characteristics
MCLOS	Manual Command to Line of Sight
MD	Material Development
MDS	Model Design Series; Mission-Design Series
MG	Machine Gun(s)
MIA	Missing in Action
MOS	Military Occupation Specialty
MPC	Military Payment Certificate
MSC	Military Sealift Command
MSTS	Military Sea Transportation Sea Service

N

NAKA	North American Kindleberger Atwood Lab (NAKA) 1.5-inch Solid Prop Aircraft Rocket
NASA	National Aeronautics and Space Administration
NATO	North Atlantic Treaty Organization
NCAI	National Congress of the American Indian
NET	New Equipment Training
NETT	New Equipment Training Team

NLF	National Liberation Front
NMAI	National Museum of the American Indian
NOAA	National Oceanic and Atmospheric Administration
NOD	Night Observation Device
NVA	North Vietnamese Army

O

OCAFF	Office of the Chief of Army Field Forces
OCS	Officer Candidate School
OPCON	Operational Control
OPD	Olfactory Personnel Detector
OPSEC	Operational Security
OPTEMPO	Operational Tempo

P

PAVN	People's Army of Vietnam
PCF	Patrol Craft Fast
POE	Ports of Embarkation
POL	Petroleum, Oil and Lubricants
PSYOPS	Psychological Operations
PTSD	Post-Traumatic Stress Disorder
PTO	Pacific Theater of Operations
PZ	Pickup Zone

R

RAF	Royal Air Force
RAID	Reconnaissance and Aerial Interdiction Detachment
R&D	Research and Development
RAN	Royal Australian Navy
R&R	Rest and Recuperation
RCN	Royal Canadian Navy
RCS	Readjustment Counseling Service
RCT	Regimental Combat Team
RIF	Reduction In Force
RFP	Request for Proposal(s)
RN	Royal Navy
ROAD	Reorganized Objective Army Division(s)
ROCID	Reorganization of the Current Infantry Division
ROK	Republic of Korea
ROKA	Republic of Korea Army
ROTC	Reserve Officer Training Corps

RPG	Rocket Propelled Grenade
RPM	Revolutions Per Minute
RR	Radio Research; Recoilless Rifle(s)
RTB	Return(ed) to Base
RVN	Republic of Vietnam

S

SEATO	Southeast Asia Treaty Organization
SEMA	Special Electronic Mission Aircraft
SF	Special Forces
SIP	Standardization Instructor Pilot
SOCOM	Special Operations Command
SOP	Standard Operating Procedure
SOS	Special Operations Squadron
SRS	Strategic Reconnaissance Squadron
SRW	Strategic Reconnaissance Wing
STOL	Short Takeoff and Landing
STRAC	Strategic Army Corps

T

T	Prefix indicating M.S.C. (MSTS) ship
TATSA	Transportation Aircraft Test and Support Activity
TC	Transportation Company/Transportation Corps
TDA	Table of Distribution and Allowances
TDY	Temporary Duty
T for C	Termination for the Convenience of the Government
TK-1/-2	Temporary Kit-1/-2
TNT	Trinitrotoluene
TO&E	Table of Organization and Equipment
TOW	Tube launched, Optically tracked, Wire guided
TTP	Total Package Procurement
TRADOC	Training and Doctrine Command
TRUMP	Tribal Class Update and Modernization Project

U

USAF	United States Air Force
USARPAC	U.S. Army Pacific
USASGV	United States Army Support Group, Vietnam
U. S. C.	United States Code
USCONARC	United States Continental Army Command

USNS	United States Navy Ship
USO	United Services Organization
USPHS	United States Public Health Service
USPTO	United States Patent and Trademark Office
UTTHCO	Utility Tactical Transport Helicopter Company

V

VA	Veterans Administration
VC	Viet Cong or Vietnamese Communist (*Viet Nam Cong-San*)
VHPA	Vietnam Helicopter Pilots Association
VHP	Veterans History Project
VIP	Very Important Person
VNAF	Vietnam Air Force
VPA	Vietnam People's Army
VR	Visual Reconnaissance
VVMF	Vietnam Veterans Memorial Fund
VTOL	Vertical Takeoff and Landing

W

WAC	Women's Army Corps
WAVES	Women Accepted for Volunteer Emergency Service
WIA	Wounded In Action
WO	Warrant Officer
WP	White Phosphorous

OTHER

11B	Infantry soldier MOS

NOTES

Forward

1. Carter Meland and David E. Wilkins, "Stereotypes in sports, chaos in federal policy," *The Star Tribune*, November 22, 2012, http://www.startribune.com/stereotypes-in-sports-chaos-in-federal-policy/180435801/.
2. "Memorandum for the Heads of Executive Departments and Agencies: Tribal Consultation," November 5, 2009, https://obamawhitehouse.archives.gov/sites/default/files/microsites/ostp/2009tribal.mem_.rel_.pdf.

Introduction

1. John Gillespie Magee, Jr. "High Flight," August 18, 1941.
2. Thomas Paone, "Plans for the Little Know Confederate Helicopter," accessed March 6, 2021, https://airandspace.si.edu/stories/editorial/plans-little-known-confederate-helicopter.
3. Ibid.
4. Walter J. Boyne, *How the Helicopter Changed Modern Warfare.* (Gretna: Pelican Publishing Company, Inc., 2011), 311.
5. Dr. James W. Williams, *A History of Army Aviation: From Its Beginnings to the War on Terror.* (Lincoln: iUniversity, Inc.), 30.
6. Additionally, during World War II, Hanna Reitsch became the only female German to obtain a captain's license, the first woman test pilot, and the only woman to receive the Iron Cross First Class, and during the final days of the Third Reich was chosen to fly into Berlin because she could pilot a helicopter. (McCombs and Worth, Op. Cit., 495.)
7. Boyne, Op. Cit., 44.
8. Richard C. Kirkland, *Tales of a Helicopter Pilot.* (Washington, D.C.: Smithsonian Institution Press, 2013), 67.
9. Robert F. Door, "The First Helicopter Rescue: Where the special operations combat rescue mission began," accessed September 17, 2018, https://www.defensemedianetwork.com/stories/first-helicopter-rescue/.
10. "Sikorsky Product History: S-47/R-4 Helicopter," accessed September 25, 2018, http://sikorskyarchives.com/S-47.php.
11. Boyne, Op. Cit., 58.
12. David T. Zabecki, "Valérie André—French MEDEVAC Pilot Flew into Enemy Fire for Rescues," *Vietnam*, (February 2021): 64.
13. Ibid.
14. "Lessons U.S. Learned in the Helicopter War," *U.S. News & World Report*, November 23, 1970, 50.
15. Ibid.
16. Ibid.

17. Otto Kreisher, "The Rise of the Helicopter During the Korean War," accessed September 23, 2018, www.historynet.com/The-rise-of-the-helicopter-during-the-Korean-War.htm.
18. Colonel Robert H. Schulz, "Looking Ahead," *United States Army Aviation Digest*, 5, no. 5 (1959): 9.
19. Charles E. Wilson, "Memorandum: Clarification of Roles and Missions to Improve the Effectiveness of Operation of the Department of Defense," *United States Army Aviation Digest*, 2, no. 12 (1956): 6.
20. Ibid., 7.
21. Ibid., 7.
22. Ibid., 8–9.
23. Schulz, Op. Cit., 10.

Army Helicopters Are Born

1. Shannon A. Brown, *Providing the Means of War: Historical Perspectives on Defense Acquisition.* (Washington, D.C.: Government Printing Office, 2005), 30–31.
2. "The Combat Developments and Research and Development Systems of the Army," *United States Army Aviation Digest*, 6, no. 3 (1960): 4.
3. Ibid., 4-5.
4. Dr. James Williams, Op. Cit., 50–51.
5. A.A. Vandergrift, as told to Robert B. Asprey, *Once A Marine, The Memoirs of General A.A. Vandergrift.* (New York: W.W. Norton & Company, Inc., 1964), 64.
6. General Lemuel C. Shepard, Jr., USMC (Ret.). Oral History. Transcript, Mr. Benis M. Frank, Interviewer. Washington, D.C.: History and Museums Division, Headquarters, U.S. Marine Corps, 1967, 153.
7. Robert Debs Heinl, Jr., *Soldiers of the Sea, The United States Marine Corps, 1775–1962.* (Annapolis, Maryland: U.S. Naval Institute, 1962), 513.
8. Shepard, Op. Cit.
9. James Maurice Gavin. "Cavalry, And I Don't Mean Horses." *Harpers*, New York, April 1954, 60.
10. Ibid.
11. Mark Albertson, "Army Aviation in Vietnam—The Rogers Board," accessed February 24, 2019, http://www.armyaviationmagazine.com/index.php/history/not-so-current-2/713-army-aviation-in-vietnam-the-rogers-board.
12. Ibid.
13. Dr. Herbert LePore, "The Role of the Helicopter in the Vietnam War," *United States Army Aviation Digest*, 1–94–4, (July/August 1994): 33.
14. Richard P. Weinert, Jr. *TRADOC Historical Monograph Series: A History of Army Aviation —1950–1952.* (Fort Monroe: U.S. Army Training and Doctrine Command, 1991), 115–116.
15. Ibid.
16. Ibid.
17. Lieutenant General John T. Tolson, *Vietnam Studies: Air Mobility 1961–1971.* (Washington, D.C.: Center for Military History Publication, 1999), 10.
18. Ibid.
19. Sergio Miller, *In Good Faith, A History of the Vietnam War Volume 1: 1945–65.* (Oxford, United Kingdom: Osprey Publishing, 2020), 155.
20. "Vietnam: A Television History," accessed August 1, 2021, https://openvault.wgbh,org/catalog/V ECAFFE3A8A60F4F28A8145B69087BD498.
21. Miller, *In Good Faith*, 161.
22. Tolson, Op. Cit., 18–19.
23. LePore, Op. Cit., 35.

24. Dr. Jacob A. Stocfisch, "The 1962 Howze Board and Army Combat Developments," RAND Arroyo Center, 1994, x.

25. Lieutenant General Hamilton H. Howze, "U.S. Army Tactical Mobility Requirements Review Board, Final Report,—Brief by the President of the Board," Fort Bragg, North Carolina, 20 August 1962, 8.

26. Ibid.

27. Major Kevin J. Dougherty, "The Evolution of Air Assault," *Joint Forces Quarterly*, (Summer 1999): 55.

28. Stocfisch, Op. Cit.

29. Ibid.

30. Virgil Ney, *Evolution of the U.S. Army Division 1939–1968*. (Fort Belvoir, Virginia: Technical Operations, Inc., January 1969), 57–93.

Identifying Army Helicopters

1. "USAAC/USAAF/USAF Aircraft Designation Systems," accessed March 15, 2020, https://www.historyofwar.org/articles/weapons_USAAF_aircraft_designations.html#3.

2. Major General Hamilton H. Howze, "The Last Three Years of Army Aviation," *United States Army Aviation Digest*, 4, no. 3 (1958): 21.

3. "Aircraft Mission-Design Series," accessed March 3, 2019, http://www.globalsecurity.org/military/systems/aircraaft/mds.htm.

4. Dr. James Williams, unpublished *Memorandum on Naming Helicopters*, August 24, 2000.

5. Crispin Burke, "Everyone Relax—The Army's Native American Helicopter Names Are Not Racist," *War is Boring*, accessed October 13, 2018, https://medium.com/war-is-boring/everyone-relax-the-armys-native-american-helicopter-names-are-not-racist-d21beb55d782.

6. Department of the Army, Army Regulation 70-28, "Assigning Popular Names to Major Items of Equipment," 4 April 1969, 1.

7. Ibid.

8. "Naming the Helicopter," accessed August 15, 2019, http://www.chinook-helicopter.com/origins/origins.html.

9. Department of the Army, Army Regulation 70-28, "Assigning Popular Names to Major Items of Equipment," 18 June 1976, 2.

10. Army Regulation 70-28, "Assigning Popular Names to Major Items of Equipment," 4 April 1969, 2.

11. Lieutenant Colonel Willard J. Hodges, Jr., Letter to Daphne Leeds, September 22, 1958.

12. Ibid.

13. SGD Daphne Leeds, Letter to Lieutenant Colonel Willard J. Hodges, Jr., September 24, 1958.

14. Major General Ronald K. Andreson, USA, Retired, email message to author, September 29, 2020.

15. A Live trademark has sufficient standing within the marketplace to block an application for the registration of a similar mark.

16. Department of Defense Directive 4120.15, "Designating and Naming Military Aerospace Vehicles," (Washington D.C.: Washington Headquarters Service, 1985), (as amended), 2.

17. Barbara Cummings, "Lakota Leaders Join Army to Welcome New Helicopter Fleet," *Army News Service*, February 20, 2008.

18. Ibid.

19. Ibid.

20. Cécile Ganteaume, *Officially Indian: Symbols That Define the United States*. (Washington, D.C.: National Museum of the American Indian, 2017), 136–137.

The Native American War Experience

1. Tom Holm, *Strong Hearts, Wounded Soldiers: Native American Veterans of the Vietnam War.* (Austin, Texas: University of Texas Press, 1996), 192.
2. Francis Flavin, Ph.D., "Native Americans and American History," accessed December 27, 2018, https://www.coursehero.com/file/22133704/native-americans/.
3. Martin J. Dougherty, *Native American Warriors: The Legendary Tribes, Their Weapons, and Fighting Techniques.* (London: Amber Books, Ltd., 2018), 213.
4. Russell F. Wigley, *History of the United States Army.* (New York: The MacMillan Company, 1967), 22.
5. Dougherty, Ibid. p. 52.
6. Ibid.
7. Herman J. Viola, *Warriors in Uniform: The Legacy of American Indian Heroism.* (Washington, D.C.: National Geographic Society, 2008), 19.
8. John C. Miller, *Origins of the American Revolution.* (Boston: Little, Brown and Company, 1959), 350.
9. Mark Hirsch, "The Promise and Peril of Alliance: From Contact to 1814," *Why We Serve: Native Americans in the United States Armed Forces,* eds. Harris, Alexandra N., Hirsch, Mark G. (Washington, D.C.: Smithsonian Institution National Museum of the American Indian, 2020), 41.
10. Harris, Op. Cit., p. 47.
11. Joseph J. Ellis, *American Creation: Triumphs and Tragedies at the Founding of the Republic.* (New York, Alfred A. Knopf, 2007), 128.
12. As President, Jefferson would guard the gradual removal of Indians that subsequent President Andrew Jackson would culminate with the Indian Removal Act of 1830.
13. "Letter from Henry Knox to George Washington, June 15th, 1789," *The Papers of George Washington Digital Edition. (*Charlottesville: University of Virginia Press, Rotunda, 2008*), 491.
14. Ellis, Op. Cit., 139.
15. Ibid.
16. The Creek Nation extended from western Georgia to northern Florida and across Alabama to eastern Mississippi.
17. Ellis, Op. Cit., 157.
18. Ibid., 156.
19. Ibid., 160.
20. Ibid., 129.
21. Donald Fixico, "A Native Nations Perspective on the War of 1812," accessed December 20, 2018, http://www.pbs.org/wned/war-of-1812/essays/native-nations-perspective/.
22. Ibid.
23. Jon Meachan, *American Lion: Andrew Jackson in the White House.* (New York: Random House, 2008), 145.
24. Martin J. Dougherty, *Native American Warriors: The Legendary Tribes, Their Weapons, and Fighting Techniques.* (London: Amber Books, Ltd., 2018), 112.
25. Ibid.
26. "The Library of Congress: A Century of Law Making for a New Nation," U. S. Congressional Documents and Debates, 1774–1875, Statutes-at-Large, 21st Congress, 1st Session, Chapter CXLVIII, 411–412.
27. "Permanent Indian Frontier," accessed September 16, 2019, https://www.nps.gov/fosc/learn/historyculture/pif.htm.
28. Robert Wooster, *The United States Army and the Making of America From Confederation to Empire, 1775–1903.* (Lawrence, Kansas: University Press of Kansas, 2021), 96.

29.

Tribe	Population East of the Mississippi	Removal Treaty	Years of Major Emigration	# Removed (%)
Choctaw	19,554	Dancing Rabbit Creek - 1831	1831–1836	12,500 (64%)
Creek	22,700	Cusseta - 1830	1834–1837	19,600 (86%)
Chickasaw	4,914	Pontotoc Creek - 1832	1837–1847	>4,000 (82%)
Cherokee	21,500	New Echota - 1835	1836–1838	20,000 (93%)
Seminole	5,000	Payne's Landing - 1832	1832–1842	2,833 (57%)

30. Wooster, Op. Cit., 156.
31. Gary Robinson and Phil Lucas, *From Warriors to Soldiers*. (Bloomington: iUniverse, Inc., 2009), 30–31.
32. Viola, Op. Cit., 32.
33. Ibid.
34. Ibid.
35. Ibid., 33.
36. Wooster, Op. Cit., 203–204.
37. A Corps of Competent Authors and Artists, *Wildlife on the Plains and the Horrors of Indian Warfare*. (New York: Arno Press, 1969), 43.
38. William H. Powell, "Soldier or Granger?" *United Service, a Monthly Review of Military and Naval Affairs 2*, (November 1889), 446–447.
39. Ibid., 448.
40. William H. Powell, "The Indian as a Soldier" *United Service, a Monthly Review of Military and Naval Affairs 3*, (November 1889), 446–447.
41. David McGormick, "A Novel Proposition: Indian Regulars in the U.S. Army in the 1890s," *Army History*, No. 114 (2020): 9, 10.2307/26863612P. 9.
42. The 1890–1891 "messiah craze" was the culmination of the Ghost Dance revivalist movement among nineteenth-century Native Americans. The latter was a ritual round-dance thought to imitate the dances of the dead to cause the renewal of the world and the return of the dead. Chief Sitting Bull, an apostle of the movement, and his people were ardent followers of the new faith and when the ardor alarmed white government agents, the government decided to arrest the chief to bring order to the reservation. During his attempted arrest on December 15, 1891, the chief was killed. The chief's followers fled to the Cheyenne River reservation to join the Miniconjou Sioux. The pursuing military massacred approximately 250 Sioux warriors and their unarmed women and children at Wounded Knee, South Dakota. The tragedy is identified as the event that ended the Indian Wars in the west.
43. McGormick, Op. Cit., 10–12.
44. Ibid.
45. The actual enlistments numbered only 780.
46. Jon Ault, *Native Americans in the Spanish American War*, accessed February 12, 2021, https://www.spanamwar.com/NativeAmericans.htm.
47. "Why We Serve: Native Americans in the United States Armed Forces—Spanish American War," accessed February 12, 2021, https://americanindian.si.edu/why-we-serve/topics/spanish-american-war/.
48. Ibid.
49. Ibid.
50. Ibid.
51. "Native Americans in the Military—World War I," accessed October 26, 2022, https://www.fcpotawatomi.com/news/native-americans-in-the-military-world-war-i/.

52. Diane Camurat, "The American Indian in the Great War: Real and Imagined, Part Two, Chapter One: The Place of the American Indians in the Military in 1917," accessed March 30, 2020, https://net.lib.byu.edu/~rdh7/wwi/comment/Cmrts/Cmrt5.html.

53. Matthew L.M. Fletcher, "A Short History of Indian Law in the Supreme Court," accessed April 6, 2020, https://www.americanbar.org/groups/crsj/publications/human_rights_magazine_home/2014_vol_40/vol--40--no--1--tribal-sovereignty/short_history_of_indian_law/.

54. "Did you Know? Oneidas Declared War on Germany in 1918," accessed April 6, 2020), https://www.oneidaindiannation.com/did-you-know-oneidas-declared-war-on-germany-in-1918/.

55. Paul C. Rosier, *Serving Their Country: American Indian Politics and Patriotism in the Twentieth Century.* (Cambridge, MA, Harvard University Press, 2009), 45.

56. Charla Bear, "American Indian Boarding Schools Haunt Many," accessed April 24, 2020, https://www.npr.org/templates/story/story.php?storyId=16516865.

57. Rosier, Op. Cit., 47.

58. Jennings C. Wise, *The Red Man in the New World Drama: A Politico-Legal Study with a Pageantry of American History.* Revised and Edited by Vine Deloria, Jr. (New York: MacMillan Publishing Company, Inc., 1974), 320.

59. "Native Voices: 1917 American Indians Volunteer for World War I," accessed December 3, 2018, https://www.nlm.nih.gov.

60. Diane Camurat, "The American Indian in the Great War: Real and Imagined, Part Two, Chapter Two: American Indian Service in WW I," accessed March 30, 2020, https://net.lib.byu.edu/~rdh7/wwi/comment/Cmrts/Cmrt6.html.

61. Ibid.

62. R. David Edmunds, Frederick E. Hoxie, and Neal Salisbury, *The People: A History of Native America.* (Boston: Houghton Mifflin, 2006), 365.

63. Dr. Daniel M. Cobb, *Native Peoples of America.* (Chantilly, Virginia: The Great Courses, 2016), 371.

64. Ibid.

65. Ibid. 372.

66. Naval History and Heritage Command, "20th Century Warriors: Native American Participation in the United States Military," accessed December 27, 2018, https://www.history.navy.mil/research/library/online-reading-room/title-list-alphabetically/t/american-indians-us-military.html.

67. "36th Infantry Division in World War I: Chapter IV – From Texas to the Marne," accessed December 5, 2018, http://www.texasmilitaryforcesmuseum.org/36division/archives/wwi/white/chap4c.htm.

68. Louis Coleman, "Thirty-Sixth Infantry Division," accessed March 15, 2020, https://www.okhistory.org/publications/enc/entry.php?entry=TH003.

69. Ibid.

70. Viola, Op. Cit. 73.

71. Code Talkers Recognition Act of 2008, Public Law 110–420, October 15, 2008.

72. "How Native Americans Code Talkers Pioneered A New Type of Military Intelligence," accessed October 26, 2022, https://www.history.com/news/world-war-is-native-american-code-talkers.

73. Ibid.

74. "How Are Sikorsky Helicopters Named?" *Sikorsky Archives News*, July 2016, 2.

75. Konnie LeMay. "A Brief History of American Indian Military Service," accessed December 5, 2018, https://newsmaven.io/indiancountrytoday/archive/a-brief-history-of-american-indian-military-service-X7hYOzquEUin095S8QpVjw/.

76. Olivia B. Waxman, "We Became Warriors Again: Why World War I Was a Surprisingly Pivotal Moment for American Indian History," accessed March 29, 2020, https://time.com/5459439/american-indians-wwi/.

77. Blake Stilwell, "Why Native American nations declared war on Germany twice," accessed April 6, 2020, https://www.wearethemighty.com/history/native-americans-twice-war-germany?rebelltitem=1#rebelltitem1.

78. Waxman, Op. Cit.
79. Ian W. Toll, *Twilight of the Gods: War in the Western Pacific, 1944–1945.* (New York: W.W. Norton & Company, 2020), 14.
80. Douglas MacArthur, *Reminiscences.* (New York: McGraw-Hill Book Company, 1964), 256.
81. The parenthetical numbers indicate the number of total awards of that decoration that the general received.
82. Dana Hedgpeth, "Recognition sought at Indian museum's veteran memorial," *The Washington Post,* Sunday, April 25, 2021, A-5.
83. Ibid.
84. The Statutes At Large of the United States of America From April 1917 to March 1919, Volume XL, Sixty-Fifth Congress, Session I, H.R. 3545, May 18, 1917, Chapter 15, Section 5.
85. Twenty-five years after an allotment of land was issued to an Indian allottee, he would be given complete, fee simple ownership of the land at which time the landowner could sell or lease it to anyone.
86. Camurat, "The Place of the American Indians in the Military in 1917," Op. Cit.
87. Vine Deloria, Jr. and Clifford M. Lytle, *American Indians. American Justice.* (Austin: University of Texas Press, 1983), 218–219.
88. Diane Camurat, "The American Indian in the Great War: Real and Imagined, Part Two, Chapter Three: American Indian Symbols in WW I," accessed March 30, 2020, https://net.lib.byu.edu/~rdh7/wwi/comment/Cmrts/Cmrt7.html.
89. Ibid.
90. Ibid.
91. Ibid.
92. J. Keith Salida, "Target Plei Mei – Hanoi's 1965 Bid to Conquer Vietnam's Western Highlands," *On Point: The Journal of Army History,* Fall 2021, Volume 17, No. 1, 36–38.
93. "Secretary of Defense. Robert McNamara, Memorandum for the President, 'Vietnam Situation,' 21 December1963," accessed September 15, 2021, https://www.mtholyoke.edu/acad/intrel/pentagon3/doc156.htm.
94. Thomas S. Helling, *The Agony of Heroes: Medical Care for America's Besieged Legions from Bataan to Khe Sanh.* (Yardley: Westholme Publishing, LLC, 2019), 343.
95. From comments made to the media by Brigadier General Richard Neal, USMC, on February 19th, 1991, in Riyadh, Saudi Arabia.
96. Kris Osborn and Ho Lin, "The Operation That Took Out Osama Bin Laden," accessed August 15, 2019, https://www.military.com/history/osama-bin-laden-operation-neptune-spear.
97. *ABC World News Tonight with David Muir,* February 10, 2022.
98. Viola, Op. Cit., 67.
99. Ibid.
100. Edwards, Op. Cit., 375.
101. "Statistics of the Vietnam War," accessed November 5, 2020, https://vhfn.org/stat.html.
102. Val Niehaus, "Native Americans in the Military—World War II (1939–45)," *Potawatomi Traveling Times,* Volume 20, Issue 16, February 15, 2015, 1.
103. Edwards, Op. Cit., 406.
104. Ibid.
105. Viola, Op. Cit., 88.
106. Ibid.
107. "Counting Coup," accessed December 15, 2018, http://plainshumanities.unl.edu/encyclopedia/doc/egp.war.013.
108. "Counting Coup on the Plains and Overseas," accessed December 15, 2018), https://centerofthewest.org/2016/07/21/counting-coup-on-the-plains-and-overseas/.
109. Joseph Medicine Crow's wartime story can be seen in a PBS video found at: http://www.pbs.org/video/2365709365/.
110. Morgan, Op. Cit., 2.

111. Paul C. Rosier, *Serving Their Country: American Indian Politics and Patriotism in the Twentieth Century*. (Cambridge, MA: Harvard University Press, 2009), 76.
112. Ibid., 78.
113. Ibid., 86.
114. Ibid.
115. Ibid.
116. Ibid., 78.
117. "Study Notes," Op. Cit.
118. "The Navajo Code Talkers," accessed December 20, 2021, available from https://p47millville. org/?s=navajo+code+talkers.
119. Ibid.
120. Carolyn A. Tyson, *A Chronology of the United States Marine Corps 1935–1946, Volume II*. (Washington, D.C.: History and Museums Division, Headquarters, U.S. Marine Corps, 1965), 54.
121. Keith Warren Lloyd, *Avenging Pearl Harbor: The Saga of America's Battleships in the Pacific War*. (Guilford: Lyons Press, 2021), 193–94.
122. Morgan, Op. Cit., 25.
123. Niehaus, Op. Cit., 3.
124. Konnie LeMay, "A Brief History of American Indian Military Service," accessed December 5, 2018, https://newsmaven.io/indiancountrytoday/archive/a-brief-history-of-american-indian-military-service-X7hYOzquEUin095S8QpVjw/.
125. Morgan, Op. Cit. 23.
126. Tom Holm, "Forgotten Warriors: American Indian Servicemen in Vietnam," *Vietnam Generation*, Volume 1: Number 2, Article 6, 56, https://digitalcommons.lasalle.edu/cgi/viewcontent. cgi?article=1016&context=vietnamgeneration.
127. Viola, Op. Cit., 144.
128. Morgan, Op. Cit.
129. Holm, Op. Cit., 58.
130. Ibid. 57–58.
131. Ibid. 58.
132. For a population of 42,000, a random survey of at least 381 respondents would be required for a 95% confidence level, a 5% margin of error, and a statistically significant result.
133. Holm, Op. Cit., 58.
134. Robinson and Lucas, Op. Cit., 7.
135. Don McCombs and Fred L. Worth, *World War II: 4,139 Strange and Fascinating Facts*. (Avenal, New Jersey: Wings Books, 1994), 162.
136. The timing and chosen battle cry strongly suggest that the movie was the popular Paramount western, Geronimo, about the Apache chief.
137. "Geronimo – Why American Paratroopers Shout the Apache Chief's Name When Jumping," https://militaryhistorynow.com/2020/09/21/geronimo-why-american-paratroopers-shout-the-apache-chiefs-name-when-jumping/.
138. "No. 121 Squadron RAF," accessed February 22, 2021, https://www.americanairmuseum.com/unit/884.
139. Thomas S. Helling, *The Agony of Heroes: Medical Care for America's Besieged Legions from Bataan to Khe Sanh*. (Yardley: Westholme, 2019), 224–225.
140. Ibid.
141. Ibid., 225.
142. John Wukovits, *Dogfight over Tokyo: The Final Air Battle of the Pacific and the Last Four Men to Die in World War II*. (New York: Da Capo Press, 2019), 92–93.
143. Ibid. 109–110.
144. 0690305021 Richard (Dick) Detra Collection, The Vietnam Center and Sam Johnson Vietnam Archives, Texas Tech University.

145. Naval History and Heritage Command, "20th Century Warriors: Native American Participation in the United States Military," Op. Cit.

146. Viola, Op. Cit., 155.

147. "Indigenous," "Indian," and "Native" are used interchangeably throughout this book. As a people, Indigenous individuals and peoples in North America do not consider the term "Indian" as a slur or affront. They also prefer that their nation's names when used be in their own language. Some of their names have been correctly used along with the more familiar usage, e.g., Sioux, Shawnee, etc.

OH-13 *Sioux*

1. Dr. Williams, Op. Cit., 55.

2. "Bell Helicopter OH-13D Sioux," accessed March 20, 2019, https://cavflight.org/index.php?option=com_content&view=article&id=13&Itemid=130.

3. "Establishing Our Own," accessed July 21, 2019, http://www.armyaviationmuseum.org/part-ii-establishing-our-own/.

4. "Bell H-13 Sioux," accessed March 21, 2019, http://yellowlegs-and-others.com/Aircraft/Aircraft_Details/Bell_H-13_Sioux_(HTL-3).html.

5. Eugene G. Piasceki, "Second Helicopter Detachment At Chang-to," accessed October 27, 2022, https://arsof-history.org/articles/v6n1_ghq_raiders_sb_helicopter.html.

6. Lieutenant Colonel Ronald Brown, *Whirlybirds: U.S. Marine Helicopters in Korea*. (Washington, D.C.: U.S. Marine Historical Center, 2003), 8, 11.

7. Ibid., 33.

8. Mark Albertson, "The Korean War—The Helicopter," accessed October 27, 2022, https://www.armyaviationmagazine.com/index.php/history/not-so-current-2/1884-the-korean-war-the-helicopter.

9. Otto Kreisher, "The Rise of the Helicopter During the Korean War," accessed August 25, 2018, https://www.historynet.com/the-rise-of-the-helicopter-during-the-korean-war.html.

10. Lieutenant Colonel Charles O. Griminger, "The Armed Helicopter Story Part I: The Origins," *United States Army Aviation Digest*, Volume 17, Number 7, July 1971, 15.

11. Walter J. Boyne, *How the Helicopter Changed Modern Warfare*. (Gretna: Pelican Publishing Company, Inc., 2011), 113.

12. Ibid.

13. Colonel Jay D. Vanderpool, "We Armed the Helicopter," *United States Army Aviation Digest*, Volume 17, Number 6, June 1971, 24.

14. Ibid., 6.

15. Lieutenant Colonel Charles O. Grimmer, "The Armed Helicopter Story Part IV: Weapons Systems (Early Experimentation)," *United States Army Aviation Digest*, Volume 17, Number 10, October 1971, 19.

16. Lieutenant Colonel Charles O. Griminger, "The Armed Helicopter Story Part III: Armed Helicopters Around the World," *United States Army Aviation Digest*, Volume 17, Number 9, September 1971, 11.

17. Ibid., 12–13.

18. James A. Warren, *Year of the Hawk: America's Descent into Vietnam, 1965*. (New York: Scribner, 2021), 222.

19. Donald Porter, "In Vietnam, These Helicopter Scouts Saw Combat Up Close: Cobras and Loaches," *Smithsonian Air & Space Magazine*, September 2017, accessed March 21, 2019, https://www.airspacemag.com/military-aviation/snakes-loaches-180964341/.

20. Ibid.

21. Ostler, Op. Cit., 24.

22. Wooster, Op. Cit., 165.
23. Ibid., 165–166.
24. McClellan, Op. Cit.
25. Robert M. Utley, *Frontier Regulars: The United States Army and the Indian: 1866–1891*. (New York: Macmillan Publishing Co., Inc., 1984), 3.
26. Utley, Op Cit., 56.
27. Ibid.
28. Ibid., 99.
29. Ibid., 107.
30. Ibid., 108.
31. Ibid.
32. Ibid., 107–110.
33. Ibid., 115.
34. Ibid., 118.
35. Ibid., 140.
36. Ibid., 169.
37. Ibid., 148.
38. Ibid., 197.
39. Ibid., 243–246.
40. Ibid., 246.
41. Ibid., 248–249.
42. Ibid., 250–251.
43. Ibid., 251.
44. United States v. Sioux Nation of Indians, 448 U.S. 371, 376 (1980) ("US v Sioux Nation").
45. Utley, Op. Cit., 254.
46. Ibid., 261.
47. Ibid., 266–267.
48. Ibid., 275.
49. Ibid., 272–283.
50. Dougherty, Op. Cit., 152.
51. Utley, Op. Cit., 299,
52. Wooster, Op. Cit., 263.
53. Ibid.
54. Utley, Op. Cit., 412.
55. Ibid., 416.
56. Ibid., 416–418.
57. Ibid., 420.

CH-19 *Chickasaw*

1. Bryan R. Swopes, "This day in Aviation—Sikorsky CH-19 Chickasaw Archives," accessed October 31, 2018, https://www.thisdayinaviation.com/tag/sikorsky-ch-19-chickasaw/.
2. Dr. Kaylene Hughes, "Army Helicopters in Korea, 1950 to '53," accessed January 23, 2019, https://www.army.mil/article/177302/army_helicopters_in_korea_1950_to_53.
3. Kreisher, Op. Cit.
4. Griminger, "Armed Helicopters Around the World," Op. Cit., 21–22.
5. Lee Jacobson and John Daniel, "S-55 Firsts," *Sikorsky Archives News*, The Igor I. Sikorsky Historical Archives Inc., July 20, 2006, 3.
6. Ron Bachman, "H-19," email to author, 2022.
7. Carter, Op. Cit., 52–53
8. Ibid., 53.

9. "Sikorsky UH-19D, Chickasaw," accessed January 22, 2019, http://www.ewarbirds.org/aircraft/uh19d.shtml.

10. Vanderpool, Op. Cit., 24.

11. Grimminger, "Part Two," Op. Cit., 17–18.

12. Ibid., 22.

13. Anton Treuer, et al., *Indian Nations of North America.* (Washington, D.C.: National Geographic, 2010), 155.

14. Ibid.

15. "Chickasaw Removal," accessed on January 25, 2019, https://www.chickasaw.net/our-nation/history.aspx.

16. Greg O'Brien, "Chickasaws: The Unconquerable People," accessed January 25, 2019, http://mshistorynow.mdah.state.ms.us/articles/8/chickasaws-the-unconquerable-people.

17. Ibid.

18. "Chickasaw Tribe," accessed August 21, 2019, https://historyofmassachusetts.org/native-american-revolutionary-war/.

19. Treuer, et al., Op. Cit., 155–156.

20. Angie Debo, *A History of the Indians of the United States.* (Norman: University of Oklahoma Press, 1970), 125.

21. Ibid.

22. Ibid., 170.

23. Ibid.

24. O'Brien, Op. Cit.

25. Debo, Op. Cit., 171–172.

26. Ibid., 182.

27. Ibid., 179.

28. Ibid.

29. Ibid., 180.

30. Richard Green, "James Adair and the Chickasaws: Part II The Way of the Warriors," accessed January 27, 2019, https://www.Chickasaw.net/Our-Nation/History/Historical-Articles/Culture/James-Adair-and-the-Chickasaws,-Part-II-The-Way-of-the-Warriors.aspx.

31. Ibid.

32. Treuer, et. al, Op. Cit., 156.

CH-21 *Shawnee*

1. Robert J. Brandt and William J. Davies, *The Piasecki H-21 Helicopter: An Illustrated History of the H-21 Helicopter and Its Designer, Frank N. Piasecki.* (Bloomington: Trafford Publishing Company, 2007), 10–14.

2. Scott Schwartz, "Helicopter Workhorse: The Piasecki H-21," accessed October 30, 2019, http://www.aviation-history.com/piasecki/h21.htm.

3. Ibid.

4. Thomas R. Messick, "The Flying Banana in Vietnam," accessed October 24, 2018, http://www.historynet.com/flying-banana-vietnam.htm.

5. Colonel Emmett F. Knight, *First in Vietnam: An Exercise in Excess of 30 Days The U.S. Army 57th Transportation Helicopter Company (Light Helicopter) (CH-21) 1961–1962.* (Williamsburg: A15 Publishing Company, LLC, 2020), 25.

6. Lieutenant Colonel G.H. Shea, "From Horses to Helicopters," *United States Aviation Digest,* Volume 1, Number 4, May 1955, 13.

7. Ibid., 44–57.

8. Griminger, "The Armed Helicopter Story-Part II: "Vanderpool's Fools," Op. Cit., 17–18.

9. Vanderpool, Op. Cit., 25–26.

10. Griminger, "The Armed Helicopter Story-Part II," Op. Cit., 17.
11. Ibid., 26.
12. Griminger, "The Armed Helicopter Story-Part III: Armed Helicopters Around the World," Op. Cit., 11.
13. "Piasecki H-21 Helicopter," accessed October 22, 2018, https://en.wikipedia.org/wiki/Piasecki_H-21#Specifications_(CH-21C).
14. "Battalion History: 71st Transportation Battalion," accessed September 28, 2019, https://transportation.army.mil/history/documents/71st%20Trans%20Bn.pdf, 11–12.
15. Ibid., 13.
16. Charles Lam Markman and Mark Sherwin, *John F. Kennedy: A Sense of Purpose*. (New York: St. Martin's Press, 1961), 179.
17. Ibid., 220–221.
18. Ibid., 226.
19. Hastings, Op. Cit., 130–131.
20. Hastings, 131.
21. "Battalion History: 93rd Transportation Company," accessed October 24, 2018, http://www.145thcab.com/History/NL13HIST.htm.
22. Shea, Op. Cit., 35.
23. Major B. D. Harber, *Logistical Support of Airmobile Operations, Republic of Vietnam (1961–1971)*. (St. Louis: U.S. Army Aviation Command, 1971), 4.
24. Major General Robert J. Brandt, *Thunderbird Lounge*. (Victoria: Trafford Publishing, 2004), 19.
25. Also known as "baby flattops" or if built by Henry Kaiser's Washington Shipyard (hull number 57 through 104) as "Kaiser Coffins." Ian W. Toll, *Twilight of the Gods: War in the Western Pacific, 1944–1945*. (New York: W.W. Norton Company, 2020), 261.
26. USNS or United States Navy Ship is a designation for a Navy ship with a civilian merchant seamen crew in the employ of the Department of the Navy.
27. During World War II, the USS *Core* (CVE-13) was used for carrier qualification exercises for new Naval Aviators such as Air Group 88 in early 1943. Wukovits, Op. Cit., 39–40, 50.
28. "Battalion History: 57th Transportation Company," accessed October 26, 2018, http://www.145thcab.com/History/NL14HIST.htm.
29. Headquarters Fort Lewis, Fort Lewis, Washington, Movement Order #3, November 8, 1961.
30. Knight, Op. Cit., 77.
31. "The 57th Transportation Company (Light Helicopter), The 98th Transportation Detachment (CHFM), and the CH-21C Shawnee 1987 Reunion Scrapbook," Fort Rucker, Alabama: Boeing Vertol Company, 26.
32. Ibid., 2, 6.
33. Brandt and Davies, Op. Cit., 69–70, 83.
34. Lieutenant General John J. Tolson, *Vietnam Studies: Airmobility 1961–1971*. (Washington, D.C.: Department of the Army, 1973), 3.
35. Raymond K. Bluhm, Jr., ed., *U.S. Army: A Complete History*. (Arlington: The Army Historical Foundation, 2004), 601.
36. The *Card* (CVE-11), *Core* (CVE-13), and *Croatan* (CVE-25) were three Bogue-class escort carriers that operated in the Atlantic against U-boats. Alan C. Cary, *Sighted Sub. Sank Same. The Navy's Air Campaign against the U-boat*. (Havertown: Casemate Publishers, 2019), 136–138.
37. Captain Charles A. Bartholomew and Commander William I. Milwee, Jr., *Mud, Muscle, and Miracles: Marine Salvage in the United States Navy*. (Washington, D.C.: Naval History & Heritage Command, 2009), 247.
38. Jon Hoppe, "The Attack on the USNS Card," accessed April 21, 2020, https://www.navalhistory.org/2015/10/07/the-attack-on-the-usns-card.
39. "The Attack on the USNS Card (T-AKV-40)," accessed April 23, 2020, https://www.navalhistory.org/2015/10/07/the-attack-on-the-usns-card.

40. Ibid.
41. "U.S. Ship is Sunk by Vietnam Reds; Crewmen Escape; The *Card*, Copter Transport, Blasted at Saigon Dock—Settles to Bottom; Old Aircraft Aboard; 'Baby Flattop' Was About to Sail," *New York Times* Archives, May 2, 1964, 1.
42. Hoppe, Op. Cit.
43. Ibid.
44. Bartholomew and Milwee, Op. Cit., 248.
45. *New York Times* Archives, Op. Cit.
46. "Viet Cong Commandos Sank an American Aircraft Carrier," accessed April 23, 2020, https://cherrieswriter.com/2017/08/15/viet-cong-commandos-sank-an-american-aircraft-carrier/.
47. Bartholomew and Milwee, Op. Cit., 250.
48. "Viet Cong Commandos Sank …," Op. Cit.
49. *New York Times Archives*, Op. Cit.
50. "The Attack on the USNS Card," Op. Cit.
51. "Viet Cong Commandos Sank …," Op. Cit.
52. Hoppe, Op. Cit.
53. Don Vaughan, "Helicopters' Debut in Vietnam," *Military Officer*, January 2022, 35.
54. Tolson, Op. Cit.
55. Thomas R. Messick, "The Day We Lost Charlie: Questions Remain for a Mission Flight Leader Following the Death of a Helicopter Pilot," *Vietnam*, 33, no. 3 (2020): 40.
56. Ibid., 71–74, 95.
57. "1987 Reunion Scrapbook," Op. Cit., 27.
58. Brandt, Op. Cit., 195.
59. Ibid., 261.
60. Ibid., 127.
61. Ibid., 93.
62. Ibid., 119.
63. Ibid., 74.
64. Tolson, Op. Cit., 25.
65. "First U.S. helicopter is shot down in Vietnam," accessed August 18, 2019, https://www.history.com/this-day-in-history/first-u-s-helicopter-is-shot-down-in-vietnam.
66. "Helicopter or incident 56-02084," accessed August 25, 2019), https://www.vhpa.org/KIA/incident/04907ACD.HTM.
67. William "Billy" James, (1LT, 33rd Transportation Company), interview with the author, June 15, 2020.
68. Ibid., 605.
69. Tolson, Op. Cit., 73.
70. Brandt, Op. Cit., 13.
71. Ibid., 19.
72. Ibid., 79, 95.
73. "33rd Transportation Company (Light Helicopter) (H21)," accessed October 24, 2018, http://www.118ahc.org/33rdtransco.htm.
74. Brandt and Davies, Op. Cit., 79.
75. LTC Bertram G. Leach, "Viet Nam 1962–63: 93rd Transport (Light Cargo Helicopter)," accessed May 30, 2019, https://www.vietnam.ttu.edu/reports/images.php?img=/images/1984/19840102001.pdf, 1.
76. Ibid., 2.
77. Brandt, Op. Cit., 95.
78. Ibid., 108.
79. "1987 Reunion Scrapbook," Op. Cit., 29.
80. Messick, Op. Cit.

81. Brandt, Op. Cit., 156–157.
82. Ibid., 157.
83. David M. Toczek, *The Battle of Ap Bac: They Did Everything But Learn From It.* (Westport: Naval Institute Press, 2001), 71.
84. Truong V. Truong, *Vietnam War: The New Legion.* (Victoria: Trafford Publishing, 2010), 419.
85. Toczek, Op. Cit., 72.
86. Neil Sheehan, *A Bright Shining Lie: John Paul Vann and American in Vietnam.* (New York: Vintage Books, 1988), 204–5, 211.
87. Toczek, Op. Cit., 72.
88. Sheehan, Op. Cit., 212.
89. Truong, Op. Cit., 351.
90. Mark Moyar, *Triumph Forsaken: The Vietnam War 1954–1965.* (New York: Cambridge University Press, 2006), 187.
91. David W. P. Elliot, *The Vietnamese War: Revolution and Social Change in the Mekong Delta 1930–1975.* (New York: M.E. Sharp, 2007), 182–183.
92. Hastings, Op. Cit., 160.
93. Moyar, Op. Cit., 188.
94. Truong, Op. Cit., 361.
95. Ibid.
96. Ibid., 368.
97. "Battalion History: 93rd Transportation Company, Op. Cit.
98. Don A. Starry, *Armored Combat in Vietnam.* (North Stratford: Avro Press, 1980), 27.
99. Elliott, Op. Cit., 183.
100. Truong, Op. Cit., 407.
101. Ibid., 412.
102. Ibid., 416.
103. Max Hastings, *Vietnam: An Epic Tragedy, 1945–1975.* (New York: HarperCollins Publishers, 2018), 162.
104. Truong, Op. Cit., 420.
105. Hastings, Op. Cit., 162–163.
106. U.S. Department of State, Office of the Historian, "Foreign Relations of the United States, 1961–1963, Volume III, Vietnam, January-August 1963," accessed June 27, 2020, https://history.state.gov/histocricaldocuments/fus/1961-63v03/d1.
107. Hastings, Op. Cit.
108. Ibid.
109. Office of the Historian, Op. Cit.
110. Ibid. Reports were from *The Washington Post* on January 3, 1963, and *The New York Times* on January 4, 1963.
111. COSVN was the North Vietnamese political and military headquarters which controlled the People's Revolutionary Party, the National Liberation Front, and the Viet Cong in southern South Vietnam.
112. Hastings, Op. Cit., 166.
113. Battalion History: 93rd Transportation Company, Op. Cit.
114. Ibid.
115. Lieutenant General John H. Hay, Jr., *Vietnam Tactical Studies: Tactical and Material Innovations.* (Washington, D.C.: Department of the Army, 2002),16–17.
116. Drew J. Scott and John Jones, "The CH-37 Mojave in Viet Nam," accessed September 28, 2019, https://www.vhpa.or/CH-37B.
117. Tolson, Op. Cit., 26.
118. Harber, Op. Cit. 19.
119. Tolson, Op. Cit., 28n.
120. "Simple Ceremony Marks Ch-21 Retirement," *The Observer*, July 25, 1964.

121. Ibid.
122. Ibid.
123. Ibid.
124. http://www.118ahc.org/33rdtransco.htm, Op. Cit.
125. Karen Waddell, *The Cold War Historical Context1951–1991, Fort Richardson, Alaska.* (Fort Collins: Colorado State University, 2003), 23.
126. A. Ross Russell, Interview, July 8, 2020.
127. Treuer, et. al., Op. Cit., 167–168.
128. Chief Glenna J. Wallace, "Proud to be Eastern Shawnee—A Brief History of the Eastern Shawnee Tribe," accessed January 29, 2019, https://www.estoo-nsn.gov/culture/brief-history/.
129. "Shawnee Tribe," accessed August 21, 2019, https://www.history of Massachusetts.org/native-american-revolutionary-war/.
130. Ibid.
131. Dougherty, Op. Cit., 86.
132. Ibid.
133. Debo, Op. Cit., 91.
134. Dougherty, Op. Cit., 88.
135. Ibid., 90.
136. Ibid., 91.
137. Treuer, et. al., Op. Cit., 54.
138. Ibid.
139. Ibid.

OH-23 *Raven*

1. Brad McNally, "Rotorcraft Pioneers, Part III: Stanley Hiller, Jr.," accessed May 10, 2019, http://www.verticalreference.com/HELIARTICLES/tabid/433/ID/2536/Rotorcraft-Pioneers-Part-III-Stanley-Hiller-Jr.aspx.
2. Stanley Hiller, Jr., *National Academy of Engineering Memorial Tributes*, 12, (2008): 148-149, https://nap.nationalacademies.org/read/12473/chapter/25.
3. Ibid.
4. "Stanley Hiller, Jr.," accessed April 24, 2019, https://www.nndb.com/people/442/000116094/.
5. McNally, Op. Cit.
6. Valerie J. Nelson, "Stanley Hiller Jr., 81; Pioneer in Helicopter Design, Rescuer of Troubled Corporations," accessed May 10, 2019, https://www.latimes.com/archives/la-xpm-2006-may-01-me-hiller1-story.html.
7. J.P. Spencer, "Whirlybirds: a history of the U.S. Helicopter Pioneers: Hiller X-2-235," accessed on May 10, 2019, http://www.aviastar.org/helicopters_eng/hiller_x-2-235.php.
8. Spencer, Op. Cit.
9. Hiller, Op. Cit.
10. McNally, Op. Cit.
11. Spencer, Op. Cit.
12. General Hamilton H. Howze, USA (Ret.), "An Appraisal of Army Aviation in Vietnam," *Army Aviation*, November 20, 1966, 19.
13. James, Op. Cit., 81–82.
14. Ibid, 82.
15. Nancy Montgomery, "Larry Colburn: The Last 'hero' of My Lai," *Stars and Stripes*, December 21, 2016.
16. Miller, No Wider War, Op. Cit., 352.
17. Stephen Wittels, "Korean Peninsula Clashes (1955–2010)," (Washington, D.C.: Council on Foreign Relations Center for Preventive Action, 2010), 4.

18. Charles Kraus, "21 Newly Translated Soviet Documents on North Korea, 1968–1969," accessed May 14, 2019, https://www.wilsoncenter.org/blog-post/21-newly-translated-soviet-documents-north-korea-1968–1969.

19. "Herman Hofstatter—POW Record," Compiled by the P.O.W. Network, accessed May 14, 2019, https://www.pownetwork.org/bios/h/hxO2.htm.

20. Major Daniel P. Bolger, *Scenes from an Unfinished War: Low-Intensity Conflict in Korea 1966–1969*. (Fort Leavenworth: Military Bookshop, 2011), 107–109.

21. Vance Gammond, "Hiller 360 / UH-12 / OH-23 1947," accessed May 16, 2019, http://www.aviastar.org/helicopters_eng/hiller_oh-23.php.

22. Darryl James, *Phoenix 13: Americal Division Artillery Air Section Helicopters in Vietnam*. (Havertown: Pen & Sword Books, 2020), 7.

23. Ira Will McComic and Jerry Barnes, "The Fort Wolters Tour Introduction," accessed on May 15, 2019, www.fwcvhpa.org/fwtour/intro.php.

24. Ibid.

25. James A. Barnes and Flavous D. Stratham, "Technical Memorandum 8–70," U.S. Army Primary Helicopter School Training Program Performance Norms, Human Engineering Laboratories, 3.

26. "Ravens in Native American Culture," accessed April 28, 2019, ww.avesnoir.com/ravens-in-native-american-culture/.

27. G. Joseph Pierron, "Little Raven: South Arapahoe Chief," accessed April 18, 2019, https://www.kshs.org/kansapedia/little-raven/17642.

28. Wally Gobetz, "Follow Colorado—Westminster: Chief Little Raven," accessed April 18, 2019, https://www.flickr.com/photos/wallyg/8217880713.

29. Loretta Fowler, "Arapaho and Cheyenne Perspectives," *American Indian Quarterly*, 39, Issue 4 (2015): 373, https://www.proquest.com/docview/1717290976.

30. Ibid.

31. Ibid., 374.

32. Ibid., 374–375.

33. Ibid., 375.

34. Ibid., 376.

35. Ibid.

36. Ibid.

37. History.com Editors, "Sand Creek Massacre," accessed April 18, 2019, https://www.history.com/this-day-in-history/sand-creek-massacre.

38. Utley, Op. Cit., 137–146.

39. Notable Native signatories to the treaties included Kiowa chiefs Satank, Satanta, Kicking Bird, Woman's Heart, and Stumbling Bear. The Comanche signers were Ten Bears, Tosawi (Silver Brosch), Horse Back, and Iron Mountain. Cheyenne's chiefs included Bull Bear, Black Kettle, Spotted Elk, Gray Beard, and Tall Bull. Little Raven and Storm were among those signing for the Arapaho.

40. Utley, Op. Cit., 138.

41. Ibid.

CH-34 *Choctaw*

1. Greg Goebel, "The Sikorsky S-55, S-56 & S-58," accessed January 9. 2019, http://www.airvectors.net/avs55.html#m1.

2. Vinny Devine, "Sikorsky Product History: S-56/HR2S-1/H-37 Helicopter," accessed September 1, 2019, https://www.sikorskyarchives.com/s+56%20HR2S-1H-37.php.

3. Stephan Wilkinson, "Dog of War," *Air & Space Magazine*, July 2001, https://www.airspacemagazine.com/military-aviation/dog-of-war-2370386/?pag2=1.

4. Ibid.

5. In 1959, Communist Party Chairman Nikita Khrushchev so enjoyed flying in President Eisenhower's Marine One, a VH-34, that he bought two of them. Ray D. Leoni and Bill Paul,

"Personal Recollections: Sikorsky Utility Helicopters, A Hard Beginning," accessed September 30, 2019, https://www.sikorskyarchives.com/Sikorsky%20Utility%20Helicopters,%20A%20Hard%20Beginning.php.

6. "Armed Helicopters Around the World," Op.Cit. 11.
7. Ibid.
8. Ibid.
9. Ibid., 23.
10. Ibid., 23–24.
11. Miller, No Wider War, Op. Cit., 31.
12. Ibid.
13. Wilkinson, Op. Cit.
14. Goebel, Op. Cit.
15. "Ugly Angel: The Huey's Flawed Predecessor," accessed September 29, 2019, https://warfarehistorynetwork.com/daily/military-history/the-uh-1-iroquois-huey-helicopter/.
16. Ibid.
17. Officially known as the Avtomat Kalashnikov (AK), it is a gas-operated, 7.62×39mm assault rifle developed in the Soviet Union by Mikhail Kalashnikov.
18. "Operation Starlite," accessed October 17, 2019, http://www.operationstarlite.com/history.html.
19. Ibid., 156.
20. Ibid., 157.
21. Ibid.
22. Ibid.
23. Ibid., 89.
24. Donald E. Wilson and Dennis C. Currie, "220th Aviation Company: Battle and Fall of A Shau, March 1966," accessed October 17, 2019, https://catkiller.org/history-1966-Battle-of-A-Shaw.pdf.
25. "Ugly Angel," Op. Cit.
26. Ibid.
27. Leoni and Paul, Op. Cit.
28. Ibid.
29. Treuer, Op. Cit., 87–88.
30. Gregory D. Smithers, Native Southerners: Indigenous History from Origins to Removal. Norman: University of Oklahoma Press, 2019, 61.
31. Ibid., 73–75.
32. Treuer, Op. Cit., 88.
33. Debo, Op. Cit., 88.
34. Ibid., 89.
35. Ibid.
36. Ibid.
37. Debo, Op. Cit., 108.
38. Smithers, Op. Cit., 140–141.
39. Ibid.
40. Ibid.
41. Ibid., 117.
42. Debo, Op. Cit., 118.
43. Dougherty, Op. Cit., 67.
44. Debo, Op. Cit., 170.

CH-37 *Mojave*

1. "Sikorsky CH-37 Mojave," accessed November 15, 2019, www.olive-drab.com.
2. "Sikorsky S-56/CH-37 Mojave/HR2S—1953," accessed November 17, 2019, http://aviastar.org/helicopters_eng_sik_3-56.php.

388 NOTES

3. Vinny Devine, "Sikorsky Product History: S-56/HR2S-1/H-37 Helicopter," accessed September 1, 2019, https://www.sikorskyarchives.com/s+56%20HR2S-1H-37.php.

4. Ibid.

5. Goebel, Op. Cit.

6. Devine, Op. Cit.

7. Ibid.

8. Unnamed table, *United States Army Aviation Digest*, 28, Issue 7 (1982): 26.

9. Lieutenant L. W. Mays, "The TATSA Story," unpublished story from the Vietnam Helicopter Pilots Association, courtesy of Scott J. Drew.

10. "Captain William J. Kossler, USCG Award," accessed December 4, 2019, https://vtol.org/awards-and-contests/vertical-flight-society-award-winners?awardID=8.

11. "H-37 Mojave to be Modernized," *United States Army Aviation Digest*, 6, no. 10 (1960): 3.

12. "Sikorsky S-56/CH-37 Mojave/HR2S," Op. Cit.

13. Ibid.

14. Ibid.

15. Goebel, Op. Cit.

16. Devine, Op. Cit.

17. James H. Willbanks, "The Evolution of the US Advisory Effort in Vietnam: Lessons Learned," accessed November 19, 2019, https://journals.lib.unb.ca/index.php/JCS/article/view/15238/24499.

18. "The special status of personnel serving in Military Assistance Groups (MAAG) results from their position as an integral part of the Embassy of the United States where they perform duty." Dieter Fleck, ed., *Handbook of the Law of Visiting Forces*. (Oxford: Oxford University Press, 2011), 102.

19. Operation SHOTGUN described here is not to be confused with the May 1966, psychological warfare Operation SHOTGUN option for a series of amphibious feints against North Vietnam's beaches to convince the North Vietnamese of an imminent U.S. invasion of the country. Hastings, Op. Cit., 321.

20. "Operation Shotgun," accessed November 19, 2019, https://www.1-14th.com/Vietnam/Misc/Operation_Shotgun.html.

21. "Operation Shotgun—1965," accessed November 19, 2019, https://www.centaursinvietnam.org/WarStories/WarDiscussion/D_OperationShotgun.html.

22. Bob Jones, "Shotgunners Training for Viet Duty," *The Honolulu Advertiser*, May 1, 1965, A-1.

23. Ibid.

24. "Shot Gun" Platoon," accessed December 4, 2019, http://www.118ahc.org/Shot%Gun%20Platoon.htm.

25. Bob Jones, "Schofield Shotgun Project Stopped," *The Honolulu Adviser*, November 12, 1965, A-1.

26. "Boxscore for 25th Infantry Division Shotgun Riders." *Honolulu Star-Bulletin*, February 9, 1966, C-3.

27. Drew and Jones, Op. Cit., 5.

28. Ibid., 74.

29. Scott J. Drew, "The CH-37 'Mojave' in Vietnam," accessed September 28, 2019, https://www.nhpa.org/CH-37B.pdf.

30. Ibid.

31. Texas Tech University, The Vietnam Center & Sam Johnson Vietnam Archives, "Vietnam: The Helicopter War," accessed September 1, 2019, https://www.vietnam.ttu.edu/exhibits/helicopter/support.php.

32. "Helicopter or Incident 55–00627," Vietnam Helicopter Pilots Association, accessed December 2, 2019, https://www.vhpa.org/.

33. Ibid.

34. Drew and Jones, Op. Cit., 77.

35. Jacob Van Staaveren, *Gradual Failure: The Air War Over North Vietnam – 1965–1966*. (Washington, D.C.: Air Force History and Museum Program, 2011), 114.

36. Ibid.

37. Maj. Gen. J.B.A. Bailey, *Field Artillery and Firepower*. (Annapolis, Naval Institute Press, 2004), 519n37.
38. Staaveren, Op. Cit., 115.
39. "NSA Spies Helped Save Drones From a Fiery Death Over Vietnam," accessed December 1, 2019, https://warisboring.com/nas-spies-helped-save-drones-from-a-fiery-death-over-vietnam/.
40. Drew and Jones, Op. Cit., 11.
41. Ibid.
42. "NSA Spies," Op. Cit.
43. Ibid., 43.
44. Ibid.
45. Major General David Ewing Ott, *Vietnam Studies: Field Artillery, 1954–1973*. (Washington, D.C. :Department of the Army, 1995), 81–82.
46. "CH-37 Mojave," accessed September 1, 2019, https://www.globalsecurity.org/military/systems/aircraft/h-37.htm.
47. Ibid.
48. Drew and Jones, Op. Cit., 29
49. Ibid.
50. Ibid
51. Ibid.
52. Specialist Four James Stansell, "Mojave Finale," *United States Army Aviation Digest*, 17, no. 2 (1971): 65.
53. Devine, Op. Cit.
54. Ibid.
55. "Dutch Springs," accessed November 18, 2019, https://www.dutchsprings.com/scuba/.
56. Treuer, 203.
57. Ibid.
58. Treuer, Op. Cit., 207.
59. Ibid.
60. Dan Michalski, "Biden to honor tribes by protecting Nevada Land," *The Washington Post*, Thursday, December 1, 2022, A1.

UH-1 *Iroquois*

1. Peter Dorland and James Nanney, *Dust Off: Army Aeromedical Evacuation in Vietnam*. (Washington, D.C.: Center of Military History United States Army, 2008), 19.
2. Ibid., 24.
3. David A. Brown, Op. Cit., 103.
4. "Bell UH-1H Iroquois 'Huey' Smokey III," accessed May 14, 2020, https://www.s.i.edu/object/nasm_A19960005000.
5. David A. Brown, Op. Cit., 98–99.
6. "HU-1A Iroquois: Designed for Frontline Service," *United States Army Aviation Digest*, 5, no. 5 (1959): 11–15.
7. Ibid.
8. Carl O. Schuster, "Arsenal: UH-1 Iroquois 'Huey' Helicopter," accessed February 22, 2020), https://www.historynet.com/arsenal-uh-1-iroquois-huey-helicopter.htm.
9. Weinert, Op. Cit., 148–150.
10. Ibid., 150–151.
11. "82nd Airborne Division: UH-1A Iroquois," accessed May 14, 2020, https://www.facebook.com/82ndAirborneDivision/posts/uh-1a-iroquois-helicopter-utility-no-1-first-entered-service-in-june-1959-and-wa/10161577498735387/.
12. Ibid., 151–152.

13. Charlie Ostick, "The Huey," accessed May 13, 2020, https://www.Whpa.org/stories/huep.pdf.
14. Patrick Henry Brady with Meghan Brady Smith, *Dead Men Flying: Victory in Viet Nam*. (Washington, D.C.: WND Books, 2012), 76.
15. Bryan R. Swopes, accessed May 12, 2019, www.thisdayinaviationhistory.com/21-apr-1944/.
16. Fred M. Duncan, "Operation Ivory Soap," *The DUSTOFFer*, (Spring/Summer 2001): 5.
17. Bluhm, Op. Cit., 602.
18. Dorland and Nanney, Op. Cit., 24.
19. Ibid.
20. Ibid., 27–28.
21. Ibid., 28.
22. Ibid., 29–30.
23. Ibid., 115–116.
24. Ibid., 116.
25. The first hour after combat injury is known as the Golden Hour, the 60 minutes from the time of injury when the most critically injured can be saved if they receive proper treatment. Brady, Op. Cit., 10.
26. "Combat Medicine in Vietnam War, Part 2 of 3," United States of America Vietnam War Commemoration, accessed May 15, 2020, http://wwwvietnamwar50th.com/education/.
27. Dorland and Nanney, Op. Cit., 116.
28. Ibid.
29. Lou Pepi, *"My Brothers Have My Back"*. (Jefferson, North Carolina: McFarland & Company, Inc., Publishers, 2018), 99–100.
30. Matthew Naythons, *The Face of Mercy: A Photographic History of Medicine at War*. (New York: Random House, 1993), 239.
31. Helling, Op. Cit., 380.
32. Ibid., 381.
33. Ronald B. Frankum, Jr. and Stephen F. Maxner, *The Vietnam War for Dummies*. (New York: Wiley Publishing, Inc, 2002).
34. Holley and Sloniker, Op. Cit., 166.
35. Ibid., 117.
36. Boyne, Op. Cit., 163.
37. Ibid.
38. David Freeman, "White Elephants," *Delta Dustoff*, accessed April 20, 2020, http://www.deltadustoff.com/Stories/WhiteElephants/tabid/86/Default.aspx.
39. Holley and Sloniker, Op. Cit., 157.
40. Chuck Franson, "Bolko Zimmer and the 'White Elephants'," *The DUSTOFFer*, (Fall/Winter 2013): 21.
41. Pullum, Op. Cit.
42. Dorland and Nanney, Op. Cit., 69.
43. Williams, Op. Cit., 117.
44. "Views From Our Readers," *United States Army Aviation Digest*, 19, no. 11 (1973): 2. This reference corrects the previously reported and widely accepted UTT activation date of July 25, 1962, to date shown above, based upon research of Department of the Army records (Mr. Warren Stark, Office of the Chief of Military History), and personnel assignment orders (Mr. Herbert Smith, Organization and Directory Branch, Office of the Adjutant General).
45. "Rocket Armed Helicopter October 1962-January 1964, Vietnam." Three-year yearbook of the UTT Helicopter Company and the 571st Transportation Detachment (Aircraft Maintenance), 4, 7.
46. Ibid., 22.
47. Charlie Ostick, "UTT in '62 and '62," accessed May 27, 2020, https://www.vhpa.org/stories/UTT62–63.pdf.
48. "145th Combat Aviation Battalion—Battalion History," accessed May 27, 2020, http://www.145thcab.com/NL48_HISTORY.html.

49. Ibid.
50. Ibid.
51. Hays, Jr., Op. Cit., 16.
52. Schuster, Op. Cit.
53. Griminger, "The Armed Helicopter Story Part IV," Op. Cit., 20.
54. Ibid., 21.
55. Vanderpool, Op. Cit., 25.
56. Lieutenant General (Ret.) Harold G. Moore and Joseph L. Galloway, *We Were Soldiers Once ... And Young: Ia Drang – The Battle that Changed the War in Viet Nam.* (New York: Random House, 1992), 60–61.
57. "118th Assault Helicopter Company," accessed February 22, 2020, http://www1118ahv. org/118thAHC.htm.
58. Ibid.
59. Ibid.
60. Ibid.
61. Tolson, Op. Cit., 204.
62. "118th Assault Helicopter Company," Op. Cit.
63. Ibid.
64. The first such system was a UH-1C gunship with an M3 rocket system mounted backward. Smoke grenades were ejected to the rear of the helicopter as it flew low and slow over the area.
65. Fog oil is petroleum-based oil specially blended to produce a dense, efficient screening smoke when vaporized and re-condensed at atmospheric temperatures.
66. Hay, Op. Cit., 95–96.
67. "118th Assault Helicopter Company," Op. Cit. and Hay, Op. Cit., 95.
68. Hay, Op. Cit., 95
69. Ibid., 96.
70. "118th Assault Helicopter Company," Op. Cit.
71. Ibid.
72. "More Aerial Intelligence Systems Used During the Vietnam War," accessed October 28, 2020, https://www.army.mil/article/151825/more_aerial_intelligence_systems_used_during_vietnam_war.
73. "Aircraft Used for Special Electronic Mission Aircraft (SEMA) in Vietnam," accessed October 28, 2020, https://ccvva.org/great-stories/army-security-agency/.
74. James, L. Gilbert, *The Most Secret War: Army Signals Intelligence in Vietnam.* (Fort Belvoir: Military History Office, US Army Intelligence and Security Command, 2003), 106.
75. "Night Vision in Vietnam," accessed November 3, 2022, https://smallarmsreview.com/night-vision-in-vietnam/#:~:text=The%20use%20of%20the%20night%20vision%20devices%20in,dream%20of%20seeing%20in%20the%20dark%20was%20fulfilled.
76. Joseph Trevithick, "The U.S. Army Built Night-Fighting Gunships to Hunt the Viet Cong," accessed March 2, 2020, https://medium.com/war-is-boring/the-u-s-army-built-night-fighting-gunships-to-hunt-the-viet-cong-35f5e4887c83.
77. Trevithick, Op. Cit.
78. Bob Chenoweth, *Warbirds Illustrated No. 47: Army Gunships in Vietnam.* (London: Arms and Armour Press, Limited, 1987), 54.
79. Hay, Op. Cit., 20–22.
80. The source of sealed beams for these light arrays was from inventories of lights available in the services' supply systems. Sources indicate that the light array was seven-sealed beam landing lights from an Air Force aircraft. Candidate sources included the Lockheed C-121A *Constellation*, the Fairchild C-123 *Provider*, and the Lockheed C-130 *Hercules*. There appears to have been no single source, but the C-130 lights appear to be the most commonly used.
81. "Firefly," *United States Army Aviation Digest*, 13, no. 11 (1967): 16–20.
82. Holley and Sloniker, Op. Cit., 40.

83. Chenoweth, Op. Cit., 67.
84. Major John D. Falcon, *The Freedom Shield*. (Havertown: Casemate Publishers, 2020), 304–306.
85. Ibid.
86. Miller, No Wider War, Op. Cit., 171.
87. Adam Rawnsley, "The Pentagon Deployed Scent Warfare in Vietnam," accessed September 8, 2021, https://warisboring.com/the-pentagon-deployed-scent-warfare-in-vietnam/#:~:text=The%20Pentagon%20Deployed%20Scent%20Warfare%20in%20Vietnam%20Electronic,basic%20requirement%20of%20any%20war%E2%80%94merely%20finding%20the%20enemy.
88. Ibid.
89. Ibid.
90. Ibid.
91. Dr. John C. Warren, *Airborne Operations in World War II, European Theater*. (Maxwell Air Force Base: Air University, 1956), 33–45, 102–115, and 181.
92. "Hitting the Silk—15 Airborne Operations Carried Out Since World War Two," accessed February 20, 2020, https://www.militaryhistorynow.com.
93. Dan Brookes and Bob Hillerby, *Shooting Vietnam: The War by its Military Photographers*. (Havertown: Pen and Swords Books, 2019), xii-xvi.
94. "See the elephant" refers to seeing more than one wants, learning a hard lesson, and also, seeing combat, especially for the first time. Found in the American Heritage Dictionary of Idioms by Christine Ammer Boston: Houghton Mifflin Harcourt Publishing Company, 1992.
95. Ibid.
96. Ibid., 226.
97. Ibid., xv.
98. "1st Cavalry Division," accessed February 8, 2020, https://first-team.us.com.
99. "Part III in the Helicopter Warfare Series: The AH-1 Cobra Gunship in Vietnam," accessed February 8, 2020, https://vietnam-war-history.com/post/helicopter-warfare/bell-ah-1-cobra-the-first-helicopter-gunship.
100. Ibid.
101. 2930503006. Vietnam Helicopter Pilots Association (VHPA) Collection: General Files, The Vietnam Center and Sam Johnson Vietnam Archive, Texas Tech University.
102. Ibid.
103. "Redstone Arsenal Historical Information: TOW System Chronology," accessed February 21, 2020, https://history.redstone.army.mil/miss-tow.html.
104. Captain S. L. Christine, "1st Combat Aerial TOW Team: Helicopter vs. Armor," *United States Army Aviation Digest*, 20, no. 2 (1974): 3–4
105. "Redstone," Op. Cit.
106. Major John C. Burns, "XM-26 TOW: Birth of the Helicopter as a Tank Buster," Master of Miliary Studies thesis, United States Marine Corps Command and Staff College, May 2, 1994, 15–16.
107. Christine, Op. Cit., 3.
108. "The Hawk's Claw: The Aerial TOW System," accessed February 21, 2020, https://www.thebattleofkontum.com/claw.html.
109. Christine, Op. Cit., 4–5.
110. "Redstone," Op. Cit.
111. Christine, Op. Cit., 4–5.
112. Ibid., 5.
113. Ibid.
114. Ibid.
115. Ibid.
116. Ibid.
117. Ibid.
118. Holley and Sloniker, Op. Cit., 160.

119. Sergeant Major Herbert A. Friedman, "PSYOP Order of Battle," accessed February 22, 2022, http://www.psywarrior.com/vietnamOBPSYOP.

120. Sergeant Major Herbert A. Friedman, "The Wondering Soul PSYOP Tape of Vietnam," accessed February 25, 2022, http://www.psywarrior.com/wanderingsoul.html.

121. Ibid.

122. "Operation Wandering Soul—Ghost Tape Number 10 and the Haunting Jungles of Vietnam," accessed February 26, 2022, https://militaryhistorynow.com/2013/10/30/trick-or-treat-the-strange-tale-of-ghost-tape-no-10/.

123. The tape can be found and heard at: Operation Wandering Soul (Ghost Tape Number 10)—Bing video.

124. Friedman, "PSYOP Order of Battle," Op. Cit.

125. J.A. Koch, *The Chieu Hoi Program in Vietnam, 1963–1971.* (Santa Monica: Rand Corporation, 1973), iii.

126. Warren, Op. Cit., 172.

127. J.D. Edwards, "Last UH-1 Huey, a 42-year military veteran retires," accessed October 12, 2019, https://www.army.mil/article/180593/last_uh_1_huey_a_42_year_military_veteran_retires.

128. Treuer, Op. Cit., 21.

129. Nies, Op. Cit., 55.

130. Park Ranger William Sawyer, "The Six Nations Confederacy During the American Revolution," accessed July 28, 2019, https://www.nps.gov/fost/learn/historyculture/the-six-nations-confederacy-during-the-american-revolution.htm#cp_JUMP_3550115.

131. Treuer, Op. Cit., 32.

132. Debo, Op. Cit., 13.

133. "Tuscarora War," accessed November 4, 2022, https://northcarolinahistory.org/encyclopedia/tuscarora-war/.

134. Ibid., 78.

135. Martin J. Dougherty, *Native American Warriors: The Legendary Tribes, Their Weapons, and Fighting Techniques.* (London: Amber Books, 2018), 55.

136. Alexandra Harris, "Cultures of War," Why We Serve, op. cit., 15.

137. Treuer, Op. Cit., 32.

138. Ibid.

139. Ibid.

140. Courtland Milloy, "When mythology replaces true history," *The Washington Post*, Wednesday, November 24, 2021, B5.

141. Terri Hansen, "How the Iroquois Great Law of Peace Shaped U.S. Democracy," accessed July 27, 2019, available from https://www.pbs.org/native-america/blogs/native-voices/how-the-iroquois-great-law-of-peace-shaped-us-democracy/?fbclid=IwAR0KQyHXSYFRPJQLpYkeec_loK_OEejHTH5JNXhtBgeVfol_BYYYQUgMOIo.

142. Debo, Op. Cit., p. 84.

143. Rebecca Beatrice Brooks, "Native Americans in the Revolutionary War," (accessed July 28, 2019); available from https://historyofmassachusetts.org/native-americans-revolutionary-war/.

144. Rick Atkins, *The British Are Coming: The War for America, Lexington to Princeton, 1775–1777.* (New York: Henry Holt and Company, 2019), 309.

145. Ibid.

146. Ibid.

147. Daugherty, Op. Cit., 85.

148. Ibid.

149. Ibid., 86.

150. Ibid., 88–90.

151. Ibid., 90.

152. Ibid.

153. Melanie L. Fernandes, "Under the auspices of peace: The Northwest Indian War and its Impact of the Early American Republic," *The Gettysburg Historical Journal*, Volume 15, Article 8, 2015, 180.

154. "We are all Americans—Native Americans in the Civil War," accessed March 29, 2020, https://www.alexandriava.gov/historic/fortward/default.aspx?id=40164.

155. Laurence M. Hauptman, *The Iroquois in the Civil War: From Battlefield to Reservation.* (Syracuse: Syracuse University Press, 1991), 145–146.

156. Diane Camurat, "The American Indian in the Great War: Real and Imagined, Part Two, Chapter Four: Consequences of the War," accessed March 30, 2020, https://net.lib.byu.edu/~rdh7/wwi/comment/Cmrts/Cmrt8.html.

157. Ibid.

158. Benjamin Shearer, editor, *Home Front Heroes: A Biographical Dictionary of Americans during Wartime.* (Westport: Greenwood Press, 2006), 704.

159. Thomas D. Morgan "Native Americans in World War II," *Army History,* no. 35 (Fall 1995), 23–24.

160. Ibid.

161. Ibid.

162. Ibid., 23.

163. James E. Seelye, Jr. and Stephen A. Littleton, Editors, *Voices of the American Indian Experience, Volume 2: 1872-Present.* (Santa Barbara: Greenwood, 2013), 548.

OH-6 *Cayuse*

1. "Light Observation Helicopters for the U.S. Army," *Interavia,* no. 12 (1965): 1, https://www.vietnam.ttu.edu/reports/images.php?img=/images/386/3860107005.pdf.

2. Ibid., 2.

3. Ibid., 3.

4. Philip Siekman, "The Big New Whirl in Helicopters," *Army Aviation Magazine,* 15, no. 5 (1966): 22–24.

5. Ibid., 24.

6. Holley and Sloniker, Op. Cit., 22–24.

7. *Interavia,* Op. Cit.

8. Siekman, Op. Cit. 24.

9. Ibid.

10. Ibid., 25.

11. *Interavia,* Op. Cit., 4.

12. Ibid.

13. Ibid.

14. James, Op. Cit., 82.

15. Ibid.

16. Donald Porter, "In Vietnam, These Helicopter Scouts Saw Combat Up Close," *Smithsonian Air & Space Magazine,* September 2017, https://www.airspacemag.com/military-aviation/snakes-loaches-180964341/.

17. Williams, Op. Cit., 134.

18. Hugh L. Mills, Jr. with Robert A. Anderson, *Low Level Hell: A Scout Pilot in the Big Red One.* (Novato: Presidio Press, 1992), 64.

19. "Legendary Pilot Observes Final Mission of OH-58 Helicopter," *Fort Polk Guardian,* May 4, 2015, https://www.thetowntalk.com/story/news/local/2015/05/04/legendary-pilot-observes-final-mission-oh-helicopter/26888113.

20. Mills, Op. Cit., 34.

21. "Legendary Pilot," Op. Cit.

22. Williams, Op. Cit., 134.

23. In 2022, the same bounty would be almost $8,000.

24. "The AH-1 Cobra Gunship in Vietnam," Part 3 in the Helicopter Warfare Series, accessed June 8, 2019, https://vietnam-war-history.com/post/helicopter-warfare/bell-ah-1-cobra-the-first-helicopter-gunship.

25. Porter, Op. Cit.
26. Specialist Four John Del Vecchio, "The Tadpole and the Snake," *Rendezvous With Destiny*, (Winter/Spring 1971): 1–2.
27. Porter, Op. Cit.
28. Del Vecchio, Op. Cit., 3.
29. Ibid.
30. Captain Matthew M. Serletic, "Aero scout … what's it all about?", *United States Army Aviation Digest*, 17, no. 2 (1971): 30–31.
31. Ibid.
32. Ibid.
33. Ibid.
34. Ibid.
35. Williams, Op. Cit., 133.
36. "Vietnam OH-58C Kiowa Helicopter," Vietnam Helicopter Museum, accessed June 9, 2019, http://www.vietnamhelicopters.org/oh-58c-kiowa/.
37. Porter, Op. Cit.
38. Debo, Op. Cit., 151.
39. "The Cayuse Indian War," accessed June 14, 2019, https://nativeamericannetroots.net/diary/839.
40. Ibid.
41. Debo, Op. Cit., 154
42. Stuart Rosebrook, "16 Destinations That Will Make You Weep," *True West Magazine*, accessed June 15, 2019, https://truewestmagazine.com/16-historical-destinations-that-will-make-you-weep/.
43. Debo, Op. Cit.
44. Ibid.
45. Ibid., 155.
46. "Whitman Massacre Trial," accessed June 17, 2019, https://sos.oregon.gov/archives/exhibits/highlights/Pages/whitman.aspx.
47. Freuer, Op. Cit., 270.
48. Ibid.
49. Debo, Op. Cit.
50. "Pacific Northwest Indian Wars," accessed October 2, 2020, https://accessgenealogy.com/idaho/pacific-northwest-indian-wars.htm.
51. Ibid.
52. Ibid.
53. Ibid.

CH-47 *Chinook*

1. Weinert, *History of Army Aviation 1950–1962*, Op. Cit., 156.
2. Ibid.
3. Tolson, Ibid., 94–96.
4. Kathleen Hanser, "In Good Company: Storied career of helicopter pioneer Frank Piasecki honored by the National Aviation Hall of Fame," *Boeing Frontiers Online*, 1, Issue 4 (2002), https://www.boeing.com/news/frontiers/archive/2002/august/i_people2.html.
5. "Boeing: Ch-47 Chinook," accessed July 17, 2019, https://www.boeing.com/history/products/CH47-chinook.page.
6. Emmett F. Knight, *The 57th Transportation Company Light Helicopter, The 98th Transportation Detachment (CHFM), and The CH-21C Shawnee*. A scrapbook prepared for the June 1987 reunion at Ft. Rucker, Alabama, The Boeing Vertol Company, 1987, 18.
7. "HILLCLIMBERS—1965," accessed September 10, 2019); available from https://www.147thhillclimbers.org/hill_site/b-214th/history1.htm.
8. Boeing: CH-47 Chinook," Op. cit.

9. Tolson, Op. cit., 94.

10. Ibid. p. 95–96.

11. Miller, *No Wider War*, Op. Cit., 102.

12. Ibid., 104.

13. Ibid.

14. Tolson, Op. Cit., 120.

15. "1st Aviation Brigade Hawk," 1, no. 1 (1967): 1.

16. Hay, Jr., Op. Cit., 19.

17. John R. Brunning, "Operation Pershing: They Rode with Custer's Ghost," accessed on May 31, 2019, https://theamericanwarrior.com/tag/operation-pershing/.

18. Tolson, 141–142.

19. Ibid.

20. Frederic C. Appel, "New Helicopters Developed for Vietnam," *The New York Times*, October 31, 1965.

21. Ibid.

22. Williams, Op. Cit., 118.

23. "Boeing-Vertol ACH-47A Guns-A-Go-Go," accessed June 4, 2019, https://www.helis.com/database/model/ACH-47A-Guns-A-Go-Go/.

24. The recoiling mass typically is the howitzer tube, muzzle brake, recoil system, breech, sights, etc. It excludes the carriage and wheels.

25. "Boeing-Vertol ACH-47A Guns-A-Go-Go," Ibid.

26. "Boeing-Vertol CH-47A Chinook," accessed June 4, 2019, https://www.helis.com/database/cn/41054/.

27. "Boeing-Vertol CH-47A Chinook," accessed June 4, 2019, https://www.helis.com/database/cn/22847/.

28. Lieutenant Commander Donald A. Mohr, "Guns-A-Go-Go 1976: A look back in time," *United States Army Aviation Digest*, 22, no. 6 (1976): 17.

29. "Boeing-Vertol CH-47A Chinook," accessed June 4, 2019, https://www.helis.com/database/cn/41055/.

30. "Boeing-Vertol CH-47A," /22847/, Op. Cit.

31. Lieutenant Commander Donald A. Mohr, "Guns-A-Go-Go 1976: A look back in time," *U.S. Army Aviation Digest*, 22, no. 6 (1976): 17.

32. "Boeing-Vertol CH-47A" - /41055/. Op. Cit.

33. "Boeing-Vertol CH-47A Chinook," accessed June 4, 2019, https://www.helis.com/database/cn/41053/.

34. Hay, Jr., Op. Cit., 14–15.

35. Williams, Op. cit., 133.

36. Hay, Jr., Op. Cit.

37. Williams, Op. cit., 159–161.

38. Ibid.

39. Wertz, Op. Cit., 34.

40. Ibid., 36.

41. Treuer, Op. Cit., 279.

42. Ibid., 283.

43. "Chinook Indian Chiefs and Leaders," accessed December 5, 2019, https:// accessgenealogy.com/native/chinook-indian-chiefs-and-leaders.htm.

44. The Corps of Discovery, a specially established unit of the United States Army, formed the nucleus of the Lewis and Clark Expedition that took place between May 1804 and September 1806. Captain Meriwether Lewis and Second Lieutenant William Clark jointly led the unit.

45. The Nez Percé chiefs warned that the Chinook intended to kill the Americans when they arrived in Chinook territory.

46. "Chinook Indians," accessed December 5, 2019, http://www.bigorrin.org/archmn-chinook.htm.

47. Freuer, Op. Cit., 295.

48. Ibid.

CH-54 *Tarhe*

1. "Sikorsky S-64 / CH-54 'Tarhe'—1962," accessed November 15, 2018, http://www.aviastar.org/helicopters_eng/sik_s-64.php.

2. Lee Jacobson, Edgar A. Guzmán, and John M. Kowalonek, *Sikorsky Archives News*, July 2007, 2.

3. Ibid.

4. Kenneth G. Munson. *Helicopters and Other Rotorcraft Since 1907*. (New York: The Macmillan Publishing Company, 1969), 154.

5. Weinert, *History of Army Aviation*, Op. Cit., 159.

6. Ibid.

7. Art Linden, "Sikorsky Product History: S-64 Skycrane (CH-54 Tarhe)," accessed November 16, 2018, https://www.sikorskyarchives.com/S-64_Product_History%20modX.php.

8. "Sikorsky S-64 / CH-54 'Tarhe'—1962," Op. Cit.

9. Chandler, Op. Cit., 29.

10. "CH-54 Skycrane Association," accessed February 8, 2019, http://www.ch54skycrane.com/.

11. Lee Jacobson, Edgar A. Guzmán, and John M. Kowalonek, Op. Cit., 5.

12. During Operation TAYLOR COMMON in I CTZ a number of M121s were first used in Vietnam supporting the 1st Marine Division and ARVN forces in December 1968. The inventory of M121s was exhaust on August 8, 1970, and the U.S. began using the 15,000 pound BLU-82 with a 12,600-pound GSX warhead.

13. CW4 James T. Chandler, "And Then There Were None!", *United States Army Aviation Digest*, 1–94–4, (1994): 30.

14. Tolson, Op. Cit. 120–121.

15. "Sweet Thing Joins Brigade," *Hawk Magazine*, 1, no. 1 (1967): 16.

16. Holley and Sloniker, Op. Cit., 113.

17. Tolson, Op. Cit., 122–123.

18. Williams, Op. Cit., 149.

19. Ibid., 187.

20. The aircraft was likely from the 478th Aviation Company with a complement of 10 aircraft out of Red Beach, north of Da Nang, which was responsible for supporting I Corps north to the DMZ and west across the mountains to the Laotian border.

21. Ibid., 160.

22. Ibid., 229–231.

23. Chandler, Op. Cit., 30.

24. Holley and Sloniker, Op. Cit., 96.

25. Chandler, Op. Cit., 30.

26. Holley and Sloniker, Op. Cit., 96.

27. Chandler, Op. Cit., 28.

28. Stephen Harding, *U.S. Army Aircraft Since 1947—An Illustrated Reference*. (Atglen: Schiffer Publishing, 1997), 207.

29. "Wyandot" is the accepted spelling; however, the tribe uses and prefers the Wyandotte spelling.

30. Charles Aubrey Buser, 'Tarhe," accessed on October 10, 2020, https://www.wyandotte-nation-com/culture/history/biographies/tarhe-grand-sachem/.

31. Treuer, Op. Cit., 193.

32. Ibid.

33. "Treaty of Greenville, 1795," accessed November 15, 2018, https://americasbesthistory.com/abhtimeline1795m.html.

34. Buser, Op. Cit.

35. To James Madison from the Chiefs of the Northwestern Indians, September 26, 1810, accessed November 14, 2018, https://founders.archives.gov/documents/Madison/03-02-02-0691.
36. Presidential Proclamation, December 21, 1814, accessed November 15, 2018, https://founders.archives.gov/documents/Madison/03-08-02-0389.
37. Lee Jacobson, Edgar A. Guzmán, and John M. Kowalonek, "*Sikorsky Archives News*," Igor I. Sikorsky Historical Archives, Inc., July 2007, 4.
38. Ibid.
39. Ibid.

OH-58 *Kiowa*

1. "This Day in Aviation: 8 December 1962," accessed November 13, 2022, https://www.thisdayinaviation.com/tag/yoh-4a/.
2. "Bell Helicopter OH-58A "Kiowa," accessed December 10, 2019, https://www.skytamer.com/Bell_OH-58A.html.
3. David A. Brown, Op. Cit., 184–185.
4. Ibid., 184.
5. Ibid., 185.
6. "Bell Helicopter OH-58 Kiowa," Op. Cit.
7. "Bell Helicopter News Information for OH-58 NETT," accessed December 10, 2019, https://vhpa.org/KIA/panel/battle/690627.HTM.
8. "OH-58C Kiowa Helicopter," accessed December 28, 2019, http://www.vietnamhelicopters.ord/oh-58c-kiowa/.
9. "US Helicopters—Helicopter Armament Subsystems Part I," accessed December 10, 2019, http://grunt-redux.atspace.eu/us_helos_weapons.htm.
10. "Silver Spurs-A Troop, 3/17th Air Cav: Troop History 1970," accessed January 8, 2020, http://northwestvets.com/spurs/317hist5.htm.
11. Ibid.
12. Ibid.
13. "Spur's OH-58 Kiowa Still Flying!," accessed January 8, 2020, http://northwestvets.com/spurs/68-16935.htm.
14. "High Times," accessed December 28, 2019, https://www.verticalmag.com/features/high-times-html/.
15. Treuer, Op. Cit., 182.
16. Judith Nies, *Native American History: A Chronology of a Culture's Vast Achievements and Their Links to World Events.* (New York: Ballantine Books, 1996), 139.
17. Alvin M. Josephy, Jr., *500 Nations.* (New York: Alfred A. Knopf, 2002), 372.
18. Wooster, Op. Cit., 236.
19. *Red River War of 1874–1875: Clash of Cultures in the Texas Panhandle.* (Austin: Texas Historical Commission), 4.
20. Josephy, Op. Cit., 374–375.
21. Ibid., 334.
22. Ibid.
23. Ibid., 206.
24. Blum, Op. Cit., 335.
25. Ibid.
26. "1SGT I-See-O "Plenty Fires Unknown," accessed July 4, 2020, https://www.findagrave.com/memorial/11740100/i_see_o-unknown.
27. "Artifact Spotlights," *Call to Duty: Newsletter of the National Campaign for the National Museum of the United States Army,* 15, no. 12 (2020): 4.
28. Ibid.
29. "I-See-O," *The Lawton Constitution*, March 13, 1927, 1.

30. Gina Cavallaro, "He's The Army: NCO Comes Home, Honors His Warrior Culture," *Army*, 70, no. 5 (2020): 14.

31. Dr. William C. Meadows, K*iowa Military Societies: Ethnohistory and Ritual*. (Norman: University of Oklahoma Press, 2010), 179.

32. Debo, Op. Cit., 289.

33. "No Veteran Left Alone," accessed December 19, 2019, http://projects.aljazeera.com/2014/native-veterans/black-leggings.

34. "Kiowa Dog-Soldiers and Warrior Societies," accessed December 20, 2019, https://www.KSHS.org/kansapedia/kiowa-social-and-political-structure/19278#dog.

35. "No Veteran Left Alone," Ibid.

Whom Shall I Send?

1. Leonard Wood, *Our Military History: Its Facts and Fallacies*. (Chicago: Reilly and Britton, 1916), 185.

2. General of the Army Douglas MacArthur, *Reminiscences*. (New York: McGraw-Hill Company, 1964), 414.

3. "Why Do Native Americans Serve?," accessed December 27, 2019, https://americanindian.si.edu/static/patriot-nations/.

4. Holm, Op. Cit., 14.

5. Ibid., 22–23.

6. Jeré Dean Franco, "Bring Them in Alive: Selective Service and Native Americans," *Journal of Ethnic Studies*, 18, Issue 3 (Fall 1990): 18–19.

7. Holm, Op. Cit., 23.

8. "Southeast Asia Collective Defense Treaty (Manila Pact), September 8, 1954." Signatories at that time were the United States, Australia, France, New Zealand, Pakistan, the Philippines, Thailand, and the United Kingdom. By a separate protocol to the treaty, Laos, Cambodia, and "the free territory under the jurisdiction of the State of Vietnam [South Vietnam]" were added to the provisions of the treaty.

9. Paul E. Eckel, "SEATO: An Ailing Alliance," *World Affairs*, 134, no. 2 (Fall 1971): 97.

10. Holm, Op. Cit., 118.

11. Shelby L. Stanton, *Green Berets at War: U.S. Army Special Forces in Southeast Asia, 1965–1975*. (New York: Ivy Books, 1985), 218–219.

12. Holm, Op. Cit., 170.

13. Ibid., 187.

14. Ibid., 190–191.

15. Ibid., 192.

16. Sam Bendickson, Interview with the author, Minneapolis, August 11, 2020.

17. To conserve weight and allow for heavier weapons and additional ammunition, most *Cayuse* units flew with only a three-man crew, AC, crew chief/gunner, and gunner.

18. Sam Bendickson, interview by author, Minneapolis, September 28, 2020.

19. Ibid.

20. Richard L. Stevens, *The Trail: A History of the Ho Chi Minh Trail and the Role of Nature in the War in Viet Nam*. (New York: Garland Publishing, Inc., 1993), xi.

21. James H. Willbanks, "Nixon's Cambodian Incursion," accessed September 28, 2020, https://www.historynet.com/nixons-cambodian-incursion.htm.

22. Ibid.

23. Ibid.

24. Melvin Robert Sheldon, Interview with the author, Tulalip, Washington, July 30, 2020.

25. Bendickson interview.

26. "Stories of Sacrifice Korean War—U.S. Army: Woodrow W. Keeble," accessed September 30, 2020, http://www.cmohs.org/recipient-detail/3135/keeble-woodrow-w.php.
27. Ibid.
28. Russell Cooata, Jr. Collection (AFC/2001/001/83012), Veterans History Project, American Folklife Center, Library of Congress.
29. Russell Cooata, Jr., interview by author, Cornville, Arizona, January 10, 2020.
30. Russell Cooata, Jr., interview with the author, February 5, 2020.
31. Letter Orders 746, Movement-Permanent Change of Station Organization/Unit, Headquarters, XXIII Airborne Corps and Fort Bragg, Fort Bragg, North Carolina 28307, dated 3 April 1967.
32. 14th Transportation Battalion Association (AM&S) (GS), 608th Transportation Company (DS), accessed May 18, 2020, http://www.14thtransbnamgs.org/608th-transportation-company.html.
33. Russell Cooata, Jr., interview by author, Cornville, Arizona, May 18, 2020.
34. Dan DeStefano, e-mail message to Donald Gatewood, August 7, 2012.
35. "First Navajo Helicopter Pilot," Star News, March 24, 1971, 35.
36. Leslie Hines, interview by author, Des Moines, Iowa, May 2, 2020.
37. Ibid.
38. Probably a Soviet-made B-10 (82 mm) or B-11 (107 mm).
39. The weapons were actually the Soviet-made 12.7 mm DShK 1938 ("*Krupnokaliberny Pulemet Degtyareva-Shpagina*, DShK"), which the Americans referred to as a .51 caliber.
40. The most likely ship was the USS Sanctuary (AH-17) which alternated with the USS Repose (AH-16) being on the line off Da Nang, Phu Bai, Chu Lai, and Dong Ha. Rear Admiral Todd Fisher, MSC, USN, Ret. Interview May 26, 2020.
41. The intermediate gearbox (42-degree gearbox) is located at the base of the vertical fin of the tail. It provides a 42-degree change of direction of the tail rotor driveshaft. The gearbox has a self-contained wet sump oil system. An oil-level sight glass, filler cap, vent, and magnetic chip detector are provided.
42. This maneuver is used to transition from forward flight to a landing on the surface when there may not be sufficient power available to sustain a hover. This maneuver is useful in some helicopters for emergency situations, such as certain tail rotor failures or stuck pedals.
43. Hines, Op. Cit.
44. Albert Bender, "Dragging Canoe's War," accessed May 22, 2020, https://www.historynet.com/dragging-canoes-war.htm.
45. "Chief Dragging Canoe," accessed May 23, 2020, https://www.aaanativearts.com/Cherokee/dragging-canoe.htm.
46. "Treaty of Sycamore Shoals," accessed May 24, 2020, http://www.self.gutenberg.org/articles/Treaty_of_Sycamore_Shoals.
47. Ibid.
48. "Chief Dragging Canoe," Op. Cit.
49. Ibid.
50. Ibid.
51. Clifford C. Mosier Collection (AFC/2001/001/30030), Veterans History Project, American Folklife Center, Library of Congress.
52. The program was also commonly referred to somewhat disparagingly by serving sailors as the "Kiddie Cruise" program.
53. Clifford Claude Mosier, interview by author, Fayetteville, Arkansas, October 27, 2020.
54. The Standardization Instructor Pilot also checks and teaches regular pilots as a means of assessing the effectiveness of the IP in the battalion.
55. Mosier interview, Op. Cit.
56. Ibid.
57. Melvin Robert Sheldon Collection (AFC/2001/001/109136), Veterans History Project, American Folklore Center, Library of Congress.

58. The Armed Forces Qualification Test (AFQT) is a component of the Armed Services Vocational Aptitude Battery (ASVAB) that assesses candidates for placement into various military jobs across all branches of the Armed Services.

59. Sheldon interview, Op. Cit.

60. Between 1966 and 1971, the NVA moved 630,000 NVA troops, 100,000 tons of rice and foodstuffs, 400,000 weapons, and 50,000 tons of ammunition down an extensive trail network from North Vietnam through Laos and onward to Cambodia and eventually South Vietnam. Thomas R. Yarborough, *A Shau Valor: American Combat Operations in the Valley of Death 1963–73.* (Havertown: Casemate, 2016), 9.

61. Operation ARC LIGHT was the conventional use of B-52 strategic bombers from the Air Force Strategic Air Command flying out of Guam, Thailand, and Okinawa from 1963 to 1973 to interdict the Ho Chi Minh Trail and other targets in support of the war in Vietnam. A typical bomb load was 60,000 pounds of a combination of 500- and 750-pound bombs.

62. Wendy Ann Church, email message to author, August 25, 2020.

63. Melvin Robert Sheldon, interview by author, Tulalip, Washington, August 6, 2020.

64. Bishop Michael F. Burbidge, "Statement for Veterans Day 2022," accessed November 10, 2022, https://www.arlingtondiocese.org/bishop/public-messages/2022/bishop-burbidge-statement-for-veterans-day/.

Some Gave All

1. George Santayana, *Soliloquies in England, and Later Soliloquies-'Tipperary'.* (London: Constable and Company, Ltd., 1922), 102.

2. U.S. Department of Veterans Affairs, "America's Wars Fact Sheet", Government Printing Office, Washington, D.C., 2018, November 2019.

3. "Casualty Status as of 10 a.m. EDT September 28, 2020," Department of Defense, September 28, 2020.

4. E.B. Potter, *Nimitz.* (Annapolis: Naval Institute Press, 1976), 445.

5. The Virtual Wall Vietnam Veterans Memorial, accessed July 25, 2016, http://www.virtualwall.org/

6. Geoffrey C. Ward, *The Vietnam War: An Intimate History.* (New York: Alfred A. Knopf, 2017), 244.

7. Lisa Gough, Editor, *Never Forget: The Story Behind the Vietnam Veterans Memorial.* (Washington, D.C.: The Vietnam Veterans Memorial Fund, 2008).

8. Ibid., 20.

9. Ibid., 30.

10. Kim Servart Theriault, "Re-membering Vietnam: War, Trauma, and "Scarring Over" After "The Wall," *The Journal of American Culture*, Volume 26, Number 4, December 2003, 421–431.

11. The video can be found on YouTube at: https://www.youtube.com/watch?v=DpJIUHssrYk&feature=youtu.be.

12. Robin Wagner-Pacifici and Barry Schwartz, "The Vietnam Veterans Memorial: Commemorating a Difficult Past," *American Journal of Sociology*, 97, no. 2 (1991): 376–420.

13. Defense Intelligence Agency Helicopter Loss database; Incident: 710610027

14. Lark, Lisa A. *All They Left Behind: Legacies of the Men and Women on the Wall.* (Evansville: M.T. Publishing Company, Inc. 2012), 102.

15. Ibid.

16. "Defense Intelligence Agency Reference Notes," Defense Intelligence Agency Helicopter Loss database MIA-POW file reference number: 1746; Incident: 71051610.

17. Defense Intelligence Agency Reference Notes, Defense Intelligence Agency; Helicopter Loss database Survivability/Vulnerability Information Analysis Center Helicopter database, Naval Safety Center. MIA-POW file reference number: 0203. Incident: 65120310.

18. Defense Intelligence Agency, Helicopter Loss database, Survivability/Vulnerability Information Analysis Center Helicopter database. Incident: 68042444.

19. Defense Intelligence Agency Helicopter Loss database and Army Aviation Safety Center database. Incident: 691028231.
20. Army Aviation Safety Center database. Incident: 0E664ACD. Accident Case: 0E664 Total Loss Accident.
21. Defense Intelligence Agency Helicopter Loss database; Survivability/Vulnerability Information Analysis Center Helicopter database. Incident: 68122727.
22. Defense Intelligence Agency, Helicopter Loss database; Army Aviation Safety Center database. Incident: 0D664ACD. Accident Case: 0D664 Total Loss Accident.
23. Defense Intelligence Agency, Helicopter Loss database; Incident: 701102021ACD. Army Aviation Safety Center database; Accident Case: 701102021 Total Loss Accident.
24. Roush, Gary, "Helicopter Losses During the Vietnam War," Vietnam Helicopter Pilots Association, February 3, 2018.
25. Falcon, Op. Cit., 315–316.
26. Lark, Ibid., 62.
27. Ibid.
28. Ibid.
29. "ASN Aircraft accident Fairchild C-123K Provider 54–0590 Khe Sanh," accessed August 24, 2018, https://aviation-safety.net/database/record.php?id=19680306-1.
30. Lark, Op, Cit.
31. Virtual Vietnam Veterans Wall of Faces Howard E. Hollar Marine Corps, accessed August 24, 2018, http://www.vvmf.org/Wall-of-Faces/23737/HOWARD-E-HOLLAR.
32. Defense Intelligence Agency, Helicopter Loss database; Incident: 70051011.
33. Defense Intelligence Agency Helicopter Loss database; Incident: 670423031ACD. Army Aviation Safety Center database; Accident: 670423031 Total loss.
34. MUSCLE SHOALS was the fourth in a series of five joint military electronic warfare operations conducted in Southeast Asia from 1967 until February 1973.
35. Department of Defense Press Release 370-03, "Missing Navy Crewmembers Found and Identified," May 27, 2003, accessed December 23, 2022, http://www.arlingtoncemetery.nt/aircrew-01181968.htm.
36. Ibid.
37. Defense Intelligence Agency Helicopter Loss database; Incident: 700905031ACD. Army Aviation Safety Center database; Accident: 700905031 Total loss or fatality.
38. Defense Intelligence Agency Helicopter Loss database; Incident: 70042555.KIA.
39. Unlike the Army, the standard USMC combat tour in Vietnam was thirteen months.
40. John Andrew Prime, "Crew Fights to Remember Shipmates," *Military Officer*, March 2019, 56.
41. "Captain Harry R. Crumley," accessed August 29, 2018, http://togetherweserved.com.
42. "Final Mission of CAPT Harry R. Crumley," August 29, 1918, http://www.vvmf.org/Wall-of-Faces/11324/HARRY-R-CRUMLEY?page=1#remembrances.
43. Defense Intelligence Agency, Helicopter Loss database; Incident: 6911155.
44. Defense Intelligence Agency Helicopter Loss database OPERA (Operations Report); Incident: 71021811.KIA.
45. "HMH-463 - History: Vietnam War," accessed October 28, 2019, https://www.wikiwand.com/en/HMH-463.
46. Charlie Block, "Barrel Bombing: a CO's View," accessed October 28, 2019), http://www.hmh-463-vietnam.com/reflections/yourstory.html#seventh%20story.
47. Epitaph by Master Sergeant Joe Gunn, *Sahara*, 1995.

Epilogue

1. "Establishing Our Own," accessed on July 21, 2019, http://www.armyaviationmuseum.org/part-ii-establishing-our-own/

2. Boyne, Op. Cit., 239–240.

3. Nathan Pfau, "AH-56 Cheyenne Still an Aircraft Way Ahead of Its Time," accessed August 27, 2019, https://www.army.mil/article/206181/ah_56_cheyenne_still_an_aircraft_way_ahead_of_ its_time.

4. Boyne, Op. Cit., 239.

5. Treuer, Op. Cit., 164.

6. Ibid., 160.

7. Ibid.

8. Ibid., 165.

9. Ibid.

10. The Seminole Tribe of Florida was never subdued nor made peace with the U.S. government.

11. Ray D. Leoni, "UTTAS Win Sparked Black Hawk Series," *Sikorsky Archives News*, January 2008, 1, 3.

12. Ibid., 7.

13. Colonel Raymond K. Blum, Jr., *U.S. Army: A Complete History*. (Alexandria: The Army Historical Foundation, 2004),163.

14. Ibid., 164.

15. Ibid.

16. Ibid., 165.

17. Ibid.

18. Ibid., 166.

19. Ibid.

20. Ibid.

21. Boyne, Op. Cit., 261.

22. Ray D. Leoni, "Sikorsky Archives-Product History: S-70A (UH-60A Black Hawk, YEH-60B SOTAS, EH-60A Quick Fix)," accessed September 2, 2019, https://www.sikorskyarchives. com/S-70A%20(UH-60A%20Black%20Hawk,%20YEH-60B%0SOTAS,%20EH-60A%20 Quick%20Fix).php.

23. "Historical Snapshot: AH-64 Apache Attack Helicopter," accessed September 3, 2019, https:// www.boeing.com/history/products/ah-64-apache.page.

24. Ibid., 204–205.

25. Debo, Op. Cit., 14–15, 17, 23, and 29.

26. Ibid., 97–98.

27. Ibid.

28. Hyslop, Op. Cit., 225.

29. Ibid., 263.

30. Ibid.

31. Ibid.

32. Ibid.

33. Boyne, Op. Cit., 243.

34. "RAH-66 Comanche," accessed September 2, 2019, https://fas.org/man/dod-101/sys/ac/rah-66. htm.

35. Jefferson Morris, "Army Cancels RAH-66 Comanche Helicopter After 20 years, $8 billion," accessed September 2, 2019, https://aviationweek.com/awin/army-cancels-rah-66-comanche-helicopter-after-20-years-8-billion.

36. Ibid.

37. Utley, Op. Cit., 4.

38. Ibid.

39. Debo, Op. Cit., 98–99.

40. Op. Cit., 130.

41. Wertz, Op. Cit., 98.

42. Debo, Op. Cit., 170–171.

43. Ibid.
44. Ibid., 171.
45. Ibid., 219.
46. Wertz, Op. Cit., 106–108.
47. "Army Acquisition Support Center—Lakota UH-72A Light Utility Helicopter (LUH)," accessed September 8, 2019, https://asc.army.mil/web/portfolio-item/lakota-uh-72a-light-utility-helicopter-luh/.
48. "UH-72 Lakota," accessed September 8, 2019, https://www.militaryfactory.com/aircraft/detail.asp?aircraft_id=400.
49. "Army Acquisition Support Center—Lakota UH-72A Light Utility Helicopter (LUH)," Op. Cit.
50. Boyne, Op. Cit., 268.
51. "UH-72A," accessed September 9, 2019, https://www.airbus.com/us/en/helicopters/military-helicopters/uh-72a.html.
52. "UH-72 Lakota," Op. Cit.
53. "UH-72A Lakota," accessed September 8, 2019, https://www.army-technology.com/projects/uh-72a-lakota/.
54. Ibid.
55. Ibid.
56. Ostler, Op. Cit., 22.
57. Treuer, Op. Cit., 163.
58. Ibid., 163–166.
59. Ibid., 152.
60. Mark Grimsley and Clifford J. Rogers, eds, *Civilians in the Path of War.* (Lincoln: University of Nebraska Press, 2002), 141.
61. "Chivington's Address on Sand Creek," *Denver Republican*, October 6, 1894.
62. Courtney A. Scott, "John M. Chivington," John M. Jennings and Chuck Steele, eds., *The Worst Military Leaders in History.* (London: Reaktion Books, 2022), 77–79.
63. Ibid., 80.
64. Ibid., 81.
65. Ibid., 152.
66. Ibid., 153.
67. Patrick Mason and Colonel Robert Barrie, "Flying Into The Future: Aviation Fleet Upgraded as Future Aircraft Are Developed," *Army*, 70, no. 8 (2020): 48.
68. "Aviation," *Army 2019–2020 Green Book*, 69, no. 10 (2019): 135.
69. Mason and Barrie, Op. Cit., 46.
70. Joe Lacdan, "Army awards contract to develop future vertical lift capability," accessed December 29, 2022, https://www.army.mil/article/262755/army_awards_contract_to_develop_future_vertical_lift_capability.
71. Jen Judson, "Sikorsky challenges U.S. Army helicopter award," accessed December 29, 2022, https://www.defensenews.com/industry/2022/12/28/lockheed-challenges-us-armys-helicopter-award/#:~:text=WASHINGTON%20%E2%80%94%20Sikorsky%20has%20filed%20a,helicopter%20procurement%20in%2040%20years.
72. Zack Rosenberg, "U.S. General Accountability Office denies Sikorsky-Boeing FLAA award protest," accessed April 12, 2023, https://www.janes.com/defence-news/news-detail/us-government-accountability-office-denies-sikorsky-boeing-flraa-award-protest.
73. Mason and Barrie, Op. Cit., 47.
74. The Commemorative Works Act - Public Law 99–652 (40 U.S. Code Chapter 89) stipulates that a military commemorative work may be authorized to commemorate a single war.
75. Heidi Zimmerman, "Vietnam Veterans Memorial Fund Changes Direction of Education Center Campaign," accessed August 22, 2019, https://www.vvmf.org/News/Vietnam-Veterans-Memorial-Fund-changes-direction-of-Education-Center-campaign/.
76. James Knotts, e-mail message to author, August 12, 2022.

77. Ibid.
78. An Act to Provide for a National Native American Veterans' Memorial, Public Law 103-384: 4067.
79. Dana Hedgpeth, "Little-known stories of 6 Native Americans who served in the U.S. Military," *The Washington Post*, April 1, 2019, B4.
80. Tara Bahrampour, "A memorial on the Mall long fought for, 'long overdue'," *The Washington Post*, Monday, January 15, 2018, B8.
81. Representative Deb Haaland of New Mexico became the first Native American cabinet member when the Senate confirmed her to be the Secretary of the Interior.
82. Levi Rickert, "Ground Broken for the Native American Veterans Memorial on National Mall in Nation's Capital," accessed September 22, 2019, http://nativenewsonline.net/currents/ground-broken-for-the-native-american-veterans-memorial-on-national-mall-in-nations-capital/.
83. Ryan P. Smith, "This Innovative Memorial Will Soon Honor Native American Veterans," accessed September 18, 2019, https://www.smithsonianmag.com/smithsonian-institution/this-innovative-memorial-soon-honor-native-american-veterans-180969060/#hiSCvj9LCbZsXwkK.99.
84. The music comes from the Smithsonian Folkways recording, *American Warriors: Songs for Indian Veterans*.
85. Darren Thompson, "Over 1,500 Native Veterans Participate in Dedication Ceremony for the National Native American Veterans Memorial," accessed November 24, 2022, https://nativenewsonline.net/currents/over-1-500-native-veterans-participate-in-dedication-ceremony-for-the-national-native-american-veterans-memorial.

Appendix A: Native American Medal of Honor Recipients

1. Congressional Medal of Honor Society, accessed April 11, 2020, http://www.cmohs.org/.
2. Alexandra N. Harris and Mark G. Hirsch. *Why We Serve: Native Americans in the United States Armed Forces*. (Washington, D.C.: Smithsonian Institution National Museum of the American Indian, 2020), 132–133.
3. Department of Veterans Affairs, "Native American Medal of Honor Recipients: World War II and Korean War," accessed April 11, 2020, https://www.va.gov/tribalgovernment/medal_of_honor_recipiants.asp.
4. "List of Native American Medal of Honor Recipients," accessed April 11, 2020, http://aycocklaw.com/files/17_WIKI_List_of_Native_American_Medal_of_Honor_Recipients.pdf.

Appendix B: Where Are They Now—Reservation Homes of Namesake Tribes

1. Anton Treuer, *Indian Nations of North America*. (Washington, D.C.: National Geographic Partners, 2010).

Appendix C: Official and Unofficial Names of Army Vietnam War Helicopters

1. Gordon L. Rottman, *U.S. Helicopter Pilot in Vietnam*. (New York: Bloomsbury Publishing Company, 2011), 53.
2. James, Op. Cit., 136.
3. Emmanuel Gustin, "Aircraft Nicknames," accessed May 2013, https://web.mit.edu/btyung/www/nickname.html.

4. "Big Ugly Fucker".

5. 5.8 as in not quite a 6 (OH-6 Ca*yuse*).

Appendix E: Characteristics and Performance of Army Vietnam War Helicopters

1. Stephen Harding. *U. S. Army Aircraft Since 1947—An Illustrated Reference*. (Atglen: Schiffer Publishing, Ltd., 1997), 35–38.

2. "Rotary Wing," *Army Aviation Magazine*, August 21, 1967, 76.

3. Ibid.

4. Harding, Op. Cit., 228–229.

5. "Rotary Wing," 50.

6. Harding, Op. Cit., 256–257.

7. Fred Hamlin and Eleanor Thayer Miller, eds. *The Aircraft Yearbook 1956*. (Washington, D.C.: Lincoln Press, Inc., 1956).

8. "Rotary Wing," Op. Cit., 62.

9. Harding. Op. Cit., 143–144.

10. "Rotary Wing," Op. Cit., 77.

11. Ibid.

12. Harding. Op. Cit., 231–232.

13. "Rotary Wing," Op. Cit., 64.

14. Ibid.

15. Harding, Op. Cit., 233–234.

16. "Rotary Wing," Op. Cit., 66.

17. Ibid.

18. Harding, Op. Cit., 43–48.

19. "Rotary Wing," Op. Cit., 79.

20. Ibid.

21. Harding, Op. Cit., 43–48.

22. "Rotary Wing," Op. Cit., 79.

23. Ibid.

24. Harding, Op. Cit., 43 – 48.

25. "Rotary Wing," 80.

26. John W.R. Taylor, ed., *Jane's All The World's Aircraft: 1975–1976*. (New York: Franklin Watts Inc., 1976), 266.

27. Taylor, Op. Cit., 266–267.

28. Ibid.

29. "UH-1M Huey," accessed August 22, 2020, https://combatairmuseum.org/aircraft/bellhueyuh1m.html.

30. Taylor, Op. Cit., 360.

31. Taylor, Op. Cit., 290–292.

32. "Rotary Wing," Op. Cit., 68.

33. Ibid.

34. Taylor, Op. Cit., 290–292.

35. Taylor, Op. Cit., 290–292

36. Harding, Op. Cit., 69–74.

37. Taylor, *Op. Cit.*, 455–456.

38. "Bell UH-1M Iroquois Huey," accessed August 19, 2020, https://www.combatairmuseum.org/aircraft/bellhueyuh1m.html.

39. Taylor, *Op. Cit.*, 271.

Acknowledgments

1. *"His lord said to him, Well done, good and faithful servant."* Rest in peace. (Mathew 25:21) The Bible passage is translated into the language of the Seminoles, Mvskoke, by Jeremy Fultz, Interim Director, Language Department of the Seminole Nation of Oklahoma. The Mvskoke words say, "Good, good work, kind one. I will see you again soon."

2. If you are a veteran and are willing to share your military experiences with future generations, in peace and war, please consider contacting the VHP Folklife Center at the LOC website: https://www.loc.gov/vets/kit.html, phone: (202) 707-4916; email: vohp@loc.gov.

3. While *On Warriors' Wings* was being published, the Warrior Spirit Consortium, including the National Indian Education Association, the Library of Congress, the Veteran's Legacy Program at the U.S. Department of Veteran's Affairs, and others, are launching the Warrior History Project to collect oral histories of Native Veterans across Indian Country. Native American Veterans interested in sharing their military service experiences with the Warrior History Project should contact Melanie Johnson at mjohnson@neia.org, 202-878-6284.

BIBLIOGRAPHY

Websites referenced in this bibliography were active at writing On Warriors' Wings. *Over time some URL links may have changed or been discontinued.*

"1SGT I-See-O "Plenty Fires Unknown." Accessed July 4, 2020, https://www.findagrave.com/memorial/11740100/i_see_o-unknown.

"*1st Aviation Brigade Hawk*." Headquarters, 1st Aviation Brigade, 1, no. 1 (1967): 1.

"1st Cavalry Division." Accessed February 8, 2020, https://first-team.us.com.

"10 More Schofield GIs Killed." Accessed November 19, 2019, http://www.themightyninth.org/photos/displayimage.php?album=42&pos=20.

"14th Transportation Battalion Association (AM&S) (GS), 608th Transportation Company (DS)." Accessed May 18, 2020, http://www.14thtransbnamgs.org/608th-transportation-company.html.

"25th Infantry Division Shotgunners." Accessed November 20, 2019, http://www.25th-infantry-div-shotgunner.com/cat%C3%A9gories/htm/.

"36th Division in World War I; Chapter 4—From Texas to the Marne." Accessed December 5, 2018, http://www.texasmilitaryforcesmuseum.org/36division/archives/wwi/white/chap4.htm.

"42 Years Ago U.S.N.S. Corpus Christi Bay." Accessed November 2, 2019, http://www.armyaviationmagazine.com/index.php/archive/looking-back-again/665-42-years-ago-usns-corpus-christi-bay.

"57th Medical Company (Air Ambulance)—"Dustoff." Accessed August 19, 2019, https://www.globalsecurity.org/military/agency/army/57med-co.htm.

"The 57th Transportation Company (Light Helicopter), The 98th Transportation Detachment (CHFM), and the CH-21C Shawnee, 1987 *Reunion Scrapbook*." Fort Rucker, Alabama: Boeing Vertol Company, 1987.

"82nd Airborne Division: UH-1A Iroquois." Accessed May 14, 2020, https://www.facebook.com/82ndAirborneDivision/posts/uh-1a-iroquois-helicopter-utility-no-1-first-entered-service-in-june-1959-and-wa/10161577498735387/.

"118th Assault Helicopter Company." Accessed February 22, 2020, http://www1118ahv.org/118thAHC.htm.

"560th Military Police." Accessed November 19, 2019, https://www.wikitree.com/wiki/Space:Vinh_Long_Army_Airfield.

"A Battle between the Kiowa and Cheyenne, 1837." Accessed December 17, 2019, https://www.wdl.org/en/item/17963/.

ABC World News Tonight with David Muir. February 10, 2022.

"Aircraft UH-1N: Marine Corps Air Station New River." Accessed March 1, 2020, https://www.newriver.marines.mil/About/Aircraft/UH-1N/.

"Aircraft Used for Special Electronic Mission Aircraft (SEMA) in Vietnam." Accessed October 28, 2020, https://ccvva.org/great-stories/army-security-agency/.

Albertson, Mark. "Army Aviation in Vietnam—The Rogers Board." Accessed February 24, 2019, http://www.armyaviationmagazine.com/index.php/history/not-so-current-2/713-army-aviation-in-vietnam-the-rogers-board.
_____. "Boeing-Vertol CH-21 Shawnee ("Flying Banana")." Accessed January 29, 2020, http://www.armyaviationmagazine.com/index.php/history/not-so-current-2/714-boeing-vertol-ch-21-shawnee-flying-banana.
_____. "Helicopters in Korea, Part 1," *Army Aviation Magazine*, 62, no. 7 (2013).
_____. "The Korean War—The Helicopter." Accessed October 27, 2022, https://www.armyaviationmagazine.com/index.php/history/not-so-current-2/1884-the-korean-war-the-helicopter.
Weiser-Alexander, Kathy. "Legends of America: Fort Buford, North Dakota." Accessed April 12, 2019, https://www.legendsofamerica.com/fort-buford-north-dakota/.
Andrade, John. *U.S. Military Aircraft Designations and Serials since 1909.* Hinckley: Midland Counties Publications, 1979.
"Apache—The Fiercest Warriors in the Southwest." Accessed September 5, 2019, https://www.legendsofamerica.com/na-apache/.
Appel, Frederic C. "New Helicopters Developed for Vietnam." *The New York Times*, October 31, 1965.
"A Proud Past: Part I—The Origins of Army Aviation." Accessed December 14, 2019, http://www.armyaviationmuseum.org/discover/.
"A Proud Past: Part II—Establishing Our Own." Accessed December 14, 2019, http://www.armyaviationmuseum.org/part-ii-establlishing-our-own/.
"A Proud Past: Part III—Coming of Age." Accessed December 14, 2019, http://www.armyaviationmuseum.org/part-iii/.
Army Aircraft Gas Turbine Engines, Subcourse AL0993, 5th Edition. Fort Eustis: US Army Aviation Logistics School.
"Army Acquisition Support Center—Lakota UH-72A Light Utility Helicopter (LUH)." Accessed September 8, 2019, https://asc.army.mil/web/portfolio-item/lakota-uh-72a-light-utility-helicopter-luh/.
Army Regulation 70-28. "Research and Development: Assigning Popular Names to Major Items of Equipment," Headquarters Department of the Army, Washington, D.C., 4 April 1969.
Army Regulation 70-28. "Research and Development: Assigning Popular Names to Major Items of Equipment," Headquarters Department of the Army, Washington, D.C., 18 June 1976.
Army Regulation 70-1. "Research, Development, and Acquisition: Army Acquisition Policy," Headquarters Department of the Army, Washington, D.C., 22 July 2011.
"Army's New Transport Helicopter." *United States Army Aviation Digest*, 5, no. 6 (1959).
"Army Warrant Class Photographs." Accessed June 5, 2019, https://www.vhpa.org/wocpics/classpics.htm.
"Artifact Spotlights." *Call to Duty: Newsletter of the National Campaign for the National Museum of the United States Army,* June 12, 2020.
Asprey, Robert B. *War in the Shadows: The Guerrilla in History, Volume I.* Garden City: Doubleday and Company, Inc., 1975.
_____. *War in the Shadows: The Guerrilla in History, Volume II.* Garden City: Doubleday and Company, Inc., 1975.
Atkins, Rick. *The British Are Coming: The War for America, Lexington to Princeton, 1775–1777.* New York: Henry Holt and Company, 2019.
Ault, Jon. "Native Americans in the Spanish American War." Accessed February 12, 2021, https://www.spanamwar.com/NativeAmericans.htm.
"Aviation." *Army 2019–2020 Green Book.* 69, no. 10, (2019).

Bahrampour, Tara. "A memorial on the Mall long fought for, 'long overdue.'" *The Washington Post*, Monday, January 15, 2018.

Bailey, Major General J.B.A. *Field Artillery and Firepower*. Annapolis: Naval Institute Press, 2004.

Barnes, Dr. Ian. *The Historical Atlas of Native Americans*. New York: Chartwell Books, 2017.

Barnes, James A., and Stratham, Flavous D. *Technical Memorandum 8–70, U.S. Army Primary Helicopter School Training Program Performance Norms*. Aberdeen Proving Groud: Human Engineering Laboratories, 1970.

Barnes, Robert. "High court still divided over prosecutions in Indian lands." *The Washington Post*, Thursday, April 28, 2022.

Bartholomew, Captain Charles A., and Milwee, Jr., Commander William I. *Mud, Muscle, and Miracles: Marine Salvage in the United States Navy*, Washington, D.C.: Naval History & Heritage Command, 2009.

Bartow, Lieutenant Colonel Dennis W. "Combat Loudspeakers: Weapons of the Battlefield Evangelists." Accessed February 21, 2022. Available from http://www.psywarrior.com/CombatLoudspeakers. html.

Bassett, Jenna. "Restricted Citizenship: The Struggle for Native American Voting Rights in Arizona." A Thesis Presented in Partial Fulfillment of the Requirements for the Degree Master of Arts, Arizona State University, Tempe, Arizona, December 2011.

"Battalion History: 57th Transportation Company. Accessed October 26, 2018," http://www.145thcab. com/History/NL14HIST.htm.

"Battalion History: 71st Transportation Battalion. Accessed September 28, 2019," https://transportation. army.mil/history/documents/71st%20Trans%20Bn.pdf.

"Battalion History: 93rd Transportation Company. Accessed October 24, 2018," http://www.145thcab. com/History/NL13HIST.htm.

Bear, Charla. "American Indian Boarding Schools Haunt Many." Accessed April 24, 2020, https://www. npr.org/templates/story/story.php?storyId=16516865.

"Bell H-13 Sioux." Accessed March 21, 2019, http://yellowlegs-and-others.com/Aircraft/Aircraft_ Details/Bell_H-13_Sioux_(HTL-3).html.

"Bell Helicopter News Information for OH-58 NETT." Accessed December 10, 2019, https://vhpa.org/ KIA/panel/battle/690627.HTM.

"Bell Helicopter OH-13D Sioux." Accessed March 20, 2019, https://cavflight.org/index. php?option=com_content&view=article&id=13&Itemid=130.

"Bell Helicopter OH-58A 'Kiowa'." Accessed December 10, 2019, https://www.skytamer.com/Bell_ OH-58A.html.

"Bell UH-1H Iroquois 'Huey' Smokey III." Accessed May 14, 2020, https://www.si.edu/object/nasm_ A19960005000.

"Bell UH-1M Iroquois Huey." Accessed August 19, 2020, https://www.combatairmuseum.org/aircraft/ bellhueyuh1m.html.

Bender, Albert. "Dragging Canoe's War." Accessed May 22, 2020, https://www.historynet.com/dragging-canoes-war.htm.

Bendickson, Sam interview with the author, 2020.

Bergman, Philip S. "Lebanon Report: Mobility Through Helicopters." *United States Army Aviation Digest*, 4, no. 11 (1958).

Berthrong, Donald J. "Struggle for Power: The Impact of Southern Cheyenne and Arapaho 'Schoolboys' on Tribal Politics." *American Indian Quarterly*, 16, no. 1 (1992): 1–24, https://doi. org/10.2307/1185602.

"BGM-71 TOW: XM-26 Huey Gunship." Accessed February 21, 2020. Available from https:// trendingnewscyberwarfare.blogspot.com/2016/02/bgm-71-tow-xm-26-huey-gunship. html.

Bittle, Jason. "NASA helicopter to take a spin on harsh, cold Mars." *The Washington Post*, February 15, 2021.

Block, Charlie. "Barrel Bombing: a CO's View." Accessed October 28, 2019, http://www.hmh-463-vietnam.com/reflections/yourstory.html#seventh%20story.

Bluhm, Raymond K., Jr. *U.S. Army: A Complete History*. Arlington: The Army Historical Foundation, 2004.

"Boeing: CH-47 Chinook." Accessed July 17, 2019, https://www.boeing.com/history/products/CH47-chinook.page.

"Boeing-Vertol CH-47A Chinook." Accessed June 4, 2019, https://www.helis.com/database/cn/41054/.

"Boeing-Vertol CH-47A Chinook." Accessed June 4, 2019, https://www.helis.com/database/cn/22847/.

"Boeing-Vertol CH-47A Chinook." Accessed June 4, 2019. Available from https://www.helis.com/database/cn/41055/.

"Boeing-Vertol CH-47A Chinook." Accessed June 4, 2019, https://www.helis.com/database/cn/41053/.

"Boeing-Vertol ACH-47A Guns-A-Go-Go." Accessed on June 4, 2019, https://www.helis.com/database/model/ACH-47A-Guns-A-Go-Go/.

Bolger, Major Daniel P. *Scenes from an Unfinished War: Low-Intensity Conflict in Korea 1966–1969*. Fort Leavenworth: Dane Publishing Company, 1991.

Bowers, David. Stephen interviews with the author, 2018–2019.

"Boxscore for 25th Infantry Division Shotgun Riders," *Honolulu Star-Bulletin*, February 9, 1966.

Boyne, Walter J. *How the Helicopter Changed Modern Warfare*. Gretna,: Pelican Publishing Company, Inc., 2011.

Brady, Patrick Henry with Smith, Meghan Brady. *Dead Men Flying: Victory in Viet Nam*. Washington, D.C.: WND Books, 2012.

Branch, Paul. "Confederate Expeditions Against New Bern." Accessed April 5, 2020, https://www.ncpedia.org/new-bern-confederate-expeditions-ag.

Brandt, Robert J., and Davies, William J. T*he Piasecki H-21 Helicopter: An Illustrated History of the H-21 Helicopter and Its Designer, Frank N. Piasecki*. Bloomington: Trafford Publishing Company, 2007.

_____. *Thunderbird Lounge-An aviator's story about one early Transportation Helicopter company, along with its sister companies as they paved the way in what was to become "A Helicopter War."* Victoria: Trafford Publishing Company, 2004.

Brewer, Jerry. "Now is the time for change." *The Washington Post,* July 3, 2020.

Britzky, Haley. "Here's why Army helicopters have Native American names." Accessed November 9, 2020, https://taskandpurpose.com/history/army-helicopters-native-american-names?mc_cid=945614d799&mc_eid=78974c86fb.

Brookes, Dan, and Hillerby, Bob. *Shooting Vietnam: The War by its Military Photographers*. Havertown: Pen and Swords Books, 2019.

Brooks, Rebecca Beatrice. "Native Americans in the Revolutionary War." Accessed July 28, 2019, https://historyofmassachusetts.org/native-americans-revolutionary-war/.

_____. "Who Fought in the French and Indian War." Accessed on December 27, 2018, http://historyofmassachusetts.org/who-fought-french-indian-war/.

Brown, David A. *The Bell Helicopter Textron Story: Changing the Way the World Flies*. Arlington: Aerorflax, Inc., 1995.

Brown, Dee Alexander. *Buy My Heart at Wounded Knee: An Indian History of the American West*. New York: Henry Holt and Company, 1970.

Brown, Shannon A. P*roviding the Means of War: Historical Perspectives on Defense Acquisition*.Washington, D.C.: Government Printing Office, 2005.

Brownlee, Romie L., and Mullen, John J. III. *Changing An Army: An Oral History of General William E. DePuy, USA Retired.* Washington, D.C.: United States Army Center of Military History, 1988.

Brunning, John R. "Operation Pershing: They Rode with Custer's Ghost." Accessed on May 31, 2019, https://theamericanwarrior.com/tag/operation-pershing/.

Burbidge, Bishop Michael F. "Statement for Veterans Day 2022." Accessed November 10, 2022, https://www.arlingtondiocese.org/bishop/public-messages/2022/bishop-burbidge-statement-for-veterans-day/.

Burns, Major John C. "XM-26 TOW: Birth of the Helicopter as a Tank Buster." Quantico: United States Marine Corps Command and Staff College, 1994.

Buser, Charles Aubrey. "Tarhe." Accessed on October 10, 2020, https://www.wyandotte-nation-com/culture/history/biographies/tarhe-grand-sachem/.

"Camp Holloway." Accessed October 26, 2018, http://my.core.com/~campholloway/unitsb1.html.

"CH-37 Mojave." Accessed September 1, 2019, https://www.globalsecurity.org/military/systems/aircraft/h-37.htm.

CH-54 Skycrane Association. Accessed February 8, 2019, http://www.ch54skycrane.com/.

Caen, Herb. "Monday-Go-Round." *San Francisco Chronicle*, November 19, 1961.

Calloway, Colin G. *The Shawnee and the War for America.* New York: Penguin Group, 2007.

Cameron, Marc. *Tom Clancy: Code of Honor.* New York: G. P. Putnam's Sons, 2019.

Camia, Major Dante A. "The Evolution of the Advanced Attack Helicopter." Thesis Master of Military Art and Science (MMAS), Fort Leavenworth: U.S. Army Command and General Staff College, 1975.

Camurat, Diane. *The American Indian in the Great War: Real and Imagined, Part Two.* "Chapter One: The Place of the American Indians in the Military in 1917." Accessed March 30, 2020, https://net.lib.byu.edu/~rdh7/wwi/comment/Cmrts/Cmrt5.html.

_____. *The American Indian in the Great War: Real and Imagined, Part Two.* "Chapter Two: American Indian Service in WW I." Accessed March 30, 2020, https://net.lib.byu.edu/~rdh7/wwi/comment/Cmrts/Cmrt6.html.

_____. *The American Indian in the Great War: Real and Imagined, Part Two.* "Chapter Three: American Indian Symbols in WW I." Accessed March 30, 2020, https://net.lib.byu.edu/~rdh7/wwi/comment/Cmrts/Cmrt7.html.

_____. *The American Indian in the Great War: Real and Imagined, Part Two,* "Chapter Four: Consequences of the War." Accessed March 30, 2020, https://net.lib.byu.edu/~rdh7/wwi/comment/Cmrts/Cmrt8.html.

Canada, Government of. "Foreign Enlistment Act." Accessed July 7, 2019, http://lois-laws.justice.gc.ca/eng/acts/F-28/FullText.html.

"Canadian Surface Combatant." Accessed April 21, 2020, https://www.canada.ca/en/department-national-defence/services/procurement/canadian-surface-combatant.html.

"Captain William J. Kossler, USCG Award." Accessed December 4, 2019, https://vtol.org/awards-and-contests/vertical-flight-society-award-winners?awardID=8.

Carpenter, Les. "Redskins' 'thorough review' of name is informal process guided by Snyder." *The Washington Post,* July 9, 2020.

Carson, James Taylor. *Searching for the Bright Path: The Mississippi Choctaws From Prehistory to Removal.* Lincoln: University of Nebraska Press, 2003.

Carter, Donald A. *Forging the Shield: The U. S. Army in Europe, 1951–1962.* Washington, D.C.: United States Army, Center of Military History, 2015.

_____. *The U.S. Army Before Vietnam 1953–1965.* Washington, D.C.: United States Army, Center of Military History, 1976.

Cavallaro, Gina. "He's The Army: NCO Comes Home, Honors His Warrior Culture." *Army,* 70, no. 5 (2020).

"Cayuse Indian Pony." Accessed June 16, 2019, http://www.equinekingdom.com/breeds/ponies/cayuse_indian_pony.htm.

"Cayuse Pony." Accessed June 16, 2019, https://www.horsebreedspictures.com/cayuse-pony.asp.

Chandler, CW4 James T. "And Then There Were None!" *United States Army Aviation Digest*, 1-94-4, (July/August 1994).

Chandler, Robert W. *War of Ideas: The U.S. Propaganda Campaign in Vietnam*. Boulder: Westview Press, 1981.

Chauvin, CWO Paul. "Here's a Closer Look into the Development of the Gas-Turbine Engine." *United States Army Aviation Digest*, 6, no. 2 (1960).

Chenoweth, Bob. *Warbirds Illustrated No. 47: Army Gunships in Vietnam*. London: Arms and Armour Press, Limited, 1987.

"Cheyenne." Accessed September 5, 2019, https://www.newworldencyclopedia.org/entry/Cheyenne.

"Chickasaw Nation." Accessed April 14, 2022, https://www.chickasaw.net/News/Press-Releases/Release/New-Book-Released-by-Chickasaw-Press-835.aspx.

"Cheyenne Tribe." Accessed September 5, 2019, https://indians.org/articles/cheyenne-tribe.html.

"Chickasaw Removal." Accessed on January 25, 2019, https://www.chickasaw.net/our-nation/history.aspx.

"Chickasaw Tribe." Accessed August 21, 2019, https://historyofmassachusetts.org/native-americans-revolutionary-war/.

"Chief Dragging Canoe." Accessed May 23, 2020, https://www.aaanativearts.com/Cherokee/dragging-canoe.htm.

"Chinook Indian Chiefs and Leaders." Accessed December 5, 2019, https://accessgenealogy.com/native/chinook-indian-chiefs-and-leaders.htm.

"Chinook Indians." Accessed December 5, 2019, http://www.bigorrin.org/archmn-chinook.htm.

"Chivington's Address on Sand Cree." *Denver Republican*, October 6, 1894.

"Choctaw Code Talkers of World War I." Accessed December 5, 2018, http://www.texasmilitaryforcesmuseum.org/choctaw/codetalkers.htm.

Choctaw Code Talkers. Accessed December 5, 2018, https://en.wikipedia.org/wiki/Choctaw_code_talkers.

"Choctaw History." Accessed November 10, 2019, http://www.choctaw.org/aboutMBCI/history/index.html.

"Choctaws Who Served in 1794." Accessed November 10, 2019, https://www.accessgenealogy.com/native/choctaws-who-served-in-1794.htm.

Christine, Captain S. L. "1st Combat Aerial TOW Team: Helicopter vs. Armor." *United States Army Aviation Digest*, 20, no. (1974).

Church, Wendy Ann. Interview with the author August 25, 2020.

Clarke, Liz. "FedEx to remove signage if Redskins don't change name." *The Washington Post*, July 11, 2020.

_____. "'End Racism,' the NFL has implored. So what about the name 'Chiefs'?" *The Washington Post*, February 6, 2021.

Cobb, Dr. Daniel M. *Native Peoples of North America*. Chantilly: The Great Courses, 2016.

"Code Talkers." Accessed December 5, 2018, https://www.choctawnation.com/history-culture/people/code-talkers.

Code Talkers Recognition Act of 2008, Pub. L. No. H.R. 4544, 31 USC 5111 (2008).

Coffelt Database of Vietnam War Casualties. Accessed February 12–14m 2022, https://www.coffeltdatabase.org/detreq2.php.

Cohen, Kate. "Indians mascots are out. The problem of cultural erasure remains." *The Washington Post*, November 23, 2022.

Collins, Charles D., Jr. *Atlas of the Sioux Wars*, Second Edition. Fort Leavenworth: Combat Studies Institute Press, October 2006.

Coleman, Louis. "Thirty-Sixth Infantry Division." Accessed March 15, 2020, https://www.okhistory.org/publications/enc/entry.php?entry=TH003.

Competent Authors and Artists, A Corps of. *Wildlife on the Plains and the Horrors of Indian Warfare*. New York: Arno Press, 1969.

Congressional Medal of Honor Society. Accessed April 11, 2020, http://www.cmohs.org/.

Converse III, Elliott Vanveltner. *History of Acquisition in the Department of Defense, Volume I: Rearming for the Cold War 1945–1960*. Washington, D.C.: Historical Office, Office of the Secretary of Defense, 2012.

Cooata, Jr, Russell. Collection (AFC/2001/001/83012). Veterans History Project, American Folklife Center, Library of Congress.

_____. Interview with the author January 10, 2020.

"Costs of War." Accessed November 20, 2022, U.S. Budgetary Costs of Post-9/11 Wars Through FY2022: $8 Trillion | Figures | Costs of War (brown.edu)

"Counting Coup." Accessed December 15, 2018, http://plainshumanities.unl.edu/encyclopedia/doc/egp.war.013.

"Counting Coup on the Plains and Overseas." Accessed December 15, 2018, https://centerofthewest.org/2016/07/21/counting-coup-on-the-plains-and-overseas/.

Crable, Major Jack. "Aircraft Recovery Using the Helicopter." *United States Army Aviation Digest*, 4, no. 10 (1958).

Crawford, Neta C. "The U.S. Budgetary Costs of the Post-9/11 Wars." *20 Years of War. A Costs of War Research Serie*s. Providence: Brown University, 2021.

Cullen, CWO Richard N. "Aircraft Availability of the Iroquois." *United States Army Aviation Digest*, 8, no. 9 (1960).

Cummings, Barbara. "Lakota Leaders Join Army to Welcome New Helicopter Fleet." *Army News Service*, February 20, 2008.

Davenport, Christian. "Launch firm helps revive NASA site." *The Washington Post*, October 3, 2020.

Debo, Angie. *A History of the Indians of the United States*. Norman: University of Oklahoma Press, 2008.

Deloria, Vine, Jr. and Lytle, Clifford M. *American Indians. American Justice*. Austin: University of Texas Press, 1983.

Del Vecchio, Specialist Four John. "The Tadpole and the Snake." *Rendezvous With Destiny*, 101st Airborne Division (Airmobile), (Winter/Spring 1971).

Department of the Army Pamphlet 70–3. "Research, Development, and Acquisition: Army Acquisition Procedures." Washington, D.C.: Headquarters Department of the Army, 2014.

Department of the Army Technical Manual TM-55-1520-206-10. *Operator's Manual Army Models OH-23D, OH-23F, and OH-23G Helicopters*. Washington, D.C.: Headquarters Department of the Army, 1965.

Department of Defense Directive 4120.15. "Designating and Naming Military Aerospace Vehicles." Washington, D.C.: Headquarters Department of Defense, 1985.

Department of Defense 4120.15-List. "Designation of Military Aerospace Vehicles." Washington, D.C.: Headquarters Department of Defense, 1987.

Department of Veterans Affairs. "Native American Medal of Honor Recipients: World War II and Korean War." Accessed April 11, 2020, https://www.va.gov/tribalgovernment/medal_of_honor_recipiants.asp.

DeStefano, Dan. E-mail to Donald Gatewood, August 7, 2012.

Devine, Vinny. "Sikorsky Product History: S-55." Accessed September 28, 2018, https://www.sikorskyarchives.com/S-55.php.

_____. "Sikorsky Product History: S-47." Accessed September 24, 2018, https://www.sikorskyarchives.com/S-47.php.

_____. "Sikorsky Product History: S-56/HR2S-1/H-37 Helicopter." Accessed September 1, 2019, https://www.sikorskyarchives.com/s+56%20HR2S-1H-37.php.

Dickerson, Katelyn. "A Tale of Two Birds." Accessed May 1, 2019, https://baldeagles.org/2017/06/04/a-tale-of-two-birds.

"Did you Know? Oneidas Declared War on Germany in 1918." Accessed March 28, 2020, https://www.oneidaindiannation.com/did-you-know-oneidas-declared-war-on-germany-in-1918.

Dierks, Jack Cameron. *A Leap to Arms: The Cuban Campaign of 1898*. New York: J.B. Lippincott Company, 1970.

Door, Robert F. "The First Helicopter Rescue: Where the special operations combat rescue mission began." Accessed September 17, 2018, https://www.defensemedianetwork.com/stories/first-helicopter-rescue/.

Dorland, Peter, and Nanney, James. *Dust Off: Army Aeromedical Evacuation In Vietnam*, Washington, D.C.: Center of Military History United States Army, 2008.

Dougherty, Major Kevin J. "The Evolution of Air Assault." *Joint Forces Quarterly*, Summer 1999.

Dougherty, Martin J. *Native American Warriors: The Legendary Tribes, Their Weapons, and Fighting Techniques*. London: Amber Books, Ltd., 2018.

Drew, Scott J., and Jones, John. "The CH-37 'Mojave' in Vietnam." Accessed September 28, 2019, https://www.nhpa.org/CH-37B.pdf.

Dunbar-Ortiz, Roxanne. *An Indigenous Peoples' History of the United States*. Beacon Press: Boston, 2014.

Duncan, Fred M. "Operation Ivory Soap." *The DUSTOFFer*, (Spring/Summer 2001).

"Dutch Springs." Accessed November 18, 2019, https://www.dutchsprings.com/scuba/.

Easterbrook, Brigadier General Ernest F. "The Increasing Requirements for Army Aviation Staff Officers." *United States Army Aviation Digest*, 4, no. 5 (1959).

Eckel, Paul E.. "SEATO: An Ailing Alliance." *World Affairs*, 134, no. 2 (Fall 1971).

Editors, History.com. "Sand Creek Massacre." Accessed April 18, 2019, https://www.history.com/this-day-in-history/sand-creek-massacre.

Edmunds, R. David. *The Shawnee Prophet*. Lincoln: University of Nebraska Press, 1985.

Edmunds, R. David, Hoxie, Frederick E., and Salisbury, Neal. *The People: A History of Native America*. Boston: Houghton Mifflin, 2007.

Edwards, J. D. "Last UH-1 Huey, a 42-year military veteran retires." Accessed October 12, 2019, https://www.army.mil/article/180593/last_uh_1_huey_a_42_year_military_veteran_retires.

Elliot, David W. P. *The Vietnamese War: Revolution and Social Change in the Mekong Delta 1930–1975*. New York: M.E. Sharp, 2007.

Ellis, Clyde. "Truly Dancing Their Own Way: Modern Revival and Diffusion of the Gourd Dance." *American Indian Quarterly*, 14, no. 1 (Winter 1990).

Ellis, Joseph J. *American Creation: Triumphs and Tragedies at the Founding of the Republic*. New York: Alfred A. Knopf, 2007.

Ellison, D. Hank. *Chemical Warfare During the Vietnam War: Riot Control Agents in Combat*, New York: Routledge, 2011.

Esposito, Colonel Vincent J., Chief Editor. *The West Point Atlas of American Wars*. New York: Frederick A. Praeger, 1959.

Epstein, Kayla, and Horton, Alex. "Soldiers could lose Medals of Honor from Wounded Knee." *The Washington Post,* December 2, 2019.

"Establishing Our Own." Accessed July 21, 2019, http://www.armyaviationmuseum.org/part-ii-establishing-our-own/.

Falcon, Major John D. *The Freedom Shield*. Havertown: Casemate Publishers, 2020.

Fall, Bernard B. *Vietnam Witness 1953–66*. New York: Frederick A. Praeger Publishers, 1968.

Fernandes, Melanie L. "Under the auspices of peace: The Northwest Indian War and its Impact of the Early American Republic." *The Gettysburg Historical Journal*, 15, Article 8 (2015).

"Firefly." *United States Army Aviation Digest*, 13, no. 11 (1967).

"First U.S. helicopter is shot down in Vietnam." Accessed August 18, 2019. Available from https://www.history.com/this-day-in-history/first-u-s-helicopter-is-shot-down-in-vietnam.

"First Navajo Helicopter Pilot." *Star-News*, March 24, 1971.

Fixico, Donald. "A Native Nations Perspective on the War of 1812." Accessed December 20, 2018, http://www.pbs.org/wned/war-of-1812/essays/native-nations-perspective/.

Flavin, Francis Ph.D. "Native Americans and American History." Accessed December 27, 2018, https://www.coursehero.com/file/22133704/native-americans/.

Fleck, Dieter, ed. *Handbook of the Law of Visiting Forces*. Oxford: Oxford University Press, 2001.

Fletcher, Matthew L. M. "A Short History of Indian Law in the Supreme Court." Accessed April 6, 2020, https://www.americanbar.org/groups/crsj/publications/human_rights_magazine_home/2014_vol_40/vol--40--no--1--tribal-sovereignty/short_history_of_indian_law/.

"Fort George National Historic Site." Accessed March 25, 2020, https://www.pc.gc.ca/en/lhn-nhs/on/fortgeorge/culture/fort-george.

"Fort Griffin and the Prairie-Plains Frontier: The Most Dangerous Prairie in Texas." Accessed December 17, 2019, https://texasbeyondhistory.net/forts/griffin/prairie.html.

"For Posterity's Sake: HMCS IROQUOIS G89 / 217." Accessed April 21, 2020, http://www.forposterityssake.ca/Navy/HMCS_IROQUOIS_G89_217.htm.

Fowler, Loretta. " Arapaho and Cheyenne Perspectives." *American Indian Quarterly*, 39, Issue 4 (2015), 364–390, https://www.proquest.com/docview/1717290976.

Franco, Jeré Dean. "Bring Them in Alive: Selective Service and Native Americans." *Journal of Ethnic Studies*, Volume 18, Issue 3 (Fall 1990).

Frank, Allen K.. "Trail of Tears." Accessed March 19, 2020, https://www.okhistory.org/publications/enc/entry.php?entry=TR003.

Frankum, Jr., Ronald B. and Maxner, Stephen F. *The Vietnam War for Dummies*. New York: Wiley Publishing, Inc., 2003.

Franson, Chuck. "Bolko Zimmer and the "White Elephants." *The DUSTOFFer*, Fall/Winter 2013.

Freeman, David. "White Elephants." *Delta Dustoff*. Accessed April 20, 2020, http://www.deltadustoff.com/Stories/WhiteElephants/tabid/86/Default.aspx.

Friedman, Sergeant Major Herbert A. "Loudspeakers at War." Accessed February 21, 2022, http://www.psywarrior.com/PSYOPLoudspeakers.html.

——————. "PSYOP Order of Battle,. Accessed February 22, 2022, http://www.psywarrior.com/vietnamOBPSYOP.

——————. "The Wandering Soul PSYOP Tape of Vietnam." Accessed February 25, 2022, http://www.psywarrior.com/wanderingsoul.html.

Gaffen, Fred. *Unknown Warriors: Canadians in the Vietnam War*. Toronto: Dundurn Press, 1990.

Gammond, Vance. "Hiller 360 / UH-12 / OH-23 1947," email. Accessed May 16, 2019, http://www.aviastar.org/helicopters_eng/hiller_oh-23.php.

Ganteaume, Cécile. *Officially Indian: Symbols That Define the United States*. Washington, D.C.: National Museum of the American Indian, 2017.

Gavin, James Maurice. "Cavalry, And I Don't Mean Horses." *Harpers*, April 1954.

"Geneva Accords of 1954." Accessed June 14, 2019, https://www.encyclopedia.com/history/dictionaries-thesauruses-pictures-and-press-releases/geneva-accords-1954.

George-Kanentiio, Doug, and Child, Brenda J. "The brutal legacy of Indian schools." *The Washington Post*, August 29, 2021.

"Geronimo—Why American Paratroopers Shout the Apache Chief's Name When Jumping." Accessed January 25, 2021, https://militaryhistorynow.com/2020/09/21/geronimo-why-american-paratroopers-shout-the-apache-chiefs-name-when-jumping/.

Gerry, David C. "Gas Turbine Powerplants For Helicopters." *United States Army Aviation Digest*, 5, no. 7 (1959).

Giap, General Vo Nguyen. B*ig Victory, Great Task, North Viet-Nam's Minister of Defense Assesses the Course of the War*. New York: Frederick A. Praeger, Publishers, 1968.

Gilbert, James L. T*he Most Secret War: Army Signals Intelligence in Vietnam*, Fort Belvoir: Military History Office, US Army Intelligence and Security Command, 2003

Gilbertson, Major Brian J. "The Native American: Warriors in the U.S. Military." The United States Marine Corps Command and Staff College, October 2011.

Glowen, Ronald P. "Timeline: Native Americans in the Inland Northwest: Wars and Treaties." Accessed 15, 2019, http://www.narhist.ewu.edu/Native_Americans/timelines/timeline_wars_treaties.html.

Gobetz, Wally. "Follow Colorado–Westminster: Chief Little Raven." Accessed April 18, 2019, https://www.flickr.com/photos/wallyg/8217880713.

Goebel, Greg. "The Sikorsky S-55, S-56 & S-58." Accessed January 9. 2019, http://www.airvectors.net/avs55.html#m1.

"Gold Mining in the Black Hills." Accessed September 8, 2019. Available from https://blackhillsvisitor.com/learn/gold-mining-in-the-black-hills/.

Goldsworthy, Ryan. "The Canadian Way: The Case of Canadian Vietnam War Veterans." Accessed July 7, 2019, http://www.journal.forces.gc.ca/vol15/no3/page48-eng.asp.

Gough, Lisa, editor. *Never Forget: The Story Behind The Vietnam Veterans Memorial*. Washington, D.C.: The Vietnam Veterans Memorial Fund, 2008.

Gover, Kevin. "Dear Dan Snyder: Don't pick a new native-inspired team name." *The Washington Post*, July 9, 2020.

Gowen, Annie. "Legal experts say landmark ruling could impact tribal disputes for decades." *The Washington Post*, July 11, 2020.

Green, Graham. "Low-Level Hell 1." Accessed October 24, 2018, http://www.werelords.com/lowlevelhell/pdf/vehicle_article_and_bibliogrpahy.pdf.

Green, Michael. *United States Military Helicopters: Rare Photographs From Wartime Archives*. Barnsley: Pen & Sword Aviation, 2017.

Green, Richard. "James Adair and the Chickasaws: Part II The Way of the Warriors." Accessed January 27, 2019, https://www.Chickasaw.net/Our-Nation/History/Historical-Articles/Culture/James-Adair-and-the-Chickasaws,-Part-II-The-Way-of-theWarriors.aspx.

Greer, Captain Curtis I., Jr. "Hurry! Send A Chopper!" *United States Army Aviation Digest*, 5, no. 10 (1959).

Gregory, Barry. V*ietnam Helicopter Handbook*. Wellingborough: Patrick Stephens, Ltd., 1988.

Griminger, Lieutenant Colonel Charles O. "The Armed Helicopter Story—Part I: The Origins." *United States Army Aviation Digest*, 17, no. 7 (1971).

_____. "The Armed Helicopter Story–Part II: Vanderpool's Fools." *United States Army Aviation Digest*, 17, no. 8 (1971).

_____. "The Armed Helicopter Story–Part III: Armed Helicopters Around the World." *United States Army Aviation Digest*, 17, no. 9 (1971).

_____. "The Armed Helicopter Story–Part IV: Weapon Systems (Early Experiments)." *United States Army Aviation Digest*, 17, no. 10 (1971).

_____. "The Armed Helicopter Story–Part V: Formal Development (Models XM-1 thru XM-50)." *United States Army Aviation Digest*, 17, no. 11 (1971).

_____. "The Armed Helicopter Story–Part VI: (Conclusion) (XM-51 thru GAU-2B/A)." *United States Army Aviation Digest*, 17, no. 12 (1971).

Grimsley, Mark and Rogers, Clifford J., eds. *Civilians in the Path of War*. Lincoln: University of Nebraska Press, 2002.

Gustin, Emmanuel. "Aircraft Nicknames." Accessed May 23, 2014, http://web.mit.edu/btyung/www/nickname.html.

"H-37 Mojave to be Modernized." *United States Army Aviation Digest*, 6, no 10 (1960).

Hagen, Dennis. "When the Sioux Ambushed Pawnee Hunters at 'Massacre Canyon.'" Accessed March 10, 2020, https://www.historynet.com/when-the-sioux-ambushed-pawnee-hunters-at-massacre-canyon.htm.

Haines, Francis. "The Northward Spread of Horses Among the Plains Indians." Accessed June 15, 2019, https://anthrosource.onlinelibrary.wiley.com/doi/pdf/10.1525/aa.1938.40.3.02a00060.

Hamlin, Fred, Miller, Fred, and Thayer, Eleanor, eds. *The Aircraft Year Book 1956*. Washington, D.C.: Lincoln Press, Inc., 1956.

Hansen, Terri. "How the Iroquois Great Law of Peace Shaped U.S. Democracy." Accessed July 27, 2019, https://www.pbs.org/native-america/blogs/native-voices/how-the-iroquois-great-law-of-peace-shaped-us-democracy/?fbclid=IwAR0KQyHXSYFRPJQLpYkeec loK_ OEej HTH5JNXhtBgeVfol_BYYYQUgMOIo.

Hanser, Kathleen. "In Good Company: Storied career of helicopter pioneer Frank Piasecki honored by the National Aviation Hall of Fame." *Boeing Frontiers Online*, 1, Issue 04 (2002), https://www.boeing.com/news/frontiers/archive/2002/august/i_people2.html.

Harber, Major B. D. *Logistical Support of Airmobile Operations, Republic of Vietnam (1961–1971)*. St. Louis: U.S. Army Aviation Command, 1971.

Harding, Stephen. *U. S. Army Aircraft Since 1947—An Illustrated Reference*. Atglen: Schiffer Publishing, Ltd., 1997.

Harris, Alexandra N., and Hirsch, Mark G. *Why We Serve: Native Americans in the United States Armed Forces*. Washington, D.C.: Smithsonian Institution National Museum of the American Indian, 2020.

Hastings, Max. *Vietnam: An Epic Tragedy, 1945–1975*. New York: HarperCollins Publishers, 2018.

Hauptman, Laurence M. "Army Logic: The Tuscarora Company in the Civil War." Accessed March 30, 2020, https://www.americanindianmagazine.org/story/army-logic-tuscarora-company-civil-war.

_____. "On The Western Front: Two Iroquois Nurses in World War I." *American Indian Magazine*, 19, No. 3 (2018), https://www.americanindianmagazine.org/story/western-front-two-iroquois-nurses-world-wari.

_____. *The Iroquois in the Civil War: From Battlefield to Reservation*. Syracuse, New York: Syracuse University Press, 1991.

Hay, Lieutenant General John Hancock, Jr.. *Vietnam Studies: Tactical and Materiel Innovations*. Washington, D.C.: Department of the Army, 1974.

Head, William Pace. *Storms Over the Mekong: Major Battles of the Vietnam War*. College Station: Texas A & M University Press, 2020.

Headquarters Fort Lewis, Fort Lewis, Washington, Movement Order #3, November 8, 1961.

Hedgpath, Dana. "A powerful dedication." *The Washington Post*, November 15, 2022.

_____. "Little-known stories of 6 Native Americans who served in the U.S. Military." *The Washington Post*, April 1, 2019.

_____. "Native American vets to get memorial." *The Washington Post*, April 1, 2019.

_____. "Recognition sought at Indian museum's veteran memorial." *The Washington Post*, April 25, 2021.

Heim, Joe. "Just Asking: Kevin Gover, Director of the American Indian Museum." *The Washington Post*, November 27, 2016.

"Helicopter or Incident 55-00627." Vietnam Helicopter Pilots Association. Accessed December 2, 2019, https://www.vhpa.org/.

"Helicopter or Incident 56-02084." Accessed August 25, 2019, file:///C:/Users/dsn19/Downloads/TEMP%20(4).HTM.

Helicopter Primary Flight Training Manual. Fort Wolters: U.S. Army Primary Helicopter School, 1968.

Helling, Thomas S.. *The Agony of Heroes: Medical Care for America's Besieged Legions from Bataan to Khe Sanh.* Yardley: Westholme Publishing, 2019.

Heinl, Robert Debs, Jr. *Soldiers of the Sea, The United States Marine Corps, 1775–1962.* Annapolis: U.S. Naval Institute, 1962.

"Her Majesty's Canadian Ship Haida." Accessed April 21, 2020, https://www.veterans.gc.ca/eng/remembrance/memorials/national-inventory-canadian-memorials/details/6739.

Higginbotham, Don., *The War of American Independence.* New York: The Macmillan Company, 1971.

Higgins, Tucker, and Mangan, Dan. "Supreme Court says eastern half of Oklahoma is Native American land." Accessed July 9, 2020, https: www.cnbc.com/2020/07/09/supreme-court- says-eastern-hoal-of-oklahoma-is-native-american-land.html.

"High Times." Accessed December 28, 2019, https://www.verticalmag.com/features/high-times-html/.

Hines, Leslie. Interview with the author, 2020.

Hirschberg, Michael J. "Briefing: An Overview of the History of Vertical and/or Short Take-Off and Landing (V/STOL) Aircraft." CENTRA Technology, Inc.

"Historical Snapshot: AH-64 Apache Attack Helicopter." Accessed September 3, 2019, https://www.boeing.com/history/products/ah-64-apache.page.

"History of Bell OH-58A Kiowa Helicopter." Accessed January 4, 2020, https://www.webcitation.org/5JR03L9GJ?url=http%3A%2F%2Fwww.161recceflt.org.au%2FUnitAircraft%2FKiowa%2Fhistory_of_bell_oh58.htm.

"History of the 8th Transportation Company." Accessed October 23, 2018, http://www.transportation.army.mil/history/documents/8th%20Trans%20Co.pdf.

"Hitting the Silk—15 Airborne Operations Carrier Out Since World War Two." Accessed February 20, 2020, https://www.militaryhistorynow.com.

"HMCS *Haida* Tribal Class Destroyer, Royal Canadian Navy." Accessed April 21, 2020, https://www.navyhistory.org.au/members-area-content/ahoy/hmcs-haida-tribal-class-destroyer-royal-canadian-navy/.

"HMCS MICMAC (R10 / 214)." Accessed April 21, 2020, https://www.facebook.com/CanadianNavyFans/photos/hmcs-micmac-r10-214hmcs-micmac-pennants-r10-and-214-was-a-tribal-class-destroyer/858891127474275/.

"HMH-463—History: Vietnam War." Accessed October 28, 2019, https://www.wikiwand.com/en/HMH-463.

"Ho Chi Minh Trail." Accessed July 26, 2020, https://u-s history.com/pages/h1875.html.

Holley, Charles, and Sloniker, Mike. *Primer on the Helicopter War.* Grapevine. Texas: Nissi Publishing, 1997.

Holm, Tom. "Forgotten Warriors: American Indian Servicemen in Vietnam." *Vietnam Generation*, 1, no. 2, Article 6. Accessed April 12, 2020, https://digitalcommons.lasalle.edu/cgi/viewcontent.cgi?article=1016&context=vietnamgeneration

——————. *Strong Hearty, Wounded Soldiers: Native American Veterans of the Vietnam War.* Austin: University of Texas Press, 1996.

——————. "The National Survey of Indian Vietnam Veterans." *Report of the Working Group on American Indian Vietnam Era Veterans*, Department of Veterans Affairs, May 1992.

Hoppe, Jon. "The Attack on the USNS *Card*." Accessed April 21, 2020, https://www.navalhistory.org/2015/10/07/the-attack-on-the-usns-card.

"How Are Sikorsky Helicopters Named?" *Sikorsky Archives News*, July 2016.

"How Native Americans Code Talkers Pioneered A New Type of Military Intelligence." Accessed October 26, 2022, https://www.history.com/news/world-war-is-native-american-code-talkers.

Howze, Major General Hamilton H. "The Last Three Years of Army Aviation." *United States Army Aviation Digest*, 4, no. 3 (1958).

Howze, Lieutenant General Hamilton H.. "U.S. Army Tactical Mobility Requirements Review Board, Final Report, Brief by The President Of The Board." Fort Bragg, 20 August 1962.

Howze, General Hamilton H., USA (Ret.). "An Appraisal of Army Aviation in Vietnam." *Army Aviation*, 15, no. 11 (1966).

Hoxie, Frederick E. *Encyclopedia of North American Indians: Native American History, Culture, and Life from Paleo-Indians to the Present*. Boston: Houghton Mifflin Harcourt, 1996.

Hoxie, Frederick and Iverson, Peter. *Indians in American History*. Hoboken: John Wiley and Sons, 2014.

Hughes, Dr. Kaylene Hughes. "Army Helicopters in Korea, 1950 to '53." Accessed January 23, 2019, https://www.army.mil/article/177302/army_helicopters_in_korea_1950_to_53.

——————. "U.S. Army Air-to-Ground (ATG) Missiles in Vietnam." Accessed February 21, 2020, https://www.army.mil/article/181893/us_army_air_to_ground_atg_missiles_vietnam.

Huston, James L. "Civil War Era." Accessed March 19, 2020, https://www.okhistory.org/publications/enc/entry.php?entryname=CIVIL%20WAR%20ERA.

Hyslop, Stephen G. *The Old West*. Washington, D.C.: National Geographic, 2015.

Iati, Marisa. "Native American tribe once forced to move by U.S. is getting some land back." *The Washington Post*, September 21, 2019.

"In flight on Sky Route 66 and the first in-flight refueling of a helicopter." Accessed March 19, 2020, https://sobchak.wordpress.com/2012/06/21/in-volo-sulla-sky-route-66-e-il-primo-rifornimento-in-volo-di-un-elicottero/.

"In Vietnam, These Helicopter Scouts Saw Combat Up Close—Cobras and Loaches, two vastly different aircraft, relied on each other to fight the enemy." Accessed March 14, 2019, https://www.airspacemag.com/military-aviation/snakes-loaches-180964341/.

"Iroquois battle Fellow Iroquois on the Niagara Frontier During the War of 1812." Accessed March 22, 2020, https://www.historynet.com/iroquois-battle-fellow-iroquois-on-the-niagara-frontier-during-the-war-of-1812.htm.

"Iroquois Class Air Defence Destroyers." Accessed April 21, 2020, https://www.naval-technology.com/projects/iroquoisclassairdefe/.

Jacobson, Lee, and Daniel, John. "S-55 Firsts." *Sikorsky Archives News*, July 2006.

Jaggers, Major James N. Jr.. "HueyCobra—Poised to Strike." 225011102 Douglas Pike Collection: Unit 03–Technology, The Vietnam Center & Sam Johnson Vietnam Archive, Texas Tech University.

James, Darryl. *Phoenix 13: Americal Division Artillery Air Section Helicopters in Vietnam*. Havertown: Pen & Sword Books, 2020.

Jenerette, Major Vandon E. "The Forgotten DMZ." *Military Review*, LXVIII, May 1988.

Jenkins, Sally. "Good riddance to all mascots that turn real people into props." *The Washington Post*, December 15, 2020.

Jevec, Adam and Lee Ann Potter. "Memorandum re the Enlistment of Navajo Indians." *Social Education* 65, 5 (September 2001).

Jones, Bob. "Schofield Shotgun Project Stopped." *The Honolulu Adviser*, November 12, 1965.

——————. "Shotgunners Training for Viet Duty." *The Honolulu Advertiser*, May 1, 1965.

——————. "3 Schofield GIs Killed, 59 Hunt "Riding Shotgun'." *The Honolulu Advertiser*, December 30, 1964.

Jones, Thomas A. "Operation Shotgun"—The 25th Infantry Division Association. Accessed November 19, 2019, https://www.1-14th.com/Vietnam/Misc/Operation_Shotgun.html.

Jordan, Julia A. "Interview of Jess Rowlodge (Arapaho)." Accessed April 18, 2019, http://amertribes.proboards.com/thread/2302/little-raven-family.

Josephy, Alvin M., Jr. *500 Nations*. New York: Alfred A. Knopf, 1994.

Judson, Jen. "Sikorsky challenges U.S. Army helicopter award." Accessed December 29, 2022, https://www.defensenews.com/industry/2022/12/28/lockheed-challenges-us-armys-helicopter-award/#:~:text=WASHINGTON%20%E2%80%94%20Sikorsky%20has%20filed%20a,helicopter%20procurement%20in%2040%20years .

Karnow, Stanley A. *Vietnam: A History*. New York: Penguin Books, 1984.

Kennicott, Philip. "A Tribute to Native American Veterans." *The Washington Post,* January 3, 2021.

Kilgore, Adam and Allen, Scott. "Sudden end of 'Redskins' was decades in the making." *The Washington Post,* July 14, 2020.

Kilgore, Adam and Stubbs, Roman. "Renaming Redskins may sway other teams." *The Washington Post,* July 12, 2020.

"Kiowa." Accessed December 13, 2019, https://spartacus-educational.com/WWkiowa.htm.

Knight, Colonel Emmett F. *First in Vietnam: An Exercise in Excess of 30 Days, The U.S. Army 57th Transportation Helicopter Company (Light Helicopter) (CH-21) 1961–1962*. Williamsburg: A15 Publishing Company, LLC, 2017.

—————————. *The 57th Transportation Company Light Helicopter, The 98th Transportation Detachment (CHFM), and The CH-21C Shawnee: A scrapbook prepared for the June 1987 reunion at Ft. Rucker, Alabama*. The Boeing Vertol Company, 1987.

Koch, J.A. "The Chieu Hoi Program in Vietnam, 1963–1971." Rand Corporation, January 1973.

Kosmidis, Pierre. "5,086: Number of Helicopters Destroyed During the Vietnam War." Accessed January 15, 2020, http://www.ww2wrecks.com/portfolio/5086-helicopter-losses-during-the-vietnam-war/.

Kraus, Charles. "21 Newly Translated Soviet Documents on North Korea, 1968–1969." Accessed May 14, 2019, https://www.wilsoncenter.org/blog-post/21-newly-translated-soviet-documents-north-korea-1968-1969.

Kreisher, Otto. "The Rise of the Helicopter During the Korean War." Accessed August 25, 2018, www.historynet.com/The-rise-of-the-helicopter-during-the-Korean-War.htm.

L, Ralph. "War Machine: Top Aircraft of the Korean War." Accessed January 24, 2019, https://militarymachine.com/korean-war-aircraft/.

Lacdan, Joe. "Army awards contract to develop future vertical lift capability." Accessed December 29, 2022, https://www.army.mil/article/262755/army_awards_contract_to_develop_future_vertical_lift_capability.

Lair, Meredith H. "The Education Center at the Wall and the Rewriting of History." *The Public Historian*, 34, no. 1 (2012).

"Lakota History and Ancestry." Accessed September 5, 2019, https://www.lakotamall.com/history-and-ancestry/.

Lane, Lieutenant Commander David A. "Hospital Ship Doctrine in the United States Navy: The HalseyEffect on Scoop-and-Sail Tactics." *Military Medicine*, 162, 1997.

Labaree, Leonard W., ed. *The Papers of Benjamin Franklin*, volume 5, July 1, 1753, through March 31, 1755. New Haven: Yale University Press, 1962.

Lark, Lisa A. *All They Left Behind: Legacies of the Men and Women on The Wall*. Evansville: M.T. Publishing Company, Inc., 2012.

Law, Mike. Interview with the author, 2020.

Leach, Lieutenant Colonel Bertram G. "Viet Nam 1962–63: 93rd Transport (Light Cargo Helicopter)." Accessed May 30, 2019, https://www.vietnam.ttu.edu/reports/images.php?img=/images/1984/19840102001.pdf.

"Legendary Pilot Observes Final Mission of OH-58 Helicopter." *Fort Polk Guardian*. Accessed January 4, 2020, https://www.thetowntalk.com/story/news/local/2015/05/04/legendary-pilot-observes-final-mission-oh-helicopter/26888113.

"OH-58A." Accessed October 28, 2019, https://mapsairmuseum.org/bell-oh-58a- kiowa/.

"OH-58C Kiowa Helicopter." Accessed December 28, 2019, http://www.vietnamhelicopters.ord/ oh-58c-kiowa/.

"Oneida Chiefs Declare War Against Hums." Accessed March 28, 2020, https://www.oneidaindiannation. com/wo-content/uploads/2017/04/WWI-Clip-copy-2.jpg.

"Operation Amigos." *United States Army Aviation Digest*, 6, no. 8, (1960).

"Operation Shotgun." Accessed November 19, 2019, https://www.1-14th.com/Vietnam/Misc/ Operation_Shotgun.html.

"Operation Shotgun—1965." Accessed November 19, 2019, https://www.centaursinvietnam.org/ WarStories/WarDiscussion/D_OperationShotgun.html.

"Operation Starlite." Accessed October 17, 2019, http://www.operationstarlite.com/history.html.

"Operation Wandering Soul—Ghost Tape Number 10 and the Haunting Jungles of Vietnam." Accessed February 26, 2022, https://militaryhistorynow.com/2013/10/30/trick-or-treat-the-strange- tale-of-ghost-tape-no-10/.

Osborn, Kris, and Lin, Ho. "The Operation That Took Out Osama Bin Laden." Accessed August 15, 2019, https://www.military.com/history/osama-bin-laden-operation-neptune-spear.

Ostick, Charlie. "The Huey." Accessed May 13, 2020, https://www.vhpa.org/stories/huep.pdf.

_____. "UTT in '62 and '62." Accessed May 29, 2020, https://www.vhpa.org/stories/ UTT62-63.pdf.

Ostler, Jeffrey. *The Plains Sioux and U.S. Colonialism from Lewis and Clark to Wounded Knee*. Cambridge: Cambridge University Press, 2004.

_____. *The Lakotas and the Black Hills*. New York: Penguin Books, 2019.

Oswalt, Lieutenant Colonel John W. "Report of the "Rogers" Board." *United States Army Aviation Digest*, 7, no. 2 (1961).

Oswalt, Wendall H. *This Land Was Their: A Study of North American Indians*. Houston: Mayfield Publishing Company, 1999.

Ott, Major General David Ewing. *Vietnam Studies: Field Artillery, 1954–1973*. Washington, D.C.: Department of the Army, 1995.

"Our History." Accessed January 24, 2019, https://www.chickasaw.net/our-nation/history.aspx.

Paone, Thomas. "Plans for the Little Know Confederate Helicopter." Accessed March 6, 2021, https:// airandspace.si.edu/stories/editorial/plans-little-known-confederate-helicopter.

"Part III in the Helicopter Warfare Series: The AH-1 Cobra Gunship in Vietnam." Accessed February 8, 2020, https://vietnam-war-history.com/post/helicopter-warfare/bell-ah-1-cobra-the-first- helicopter-gunship.

Pate, James P. "Oklahoma History: Chickasaw." Accessed January 24, 2019, https://www.okhistory/ publications/enc/entry.php?entry=CH033.

Pearson, Lieutenant General Willard. *Vietnam Studies The War in the Northern Provinces 1966–1968*. Washington, D.C.: Army Center for Military History, 1975.

Pepi, Lou. *"My Brothers Have My Back."* Jefferson: McFarland & Company, Inc., Publishers, 2018.

Perdue, Theda and Green, Michael D. *North American Indians: A very short introduction*. New York: Oxford University Press, 2011.

"Permanent Indian Frontier." Accessed September 16, 2019, https://www.nps.gov/fosc/learn/ historyculture/pif.htm.

Pfau, Nathan. "AH-56 Cheyenne Still an Aircraft Way Ahead of Its Time." Accessed August 27, 2019, https://www.army.mil/article/206181/ah_56_cheyenne_still_an_aircraft_way_ahead_of_its_ time.

"Phips Bounty Proclamation." Accessed July 8, 2020, https://upstanderproject.org/firslight/phips.

Piasecki, Eugene G. "Second Helicopter Detachment At Chang-to." Accessed October 27, 2022, https:// arsof-history.org/articles/v6n1_ghq_raiders_sb_helicopter.html.

Pierron, G. Joseph. "Little Raven: South Arapahoe Chief." Accessed April 18, 2019, https://www.kshs.org/kansapedia/little-raven/17642.

Poole, Robert M. *On Hallowed Ground: The Story of Arlington National Cemetery.* New York: Walker & Company, 2009.

Pope, Cassie. "6 Facts About the Huey Helicopter." Accessed January 20, 2020, https://www.historyhit.com/facts-huey-helicopter/.

Porter, Donald. "In Vietnam, These Helicopter Scouts Saw Combat Up Close: Cobras and Loaches." *Air & Space Magazine*, September 2017, https://www.airspacemag.com/military-aviation/snakes-loaches-180964341/.

Powell, William H. "Soldier or Granger?" *United Service, a Monthly Review of Military and Naval Affairs*, 2, (November 1889).

_____. "The Indian as a Soldier." *United Service, a Monthly Review of Military and Naval Affairs*, 3, (November 1889).

"Presidential Proclamation, 21 December 1814." *Founders Online.* National Archives, last modified June 13, 2018, http://founders.archives.gov/documents/Madison/03-08-02-0389. [Original source: *The Papers of James Madison*, Presidential Series, vol. 8, July 1814–18 February 1815 and supplement December 1779–18 April 1814, ed. Angela Kreider, J. C. A. Stagg, Mary Parke Johnson, Anne Mandeville Colony, and Katherine E. Harbury. Charlottesville: University of Virginia Press, 2015, pp. 455–461.]

"Prisoner of War Record—"Herman Hofstatter." Compiled by P.O.W. Network. Accessed May 14, 2019, https://www.pownetwork.org/bios/h/hx02.htm.

Prime, John Andrew. "Crew Fights to Remember Shipmates." *Military Officer*, March 2019.

Pullum, Ignacio. "The UH-1 Iroquois "Huey" Helicopter." Accessed March 1, 2020, https://warfarehistorynetwork.com/2016/09/19/the-uh-1-iroquois-huey-helicopter/.

"RAH-66 Comanche." Accessed September 2, 2019, https://fas.org/man/dod-101/sys/ac/rah-66.htm.

"Ravens in Native American Culture." Accessed April 28, 2019, www.avesnoir.com/ravens-in-native-american-culture/.

Rawnsley, Adam. "The Pentagon Deployed Scent Warfare in Vietnam." Accessed September 8, 2021, https://warisboring.com/the-pentagon-deployed-scent-warfare-in-vietnam/#:~:text=The%20Pentagon%20Deployed%20Scent%20Warfare%20in%20Vietnam%20Electronic,basic%20requirement%20of%20any%20war%E2%80%94merely%20finding%20the%20enemy.

Red River War of 1874–1875: Clash of Cultures in the Texas Panhandle. Austin, Texas: Texas Historical Commission.

"Redstone Arsenal Historical Information: TOW System Chronology." Accessed February 21, 2020, https://history.redstone.army.mil/miss-tow.html.

"Report on the Reorganization of the Department of the Army." Department of the Army, Washington, D.C., December 1961.

Rickert, Levi. "Ground Broken for the Native American Veterans Memorial on National Mall in Nation's Capital." Accessed September 22, 2019, http://nativenewsonline.net/currents/ground-broken-for-the-native-american-veterans-memorial-on-national-mall-in-nations-capital/.

"Riding Shotgun on a Huey—1966." Accessed November 20, 2019, https://www.guns.com/news/2018/12/riding-shotgun-on-a-huey-1966-army-training-film-on-door-gunners-video.

Robinson, Gary, and Lucas, Phil. *From Warriors to Soldiers.* Bloomington: iUniverse, Inc., 2009.

"Rocket Armed Helicopter October 1962–January 1964, Vietnam." Three year yearbook of the UTT Helicopter Company and the 571st Transportation Detachment (Aircraft Maintenance).

Sink, Colonel R. F. "Memorandum to Soldiers of the 506th Parachute Infantry." Fort Benning, Georgia, December 18, 1942.

Sleeper-Smith, Susan, Barr, Juliana, O'Brien Jean M., and Shoemaker, Nancy. *Why You Can't Teach United States History Without American Indians.* Chapel Hill: University of North Carolina Press, 2015.

"Small Arms Survey Research Notes: Recoilless Rifles." *Small Arms Survey,* Research Note 55, December 2015. Geneva, Switzerland.

Smith, CW2 Bobby D. "Let Us Not Give Up the Flare." *United States Army Aviation Digest,* 15, no. 2 (1969).

Smith, Charles R. "Plane Crashes in Hong Kong Harbor, 58 Marines Killed." *Dunkirk Observer,* August 24, 1965.

Smith, Ryan P. "This Innovative Memorial Will Soon Honor Native American Veterans." Accessed September 18, 2019, https://www.smithsonianmag.com/smithsonian-institution/this-innovative-memorial-soon-honor-native-american-veterans-180969060/#hiSCvj9LCbZsXwkK.99.

Smithers, Gregory D. *Native Southerners: Indigenous History from Origins to Removal.* Norman: University of Oklahoma Press, 2019.

"Smoke Ship Mission." Accessed February 21, 2020, https://www.si.edu/object/nasm_A19960005000.

Sotham, John. "Huey—If you remember Vietnam, you remember the Bell UH-1." Accessed January 19, 2020. Available from https://www.airspacemag.com/military-aviation/huey-1023487/?all.

"Spain declares war against Great Britain." Accessed August 21, 2019, https://www.history.com/this-day-in-history/spain-declares-war-against-great-britain.

Spector, Ronald H. *United States Army in Vietnam—Advice and Support: The Early Years 1941–1960.* Washington, D.C.: United States Army Center of Military History, 1985.

Spencer, J.P. "Whirlybirds: a history of the U.S. Helicopter Pioneers: Hiller X-2-235." Accessed on May 10, 2019, http://www.aviastar.org/helicopters_eng/hiller_x-2-235.php.

"Spur's OH-58 Kiowa Still Flying!" Accessed January 8, 2020, http://northwestvets.com/spurs/68-16935.htm.

"Stanley Hiller, Jr." *Memorial Tributes.* National Academy of Engineering, 12 (2008), 10.17226/12473.

Stansell, Specialist Four. "Mojave Finale." *United States Army Aviation Digest,* 17, no. 2 (1971).

Stanton, Shelby L. *Green Berets at War: U.S. Army Special Forces in Southeast Asia, 1965–1975.* New York: Ivy Books, 1985.

Starry, Don A. *Armored Combat in Vietnam.* North Stratford: Avro Press, 1980.

"Statistics of the Vietnam War." Accessed November 5, 2020, https://vhfn.org/stat.html.

Steven Albert Collection (AFC/2001/001/66796). Veterans History Project. American Folklore Center, Library of Congress.

Stevens, Richard L. *The Trail: A History of the Ho Chi Minh Trail and the Role of Nature in the War in Viet Nam.* New York: Garland Publishing, Inc., 1993.

Stewart, Richard W., ed. *American Military History, Volume 1, The United States Army and the Forging of a Nation, 1775–1917.* Washington, D.C.: U.S. Army Center of Military History, 2005.

Stilwell, Blake. "Why Native American nations declared war on Germany twice." Accessed April 6, 2020, https://www.wearethemighty.com/history/native-americans-twice-war-germany?rebelltitem=1#rebelltitem1.

Stocfisch, Dr. Jacob A. "The 1962 Howze Board and Army Combat Developments." Santa Monica, California: The RAND Arroyo Center, 1994.

"Story of the Peacemaker." Accessed September 27, 2020, https://i36466.wixsite.com/learninglonghouse/peacemaker#:~:text=It%2)was%20a%20terrible%20time,a%20Seneca%20woman%20named20Jigonsaseh.

Stubbs, Roman. "As Redskins review name, Native American groups feel left out." *The Washington Post*, July 8, 2020.

"Study Notes—Native Americans and the U.S. Military." Accessed December 28, 2018, http://www.users.miamioh.edu/johnso58/246SNmilitary.html.

Sultzman, Lee. "Chickasaw History." Accessed January 25, 2019, http://www.tolatsga.org/chick.html.

Summers, Colonel Harry G., Jr. *On Strategy: The Vietnam War in Context*. Carlisle Barracks: Strategic Studies Institute, U.S. Army War College, 1981.

"Sweet Thing Joins Brigade." *Hawk Magazine*, 1, no. 1 (1967).

Swopes, Bryan R. "This day in Aviation—Sikorsky CH-19 Chickasaw Archives." Accessed October 31, 2018, https://www.thisdayinaviation.com/tag/sikorsky-ch-19-chickasaw/.

Syllabus, Maine Community Health Options *v*. United States, Washington, D.C.: Supreme Court of the United States, April 27, 2020.

Tate, Cassandra. "Cayuse Indians." Accessed June 12, 2019, https://www.historylink.org/File/10365.

Taylor, John W.R. ed. *Jane's All The World's Aircraft: 1975–1976*. New York: Franklin Watts Inc., 1976.

Taylor, William Alexander. *Centennial History of Columbus and Franklin County, Ohio*. Chicago: S.J. Clarke Publishing Company, 1909.

Telford, Taylor. "Cherokee Nation asks Jeep to rename vehicles." *The Washington Post*, February 23, 2021.

"The AH-1 Cobra Gunship in Vietnam." Part 3 in the *Helicopter Warfare Series*. Accessed June 8, 2019, https://vietnam-war-history.com/post/helicopter-warfare/bell-ah-1-cobra-the-first-helicopter-gunship.

"The Arapaho Arrive: Two Nations on One Reservation." Accessed September 9, 2019, https://www.wyohistory.org/encyclopedia/arapaho-arrive-two-nations-one-reservation.

"The Attack on the USNS Card (T-AKV-40)." Accessed April 23, 2020, https://www.navalhistory.org/2015/10/07/the-attack-on-the-usns-card.

"The Canadian Contribution—The Korean War." Accessed September 27, 2020, https://www.veterans.gc.ca/eng/remembrance/those-who-served/indigenous-veterans/native-soldiers/korea_response.

"The Cayuse Indian War." Accessed June 14, 2019, https://nativeamericannetroots.net/diary/839.

"The Choctaw Nation of Oklahoma." Accessed November 10, 2019, https://sde.ok.gov/sites/ok.gov.sde/files/documents/files/Tribes_of_OK_Education%20Guide_Choctaw_Nation.pdf.

"The Combat Development and Research and Development Systems of the Army," *United States Army Aviation Digest*, 6, no. 3 (1960).

"The Confederated Tribes of the Umatilla Indian Reservation." Accessed June 15, 2019, https://www.critfc.org/member_tribes_overview/the-confederated-tribes-of-the-umatilla-indian-reservation/.

"The Flying Crane." *United States Army Aviation Digest*, 5, no. 11 (1959).

"The Hawk's Claw: The Aerial TOW System." Accessed February 21, 2020, https://www.thebattleofkontum.com/claw.html.

"The Kiowa Tribe." Accessed December 17, 2019, https://www.warpaths2peacepipes.com/indian-tribes/kiowa-tribe.htm.

"The Navajo Code Talkers." Accessed December 20, 2021, https://p47millville.org/?s=navajo+code+talkers.

The People of the River." Accessed November 12, 2019, https://www.fortmojaveindiantribe.com/about-us/.

"The Reservation System." Accessed October 26, 2022, https://www.khanacademy.org/humanities/us-history/the-gilded-age/american-west/a/the-reservation-system.

The Statutes At Large of the United States of America From April 1917 to March 1919, Volume XL, Sixty-Fifth Congress, Session I, H.R. 3545, May 18, 1917, Chapter 15, Section 5.

Theriault, Kim Servant. "Re-membering Vietnam: War, Trauma, and 'Scarring Over' After 'The Wall'." *The Journal of American Culture*, 26, no. 4 (2003).

"The Umatilla Indian Tribe." Accessed June 15, 2019, https://www.u-s-history.com/pages/h1540.html.

"This Day in History-April 06: Black Hawk War Begins." Accessed September 3, 2019, https://www.history.com/this-day-in-history/black-hawk-war-begins.

"This Day in History: June 2, 1924." The Indian Citizenship Act. Accessed December 5, 2018, https://www.history.com/this-day-in-history/the-indian-citizenship-act.

"This Day in Aviation: 8 December 1962." Accessed November 13, 2022, https://www.thisdayinaviation.com/tag/yoh-4a/.

"This WWII-era ship got new life fixing helicopters in Vietnam." Accessed November 2, 2019, https://www.wearethemighty.com/usns-corpus-christi-bay-albemarle.

Thomas, CWO Ben G. "Why Tandem?" *United States Army Aviation Digest*, 6, no. 4 (1960).

Toczek, David M. *The Battle of Ap Bac: They Did Everything But Learn From It*. Westport: Naval Institute Press, 2001.

"To James Madison from the Chiefs of the Northwestern Indians, 26 September 1810." *Founders Online*, National Archives, last modified June 13, 2018, http://founders.archives.gov/documents/Madison/03-02-02-0691. [Original source: *The Papers of James Madison*, Presidential Series, vol. 2, 1 October 1809–2 November 1810, ed. J. C. A. Stagg, Jeanne Kerr Cross, and Susan Holbrook Perdue. Charlottesville: University Press of Virginia, 1992, pp. 554–559.]

Toll, Ian W. *Twilight of the Gods: War in the Western Pacific, 1944–1945*. New York: W.W. Norton & Company, 2020.

Tolson, Lieutenant General John T. *Vietnam Studies: Air Mobility 1961–1971*. Washington, D.C.: Government Printing Office, 1973.

"Missile: Tow." Accessed February 20, 2020, https://history.redstone.army.mil/miss-tow.html.

Townsend, Kenneth William. *World War II and the American Indian*. Albuquerque: University of New Mexico Press, 2000.

"Transitioning into the CH-54." *United States Army Aviation Digest*, 14, no. 2 (1968).

Treaty of Greenville, August 3, 1795 - Full Text. Accessed November 15, 2018; Available from https://americasbesthistory.com/abhtimeline1795m.html.

"Treaty of Sycamore Shoals." Accessed May 24, 2020. Available from http://www.self.gutenberg.org/articles/Treaty_of_Sycamore_Shoals.

Trevithick, Joseph. "The U.S. Army Built Night-Fighting Gunships to Hunt the Viet Cong." Accessed March 2, 2020. Available from https://medium.com/war-is-boring/the-u-s-army-built-night-fighting-gunships-to-hunt-the-viet-cong-35f5e4887c83.

"Tribal Warfare: The 1935 Tribal Class Destroyer Design in Commonwealth Service." Accessed April 21, 2020. Available from https://www.navy.gov.au/sites/default/files/documents/Pfennigwerth_-_Tribal_Warfare.pdf.

"A 'Redskin' Is the Scalped Head of a Native American, Sold, Like a Pelt, for Cash: What a word means to my family." Accessed July 7, 2020. Available from https://www.esquire.com/news-politics/news/a29445/true-redskins-meaning.

Treuer, Anton, Frazer, Teri, Hill, Rick, et.al. *Indian Nations of North America*. Washington, D.C.: National Geographic Partners, 2010.

Truong, V. *Vietnam War: The New Legion*. Victoria: Trafford Publishing, 2010.

Tucker, Spencer C., ed. *The Encyclopedia of the Wars and the Early American Republic, 1783–1812: A Political, Social, and Military History, United States*. Santa Barbara: ABC-CLIO, 2013.

Tuttle, Ian. "Why Can't They Name Attack Helicopters After Hippies?" Accessed June 9, 2019. Available from http://www.nationalreview.com/article/381813/why-cant-they-name-attack-helicopters-afterhippies-ian-tuttle.

Tyler, Commander David G. "The Leverage of Technology: The Evolution of Armed Helicopters in Vietnam." *The Military Review*, Fort Leavenworth, Kansas: U.S. Army Combined Arms Center, August 2003.

Tyson, Carolyn A. *A Chronology of the United States Marine Corps 1935–1946, Volume II*. Washington, D.C.: History and Museums Division, Headquarters, U.S. Marine Corps, 1965.

"Ugly Angel: The Huey's Flawed Predecessor." Accessed September 29, 2019. Available from https://warfarehistorynetwork.com/daily/military-history/the-uh-1-iroquois-huey-helicopter/.

"UH-1M Huey." Accessed August 22, 2020. Available from https://combatairmuseum.org/aircraft/bellhueyuh1m.html.

"UH-72A." Accessed September 9, 2019. Available from https://www.airbus.com/us/en/helicopters/military-helicopters/uh-72a.html.

"UH-72A Lakota." Accessed September 8, 2019. Available from https://www.army-technology.com/projects/uh-72a-lakota/.

"UH-72 Lakota." Accessed September 8, 2019. Available from https://www.militaryfactory.com/aircraft/detail.asp?aircraft_id=400.

"U.S. Army Bell H-13 Sioux Helicopter." Accessed March 14, 2019. Available from http://www.acquacollectibles.com/challenge-coins/u-s-army-bell-h-13-sioux-helicopter-vietnam-veteran-challenge-coin.html.

United States Army Board of Aviation Accident Research. "Getting To Know The Iroquois." *United States Army Aviation Digest*, Volume 6, Number 6, Fort Rucker, Alabama, June 1960.

United States Army Military Police Board. "MP With Wings." *United States Army Aviation Digest*, Volume 5, Number 3, Fort Rucker, Alabama, March 1959.

"USAAC/USAAF/USAF Aircraft Designation Systems." Accessed March 15, 2020. Available from http://www.historyofwar.org/articles/weapons_USAAF_aircraft_designations.html#3.

Unnamed table, *United States Army Aviation Digest*, Volume 28, Issue 7, July 1982.

"U.S. Army Primary Helicopter Center/School." Accessed May 16, 2019. Available from https://www.fortwolters.com/USAPHS.html.

"US Helicopters - Helicopter Armament Subsystems Part I." Accessed December 10, 2019. Available from http://grunt-redux.atspace.eu/us_helos_weapons.htm.

"U.S.S. *Card*." Accessed October 25, 2018. Available from https://en.wikipedia.org/wiki/USS_Card#Vietnam_War.

"U.S.N.S. *Core*." Accessed October 25, 2018, https://www.google.com/search?ei=IXPSW8vXJIOBzwLa56OQBg&q=uss+Core&oq=uss+Core&gs_l=psyab.3.0.0j0i10l9.12584.13397..16196...0.0..0.99.320.4......0....1..gwswiz.......0i71j0i67j0i131.g6y0izFVtk0.

"U.S.N.S. *Corpus Christi Bay* Returns after Six-Year Tour in USARV." Accessed November 2, 2019, http://armyaviationmagazine.com/index.php/history/not-so-current-2/1622-usnu-corpus-christi-bay-returns-after-six-year-tour-in-usarv.

"U.S.S. *Croatan*." Accessed October 25, 2018, http://www.hullnumber.com/CVE-25.

"U.S.S. *Princeton*." Accessed October 25, 2018, http://www.navsource.org/archives/10/11/1105.htm.

"U.S. Ship is Sunk by Vietnam Reds; Crewmen Escape; The Card, Copter Transport, Blasted at Saigon Dock—Settles to Bottom; Old Aircraft Aboard; 'Baby Flattop' Was About to Sail." *New York Times Archives*, May 2, 1964.

Utley, Robert M. *Frontier Regulars: The United States Army and the Indian: 1866–1891*. New York: Macmillan Publishing Co., Inc., 1972.

Northern California Citizenship Project. "United States Voting Rights Timeline: Mobilize the Immigrant Vote 2004," 2004.

Vance, William E. "Coast to Coast in An H-21." *United States Army Aviation Digest*, 2, no. 10 (1956).

———, "History of Army Aviation." *United States Army Aviation Digest*, 3, no. 6 (1957).

———, "Saber in the Sky." *United States Army Aviation Digest*, 5, no. 8 (1959).

Vandergrift, A. A., and Asprey, Robert B. *Once a Marine, The Memoirs of General A.A. Vandergrift*. New York: W.W. Norton & Company, Inc. 1964.

Vanderpool, Colonel Jay D. "We Armed The Helicopter." *United States Army Aviation Digest*, 17, no. 6 (1971).

Van Stavveren, Jacob. *Gradual Failure: The Air War Over North Vietnam 1965–1966*. Washington, D.C.: Air Force History and Museum Program, 2011.

Varga, Theresa. "What's in a name? More than what the polls show." *The Washington Post*, July 9, 2020.

Vaughan, Don. "Helicopters' Debut in Vietnam." *Military Officer*, January 2022.

"Viet Cong Commandos Sank an American Aircraft Carrier." Accessed April 23, 2020, https://cherrieswriter.com/2017/08/15/viet-cong-commandos-sank-an-american-aircraft-carrier/.

"Vietnam: A Television History." Accessed August 1, 2021, https://openvault.wgbh,org/catalog/V ECAFFE3A8A60F4F28A8145B69087BD498.

"Vietnam: Mounted Combat." Accessed February 21, 2020, http: webdoc.sub.gwdg.de/ebook/p/2005/CMH_2/www.army.mil/cmh-pg/books/Vietnam/ mounted/chapter8html.

"Vietnam OH-58C Kiowa Helicopter." Vietnam Helicopter Museum. Accessed June 9, 2019, http://www.vietnamhelicopters.org/oh-58c-kiowa/.

"Vietnam: The Helicopter War." Accessed February 25, 2020, https://www.vietnam.ttu.edu/exhibits/helicopter/support.php.

Vietnam Veterans Memorial, Directory of Names. Washington, D.C.: Vietnam Veterans Memorial Fund, Inc., May 2007.

Vogel, Virgil J. *The Indian in American History*. Chicago: Integrated Education Associates, 1969.

Viola, Herman J. *Warriors in Uniform: The Legacy of American Indian Heroism*. Washington, D.C.: National Geographic Society, 2008.

Voigt, Matthias. "Indigenous Experiences of War (USA)." Accessed March 29, 2020, https://encyclopedia.1914–1918 online.net/article/indigenous_experiences_of_war_usa.

von Kann, Brigadier General Clifton F. "The Real Goal of Army Aviation." *United States Army Aviation Digest*, 6, no. 3 (1960).

"Wabanaki Timeline." Accessed July 8, 2020, http://archive.abbemuseum.org/research/wabanaki/timeline/proclamation.html.

Waddell. Karen. *The Cold War Historical Context 1951–1991 Fort Richardson, Alaska, United States Army Alaska*. Fort Collins: Colorado State University, March 2003.

Wallace., Chief Glenna J. "Proud to Be Eastern Shawnee—A Brief History of the Eastern Shawnee Tribe." Accessed January 29, 2019, https://www.estoo-nsn.gov/culture/brief-history/.

Ward, Geoffrey C. *The Vietnam War: An Intimate History*. New York: Alfred A. Knopf, 2017.

Warden, Amy. "There is one less child in this cemetery." *The Washington Post*, June 28, 2021.

Warnick, William L., and Jones, Warrant Officer Derryl. *Research Product: Aeroscout Pilot and Aeroscout Observer Responses to the Air Cavalry Tactical Information Survey*. Fort Knox: Human Resources Research Organization, Division 2, 1972.

Warren, James A. *The Year of the Hawk: America's Descent into Vietnam, 1965*. New York: Scribner, 2021.

Warren, Dr. John C. *Airborne Operations in World War II, European Theater*. Maxwell Air Force Base: Air University, 1956.

Waxman, Olivia B. "We Became Warriors Again: Why World War I Was a Surprisingly Pivotal Moment for American Indian History." Accessed March 29, 2020, https://time.com/5459439/american-indians-wwi/.

"We are all Americans—Native Americans in the Civil War." Accessed March 29, 2020, https://www.alexandriava.gov/historic/forward/default.aspx?id=40164.

Weinert, Richard P. Jr. *TRADOC Historical Monograph Series: A History of Army Aviation—1950–1962*. Fort Monroe: U.S. Army Training and Doctrine Command, 1991.

——————. *History of Army Aviation 1950–1962, Phase II 1955–1962*. Fort Monroe: Headquarters U.S. Army Training and Doctrine Command, November 1976.

Weiser, Kathy. "Legends of America: Arapaho—Great Buffalo Hunters of the Plains." Accessed September 9, 2019, https://www.legendsofamerica.com/na-arapaho/.

_____. "Legends of America: Battle of Sand Hollows, Washington." Accessed June 14, 2019, https://www.legendsofamerica.com/battle-sand-hollows-washington/.

_____. "Legends of America: Chief Victorio—Fighting for Ancestral Lands." Accessed September 7, 2019, https://www.legendsofamerica.com/na-victorio/.

_____. "Legends of America: Forts Across the United States." Accessed March 25, 2019, https://www.legendsofamerica.com/we-fortlist/.

_____. "Legends of America: Indian Conflicts of Washington." Accessed April 24, 2020, https://www.legendsofamerica.com/wa-indianconflicts/.

_____. "Legends of America: Lakota, Dakota, Nakota—The Great Sioux Nation." Accessed January 3, 2019, http://www.snowowl.com/peoplessioux.html.

_____. "Legends of America: Red Cloud's War in Wyoming & Montana." Accessed September 8, 2019, https://www.legendsofamerica.com/red-clouds-war/.

_____. "Legends of America: The Cayuse War—Revenge for the Measles." Accessed June 14, 2019, https://www.legendsofamerica.com/na-cayusewar/.

Weiser-Alexander, Kathy. "Legends of America: The Shawnee Indian Tribe." Accessed January 20, 2019, https://www.legendsofamerica.com/shawnee-indians/2/.

Wertz, Jay. *The First Americans: The History of the Indigenous North Americans*. London: Sevenoaks Books, 2018.

"Whitman Massacre Trial." Accessed June 17, 2019, https://sos.oregon.gov/archives/exhibits/highlights/Pages/whitman.aspx.

"Why Do Native Americans Serve?" Accessed December 27, 2019, https://americanindian.si/edu/static/patriot-nations/.

"Why We Serve: Native Americans in the United States Armed Forces—Spanish American War." Accessed February 12, 2021, https://americanindian.si.edu/why-we-serve/topics/spanis-american-war/.

Wigley, Russell F. *History of the United States Army*. New York: The Macmillan Company, 1967.

Wilhite, Ray. Interviews with the author, 2019–2020.

Wilkinson, Stephen. "Dog of War." Accessed November 10, 2019, https://www.airspacemag.com/military-aviation/dog-of-war-2370386/?page=1.

Willbanks, James H. "Nixon's Cambodian Incursion." Accessed September 28, 2020, https://www.historynet.com/nixons-cambodian-incursion.htm.

_____. "The Evolution of the US Advisory Effort in Vietnam: Lessons Learned." Accessed November 19, 2019, https://journals.lib.unb.ca/index.php/JCS/article/view/15238/24499.

Williams, Dr. James W. *A History of Army Aviation: From Its Beginnings to the War on Terror*. Lincoln: iUniversity, Inc., 2005.

Wilson, Charles E. "Memorandum: Clarification of Roles and Missions to Improve the Effectiveness of Operation of the Department of Defense." *United States Army Aviation Digest*, 2, no. 12 (1956).

Wilson, Donald E., and Currie, Dennis C. "220th Aviation Company: Battle and Fall of A Shau, March 1966." Accessed October 17, 2019, https://catkiller.org/history-1966-Battle-of-A-Shaw.pdf.

Wilson, George C. "DOD Approves Army Air Assault Concept." *Aviation Week & Space Technology*, April 26, 1965.

Wilson, S. Brian. *Don't Thank Me for My Service: My Viet Nam Awakening to the Long History of U.S. Lies*. Atlanta: Clarity Press, Inc. 2018.

Wise, Jennings C. *The Red Man in the New World Drama: A Politico-Legal Study with a Pageantry of American History*, Revised and Edited by Vine Deloria, Jr. New York: MacMillan Publishing Company, Inc., 1974.

Wittels, Stephen. "Korean Peninsula Clashes (1955–2010)." Washington, D.C.: Council on Foreign Relations Center for Preventive Action, December 2010.

Wolf, Richard and Johnson, Kevin. "Eastern Oklahoma deemed Native territory." *USA Today,* July 10–12, 2020.

Wood, Christina. "A Legacy of Service: American Indians have served with distinction in the U.S. military." *Military Officer*, 19, Issue 11 (2021).

Wood, Leonard. *Our Military History: Its Facts and Fallacies*. Chicago: Reilly and Britton, 1916.

Wooster, Robert. *The United States Army and the Making of America: From Confederation toEmpire, 1775–1903*. Lawrence: University Press of Kansas, 2021.,

Wukovits, John. *Dogfight over Tokyo: The Final Air Battle of the Pacific and the Last Four Men to Die in World War II*. New York: Da Capo Press, 2019.

Zark, Brian. "Use of Native American Tribal Names as Marks." *American Indian Law Journal*, III, Issue II (Spring 2015).

Zabecki, David T. "Valéri Andre: French MEDEVAC Pilot Flew into Enemy Fire for Rescues." *Vietnam,* (February 2021.)

Zimmerman, Heidi. "Vietnam Veterans Memorial Fund Changes Direction of Education Center Campaign." Accessed August 22, 2019, https://www.vvmf.org/News/Vietnam-Veterans-Memorial-Fund-changes-direction-of-Education-Center-campaign/.

ACKNOWLEDGMENTS

Many people have helped me to a greater or lesser extent over the years I spent on this book. To try to name all of them would consume innumerable pages and expose me to omissions through human error. I have chosen to confine myself to those who made significant contributions.

Unlike many other authors, I begin my acknowledgments by recognizing my family's impact at the beginning, remembering the briefer's maxim, BLUF, bottom line up front. As I suggested in the forward, *On Warriors' Wings* is as much the culmination of my journey as it is a tribute to the legacy of those who served in the air or inspired the aircraft's official moniker. Throughout my twenty-eight-year Army career, Sharon and our children, Donna and David, were always there through the good and the challenging, the seemingly unending separations, the joyous home-comings, and the thirty-five home relocations. Their steadfast encouragement and support during the years behind this are beyond expression. They made it possible for anything I may have accomplished, actualizing my childhood dream of being an Army officer.

The realization of this book would not have been possible without the generous contributions of innumerable people who shared an interest in Army helicopter aviation, its role in the Vietnam War, and the long-overdue acknowledgment and recognition of Native American veterans not only of Vietnam, but also in all of America's military conflicts in which they participated and continue to participate in today. I am indebted to all who helped me make this scholarly journey.

The Vietnam Helicopter Pilots Association (VHPA) and its veteran members were selfless in their willingness to fix my compass heading and open their vast treasure trove of data, first-person experiences, photographs, and insights that were always at their fingertips. A simple inquiry to their magazine's readership always brought a flood of flight and wartime experiences. I am particularly indebted to the generosity of their time, experiences, and readiness to assist of VHPA's Scott Drew, Mike Law, Gary Roush, and Ray Wilhite. These men and their organization are a national resource of information on America's helicopter war which they broadly share throughout the community.

No historical perspective is complete without its pilgrimage through the United States Army Aviation Center and the Army Aviation Museum at Fort Rucker, Alabama. I was fortunate to find a comrade-in-arms in the curator of the Museum,

Robert Mitchell, who was unstoppable in his efforts to share what the museum had to offer for this effort and his own experiences and glimpses into Army aviation history. One of the titans of Army Aviation and someone I am proud to know and at the same time humbled to call a friend was immensely helpful throughout the eight years of bringing this book to life. The consummate professional aviator and leader, Major General Carl H. McNair, Jr., USA, Ret. was always ready with the cockpit, senior Army-level, and historical perspectives found in this book. Regrettably, General McNair passed away mere months before *On Warriors' Wings* release.

The details of the Vietnam War and the aviation exploits of the eleven helicopters included in this volume and their pilots and crews would be quite incomplete without the men dedicated to the linage of their unit, the legacy of their aircraft, and who were willing to reduce it all to unit newsletters, unit history websites, and the printed page. Each excursion into the depths of an aviation unit's experiences in the Vietnam War was more exciting than the last, filled with authoritative color and commentary, moments of sheer terror, and instances of lightheartedness. I am forever indebted to the Army and Marine Corps aviation units of Vietnam and their veterans who diligently recorded their history of service and sacrifice on their websites, which were valuable in telling the *On Warriors' Wings* story.

Most white men do not naturally appreciate the service, sacrifice, and courage of America's Native American population over the centuries in our nation's service. I was extremely fortunate to have the enduring support of a Native Warrior of the Seminole Tribe of Florida, David Stephen Bowers, and his wife, Elizabeth Bowers Bates. Through their efforts, I gained a broader comprehension of their people's proud and courageous traditions. With their encouragement, I undertook the Native American portion of this project. Their efforts will soon culminate in the Seminole Tribe of Florida's Memorial to Native Veterans of Vietnam, including a statue of Stephen, who proudly served with the 173rd Airborne Brigade. As my manuscript neared completion, a great sadness descended as the Almighty Father called Stephen home far too early. He will forever be missed but never forgotten. "*Heres, votive here, kind one. Hvtvm cehecares.*"[1]

Writing about Native Americans is not to be taken lightly or without an understanding that arises from years of continuous study and observation. *On Warriors' Wings* benefitted from the collective knowledge of three Native American scholars: Herman J. Viola, Ph.D., Jimmie R. McClellan, Ph.D., and Michael Oblinger, Ph.D. Each is a prominent Native American historian. Their efforts ensured the accuracy of the portrayal of the Indigenous content, the respectful accounting of tribal traditions, and the Native American historical legacy. They gave of their knowledge and experience to ensure the accuracy of the Native American content, the respectful accounting of tribal traditions and history, and an accuracy derived from credible sources and befitting the proud history and heritage of the tribes and chiefs for whom the eleven Vietnam Army helicopters were named.

My friends, colleagues, and fellow volunteers at the Vietnam Veterans Memorial Fund including Colonel Stephen Delp, USA, Ret. and Timothy Tetz, were invaluable in their assistance and access to the information that the reader found in the chapter entitled, Some Gave All. They and their organization continue to keep the memories of the fallen of the Vietnam War alive daily through the care and support of the Vietnam Veterans Memorial, the Traveling Wall that Heals, and their commemorative ceremonies. I and all Vietnam veterans are continuously in your debt.

There is a rapidly growing resource that deserves greater awareness and appreciation not only by historians and scholars but also by the everyday American citizen. That is the Veterans History Project (VHP),[2] a program of the American Folklife Center in the Library of Congress (LOC).[3] The project is charged with collecting and preserving oral histories and documentary materials from veterans of World War I through the current conflicts. I was indeed fortunate to work with and obtain the willing assistance of Colonel Robert W. "Bob" Patrick, USA, Ret., the then Director of the VHP, current Director Karen Lloyd, and their staff as I searched for Native American Veterans of Vietnam among their oral histories. They were aviators and crew members of the Native American named helicopters included in this volume. While I found several oral histories that satisfied these criteria, the almost eighty Native American oral histories of Vietnam Veterans were an eye-opening experience. They revealed how little I know about the larger Vietnam experience beyond my little piece of the war. I commend the VHP library to anyone who wants to know about the wartime experience and how the men and women who endured it matured, grew and changed.

On Warriors' Wings would not be complete without the first person's accounts of the aviators and crew members who shared them in the chapter "Whom Shall I Send." Each veteran shared a piece of himself as he relived those months and years of service. In some cases, family members added their perspectives or told the story of a veteran who died years after returning from Vietnam. As the book's reading reflects, Native American warriors are a humble people, reluctant to share their wartime exploits, choosing instead to confine their telling to members of their Tribe, Nation, or warrior clan. The acknowledgment or recognition they garner from their people is all they desire. So, for these men to share their wartime experiences willingly or reluctantly is even more remarkable; I pray they will all find this volume worthy of sharing their stories, service, and sacrifice.

I am indebted to aviation artist and Vietnam War veteran Joe Kline who generously adapted his work "Army Aviation" to make the cover of this volume. His work including my cover, are emblematic of his creative philosophy, "to best tell the soldier's story, you had to fight by his side."

This volume owes a great thanks to the archivists from the National Museum of the American Indian and The Vietnam Center and Sam Johnson Vietnam Archives from Texas Tech University, without whom the fullness of the history recorded herein would not be complete.

After almost three decades of active military service in both command and staff positions, the rigors of high school and college composition and writing classes become somewhat malleable to respond to "the needs of the service." My manuscript presented a daunting challenge requiring a herculean effort by the editors of Global Collective Publishers and especially Curtis Key. His masterful touch uncluttered my thoughts and expressions, releasing an immensely improved and more readable volume. Likewise, the GCP team was creative and artistic in presenting the volume now completed.

Again, thank you to one and all.

INDEX